ARTHUR RIMBAUD

ARTHUR RIMBAUD

PRESENCE OF AN ENIGMA

Jean-Luc Steinmetz

TRANSLATED BY

Jon Graham

WELCOME RAIN PUBLISHERS

ARTHUR RIMBAUD: PRESENCE OF AN ENIGMA by Jean-Luc Steinmetz
Originally published in France as *Arthur Rimbaud, une question de présence*

Illustration credits: 2, 4, 5, 6, 8, 11, 12, 13, 14, 17, 18, 19, 20, 21 courtesy of the Musée-Bibliothèque Rimbaud, Charleville-Mézières; 1 courtesy of the Bibliothèque Nationale, Paris; 7 courtesy of the Musée d'Orsay, Paris; 9, 10, 15, 16 courtesy of the Bibliothèque d'art et d'archéologie Jacques Doucet, Paris.

Welcome Rain Publishers would like to thank the French Ministry of Culture and the Musée-Bibliothèque Rimbaud, Charleville-Mézières for their assistance with this translation.

Library of Congress CIP data available from the publisher.

Direct any inquiries to
Welcome Rain Publishers LLC,
225 West 35th Street, Suite 1100
New York, NY 10001.

ISBN 1-56649-106-1

Manufactured in the United States
of America by BLAZE I.P.I.

First Edition January 2001

1   3   5   7   9   10   8   6   4   2

For Kuréha Yuguré
in the leaves of dusk
in the Dawn of summer

"Life is a farce we all must lead."
RIMBAUD (*A Season in Hell*)

CONTENTS

RIMBAUD'S LEGEND ENDURES. HIS TEMPERAMENT AND THE SCANDALS HE loved to create are partially responsible, as is the deliberate self-effacement he undertook later in life. Perhaps in Rimbaud's case it would be better to focus on his work. However, one may even wonder if he himself really wanted his work (with the exception of *Une saison en enfer*, which he published only to renounce soon afterwards) to reach us. Rimbaud's lack of interest in his creative output and his obstinate desire to go through life at record speed have turned him into a "character" standing in defiance of literature and, in certain ways, of posterity. Posterity, however, has been all the more curious to know the man as he relinquished only a few rare tokens it could use for getting its bearings on a route that seems to coincide with some secret design.

There are numerous biographies of Rimbaud. All have sought to fill the obvious gaps and resurrect a man who arrived from all time and was on his way everywhere.[1] If Proust, in *Contre Sainte-Beuve*, could assert, "A book is the product of an ego other than the one we display in our habits, society, and our vices,"[2] then Rimbaud, merely through his way of living, unwittingly forged a kind of example. His gestures and deeds have spread a violent lesson concerning what some have called "poetry in action," a vital conduct diametrically opposed to artistic quests carried out in the security of reasonable and quiet lives. Even if the facts of Rimbaud's life are regarded as being of negligible importance, his biography nonetheless harbors the awesome energy that animated Rimbaud and made him a vagabond, a traveler, an individual with no permanent address, in short, a displaced person and, to use Mallarmé's famous description, a "considerable passerby."[3] Neither Tristan Tzara, attentive to poetry as "a mental activity" and not a "means of expression,"[4] nor Henry Miller, eager to see him as an alter ego,[5] nor the American poets of the Beat generation, for whom he was a posthumous mentor, reduced Rimbaud to his writings. The majority of writers and literary historians have

understood that the entirety of his work includes not only poems, the chap-
book *Une saison en enfer*, and *Illuminations*, but also a certain thought process for which the texts simply translate one of his phases, momentarily
borrowing the path of art. Félix Fénéon, introducing *Illuminations* in 1886,
unhesitatingly declared them "above all literature."[6] Certainly this was an
exaggeration, and yet it acknowledged that for Rimbaud the act of writing
was comparable to a vehement magical act whose first aim was to modify the
order of reality. As a writer, Rimbaud nevertheless occupied a precarious position in the cultural world, since his poetry responded less to an artistic intention than to a vertiginous ambition to change the measures of this world.

Rimbaud's story clearly shows the development of a desire that will
nonetheless remain remote to us, like the highlights of a landscape to which
we will never have access, save through an approximate perspective. This
impression, however, is set apart from a whole or, better, a development, an
enlargement in which poetry, mirroring adolescence, would have signified
primarily a passage. Rimbaud—if one accepts at all what this name conceals—is not restricted to his writings, and those individuals who believe—in
the name of a formalist precision verging on the obvious—that an author
holds himself entirely within his work and nowhere else[7] (here is Proust's
ego) are wrong in this instance. Work and art, soon challenged by Rimbaud,
were denied in the particular process of his obstinate desire to take on various
roles and borrow different avatars in the hope of finally achieving his objective (which in any case remained inaccessible). The numerous premonitory
phrases that saturate *Une saison en enfer* do not indicate any awareness on their
author's part of his destiny. Rather, they suggest a partially unconscious aim
that pointed Rimbaud toward a future in which he would find only obstacles
and deceptions. To study his life is to understand this movement, this constant drive. On these grounds, what is called his "silence" forms part of his
trajectory; it is confirmation of the hyperbolic attempt. The "dreamed-of dis-
engagement," affirmed in the poems, is realized in this way: a mute result that
is due in no way to the luck of circumstance, but to a "moral" intention.

In composing a new biography of Rimbaud I did not set out to scrutinize
the characteristics of a man in order to chart their appearance in his texts.
Nor did I attempt to make these texts dependent upon geographical, atavistic,
or social conditions. In fact, Rimbaud the individual calls these types of causes

into question. Unique in his renunciation of literature, he pursued a project far from all artistic temptation. based more on sensitivity than intelligibility. Within him, literature—believable for one absolute moment, then felt as a fundamental deception—is surpassed,[8] then annihilated, for the benefit of a form of behavior that was more adventurous and apparently more real, though it derives from the same desire that possesses an individual with a dramatic and marvelous sense of dissatisfaction.

In recognition of Rimbaud's momentum that never found its just compensation, his biographers have redoubled their efforts, unaware that they were attempting the impossible. These biographies are devotions wherein each author provides a demonstration of *his* Rimbaud. Rimbaud has quickly gone from being a figure of desire to an identificatory snare.[9] Étiemble—with a meticulous attention to detail bordering on irony—has provided an excellent analysis of these works,[10] which have each erected an idol to their own measure. The first in this long line was without doubt Pierre Dufour's[11] edifying attempt at a biography. Here Dufour, alias Paterne Berrichon and the husband of Rimbaud's youngest sister, Isabelle, boldly declared: "By way of biography, I accept but one theme: my own. I refute all others as mendacious and offensive."[12] Rimbaud has become the property of biographers who found much to say where he said little. The biographies of the poet of "Le bateau ivre" are inevitably disappointing because of their inability to remain at the height of a desire, that while concealed, has provided numerous signs of its existence. Even one of the more inspired books, written by Enid Starkie[13] (called a "blue-stocking in a petticoat" by Claudel), developed hypotheses harmful to Rimbaud's memory, such as the one portraying him as a slaver. The unjustly forgotten biography by Pierre Arnoult[14] has merit—despite the errors it contains—for the alacrity of its style and its author's ambition to recount Rimbaud's life "like the life of a well-known and passionately admired friend." A more recent example, the work of Pierre Petitfils[15] records every fact, even the least important, to such an extent that Rimbaud's work is barely taken into account. Monsieur Petitfils takes issue with those "whose heads are so filled by ideology that they have lost sight of the flesh-and-blood individual," but did he himself dare discuss the impetuous nature of this flesh and blood individual? The latest book, Alain Borer's *Rimbaud en Abyssinie*,[16] justly praised by the press, has been thrust forward as one book that, while not avoiding narcissism, does provide a better understanding of Rimbaldian desire. Eager to eliminate chronology (that "old moon" of an outdated criticism), Borer pulls his readers into a real-life theme in which Rimbaud escapes from time's elapsing into a system of reruns and repetitions. Everything, subtly caught in a grid of reconciliations, enters into the framework of a universe that has been too judiciously balanced. To get right to the theory of two Rimbauds[17]—the one who writes, and the one who is silent—a logical continuity has been established throughout his life from childhood. Here the poet has become so faithful to himself that all contradictions, hesitations, and regrets have been removed.

Such precedents have a great deal to teach. I wouldn't venture to take my place in their wake if I hadn't first edited his work[18] and realized it wasn't enough. I don't regard biography as a supplementary tool but rather as the best means of intellectually embracing a composite figure who is extended by means of his texts and beyond—via his gestures, actions, attitudes, thought processes, and appearances that have all been more or less independently claimed or vouched for.

Since 1980 almost all documents permitting the precise reconstruction of the Rimbaldian trajectory have been inventoried.[19] We can always hope more will be discovered, though, no matter how slim the chances. It is certainly not enough simply to put this material in order. Here, when possible, interpretation seems called for, not the serene impassivity of a records clerk. I am not seeking, however, to create an individual who is too easily understood and effortlessly superimposed upon the fantasies he has already created in the contemporary imagination. Nor have I sought some kind of pseudo-objectivity any more than I sought to impose a verifiable image that would add an additional face to the gangster-seer-homosexual-initiate-explorer–totem pole. What is most important is to note the manner in which Rimbaud created his own legend. Nothing is missing from the many volumes of Étiemble's *Le Mythe de Rimbaud*, save precisely that volume in which the Charleville student, Parisian pedestrian, London exile, and the Javanese, Aden, and Harari businessman could be seen manufacturing his appearance and projecting his role. Rimbaud's double is not so much that individual of the same name who lived in the vicinity of Aden at the same time he did (and of whose existence he was aware) than this *other* he always wanted to be and pursued ceaselessly as if it were necessary for him to strip off his most recognizable outward appearance in order to conquer his hidden truth. One writes Rimbaud's biography with the idea of creating a close resemblance as a substitute for the real person. One also witnesses the birth of this other he carried within as his secret "genius." I therefore found it necessary, following much reflection, to recognize that the ring of legends surrounding him were not the accumulation or sedimentation of rumor but the response to his own most heartfelt desire at those times he was grappling with his idealized projections or giving in to a spirit of mystification that somewhat allowed him to make light of a crushing reality.

A curious rhetorical exercise awaits all those who concern themselves with writing the life of Rimbaud. This is the need to "do something with" a certain number of extremely familiar anecdotes and judging their content. We all walk here on trails that have been duly marked off through an organization of retrieved words as opposed to a now verifiable physical reality. What remains is what has disappeared as deposits in the form of various written objects: his work, his letters, official documents. What it comes down to is the composition of a palimpsest-like narrative that is novel only through the distinctive manner in which it has been reworked, reconstructed, and reexamined. Here there are constant deviations and numerous little differences. Yet it is still the same story. Here Rimbaud becomes another story, a kind of interpretive narrative. I have not thought it necessary to say where Rimbaud is leading us or even to declare that he is leading us anywhere. The main concern was the avoidance of two reefs: one the almost detective-like report and the other the overburdened narrative that uses this subterfuge to discuss the author's personal delusions. "I am hidden and I am not," as Rimbaud says in *Une saison en enfer*. Perhaps it is appropriate for his narrator to occupy an equally spectral position. The "subject" he makes visible through his writing is the same one to whom he also gives birth from page to page as a character and, more important, a necessity that is more meaningful for the biographer to follow than to form.

A biography is a question of presence. For that reason the present tense is predominant in this work, not as the ploy of a realist novelist but in order to maintain the urgency needed to keep pace with the "promeneux" (this marvelously appropriate Ardennais word [meaning "walker"—translator] was given to me by André Dhôtel). Until now most biographers have carried Rimbaud back to the past and recounted his life in the imperfect or past tense, which dismisses the immediacy of his itinerary or slips it into the strata of a cultural memory. I, on the contrary, find it desirable to situate him in the quick of the event (whether it be a dead end or a transition), at that very moment he is readying himself to pierce "the sky reddening like a wall."[20]

On the other hand I have decided to make do without another easy realist technique that makes the characters of a "life" converse together. This is an uncalled-for "stage trick" that often turns otherwise well documented books into sensationalist biographical novels. I also decided to cite only short extracts from his texts (one should obviously read them in a separate collection), especially his correspondence, which contains certain letters that, though marvelous, would break the flow of the narrative (how for example would one integrate *in extenso* the illustrious letter of the seer?). However, I have not refrained from turning to this correspondence quite often in order to reconstruct the last period of Rimbaud's life (1880–1891),[21] when he was a businessman in Aden and Harar. Who doesn't have the impression that Rimbaud, at the threshold of these years, which are sometimes considered negligible and by virtue of that judgment liable to a certain occultation, had precisely reached the very place place long foretold as the final strand in a web of fateful actions and words? Over the course of his letters the hours of Aden and Harar echo like unimpeachable oaths. They draw us painfully close to a Rimbaud whose reasons to live were gradually escaping him and over whom absurdity was gaining complete possession. Henceforth he was only a driven man living out numerous schemes that were all working equally toward his undoing.

Once this book has been read, a review will no doubt be in order. Here again Rimbaud has been only a series of living images that raise questions, but also a reconstruction that can be regarded as certain without necessarily being credible. Here again someone's "destiny" has been traced. Are we to think, in recollection of Sartre's *Baudelaire* that Rimbaud lived the life he deserved?[22] After the fact, when the picture is complete, one will no doubt bring up a series of motives, departures, and returns (a shuttle?)—it is not always enough to explain the poetic instinct but it does testify to the ever desirable, ever in-question area always out there.

There are not two Rimbauds determined by an invisible equator of a proven silence. There is one Rimbaud who is always on the move, lured into the future by the forever evasive nature of the object of desire, the object he has lost. His life is a movement that intentionally loses itself. His poetry remains to the side, stable in its lines and verses but as firmly set moments of vertigo. Then as now the end result is an expenditure: the modalities of a breakaway and efforts toward a freedom that would allow him to know himself thoroughly and experience his life as pleasure, even when chained to human toil.

Today, once again, "with "both fists in our pockets," each of us resumes his journey with the crazy notion of finally reaching who we think we truly are, on the far side of the horizon.

PART I

A SCHOOLBOY
FROM CHARLEVILLE

PIECES OF CHILDHOOD

I WON'T BE GOING TO CHARLEVILLE THIS TIME. I WON'T BE CROSSING THE square by the station where his bust is erected. I won't be taking the now almost familiar route by rue Thiers (formerly rue Napoléon) where he was born; rue Bourbon where he spent the earliest days of his childhood, and 5 bis quai de la Madeleine[1] (dubbed the "Madelomphe" by Verlaine) where he wrote "Le Bateau ivre." I won't be passing through place Ducale nor entering the Library of the Sitters, which overlooks place de l'Agriculture, or the school where he was once once one of the most promising pupils. Nor will I enter the Old Mill, the superb edifice with the high roof that has become his museum. I won't be gazing into the Meuse, whose currents inspire reveries. This is where he spent his early life, and these are the places that fenced him in, from which he escaped through the energy of a will merged with poetry. But to return there personally as an avid, attentive observer will actually serve little purpose except for the stark verification of his absence. During his life Rimbaud questioned the validity of his presence, feeling he might be invisible, in spite of the scandals he provoked and the curious glances he attracted. "Some of those I've encountered perhaps haven't seen me." Both truth and legend, he now forms one image. It is in fact his absence we feel, and the reality of Charleville only confirms it in its compliance with an insurmontable distance, with the movement of an impossible confiscation.

I went there in search of a man; what I encountered was only a fiction composed of his works, letters, and those official documents that, though meant to be exact, are only an approximation. Assuredly what binds these writings together is the thread of a life, but a life whose principle was based on running away and taking off. A life that took place as a phenomenon of violent radiance like the blue rays of "his" eyes.

The first written traces concerning the person who remains a "hand with the pen"[2] as well as a forward march, consists, as it should, of a birth certificate[3] and a baptism record. No one escapes their ancestry. Like everyone else, the future wanderer was subject to genetic laws that left a lasting effect upon his body and speech. Parents are always the artisans of a destiny: they remain in the individual as genes and the hell of necessity.

> In the year eighteen hundred and fifty-four on the day of October 20, at five hours in the evening appearing before me, François Dominique Eugène Le Marle, appointed deputy filling the duties of an officer of the civil government of the town of Charleville, second arrondissement of the Ardennes department, Jean-Nicolas Cuif, age fifty-six, property owner and resident of Charleville who has declared before me that Marie Catherine Vitalie Cuif, age twenty-nine, without profession, wife of Frédéric Rimbaud, age forty, infantry captain of the forty-seventh regiment in the garrison at Lyon, where he resides, has given birth, in this town, on this twentieth day of the present month, in the house of the aforesaid Jean-Nicolas Cuif, rue Napoleon, in the Notre Dame quarter, an infant of male sex, whom she has presented to us and to whom she has given the fore-names of Jean-Nicolas Arthur, said declaration and presentation made in the presence of Prosper Letellier, age thirty-six, bookseller, and Jean-Baptiste Hémery, age thirty-nine, employee of the town hall, residing in Charleville. Following upon which we have read the present certificate and the aforesaid individuals and witnesses have signed it with us.
>
> Cuif,   Hémery,
>
> Letellier,   Le Marle.

From this moment forward Arthur's father, Captain Rimbaud, then garrisoned in Lyon, would be conspicuous by his absence. What could have been merely a inconsequential token event would grow into a major irritatant that would eventually force the couple to part. Rimbaud, on the day his birth was announced, just as a month later, November 20, when he was baptized, was placed entirely in the world of the Cuif family. Neither he nor his brother and sisters would ever know his paternal family.

Paterne Berrichon, relying on the memories of his mother-in-law, Madame Rimbaud, describes Frédéric Rimbaud as "a man of average height, fair-haired, with a high forehead, blue eyes, a short, slightly turned-up nose, a full mouth, sporting, as was then the fashion, a mustache, and imperial."[4] Born in Dôle on October 7, 1814,[5] to a farmer's daughter and a master tailor, he chose to enter the military profession when he reached the age of eighteen. Systematically moving through the ranks, he was sent to serve in Algeria in 1841. This was at the height of the colonial period. French troops, under the command of Marechal Bugeaud, were then combatting the forces of Abd el-Kader. In 1845 Frédéric Rimbaud was promoted to the rank of second lieutenant, then named head of the Arab Office of Sebdou, thirty miles from Tlemcem, in Oranie. His duties were essentially administrative. He was required to write up reports on a wide array of problems, a task he performed zealously and that others—I am thinking here of the little known Lycanthrope, Pétrus Borel,[6] who, starting in 1846 was an inspector of colonization in Mostaganem—saw as a real chore. It is not merely an idle fancy to imagine the two men meeting, but Frédéric Rimbaud was not a poet and Pétrus had no talent as an administrator. Thus fates are woven. While Borel was still composing his *Léthargie de la Muse* in his Castel of High Thought, Frédéric was single-mindedly recording numerous reports, and when the manufacture of these did not prove sufficient, writing a *Traité d'eloquence militaire*, out of a need for diversion as much as personal conviction, it may lead one to believe his speech was as lively as his pen. This specialized form of literature was not as rare as is commonly believed, and many officers from Bugeaud's entourage, priding themselves on eloquence, have left works in which their rhetorical gifts shine conspicuously.[7] Frédéric definitely possessed above-average intelligence. Furthermore, he held on to his texts, written during his leisure time in a remote and barely pacified Algeria, and brought them to Charleville, where he would later leave them.[8] Rimbaud would have leafed through these papers as a child, but other pages covered with unusual letters soon drew his attention: an Arab dictionary annotated in his father's hand: "Arab papers" in which he found a "notebook entitled 'Jokes, Word Games, etc.,' and a 'collection of dialogues and songs useful to those learning the language.'"[9]

After the revolution of 1848 the troops of Oran, to which Lieutenant Rimbaud's battalion belonged, threw their support to the Republic. Frédéric remained at this posting until 1850, at which time he returned to France. Two years later he was promoted to captain of the 47th Regiment line infantry. It is still hard to imagine how this soldier who spent the bulk of his career abroad was able to meet a young Ardennais resident who had remained faithfully rooted in her native province. But military life had him frequently changing garrisons. And so it was that in 1852 we find him posted to Mézières, a town so close to Charleville that today they have become twin towns. At Charleville's place de la Musique, a military band—swinging their red shakos amid gleaming brass instruments—sometimes performed on Sunday as family entertainment. Vitalie Cuif, a young woman of twenty-eight years of age and a newcomer to city life, found this an acceptable diversion. She was a large, serious woman, whose reserve and beautiful blue eyes could prove quite enticing.[10] The captain noticed her. They made each other's acquaintance according to standard decorum and in all likelihood thanks to the efforts of intermediaries anxious to unite them.

Born on March 10, 1825, in the hamlet of Roche (the canton of Artigny) thirty miles from Charleville, Vitalie didn't have a happy childhood.[11] She lost her mother when she was five and since then lived most of her life in the company of her father, Jean-Nicolas Cuif, and her brothers, Jean-Charles Félix, born in 1824, and Charles-Auguste, born in 1830. She soon replaced her deceased mother in taking charge of the domestic duties, duties that would absorb her the rest of her life.

The Cuifs were an honorable peasant family whose roots can be traced back to before the Revolution. In *Une Saison en enfer* Rimbaud shamelessly declared, "I have always been of an inferior race." The fact remains that his ancestors were far from penurious. Jean-Baptiste Cuif, his maternal great-grandfather, owned the farm of Fontenilles, an ancient convent. Over the years he had increased his fortune, buying land in the neighboring communities of Voncq and Chuffilly. He settled in Roche, which was passed on to his son, then his grandson, Jean-Nicolas, and where the children of this latter grew up. But while Vitalie was diligent and guided by a flawless moral sense from her earliest childhood, her brothers were distinguished for their dissolute behavior. In 1841, at the age of seventeen, Jean-Charles Félix left the Ardennes region to escape a sordid affair that threatened to send him to prison, and enlisted for service in Algeria at the same time Lieutenant Rimbaud was there. He only returned after Vitalie's marriage, at which time his sunburned complexion earned him the nickname "the African" throughout the canton, a name that for us has such premonitory overtones. Charles-Auguste hardly ever lifted a hand to work except to finance his drinking binges. Nevertheless he married in 1852. The new couple's presence at the farm seems to have created disputes that subsequently compelled Vitalie to leave. Her father, Jean-Nicolas gave Roche to Charles-Auguste to get as much as he could out of the farm and provide his daughter a good dowry. They both left Roche for Charleville and moved into the second floor of 12 rue Napoléon in the Notre Dame quarter near the center of the town. Shortly afterward Charles, incapable of managing his property, sank into alcoholism, abandoned his wife, and sold the farm to "the African," who had returned in 1854, following a long and mysterious absence. Henceforth he wandered like a vagabond throughout the department, working here and there as a farm hand. It would seem alcohol preserved him since he did not die until 1924, after leading a mule-headed, good-for-nothing existence. Colonel Godchot, one of Rimbaud's biographers, insisted that the Cuifs were a fault-finding and undisciplined lot.[12] It ran in Rimbaud's family! But most likely Arthur knew his uncles only through rumor, as his mother undoubtedly refused to speak about them. Certainly laziness, drunkenness, and vagrancy form "headings" in Rimbaud's life but they cannot be made dependent on such an improbable atavism. Everything leads one to believe that his later advocation of a "reasoned derangement of all the senses" as a poetic method owed nothing to the sad examples of Charles the drunkard and Felix "the African." On the other hand, it is certain that his mother was a permanent symbol of the tedious, sedentary lifestyle in a home where habit ruled so strongly that all dreams and hopes were stifled.

Indeed, there could be nothing less adventurous than the years she spent at Roche: she was a schoolgirl; the young mistress of the home soon to be exhausted by her housekeeping duties; and a field hand in summer, when she worked alongside the men harvesting and haymaking. However, her arrival in Charleville marked her joyless universe with an unexpected transformation, and her meeting with Frédéric replaced her normal resignation with happiness. By all accounts the two betrothed suited one another. The wedding accordingly took place in February 1853. She brought with her a considerable dowry (30,000 old francs), to which were soon added the revenues from Roche.[13] The captain was a fine figure of a man with a career. She loved this older soldier, and, after years spent in African solitude, he had hopes of finding a peaceful retirement in affectionate surroundings.

Nine months after their wedding the sturdy Frédéric is born. His destiny would certainly be much less brilliant than his brother's, but his life will last much longer! Captain Rimbaud is sent to the garrison in Lyon in May 1853. During a brief leave he returns, just long enough to father a second child, Jean-Nicolas Arthur the poet, but he is not present for his birth. At that time he is preparing to depart for Crimea where Napoleon III and the English in opposition to Nicholas I are attempting to settle the thorny question of the East by force. Every day Madame Rimbaud follows the agonizing progress of that audacious campaign in the papers and through the postcards she receives. Rimbaud was too young and probably didn't retain even the slightest memory of it, but he may have later seen an engraving of the Battle of Inkerman (in which his father didn't take part) at home. In any event, he would happily display such a picture adorning the wall of a bourgeois salon—that of the honorable Monsieur Labinette—in the ironic "Une Coeur sous une soutane."[14]

The couple therefore experienced a forced separation, a prelude to several more that would eventually break them up for good. With each passing day, Vitalie's dream of a happy life slowly vanished. Once more she was forced to perform the chores incumbent on a single woman saddled with several young children. The captain finally returns safe and sound, but to see his wife and sons for only a week's time as he is posted to Grenoble on his return—the duties and rigors of military life. From this short stay the first Vitalie is born, dying at the age of three months. A year later, during May 1858, another Vitalie sees the light of day as the result of another brief visit by the captain. The eldest of Rimbaud's sisters, she will not survive adolescence, but Rimbaud would bear a great deal of affection for her and she constitutes one of the most naive and authentic witnesses to the deeds and gestures of the poet (almost without his knowing) because of the diary she kept between 1873 and 1875.

The unrelievedly gray and monotonous years brought their share of births and deaths. Jean-Nicolas dies in July 1855; Madame Rimbaud feels it deeply and will often mention this "good father." She misses him by far over all the others she has lost. From him she inheirits the farm of Roche (which she will soon rent to various farmers). She makes a momentous decision shortly after his death, once the harvests are in. Leaving her children in a neighbor's care, she rejoins her husband at the Schlettstadt garrison near Strasbourg. There she spends several days with him. This is a surprising gesture from a woman with such a bad-tempered reputation. It could be regarded as a violent request for love that had to be quickly repressed. The captain was a procreator rather than a lover. In July 1860 Isabelle was born from his labors. She was the sister destined to become Rimbaud's biographer and the constructor of his legend.

In spite of this short-lived journey Madame Rimbaud is quickly drawn back into the exhausting routine of everyday life. Her four children leave her no rest. The eldest is seven years old, the youngest still in the cradle. As the apartment can no longer hold her small family, she leaves it for 73 rue Bourbon in a working-class neighborhood. Over the following years, similar moves would occur at a brisk pace, as Madame can never find lodging to her satisfaction. Since Vitalie's stay in Strasbourg the captain appears less and less frequently at the family home. But, much as it is needed, his rare presence doesn't bring any happiness to the family heart. He couldn't tolerate his children, whom he barely knew, and he got along poorly with his wife. Everything served as an excuse for a quarrel with this "mobile character who was by turn indolent and violent."[15] From these numerous disputes Arthur, who was then six years old, retained a curious memory according to his future friend Ernest Delahaye. A silver bowl was placed on a sideboard in their home; one night his father had furiously grabbed the object then hurled it to the floor, "where it bounced and made music."[16] He then picked it back up and replaced it on the sideboard. Madame Rimbaud, not wishing to be outdone in displays of irritability, immediately took hold of the bowl and threw it to the floor as well. It was a scene of absurd violence in which each participant attempted to assert his or her rights. It is surprising to find it deposited as it was in Rimbaud's memory, but behind this screen of memory it is undoubtedly prudent to suspect a scene more real, and perhaps more unpleasant than the one the child buried in his mind. Rimbaud, for whom this should have been a painful experience, retained only a repetitive impression dominated by the pleasure of a certain "music," which likely conceals the fallout of a bitter squabble.

Transferred to Cambrai in June 1860, which allowed him to be closer to his family, the captain instead definitively broke with the family he had created but with whom he had never formed any solid attachment. The couple didn't divorce but separated. Following Frédéric's death on November 17, 1878, Vitalie, moreover, drew a widow's pension from the army. She then seems to have attempted to erase every trace of this non-husband she had failed to hold, but who in all likelihood never loved her and saw her only as bait—thanks to her small fortune—for the trap in which he had been caught. They were of opposite temperments. The soldier accustomed to changing billets couldn't understand the thrifty, pious countrywoman with no horizons. However, a letter written by Madame Rimbaud toward the end of her life[17] recalls in melancholy terms the early days of her marriage when there bloomed a moment of happiness: "There are a lot of soldiers passing through here, which inspires very strong feelings in memory of your father with whom I would have been happy *if I had not had certain children that caused me so much suffering.*" An abrupt fit of memory. The italicized part of the sentence seems to indicate that Vitalie would have been happy if only she hadn't become a mother! Obviously, there is no reason to believe this; this late and underhand manner of excusing her fugitive husband in no way excuses his conduct. Madame Rimbaud should have known that soldiers are only made for passing through!

This departure of his father was felt more strongly than has been thought by Rimbaud, who viewed it as some kind of injust punishment. It caused certain images to arise that formed an objective part of his life. That is, if it is true that a life is also a group of fictions composed by the individual's interior dynamic.

He interrogates his memory in several poems, specifically the poem that bears that word as its title. It paints a strange and disturbing scene in which names and figures can be seen forming through the course of the words that also follow the course of a river. Whoever reads "Memoire" has the impression of looking through a windowpane. At times the reader feels a need to wipe away the condensation building up on the glass. Rimbaud exhumes visions reworked by his unconscious mind: the rampart of a city "For whom a maiden was the defender," Madame, himself, young girls, books bound in Moroccan leather, a meadow. Within this dreamlike atmosphere certain phrases that have an evocative value, even if one is unaware of what they truly conceal become detached:

> Madame se tient trop debout dans la prairie
> prochaine où neigent les fils de travail; l'ombrelle
> aux doigts; foulant l'ombelle; trop fière pour elle;
> des enfants lisant dans la verdure fleurie

> leur livre de maroquin rouge! Hélas, Lui, comme
> mille anges blancs qui se séparent sur la route,
> s'éloigne par-delà la Montagne! Elle, toute
> froide, et noire, court! après le départ de l'homme!

> Madame stands too straight in the meadow
> near to where the threads of the work snow down; her parasol
> in her fingers; trampling the umbel; too proud for her;
> children reading in the flower-filled grass

> their book of red moroccan. Alas, he like
> a thousand white angels separating on the road,
> withdraws beyond the mountain! She, all
> cold, and dark, runs! after the departing man!"

It is impossible not to see this as the staging of a scene Rimbaud had perhaps never lived[18] but which he tried to set as a kind of photographic slide for oneiric usage. In a certain respect his life is also the interpretation that he gave it when he found explanations lacking. This one-way departure and the question raised by the man retreating on the road who gradually dissipated into a clear mist beyond a mountain that could simply be the Mount Olympus, whose modest heights dominate Charleville, survived in his memory as it did in that of his mother and sisters. What was left now, rue Bourbon? The young girls in their "green faded dresses," says the same fantasy text, the children holding red leather-bound books in their hands, similar to those awarded at the end of the school year. A decisive moment revised and corrected by the adolescent Rimbaud, who supplies no commentary but inscribes in black and white the same motif around which a "memory" is formed. Rimbaud's memory is constructed out of what he remembers and what he forgets. This departure (which no one could dare call inaugural) is on the verge of being forgotten. In it the father breaks the conjugal ties and leaves the mother the painful task of replacing him, which she does more in a spirit of rancor than regret. The captain even inspired a scenario by Rimbaud that often goes unmentioned because it is obscene. It so happens that Rimbaud's memory, when inspiring his writings, does not ignore the fact that childhood is made up of sexual impressions. When, he rhymes his "Remembrances du vieillard idiot" in the *Album zutique* which contains poems of burlesque inspiration he tried, of course, to distinguish himself from the person speaking, but he took advantage of this to relive certain unadmissible childhood events: "I dream of my father sometimes"; "Because a father is disturbing;" "His knee, sometimes coaxing; his pants whose fly my finger longed to open." Rimbaud is undoubtedly exaggerating. His poem authorizes a provocative, higher bid. We can imagine, though (it pleased him to let us imagine), a homosexual temptation that would not have been inconsequential. The absence of his father's speech echoed throughout his daily life. In the place of his empty presence another body formed.

After Frédéric's departure Madame Rimbaud became even more authoritarian, a comforting role for her. Certainly the spirit of fantasy, even the simplest indulgence, had always been absent from her, but we should take into account the domestic misfortunes that weighed her down. The trials of her childhood had toughened her. The failure of her marriage destroyed her most beautiful illusions. Rimbaud has always left us with the silhouette of the "mother of duty" holding a Bible in her hand. This is how she should be situated in the world of his childhood: severe and dogmatic, putting her trust in morality and religion amid of so many disappointments. Later in life, Rimbaud would never be at a loss for harsh, mocking words for her: the *mother*, the *daromphe*, the *mouth of shadow.*

From 1860 on, the life of the household depends entirely upon her energy, her will—an unsmiling will, it is true, as if, henceforth, she saw before her a gray world of irremissible tasks and desires deferred. At the age of thirty-five Vitalie is like a widow. She makes a duty out of raising her four children as best she can in order for them to attain a more respectable place in society—

well-to-do certainly—one that is superior to the peasant's milieu she knew as a child. She therefore exerts herself to give her sons and daughters a perfect education. They represent her hopes and reason to live.

Still an adolescent, Rimbaud will not forget the claustrophobic atmosphere of rue Bourbon. Here we need to read his "Les Poètes des sept ans" again. It is a veritable retrospective film lacking neither tastes nor smells. The poem unfolds to the rhythm of the seasons: "wan Sundays of December" in which time doesn't pass, days of the Lord whose greatest amusement is the mass, or else torrid summer afternoons during which the child seeks shelter in the shadows. We witness here the awakening of a solitude and a revolt. The people surrounding Rimbaud become his characters. First of these is the giant, all-powerful mother against whom he will collide all his life and who will always be there to listen to him uncomprehendingly, the womb from which he fell as an "ape of a man,"[19] a "mouth of shadow,"[20] and later on a mailbox that collected his African curses. Rimbaud takes snapshots, captures outbursts. Rimbaud, the stubborn child, the child who hurls his insults from the top of the stairs, the mocking and the lying child. And the encounter of two blue-eyed gazes, one wishing to make the other acknowledge that which is unacknowledgeable in life. And then—because the isolated Rimbaud is a fraternal being—there is the feeling that emanates from the working-class neighborhood where he lives, with its smock-clad workers, its crowds reacting to the news announced by drum and town crier, those obscure beings loved by Hugo and Zola, those anonymous human floods, future cannon fodder, future labor pools, workers today and revolutionaries gunned down tomorrow. Then, always emerging from these dark days were the poor children "stinking of diarrhea," clad in rags, whom he will love again in "Les Effarés" and for whom he has a compassion his mother deems "sordid."

At seven years of age Rimbaud is a poet and very much at home in his own depths, in the dawning experience of words and vision, when the emptiness becomes even hollower before him and starts vibrating with voices and images. It was through good fortune that his universe was not reduced to the four walls of a room or to the streets of Charleville; he found himself able to set sail in any open book. Rimbaud absorbed what he needed from everything: newspapers, magazines, serials. Though he had hardly begun to read and write, in answer to the boredom of the town he invented fragments of novels and plotted out narratives of fabulous adventures. Here he discovered an atmosphere truer than life, the extraordinary energy of a freedom with which he could resist the disgust that was already assailing him, stirring him up.

THE HUMANITIES

NOW ON HER OWN, MADAME RIMBAUD WOULD DEVOTE HERSELF TO HER children's education. Though she herself possessed only meagre intellectual abilities she was not lacking in ambition. Her efforts were devoted to her sons in particular. As a mother concerned with their future she wanted them to have the best possible education. In 1862 Arthur and Frédéric were placed as day students at the Institution Rossat on 11 rue de l'Arquebuse, an establishment that then had more than three hundred students and a superior reputation to that of a *collège*. Decidedly modern, it provided professional training as well as the traditional classical education. Rimbaud begins his studies in the ninth form.[21] His intelligence and precociousness quickly attracts attention. Each year he amasses more prizes. Are these sufficient grounds for regarding him as a model student? The surviving documents from that era, except for the appropriately eloquent honors rolls, reveal a playful child who was already a poet. With his elder brother Frédéric, a robust child with a gentle, easygoing nature, Arthur has fun like all boys his age, despite the strict, eagle eye of his mother. For them, school isn't just a new form of prison. On the contrary, it allows them to escape from under the crushing maternal thumb and play to their heart's content. Rimbaud for one finds the school atmosphere an ideal opportunity for evasion, and quickly grasps that books provide an inexhaustible resource in this regard. But beyond books he discovers the very essence of knowledge which embraces the world at first then opens it infinitely. It doesn't take Rimbaud long to discover the astonishing freedom of creation: making something from nothing or building a universe out of merely a few scraps and fragments.

He starts making up fake homework in a notebook[22] to fool his mother's constant vigilance and manufactures "his anthology" of preferred texts right alongside. He still writes timidly, almost as if in spite of himself, not knowing when copying it over if he is not already expresseing himself using someone else's phrasing, having slightly modified its syntactical inflexion and changed a few words. He reproduces passages from Cicero and the Latin poet Phaedrus, whose fables he is now learning (*"ego nominor leo"*). He reveres the dreamer La Fontaine and also writes a Latin version of his fable "'The Ant and the Grasshopper." To this he adds several portraits of renowned men of Antiquity such as Aristomenes, Cato, Croesus, all directly inspired by the *De viris illustribus*, or the classroom Plutarch. He pens passages from the Bible on Adam and Eve in Paradise, and the shepherd Abel. He also extracts a pretty *cuadro* on the flies of strawberry flowers from the *Études de la nature* by Brother Bernardin de Saint-Pierre. A real subject for recital. The style is precise as required by entomological curiosities. Rimbaud, the great recopier, doesn't hesitate to sign some of these texts with a flourish: "Arthur," "Rimbaud Arthur," "Arthur Rimbaud of Charleville."

Among these pieces chosen for his personal use he does however slip in an original composition due to his talent alone, a fictional text of two pages. It is untitled but already displays some ambition, since it begins fairly pompously with a "prologue." Here he recounts the story of his own life. Like all beginners he himself is the first object that grabs his attention. Arthur thus enters literature as if everything had already been completed. Rimbaud the child traces the novel of what he has lived and shows us its truth. Of course he acts as a connoisseur and makes use of artifices that have already proven their worth, for example, the ruse of a dream: "I slept but not without slaking my thirst with the water from a stream." He transposes his life into a curious past: "I dreamt that I was born in Reims in the year 1503." This river water does not summon forgetfulness like that from the Lethe, on the contrary, it reawakens very remote memories. A strange date, that of 1503 under the rule of Louis XII. Our young author tumbles into the historical novel like the early Flaubert. As for the holy city of Reims, it was without doubt the most prestigious of those neighboring Charleville and it is quite conceivable that the young poet wished to place himself under the protective shadow of its cathedral. The following part of the story offers a very gripping "version" of his ideal family. Here Rimbaud corrects his biography. He invents a father who is an "officer in the king's armies," "large, slender," "from forty-eight to fifty years of age," like Frédéric at the time he wed Vitalie Cuif, a man of a "lively, fiery, often angry nature." It would seem these few phrases are an absolutely true-to-life portrayal. However, Rimbaud transformed his mother into another woman who was "gentle, calm, frightened at the least thing." She is completely transformed here in accordance with his ideal vision of her. "She was so mild-mannered that my father took pleasure with her as if she were a little girl." Reading more deeply into this description, one understands that the calm extolled by Rimbaud corresponds in fact to Madame Rimbaud's cold nature and the total absence of fantasy in her character. The rest of the story is not lacking in malice. He blames schooling. What good is Latin, Greek, historical knowledge? Rimbaud slyly enjoyed mocking the academic milieu of which he was such a brilliant example. His mother believed he was busy with homework while he was scribbling out for his own pleasure a story he impudently concludes with the phrase "me, I will be a stockholder." The child penning this ironic future did not foresee the oppresive rule of work and the long years in the desert that lay in store for him. For the moment he is living a completely carefree existence in which the power of illusion transforms the forms of reality at his pleasure.

Rimbaud, the advocate of study—what could be more natural!—was also the advocate of fun and games. The same notebook contains a series of drawings wittily entitled "Pleasures of Youth" which provides an ironic perception of childhood amusements. It is not hard to see the games he played with his brother and sisters here, unless the little girl portrayed in the first and second drawing is that "daughter of the workers next door" whose buttocks he bit in "Les Poètes de sept ans," "because she never wore panties." It is a real collection of childhood marvels: a kid pushing a sleigh (it snows a lot in Charleville). A little girl proclaiming herself "Queen of the North"; the boy, a more realistic hero of the Jules Verne variety, is nervously saying, "We are about to sink." In one drawing a chair is hung from a door handle. The same little girl from the previous drawing is perched on it precariously. The boy is advising her in northern slang to "hold on a sec." In another game Arthur puts on his school uniform and pretends to say Mass with his face hidden behind a large book. Vitalie and Isabelle are kneeling before him. One of them is brandishing a doll and irreverently shouting, "This thing needs to be baptized." "Agriculture" is a vignette depicting a plant posed on a windowsill that induces astonishment or pride in spectators. "Navigation" commemorates a more dangerous game to which the two brothers were then readily

devoting their energies. Here, the smaller of the two freshwater sailors is lift-
ing his arms toward heaven and crying "Help!" A true detail? Later on, Delahaye, our most reliable witness when it comes to evoking Rimbaud's youth,
always asserted that when he was a young *collégien*, the young brothers would
amuse themselves tugging a barge back and forth across the Meuse by pulling
on its mooring chain.[23] Overly perspicacious minds haven't failed to compare
this diversion to the future verses of "Le Bateau ivre." Instead let's leave these
schoolboys innocently bickering on their craft, momentarily elated at leaving
the shore, but anxious about the pitching caused by their disorderly movements, or else dazzled by their reflections in the constantly rushing waters.

To the contrary of Frédéric, who was beginning to assert his vocation as a
dunce, Arthur distinguishes himself at the Institution Rossat with his excellent schoolwork and lively wit. In the eighth form he obtains the prize of
honor. His talents as a Latinist are noted (grammar and theme) in the seventh,
but he also counts among his school prizes an honorable mention for calcu-
lus. Every year his diligence is rewarded by a great many books "in red
moroccan" of an exemplary morality. Some pleasant surprises can be found
leafing through the well-meaning passages that weigh down these educa-
tional pieces of prose. Several titles attract attention among the volumes
rediscovered by P. Berrichon.[24] We can safely ignore the *Beautés du spectacle de
la nature* by the Abbé Pluch, an eighteenth-century providentialist and instead
latch on to the *Robinsons français* or the *Robinson de la jeunesse*. Rimbaud,
amply provided with desert island colonizers, manufactures from them a
verb for sentimental purposes: "The wild heart Robinsons through novels."[25]
Yes, novels are dream traps and master smugglers of other places. Nothing
matches their unverifiable distances for placing a golden age where "delighted
freedom," that which was one day stolen from men, is shining, gleaming yonder in those wide-open spaces that the pioneers were beginning to discover.
But Rimbaud wasn't safe from contradictions. He had written: "I will be a
stockholder." It certainly calls for a less modest ambition to conquer the
West, as extolled by Mayne Raid, another classical author for the young
chronicling the saga of America's untamed lands in the footsteps of James
Fenimore Cooper.

For the moment he is a relentless reader, a budding poet or novelist (he
finds this prospect exhilarating), an obedient son whose emerging personality

already distinguishes him from others, a fact Madame Rimbaud notes with pride. Her pride in her children is revealed by the impeccable procession they formed going to eleven o'clock mass on Sundays. The two girls would head up this parade, followed by their brothers, with Madame Rimbaud bringing up the rear. The Carolopolitans didn't jeer out loud at this solemn spectacle but instead laughed up their sleeves. Vitalie spends no time with anyone outside her immediate family. Stubborn in her isolation and embittered by the impossible failure of her marriage, her pride is all that holds her together. She is unshakable, a stranger to tears. Arthur, who shares every child's dream of a tender mother, nonetheless feels her suppressed sorrow is appropriate. He may not find the affection he seeks, but understands the reason for its absence. So books, study, the vast continent of ancient languages, and poets become substitutes for the tender words he longed to hear and the truly happy gaze he longed to encounter.

In October 1864, Rimbaud enters the sixth form. In the class photo taken that year, Rimbaud, seated with his kepi on his knees and strapped in his uniform, stares at the cameraman, looking sullen and discontented, as if irritated that such a ceremony has been foisted upon him. For reasons we don't know and possibly pertaining to the quality of teaching offered at the Institution Rossat[26] (which many then thought too progressive), he is enrolled in the *collège*, along with Fréderic, after Easter 1865. This will be his introduction to the strict secondary studies of that time. In addition to the mandatory religious instruction, the scholastic program continued to develop the student's reverence for Greek and Latin antiquity. Other areas of study, notably the sciences, often were neglected. The school's primary task was the molding of an elite who would become tomorrow's leaders. In those days it was thought that the art of writing and speaking well was essential. The schools used a two-part procedure to impose their authority on the still-malleable minds in their care. In the first phase (which lasted until the third form), the teachers strove to instill the French language and style with the use of illustrious models. The students simply reproduced the original texts assigned by the teacher. Dictation, reading, and recital were the principal elements of such a pedagogy. In the second phase these original texts were translated various ways to teach students grammar and the logical workings of the language. Of course there was no question of any student commentary upon the texts they studied.

Implicitly considered perfect and beyond criticism, they belonged to the sacrosanct patrimony of studies. The author selection enforces a dominant ideology that is in accord—do I need to make this clear?—with the mentality of the established order. From the sixth form to the third the students were therefore condemned to repeat through various procedures what had been written and thought by the Ancients, who were regarded as an unrivaled reference. Since the genius of the French language had its source in Greek and Latin, generations of school-boys had to slake their thirst from the same sad and reverential manuals. Rimbaud undoubtedly owned the *Éléments de la grammaire latine et de la grammaire français* by the Abbé Lhomond, choice morsels from the *Epitome*, and the inevitable *Gradus* crammed with ready-made formulas for fashioning beautiful Latin hexameters. Exercises of French dissertation appeared, starting only with the third form. The work primarily consisted of imitating the appropriate models, which allowed for the handling of *topoi* (the commonplaces that involve the treatment of a subject) and the emphasis of tropes (rhetorical figures).

The Charleville *collège* certainly gave a better impression than did the Institution Rossat, even though its interior was dilapidated and shabby.[*] It looked over place du Saint-Sépulcre (today it is place de l'Agriculture) and occupied the ground floor (the municipal library was on the second floor) of a building of an ancient congregation of Sepulcrines dispersed by the Revolution. It was flanked by a seminary and a chapel. The convent of the canonesses, who had returned in 1828, abutted its right corner. On the other side of the square were several bourgeois houses and some tannery buildings overlooking the Meuse. This is what Rimbaud saw when entering or leaving by the *collège's* stately porch. Arthur and Frédéric arrived together from 13 cours d'Orleans, where they now lived (in 1866, Madame Rimbaud moved the family to 20 rue Forest). They were no longer in the same class. Frédéric's penchant for study was of the most modest degree while Arthur earned top honors for his efforts. But both brothers were identifiable at a glance by the identical severity of their dress. They wore bowler hats, black jackets that contrasted sharply with the impeccable whiteness of their shirts, and pants of

---

[*]The buildings were restored in 1866–1867 with the arrival of the new principal, Monsieur Desdouet.

slate blue cloth.[27] This sober attire would not change over the years. The bowler hats especially smack of an excessive severity. Frédéric quickly exchanged this head gear for the kepi worn by his fellow students, but Arthur, who detested uniforms, ostentatiously kept his. In addition, each of the boys always sported an umbrella, regardless of the weather.

During the second trimester of the sixth form in 1865, Rimbaud is placed at the head of the class, where he soon distinguishes himself by an analytical summary of ancient history that astounds his teacher, Monsieur Crouet. This exceptional schoolwork makes the rounds of the school and the principal, Monsieur Malard, congratulates its author.[28] This occurs perhaps at the same time Rimbaud maliciously notes in his secret journal that knowing the history of "Chinalon, Nabopolassar, Darius, Cyrus, Alexander, and other cronies notable for their diabolical names" was nothing less than torture. This is quite revealing of the double nature, even duplicity, he was not averse to using. We can be sure that he was now fully aware of the game imposed society forces the individual to play and that he strove to provide himself with an agreeable facade while feeling on the inside the first flames of an inextinguishable revolt.

In the fourth form he fell under the strict authority of the old Monsieur Pérette, saddled with the nickname of "Père Bos," for which several Rimbaldian biographers have desperately sought a plausible explanation. The bafflement this has caused is hardly warranted. Père Bos was undoubtedly one of those shortsighted instructors, completely convinced of their own knowledge and importance who are always suspicious of precocious intellects whose clarity is so blinding it remains invisible. Pérette, no doubt favorably forewarned of Rimbaud, turned his nose up before the alleged prodigy. And when the principal boasted of the merits of this remarkable recruit (assuredly a future student at the Ecole Normale Supérieur in Paris!), he would have gotten this reply: "All you could wish for! His eyes and his smile don't please me. I tell you he's going to come to a bad end!"[29] A superb gift of prophesy! This Carolopolitan Cassandra would not have been remembered by posterity but for his illustrious pupil, who did, in fact come to a bad end, but went on in a much better fashion. Notwithstanding, Rimbaud didn't detest this hardworking boor who revealed to him such unforgettable works of beauty as Virgil's *Aeneid* and Ovid's *Metamorphoses*, and most important, initiated him into the rudiments of Latin versification. This exercise has been forgotten in our time but was once a chore to which the youth of *lycées* and *collèges* had to comply meekly. This other language, with its turns of phrase and vocabulary, was of great importance for Rimbaud. The compositions in dactylic hexameters on assigned topics required stutents to observe numerous constraints and forced them to perceive the structure of words, even their tiniest components, as well as the value of the shortest syllable. The Rimbaud of 1867 excelled in these academic exercises, which appear to have hastened the first stirrings of his genius.

One event marks this year. I am referring to the inevitable first communion that no well-meaning family could afford to neglect. The children, their souls polished by the priests, incessantly whitewashed their consciences. For several weeks, they were possessed by desire for saintliness. Rimbaud didn't escape these fleeting surges of naive mysticism. His mother attired him in new clothes. The great day with its ritual arrived. No doubt some members of the Cuif family from the area had been invited for the occasion, but not the undesirable Charles, who had too great a penchant for profane libations. Arthur and Frédéric posed before the photographer, Monsieur Jacoby[30] wearing white gloves and white armbands. Each is holding his book for mass. Both have their hair slicked down with sugar water and well combed with an implacable part. Frédéric is standing up, and Arthur is seated, staring straight ahead with a disturbing curiosity.

One testimony survives concerning the religious Rimbaud of that time. One Sunday, as the students were leaving chapel (this account is from Delahaye) the older students, taking advantage of the absence of the class monitor, played around, spraying one another in the face with holy water from the font. Rimbaud, all alone and with all his thirteen-year-old strength, hurled himself on his impious classmates and tried to put an end to their sacrilegious behavior, until a monitor arrived who gave the major guilty parties harsh detentions. From this quarrel, Arthur momentarily earned the nickname of the "little hypocrite,"[31] a label his adolescent rebellion soon made debatable.

There is nothing more monotonous than academic life despite the uproars raised by the students, the sometimes laughable professors, and the race for top honors. In the third form, Arthur hears the teaching of Father Ariste Lhéritier, who swore only by Boileau, he whom the romantics described as "antiphlogistic." They may just as well have said killjoy. Out of bravado Rimbaud allegedly handed in a sort of pastiche of "Repas ridicule" and "Lutrin." He is also said to have composed a style of critical study outdoing the requirements of the author of the *Art poétique* and even made an effort to pick out a few minor errors in the works of the "legislator of Parnassus" himself. In fact, he confined himself to shortening the long notice to a manual of *Études littéraires.*[32] His talent as a Latinist also found opportunity to give itself free scope in a more audacious endeavor. Knowing that the young imperial prince was about to take his first communion, Rimbaud sent him an epistle in Latin verse, the contents of which are not known, incidentally. A certain Jolly, who was one of Arthur's schoolmates, recounts the anecdote in a letter to his brother:[33]

> You no doubt know the Rimbauds; one of them (he who is now in the third) just sent a letter in sixty Latin verses to the little imperial prince concerning his first communion. He kept this in the greatest secrecy and hadn't even shown his verses to his teacher; he also made some mistakes seasoned with a few false verses. The prince's private tutor just responded to him by telling him that His Majesty's child was touched by this letter, that like him he was a student and with good heart excused him his false verses. That was a sharp lesson for our Rimbault [*sic*], who wanted to make an impulsive act showing off his cleverness. The principal paid him no compliments.

This missive proves many things. It indicates an independent temperament, great self-assurance already (Rimbaud believes in what Jolly called his "cleverness"), and finally, the birth of an ambition that does not deny the kindred approaches of poets then in vogue. Rimbaud in no way writes for himself alone. He strives to make himself known— for him, a way of life. As withdrawn and uncommunicative as he may be, he still feels a need for attention from the other to exist. As his studies filled his well-formed head he took advantage of them; he had his piece to say and he said it. Soon he began to express himself in those Latin verse compositions that are the first fictional works allowed (in another language). He thus avoided the ridicule of the neophyte versifiers, but not without putting a little of himself to the test.

It is now 1869. Madame Rimbaud again changes apartments.[34] This time she moves to 5 *bis* quai de la Madeleine, on the banks of the Meuse, quite close to the *collège*—which can only facilitate Arthur's studies. This house still exists. It is open to visitors, a plaque has been mounted on it, and the great Beat generation figure Allen Ginsberg clearly saw the poet's ghost when sleeping there in 1982, a fact he later confided to several of us on the road to Roche.[35] There is nothing inviting about its great black facade but in spite of the busy road named quai Arthur-Rimbaud that separates the building from the riverbank, one can see a part of the landscape that Rimbaud saw on a daily basis from the ground floor when he wasn't in his own room, which looked out over an inner courtyard: the movement of the river, the passage of the seasons on the trees, the high walls of the Old Mill. And further on, if one closes one's eyes and dreams, are the sea, voyages, escape.

Rimbaud's new professor, when he enters the second, is not at all like the strict, irritable Lhéritier. Monsieur Duprez is a young man, a fan of the Romantics, certainly not the most unbridled ones, but Hugo, Lamartine, and the Musset of *La Nuit de mai*. For Rimbaud, henceforth a victim of his reputation as the head of his class, only outdoing what he had already done was permissible. On November 6, Duprez gives an assignment of writing Latin verses starting with an ode by Horace in which the old poet evokes his childhood and the beginnings of his vocation. It is no difficult task for Rimbaud to compose "a schoolboy's reverie." "Ver erat" (This was spring.) A word to the wise is enough! The schoolboy (whom he invents) forgets the dull school and charmless lessons of the teacher (*tristia verba magistri*). The rest of the assignment develops a melodious vision that ends with Apollo appearing to the dreamer and inscribing on his head these words in capital letters: TU VATES ERIS ("You will be a poet"). This imaginary scene in which Rimbaud perhaps gives himself a coronation lacks simplicity but how could writing in dactylic hexameter have any other result! The academic jury awarded him the prize despite some impertinent remarks he let fall in this strict exercise. For the first time in his life Rimbaud is published—for having said better than others that he would be a poet. The poetic review is called, in very academic fashion, the *Moniteur de l'enseignement secondaire. Bulletin officiel de l'académie de Douai*, a title that is a bit long and one with which the Parnassians would hardly have been familiar. The work is signed on three printed lines: "RIMBAUD, Arthur, private day student of the collège of Charleville, born in Charleville, October 20, 1854." While still in Monsieur Duprez's class, the Latin scholar emeritus will repeat his crime with an improvisation based on a poem by Nîmes author Jules Reboul. This is a very moving piece that recounts the death of a child torn too soon from the affections of his family, but who appears to his mother in the form of an angel. This modest work of poetry will have such an effect on him that, faithful to the doctrine of imitation advised by his teachers, he will use it as inspiration for the first of his works written in French, "Les Étrennes des orphelins."

However Rimbaud was not only a reserved and studious schoolboy; he had several friends with whom he already was discussing literature. As the *collège's* star pupil he was quite intimidating. The young Ernest Delahaye, who came from Mézières and fooled around in class on the same bench as Frédéric, had heard his neighbor speak of the prodigy: "My brother is splendid!" an adjective then in vogue and which a great literary mind, Jean Paulhan, would be happy to use later. After several false starts Delahaye made Arthur's acquaintance; as is known, they became good friends. The nature or power of fate is such that Rimbaud would soon be frequenting the company of his La Boétie, his inseparable witness. They were soon joined by Labarrière, a fellow student who was courting the Muse and burning to recite his verses to his friends. Thus formed, unbeknownst to Madame Rimbaud, a small group in which, of course, Arthur acted as chief and ringleader. He and his confederates now took long walks in the areas surrounding Charleville or else strolled through the streets of the town and on place Ducale, where one day an American circus strayed, dazzling them all evening with its unseemly pomp.[36] They casually discussed books, politics, and lively girls (less is known regarding this subject). They carefully read the newspapers. Later they would attempt to become contributors.

In addition to the family-oriented *Revue pour tous*, *La Veillée des chamières*, and the attractive *Magasin pittoresque*, one of the great dream purveyors of the time, they are quite familiar with the Parisian sheets that reached Charleville. Opposition journals had multiplied since 1868, when the new press law was proclaimed by the liberal Empire. Some of the more striking were *Le Réveil*, *Le Rappel* (organ of the Radical Democrats founded by Hugo), the baton of which was soon picked up by *La Marseillaise*, and especially the extraordinary

Lanterne of Rochefort, a small booklet about sixty pages long with a red-orange cover, whose first issue began with this phrase: "France contains thirty-six million subjects, not counting the subjects of discontent." To these were added *Le Figaro* of Villemessant and *Le Petit Journal* for the serials they provided, and many illustrious satirical publications such as *La Charge*, *Le Charivari* (available continuously since 1830), *L'Éclipse*, and the "marvelocerous" *Lanterne de Boquillon* in which the brave soldier writing to his fellow rustics accumulated "incorrect liaisons" in a language so droll that Rimbaud quite naturally adopted it to garnish his everyday conversations.

The world of the *collège* formed a prisonlike milieu in which the flowers of rhetoric bloomed and sometimes withered. The outside world smells of life, free air, but a life that keeps its secrets. Rimbaud and his friends are not ignorant to the realities of misery. He has seen it up close in the Bourbon quarter. Every Sunday he passes by the indigents parked on the pew for the poor. He knows the hard toil of the workers, the "smocks," and the thankless tasks of women. At fourteen years of age he already has some ideas on the subject of politics. He who once wrote, perhaps hypocritically, to the young prince imperial now declares to Ernest Delahaye that Napoleon III, now saddled with the nickname "Badinguet" by his opponents, deserves to be sent to the galleys[37] and that the Empire is a bunch of rogues. He admires *Les Châtiments*. Hugo remains over on his island, a larger-than-life figure of poetry and exile. When Delahaye proudly informs him that he had read the tract *La Lanterne* in a Belgian cabaret, Rimbaud exults.[38] Since the debut of this publication in May 1868, each issue had been met with legal proceedings. And in an assignment given by Abbé Vilhème, his history professor, he proclaimed like a true bousingot[*]: "Robespierre, Saint-Just, Couthon, the *young* await you."

Literature also was discussed. Sheltered by the walls of Charleville were several bookstores among which was the Jolly establishment at the corner of place Ducale and the rue du Moulin. Arthur never had any money, but he skimmed through the books there or consulted those his friend Labarrière bought and then generously passed on to him. He was especially interested in *Parnasse contemporain*. This publication appeared in the form of thirty-two-

---

[*]The name given to young anarchists in France around the time of 1830—translator's note.

page booklets with blue covers, and had been published regularly since 1866 by Alphonse Lemerre, the publisher in passage Choiseul in Paris who had gathered around him the best poets of the new generation. Here Rimbaud discovered the recent works of Théophile Gautier, *L'Exil des dieux* of Banville, the first sonnets of Heredia, Leconte de Lisle, and, in the fifth booklet—a surprise choice—fifteen new *Fleurs du Mal* by Baudelaire.* Since 1869, a new, more substantial series was being published. Several of the pamphlets passed on by Labarrière that were carefully annotated by Rimbaud—who indicated his reservations and preferences in the margins—have been discovered.[39] The first issue consisted of "Kaïn" by Leconte de Lisle, a large composition that greatly inspired Arthur. He marked ninety-two of the poem's hundred verses with a vertical line indicating their appeal to him. In the second issue, partially devoted to Théodore de Banville, Arthur admired "La Cithare," especially for its final verses. On the other hand, "Les Ballades joyeuses" and "Comédie" by the same author seem to have left him indifferent. The third issue contains a jumbled assortment of poems by Sully-Prudhomme, Verlaine, Ernest d'Hervilly, Lefébure, and Madame Blanchecotte. Rimbaud appreciates Verlaine's work but makes fun of the verses of the poetess and derisively corrects some of them. *"J'ai porté bien lourd mon chagrin dernier"* becomes under his pen: *"J'ai porté bien lourd mon chignon dernier."***

One year followed the next in this sleepy little town. Nothing happened. The courses at school flowed as impertubably as the Meuse. Principal Monsieur Desdouet continued to place all the school's hopes on Rimbaud. With Madame Rimbaud's permission he was now given private lessons. This "gifted child" was being prepared. He was not actually regarded as a Lamartine in the making in that up to then he was noted less for his French compositions than for his excellent and prize-winning Latin verse. At the end of the second form he once again distinguished himself on the most laconic subject:

---

*These were "Épigraphe pour un livre condamné," "L'Examen de minuit," "Madrigal triste," "À une Malabaraise, "L''Avertisseur," "Hymne," "La Voix," "Le Rebelle," "Le Jet d'eau," "Les Yeux de Berthe," "La Rançon," "Bien loin d'ici," "Recueillement," "Le Gouffre," and "Les Plaintes d'un Icare."

**My latest grief has been a heavy burden for me" is replaced by "My latest bun is a heavy burden to me"—translator's note.

"Abd el-Kader."[40] This one evoked many historical memories. Lieutenant Rimbaud himself had written this name countless times in his reports from Sebdu. Over a period of six hours without stop Arthur composed ninety-three hexamaters that he prefaced with a classic epigraph borrowed from Jean-Louis Guez de Balzac: "Providence sometimes has the same man reappear in several centuries." A pretty remark, but hardly prudent when applied to Rimbaud himself! It at least served his immediate purpose in that, as an expert student of ancient history, he sought to establish a scholarly parallel between Abd el-Kader and his ancestor Jugurtha. To conclude his assignment, he didn't neglect to flatter the Emperor, who in 1853 had finally freed the Kabylian sovereign held prisoner in France since his final defeat. "Deliver yourself, my son, to the new God," counsels Jugurtha to his modern successor. In fact the Rimbaud writing these verses had no such belief in the *"novo Deo"* whom he regarded more as a tyrant oppressing France. A year later he won't have enough harsh words to denounce Napoleon III, the "Pale Man," who was drunk from twenty years of power during the course of which he had wished to "blow out freedom" "like a candle."[41]

A PROFESSOR
NAMED IZAMBARD

FOLLOWING THE AUGUST-SEPTEMBER VACATION OF 1869, WHICH WE ASSUME was uneventful (it is not known if the Rimbaud children went to the farm in Roche during that period) Rimbaud enters the *première*. This is the famous first form, whose name (rhétorique)* is in itself a complete curriculum. His professor is Monsieur Feuillâtre. Rimbaud begins to write his first poems. He has already noted that the *Revue pour tous* sometimes publishes texts by its readers. For the upcoming New Year's festivities, he conceives his "Les Étrennes des orphelins," a long poem in five parts that is strongly influenced by Victor Hugo's "Pauvre Gens" and Reboul's "L'Ange du Berceau." Beauties, alongside the obvious missteps, are scattered throughout. His secret tenderness and sympathy are paramount in these verses that trace an intimate scene taken straight from his own life. Two children are abandoned in a room. Their father is far away and their mother has just died. The orphans are recalling happier New Years of times past and believe that the funeral decorations, inscribed to them with the words of remembrance "To Our Mother" are the new toys given them for this occasion. In this moving, compassionate poem, abandonment and illusion assume their full meaning. This is the first Rimbaud to find his voice, preceding the poet who will seek to transform the realities of life into a magical art. Favorably impressed, the editors of *Revue pour tous* advise the author—with a short paragraph inserted in the newspaper—to reduce his piece by one-third if he wishes for it to be used. Rimbaud decides to attempt several cuts and on January 2, 1870, has the pleasure of seeing himself published—an event in which Madame Rimbaud herself cannot help but rejoice. Arthur the grind clearly sees that

---

*What is now called *classe de première* was in the nineteenth century called the *rhétorique*, meaning "rhetoric"—translator's note.

---

embarking upon a literary career will not be so difficult if he knocks on the right doors.

The same month Monsieur Feuillâtre is transferred to another school. He is replaced by Georges Izambard, a young twenty-one-year-old teacher.[42] An arts graduate, his previous posting had been in Hazebrouck, an area close to his adopted town of Douai, where he had been raised by his maiden aunts, the Gindres. His pudgy face is framed by sideburns, and often lit up by a benevolent gaze sparkling behind a pair of pince-nez. Hardly a strict pedant, he was rather a simple-mannered and quite likable individual. He immediately catches his students' interest and even stirs their passion. Before meeting Rimbaud, he had heard boasts of his skills from Monsieur Desdouet, who never shrank from any opportunity to sing his praises. But it isn't the "monster of the competitions" and excellent student who arouses his interest, but rather an awakening mind ready to be launched toward the wonders of poetry. Rimbaud, whose later ingratitude toward Izambard will be all too evident (this was his customary conduct toward those who befriended him), feels he has finally found an adult who truly understands him, listens to him, and takes his literary projects seriously. In Izambard he has met a kind of older brother whose erudite learning hasn't smothered his curiosity for life and, while certainly constrained by the strictness of the teaching profession, is a lover of the nobler arts and, like Rimbaud, capable of secret revolts against the opulent society of the Second Empire. A close accord seems to have existed from the outset between the professor and the student. This often destructive kind of relationship created the best possible results in but a few months' time. Izambard, whose retiring personality is by no means a sign of mediocrity, provides the indispensable encouragement Rimbaud needs in his first bursts of creative joy. Until then Delahaye had been the friend, and a kind of alter ego and lesser genius. Izambard's value is that of an accompanist, someone who takes the least possible advantage of the mentor role he would have been able to play. While guiding Rimbaud with his critical impressions as his first reader, he experiences an irresistible attraction to this neophyte poet whom he does not view as a disciple, and in whom he senses the outline of an adventure—whose outcome may become either pitiful or prodigious.

Still proud of his "Les Étrennes des orphelins," not so much for its true merits as for the fact of its publication, Rimbaud is now taking seriously what had been at the beginning only a game. A game that was undoubtedly more abstract than others but just as satisfying: writing. The texts selected as subjects of French composition are a constant source of creativity for him. Where he is called upon to imitate, he rapidly invents. Certain examples of his schoolwork continue to plagiarize their models: for example, his "Lettre de Charles d'Orléans à Louis XI pour demander la libération de François Villon, prisonnier à Blois."* He composes a cento out of a web of quotations adroitly strung together in a medieval language straight from Villon himself, whose works Rimbaud has paged through.

In the sealed environment of Charleville, books circulate like rare oxygen for captive thoughts. Izambard lends several volumes to Rimbaud because he knows the maternal library is extremely poor. Arthur finds himself briefly in possession of Theodore de Banville's *Gringoire*, a smart comedy in prose of which he particularly likes the ballad of the "Verger du roi Louis," and *Notre-Dame de Paris*, of which certain daring descriptions, such as Esmeralda's loves, hold his most enthusiastic attentions. However, nothing gets past Madame Rimbaud. Coming across this novel that she moreover mistakes for *Les Misérables*, she sees only the author's name: Victor Hugo[43] the Republican, the outlaw, the man who spits upon the Emperor and hurls his irascible *Châtiments* from his island. She immediately sends a letter to Izambard requesting he keep a better eye on the books he lends his students and returns the incriminating volume to the principal. Izambard is then ordered by the principal to apologize to Madame Rimbaud. She first greets him with a lesson on political submission condemning the socialist Hugo, terror of the Throne and Altar. While listening to her unflinchingly, Izambard discovers the restrictive environment in which his pupil lives. It gives him a greater understanding of Rimbaud's revolt and astonishing lucidity.

Indeed, the assignments he now hands out transform as if by magic under his student's pen into poems regularly deposited on the teacher's chair at the end of the lesson. During this effervescent period Rimbaud, with singular precision in a never before heard language (despite the imitative features it contains), demonstrates his total mastery of a vision that blends dreams and

---

*"Charles d'Orléans' letter to Louis XI Requesting the Release of François Villon, Held Prisoner in Blois."—translator's note.

reality. In the wake of his "Letter to Charles d'Orléans," he soon composes not a ballad but a hanged men's dance in which the shadow of Saladin, one of the "always moving spirits" from Dante's *Inferno*, can be seen. This frenetic tableau of a macabre strength proves he has read Baudelaire at this time, if only the pieces published in the *Parnasse* of 1866. His poems don't seek to stubbornly speak of languid sorrows and the fevers of adolescence. They are not intended as remedies or balms. Their worth lies in the perfection and rightness of the words and the unforeseen quality of their images. They can also be animated by a satiric spirit, such as in "Le Châtiment de Tartuffe," which begins to sketch out one of those grotesques that the skillful silhouetist Rimbaud will later parade before us. Sometimes the canvas of a composition in Latin verse, such as his "Ophélie" inspired by Shakespeare, inspires melancholic and passionate stanzas whose color illuminates texts that echo the accent of a limitless freedom as vast as the sky. The air of bewilderment he borrows from Hugo is his means of discovering another space beyond words and forms. These first attempts take on the air of masterpieces. Moreover, their perfection leaves Rimbaud with only one solution if he wishes to continue writing: to go further and surpass poetry itself.

Encouraged by Izambard's understanding, Rimbaud also begins to refine that dark sense of humor he will retain for the rest of his life. For the moment he limits himself to detecting the shortcomings of his contemporaries, that community of adults he too will soon join. This talented draftsman draws his caricatures in a notebook or on the pages of an old atlas when opportunity arises.[44] Reality, which he can no longer tolerate except when he's turned it into a game, soon furnishes him with the subject of one of his most successful caricatures. This time he writes it.

The *collège* of Charleville had welcomed the students of the neighboring seminary[45] to its classes since 1808. They took the same courses as the regular students. The competitive atmosphere that resulted often degenerated into outright hostility between the two camps and Rimbaud, the star pupil of the *collège*, quite naturally transformed himself into the champion of his classmates, who were also less numerous than the others. Annoyed at this overcrowding and animated by his recent study of *Tartuffe* (the man in black with clerical bands), as well as additionally inspired by his reading of Lamartine's *Jocelyn*, Rimbaud improvised a prose piece in the guise of a poet seminarian's notebook. Its "author" is completely overcome by his recent meeting with a foolish young girl with the delicious name of "Thimothina Labinette at his parents' representative in town." He entitles these "intimate thoughts" "Un coeur sous une soutane." They testify to a talent for observation that makes us regret the rarity of works by Rimbaud the storyteller. There can be no doubt that we are in the presence of a brilliant schoolboy who takes hold of tiny events and transforms them into comic situations with scintillating verve. Of course he is only attacking his neighbors the seminarians and priests whose unctuousness and dubious morals he mocks. He is not yet the absolute denigrator of society.

During these months of total creativity, Rimbaud shapes himself as a poet in tune with his growing body and his expanding senses that are soaking in the world in their fashion. He hesitates between tones, experiments, enters the rigorous realm of prosody with an astonishing freshness, even if his head is stuffed full with cultural souvenirs, among which are books his mother would have condemned even more rigorously than *Les Misérables*. Izambard has lent him Baudelaire's *Les Fleurs du Mal* and undoubtedly other volumes from the *Complete Works*, which were then published by Michel Lévy. Baudelaire provides him the key to a universe of both heaven and hell in which true poetry demonstrates its fundamental, inevitable cruelty. The term "seer" in Gautier's preface strikes Rimbaud in particular. He marvels over the *Paradis artificiels* and comes to a total standstill before the rigorous singularity of the *Petits poëmes en prose*. Izambard even entrusts him with extremely obscure collections, for example, *Les Vignes folles* by Albert Glatigny,[46] a cursed poet before the fact, a wandering minstrel by trade, a mad lover by temperament, and a poet to the ends of his black fingernails. However, still under the spell of the style of Hugo (that of the author of *La Légende des siècles*), Arthur wishes to try his hand at the great historical tableaus and hammers out his "Forgeron"—ample proof of his sympathy for the sans-culottes of 1792 who demanded the head of Louis XVI. He is inspired by an engraving illustrating a page in Thiers's *The History of the French Revolution* depicting the butcher Legendre on the night of August 10, 1792, seeking to adorn the head of the sovereign with the famous red cap (with which Hugo wanted to adorn the dictionary). Ominously Arthur takes the part of "the riffraff." The good student is already rising in revolt and not only against his mother, the *collège*, and the priests. He desires the fall of the Empire. He will not have to wait long for this collapse.

However, during the same months he dabbles in the mythological genre because of his great interest in the new school revealed to him by the *Parnasse contemporain*. "Credo in unam,"[*] a blasphemous title, parodies Catholic ritual and draws an almost erotic image of woman. No doubt Rimbaud has not yet experienced physical love, but he knows how to speak to us with a surprising sensuality about the awakening of nature and its vernal power. With the luxuriance of Banville and the ideas of Musset, he turns back to the gods of paganism and attacks the gloomy religion of the crucified one—a rebellion he will soon accentuate in poems of pure blasphemy. Original in his use of words, he is less so in the ideas he develops. These are traced from the grand Parnassian themes displayed previously in the art-for- art's-sake poetry of Gautier and the vast compositions of Leconte de Lisle. Next to these pieces, definitely weighed down by the ambition animating them, he creates some admirable short verses. Among them are the two quatrains of "Sensation" in which rhetoric is abandoned for a true relationship with the moment expressed in a subtle fashion, even if this moment is primarily the formation of an impossible image by words. The future Rimbaud can be found here using the future tense to launch his phrases into the verbal realm, where they are further propelled by the outline:

SENSATION

Par les soirs bleus d'été, j'irai dans les sentiers,
Picoté par les blés, fouler l'herbe menue:
Rêveur, j'en sentirai la fraîcheur à mes pieds.
Je laisserai le vent baigner ma tête nue.

Je ne parlerai pas, je ne penserais rien:
Mais l'amour infini me montera dans l'âme,
Et j'irai loin, bien loin, comme un bohémien,
Par la Nature,—heureux comme avec une femme.

---

[*]Now titled "Soleil et Chair"—Translator's note.

On blue summer evenings, I will follow the paths
Pricked by the wheat, I tread over the short grass
Dreaming, I will feel its coolness on my feet
I will let the wind bathe my bare head.

I will not speak, I will think of nothing:
But infinite love will rise in my soul;
And I will go far, far away, like a Bohemian,
Through the countryside—happy as if I were with a woman.

A poem of intoxication certainly (like that of flower-crowned Ophelia before she drowned), but essentially this is a victory for the very simplicity of poetry when Rimbaud says "pricked by the wheat," when he suddenly notices that the grass is "short." He gives expression to his longing for escape. At first it is a simple promenade no different from other walks in the surrounding areas of Roche, but then for a moment the bar of the horizon is surmounted: one is suddenly far away, the village steeples are now invisible. Rimbaud, in the future tense, takes a deep breath to launch himself into this breach and project himself into his beloved silhouette—the Bohemian, Nodier's king of the seven castles, or the man of the "prophetic tribe" praised by Baudelaire. It is enough to read this Rimbaud from the spring of 1870 to know that the adolescent is in complete possession of his means and that, despite the revolt of "Le Forgeron," he feels the appeal of a completely natural beauty quite different from the illustrious marbles embodying that of the Greeks.

Love? The *collège* student, not yet sixteen year's old, was of the same mind on this subject as Delahaye and Labarrière. He invents several lively, airy poems, which proves he had already read Verlaine at around this time. "Première Soirée" and "Les Reparties de Nina" are addressed directly to a young girl and recount a scene of seduction that would have earned him a couple smacks if discovered by Madame Rimbaud. With his forehead pressed against the windowpane in reverie and watching the new leaves stirring on the trees, he attempts some gestures and imagines some mutinous lines. Does he walk in the countryside toward an impossible bliss, toward kindness— a word that often reappears under his pen as if to conjure away all manner of misfortune—with the same glimpse of the street he has while walking to the *collège* or along the banks of the Meuse? The tense is always future, scattered with conditionals. Only the last verse, Nina's reply, brings us back to reality: "And my office." Rimbaud wants no part of a near setback and always keeps a dream in reserve to make up for a temporary defeat. He also sometimes touches on more dismal areas. In his more secret poems he destroys the happy images he erects in others with such audacious confidence. In his "Venus Anadyomene," who is "hideously beautiful with an ulcer on her anus," he ravages with rare violence the woman who is the very epitome of beauty.

The month of May, the month of love, is also the month of birth. "Tu vates eris," "You will be a poet," he once wrote in a Latin verse composition. Confident of his genius, he addressed a letter to Theodore de Banville, a recognized master. Despite his celebrity, Banville, was by no means a pontificator. In tandem with several others he looked after the fortunes of *Parnasse contemporain*. He had originally lived the life of a bohemian and frequented Baudelaire, who thought highly of him. His poetry pursued a trend inaugurated by Gautier that played marvelously with rhyme in an atmosphere of eternal fantasy. This work moved Rimbaud with its jubilation and virtuosity. On May 24, 1870, Arthur wrote to the "Dear Master," in a lively and playful style. At times he confused the trends: "The poet is a Parnassian," he asserted without hesitation; but he also considered Banville a "true Romantic," a descendant of Ronsard, "a brother of our masters from 1830." His desire? He didn't take pains to conceal it: to be published in the latest edition of the famous *Parnasse contemporain*, a sort of permanent anthology that would assure him precocious consecration, before he had even put together a collection of his verse. Hence his sending of "Credo in unam" which would then become (of this he had no doubt) the poet's Credo. He included two carefully copied-over quatrains of "Sensation" and his "Ophélie."

There is no need to insist on the impatience with which he must have awaited a response. He had simply written the address of Alphonse Lemerre, 47 passage Choiseul, on the envelope. We know Banville responded.[47] But it isn't known in what terms. Though he hardly would have discouraged the author. The poems weren't accepted, though, and the disappointed Rimbaud felt no obligation to inform his friends and family of this illustrious but undoubtedly reserved and prudent reply.

The wonderfully tentative poetic exercises to which he then turns his attention do not distract him from his studies. He gives Izambard complete satisfaction when he again wins first prize in Latin verse composition in the academic competition and Monsieur Desdouet rewards him with a copy of La Bruyère's *Les Caractères*, which he dedicated personally.[48] In June he again takes part in a competition. This time the subject is Sancho Panza bemoaning his dead ass.[49] Arthur had also excelled with a Latin translation, "Invocation of Venus." But in this instance he had recourse to a low ruse that went unnoticed by the teachers. In fact he copied over a recent verse translation of Sully-Prudhomme, merely improving it to his liking. His graders—we have to believe—were not assiduous readers of the Parnassians. Rimbaud was able to fool them at little cost.

However, the school year drew toward its end. Enjoying greater freedom, granted despite his mother's recriminations, Rimbaud scoured Charleville from one end to the other with Delahaye and often accompanied his friend to Mézières. While en route they exchanged many ideas that Delahaye later claimed to have preserved in his memory. On Sundays they would go listen to the military concerts at place de la Gare. On July 10, 1870, the Sixth Regiment plays, among other captivating pieces, the "Polka-Mazurka of the Fifers." It is hot. The bourgeois gentlemen poke the sand with their canes and talk about treaties because relations with Prussia are becoming more and more strained. Couples stroll across the avenues. The *pioupious*[*] are courting the maids. Rimbaud takes it all in with a glance. This world he detests so heartily, this world of anti-poetry, is all there, reduced to several "types." Routine and vile serenity. Harmonious oompahs that arouse his scorn. In a corner of the picture he can be spotted like a scruffy student (those of whom Vallès will soon speak), following the "lively young girls" with his eyes. During these first days of summer did he experience the semblance of an idyll? His attentive companion Delahaye states that meetings were arranged with a young girl of good family.[50] In a poem dated September 29, 1870 (probable date of the cleaned-up version), Rimbaud will attempt to repeat his "novel." The young lady walks next to her father, some Monsieur Prudhomme type wearing an enormous

---

[*]*Pioupious* are the common French foot soldier of the era, distinguished by their red leggings—translator's note.

---

detachable collar like those in which the caricaturist Daumier buried the chins of his worthies. She wore adorable "little boots." Arthur plays the bashful lover, though he "puts on airs," drinks beer, writes some verses for his beauty that he dubs "cavatinas," and his exercises of style were briefly appreciated. He is "rented until the month of August" a commingling of rental and praise!* After which the idyll is ended.

Now that the school year is over his ties with Izambard are strengthened. Younger and elder are hardly five years apart and both possess an ardent love for literature. In the evening Arthur walks his deferential friend back to his apartment "*sous les allées.*" Often they get together there with Deverrière, professor of rhetoric at the Institution Rossat, and Caroline Gindre, one of Izambard's aunts, who has come to spend several days at the home of her godson this July.[51] Deverrière is a jovial, cultivated young man who is an enthusiast of liberal ideas—as will be shown by his subsequent career—and journalism. Mademoiselle Gindre brings to mind another resident of Douai: Marceline Desbordes-Valmore whose works will later claim Rimbaud's attention. But these pleasant days won't last, and without waiting for Rimbaud's triumph at the awarding of the prize on August 6, 1870, Izambard leaves Charleville with Deverrière, whom he has invited to stay for several weeks. Rimbaud sadly accompanies them to the station to bid them farewell.

Notwithstanding, the time was no longer right for poetry or even the charms of friendship. On July 19 imperial France declared war on Prussia. The emperor's boastful gesture would cost his regime dearly and fatally. The people, especially those living close to the border, were now in a state of great unease. The residents of Charleville were among these latter. The citadel of Mézières filled with armed troops. In fact, the declaration of war under a false pretext sought to restore—following a quick campaign—the prestige of the Empire that recent social disturbances (for example, the demonstrations on the occasion of the burial of Victor Noir) had weakened considerably, despite the illusory plebiscite of May 8. The entire army was ready—or so it was said. Victory was not in doubt. Émile Ollivier asserted that the enemy could be confronted with an "easy heart." Already revenge-minded, the Bonapartist

---

*The word play here is not translatable. The verb *louer* means both to rent and to praise—translator's note.

newspapers blew on the embers. Certain hack journalists such as Granier de Cassagnac and his father didn't hesitate to contrive impossible combinations to sharpen the bellicose mood of their readers. They went so far as to evoke the heroism of the sans-culottes. Rimbaud, after reading their stupid comparison in *Le Pays*, writes "Morts de quatre-vingt-douze et quatre-vingt-treize," in which he tactfully recalls the "millions of Christs with dark, tender eyes" of the armies of the Republic. By upping the ante of the beliefs he expressed in "Le Forgeron," Rimbaud demonstrates his admiration for the revolutionaries. Shortly before Izambard's departure, he had shown this sonnet to his friend, a fellow antibonapartist, who had admired its polemical tone and rightful resentment.

He must now exhaust the long vacation period stretching before him on a day-by-day basis. A delivery from Paris momentarily diverts his attention, the satirical journal *La Charge* has accepted and published his poem "Trois Baisers":* "She had very little clothing on." But what is the point of such trifles when people speak only about the war and the dead. He keeps up with events and is even spellbound by the catastrophic news. By good fortune Izambard gave him permission to visit his apartment whenever he pleases to make use of his extensive library. He has only to request the key from the owners.[52] Many wonders await him in this haven. He devours everything, completely at random and with no preconceived notions.[53] There are keepsakes such as *Le Diable à Paris* published by Hetzel, whose whimsical drawings by Grandville hardly enthrall him, and popular novels such as *Costal l'Indien* by Gabriel Ferry, an adventure tale that André Breton will receive as a prize in primary school years later, and *La Robe de Nessus* by Amédée Achard. He pages through the Gustave Doré illustrated Don Quixote and even reads the bottom of the barrel with Sully-Prudhomme's *Les Epreuves*. He even sinks so low as to read *Les Glaneuses* by Paul Demeny, a work of afflictive banality. Yet Izambard has spoken to him about the novice Demeny who was one of his friends from Douai. Rimbaud could become acquainted with him when the time came. He also buys a few books. His mother may have provided him with a little money or, as a less elegant solution, he sold several of the books lent him in order to read new ones. Furthermore, he does not refrain from

---

*The original title of *"Première soirée."*

stealing out of bookstore display windows should the opportunity arise. This is how he obtains*Les Rayons perdus* by Louisa Siefert. This book was very talked about in 1870, and only in 1870. He admires this work of a noteworthy insipidity, proof that his tastes are not yet established and that he can still be moved by sentimental and hackneyed old stories, just as later he will find naive refrains enchanting. He loads his shelves with other works: *Florise* and *Les Exilés* by Banville, *Les Nuits persanes* by another poet, Armand Renaud, *Les Couleuvres* by Louis Veuillot the polemicist, an issue of the critic Pontmartin's *Nouveaux Samedis*, and finally some incomplete *Parnasse contemporain* pamphlets. Next to these hardly sustainable feelings of admiration, he has already taken note of the mutinous originality of the Verlaine of *Fêtes galantes*.

But aside from the pleasure he derives from these readings, Rimbaud finds his isolation barely tolerable, as he would rather be sharing everything he is thinking and writing. The letter he sends to Izambard on August 25 sparkles with scorn and vitality: "My native town is the most supremely idiotic of all small provincial towns. I am disoriented, ill, furious, stupid, dumbstruck; I had hoped for sunbaths, endless walks, rest, travel, adventure, bohemian escapades in short; I had especially hoped for newspapers and books. But nothing! Nothing!" Charleville, threatened, encumbered with soldiers, became a grotesque place: "Because it sees two or three hundred *pioupious* rambling about its streets, this benighted populace gesticulates like a bully-boy Prudhomme, quite a difference from the besieged of Metz and Strasbourg. It's terrifying, retired grocers wearing their uniforms again. It's shocking to see what sex appeal this has—notaries, glaziers, tax collectors, carpenters, and all the big-bellied who, *chassepot* over their hearts, are patrolling the gates of Mézières; my country is rising up! I prefer to see it seated; don't get all riled up! that's my principle." Peerless lucidity from Rimbaud, who certainly didn't take after his father (then in retreat to Dijon but still wanting to take on the Prussians).[54]

His satiric vision restores in chic terms the laughable bustle of that era's braggarts flaunting cheap heroism. He discovers the horrors of war and pities the "cannon fodder" handed over to the German armies, even if the majority of the French, from bourgeois gentlemen to workers, had only one cry at first: "To Berlin! To Berlin!" a wretched, swaggering motto that in several months the assailant would render null and void by reaching Paris. Hostile to an emperor who in his opinion was only an "old itch," Rimbaud henceforth notes on a daily basis the errors in which the French army, concentrated specifically in the Ardennes region, are getting entangled. MacMahon seeks now to join with Bazaine, still obstinately billeted in Metz. On August 25 he goes to Vouziers. All of Charleville watches these troop movements. Some people even saw Napoleon III. Undermined by his suffering from kidney stones, he fights the pain with daily doses of opium. His pale and made-up face is frightening, like a visible premonition of disaster. The peasants sometimes ask the soldiers where their long columns are heading, and the veterans, who triumphed at Malakoff or Solferino, yell back with no pretense: "To the slaughterhouse!" In the closing days of summer, Rimbaud, who often with his friend Delahaye, went as far afield as Mézières, site of resistance against the Prussian advance, composed the calm and tragic tableau of his "Dormeur du Val." A young man slightly older than he appears to be relaxing in "the cool blue watercress." But the cradle of greenery in which he is sleeping reveals—by the very movement of the poem that draws the reader near—the two red holes he is wearing on his right side. Rimbaud's revolt is no longer just a rowdy activity or a frenzy that has no point of implementation: it overflows with humanity and justice.

He reads the news ardently, at least what news makes it to Charleville to be dispensed by the traditionalist and jingoistic *Courrier des Ardennes*. He knows though that not everyone accepts this war. It has been condemned in Paris by the members of the Internationale. The president of the Council, Émile Ollivier, the "comrade in glasses,"[55] had confidently announced it but the Prussian army turned out to be stronger and better trained. To tell the truth, Moltke and Bismark had only been waiting for the chance to attack the French army and demonstrate their superiority. A first engagement with the enemy on August 2 was rewarded by a minor success that was quickly transformed into a "stunning victory" in images of Epinal. But after this lucky day in Sarrebrücken, the French troops suffered defeat after defeat, in Wissemburg, Reichschoffen (despite the heroic charge made by MaMahon's cuirassiers), Forbach, and Saint-Privat, where Bazaine came ever so close to carrying the day. He was now staying put in Metz, acting as if he believed it possible to join the emperor's troops with his own. In fact he was saving himself for a political future that his cunning could not guarantee him.

Irreversible disaster was approaching while the empire vacillated; a new era was traced out on a horizon of fear and blood.

To speak of Rimbaud is to inevitably speak of his episodes of running away; it so happens that he was not the first child of Ma Rimbe's who sought to desert the family dwelling. At the time the victory at Sarrebrücken supported the illusion of an easy victory, Arthur's elder brother Frédéric had dogged the steps of a regiment of infantrymen crossing through Charleville. He had joined their ranks and followed them in the direction of Metz, heeding only his precocious patriotism. The soldiers quickly adopted this unexpected recruit and entrusted him with minor tasks. Frédéric will only get back to 5 *bis* quai de la Madeleine only in November, when all military hopes for the eastern front had been annihilated. Even if this anecdote should be mentioned only with the greatest reservations it may be useful to take it into account to better explain Rimbaud's own wanderings. Delahaye relates it with the utmost conviction and it allows one to presume a spontaneous audacity in Frédéric that for his younger brother would not have been inconsequential.

At the end of the month of August, having exhausted all his books, Rimbaud decides to leave. He could have run away quietly to rejoin his friends in Douai, safe from any danger. But now he's looking further ahead. He seems to have been contemplating this scheme from the twenty-fifth, at least it would seem so from the postscript in one of his letters to Izambard: "Soon, revelations on the life I that am going to lead after . . . vacation." His correspondent may have wondered about the ellipsis points that maliciously interrupted the wording of the phrase. For Arthur, deprived of all news and sensing the imminent collapse of the empire, one action is imperative: go to Paris. He has no money and getting there on foot will definitely take too long, not to mention the insecurity of the countryside. So he sells some books— Izambard's or school prizes—and takes the train. Isabelle Rimbaud's husband, Berrichon, has provided a specific version of this moment. Madame Rimbaud, as she did every day in the summer, would have taken her children on a walk along the banks of the Meuse, where her son easily gave her the slip. The poem "Mémoire" is supposedly a reflection of the circumstances surrounding this abrupt departure.[56] Nothing else supports his opinion. Still the fact remains that Rimbaud premeditatedly climbed aboard a train at the

Charleville station. Trains were rare. War rendered the means of connection all the more hazardous as the battle of Sedan, some twelve miles from there, was taking place at that very moment in the worst conditions for MacMahon and the emperor, who had been caught in the trap of its citadel that the enemy had quickly surrounded. Since the direct line to the capital was cut, Rimbaud had to follow another route and go up by the northern railway into Belgium. His money was dwindling and Paris was getting farther away. At Charleroi he had only a small amount remaining, just enough to go down as far as Saint Quentin. But desire overpowered him and he continued beyond that point without a ticket. However, police surveillance had been intensified. Spies were feared. In Paris train tickets were scrupulously verified. Getting off at the Gare du Nord, Arthur didn't escape the ticket checkpoint and he who thought he had found the path to freedom instead found himself apprehended and led between two gendarmes to the prefecture, where he was interrogated. He lied about his age, declaring, as he did in his letter to Banville, that he was seventeen. He was forced to confess that he didn't know anyone in the capital. From that point he was considered a vagrant, a vagabond. And the fact that he came from Charleville—practically a border town—aggravated his case and made him suspect. Following a quick interrogation, during which he showed some impertinence to the examining magistrate (such are Izambard's remarks, inspired by Rimbaud himself, who perhaps was bragging), he was conducted to boulevard Mazas (Diderot, today) and the famous prison of the same name. Perpetrators of serious crimes were incarcerated here. Rimbaud became nervous, and rightly so. After the standard shower and disinfection, he obtained writing materials and sent several letters: one to the imperial procurator (but, at that very moment, the defeat at Sedan had doomed the empire), one to the police inspector of Charleville, one to his mother, and lastly one to Georges Izambard, in whom he especially places his confidence for he fears, and for good reason, the reprisals of the *mother*. It is clear that he found in this young professor turned friend all the emotional support that until then had been lacking in his life: "*My hope is in you* as in my mother; you have always been as a brother to me"; "I love you as a brother, I shall love you as a father." An urgent request, an almost frantic appeal: "If you receive no more news from me by Wednesday, before the train that leaves Douai for Paris, *take that train, come here to reclaim*

43

me by letter, or by presenting yourself to the procurator to intercede, *to vouch for me, and to pay my debt! Do all that you can.*[. . .]" Izambard, then on vacation in Douai, was alarmed by this communication. He immediately did what was necessary for Rimbaud's freedom, paid the debt of thirteen francs and, in this instance, demonstrated the most generous devotion. Several days later, Arthur, freed from prison, arrives at the station of Douai,[57] as direct connections to Charleville from Paris are still impossible. The traveler was expected. He had just lived his first adventure. An adventure he can now continue under the best auspices, since he was welcomed by Izambard's aunts to the rue de l'Abbaye-aux-Prés, in a quiet district of the town where they owned a pleasant home. Rimbaud already knew Caroline, whose two sisters he now met (did all three become "Les Chercheuses de poux" under his pen, diligently seeking to clean his hair of the vermin picked up at Mazas?). Rimbaud found himself in congenial company with them as well as with Izambard and Deverrière. Subjects for conversation weren't lacking, all the more so as during the fugitive's incarceration, the Empire had definitively fallen. Napoleon III had been vanquished at Sedan. The republic had been proclaimed on September 4. In Paris, the crowd massed on the place de l'Hôtel-de-Ville and cheered Rochefort, Flourens, and other illustrious war resistors at the very moment that Rimbaud was imprisoned in the same neighborhood. A government of National Defense headed by General Trochu was concerned with more urgent matters. The situation remained confused, however. The different political parties were weighing their chances before the future elections for the National Assembly. Resistance was organizing with the greatest difficulty.

Meanwhile, starved for reading material, Rimbaud, comfortably settled in a room on the third floor of the house, at first dips as he pleases into the large library located there. One day, Izambard sees him with a book of Montaigne in hand, dazzled by several phrases concerning poetic inspiration: "The poet, seated on the tripod of the Muses, furiously pours forth all that enters his mouth, like the gargoyle of a fountain, and there escapes from him things of diverse substance, contrary substance, and an uneven flow." Will Rimbaud be thinking of such expressions later, when he speaks about "the reasoned derangement of all the senses"? During his stay in Douai, he will repeat these few lines so often, like a password, that sixty years later, Izambard, from having heard them persistently drummed into his ears, will still hold them in his memory.

The occupations of the "vacationer" were not confined—one would guess—to long periods of reading, shut away in a room. Far from maternal surveillance, his primary sensation was one of marvelous liberty. Despite the remonstrations of his mother, who was already harassing him to return in haste to Charleville, he didn't care one whit about returning to his "supremely idiotic" town. He liked Douai; a certain agitation animated the town. The national guard had been reestablished throughout the whole of France. Izambard, exempt from military service because of myopia, didn't hesitate to enlist. Rimbaud, who wasn't old enough to take up arms, accompanied him. But, for lack of real rifles, the drills were performed with brooms! Outraged, Rimbaud wrote a protest letter in a truer administrative style than is permissible. A "mumbled jargon" is how Izambard excellently describes it. Rimbaud's former professor was the keeper of this extraordinary document intended for the mayor, Monsieur Maurice, but which didn't reach him for want of signatures of bona fide petitioners.[58]

Public life was reestablished. In Douai, Rimbaud, Izambard, and Deverrière made certain to attend the preparatory meetings for the next municipal elections. A diverse assembly was held Friday, the twenty-third of September on rue d'Esquerchin. Certain candidates, most often known for their reactionary political opinions, did not hesitate to place their names on several slates (of which one was the party of "appeasement!"). Soon, though, following a series of violent discussions, their strategy was discovered and a single slate called "democratic" was formed. With caustic concision Rimbaud wrote up an account of this meeting and submitted it to the *Libéral du Nord* (a small newspaper of which Izambard was head editor for the moment), which will publish it as a brief article on the "local news" page. This was his journalistic debut. He will make yet many more such attempts, though from what we know most were doomed to failure.

The situation France was going through (this ambiance of drifting, uncertainty, waiting) was well matched to Rimbaud's idleness. To a certain extent, it coincided with those great appeals that echo through adolescence, a time of premonition and uneasy hopes. He had not abandoned poetry, far from it! And Izambard had introduced him to one of his friends, a twenty-six-year old poet named Paul Demeny, whose first book, *Les Glaneuses*,[60] published in Paris by the Librairie Artistique,[*] Rimbaud had casually paged through. Rimbaud certainly retained nothing from these mediocre pages in which poetry is reduced to a strict observance of the rules of prosody. But Demeny had had the honors of being published. The publisher was also a friend of the family, which might explain the reason this book, despite its obvious infelicities, was published. Arthur, more interested by these material opportunities than Demeny's literary ideas, did not hesitate to copy over all the poems that he had written to this point and knew by heart for him. Settled into his third-floor room, he covers large sheets of paper with painstaking penmanship and thus creates his first collection of verse. But he does not have the time to finish it. Madame Rimbaud, who had already written Izambard a threatening letter on September 16, sends him an even angrier missive[61] a week later. She finds it inconceivable that her son could still be delaying his return. She even begins to think that he may have run away again: "On the other hand the police are taking steps to find out where he has gone, and I greatly fear that before the receipt of this present letter, the little scamp will get himself arrested a second time, but in that case he won't need to return anymore, for I swear on my life that I will not take him in again." Rimbaud knows that his mother does not "swear" in vain. By obstinately clinging to his short-lived happiness he was taking a strong risk of becoming a man without a family, like his Uncle Charles, whom Madame refuses to see. Understanding the gravity of the situation, Izambard advises him to return. To soften the blow he proposes to accompany him, as he has to get back his books "sous les allées." However, he planned to leave soon after (a patriotic Republican, he had in fact taken leave from his post, and though exempted, had enlisted in the mobilization of the northern region).

The trip takes longer than expected. To reach Charleville, one has to go through Belgium. One can imagine the mood of the *mother*, awaiting her son. Luckily Izambard took him back to the family residence, which initially sparing him from the backlash of her built-up anger. Rimbaud felt no need to get

---

[*]Demeny also provided this publishing house with a one-act comedy, *La Flèche de Diane*, 1870.

off easy, however. In any case, complaining about it would have been a repudiation of his desire for freedom that was worth the incurrence of such trials.

Once again, it is necessary for him to learn to live with boredom. He misses Douai. He impatiently awaits the news from Paris, where the conflicts between exacerbated republicans and partisans of law and order, between proletariat and bourgeoisie, worsen on a daily basis. This is the moment Rimbaud makes his choice. He will be the incorrigible one. October is when he crossed the invisible frontier that made him a major rebel. Henceforth he knows he is moving into the unknown. Without alerting either Izambard or Deverrière of his intentions, nor paying any more heed to the maternal lectures, he again takes to the road. His mother thinks that he has relapsed into evil ways and is headed for Paris again. But with what money? She hastily consults Izambard, who, wishing to visit the battlefield of Sedan, had not yet returned to Douai and is stupefied by his former student's audacity. We have some idea of the vagabond's itinerary, however. Rimbaud left for Fumay to see one of his friends. His disappearance took place on either the sixth or seventh of October. It is now the eighth. Izambard, more devoted than is wise to the elusive Arthur, starts off on the "rambler's" trail.

Rimbaud, little concerned with the pursuit he risked provoking, willingly responds to this call to travel that will spur him on for the rest of his life. The elsewhere takes shape and blows in his face. "But how salubrious is the wind!" he will later say. What is he looking for? To get away? But it is just as much to get somewhere. To be en route toward an unknown destination whose incandescent beauty he foresees. What is yonder? Ophelia? Nature? The father who one day disappeared on the wide-open road? Certainly, his odyssey is still only a fantasy and his vagabonding has several secure stopovers in reserve.[62] First is the home of Billuart in Fumay, a small town of slate buildings located on a bend of the Meuse. He arrived there perhaps by train, since his poem "Rêvé pour l'hiver," dated October 7, bears the precision "On board." It is dedicated to a mysterious "Her," followed by three asterisks, which seems to correspond to the girl who was the recent inspiration for "Roman," and even "Première Soirée." This (irregular) sonnet is nevertheless a dream and the Rimbaldian tense, the future tense, is dominant here in effrontery and temporary solution. The Billuart family gives the school egghead boasted of by the son of the household their hospitality for a night. Rimbaud does not linger in this charming town, whose Spanish-style houses border the embankment of the Meuse, but in true Bohemian style pursues his route on foot in the direction of Vireux, where he counts on being housed by another schoolmate, Arthur Binard. He stays there only a short while; still following the river, he reaches the river port of Givet in the evening. The town is dominated by one of Vauban's citadels. Seagulls sport with one another over the water, where barges pass. Rimbaud sleeps there, invited to stay at a barracks of the state security police. In his own way he is leading the bohemian life, not the Parisian and miserable one of Murger (he will have plenty of time to become acquainted with that style), but that of a rover protected in heaven by the Big Dipper and the rustling of the stars, a new version of the music of the spheres. The next day he crosses the border without any further mishaps and by the end of the afternoon reaches Charleroi. Binard had given him a little money. He passes before an establishment with the surprising sign: "Au Cabaret-Vert." In fact whoever enters there takes a bath in the color green: all the furniture inside is painted that color. Starving, he orders a solid meal: bread and butter, some ham still warm and flavored with a clove of garlic, all washed down by a tall mug of beer. Momentarily lending a face to the Muse is a sweet and lusty waitress with enormous tits who finds this boy of sixteen attractive. It is a marvelously Rimbaldian moment of simple joy, a single stage of an exhausting itinerary that only death will halt. It is five o'clock in the evening. Rimbaud could find love. At his table, the entire future stretches before him. Nothing is lost, nothing yet. And he writes his poem in a single line in the color of the time.

In Charleroi, he planned on negotiating with Senator Xavier des Essarts, the owner of the local paper. With the wealth of his experience behind him *in partibus* as a gossip columnist at the *Libéral du Nord*, he wishes to be hired as an editor. According to Izambard, hot on the trail of Rimbaud, the young man aired highly abusive opinions about the leading figures of the day to this des Essarts, who was first attentive to the words of this adolescent he had cordially invited to share his table. Shocked, des Essarts politely asked him to leave. There was nothing left for him to do but pursue his headlong flight. Brussels was not far and no doubt he was clever enough to sneak aboard a train again. Definitely on foreign ground, his feet burning from boots that were too tight, he finally enters a city where he knows only one single address that he heard mentioned by chance during a conversation between Izambard and Deverrière: that of Paul Durand. He finds the street, knocks at the door, and mentions his friend's name. At once he is affably received. He is housed and fed for two days. When he takes his departure, to visit Belgium and round out his education—so he claims (and it is not a complete lie)—he is clad in clean clothes, a new tie, and has money in his pocket. Perhaps he has seen enough, though. In any event he finishes his journey and returns not to Charleville—that would have been too easy—but to the Gindre home, where he hopes to see Izambard again. In fact, that latter who had laboriously followed his trail, finds him there following a detour to Brussels. Again Rimbaud invites himself to the rue de l'Abbaye-aux-Prés and spends time with Demeny. The evenings extend into the late hours discussing politics and literature. Everyone is talking about Bazaine's shameful capitulation. When he finds enough time (but he knows full well that his mother, finally assured of his presence in Douai, will not delay in making her presence felt), Rimbaud finishes the notebook that he had half filled in September. He adds to it all of his most recent poems, a grouping of sonnets that reconstruct several moments of his vagabonding. Madame Rimbaud storms in the distance. A letter addressed to Izambard (one can imagine in what tone) enjoins this latter not to return the scamp as on the first occasion (the result was so deplorable that nobody would want to repeat that experience), but to place him in the hands of "the authorities" who will repatriate the juvenile delinquent at the expense of the state. Izambard forces Rimbaud to listen to reason; he balks but once again resolves to bid farewell to the Gindres. He is then entrusted to the police. The teacher and the student shake hands as comrades. They had no way of knowing this would be the last time they saw each other. For almost a year letters will maintain the ties of a friendship that will be revealed as more and more fragile as their literary opinions grow further apart and as Rimbaud, won over to the ideas of the Commune, gains confidence and assumes an air of superb intransigence.

HISTORY

RIMBAUD'S RETURN TO CHARLEVILLE HAD EVERY APPEARANCE OF AN admission of defeat. He had balked and shaken off the yoke but the force of things had proven too strong. However, he had gleaned some images of "free freedom" that he would hold forever. Some of them will later enamel the *Illuminations* but for the time being his situation is hopeless. He finds himself back in the same town busy with its mediocre resolutions among an inept bourgeoisie from whom he increasingly sought to distinguish himself, for example, by keeping his hair long, which attracted sarcastic comments from passersby. He paced back and forth across place Ducale and through the streets encumbered by armed soldiers. There was no longer any question of devoting himself to Greek or Latin. He knew their secrets. And what good were these studies of the humanities now? The burden of war and vigorous political polemics had abruptly rendered so many years of study in ignorance of reality null and void. Rimbaud, completely immersed in the present, now scorns mythology and the gods of Parnassus. In any case it will be a long time before courses resume at the *collège*. However, Madame Rimbaud, with her characteristic kindness, had already informed her son of her plans to send him to boarding school at the start of the next year to mend his ways, an insupportable prospect for one who has just tasted the joys of full independence.

He quickly sends a letter to Izambard, who still understands him so well: "I am dying, I am decomposing in dullness, in wretchedness, in grayness. What do you expect? I am bent upon the adoration of free freedom and . . . so many things, that 'it's cause to be pitied,' wouldn't you think?" Torn between his desire to clear out once and for all and the necessity of keeping the promises he made, Rimbaud emphasizes the need for affection flooding him, though until now he has experienced only the "deserts of love"[*] and the indifference of women. "If it were a question of doing something for you I would die to do so—I give you my word." And he signs it as "this 'heartless' Rimbaud. A quote? Somebody else's description of him that he repeats to his own detriment? Has the true nature of the passion and almost amorous complicity that drew Rimbaud and Izambard together been truly assessed? Izambard will not mention it, perhaps out of innocence. However, Rimbaud will discover the inverse form of physical love later!

Now a resigned prisoner of the whims of history, all he can do is wait. He chooses to devote himself to some serious idleness, something that is not always without merit for a poet. In this stretch of time interrupted by alerts and "franc-tirades"[**] (as he calls them), he discovers another time, that of the poem, which deducts from daily life its share of sights and surprises, and transforms them as if with a magic lantern. Although prey to boredom, Rimbaud remains a reality detector with a constantly active mind. His idleness is a method of opening himself to curiosity, thirst, or depravity, among other things. We will see his cultivation of these variants, giving to laziness its share of invented wonders.

Though he unfortunately no longer sees Izambard, he does continue to frequent the journalist Deverrière, with all the necessary precautions. He also has plans to renew ties with his friend Delahaye. All of Charleville had gloated over the recent jaunts of little Rimbaud. The perfect student was now a poor rascal; many families forbid their sons to have anything more to do with this poor specimen who put on bohemian airs with his long hair falling to his shoulders, a Gambier at his lips, and a rebellious attitude. On a beautiful November afternoon,[65] Arthur walks to Mézières, where he enters Madame Delahaye's grocery store. Ernest, known as Delahuppe, is there. The two friends fall into each other's arms. They have so much to tell each other. The delighted Delahaye accompanies Arthur all way back to the quai de la

---

[*] The sheets of text by Rimbaud bearing this title are difficult to date. Although they note the dreams of "a very young man," dreams dominated by women, servants or socialites, it is likely that they were written in a later period: 1872 or 1873.

[**] A pun on the French words *franc-tireur* ("irregular combatant," "maverick") and tirade ("soliloquoy," "tirade")—translator's note.

Madeleine. Taking countless detours to lengthen the pleasure they have in each other's company, they exchange impressions of recent events and talk casually about whatever comes to mind. If Delahaye, although quite reluctantly, has been placed in an ideal position—Mézières, a fortified city, was indeed one of the objectives of the Prussian offensive—Rimbaud, for his part, is still enchanted by the ups and downs of his recent travels. Henceforth they will frequently see each other.

The *collège* is still closed, allowing them to take endless hikes together. From Mézières they head toward Saint-Julien, traversing an entire complex of fortifications, and enter the "Bois d'Amour," where they smoke cigarettes that they roll with great care (twelve grams of tobacco being worth twenty centimes). Rimbaud recites the poems from his Douai notebook or else, like a magician, pulls from his pocket the latest books he loves: novels such as *Hard Times* by Dickens, *Madame Bovary* by Flaubert, *Les Amoureux de Sainte-Périne* by Champfleury. Rimbaud at this time seems to be devoting all his attention to a realistic style of expression: the precise observation, the ironic description of human foibles, the caricature. This Rimbaud is not very well known yet he definitely existed. It is his voice we hear in the majority of poems Rimbaud composed between the autumn of 1870 and the summer of 1871. For the moment he appears to be fascinated by the very essence of life, never as a cause for melancholy because of its perpetual flight, but captured, rigorously harnessed, and stripped down to the profound energy that animates it. To hearten themselves, the *collégiens* on forced vacation also reread the verses of Rimbaud's popular edition of *Les Chatiments*: a blue brochure with tiny letters.

In Charleville several original minds entered political life. As in Douai, the creation of the republic had provoked the appearance of many local papers. To counter the *Courrier des Ardennes* representing the most conservative camp of the bourgeoisie, the clearly rebellious *Le Progrès des Ardennes* was started. It was headed by Monsieur Jacoby, a "character" and old neighbor of Rimbaud's family when they lived on rue Forest. Monsieur Jacoby exercised the still uncommon and rather mysterious profession of photographer. After the December 2 coup d'état, his anti-bonapartist opinions had gotten him banished. He could now finally get his revenge by starting a democratic newspaper. Rimbaud, decidedly seduced by journalism (but for him it is a means of publishing his poems—he hasn't forgotten his previous submissions to the *Revue pour Tous* or to *La Charge*), first expedites several verses to the editor. This latter lets him know by a brief article that the time is not suited for "rustic tunes from a panpipe" (Delahaye remembered this expression). Undiscouraged, the two companions, who now haunt a gardener's cabin they discovered near the Bois d'Amour, enthusiastically concoct some satiric articles. Rimbaud rustles up a sort of mocking story: a drunken Bismarck is looking at a map of Europe. Through jerky gestures he indicates the city of Paris, sets his pipe down on that part of the map, nods off under the effect of the alcohol, and soon wakes up with his nose stuck into the still burning bowl of his pipe. Delahaye admits to having made some straightforward remarks about Bazain's treason. The two sidekicks are careful to use pseudonyms: Charles Dhayle for Delahaye, Jean Baudry for Rimbaud, who claims thereby to embody the magnanimous hero of a then popular play by Auguste Vacquerie.[66] In his own way he wished to be a righter of wrongs. Jacoby, who little appreciated these dissimulations, wishes to force the mysterious authors to unmask themselves; he therefore publishes a polite little note in his paper: "Messieurs Jean Baudry and Charles Dhayle. Your articles interest me, but lower the flap of your mask a little, if you please."

Arthur and Delahaye perhaps would have consented to this when a new event shook up the fragile security of daily life. Following fruitless negotiations the Prussians attack the citadel of Mézières, which they light up with a new kind of fireworks at this year's end. Shells rain down on the old town, caving in the roofs of the houses and toppling their walls. The dead are piled in the streets. The worst is feared in Charleville, which the enemy has spared to this point. Two days after the bombardment, the journal *L'Étoile belge* lists the entire Delahaye family among the victims. Alarmed, Rimbaud makes his way to Mézières. He takes note of the ruins but luckily finds his friend. The bombardment has destroyed the family's grocery and damaged many homes, though. Among them is the Devin printing shop where *Le Progrès des Ardennes* had resided. But Devin, a small-scale phoenix, would soon be reborn from its ashes.

Over the following days, Rimbaud, left to his own devices, goes to the village of Prix, where the stricken Delahaye family had taken refuge, then to the closer hamlet of Theaux, where they settled next. The weather is severe. The streams have iced over. Often it snows. What does it matter! The friends tramp about the surrounding countryside: Warcq, Evigny, Warnécourt. They often cross the paths of Prussian army *"tringlots."** Rimbaud recites new poems to his companion, some of them dedicated to the war dead, such as "Les Corbeaux," others of a scatological vein like those "Accroupissments" in which Brother Milotus listens to his tripes twittering in the moonlight. They also air their opinions on current events. Despite a heroic but poorly organized resistance, the Prussians have reached the area around the capital and are bombing Paris. At the announcement of this news (but one is never sure of anything one hears), the majority of the French believe the end of the Republic is imminent and territory will soon be handed over to the enemy. On January 28, in order to save Paris, the armistice is signed to the shame of the people. Favre, by signing the official document, blinks and spills an "aqueduct" of crocodile tears.

The February 8 legislative elections clearly emphasize the difference between the provinces, the conservative-leaning "countryfolk," and the large cities carried by the republican left but not the "reds," comprised of the Blanquists, and other radical groups. The National Assembly, which meets in Bordeaux, now contains 400 royalists, the Gentlemen of Kerdrel of whom Rimbaud will soon speak. The republicans are less numerous by half.

On February 17, the small-minded Thiers, whose *Histoire de la Révolution française* Rimbaud had read, was named the head of the executive branch of power. The county, exhausted and bled dry, undergoes a humiliating period it will not be able to tolerate for long. The proletariat and the republicans feel they have been deceived by the government, which they think has entered into secret agreement with the enemy to crush the revolutionary party that had been advancing its claims to power over the previous year.

When the Parisian delegates learned of the decision to abandon the eastern provinces of Alsace and Lorraine to the Prussians they resigned, not out of a jingoistic reaction, but to protest the increasingly bourgeois defeatism of a majority ready to make any compromise. As poorly informed as he may have been in Charleville, Rimbaud knew the facts. His admiration for the Parisians grows with his knowledge of the wind of revolt that has been long

---

*Slang for "soldier" in French—Translator's note.

blowing over "the holy city." Attempts to snuff it out have been made since October 1870. The government of National Defense fought it with more tenacity than the enemy. But the word "Commune" already carried all the hopes of the workers and the little people. Félix Pyat coined the word in the September 20, 1870, issue of *Le Combat*. It was taken up enthusiastically at various demonstrations of the extreme left. On October 31, following Bazaine's surrender, the mob led by Vaillant, Flourens, and Blanqui had invaded the Hôtel de Ville, while at Versailles, Monsieur Thiers—him already!—was vainly trying to negotiate a first armistice. A slightly greater effort would have ensured the installation of a Committee for Public Safety, but the red leaders were incable of finding agreement and the government they threatened was delivered from receiving its just desserts by the battalions in its pay.

In February 1871, with the Charleville *collège* then serving as a military hospital, some courses resumed in the building housing the municipal theater.[68] Rimbaud, claiming that he is hardly suited for "treading the boards," momentarily envisions retiring like a hermit to a quarry cave in the Romery woods, where he and Delahaye meet to smoke their pipes and read poems. Soon he makes the more radical decision to abandon the family home and, following to the perfectly rehearsed scenario of the previous year, takes the train to Paris, impatient to know what is happening there, and to be where the action is. Did he have some scheme for finding work there? Had Demeny provided him with some advantageous addresses?[69] Later letters allow this assumption.

Getting off the train at the Gare de Strasbourg on February 25, he is under the impression that the energy of his revolt will find kindred spirits. He lives his first days there alarmingly out of touch with reality. He finds an uneasy Paris threatened by the enemy and betrayed by its leaders. The national guard are patrolling almost everywhere. These units have not had their weapons taken from them whereas the regular army has been stripped of their weapons in conformance with the articles of the armistice. This reserve of men, often equipped with chassepots, an excellent rifle model taken from the regular troops themselves, gives the streets of the city a singular appearance. The architectural grandeur of the monuments may escape Rimbaud but not this atmosphere of civil war. He enters cafés in which new world–building fanatics are holding forth. Over the zinc counters people are working out the details for harmonious tomorrows and insulting the incompetent members of the Assembly in crude terms. Idealism and rage. Keen delights and fierce words. He makes a good assessment of what is the people's true strength and the desire for justice that lashes their minds. However his last sous are quickly spent. In several days he touches bottom. He is dying of hunger, as are most people. There is a shortage of foodstuffs. It is freezing cold out. Carts are crossing over the ice -locked Seine. His stomach empty and his face filthy, he sleeps with the down and out under bridges, on barges, and even a pile of coal. He does remember André Gill, whose drawings he admired in *La Lune* and *L'Éclipse*. Risking his all, he goes to the artist's home whose address someone had sent him. By chance this latter individual never locked his studio; Rimbaud enters, stretches out on a bench, and falls asleep. A while later the master of the house returns home to find this stranger, whom he awakens and asks for an explanation. Rimbaud tells him his story. Gill truly wishes to believe him but sends him away, though not without first giving him ten francs.[70]

It is quite significant to see the Rimbaud of this period avidly seeking to frequent caricaturists as well as poets. In his writings from that time he sought nothing so much as to compete with them. And when he wanders in the press district, he dreams of finding a place in the immense swarm of journals of the day. Ephemeral words of course, but strong and full of life. A nightmare world is collapsing. Another is being built with strokes of desire, idealism, anger, and vengeance. These are reflected in the mocking or enraged lines of the drawings, the fierce and hilarious caricatures, the pages with their cramped type of the pamphlets and lampoons, the revolutionary bombast, the provocations, and the prophetic flights of fancy that take themselves for the harbingers of the coming era where universal justice will reign. He views Paris, with its display windows of bookstores and newspaper kiosks, like a penniless child pressing his nose against the window of a candy store. He undoubtedly made a reconnaissance of rue des Petits Champs and passage Choiseul with the hope of glimpsing several Parnassian gentlemen. But the Parnassians have been, to say the least, overtaken by events. Each dutifully churns out a patriotic poem. Mendès rhymes "La Colère d'un franc-tireur," François Coppée, the "Lettre d'un mobile breton" (that was read aloud in the theaters), André Theuriet evokes "L'Invasion," Leconte de Lisle composes an ambitious work, "Le Sacre de Paris." What could Rimbaud expect from any of them? In the midst of all this patriotic hodgepodge he happily happens across a booklet by Glatigny, whose "Les Flèches d'or" he already loves. Glatigny now offers the "New Châtiments" entitled "Le Fer Rouge." Elsewhere, at 18 rue Bonaparte, Rimbaud, with beating heart, crosses the doorway of the famous Librairie Artistique, which had published *Les Glaneuses* by Demeny. They ask him for news of this author, who has just gotten married. Rimbaud, although making all concessions to proper manners, takes this opportunity to submit a manuscript of his latest poems, for wasn't it there that he wished to be published in his turn? The letter he will subsequently send Demeny will not breathe a word of this. In the troubled city, hunger gnawing at his belly, he regretfully ascertains that the literary world is no longer what he believed it to be; henceforth each recounts *"his* siege." Fortunately there are free, violent, and anti-establishment newspapers: Rochefort's *Le Mot d'Ordre* and Vallès's *Le Cri du peuple*, which he sincerely admires. But the fantasies that Eugène Vermersch provided in short-lived journals such as the new *Père Duchêne** prompted Rimbaud's greatest enthusiasm. Meeting him would have spared Rimbaud several months of fruitless wanderings and suppressed rage. But it was never said that Rimbaud would rush through his life in this way. Besides, Vermersch had better things to do than converse with a kid from Charleville.

Rimbaud, who has traversed the streets of the capital without truly meeting any kindred spirit, sees his resources dwindling. He is on the point of making "the final croak" (for the first time)! Rather than join with some band of marauders he prefers to return home with one final burst of energy that tears him out of the world of misery in which he was foundering. He therefore returns to Charleville on foot. This is no longer an enchanting bohemian autumn escapade but a long lonely road in the cold. "On the roads, during winter nights, without home, without clothes, without bread, a voice gripped my frozen heart: Weakness or strength, there you are, it is strength."[71] Passing through the gates of the town was enough to immediately feel the need to leave again. Forgotten are the misery and famished strollings in Paris; he is once again certain his place is there, whatever the cost.

---

*These publications were suspended by the decree of March 11, 1871. They will continue to appear nonetheless.

He has hardly returned when France learns of the extraordinary eruption of the Commune, proclaimed in Paris on March 18. The people in power. The riffraff in the Hôtel de Ville. The proscribed become kings. Rimbaud reacts with enthusiasm. Delahaye portrays him arriving in Theux, where he had taken refuge and hurling a triumphant: "That's it!" Then the two friends agree to go to Charleville to mock its bourgeois inhabitants stunned by such news. They hasten to cry to all present, and not without a certain swagger: "Order is vanquished!" Their fellow citizens are so appalled, they are incapable of responding to these provocateurs. Arthur had just barely missed the insurrection. At least he would soon be celebrating it in his poems. Fortunately the press provided some bits of news, though prudently phrased of course. He comes to his own conclusions and launches into long, impassioned discussions with Delahaye, Labarrière, and several other friends. They all believe the hour of freedom has arrived. After 1830 and 1848, which had been confiscated by authoritarian powers, what revenge! A world renewed. It could no longer overlook the formidable disarray of this Commune in which goodwill collided with factional struggles. The people, overflowing with mad and generous ideas, were poorly equipped to lead their victory but a violent dream flooding France from all sides enflamed the popular imagination and infinitely enlarged the field of possibilities.

Rimbaud has to pretend to be working since he refuses to take any courses at the *collège* that had reopened its doors in April.[72] There is at least one person he has to keep hoodwinked. He thinks journalism might offer him a road to salvation, although his prior experiences in this realm all had resulted in failure. But numerous reasons could be found for these earlier, unsuccessful attempts and he is encouraged by what he has just seen in Paris. He therefore asks Jacoby, who has just relaunched *Le Progrès des Ardennes*, to make a place for his journalistic debut. He is entrusted with the opening of the correspondence as a beginning position but sees his hopes fly away once again when the journal is suspended from publication on April 17, five days after he started work.

It is not at all rash to think his overriding desire at this time was to be taking part in this precedent-setting event in which the very spirit of freedom was triumphing over numerous plots and snares. However, his recent attempt to run away prevented him from acting as quickly as he would have liked.

Rimbaud's participation in the Commune continues to pose a problem. Through a unique paradox it appears to be so self-evident that doubts have been cast on the testimonies attesting to it. Delahaye, whose statements are almost always credible, has furnished precise information later corroborated by Verlaine and Paterne Berrichon.[73] Rimbaud sent a letter on April 17 to Demeny in which he recounted his latest escapade. Less than a month later—we know this through his letters of May 13 and 15[*] addressed to Izambard and Demeny—he is still (or back?) in Charleville. The Paris Commune will come to an end following the Bloody Week of May 21 to 28. So there are two strongly circumscribed periods of time—April 17 to May 12, and May 15 to May 28—during which he could have gone to Paris and demonstrated his solidarity with the insurgents in person. Delahaye's remarks on this, despite certain details, remain vague. He himself had gone to Normandy with his family during the first two weeks of April and wouldn't return to the Ardennes until the end of May. During all this time he was thus unable to see Rimbaud, which is assuredly the explanation for the gaps in his memory. His remarks deserve serious consideration, however, as later testimony confirms them.

With rail communications again interrupted, Rimbaud, always in need of money, would have set off on foot for the "holy city" of the west. Confident in his luck, he hopes to find some charitable soul along his way who will give him something to eat. In addition, he doesn't overlook the fact that federal troops are given remuneration: thirty sous a day, almost nothing, but if his enlistment is accepted in Paris he will have something to subsist on, enough to escape the frightful misery he had known during the previous month. He resolutely takes the road. The 150-mile journey has no terrors for him. He has experience and perhaps knows, like hobos, the location of certain caches and secure spots. While en route he is picked up by a tipsy cart driver. Sitting side by side they talk politics and the peasant asks the tramp to do a quick sketch for his son. Rimbaud jots down a hilariously funny Monsieur Thiers in the style of caricatures then in vogue. After five or six days of walking he finally arrives within sight of the capital and manages to obtain entry into the insurgent city. He crosses the path of men in arms, traverses the barricades, and is

---

[*]However the May 15 letter ends with these words: "Quick, for in eight days I will be in Paris, perhaps."

59

intoxicated by an atmosphere that is equal parts of fear and joy; those who have remained in Paris in the rebellious districts move about in a world of dangerous freedom. The government has taken refuge in Versailles and considers the Popular Committee to be a band of miscreants. The ministers are convinced they must act and force the rebels to surrender. *Intra muros* numerous cannons and rifles are in evidence. But not food, which is increasingly scarce. What does it matter! Rimbaud is a regular customer in the world of hunger. Moreover, he has a simple scheme of enlisting in a group of franctireurs, one of the military units assembled during the first months of the siege. The Commune certainly needed men, but it could hardly rely on inexperienced youths and marginal individuals whose adherence was most likely motivated by the prospects of a paycheck and food rations. According to Rimbaud's remarks reported by Delahaye, nobody raised any objection to his enlistment in a commando squad. He presented himself as a young partisan who had come from the countryside to defend the cause of the people. He is applauded; making the rounds of his new comrades, he collects in his kepi the stupendous sum of twenty-one francs, which he is quick to spend on the very people who had just welcomed him so generously. All this high society, which includes zouaves and foot soldiers as well as soldiers from the 88th Regiment, the same regiment that had refused to fire on the people of Montmartre, is sent to the Babylon barracks where they eat and sleep. Military drills are performed to instruct the new arrivals in the handling of arms. The vets already know what's what. Verlaine will later make a very laconic allusion to this time, recalling that Rimbaud's companions were "the vengeful waves of Flourens,"[74] who was one of the very first insurgents. A trifle coquettishly he will also make clear that these "white-belted Ephebes" pronounced the revolutionary's name as "Florence." In the barrack rooms Rimbaud experiences a disgusting promiscuity that is not at all heroic. Nevertheless he makes a friend among the soldiers of the 88th. Days pass in waiting. News is peddled, then denied. Freedom in remission has a taste of fever. Is this the moment at which it is necessary to situate an episode that is sometimes emphasized by his biographers, and sometimes considered as pure fiction or passed over in silence? Delahaye doesn't mention it. But Paterne Berrichon, always in accordance with a strictly biographical interpretation of the texts, maintains that the poem "Le Coeur supplicié" would describe a drunken orgy witnessed by the author:[75]

> *Mon triste coeur bave à la poupe,*
> *Mon coeur est plein de caporal:*
> *Ils y lancent des jets de soupe[. . .]*

> My poor heart slobbers at the poop,
> My heart covered with tobacco spit:
> They spew streams of soup at it

Berrichon's false certainties led him to commit many errors. Nevertheless, the poems written by Rimbaud in 1871 are, for the most part, neither completely true nor completely fictitious. He simply takes a greater or smaller distance with respect to reality. "Le Coeur supplicié" is definitely one in which he takes the greatest, in that he made use of it to illustrate the first "letter of the seer," as it is known that he sent it to Izambard on May 13. He will copy it over for Demeny under the title "Le Coeur du pitre" in June. He will also send it to Verlaine, this time entitled "Le Coeur volé," during the autumn of 1871. He therefore considers it a masterful work and highly significant of his new art. So what are these satiric triplets recounting? A story of a disgrace that affected him personally: a corporal, *pioupious* with erections, "ithyphallics," have debauched him, they have stolen his heart. He definitely didn't draw a picture like this out of simple poetic preference. We can certainly find here the pain of the Baudelarean albatross mocked by the crew members. But the military universe depicted by the poet appears especially close to the environment he would have experienced at that time in the Babylon barracks (presuming that he went there). Nothing forbids the thought that he was a victim of some violent sodomistic episodes (unless he was only a mere spectator), and some base, virile actions that corrupted his youth. Delahaye and especially Izambard, who had several scores to settle with Berrichon (Madame Rimbaud's son-in-law and authorized biographer because of his wife, the intransigent guardian sister Isabelle), have contested such a realistic interpretation.[76] There is a law of silence in certain cases. What "Le Coeur supplicié" appears to reveal nevertheless preserves its mystery. It will be noted that Rimbaud displays his misogyny more deliberately from this moment. It would certainly be hard to take the position that a homosexual rape of which he was ashamed simultaneously had the power of converting him to the pleasures of love between men. It would at least seem that "Le Coeur supplicié" offered so conspicuously by Rimbaud to his correspondents had the value of a revelation for him. As a result perhaps too much was made of it! Because of this bare-faced, public confession his veracity becomes suspect and we remain incredulous before the ostentatious depiction of a traumatic event that is probable without being certain.

The drinking binges, the smoke-filled sleeping quarters, the uproar of the barracks hardly distracted the franc-tireurs avid for more memorable activities. However, the confrontations at the gates of the city were becoming more violent; it was sensed that the isolated Commune would not hold on much longer and that those presumed guilty would be severely punished. Rimbaud therefore flees around fifteen days before the Bloody Week, if we are to believe Delahaye, furthermore recalling, and rightfully so, that the deserter had no reason to boast about his defection. Arthur could have related the true story to his closest confident, without necessarily having to repeat it to others such as Izambard. For his part, somewhat troubled by his total ignorance of this period of Rimbaud's life, Izambard will claim that Rimbaud invented his adventures to maintain his role as a militant Communard, a role he had adopted March 18, the day on which the insurrectional government had been proclaimed.

After several days of forced marches through Villiers-Cotterêts, Soissons, Reims, and Rethel, where he experienced various adventures not worth describing, Rimbaud finally reaches Charleville the inevitable.

RIMBAUD AGAIN FINDS HIMSELF IN TROUBLED WATERS WITH HIS MOTHER, who is now constantly harassing him to find a job. Though keeping abreast of all the daily news concerning this Commune now living out its final days in fear and enthusiasm, he frequents the library even more assiduously than he did in the past. His thoughts turn to Paris during the hours of the final battle and inspire him to write what he derisively calls a "topical psalm," a "Chant de guerre parisien," which depicts a burlesque confrontation. The "they" he speaks of are the Thiers and the Picards—worthless "cupids" flying over the spring flowers—and Jules Favre crying his crocodile tears. On the other side are his fellow revelers and insurgents. Rimbaud the survivor sees the civil war in a strange fashion. Did he even take the grievous confrontations then taking place between city and rural dwellers seriously? This ironic war song certainly does not foresee the massacres of the Bloody Week. There is no little egotism in Rimbaud's poem, even if he does evoke the lake "with reddened waters" of blood in one verse.

His creative powers thereby developed in tune to the large insurrectional machine that turned in the capital come what may, and with the new season while he waited for "the time of cherries falling on the leaf like drops of blood." He lives in an atmosphere of violence, the energy that stimulates spring and strongly scented flowers. He will determine the time of his own birth. Unless he feels it mounting inside like a sexual spasm. Everything he writes now is marked by sarcasm, the desire for mad freedom and the astonishing presence of his body tightly embracing a language of humor poured into words, a sap of adjectives, and a juice of neologisms, because the tongue itself must become other, like the Commune will regenerate exhausted history with a renewal of sap.

This rather short, frail, easily embarassed boy (he then measures five foot three) has still not known a woman. Yet his angelic face had undoubtedly

63

seduced some young passerby. Delahaye, Pierquin,[77] and all his other friends will remember several choice anecdotes about a fifteen-year-old-lover who accompanied the adolescent runaway. She would have refused to follow him to Paris (which would better explain one of his escapades)? He assuredly had love affairs, but "small ones" as he puts it so simply—that is to say of little importance, and it requires all the imagination of a Louis Pierquin to believe that Rimbaud was still thinking on his deathbed of a young girl he would have loved during this year. It is better to listen to the hate expressed by the main character reviewing the jeering girls of Charleville. He dismisses all those girls who once could have offered him any illusions as blue-eyed, blond, black-haired, or red-haired "uglies." He has since discovered that Woman, despite her sweetness, primarily conceals a heap of entrails. He can expect nothing from this "sister of charity."[78]

His satirical, sharpened eye is ever ready to transform all who displease him into grotesques; among the "heads" he takes are customs officials, the seated men in the library, the poor in church. He gives a patina of disturbing colors to all the ultimate variants of romantic physiologies. One of his friends of this time, a certain Ernest Millot, had a priest among his relatives. This, as well as the seminary teachers and their students, is the inspiration for his portrayal of a Brother "Milotus," who looks through the skylight at "Venus in the deep sky," while squatting with his hand on the handle of a chamberpot.[79] He discovers the singularity of a poetry that blends lyricism and scatology. Bolder than the Baudelaire of "Une Charogne," he says the hideous and grafts words on bodies that he makes speak according to a truth that digs more deeply into reality. He unbinds the surfaces where realism gets caught; he explores an unknown site that owes nothing to dream but is the force or energy of beings and things still hidden.

May 13, 1871: the Commune is still holding on. Rimbaud, far from Paris, is champing at the bit. His head is crammed with images of streets on full alert as well as those from the many books he is now devouring at the library, despite the disapproval shown him by their jealous guardian, Monsieur Jean Hubert, a former teacher of rhetoric and logic (vulgarly nicknamed "Saint-Hubert-cul"* by Delahaye and Rimbaud).[80] He has also just received a letter

---

*Saint Hubert ass—translator's note.

from Izambard, who has been seeking to return to the teaching profession following the January armistice. In April he had turned down a job as tutor in Saint Petersburg, where his brother lived—this would have been a great adventure!—and sensibly accepted a position as a part-time teacher at the lycée in Douai. So he wouldn't be getting away from his little town. Could Rimbaud congratulate him for accepting such a restricted destiny? "Here you are a professor again." But his return letter[81] doesn't confine itself to simple reproaches. Extraordinary projects take shape there that certainly owe much to circumstances. Rimbaud elatedly and vehemently enumerates a list of his intentions, profound lightning flashes that have not yet ceased illuminating the shadowy land of poetry. Countless exegeses have attempted to analyze them. A challenging vision extends there that by all the evidence challenged Rimbaud himself. He *reveals* absolutely and with no assistance. This occurs during a transitional historical moment—equally exceptional for him—that he accepts as the equivalent of a command. His letter to Izambard inscribes a line of demarcation between the "incorrigible" professor and the poet who, adopting a diametrically opposed attitude, follows a strange principle based on getting into a bad rut or downslide. A master magician, an expert comedian in making faces (as will be seen with Verlaine) or savage grimaces, Rimbaud chooses to act badly, to deprave himself. Furthermore, all this staging coincides with the search for his own identity, the famous juvenile identity crisis for which he provides the "genius" solution. In the general disarray France was experiencing he could have limited his seventeen-year-old cynicism to summary eccentricities: holding forth in the cafés, wearing his hair long, smoking his Gambier pipe upside down, covering the walls of Charleville with indecent inscriptions. Yet Rimbaud significantly linked this conduct to the poetic experience and hunted down every vague idea in this domain. The Commune assuredly placed him in a state of urgency, precipitated his intuitions, and brought his poetry to a fever pitch, forcing it to change. Rimbaud makes a clear distinction between the patient workers, the bureaucrats like Izambard, and the real workers (those he will soon admiringly label "horrible"), the proletarians and Communards at whose sides he wishes to be, even if there is no question for him of writing a poetry of political commitment. And it is as a worker (of language) that he draws another contrast between objective poetry and subjective poetry. He is actually speaking to

65

Izambard not only as his professor but as a person who sometimes passed on some banal attempts at poetry. In his mind the term "subjective poetry" targets the sentimental bagatelles composed by his correspondent. He, on the other hand, identifies with a new, lucid, severe, and even harsh objectivity. He draws near the Parnassian doctrine only in appearance: its worship of forms and impersonal themes that didn't exclude a real sensuality when necessary, as shown in Banville's work. In the same era (or almost), Isidore Ducasse also took issue with Musset's followers, the eulogists of the states of the soul[82] and sought a "science of poetry" in an almost geometrical terminology. The Commune convinced Rimbaud to assault language by the influx of a disfiguring and satiric intention well illustrated by his *"Le Coeur supplicié,"* a significant inclusion with his May 13th letter. In fact his objectivity has nothing in common with impassivity, as one might think. It is prompted by an *objective* constructed from a specific work that aims to transform the individual himself. Furthermore, Rimbaud is not about to let a little thing like a contradiction stop him. He sheds doubt upon the illustrious Cartesian cogito "I think therefore I am," but replaces it with "one thinks me." But who is he speaking of? What is the other of "I is another," an illustrious but now secondhand formula that seems to have been conceived after the fact to justify the conjectures of psychoanalysis? The more closely one looks at this inaugural letter and the discoveries it suggests, the less clearly these discoveries are actually demonstrated there; his phrases vanish in a fulgurant stream. The evidence illuminates the discoverer so strongly that he doesn't explain, he takes note.

Isabelle made her first communion the day after this letter to Izambard was written.[83] Rimbaud had to attend the ceremony and its follow-up events. He will remember it, yet he was hardly of any mind for these *mysticalities.* He had also taken his pen back in hand on May 15, still preoccupied by his singular manifesto that he now wished to send to Paul Demeny. This second letter is actually the one traditionally designated as the "letter of the seer." The word appeared in the first letter and reappears here. The long development to which Rimbaud abandons himself, the three poems chanted within ("Chant de guerre parisien," "Mes Petites amoureuses," "Accroupissements") are ample proof of his inner conviction that he has "invented" a new poetic continent.

Such an exposition bubbling with life had no impact on the poets of his generation in that it would remain unknown until 1912.[84] His very late influence would be exercised only upon the surrealists and the members of the Grand Jeu group who felt he had anticipated their own theoretical conjectures. Rimbaud wrote the "letter of the seer" with no concern for intellectual posturing, nor even of tossing out some crumbs of a consistent poetic art. He retraces the history of poetry with the impetuosity of youth, although he often reaches some very summary judgments. Everything here comes under the jurisdiction of intuition even if—trying to give order to his thoughts—he makes distinctions between Greek poetry that gives rhythm to action, Romantic poetry (preceded by a long period of "rhymed prose"), and lastly modern poetry heralded by the second generation of Romantics, such as Gautier, Leconte de Lisle, and Banville. Rimbaud is delineating the panorama of his preferences. It is perfectly acceptable if he doesn't provide footnotes as the collaborators on the review *Littérature* will do in 1921.[85]

He spares Hugo (though not without reservations), reviles Musset, and deifies Baudelaire. He reproaches even the greatest poets though for using the "old form," although the poems he inserts are far from presenting the categorical upheaval he proclaims. It is quite difficult to perceive just what he is imagining at this stage of his life. Not only does he redefine the word *seer*, he uses to explain to Izambard the role of the poet,[86] but his entire letter is presented like a vision. It foretells and holds itself "in advance" within an augural zone. He carefully repeats his formula of "I is another," which he interprets in terms of "depths," a face hiding in the wings of the theater of personal expression of an intimate truth. He has a presentiment of an unlooked-for solution, provided by language itself, to the virtualities of human thought. There is a method for this: the "long, immense, and reasoned *derangement of all the senses*." To break with habit, quit styles of conventional logic, discover new routes, make oneself monstrous, to head for the worst. In the final analysis he is announcing a formidable salvation through words and a multiplication of progress that he adds not without positivism because he wishes to save humanity (naive legend) like Prometheus—which doesn't stop him from choosing the negative path of depravity. His idea of a poetry "in advance" repeats the steps of the magi poets: Lamartine, Hugo, who were also each accompanied by a revolution: 1830, 1848, 1871. But Rimbaud will be neither a deputy nor a candidate for the presidency of the republic. His political career can be readily summed up: he will quickly abandon the party, several months commitment to the weak means of journalism, and the illusionary drafting of a communist Constitution[87] attributed to him by Delahaye's memory but of which nothing remains. The mythic world, the certainties predicted by the Norns,[88] will demand a great deal more of his attention.

Rimbaud undoubtedly was waiting for his correspondents' reaction to the two "bombs" he had sent them, veritable revolutionary pamphlets whose importance he felt would not escape them. Demeny, although favored with a good dozen pages, doesn't even bother to reply. Izambard, quite angry at being sent packing by his student whose lesson he hardly accepted and little convinced of Rimbaud's great designs as illustrated by "Le Coeur supplicié," replies with a mocking epistle and violent parody, *"La Muse des méphitiques"*:[89]

> *Viens sur mon coeur, Muse des Méphitiques,*
> *Et roucoulons comme deux amoureux.*
> *Pour bafouer toutes les esthétiques,*
> *Viens dans mes bras, Muse des Méphitiques.*

> Come over my heart, Muse of the Mephitic Ones,
> And let's bill and coo like two lovers.
> To ridicule all the aesthetes,
> Come into my arms, Muse of the Mephitic Ones.

He didn't recognize the novelty of "Le Coeur supplicié" which he found a suffocatingly bizarre text. He mocked it facetiously in the tone of the *Parnassiculet contemporain*,[90] which had made fun of the verses of the budding Parnassians since 1866.

Several days later people would learn of the events of the Bloody Week, the futile heroics of the reds, the battles in the streets, the final repression. In seven days the Commune had been overturned and flattened like Carthage. The Versailles forces had massacred the insurgents. Thousands were said to have been killed, shot down en masse with no preliminary trials. Those who had not fled in time and yet managed to survive the slaughter now found themselves in the hulks.[91] Others, such as Louise Michel, were deported to New Caledonia. Thinking of these active, strong women whose courage he admired (not at all like the "uglies" under the tree with tender shoots!), Rimbaud writes "Les Mains de Jeanne-Marie," hands he now imagines impris-

68

oned in a "chain of clear rings." The poem is a new idea that reflects the incendiary gleams of the insurrection but uses an old form as its template: Théophile Gautier's "Etudes de mains." The Commune remained inside him with the strength of a violent dream of love. They had come within a hair's breadth of the miracle: pure freedom! In a mood of black resignation he composes "Paris se repeuple." The beautiful city, the Holy City, is again invaded by those who had fled: "Syphilitics, dwarves." The city had been set on fire and washed with blood. The Parisians had inventoried their ruins and burnt palaces: the General Accounting Office, the Palais-Royal, the Hôtel de Ville. The "incendiary reflections" had been avoided and "the old men, puppets, lackeys" are all now returning and whooping it up over Paris the "whore."

Skeptical and furious, Rimbaud henceforth gets paid off in bocks and girls[92] ("girls" in this instance refers to small bottles of beer). He lives in idleness like "an angel with the hands of a barber." His mother, weary of constantly remonstrating with him, washes her hands of this intractable son who hangs around in cafés and frequents the Republican elite like Perrin and Deverrière, individuals known for their progressive opinions and who are more interested in their journalistic projects than the courses they teach. Henri Perrin, a "militant radical," had first taught at the *collège* where Delahaye had been one of his students. But he had resigned his position after Easter. Izambard's close friend Deverrière continued to teach at the Institution Rossat but his talents as a pen pusher took up most of his time. They would all meet at the comfortable Café de l'Univers facing the Square de la Gare and discuss remaking the world. Rimbaud read several satirical little pieces inspired by Vermersch and Vallès to Perrin, who was launching a new journal, *Le Nord-Est*. Shortly after the appearance of the first issue, he would even favor him with a long poem "La Plainte des épiciers,"[93] in which, pretending to be a small Carolopolitan businessman, he attacks Perrin, who is in the habit of humorously pillorying all such affluent mediocrities. Such attempts with their whiff of scandal did not have the good fortune to please the new journalists and in retaliation Rimbaud would cover a few Charleville walls with a SHIT ON PERRIN. He would later contaminate the language of Verlaine with similar phrases.* Such summary graffiti is not enough to satisfy him, and

---

*Several very ostentatious "Shit on God" inscriptions will also be attributed to him.

Delahaye and Izambard remember him scratching out verses with the most surprising mediums. When leaving the Gindres' home he wrote a short good-bye poem on their door, soon covered over, alas, by a thick coat of paint.[94] On another occasion he allegedly inscribed an eight-line verse of his own invention under the attic roof of the belltower of the church Notre-Dame-de-l'Espérance in Mézières to commemorate his comical discovery of a chamberpot absurdly placed in this lofty place.[95]

Though Rimbaud seems to be living in a state of complete idleness at this time, he is nonetheless constantly writing letters and poems. He knows quite well that the time has come for him to prove himself. He is weighed down, however, by the laziness he has made a principle. His obsession with work as a veritable punishment from God will plague him until the day he dies. Harassed by his mother, as "inflexible as seventy-three steel-helmeted administrations,"[96] whose sole desire is to see him employed, enraptured by his latest inspirations and prey to an inner calling that closely resembles a vocation, he multiplies the itineraries for becoming this *poet* whose function he feels is so necessary at this moment when society, shaken to its deepest foundations, is entering a new era. Certainly the newborn Third Republic, still soiled with the blood of the proletariat, has nothing worthwhile to say to him, but he already has thought ahead to a luminous future in which universal justice will finally shine. The Rimbaud who hangs out on the streets with Ernest Delahaye and takes long excursions to the outskirts of Charleville has but one passion: poetry, for which he invents an apparently lazy lifestyle that is actually a blend of actions, meditation, frenzied intention, and experience on the move. Nonetheless, in the midst of so many discoveries, he feels intensely alone and incapable of communicating his dream. Demeny does not bother to answer him. Izambard has not taken him seriously. To tell the truth, what could he expect from his former friends in whom he had momentarily placed his hopes?

Toward the end of that school year Henri Perrin, now editor of *Nord-Est*, was replaced by another professor. The newcomer, Edouard Chanal,[97] was a Lorraine native with a placid face, blond beard, and blue eyes. Well-liked by his students, among whom was Delahaye, he taught them to appreciate Villon, Marot, and Ronsard. Through Delahaye, Rimbaud was aware of the virtues of this new arrival and briefly fantasized about confiding in him. A meeting was contrived, promoted by a "planned" stoke of chance, but on the verge of approaching him, Rimbaud refused to take the plunge. This is a good illustration of his shyness—the ever-present understudy of his revolt—and taste for scandal. This adolescent captive, prey to the mirages of his genius and perpetually ill at ease because he dreamed so much of freedom, felt a need to speak to others of the elements of his spiritual geography: clairvoyance, "collapses, routs, and pity." When, he composes his "Poètes de sept ans" at 5 bis quai de la Madeleine, not only is he orchestrating the upsurge of his memories, but describing himself at that very moment tracing out the contours of his thought: desires for freedom, heavy ocher skies, maritime odysseys, a complete universe of *absolute exoticism.* In its own way Charleville erected the walls of an invisible prison. Nothing could better depict a closed world than place Ducale, despite its marvelous layout. Strolls through town always led back there. However Rimbaud's feet, taking the rue du Petit-Bois, led him increasingly to the Café Dutherme, the hangout of one very singular drinker who seems to have stepped straight out of a Flemish painting. Auguste Bretagne is a man with an enormous potbelly, heavy jowls spilling over his shirt collar, and black sideburns framing a pink face,[98] who empties one mug after another while smoking his pipe. The man is a complete introvert. He comes to the café every day when he leaves the sugar works where he performs the very mediocre tasks of a head clerk of indirect taxation; in other words he is a "bar rat." At the age of thirty-five he cuts an odd figure, about whom contradictory and often unpleasant rumors are flying. Though not very outgoing, he sometimes delivers curious speeches that blend notions of occultism and magic. He collects old books, plays the violin, and will cross swords on political matters if goaded. Izambard made his acquaintance during the past year when the two men took their meals in the same boarding-house. There is no doubt Rimbaud was introduced to him, yet he remains an enigmatic figure in Rimbaud's life. The little we know of him allows him to be held responsible for a "parallel" education in which he would have acquainted Rimbaud with the forbidden texts of white and black magic, revolutionary pamphlets, and so forth. The biographers, otherwise discreet in his regard, have given him an extensible role that fills a gap just so and provides an answer to the question raised by Rimbaud's presumed connection to occultism. All poets are misrepresented in this way by different delusional interpretations. For the difficulties posed by texts that are beyond them, there are always ingenious minds that discern therein the signs of an "initiation." Auguste Bretagne would thus permit the genesis of the future "Sonnet des voyelles" to be explained! Anticlerical, but with an impassioned interest in mysticism, he liked to caricature clerics. This great specialty of his had earned him the paradoxical nickname of "the priest." His opinions, when he deigned to venture them, were proof of an anarchistic and jubilant mentality. Rimbaud's depraved ways enlivened his normally imperturbable expression. Each understood the other to a wonderful extent, even when they had nothing to say and just sat silently, watching the passage of time. Bretagne saw the cynical adolescent engaged upon the perilous path of poetry, to which he certainly preferred music. An excellent violinist he would occasionally have some fellow musicians over to his home. Sometimes Rimbaud attended these chamber music concerts. At times he would recite his poems. Bretagne encouraged him without really having any idea of their value. For his part, he was satisfied with the *Poèmes saturniens* of Verlaine, whom he had known before in 1868 and 1869, when he worked at the Dehée Sugarworks in Fampoux, not far from Arras.[99] Verlaine, who was there visiting his maternal uncle, had forged a tavern friendship with the "bar rat," and Bretagne, also a good violist, had even played a duo with Charles de Sivry, who while visiting Verlaine, had borrowed the church harmonium to play Wagner, Hervé, and "all the swings" from Nina de Villard's (a Parisian salon popular with the Bohemian artists of the time). Bretagne will even show Rimbaud his odd present from Verlaine, the inkstand the poet had used to write *Poèmes saturniens*. Rimbaud couldn't help but be delighted by such coincidences. Looking at it from this angle, one may be surprised that the man from the sugar works did not urge him to write the author of *Fêtes galantes* sooner. In fact Rimbaud would not make that decision until the end of that August.[100]

Though Rimbaud happily spends time with Deverrière and especially Bretagne, he nonetheless continues to see the faithful Delahaye. When summer arrives the "walkers" resume their wanderings again. Rimbaud finds makeshift excuses to reassure his mother, who is constantly storming after him, and Delahaye has no compunctions about skipping class. They make regular arrangements to meet at the corner of rue du Moulin and quai de la Madeleine near the *collège*. From there they set off on long walks to Saint-Laurent and Gernelle, and to the hill of Aiglemont tinkling with the hammers of the nail makers. Rich with a thin sou, they would share a beer at Chez Chesnaux. At times their expeditions led them almost nine miles through the forest, in the direction of Passemange. They cross over into Belgium, free as the air except for a mandatory disinfection—a less than pleasing operation—in an ad hoc shed (there was, in fact, a fear of foot-and-mouth disease that was then rampant in the French Ardennes). They push on a bit further just to provide a motive for their escapade, buying packs of tobacco whose wrapper inscription, "Manufacture de Thomas Philippe," delights them. In the woods on the return trip they encounter customs officials who say "For God's sake" and "Nothing doing." This is not the first time Rimbaud has crossed the border but the emotion that grips him is just as intense. Independence, escape, a feeling of somewhere else. Keenly interested in poetry, the two companions travel over hill and dale reciting verse. Rimbaud sometimes mixes his with those by the authors of the *Parnasse contemporain*, which he knows by heart. At this time he very much admires Léon Dierx (and his *Vieux Solitaire*), an intimate of Verlaine and hope of the new generation. His May 15 letter to Paul Demeny recognizes two seers in the current school, Mérat and Verlaine. But on June 20 it is to Jean Aicard that he mails (care of Lemerre) a copy of his "Effarés,"[101] which he proposes to exchange for the other's "Les Rébellions," which had just been published.

So he doesn't hesitate to knock on doors. Not only does he see himself as a poet, but he wishes to be recognized as one. He seeks to display his works by every available means, and when he isn't making great tours of the countryside with Delahaye, he is carefully recopying and dispatching his poems to Paris and beyond. His faith in the Demeny connection to the Librairie Artistique has not quite died. Irritated at his correspondent's failure to respond to his previous letter in which he had expounded on his developing theory, he sends him a new letter containing "Les Poètes de sept ans" and "Les Pauvres a l'église." He adds "Le Coeur du pitre," the former "Coeur supplicié," which had already illustrated the first letter of "seer" sent to Izambard. Furthermore, he is concerned about giving an impression of entering a new creative phase and peremptorily asks Demeny to "burn the pages of the notebook" that he put together for him in Douai in October 1870. He is not one to accumulate things. It is a question of speed, a resourceful pace that keeps making progress. He therefore proceeds to his own metamorphoses himself, making sure that the cast-off skins from his molt are definitively destroyed. It's then

all over and done with. He nevertheless spares one poem, not the most striking, but the one that in his eyes perhaps is the most successful: "Les Effarés,"
which he has already sent (as we have seen) to Jean Aicard and which he will
also send to Verlaine. All the activities he engaged in during these few months
should not be found surprising. They were only a pastime. In contrast, he
fully devotes himself to poetry. He believes in the poet's mission in which he
feels he must win his place.

Recalling Banville's response of the year before when he had favored the
master with his "Credo in unam," he goes on the offensive again. In a very
strange manner though, for what could the author of *Les Stalactites* think of
the long poem he intends for him? Rimbaud signs it "Alcide Bava," or in other
words Hercules (nicknamed Alcide, "the strong one," by the ancients), who
spat out this text. Arthur never made up a pseudonym that sounded
anything like his real name. It brings to mind the Jean Baudry that he assumed
for his first journalism attempts. The title, "Ce qu'on dit au Poète à propos
de fleurs," conceals a lesson in style under a joke, a veritable mocking art of
poetry in gamboling octosyllables, that completes the seer letters to perfection
with just a touch of dogmatism. What does Rimbaud wish to demonstrate?
That the preeminent poetic themes, like rivers, should be treated in an original
way and that it is time to emerge from vegetal and vegetative repetitions. He
does not refrain from carrying his polemical theory to absurd heights. In this
period of progress it is necessary to sing of useful plants, tobacco, cotton, and
rose madder.* But we are mistaken to view this as his conception of the poet's
mission and the ending clearly demonstrates that it is far more important for
him to create unheard-of flowers with his words. The tone is derisive and
taunting; Banville may well have found it annoying. *In fine* Rimbaud takes the
precaution of writing: "I will always love the verses of Banville,"[102] and those
who have seen this missive as only a facetious gesture in which he is making
fun of its addressee have gotten only a poor idea of its true scale. In all likelihood Rimbaud is addressing the other Banville here, the eccentric admired by
Baudelaire, the virtuoso of *Odes funambulesques*, who this parody doesn't
totally spare, it's true, but he hoped to have the reading of a fellow conspirator
from the master. Offensively dated "July 14, 1871," his text celebrates a libera-

---

*For the purpose of dyes—translator's note.

tion in its way. The end of the letter (to which he expected an answer) gave Bretagne's address, a necessary precaution as it was out of the question that the *mother** be informed of the increased attempts that he was insolently making to finally secure a name for himself.

Furthermore, each day sees new verses born from his pen, forged by the strange clairvoyance that possesses him. Rimbaud does not disclose to us the space of an intimate dream as much a reality that has been looked at anew, transmuted, and exacerbated with completely different means than those used by his naturalist contemporaries. What falls under his eyes becomes the object of an ardent metamorphosis at the end of which reconstructed objects, beings, and landscapes emerge. It testifies to an accelerated sensation and he performs real acts of magic where our eyes only manage to see the common presence of things. In his "Les Poètes de sept ans," he had spoken of himself, his suppressed rages, his imagination. In "Les Premièrs Communions," he attacks the mediocre rites of religion. "Truly, it's stupid . . ." He creates while he is describing, and this poetic narrative relates the entire history of women subjugated by the prohibitions of the Catholic religion. The well-behaved communicant experiences the awakening of mad desires out in the open. Rimbaud surrounds the quotidian, then traverses it. He could have been another Coppée[†]; but his realism surpasses all realism, his revolt brightens and radically illuminates words. This is also the inspiration for his "L'Homme juste," of which we unfortunately have no more than a few fragments. Hugo, the exile of Guernsey, "Beard of the family and fist of the city," is the object of a rude attack here. Still indignant at the thought of the martyrs of the Commune, Rimbaud could hardly accept the compromise chosen by the author of *Les Châtiments* who had published three poems calling on the forces of Versailles and the Communards to reconcile in *Le Rappel* of April 19 and May 7. He scoffs at this Just Man, too sure of his reason and oblivious of the necessary vengeance.

The summer grew old. In Charleville, Rimbaud was going around in circles. He had definitely resolved not to set foot back in *collège* but he was still jobless. The first issue of Perrin's and Deverrière's *Nord-Est* came out in early

---

[*]English in the original. All subsequent appearances of Rimbaud's reference to his mother in English will be italicized—translator's note.

[†]French author François Coppée (1842–1908) who wrote *Les Humbles*—translator's note.

July, but he no longer maintained any illusions in that regard. None of his texts would be accepted there, unless he radically changed his style, which he refused to do.* The hours pass, with Delahaye or the taciturn Bretagne philosophically smoking his pipe. Killing time! On August 28, anxious, ignored, and faced with an uncertain future, he draws a picture of his situation for his friend Demeny (who was far away and hardly won over to his ideas):

> For more than a year I have given up ordinary life for what you know. Encaged in this Ardennes countryside that no words can describe, seeing not a soul, absorbed by an infamous, inept, obstinate, and mysterious work, only answering questions and the most vulgar and wicked apostrophes with silence, showing myself worthy in my extra-legal position, I have ended by provoking atrocious resolutions from a mother as inflexible as seventy-three administrations with steel helmets.

It could not be put any better. Rimbaud knew himself—and knew his "work," which he labels with surprising epithets, the least of which deserves prolonged examination. But he has touched bottom and the idleness painfully necessary to his monstrous transformation cannot go on much longer. Demeny had once mentioned the possibility of a job in Paris as a worker at fifteen sous a day. Of course he would prefer "less absorbing" occupations. During this same time Mallarmé was exhausting himself learning the English language. Was Rimbaud still thinking of obtaining some remunerative employment at the Librairie Artistique on rue Bonaparte, where he had gone in February? In any event, he had almost reached the end of his rope. No more solutions presented themselves to temper his anxieties. Buried within himself and experiencing terrible fits of rage, he lived in a state of profound distress. "Father" Bretagne grew alarmed about his protégé's sneaking out of

---

*One thinks to have found a text by Rimbaud in the issue of September 16, 1871: *Lettre du baron de Petdechèvre à son secrétaire au château de Saint-Magloire* (see *O.C., Pl.,* pp. 227–230). This anticommunard article signed "Jean Marcel," is presented there as taken from the *Progrès [des Ardennes].* The majority of Rimbaud's editors have pronounced against this attribution (see A. Adams and A. Guyaux). It was defended through by P. Petitfils (*Rimbaud,* p. 130) and S. Murphy (*Bulletin du Centre culturel Arthur-Rimbaud,* no. 10. September 1986, pp. 39–46).

the house in order to drink with him for an hour at the seedy Café Dutherme. He brought up Verlaine's name again.

The imperturbable drinker finally entrusts Rimbaud with the poet's address. Why did he wait so long, you may ask? Now, it is certain that Rimbaud only dared correspond with the "seer" of Parnassus quite late, although he had made a number of fruitless attempts with other individuals. Bretagne bore some responsibility for this, but nothing until now allows any understanding of this wasted time or the opportunity provided by this late endeavor. For Rimbaud, Verlaine constituted his last chance. He was hoping for more than simple words of appreciation and encouragement from him. After the exhausting experience of this latest summer spent in Charleville, he wished to abandon the Ardennes town definitively, escape maternal surveillance, and live a free life of total poetry. Ready to make his appeal to Verlaine, he quickly informed his friend Delahaye of his intentions and, supplied with pen and paper, they soon reached the Café Dutherme where the obliging owner put a large table at their disposal. Rimbaud wants Verlaine to judge him by his works, therefore they have to be copied out in excellent handwriting. The obliging Delahaye, his forever faithful admirer, offers to do this for him and, applying himself to his task writes them out in *petite ronde* (the letters that come closest to printshop letters) under Rimbaud's dictation. Definitely an historic moment that has its place among others whose light we would like to capture. Life continued around them as if nothing were out of the ordinary. The noises of the passersby sometimes broke the silence of the room in which Rimbaud's voice echoed. In a way Delahaye's pen was tracing the first lines of a destiny. Rimbaud, if we are to believe his part-time secretary,[103] would have sent five texts with this letter: "Les Effarés," "Accroupissements," "Les Douaniers," "Le Coeur volé," and "Les Assis," all recent works, except for the first, which he had also just sent to J. Aicard. He still held "Le Coeur volé" in high regard, as he did "Accroupissements," which can be found in one of the letters of the seer. We are certainly indebted here to Delahaye's memory, assuredly more exact than that of Verlaine who only remembered "Les Effarés" and "Les Premières Communions" from Rimbaud's two letters.[104] Reassured by his scribe's perfect copies, Rimbaud in turn takes up his pen and recounts the misery and poetry of his life: running away to Paris, failed schemes, clairvoyance deferred. With a bit of impatience, he describes himself as a "little crass," an explicit variation of his self-depraved nature, and promises, if given hospitality in the capital, to be "less bother than a Zanetto." This expression particularly struck Verlaine.[105] The Zanetto in question is an allusion to the young and seductive Bohemian played by Sarah Bernhardt in a play by François Coppée, *Le Passant*, which in 1869 had witnessed the first triumph of the little group destined to become the Parnassians. Connivance oblige! Bretagne kindly adds several lines of greetings to the addressee and praise for the extraordinary merits of his protégé. The letter is quickly posted. Rimbaud had finally dared to address the sole poet whose originality he recognized (despite some excessive liberties).[106] Verlaine the individual had been described to him by Bretagne as an unreserved drinker, little mindful of convention, a Bohemian who had returned to the fold for a time, but was constantly tempted by absinthe. How they had drunk the "breune" and the "chelblinque," not to mention the "gnief" and the "bistouilles,"* when Verlaine, had visited the home of his uncle, the sugar producer Julien Dehée, during his summer vacation! Rimbaud, who believed in his poems, nonetheless experienced some apprehension at the thought of being read by the poet of *Les Fêtes galantes.*

Two days go by; incensed from waiting, at the end of his patience, and wishing to win the support of his reader once and for all, he sends another series of poems, again handwritten by Delahaye: "Mes petites amoureuses," "Paris se repeuple" (Verlaine had been a Communard, hadn't he!), and "Les Premières Communions." Verlaine's memories do lack clarity. Whether Rimbaud's first letter to him had been addressed to rue Nicolet in Montmartre, the home of his in-laws, then expedited to the Pas de Calais,[107] where he was then on vacation (it is from there he would have responded to Rimbaud, making apologies for the delay), or whether he found this mail at Lemerre's on his return to the capital, the fact is that he responded as quickly as possible to this unknown correspondent, whose violently original creation was a surprising discovery. He doesn't hesitate to tell Rimbaud that he admires his texts and that he finds him "prodigiously well armed for battle,"[108] that's to say ready to lead the combat for the new poetry. The war, which Rimbaud had failed to wage as a *franc-tireur*, he would this time carry into the ranks of the singing

---

*Verlaine's slang for cheap wines and rotgut.

poets of "flowers for glasses." Without a doubt he was portrayed as a dark rebel, a wild man in the style of Petrus Borel. Verlaine, the Saturnian, remembering that fanatic from the years around 1830, answers him in the same tone: I have a whiff of your lycanthropy.[109] Furthermore he has closely read the pieces he received. Some shocked him by their neologisms: the *"pialats ronds"* [round staring eyes] in "Mes Petite Amoureuses," the *"rosiers fuireux"* [rambling rosebushes] in "Les Premièrs Communions," or the misuse of medical terms, as if the author had the ambition of providing an ultra-Baudelairean anatomy lesson. The *"culs en ronds"* [their rounded asses] from "Les Effarés" did not earn his commendations either, even though he himself had published some extremely indecent poems ("Les Amies"), in Belgium under the pseudonym Pablo de Herlagnez.[110] Other letters would follow. But Verlaine was already circulating the manna from Charleville. It isn't long before his companions from passage Choiseul, the Café du Gaz, and the reunions at Nina's: the Cros brothers, Camille Pelletan, Gustave Rivet, Philippe Burty, receive the sacrament from the cult of Rimbaud. All are in agreement on the matter of welcoming this adolescent rebel with pockets full of poems. A final letter implores him: "Come, dear great soul, we are summoning you, we are waiting for you."[111] It isn't certain that Rimbaud appreciated being a soul, but the invitation was important. Everything went perfectly, ensuring that this trip to Paris wouldn't be limited to a few miserable days spent in the streets looking in bookstore windows and collecting a few scraps to ease his hunger. Rimbaud now realizes that he can make his way in the great city of poets with the unusual Verlaine as his godfather.

Before his departure on a sojourn, whose stakes he can easily assess, he composes "Le Bateau ivre," as much out of conviction as to supply additional proof of his talent. This is the poem that will always be associated with his name. Between its motivation to what makes its subject explicable, there is all the mystery that separates the creation from what made its birth possible. "Le Bateau ivre" alone is enough to make Rimbaud significant. It has become one with his body. The veritable example of clairvoyance (a word that he will never write) appears there. Rimbaud pierces the "sky reddening like a wall." Here he sees in all clarity "what men have thought they saw." If this poem betrays the sure knowledge of an expert rhetorician, it primarily carries an orchestra of sensation and color with its cargo of extraordinary elements. A month previously Rimbaud had repeated to Delahaye the strophes of "Vieux Solitaire"[112] by Dierx: "I am like a hulk without yards or masts." But there is no "like," or "such as" here. The ship, or boat rather, a modern Argo, speaks in oracular verses. Allegory? Without a doubt. It is that of life breaking its moorings and attaining the Great Unknown. The beginning nevertheless commences with a subtle dig against the Parnassians, who were then called the Impassive Ones because of their cold and impersonal poems:

> *Comme je descendais des Fleuves impassibles,*
> *Je ne me sentais plus guidé par les haleurs:*
> *Des Peaux-Rouges criards les avaient pris pour cibles*
> *Les ayant cloués nus aux poteaux de couleurs.*

> As I came down the impassive Rivers,
> I no longer felt myself guided by the haulers!
> Screaming redskins had used them for targets,
> And had nailed them naked to colored stakes.

The savages destroy civilization's timid measures. The poem of the sea opens irresistibly downstream. However the Meuse—as seen from the Rimbaud home—is flowing slowly here. It is a moving symbol of an unforeseeable future.

On the beautiful September afternoon the day before his departure, Rimbaud reads the astounding verses to Delahaye. They are near the entry to the Fortemps Woods. Sunlight plays on the foliage. Though ready to leave, Rimbaud is still anxious. Does society need seers? And what do Verlaine and the others, so eager to see him but no doubt so different from him, have in store for him? We are not very knowledgeable about the conditions in which this departure that followed on so many returns and destroyed hopes took place. Bolstered by Verlaine's letters, can Rimbaud succeed in convincing his mother that a destiny as a writer awaited him? She was certainly not one of those people who believed in men of letters. Later Isabelle will assure us that she detested literature.[113]

That being the case, should we prefer the version provided by Delahaye? Rimbaud would have garnered great satisfaction from once more escaping the *mother.* Enriched with a gold louis generously bestowed upon him by Dev-errière or Bretagne, weighed down by only his poems, he buys a third-class ticket with the money order sent by Verlaine.[114] His friends have accompanied him. They cross the square where everything—trees and flowers—is in order. At the last moment he wonders if the adventure in which he is engaged will not resemble the voyage of his drunken boat, called toward unheard-of lands, but condemned at the end of the race to the cruelest kind of dissatisfaction. It is too late to pull back, though. And Charleville, which he condemns once and for all to execration, disappears in the distance.

PART II

WITH THE
"PITIFUL BROTHER"

IN THE LAND OF THE
"VILAINS BONSHOMMES"

RIMBAUD'S BIOGRAPHY COULD BE PLACED UNDER THE SIGN OF PASSAGE. This is not a retrospective illusion but a reality that aids us to better determine the full scope of letters and encounters. A time always comes when he takes off, cuts things short, grows a new skin. A particular scansion is born from these partings that informs us about the manner in which he lived time and lived in his times, about his connections and separations, and his constant hope for escape and a means of "getting by." The few hours separating Charleville from Paris are also a large temporal border. Rimbaud's future experience will mark him irreversibly, but he will also display an enigmatic fidelity to the places he cursed and yet never truly abandoned: the "idiotic town" of Charleville and Roche, the "lair of wolves."

Verlaine was impatiently awaiting him in Paris. He and some friends had analyzed the verses from this astonishing and impertinent poet. Charles Cros was particularly intrigued by this unusual talent, and his curiosity drove him to accompany Verlaine to the Gare de Strasbourg (the current Gare de l'Est) to welcome the new arrival. The two men missed him, though, either because they got there too late or because they did not recognize him in the crowd of travelers (the more likely possibility). We have to prefer this second hypothesis in which the irony of fate is so visible. Who today would not recognize Rimbaud in a train station? But at the time he did not stand out among all the other arriving passengers, as he was not all that conspicuous despite his being younger than his fellow travelers. What did he look like then? Verlaine remembered "a real child's head, plump-cheeked and young, atop the large, bony and somewhat clumsy body of a still-growing adolescent whose voice, with its strong, almost patois-speaking,* Ardennais accent, had the high and low tones of a boy whose voice was breaking."[1] His extremely young wife, Mathilde would later speak less affably of "a large, sturdy boy with a reddened face, a peasant. He looked like an overgrown schoolboy, because his pants were too short and revealed his blue cotton socks, most likely knit by his mother. His hair was long and wild, he was wearing a cord tie, and he had a slovenly appearance. His eyes were blue and quite handsome, but they had a sly expression that in our indulgence we mistook for shyness."[2] How unfair of ultra-fashionable Mathilde to fault Rimbaud his lack of elegant attire! But her woman's eyes (as well as those of a wife who would always bear a grudge against this intruder) caught certain details that escaped Verlaine—as could well be imagined: the blue cotton socks, for example, that are almost the equivalent of Van Gogh's poor shoes. His gaze was hardly an object of admiration, either. She saw only malice in it. Rimbaud had similarly accused himself of such duplicity when he described himself in the words of the "seven-year-old poet." Later he will simply say: "I got my blue-white eyes from my Gallic ancestors."[3]

Rimbaud resigns himself to the fact that no one is waiting to meet him and makes the long walk to the foot of Montmartre. Three-quarters of an hour later, after asking for directions several times, he finally reaches 14 rue Nicolet. It is there in fact that Verlaine has somewhat inconsiderately promised to put him up. The dwelling is a two-story, bourgeois town house surrounded by a garden, stables, and outbuildings[4] belonging to the independently wealthy Monsieur de Mauté. Verlaine is housed there by his in-laws, whose sixteen-year-old daughter Mathilde, he has recently wed. She is expecting a child and Rimbaud doesn't arrive exactly at the most opportune moment, but his host's promises are his only option. We can imagine the impression he made on the young girl and her mother when he appeared at the door. However, his extreme youth served to excuse him.

---

*The linguist Michel Tamine relayed to me in specialist terminology the most remarkable characteristics of the Ardennes speaking style: a tendency to velarize the frontal [*a*], a disorganization of open *è* and closed *é*, a confusion of the glides [w] and [y] ("huit" is pronounced "oui" and inversely "oui" becomes "ui"), eventually hard to distinguish [*ã*] and [*õ*] in words like "blanc," "blond," etc.

They welcome him into a small salon with Louis-Philippe furnishings on the ground floor. Verlaine and Cros arrive shortly thereafter. Great is their stupefaction before this constrained, almost sullen visitor. Rimbaud in turn sees their faces for the first time: Verlaine, already balding despite being only twenty-seven, is bearded and has prominent Mongol cheekbones.[5] Cros has roguish features, an elegant mustache, and a sparkling eye. A meal is soon served, during which Cros does not refrain from interrogating their guest, who responds to this examination quite reluctantly. Rimbaud is a shy individual, also capable of inexplicable displays of rudeness. On the first meeting, he does not confide in anyone. As an adult he will be the same close-mouthed person he was as a youth. One single phrase survives from his remarks, an absurd fragment that will linger in Verlaine's memory as if to mock oblivion. It is from these nothings that one reconstructs a life (as if with thread)! They are valuable for what they are: an involuntary affront. While sulkily responding to the questions asked him, Rimbaud, on seeing Gatineau, the dog of the house (animals are a refuge for the shy on such occasions), blurts out: "Dogs are liberals!"[6] It is a sparse, politically tinged oracle whose exact meaning remains unclear. With this, weary from his journey, he goes upstairs to sleep in the room reserved for him, where he finds the portrait of an ancestor who inquisitorially glares at him. The next day he will ask that it be taken down from the wall. Charles Cros takes his leave. Verlaine returns to his room, which adjoins Mathilde's, more astonished by the presence in his home of this adolescent from Charleville than he will be by the birth of his own son several days later.

On the next day, the two poets—lets restore them this crucial role—confide to each other the highlights of their existence. Rimbaud tells of his flights, his disappointed hopes, the discovery of his vocation as a seer. Verlaine speaks of his beginnings as a Parnassian[7] before the word had even been invented and Louis-Xavier was publishing the short-lived review *L'Art*. In 1866 the group was already formed. And though Victor Hugo hadn't wished to give them his seal of approval, other great elders had offered these neophytes their patronage. Gautier supported them. The high and mighty Leconte de Lisle, the spirit of impassivity itself, was their close friend and they sometimes visited him at his apartment in the Invalides quarter. There they would often find José-Maria de Heredia, a Spaniard from Havana and crafter of sonnets;

Catulle Mendès, whose Swedenborgian *Philoméla* had been a literary event; Coppée, who resembled Bonaparte and was already composing very simple poems that were a foreshadowing of his *Intimités*; Dierx, Valade (one of the witnesses at Verlaine's wedding), and the superb Villiers de l'Isle-Adam, "playing a naive Hamlet," who possessed a profound intelligence formed from the thought of Hegel and was an excellent storyteller as well. Their affinities outweighed their individual differences. This union had been strengthened when they joined in support of a play by the Goncourts, *Henriette Maréchal*. This was certainly not their battle of *Hernani*, but as the play had been sharply criticized, they made certain to give it extravagant ovations night after night. People had taken note of them on this occasion.

Though *L'Art* was forced to sink with all hands, Ricard's ambitions had not sunk with it. Soon after he presented the young Alphonse Lemerre, a Norman bookseller who had established a small store at 47 passage Choiseul, with his idea of creating a permanently appearing anthology whose first working title was the very banal *Les Poètes contemporains*. Fortunately, others preferred *La Parnasse contemporain* to his choice (a reference to the old poetry collections published during the Renaissance). The publication appeared in installments. Nothing to attract the wrath of the critics was found in the first issue, which opened with five poems by Gautier, followed by Banville's great work, *L'Exil des dieux*, and the sonnets of Heredia, nor in the second issue devoted entirely to Leconte de Lisle. The same did not hold true for the fourth issue in which Catulle Mendès's "Le Mystère du lotus," which on a first reading, with its confused references to Hindu mythology, gives an annoying impression of hodge podge. This was enough for Barbey d'Aurevilly, the "constable of Letters," to take up his most elegant pen and brand all the writers enlisted under Lemerre's *Fac et spera* ensign with the name of Parnassians, an appellation that stuck. The following issues introduced to the public some high-quality poets: intimists such as the Coppée of *Les Promenades et Intérieurs* and moralists like Sully-Prudhomme. Among the surprises were Verlaine himself and his colleagues from the Hôtel de Ville: Dierx and Valade who, after putting in their day at the office, would gather at the Café du Gaz to read their verses composed under the benevolent auspices of the administration. For four years Verlaine's work had been evolving in this milieu in which the spirit of fantasy allied with the quest for beauty, a panacea so well represented by Banville's work. Their meetings were numerous and gay, whether in the mezzanine of passage Choiseul or in the homes of such extremely beautiful patrons like Nina de Callias who was in love with Charles Cros and gave exquisite parties. Sometimes a meal would draw them together as well. The dinners of the Vilains Bonshommes,[8] a name they had daringly adopted following the performance of *Le Passant*, a wildly successful play by Coppée staged at the Odeon Theater, had been inaugurated recently. The *Nain jaune* theater columnist Cochinat had coined this name for them and they quickly transformed his insult into a veritable symbol of self-promotion. Verlaine has promised Rimbaud he will present him in all these exalted places of poetry. He has already announced his imminent arrival and passed around some of his poems.

As Rimbaud was surprised at his host's complete availability, Verlaine was compelled to admit to him that he was no longer working. He had been dismissed[8bis] from his job as a scheduling clerk after the Commune, leaving him complete freedom for writing. Moved by his Republican convictions, he had joined the National Guard during the period of the Commune and held a position of some responsibility. He was soon named "head of the press bureau," a relaxing occupation that consisted of reading "all the articles that were favorable or hostile" to the insurgents in the newspapers and writing refutations when called for. Now the repression following the Bloody Week had struck indiscriminately, and Mathilde's half-brother Charles de Sivry—a decent musician and hardly a militant—had been arrested because of his contacts with several insurgents and deported to the camp of Satory. Verlaine feared the worst. For the moment he was living on what money his mother could spare him, and he received room, board, and laundry at the home of the Mautés, who did their best to help the young couple. His marriage was most likely a love match following a turbulent youth that included frequentation of brothels, maybe some platonic homosexual relationships, and immoderate consumption of alcohol. At the very least, he viewed it as an opportunity to settle down. But the Commune period buried such good resolutions. He had started to drink again and hang out with hoodlums. After the Bloody Week, with Mathilde pregnant and Verlaine in fear of prosecution, the young couple had left for three months "to recuperate in the country" at the home of his uncle Julien Dehée, the Fampoux sugar producer,[9] whom

Bretagne also knew. They also went to the home of Verlaine's cousins, the Dujardins, in Lécluze. This September they had just returned to Paris for the birth of the child. Mathilde's father, Monsieur Mauté, had been absent some time hunting on his lands, which made it all the easier for Verlaine to invite Rimbaud. But his father-in-law would be returning soon and there was no guarantee that the new arrival would benefit much longer from the hospitality now so generously granted him.

Although Rimbaud had been warmly welcomed, it isn't difficult for the traveler to guess at the precarious nature of his situation. He takes Verlaine's measure—on whom he had conferred the title of "seer" from afar—with his customary lucidity. The author of Les Fêtes galantes, and La Bonne Chanson (composed for Mathilde that very year) is mired in a domestic life that Rimbaud has no use for. He finds pleasure in opposing this world of duties and necessities with an offhand manner. He acts with indifference toward Mathilde, who is in the final weeks of her pregnancy, and refuses to do anyone the slightest favor. He spends a great deal of time casually lying on the steps outside the house warming himself under the autumn sun. One day, surrendering to the irritating habit he had picked up in Charleville, he steals an ivory crucifix belonging to the family. He planned on selling it, no doubt for the purpose of acquiring some books or new clothes.[10] The dependent state in which he was forced to live hardly suited him.

However, Verlaine, whose weakness of character, intemperance, and taste for idleness were revealed to Rimbaud a little more each day, took him on the rounds throughout Paris: Chez Battur (a restaurant on rue des Martyrs, where he was given the nickname of the boy Baptist), the Rat Mort, the Café de Madrid, the Café au Suède, the Café au Gaz facing the Hôtel de Ville, and the Café au Delta. The two men went from drink to drink (especially absinthes) passionately discussing the future of poetry. Did Rimbaud repeat the terms of his famous letters from the month of May that Verlaine knew nothing about? Verlaine's memory recalls opinions that Rimbaud may not have held at this specific time, since he remembers conversations concerning free verse and various experiments in prose. Rimbaud's creations from this time remain quite mysterious. They existed, but only fragments remain, giving us only a very approximate idea of their true nature.

Their frequenting of the establishments in the Latin Quarter or on the boulevards, as well as the most no-name wine shops, could not go on for long without the worst consequences. Four days after the birth of his son Georges (born October 30), Verlaine returned quite late to rue Nicolet in a state of extreme drunkenness.[11] Completely dressed and still wearing his hat, he stretched out on the conjugal bed with his feet on the pillow. Mathilde could not help but observe Rimbaud's detestable influence. The two partners had ears only for each other. Verlaine succumbed again to his penchant for drinking binges, so painfully kept under control during the first months of his marriage. In addition, his homosexual desires that had already emerged in *collège* and most recently drawn him toward Lucien Viotti (an old *lycée* companion killed during the Commune), reawakened and pulled him toward Rimbaud.[12] The artless nature of the young Ardennais, even his rustic uncouthness and paradoxical "innocence," could only seduce him. Rimbaud, who had mocked the insidious brushing touches of the priests lusting after the young seminarians in "Un coeur sous une soutane," was not ignorant of this forbidden love that may have been violently forced upon him by the *francs-tireurs* of the Babylon barracks or whose unusual pleasures Bretagne may also have extolled the to him. He strove to convince Verlaine to engage in a lifestyle assuring access to "clairvoyance." The recommended solution—as will be recalled—is the cultivation of monstrosities. Self-depravity thus furnishes the companions a reverse method, a self-transformation of the individual with the objective of renewing poetry. Slovenly appearance (anti-Dandyism), numerous drinking binges, a hurtful sincerity, sarcasm, and the contrary practice of love form the elements of a program that may or may not have been rigorously followed during this period. The eyewitnesses always paint an image of a disturbing, cruelly joking, violent, and extremist Rimbaud. He is heard swearing without restraint. He is witnessed threatening to kill various people, blowing tobacco smoke up the nostrils of an innocent coach horse,[13] and trashing the lodgings put at his disposal. To tell the truth, it is less interesting to recount these anecdotes in great detail than to spot a form of character or resolution behind them. Rimbaud seeks to displease. In Charleville and Douai, he had once wished to attract the good graces of an Izambard (with whom he broke off relations), a Demeny, a Bretagne. Now he strives to shock those who help him. Like a koan master,[14] he seeks to awaken the other through violence or the seemingly absurd. It is easy to see that he is then viciously profiting from his newfound freedom (it is not known if he shared news of his life then with his mother), and that he is administering, as if in spite of himself, some lessons in *savoir-vivre* to those he considers to be merely going through the motions of living.

Thus bullied Verlaine, became more and more attached to him. Rimbaud both used and abused him; their relationship took an ostensibly scandalous turn. Hadn't the two friends dared to offer their arms to each other (almost certainly out of bravado) during the intermission of the première of *Le Bois* by Glatigny, with all Paris in attendance! The journalists on this November 15 couldn't help but note the adolescent with the eyes of "an exiled angel," and the following day Edmond Lepelletier, a long-standing friend of Paul's, did not hesitate to write in *Le Peuple souverain* (which he signed with the pseudonym Gaston Valentin) that seen "circulating and chatting in the foyer [. . .] were the *saturnalian* poet Paul Verlaine arm in arm with a charming young person: Mademoiselle Rimbaud."[15] A sarcastic warning that may have alarmed Verlaine if he had not chosen to laugh at it. He was following a practice of scandal, basically little different from that of the Jeune-France of 1830, but it was less out of a poetic design than from opposition to the bourgeoisie, for getting out of the common rut in which he feared otherwise becoming bogged down.

Full of pride from his discovery, he does not dream of keeping the "strange beast" for himself alone. He had promised Rimbaud. He would make him known. He therefore introduces him to Valade, Aicard, Merat (known as Tricks Death), an excellent draughtsman Jean Forain (known as Gavroche[*]), and an extremely young man full of verve and talent, Camille Pelletan. These are his closest friends, unlike the Parnassians in certain respects. Though drawn together by their mutual esteem for the *Parnasse*, they each assert the force of their individual personalities. Friendship unites them as much as poetry. Rimbaud is soon brought to the home of Banville to whom he read his "Le Bateau ivre." The master admires it but not without offering some well-meaning formal criticisms. Why have a boat speak (it would have been

---

[*] Meaning "ragamuffin"—translator's note.

---

better, in his opinion, to say a "vessel"[16])? Rimbaud, furious, finds nothing better to do when leaving but grumble a suppressed and caustic "Old jerk!"

He had undoubtedly already recited his "Bateau ivre"—for which he has such high expectations and which in his eyes constitutes a probationary text—at one of the dinners of the Vilains Bonshommes shortly following his arrival. Our literary history swarms with these little societies faithful to ancient traditions: the Bacchic reunions of the poets of the Pléiade in Arcueil, the songwriters of Caveau, and so on. The term *Vilains Bonshommes* came, as we have seen, from a sarcastic expression bestowed by Victor Cochinat (known as Bamboula[17]) on Coppée's supporters who had attended the premiere of *Le Passant* on January 14, 1869. In fact the Vilains Bonshommes continued the tradition of the Swans Dinners that already brought together certain Parnassians. Most often they met at the Hôtel Camoëns on the Rue Cassette, near the current Saint-Germain-des-Prés, or at the restaurant Les Mille-Colonnes, under the arcades of the Palais-Royal on rue Montpensier. From August to December 1871 they met at Chez Ferdinand Denogeant, "a restaurant with meals at set prices" and "wines at retail cost." The friends (about thirty guests) all contributed toward an adequate meal, with plenty to wash it down (it goes without saying). An invitation decorated with a callipygus woman (by Félix Régamey) alerted each member to the day of the reunion. Verlaine brought Rimbaud, who read his "Bateau ivre" following the other recitals. Its effect was considerable, even if we shouldn't get carried away by its success, as the gathering was quite naturally well disposed toward the new arrival. But the letter written by Léon Valade on October 5, 1871, to Émile Blémont,[18] then in England, constitutes an exceptional document that clearly shows how strongly Rimbaud struck his audience:

> You certainly missed out by not attending at the last dinner of the Affreux Bonshommes. There, a most *outrageous* poet, not yet eighteen, named Arthur Rimbaud, was exhibited, under the auspices of Verlaine, his inventor and, in my opinion, his John the Baptist on the Left Bank. Big hands, big feet, a completely babyish face that could be that of a thirteen-year-old boy, deep blue eyes, a temperament more wild than shy, such is this kid, whose imagination full of unheard-of powers and corruptions has fascinated and terrified our friends.

"What a great subject for a preacher!" Soury exclaimed. D'Hervilly said: "Jesus in the midst of the doctors." "It is the Devil!" Maître declared to me, which led me to coin this newer and better description: "The devil in the midst of the doctors." I cannot provide you the poet's life story. You should know only that he has just come from Charleville with the firm intention of never returning to his home or family.

Come, you will be able to see his verses and judge for yourself. Barring the millstone that Fate so often holds in reserve to weight our heads, *this is a genius rising.* This is the cold expression of an opinion I've had three weeks to think over and not a passing fancy.

Valade could not know that the millstone would long weigh on this head that would later refrain from speaking of its own volition. Several of those in attendance at this reading have retained equally vivid memories of it, and Jules Claretie uses strangely similar language to describe him to one of his correspondents.[20] Of course, we would be mistaken to think Rimbaud seduced everyone. Verlaine will recall a decade later that the great Parnassians who sought to make his acquaintance, often through simply granting him an interview, didn't react so warmly in his favor. The youngest poets—those least subservient to the struggles between the various schools—admired him, whereas the more highly placed suspected him of being some sort of illusionist or "con man." As François Coppée would say quite frankly, a "successful shirker[21] or worse, a second-rate Petrus Borel, a failed Romantic, a skilled amateur of racket and daydreams, which is Catulle Mendès's judgment in his *Rapport sur le mouvement poétique français de 1867 à 1900.*[22] Among the occasional guests at the dinners of the Vilains Bonshommes, Mallarmé—destined to become the most illustrious of all—will retain an unusual recollection of Rimbaud. It is the poet's hands that seem to have stayed in his memory, like a fragment fallen from an Orphic body. He describes them, in fact, "as something proudly or foully sprouting from a daughter of the common folk, I add to his laundryman status, because of his large hands and their transition from hot to cold reddened by chilblains. Which indicated yet more terrible vocations to belong to a boy."[23] Mallarmé obviously kept in mind what Verlaine had written about Rimbaud in 1883 when he edited his text. What is important for our purposes is that he saw Rimbaud like a sort of

Jeanne-Marie or Gervaise, like a laundrywoman at the Goutte d'Or with chilblain-covered hands that abruptly confer a violent strangeness to the task of writing.

Despite the promises he had made to Verlaine, Rimbaud, the apprentice vagabond, couldn't stay in one place for long. Verlaine would later recall that his protégé benefited "from the most amiable, largest . . . and most *circular* hospitality."[24] Following the poet during the autumn and winter of 1871 will quickly make one dizzy. With the return of Verlaine's father-in-law, he left the Mautés' town house. The recent birth of the little Georges occupied the minds of those there more than this intruder, who Mathilde and her half-brother Charles de Sivry felt had dubious morals, even when making allowances for youthful indiscretions. Verlaine then entreated his friends to shelter the needy one, "the turn of each (coming) on a day-to-day basis during the costly and glacial season."[25] Charles Cros, who had attended the landing of the prodigy, was the first to take him under his roof. His solid friendship for Verlaine and the sincere admiration he bore the newcomer explains this spontaneous act of generosity. He was then renting a kind of studio at 13 rue Séguier, not far from the quai des Grands-Augustins[26] that served as a bachelor pad as well as a laboratory. Cros pursued research there that wasn't inspired only by the "science of love."[27] An original scholar, he hadn't yet discovered the principles of color photography or the phonograph, but was seeking to fabricate synthetic gem stones. He was eventually successful at this and never hesitated to assume enormous expenditures to achieve his goals. He also lived in this lodging where he put up needy artists. He wasn't the sole occupant of the space, though, in that a certain Penoutet—a painter of realistic seascapes who had been given the sobriquet of Michel de l'Hay— sometimes worked there.

Cros was a mentally distinguished enthusiast of the unusual, a "seer" in his own way and an alchemist of fantasy. He also composed sharp-witted, beautiful, and disillusioned poems of a profound lightness such as Nerval wrote. He had already written much of his *Le Coffret de santal*. But he cultivated a sense of happiness—though certainly tinged with melancholy—that annoyed the gloomy and unpredictable Rimbaud who was so profoundly misanthropic. In any case, Cros was unable to look after the boy he had housed so cordially much longer. It seems that Rimbaud went out of his way to behave toward his host in an intolerable way, tearing out—this at least is what Gustave Kahn says—the pages from a collection of *L'Artiste* that had been carefully saved by Cros because it contained some of his poems. Rimbaud took them for a very simple, too simple use![27] On another occasion, when Cros hospitably cleaned Rimbaud's shoes, the latter expressly went out into the street to make them as filthy as before. His vexing conduct and sarcastic remarks doomed his situation there. The young man from Charleville remained faithful to himself in derision and boorish behavior. It isn't reported that Cros showed him the door but Rimbaud must have realized that his inflammatory little game had reached its limits.

From what we know, Rimbaud, upset with everything and irritated by what he found in the world of poets, as well as embittered by Verlaine, who was still bound to his family whereas he had had the courage to cut his bridges, soon precipitated himself into the worst kind of bohemianism and went back to those wretches among whom he had lived one or two weeks during the month of February 1871. It is in their company, near the place Maubert, that Verlaine, alarmed by his absence, will find him after days of searching. With what words could he convince him to return, not to the straight path, but to rejoin his fellows, that is, the poets who had disappointed him so? It was no doubt on Verlaine's initiative that various friends decided to put together a collection to help Rimbaud and provide him a kind of "income" (three francs a day!) in order for him to "devote himself to his great art, with no concern for the result." A letter from Charles Cros, decidedly lacking in spite, asks Gustave Pradelle's participation and neatly puts the name of the subsidized one as "the foster child of the Muses."[28] In addition, Théodore de Banville, a close friend of Verlaine's, who didn't forget that Rimbaud had first applied to him as a veritable savior, proposed to house him in a maid's room attached to his apartment at 10 rue de Buci, near the Odéon. They took pains to make him welcome, but Rimbaud—who had caught lice from his contact with the bums—found nothing better to do than strip off his clothes and appear naked at the window the first day he was there. The scandalized neighbors complained, and Banville was forced to remonstrate with his guest who won't remain long at this completely makeshift refuge.[29] Much worse was subsequently told about his unpleasant conduct toward the author of *Gringoire*. But should we believe Rodolphe Darzens, for example, the original prefacer of *Reliquaire* who diligently collected every piece of gossip?[30] It is more than certain that these numerous acts of bizarre, often ostentatious behavior corresponded to a much deeper intent for Rimbaud. Its continuity has to be taken under consideration, for it then allows the affirmation of a lifestyle to be heard.

In October, Charles Cros—who we find mixed up in Rimbaud's Parisian life of 1871 almost as much as Verlaine—takes the initiative to create a meeting spot for his friends. The opportunity was provided him by the availibility of a room at the Hôtel des Étrangers, an establishment that occupied the corner of rue Racine and rue de l'École de Médecine and looked out over boulevard Saint Michel in the heart of the Latin Quarter. The room was located on the fourth floor, if we are to believe the vignette in the *Album zutique*[31] portraying the building. However, when Ernest Delahaye came to visit Rimbaud in November, he found him in the mezzanine of the hotel, and his *Souvenirs* assert that this is where the meetings of the group took place.[32] Rimbaud found an entirely temporary home there. It isn't certain that it was reserved specifically for him, because, as the upright piano set against the wall attested, it first went to the musician Cabaner. Cabaner, whose scrawny face ("Jesus Christ after three years of absinthe,"[33] said Verlaine) had had the honor of being painted by Manet, was one of the characters of the quarter.

> Cut by an unyielding and straight part
> His long, straight hair sticks to his forehead;
> His wild and stiff beard has the suspect redness
> Of Dante's having seen what no other will see.[34]

He had pursued his studies at the conservatory, where he had been the student of Marmontel. But since then, celebrity shunning him (for he only composed bluettes), he had led a miserable life as an accompanist in low-class music halls and pubs. Thirty-seven years of age, his health was already seriously compromised by tuberculosis. A friend of Verlaine's brother-in-law, Charles de Sivry, he had set the works of many poets to music, going from the serious—Banville's "Niobe," to the comic, "Le Hareng saur" by Charles Cros. He inspired sympathy and mockery by turns. Furthermore, he had grown accustomed to being the butt of the group's jokes (in which no malice was intended). The influence he had on Rimbaud is difficult to assess, it is probable that during the course of their brief cohabitation the two men shared many discussions that went beyond the ordinary and lost them in incredible speculations. No doubt he introduced Rimbaud to a kind of music quite different from that played by the Charleville town band, and which is a superlative forecast of the *Illuminations* (in which it does not figure only as a simple metaphor). Cabaner was the Parisian counterpart for Rimbaud of that bizarre initiator: Auguste Bretagne. An unexpected discovery has been made of "Le Sonnet des sept nombres"[35] written in his hand, a quasi-kabbalistic work dedicated "to Rimbald." Cabaner develops here the visions evoked by each note of the scale. He had composed a song along the same vein that takes the newcomer to task: "What are you doing in Paris, poet / come from Charleville?" The refrain of this "scie,"* which consists of no less than seven couplets, shows Rimbaud's state of mind at that time: "Child, what are you doing on earth? / —I wait, I wait, I wait! . . ." From verse to verse, Cabaner evokes with ironic insistence the "poor mother" abandoned in Charleville, proof that Rimbaud had recounted his personal history to him and provided details of the one he now nicknamed the *"daromphe,"* or in other words the mistress, she who makes the law. The goodhearted Cabaner wrote this bluette without concealing his tender feelings for "the child." He was said to be attracted both by Venus and Cupid; the end of the song leaves little doubt concerning his tastes: "It was to sound your nature, / Child, that I spoke to you thus, / But I would offer you food, / Clothing, . . . bed . . . if you wanted." It was never said that he managed to "sound the nature" of Rimbaud!

The club, formed thereby in an inorganic fashion, had only an ephemeral existence. The traces it left were numerous, though, starting with those contained in the *Album zutique*, in which all (or almost all) of the members wrote poems of a parodic and most often scatological nature. It seems that the regulars of the Hôtel des Étrangers were unanimous in choosing to call themselves by the unusual term *Zutistes*. The word is not too strong. Compared to the other more displeasing swear words that Rimbaud gladly uttered, zut! [equivalent to "damn"—translator's note] remains good form. It wasn't used as readily then as now, but its use goes back to the glory days of Roman-

---

* A practical joke repeated endlessly—translator's note.

---

ticism when Borel, for example, had one of the characters in his novella *Passereau* say: *"Zuth et bran pour les Prussiens!* [Damn and shit for the Prussians!][36] The *Zutistes* used it to show that they reviled the society in which they led low-key lives. They were the forerunners of pleiads of marginal mindsets, bohemian and contentious artists, longhairs, hydropaths, and others. The *Zutistes* express a moment, an episodic mentality. They allow the foretaste of a strong period in literature, but they seem to have had anxieties about creating works, although less than the future Dadaists. For the pleasure of meeting one another far from honest folk and philistines, a makeshift community was formed, given concrete shape by a locale: Cabaner and Rimbaud's room, a book: the famous *Album*, and some very simple rituals like drinking—often more than reasonable—and sometimes taking hashish— attested to by several phrases in the *Album* and in the tale of Ernest Delahaye, who had come to Paris to see Rimbaud and found him discomfited from having taken that drug for which Baudelaire and Gautier had already expressed their appreciation.

The *Album*, an extraordinary testimony that came down to us almost miraculously (no miracle, for it was carefully preserved by the actor Coquelin the younger, the regular interpreter of Charles Cros's monlogues) conjures up a singular ambiance. The first page notably, following the fantastic drawing by Antoine Cros that opens the book, merits being cited.

OPINION OF THE CIRCLE

(MÉRAT.) Five sous! It's ruinous! Asking me for five sous?
Insolents, the lot! . . . (Penoutet.) Old chap! I've just come from the Café Riche;
I saw Catulle . . . (Keck.) Me, I would like to be rich—

(VERLAINE) Cabaner, some fire wa . . . (H. Cros.) Gentlemen, you are loaded!

(VALADE.) The devil, not so much noise! The woman downstairs
Is giving birth . . . (Miret.) Have you seen the article on Austria
In my review? . . . (Mercier) Horrors! gentlemen, Cabaner is cheating on the
refreshments! (Cabaner) I . . . can . . . not answer everyone!

(GILL.) I am not drinking, I'm paying! Go look for something to drink,
Here are ten sous! (A. Cros.) Yes! Yes! Mérat, do me the honor of believing

---

this, / Zutism is the real name of the circle! (Ch. Cros.) In truth,
I am the authority! Authority is me . . .

(JACQUET.) No one is playing the piano! it is vexing for one to waste
His time, Mercier, play the Joyous Viv . . . (Rimbaud.) Ah! shit!

In these remarks of the circle (signed "Léon Valade" and "J. Keck"), all the friends are speaking to the company at large. Familiar names are seen there, including that of Mérat, who wasn't yet angry with Rimbaud, as will be seen later on. Some of them were only shooting stars, though. We know nothing of Miret, who claims to have a review. Jean Keck is hardly any better known. On the other hand, we have already met Pénoutet sharing Charles Cros's studio. Cros appears as the uncontested leader. He is fittingly surrounded by his brothers: Antoine the doctor and Henri the wax sculptor. Mercier occupies a more modest place. He will later direct the *Revue du Monde nouveau* in which Mallarmé's "Le Démon de l'Analogie" will be published. Especially notable at the heart of this unusual cenacle are Verlaine and Valade, both former table companions at the agapes of the Vilains Bonshommes, and André Gill, the caricaturist who Rimbaud may have remembered meeting a year earlier when, in a wretched state, he had sought shelter at the painter's studio. The colorful *Album zutique* is not simply a source of information about the activities of some eccentrics, it betrays the profound transformations that were affecting poetic milieus of that era. The Parnassians, barely gathered around their editor Alphonse Lemerre, had been dispersed. The war of 1870 and the Commune had necessarily created rifts. The partisans of the insurgents such as Verlaine and Valade now refused any contact with those who had more or less allied with those in power. Leconte de Lisle and Heredia had conducted themselves like haughty bourgeois. Their poetry, when all was said and done, was in the same vein as their political opinions: hieratic in character, conventional in ideas, and rigid in form. Elsewhere, the good François Coppée, whose well-meaning "La Grève du forgeron" earned him their reproaches, had revealed the down-to-earth nature of his talent and the lack of imagination in his "humble efforts" with works like his *Promenades et Intérieurs* that bordered on incompetence. (Verlaine, when he was in Fampoux in July 1871, had sent Valade two ten-line poems in this style, obviously written as parodies.) Lastly, several delicate young poets irritated these outspoken drinkers and unrepentant eccentrics with their simpering ways. Ratisbonne wasn't done exploiting the lucrative vein of his "Comédie enfantine"; Alphonse Daudet celebrated those souls oversensitive to the cold. All the pieces in the *Album zutique* present a mocking indictment against poetry that is too beautiful, which they gleefully counter with the realities of the lower body staged comically to make the advocates of a sanitized and contrived beauty more worldly-wise. It was certainly not out of a concern to open the path to a future poetry that the *Zutistes* composed their superb mockeries. It would be wrong to regard these works only as an insignificant amusement, though. Their fashion of emphasizing the literary tics of their victims finds its counterpart in the scouring violence of the prodigious rebel of Letters who was Isidore Ducasse (who died an unknown in November 1870). Verlaine, Rimbaud, Valade (who didn't keep his promise) figure among the most assiduous collaborators of this singular visitor's book. Sometimes Coppée inspired their creation of a *cuadro* of an accomplished humor in praise of a triumphant mediocrity, sometimes they skillfully dashed off monosyllabic sonnets in which the French language is put to a severe test. Rimbaud provides some unusual wonders, his sparkling magic gilds the rebel and slangy words with which he shapes certain poems. He writes a sonnet in collaboration with Verlaine[37] that says much about the awakening of his sexuality, stimulated by the reading of licentious books such as those *Joyeusetés galantes et autres de vidame Bonaventure de la Braguette*,[38] which the excellent Glatigny had published illicitly in Brussels. In imitation of Mérat, who had celebrated the parts of the female body in his collection *L'Idole*,[39] Rimbaud composed an extremely artistic celebration of the "Asshole" with Verlaine. "Our buttocks are not theirs," notes the first verse, subsequently establishing a close and shameless companionship between the text's actors. But the most remarkable piece from this very unorthodox anthology remains "Les Remembrances du vieillard idiot," signed "François Coppée," but clearly Rimbaud's by right. This time, the parodist seeks less to imitate his model than to create a somber, suffocating atmosphere in which the mysteries of sexuality and the troubled feelings they provoke are described with an astonishing precision, one that is sometimes revealed in dreams. Rimbaud, who is no longer seeking to provoke laughter, gives here an inadmissible sequel to his "Poètes de sept ans" and

"Les Premières Communions." He shows that one can start from the lowest point, out of mud and dust, humors and sweat, to attain a kind of hallucinatory verity. The *Album zutique*, which seemingly gathered together so many derisory poems, defiantly proves that the literary adventure goes on in its fashion. Serious political problems had changed the measures of life. It was no longer possible to continue as before. "Let's make a clean slate of the past," shouted Eugène Pottier's *Internationale* with incisive authority. In the malaise of the newly restored daily life, in the exhausting pinstripe fabric of the passing days, a lively impertinence still stimulated the former advocates of the popular movement—whether political sympathizers or poets—ready for a "renaissance," a title which would be picked up by Émile Blémont a year later as the name for his review that will be too well-behaved for the turbulent Rimbaud.

The meetings in Cabaner's "pad" would last only a short while, even if the activities of the *Zutistes* seem to have been extended under various appellations. Later, another group, the so-called *vivants*, would form and bring together the members of a new Bohemian milieu following hard on the heels of the 1871 group. The poems by Rimbaud inscribed in the astonishing *Album* prove that he had not stopped writing. Certainly the nomadic life he led, going from temporary lodgings to makeshift accommodations, did not allow him to devote himself to the composition of a far-ranging work—as was desired, without being under any illusions, by those who had contributed to ensuring he was free of any material needs. But it was not in his temperament to set off on long-winded works. His creative times smack of the storm, they are times of speed and urgency. He had come to Paris with "Le Bateau ivre." He had made this poem known and it had been admired. Verlaine, attentive to what he was doing, made sure to copy over all the texts of his protégé.

Thus we have at our disposal a small "folder" containing the poems that Rimbaud still held in esteem by the end of 1871. Those that he had sent Verlaine, written by Delahaye in his best handwriting, can be found there. Others have been added, which we can reasonably assume were created during his Parisian sojourn. At the time he had made a gift of several poems to his new friends, offering "Voyelles" and no doubt "Les Corbeaux" (which he will soon disown) to Blémont, to Valade he gives "Oraison de soir,"[40] which bears a great resemblance to the joys of the *Album zutique*. Verlaine will record a

"Tête de faune," which is quite close to the "Faune" he had provided in his *Fêtes galantes*. It is generally accepted that this was the time Rimbaud wrote the sonnet "Voyelles," destined to stupefy several generations of readers and earn its author as much sarcasm as admiration. Must we assume Cabaner's influence here as Pierre Petitfils does?[41] But Cabaner dedicated his "Sonnet des sept nombres" to "Rimbald," as if in recollection of the text written by his roommate and not to supply him with a model. In the roman à clef *Dinah Samuel*[42] (these were very popular with writers of that time—later, Mendès will unveil the salon of Nina de Villard in his *Maison de la vieille*[43]), Félicien Champsaur, an intimate of these bohemians, would provide some revelations about the *Zutistes*. Cabaner is portrayed there under the name of Rapenès. He is shown professing a theory of correspondences that borrows certain intuitions of Swedenborg (read by Balzac, Gautier, and Baudelaire), but also some musical experiments attempted in the eighteenth century by Father Castel, author of a *Clavecin oculaire*. Rimbaud himself appears under the pseudonym of Arthur Cimber and recites his "Chercheuses de poux," a piece he must have written at this time and not at the time of his return from Mazas in September 1870, as believed by Izambard. In the illustrious sonnet of "Voyelles," Rimbaud continues to be inspired by the ideas expressed in his letters of May 1871. It expresses the confusion of meanings and proposes the first rudiments of research on the letters of the alphabet that can lead even to madness.[44]

> A noir, E blanc, I rouge, U vert, O bleu: voyelles,
> Je dirai quelque jour vos naissances latentes:

> A black, E white, I red, U green, O blue: vowels,
> Someday I will speak of your latent origins:

Many ingenious and ingenuous interpretations of this surprising poem will be proposed! To start, the main witness Verlaine seems to have wished to neutralize once and for all any interpretation by declaring with a kind of misplaced detachment: "[. . .] the famous sonnet of "Voyelles" [which] never had in Rimbaud's mind, but the conceit, how justified! of making, to his taste [. . .] quite simply fourteen of the most beautiful verses in any language."[45] These overly categorical remarks were obviously unconvincing. A comparative reading leads one rather to think that Rimbaud constructed his "Voyelles"—

profound reveries on language—on the model of Baudelaire's "Phares": "Delacroix, lake of blood haunted by evil angels." There, where Baudelaire placed the name of an artist, then analogically developed what the work of that artist suggested to him, Rimbaud announced a vowel and formulated the visions it inspired in him. Still, according to Verlaine, a considerable witness, Rimbaud would have fashioned his most beautiful poem around this same time, "Les Veilleurs," about which we know nothing. Verlaine shows himself incapable of reconstituting it from memory (even though he will remember "Paris se repeuple" in its entirety), but he got the strongest impression from it. "It is [he should have said "it was"] written with such a vibration, a breadth, a sacred sadness! And written with such an accent of sublime desolation that in truth I dare believe it the most beautiful thing written by M. Arthur Rimbaud, by a large margin.[46] His first attempts at prose poems (in the style of Baudelaire, Delahaye tells us) would also date from this vague time. So just what was this "Chasse spirituelle" of several dozen pages that was long in Verlaine's possession, then seized by Mathilde and lost ever since?[47]

It appears that Rimbaud was not content simply to spend his time in cafés and play dirty tricks on those who displeased him. He also wrote. Unfortunately his life as a vagabond only provided the most favorable conditions toward the dispersal of his manuscripts, even their irreparable loss. It is possible however that, far from wishing to devote himself to poetry alone, he had sought some precarious employment. A testimony from Henri Mercier, one of the *Zutistes*, gives the impression that he hadn't renounced his dream of becoming a journalist. In fact Mercier recalled offering him a blue velvet suit so that he could decently present himself to the head editor of *Le Figaro*, a newspaper for which he wrote some topical prose pieces: "Les Nuits blanches," "Le Bureau des cocardiers," etc. This information remains unique, but in no way contradicts the projects that had commandeered him so many times in Charleville.

After the closing of the Club des Zutistes, the perpetual motion of Rimbaud's life would get acquainted with a new decor. He strove to remain as long as possible in the burning, wretched, marvelous Paris of workers and poets. Verlaine again sees to finding him accommodation. He finds a garret for his friend in a poor building at the corner of rue Campagne-Première and boulevard d'Enfer in the neighborhood of the Montparnasse cemetery. The ground floor is occupied by the store of a shopkeeper of all manner of goods, a baker, and wine merchant named *Trépied*.[49] Artists were beginning to establish their studios in this quarter. Verlaine also had recently introduced Rimbaud to Jean-Louis Forain, who owed his nickname of Gavroche to his Parisian urchin appearance. The poet of the *Fêtes galantes* loved to promenade ostensibly escorted by these two young men who could only be taken for classic ephebes from a distance. He broad-mindedly awarded them pet names: the little brown cat for Forain, the little blond cat for Rimbaud.[50] Completely absorbed by his desires and propensities, and encouraged by the mad freedom preached by Rimbaud, he deserts his family. His rowdy and vindictive returns home late at night (once, overcome by drink, he threatened to kill his wife and son) alarm his entourage and his mother, who sees full well that alcohol is again disturbing his reason. It is also quite obvious that he is continuing to support Rimbaud. Since the latter's arrival, he had dissipated considerable sums of money that could only be explained by donations to his protégé.

On the evening of December 13[51] Verlaine arrives at rue Nicolet with Rimbaud and Forain, whom he puts up in his room for the night. He leaves for the Ardennes quite early the next morning. He had left instructions that his two friends be looked after, but these latter, hardly disposed to profit any longer from such bizarrely imposed hospitality, also leave the premises at dawn. The steps taken by Verlaine and his impromptu departure are of a surprising nature. In fact, at the end of his resources, he went to claim from the notary in Paliseul the portion of the inheritance that had been left to him by his aunt Louise Grandjean, who had died March 22, 1869. She had been his godmother, who had diligently sought to separate him from his bad companions in Paris, and had dreamed of his marrying a woman from Ardennes. We can easily guess what use he now intends for this money. He will also spend the New Year's holiday at the home of some friends in Paliseul, without making any additional effort to return to the capital with its family scenes and his demanding lover.[52] He, too, was apt to surrender to his vagabond moods. His pilgrimages will next lead him to the Meuse valley. He is seen in Charleville, where he meets Delahaye, with whom he had gotten along famously when the latter had come to Paris, and also at the Café de l'Univers and the goodhearted Bretagne, his old crony from Fampoux, Rimbaud 's mentor *in partibus*. He caricatures Bretagne's pleasant face in a very daring letter, in

which he announces to Charles de Sivry all the pleasure that the clerk of indirect taxation, but especially the excellent viola player, would have in seeing
him again.[53] In Charleville, which Verlaine is undoubtedly seeing for the first
time—and we can easily picture the reconnaissance he made beneath the
windows of 5 *bis* quai de la Madeleine—he gets to know all those of whom
Arthur has spoken.

He has discussions with Deverrière, distinguished intellect, good republican, a brother, and Perrin, director of *Nord-Est*. With these new "camaraux,"[54] he doesn't hesitate to take long excursions in the countryside:

> *Le vent du côteau*
> *La Meuse, la goutte*
> *Qu'on boit sur la route*
> *À chaque écriteau,*
> *Les sèves qu'on hume,*
> *Les pipes qu'on fume!*[55][*]

Thus, Verlaine, in contrast to Rimbaud, who came to Paris to see the literary figures in vogue, now frequented the company of strange individuals,
eccentrics of whom he could expect nothing but friendship, learned para-
doxes, and good, cheap meals.

During this time, Rimbaud spends some anxious days. He is in need of
money, as the small reserve that Verlaine had left him has run out. He still sees
the *Zutistes*, teases Cabaner, tries his hand at argot with André Gill. At the
Louvre, accompanying Forain, who was copying famous works there, he
does not hide the fact that he would have preferred that the Commune
burned these obsolete beauties and useless relics. Such opinions, recounted
by Forain himself,[56] give the impression that the pictoral universe hardly mat-
tered to him. This may be viewed as surprising in light of *Illuminations*. But
such poems depend more on the activity of an inner vision than the perception of real sights. Rimbaud the seer, like the blind Homer, detects the future
more than he registers the present. His reservations concerning painting will

---

[*]The wind from the hillside, / The Meuse, the drop /That we drink on the route / At
each sign, / The saps we breathe in, / The pipes we smoke.

---

not prevent him from being used as a model by a certain Alfred-Jean Garnier, a minor painter in the Montparnasse quarter. The resulting portrait will moreover bear two dates. One indicates that it was executed in 1872, "Bd d'Enfer facing the gate of the Montparnasse Cemetery," which is to say "Rue Campe," as Rimbaud would say to designate his residence, his encampment; the other, on the front, says "1873."[57] The technique is crude, and the subject's features lack resemblance. They portray a Rimbaud who is bony, aged, and morose, as if overwhelmed.

The just beginning year of 1872 still had the greatest uncertainty in store for him. Paul had attained his objective, and the money he brought back would help their scheme for a new life, but Rimbaud, entirely dependent on him, spent hours waiting for him ("Idle youth / Enslaved by everything," he will write later), while Mathilde, hoping to save her marriage, made arrangements for her husband to regain the job he had lost following the Commune. Thanks to certain connections, it appeared possible. However, during a lunch to which Madame Verlaine had invited the office head, who could arrange this reinstatement, a drunken Verlaine had behaved in such deplorable fashion that there was no longer anything to be hoped for in that regard. He also was actively practicing self-depravity. Each day Rimbaud whispered his bad counsel to him and, seduced by this adolescent of inspired impertinence, he surrendered to him all the more willingly because of the closeness already established between them by their sexual relationships. Aside from the "Sonnet du Trou du Cul" (most likely dating from this time), nothing has come from Rimbaud's pen to imply his homosexuality. It should first be viewed as an element to which he acquiesced because it was contained in a system of "reasoned derangement." As for Verlaine, completely absorbed by his saturnian bias, his behavior no doubt came more under the heading of recidivism. A poem he wrote later in the prison at Mons will recall this period in explicit fashion, in that it bears the precise detail: "Concerning a room on rue Campagne-Première, in Paris, January, 1872." "Le Poète et la Muse"[58] retraces the ugliness of that miserable lodging. "O room, have you kept their ridiculous spectres, / full of dirty sunlight and spiderwebs?" he also shamelessly evokes the "nights of Hercules," about which one can make no illusion. But immediately—and Verlaine completely sticks to this denial, this long-suffering culpability—the moral entreaty returns, as if to remove the fault forever:

—

"May one hear it as they please, it isn't that: / You understand nothing of the way things are, good folk." We will reluctantly reproach Verlaine for these few verses. What are these "things"? What is this "that"? With these "things" and this "that," Verlaine and Rimbaud's life was shaped, full of culpability or a savage ingenuity.

On his return from Paliseul in January 1872, Verlaine seems to have done everything in his power to destroy his marriage. His passion for Rimbaud carries him off. Noctambulism, drunkenness, he gluttonously devotes himself to all his old demons. His returns to rue Nicolet take on the air of fistfights. On each occasion he "invents" scenes. Sometimes he threatens Mathilde with a lit match and tries to burn her hair, sometimes he beats her unmercifully, like an inebriated ragpicker. The crowning blow occurs one night when he attacks the little Georges, hurling him violently onto the bed, and then, to silence Mathilde's cries for help, attempts—according to her version of events—to strangle her.[59] On the next day, Verlaine having fled that same night to sleep at his mother's, the young woman leaves with her father and child for a spot far from Paris.[60] Two days later, Verlaine reappears at rue Nicolet. He notes their absence and Madame Mauté at first refrains from telling him where they are. He capriciously seeks to renew ties with his wife but when she assures him by letters that her return is dependent upon Rimbaud's departure, he becomes annoyed and refuses to bow to such demands. In his *Confessions*, pretending not to understand her, he will again accuse her of jealousy toward his friend: "In principle it was not even a question [why does he make this reservation for himself?] of some sort of attachment or fellow feeling [. . .] but more of an admiration, and the extreme astonishment that arose when faced by this sixteen-year-old urchin who had already written things that are, as Fénéon puts it most excellently, 'perhaps above literature' . . ."[61]

Meanwhile, the famous dinners of the Vilains Bonshommes continue with Rimbaud and Verlaine in attendance. One evening,[62] driven to distraction from hearing a certain Auguste Creissels read his insipid "Sonnet de combat,"[63] Rimbaud protests by punctuating the verses of the reading with repeated shouts of "Shit!" Étienne Carjat, wishing to defend the insulted individual, calls the insulter a "little toad,"[64] whereupon this latter takes possession of Verlaine's cane-sword and lightly scratches the one who had dared insult him so.[65] All at once he has made himself an undesirable in the sole milieu that still tolerates him. He had wished to impose his law too quickly, when he was only a talented urchin who had recently arrived from Charleville. However, shortly after his arrival, one of Verlaine's first concerns had been to take him to the studio of this same Carjat so that the former director of *Boulevard*[66] could immortalize the young poet. What remains of that session is one of Rimbaud's best-known photos. He appears to us enclosed in an oval: he seems almost frail in his correct attire. He is full-faced, with a strong chin; the abundant hair of the previous summer has since been trimmed and sticks out in cowlicks poorly disciplined by a comb. His gaze is the most arresting aspect of this portrait. It is clear, haughtily sad, and scrutinizing an imaginary object outside the picture that passes far beyond the spectator; it is quite other-worldly. If Rimbaud is confounded with "Le Bateau ivre," he is also this portrait, forever frozen in dream and lucidity on a background as gray as the sky.

Rimbaud's aggressive gesture against Carjat would have other unfortunate consequences. It was then customary for painters to paint studio scenes that grouped together illustrious friends and models. For example, Baudelaire is depicted reading a book in Courbet's painting *L'Atelier* (he was originally accompanied by Jeanne Duval but later had her erased from the scene). Fantin-Latour, who shared the hopes of young literature, had the idea to paint groups of artists. He had first laid out a *Hommage à Delacroix*. He now wishes to portray Baudelaire's disciples gathered together beneath a portrait of the poet of *Les Fleurs du mal*. Now as those he had solicited first were for various reasons unavailable, he decides to select some minor celebrities and turns to those who frequent the dinners of the Vilains Bonshommes, which he also attends at times. The painting[67] shows them at the end of a meal. The foreground is occupied by a corner of the table covered with a white linen on which are posed a decanter, glasses, and cups. Behind, from left to right, seated or standing, are Verlaine, Rimbaud, Pelletan, Valade, d'Hervilly, Blémont, Pierre Elzéar, and Jean Aicard. Yet the composition appears unbalanced. The bouquet of flowers on the right is hardly imposing; in fact it replaces a ninth confederate, Albert Mérat, who refused to be depicted in this group following Rimbaud's altercation with Carjat. Those who remain in this *Coin de table* (the definitive name given this work), have adopted constrained poses; they give the impression of not knowing one another at all. In profile or in full face, each has the air of being solely concerned with his own image.

Verlaine's embossed Kalmuk face, with its premature baldness, is revealed in three-quarter profile. In this uptight group Rimbaud's face attracts attention. The pose is traditional, but the head, supported by a reddened hand, portrays the pensive beauty of youth. His hair has grown back into a state of romantic disorder since Carjat's photo. Nevertheless, Verlaine will not see an absolute resemblance here and will himself recall, for additional authenticity, that "a sort of tenderness gleamed and smiled in those cruel, clear blue eyes and that strong mouth with its bitter grimace."[68] With this grouping, so incongrous in appearance, Fantin-Latour nonetheless restored the faithful companions of the "saturnian" poet and those second-class individuals who would make a lasting appearance in the short literary life of Rimbaud. Furthermore, on several occasions Rimbaud had consented to go to the studio on rue des Batignolles, where the painter did an admirable gouache of him in preparation for this painting. Finished, but not without problems—Fantin will be forced to remove the figure of Mérat at the last moment—the canvas will be exhibited at the salon in March 1872 and will provide a model for numerous parodic sketches in the satiric press for use in depicting similar groupings.[69]

In the midst of these events, Verlaine is still preoccupied by the flight of Mathilde. Yet he refuses all the compromises proposed to him. However, a demand for separation is soon drawn up by an attorney, accompanied by a medical certificate attesting to the blows and wounds that Mathilde had received. On February 10, Verlaine is summoned to appear in court. With this impending, he finally acts. Immediately he writes his wife that he gives in to her arguments and promises her that he will send Rimbaud away. We can imagine the discussion he had with the latter to convince him to return to his native Ardennes. We can hear his interlocutor's sarcastic comments even now. But as he has no money at his disposal, Rimbaud cannot close ranks. He will have to leave as soon as possible, for home or somewhere close, since Verlaine, with an undoubtedly thoughtful intention, takes pains—it seems—to send him not directly to Charleville, but to one of his relatives' homes in Arras, swearing to call him back as soon as possible.[70] Mathilde, now assured of her supremacy, does not delay in returning. When the inconvenient one catches the train at the Gare du Nord with rage in his heart, he knows that the history of "lying couples"[71] easily parasites the ambitions of poetic life. Once more, the drunken boat will be bumping against the banks of his native port.

MARTYRDOM, PRAYERS,
AND THE WAY OF THE CROSS

WE CURRENTLY KNOW NOTHING ABOUT RIMBAUD'S STAY IN ARRAS AND THE surrounding area, but it is more than likely that he stayed with a member of Verlaine's maternal family, the Dehées. According to Delahaye, toward the end of 1871, Madame Rimbaud recieved an anonymous letter informing her of son's misconduct. Who would have had the motive to send this letter if not the Mautés themselves, eager to rid their son-in-law of this parasite? It is possible Rimbaud surrendered to her pleas and threats to return at the very moment Verlaine was seeking to get rid of him temporarily, and that he did return, though not directly, to Charleville.

Back in his "supremely idiotic" town, he was still totally opposed to finding work and returning to the straight and narrow. Intoxicated by an absolutely useless freedom, he concentrated on visiting old friends (Delahaye, Deverrière, Bretagne), and telling scandalous stories to the young people frequenting the cafés, among whom he began to gain a serious reputation as an incorrigible bohemian. Among the unsavory anecdotes circulating about him, one is particularly revealing about his instinct for provocation. On seeing the stray dogs that wandered by while he was sitting at a table drinking a beer, he is supposed to have said—loudly and clearly—that he would sometimes take one home to subject it to the "ultimate outrage."[72] No doubt about it, Rimbaud had thought long and hard about the canine tribe since his remark about the dog Gatineau! However, his remarks—one would hope—did not always confine themselves to such boasts. Reflective of this, Delahaye states that Rimbaud was carrying out several different poetic projects during February 1872. Rimbaud would soon return to Paris. The two months he had spent in the Ardennes are currently burdened by his biographers with a large number of heteroclite creations: "new" verse, the first *Illuminations*, other endeavors in prose—which is demonstrative, in fact, of the total uncertainty that

---

111

exists when it comes to dating such texts. It remains difficult to form an opinion on this supposedly fertile period, but which could not have reasonably consolidated all the multiple shelves of Rimbaldian poetry in its extreme brevity. If we rely on Delahaye, there are several, sometimes contradictory pieces of information that are important to keep in mind.

Following his reading of Michelet and his *Histoire de France*, Rimbaud would have gotten the idea to write a series of narratives evoking certain images of bygone days. Delahaye declares that he crafted a collection of prose poems. Their title, *Photographies des temps passés*,[73] was perhaps inspired by this relatively new art of which he had met several adepts in the persons of Carjat ("the late Carjat," the man he had wished to kill with a cane-sword) and the inventor Charles Cros. Were these "photographs" perhaps forerunners of the *painted plates* [English in original] of the *Illuminations*? Rimbaud wanted to give "magnificent History" a concrete form as he liked to state repeatedly. Hence several visions retained in Delahaye's memory: an evocation of the Middle Ages, "stars of blood and a gold cuirass," a figure from the classical eighteenth century, "wearing a cope and gold miter," and perhaps several pieces of biblical prose, such as Jesus at the pool of Bethsaida. Delahaye's assertion, though unverifiable, deserves to be taken into consideration, if only by virtue of the testimony it brings to bear on that form of writing with which Rimbaud seems to have always experimented. *Une saison en enfer* will bring this poet's prose underlying his beautiful verses luminously to the surface. As unpublished works were discovered, Delahaye would modify the tone of his memories. But he never took back what he said concerning these memorial *Photographies*.

A number of things show that Rimbaud also directed his efforts toward other kinds of research. Through the letters he sent to Verlaine and the latter's responses, it is possible to reconstruct some of the interests he had at this time. He was then spending a good amount of time in the municipal library, and though busy with his discovery of Michelet's *Histoire*, he also took an equal interest in literary forms that apparently were quite foreign to his poems of 1871.

For example, he skimmed the ariettas of Favart, a poet of the eighteenth century and author of naive libretti. His stories about shepherds and shepherdesses, rustic altercations, and their accompanying songs are the first examples of musical comedies. Seduced by these superannuated rhythms, he will send the words and music of the *Ariette oubliée* to Verlaine, which Paul will have sight-read by his brother-in-law, Charles de Sivry.[74] People have been surprised—overly, no doubt—at Rimbaud's unexpected interest in Favart. It is less surprising than one would think, if we recall that Verlaine himself had earlier published his *Fêtes galantes*, placed entirely under the sign of the light and melancholy century of Watteau. The Goncourts had just brought out some essays on the art of this time as well.[75] Rimbaud, although little seduced by painting, nonetheless kept in mind the very fine prosodic successes of his friend. This is definitely a continuation and not a rupture. The Rimbaud of this era—for the little his correspondence allows him to be understood— seems to be foreseeing a new poetics. It will forever be a mystery to us unless texts that are theoretically lost resurface. Verlaine stored the letters from Charleville in a desk at the house on rue Nicolet; he will provide a brief description of them at a later date.[76] We will see that Mathilde took posses- sion of them, entrusted them to an attorney, and burned the ones that appeared the most risqué. She would subsequently declare that all the poems she found there corresponded to texts she saw published later on.[77] In spite of her remarks, it seems likely she was responsible for the disappearance of a certain number of Rimbaud's poetic works, among them, the manuscript of the famous "Chasse spirituelle," a title that stirs the imagination with its aptness and ambition. Verlaine attached the greatest importance to it and regarded it as one of Rimbaud's most beautiful achievements. But was the notebook that contained it sent to him from Charleville?

Rimbaud certainly didn't stop working during his Ardennes exile, even though he refused to take any kind of paying job, much to his mother's dis- may. When he wasn't roaming the neighborhood and haunting the taverns where he slaked an ever more burning thirst—for he was now accustomed to stronger alcoholic beverages—he was reading or writing in his room on the quai de la Madeleine. To the *mother's* remark that this would lead nowhere, he had—according to Paterne Berrichon[78]—this splendid reply: "Too bad, I write, I have to." We have seen what these endeavors may have been. We should also add another group of poems, several of which survive and which Rimbaud most likely copied over and postdated on his return to Paris. Ver- laine, in a missive from April 1872, asked Rimbaud to send his "bad!!!! verses," and his "prayers(!!!)."[79] Several lines further on he repeats this distinction more precisely: "Old verses" and "new prayers." The old verses were therefore considered "bad" by their author—would Verlaine be questioning this, in that he accompanies this judgment with four exclamation points indicating his disagreement? Was Rimbaud then concentrating on the creation of unusual "prayers" to symbolize his status as a condemned man suffering through the martyrdom of a separation that he deemed unjust? In an article that appeared in October 1895 in *The Senate*, Verlaine recalls a collection by Rimbaud, *Études néantes*, that never saw the light of day, and he will point out that the seventeen-year-old poet was quite cognizant of assonance and rhythms that he called "nothings." The poetry of Rimbaud most certainly experienced a profound transformation in these few months. The texts that are habitually named the "new verses," for no absolutely pertinent reason, were undoubtedly born during this spring. It is a tricky business pinpointing those that would have been fashioned in Charleville, at least by relying solely on a few referential elements. However, this perfunctory solution should never be entirely omitted from consideration.

One thing is obvious: the notable difference between the "old verses" ("Voyelles" and "Le Bateau ivre" should be included among these) that still use the alexandrine and the so-called new verses, which apply very different techniques. However, each poem from this period (which undoubtedly extends far beyond this forced sojourn in Charleville) seems to have been the object of a specific treatment. Rimbaud invents on a daily basis, and gradually we are left only to imagine this seemingly dead time in which his creation multiplied. Solitude and imaginative faculties. The whole carried off by an irresistible impetus. In this manner, following the Parisian adventure (that had already burdened him on several occasions with bitterness and new decisions to make) an unforeseeable Rimbaud suddenly appears at the antipodes of the Parnassians and its academicism, receptive in certain respects to Verlaine's remarks on the refinement of vocabulary, search of short meters, harmonic claudication, musicality (there has been a general reluctance to accept this). But where the Verlainian temperament rises only to the *chanson grise*, Rimbaud goes further. As always, he goes beyond, with his trademark primitivism and strength, which briefly made him a simpleton-hyena in quest of a mad innocence—that of the beasts, the moles, the wolves, or even a black man

---

who gives himself to the sun, the "god of fire." In the "Alchimie du verbe," from *Une saison en enfer*, he will become his own biographer relating this very experience, which he says lasted several months. He recounts the story of one of his follies. It corresponds, in fact, to the later outcome of the seer letters. But these were mortgaged by the Commune, whereas in his new verse Rimbaud forgets history. He is on the same wavelength as eternity. We should refrain from raising what was only a transitory experience to a mythic dimension. Rimbaud's "moments" now extend beyond our common measures, but he lived these common measures and surpassed them only through persistent effort.

Far from Verlaine, who he had already embarked upon a way of life, a "way of the cross"[80] with its painful stations, in order to finally assure him that coveted state of "child of the sun"; far from an imposed job to which he refused to bow—"Work is further from me than my fingernail is from my eye. Shit for me! Shit for me!"[81]—he lived in a very special atmosphere that he created for himself. It is not derangement as much as it is an alternately seized and relinquished *desperate enchantment*, a premonition of the nothingness that results when the negative phase leads to freedom, flight, and the "dreamed of disengagment." Our perspective in some of his poems, presumed to have been written at this time, is as if from a background that acts like a referential substratum. Neighborhood ballads of Charleville, countrysides of ancient days, banks of the Meuse, all ensorceled by an alchemical transposition. Sometimes he finds himself in a strange no-man's-land, "far from the birds, the herds, the villagers." At his feet flows the young Oise, where hallucinatory reflections stream past. It sweeps him away to exotic lands where soon, like Gauguin and many defectors from Europe, he will have his adventurer's hut and wineskin full of a "bland, gold liquor that makes one sweat"; sometimes it's another river—the Semoy no doubt—that becomes the red "River of Cassis," transmuting the blood of yesteryear's dead. "Les Corbeaux" forms and transforms an empty scene in which he is once again far from everything, carried off by only the wind. In Rimbaud we hear what direction he is walking and, connected to his lone march on the wide-open road, a kind of song for undoing misfortune, a refrain-viaticum in which isolation speaks as if it were intoxicated. We constantly truly find ourselves here in his fiction, and even more so in the fiction that creates him, the one he uses to daily shape himself.

Another proof is provided by "Mémoire" which some regard as his recollection of the first time he ran away to Paris and others have seen as the fantastically restored departure of his father. But what we read as his priority here is the marvelous nature of a poetic perspective that is insensitive to pity, and uplifted by the words and cruelty of a memory in which the individual finds his purpose against the grain, in the very word that forms and illuminates him.

The biographical tonality remains compatible with the ardent prosodic research to which his poems testify: exploration of the irregular that proceeds from Verlaine himself, but also stems from even more unexpected authors such as Marceline Desbordes-Valmore. Hungering and thirsting for another existence than the one he still must lead, Rimbaud reviews his frustrated desires. "Comédie de la soif" constructs a style of satirical drama in which voices call out to him. His grandparents from Roche, the ancestors who drink coffee on Sunday after visiting the cemetery to look after their dead, as Madame Rimbaud will so faithfully and morbidly do. The Parnassians lost in their dreams of purity, their frozen ideals. The Vilains Bonshommes, enthusiasts of bitters and symbolic inventions: "Nature of the living pillars." Rimbaud, with the impertinence he has already shown when speaking of flowers—a theme harped upon—asserts that he prefers the water "cows drink" to civilized or metaphysical beverages. And on those occasions he takes delight in imagining a universe that will finally be hospitable to him, still best evoked by the green inn of Charleroi where he was served a meal—and kissed—by a girl with enormous breasts one October day. "Comédie de la soif," then, or "Fêtes de la faim." They reveal in almost straightforward fashion the immense desires that possessed him and will ceaselessly haunt him during those months while, strong in his severity and vision of infinity, he swears inside against any aesthetic doctrine fallen into rags: "If I have any taste, it is hardly but for the earth and stones." Few prayers in all of that except in "Honte" (which may not date from this time). Sometimes he does write hymnlike poems that imitate the spiritual songs of Madame Guyon (another author he possibly read). The *Fêtes de la patience* is conceived under the influence of a simple and fervent poetry stoked by despair. "Bannières de mai" is reminiscent of the rogations chanted during the course of long processions to country chapels. The very strange "Âge d'or" expresses in the form of a hymn (with a refrain), the intimate debate that goes on inside every man:

Quelqu'une des voix
Toujours angéliques
—Il s'agit de moi—
Vertement s'explique:

One of the voices,
always angelic,
—it was talking of me—
Sharply expressing itself:

An explanation that nonetheless preserves a fundamental mystery, the very one upon which his personality is constructed. The "Chanson de la plus haute tour," which one could easily attribute to a Saint Anne spying the salutary dawn, but is also reminiscent of the story of Blue Beard, asks: "Can one pray / to the Virgin Mary?" and depicts Rimbaud's precarious situation none better:

Oisive jeunesse
À tout asservie,
Par délicatesse,
J'ai perdu ma vie.

Idle youth
Enslaved by all,
Through too much sensitivity
I have wasted my life.

Indeed nothing could provide a better picture of his state during the beginning of this spring 1872. He appears idle even if poetry and its secret demands remain. And by the same token, he languishes in servitude, his material dependence on Verlaine, from whom he was awaiting a sign to return to Paris.

Verlaine's letters provide a good glimpse of the spiritual struggles taking place then. Rimbaud had returned to the charge, proposing his program of the seer, Verlaine was the soul of prudence, even if he was aware of the "martyrdom"[82] the adolescent was undergoing for his still imprisoned dreams. On April 2 he announced that he had moved some furniture, "things," papers, objects left behind, from "rue Campe" and, going one better than his correspondent, who at the very moment was discovering the light-heartedness of Favart's *Ariettes*, was also swearing that the universe was entirely made of shit, and in turn covered the names of their more or less repudiated mutual friends with filth. A fine conspiratorial alexandrine!

Shit on Mérat—Chanal—Périn, Guérin! and Laure!

An execration that the pests from Charleville and Paris even aimed at Edmond Lepelletier's devoted sister Laure, who Rimbaud had once met at a dinner, destined to end badly as so many others before it.[83]

In mid-March, responsive to the promises that had been kept, Mathilde returned. Seeing his marriage was "back on its feet," all that remained was for Verlaine to reconcile with Rimbaud in complete hypocrisy. For appearances' sake, he had found a job at the Belgian Insurance Company of Lloyds, but dreamed primarily of bringing about the return of the one he desired with all his heart and body.* A slave to his passion, he would reveal his total readiness to resume life with Rimbaud. He gave the appearance of being subservient to the latter's wishes:

Write to me care of Gavroche and inform me of my duties, the life you intend for us to lead, the joys, the pangs, the hypocrisies, the cynicisms that will be called for: I, all yours, all you—the knowledge!—send this care of Gavroche [. . .] A final recommendation: on your return, grab me at once in such a way that we can't be shaken apart—and you can do it so well!

Rimbaud could finally believe the game won, never mind the recent bureaucrat's job found by Verlaine. Nothing could be clearer, in any case, than the assent he was given for a program for existence, one that would later be spelled out in "Vagabonds" (one of the *Illuminations*): "I had [. . .] sworn to restore him to his original state as a child of the sun." Rimbaud followed an intention, a duty, a necessity. Hence the terms of Verlaine's letter enlisting in the adventure. Guaranteed depravity and the conquest of a higher reality. It

---

* The pun made here on the homonym of corps (body) and coeur (heart) is not read-ily translatable—translator's note.

wasn't simply a question of a simple poetic companionship but a love story under construction in which the overly weak lover begs to be treated harshly so that he does not slip back into his old errors. The bewitched Verlaine now lived at the whim of Rimbaud, who haunted even his dreams.[84] One night, he saw him as a *child molestor*, without perhaps suspecting that this infant was none other than himself—given over to the fertile martyrdom imposed upon him by this damned soul. Another time he dreamed of an *all goldez* [*sic*] Rimbaud, that is to say, covered in gold like an idol, but also as object of his homosexual passion.

At the beginning of May, while seated in the Café de Cluny and waiting for his dear friend Forain, Verlaine speeds a last missive to Charleville.[85] The return of the "exiled angel" is imminent. The cost of the train ticket is going to be expedited to him. Then, in several phrases suited to arouse Rimbaud's interest, he allows him a glimpse of a plot planned against a certain gentleman in whom it would be no exaggeration to see his father-in-law: "We are conspiring against someone you know some *spirited acts of revenge*. On your return, if the prospect amuses you, some tigrish things will take place." The vengeance planned against Monsieur Mauté—"the tigrish things"—are moreover hinted at several lines later, with no very clear idea given of what was going on. All would indeed depend on "someone very consequential in Madrid," a very bizarre expression, but one that Rimbaud as a regular of the Café du Madrid could easily decipher, in that Verlaine spent time there with Antoine de Tounens,[86] an original who claimed to be king of Patagonia and generously gave away lands from his chimerical state, as well as the titles of nobility that went with them. In any event, the "tigrish" projects had no known consequences.

From the depths of his fatidic Ardennes, Rimbaud can therefore see, to his great satisfaction, the time of his enforced exile coming to an end. On receiving the money from Verlaine, he takes the train to Paris without necessarily informing his mother of the fact (the mail he received didn't come to his family residence, but to the home of the sympathetic Bretagne, his accomplice in all escapades). Upon his arrival he is given lodging in a garret on rue Monsieur-le-Prince, still in the middle of the Latin Quarter. From his window he can see the main courtyard of the Lycée Saint-Louis and its century-old trees.[87] He finds himself in a familiar environment. Rue Racine is just several hundred yards away. His neighbors are young bohemians, poets like Raoul Ponchon, a recent arrival to the capital; the bushy-headed Jean Richepin, a recent graduate from the École Normale Superièure, but highly interested in argot, hanging out with beggars and dreaming of ancient filibustering; and painters like a certain Jolibois, called "the Apple," a specialist of still-lifes who would subsequently excite less notice than Cézanne! The erratic lifestyle picks up where it left off, the daily drinking binges, the meetings with Forain ("the little brown cat"), or the Cros brothers on whom Rimbaud enjoys playing a tasteless prank one day. He pours sulfuric acid in Charles's glass while he was momentarily absent—an anecdote worthy of Alphonse Allais, and which presumes the juvenile delinquent had access to his victim's own chemicals. However, with the smitten Verlaine Rimbaud either smirks or scratches; he becomes unbearable and displays all the whims of the little mistress: fits of rage, petty demands, jealousies. The "way of the cross" begins. The dangerous life. Growing up fast, in total revolt, and completely intoxicated by freedom, he divides his time between resolute idleness, attempts at writing, and passionate discussions lasting late into nights liberally watered with curaçao bitters and absinthes. Squabbles erupt as well. Rimbaud now carries a crude, sharp, clasp knife worthy of a full-fledged hooligan with which he threatens people at the slightest provocation. One day, in an act of retaliation, he lacerates Verlaine's hands and wounds his thigh.[88] Soon after, Verlaine, invited to dine at his mother's with Mathilde, terrorizes his wife with a knife, as if in imitation of his lover's alarming bloodlust.

Mathilde will be very quickly informed of Rimbaud's return. Ernest d'Hervilly, one of the figures in *Coin de table*, had seen him in the Passage Jouffroy and thought it wise to warn the "little wife."[89] Blinded by his passion, Verlaine increasingly neglects his marriage. Because of Rimbaud's urging him to break with his wife, he often neglects to return home to rue Nicolet and spends the night with his companion. One day he carries his son off to his mother's home. He will return him to Mathilde the following day.[90] On another occasion, he arrives with Rimbaud completely unannounced at rue Lecluse and demands that Madame Verlaine feed and house them. It was definitely time for Rimbaud to move on. Rue Victor-Cousin, two steps from the Sorbonne is where he will soon be lodging, at the Hôtel de Cluny, an establishment that still exists today. The preceding month, he had cleaned up certain texts he had brought back from Charleville, and written others. In the series *Fêtes de la patience* (meaning his patience), before Verlaine and Mathilde's separation, he "waited" (as Cabaner had clearly seen), for the hour in which "real life" would finally be lived. He experiences some inexpressible moments of happiness in this marasmus, even though he has already moved forward into his spiritual odyssey. Alone, and for all our benefit henceforth, he attends perfect nuptials within the confines of his inner horizon:

> *Elle est retrouvée.*
> *Quoi?—L'Éternité.*
> *C'est la mer allée*
> *Avec le soleil.*

> It has been found again.
> What? Eternity.
> It is the sea gone out
> With the sun.

All cruelty abandoned, all lycanthropy stripped away, he has bursts of total adhesion with the world, a "fatality for happiness." At four o'clock on a summer morning, a warm feeling allows him to see the workers already filling the streets as marvelous beings, constructing a fabulous architecture. The human toil that follows is a promise of universal love, under the tutelage of Venus, queen of the Shepherds. Here he has momentarily happened into an idyllic world, not far from Arcadia. Other times he feels that this transporting happiness is of an exceedingly precarious nature and responds to what is only an illusion of his senses. The couple that he forms for the worst with Verlaine also rests on experiences of unbridled sexuality that leave him all too often with a taste of disenchantment at dawn, when the angelus drowns out the stupidly victorious cries of the amorous rooster, proud of his prowess. Verlaine, subjugated by the adolescent who had offered himself to him and whom he had boldly made his familiar, will celebrate the work of flesh in terms that won't fool anyone and reveal, for once, thanks to a private text, the nature of his passion:

LE BON DISCIPLE

Je suis élu, je suis damné!
Un grand souffle inconnu m'entoure.
Ô terreur! Parce, Domine!

Quel Ange dur ainsi me bourre
Entre les épaules, tandis
Que je m'envole aus Paradis?

Fièvre adorablement maligne,
Bon délire, benoît effroi.
Je suis martyr et je suis roi.
Faucon je plane et je meurs Cygne!

Toi le Jaloux qui m'as fait signe,
[Or] me voici, voici tout moi!
Vers toi je rampe encore indigne.
—Monte sur mes reins et trépigne!
                    May 72.

I am chosen, I am damned!
A great unknown breath of air surrounds me.
O terror! *Parce Domini!*

What harsh Angel rams me like this
Between my shoulders, whilst
I fly up to Paradise?

Adorably malignant fever,
Good delirium, blessed fear,
I am martyr and I am king
Falcon I soar and Swan I die!

You, the Jealous One who beckoned to me,
(But then!) I am here, all of me!
Toward you I crawl still unworthy!
—Mount on my back and stamp!
                    May 72

———

122

This inverse sonnet[91] (which will be seized a year later from Rimbaud's wallet during the Brussels affair), is a complete confession, or better yet, a celebration. It reveals the ambivalence of its author, Verlaine, who still felt ambiguous feelings of guilt for what could have been a totally engaging, joyful passion. But he was also gripped by fear of the unknown, fear of a future whose tragic outcome he was far from guessing. Elevation by sexual relations, flight and fall, as well as the ambiguity of these passive and active roles represented by the falcon (the minor wordplay here is of course intentional) and the swan. However, this act was the concern of an angel, a question of choice. And Rimbaud symbolized this real angel just like the student Danglos who appeared to Paul Gérard one snowy evening in Cocteau's *Les Enfants terribles*.[92] The most subtle form of connivance united them where mysticism, eroticism, and poetic quest merged them closely together in body and word.

Rimbaud's room looked out over an endless courtyard. The summer heat is exhausting. He spends his nights drinking water ("Comédie de la soif") while waiting for the cafés to open. During the course of one of these vigils when Verlaine is unable to stay the night, he takes up his pen and writes a long letter to his friend Delahaye, whom he'd left barely two months before:

Parshit, Junphe 72

My friend,

Yes, surprising is existence in the Ardenuous cosmorama. The province where you eat flour and mud, where you drink regional wine and local beer, is not what [I] miss. You are right to denounce it without letup. But this place: distillation, compromise, all narrowness; and the oppressive summer; the heat is not constant, but seeing that good weather is in everyone's interest, and that everyone is a swine, I hate the summer, which kills me when it makes even a small appearance. I am so thirsty that I am scared of gangrene; the Belgian and Ardennes rivers and caves, those are what I miss.

There is a drinking place here I like, though. Long live the Academy of Absomphe,* in spite of its ill-tempered waiters! It is the most tremulous

* Otherwise known as the Academy of Absinthe at 176 rue Saint-Jacques, which had forty barrels lining its walls. This song can be found in Félix Régamey's book, *Verlaine dessinateur*, Fleury, p. 11:

and delicate of attires, this drunkenness brought about by virtue of this sage of the glaciers, absomphe. But for sleeping in shit later!

Still the same griping, what! What is certain is: shit on Perrin. And on the bar of the universe, whether it faces the square or not. But I'm not cursing the universe, though. I wish very strongly for the Ardennes to be occupied and pressured more and more excessively. But all this is still ordinary.

The important thing is that you must be very tormented, perhaps you'd be right to walk and read a lot. A reason in any case not to lock yourself up in offices and homes. Stupefactions must take place far from such places. I am far from peddling balms, but don't think habits offer any consolations on despicable days.

I work at night now. From midnight to five in the morning. Last month, my room, in rue Monsieur-le-Prince, looked out over a garden of the Lycée Saint-Louis. There were enormous trees beneath my narrow window. At three in the morning, the candle faded: all the birds cry at once in the trees: it's over. No more work. I had to look at the trees, the skies, gripped by that inexpressible hour, the first in the morning. I saw the lycée dormitories, absolutely mute. And already the disjointed,

---

Dans la ville de Paris
M . . . M . . . pour Versailles
Dans la ville de Paris
Y'a deux académies

L'un ousqui sont quarante
Qui vivent de leurs rentes!
L'autre au Quartier Latin
Qui s'tient chez le chand d'vin!

In the city of Paris
Shit Shit for Versailles
In the city of Paris
There are two academies

The one has forty
who live off their stocks
The other in the Latin Quarter
relies on the wine merchants!

---

sonorous, delicious noise of the tip carts on the boulevards. I smoked my hammer pipe, spitting on the tiles, for my room was a garret. At five o'clock I went down to buy bread; it was time. Workers were walking everywhere. This is the time, for me, to get drunk at the wine merchants; I came home to eat, and went to bed at seven in the morning, when the sun causes the wood lice to emerge from under the tiles. The early-summer mornings and December evenings are what have always delighted me here.

But at the moment, I have a nice room, over an endless courtyard but three square meters.—rue Victor-Cousin forms a corner on place de la Sorbonne next to the Café du Bas-Rhin and opens onto rue Soufflot at the other end.—There, I drink water all night, I don't see the morning, and I don't sleep, I suffocate. So, there you have it!

Your claims will certainly be given their full due! Don't forget to shit on *La Renaissance*, the literary and artistic revue, if you come across it. So far I've managed to avoid the pesterings of emigrant Charleshits. So shit on the seasons. And colrage.
Courage.

A.R.

A superb page that lets us enter the writer's *dark room*, literally, the place where he waits but also listens and invents.

Rimbaud will extract other marvels from daily life as is his wont. Between the lines, a couple: "Jeune Ménage." While his room is open to the "turquoise blue" sky, he lays out a little enchantment, quite close to Verlainian naivetés, and enjoys disturbing the groom like a young bride. He sneaks in by their bedside in the form of a "cunning rat" or a "pale will-o'-the-wisp." Is he thinking of Mathilde, or even the "young couple" he forms with Verlaine, far from all familial holds, free in the ardent mêlée of vowels? "At night, oh, beloved, the honeymoon / Will gather their smiles [. . .]"

During the empty hours he will leaf through books, find diversion in the discovery of new caricaturists, and skim through reviews. One of these has just come into being under the tutelage of Émile Blémont, a former admirer to whom he had given a copy of the sonnet "Voyelles." Now, in the first issue of this *Renaissance littéraire et artistique*,[93] he finds under the premonitory title of *"Romances sans paroles"* a poem by Verlaine: "It is a langurous ecstasy, / It is an amorous fatigue," that not only seems to recall their liason, but comes quite close to applying the elements of the new poetics he has just discovered. He also notes a quote from Favart used as an epigraph taken from the same "Ariette oubliée" he had sent to Verlaine the past month. Then on June 29, Verlaine backslides. He presents a short "arietta" during which Rimbaud clearly recognizes Mathilde at the piano lightly running her "frail" hands over the keyboard.

Yet his quarrels and reconciliations with Paul risk becoming a meaningless routine. So Rimbaud, with that haste that always seems to carry him off, decides to force fate. He writes a severance letter that he allegedly carried to Verlaine's home on Sunday July 7, a step that seems to imply he was expecting something. At the very moment he was preparing to drop the letter at rue Nicolet, Verlaine emerged from the house; he was on his way to the home of Antoine Cros—friend and family doctor—to ask him to come care for Mathilde, who was suffering from a splitting headache. Such at least is the version given by Mathilde herself, who expressly states: "We hadn't quarreled the night before; my husband kissed me affectionately before leaving. He would never come back!"[94] It is likely that the unexpected encounter with Rimbaud took place shortly thereafter. The rest of Mathilde's story tells us that when Verlaine didn't return, they went in search of him the next day and learned from his employer that he had been absent for more than a week.[95] This absence, little noted by the biographers, would seem to demonstrate (if we take it at face value) that Verlaine had already decided to change his life— which does not imply that he was ready to leave his family. The fact remains that it was on this day in July 1872 that he yielded to Rimbaud's entreaties, that he gave in once and for all to the "seer's" arguments. He split his life in two this way, henceforth dooming himself to a slope of perdition. For Rimbaud the important thing was quite simply to leave. As if it were enough to go away to discover the unknown! Rimbaud will be a travel addict; he confronts the unknown fearlessly, and with a surprising and infectious confidence, never seeing that "Death, the old captain"[96] is often helping to weigh anchor.

For the moment the two men, free as the wind, are hastening to leave the places where they have been so liberally slandered. The couple departs, "deaf to the vulgar words of all sorts, / unreachable by vile laughter." Verlaine will later write of their escapade in his "Laeti et errabundi" ("joyous and tramps"[97]), which opposes Baudelaire's "Maesta et errabunda":

> *Nous avions laissé sans emoi*
> *Tous impediments dans Paris,*
> *Lui quelques sot bernés, et moi*
> *Certaine princesse Souris,*

> We have unabashedly left
> All impediments in Paris,
> He some duped fools, and I
> A certain Princess Mouse,

It is all too clear who the princess was. Less easy to understand are the duped fools (Monsieur Mauté?) to whom the poem makes allusion. From rue Nicolet their steps lead them to the Gare du Nord, where they plan to catch a train to Arras[98] and no doubt Belgium. Nothing forbids the idea they went by Madame Verlaine's to borrow some money. It would seem a necessary explanation for the months of idleness that follow. Verlaine's conduct would thus have been more premeditated than previously thought and his unforeseen encounter with Rimbaud was only an excuse for deceiving posterity. "We made the train around ten that evening and arrived by daybreak," Verlaine recounts in *"Mes prisons"*. It is quite early when they reach Arras, which he knows well as it is the native town of his maternal family, the Dehées. He was thus counting on a warm welcome from some good-hearted folk, a procedure Rimbaud made one of his specialties. While waiting to move on to more serious matters, they decide first to get something to eat at the station's cafeteria and, surrendering to one of those childish impulses that will transform them on more than one occasion into irresponsible children, think to astonish or disturb some morning customers. One of these especially draws their attention because of his cantankerous appearance, "a poorly dressed, almost elderly fellow wearing a worn-out straw hat over a rather badly shaved, silly, sneaky face." They see that this individual is listening to their conversation and the ill-advised idea occurs to them to pepper it with ambiguous words that will give him the impression he's overhearing a murder plot. The man, an informer for the authorities, disappears and soon returns flanked by two policemen who unceremoniously arrest the suspects. What follows is a bona fide interrogation. Fortunately, Verlaine and Rimbaud have their papers and their motive will be understood. The procurator, realizing he was only dealing with some naughty pranksters, limits his final remarks simply to telling the arresting officers: "You will accompany these two individuals back to the station, where they must get on the first train back to Paris." Free, the defendants will fraternize at the bar with the cops charged with escorting them.

As in the epic moments of Genesis, Verlaine and Rimbaud will have to make two attempts to achieve their enterprise. On leaving Arras, they had no choice but to get back to Paris. Once they arrive at the Gare du Nord, they make their way to the Gare du Strasbourg, a necessary variant for an itinerary that now sought to reach Belgium by any means available. With a special talent for landing in the wolf's mouth and for mocking those who can make it cost them, they nevertheless agree to a stop in the "good town" of Charleville,[99] without seriously considering the impracticality of such a stop. As inobtrusively as possible (but Arthur the runaway and young, failed hope of the collège is recognized), they make their way to Bretagne's door. He invites them in, delighted to see they are continuing this regular novel that he had facilitated in his way. After a good meal, he proposes a solution to the fugitive's wanderings, a solution that perhaps they themselves suggested. He convinces one of his neighbors to take them by carriole to a spot on the border much used by smugglers, undoubtedly in the forest near Gespunsart. Legend says that Bretagne introduced Verlaine and Rimbaud to their providential coachmen as "two priests who were his friends." The crossing of the border fills the travelers with a voluptuous happiness, even if the landscape hardly changes from one side of the frontier to the other. They see the same wooded Ardennes valleys and the languid course of the Meuse but they feel a kind of marvelous lightness: the "soles of the wind." The past is abruptly left behind. Leaving France for them was to miraculously untie the thread of an insoluble situation, allowing them to enter the land of poetry and live their love without fear. However, their simple stopover in Charleville has not escaped the notice of the daromphe. Some malicious town dweller has the pleasure of alerting her that her son was seen near Bretagne's home in the company of a bizarre individual. This time, Madame Rimbaud no longer gives her incorrigible son the benefit of the doubt and unhesitatingly puts the police on his trail. A highly confidential file, later found in the official archives, announces that on behalf of V. (meaning *Veuve*, "widow") Rimbaud, inquiries have been undertaken that have finally allowed the runaway to be located.[100] Inquiries that were vague enough for neither Rimbaud nor his companion to have been truly alarmed by them.

It is pleasant to muse on these distinctive moments of intense poetry that the wanderers experienced. At the speed of the peaceful train on which they found a seat, they now discover towns that seem to have emerged from their dreams. While crossing through Walcourt, Verlaine hums some verses:[101]

> *Briques et tuiles*
> *Ô les charmants*
> *Petits asiles*
> *Pour les amants!*

> Bricks and tiles,
> O the charming
> Little asylums
> For lovers!

The landscape is blooming with hops. As if transported by the wind of happiness the voyage continues,:

> *Gares prochaines,*
> *Gais chemins grands . . .*
> *Quelles aubaines,*
> *Bons juifs errants!*

> Stations upcoming
> Gay, wide paths . . .
> What bargains,
> Good wandering Jews!

Yes, they are Isaac Laquedems traversing the world in the name of poetic or erotic inevitability. They now pass—"the thundering rail stations"— through gloomy Charleroi, which reminds Rimbaud of the Cabaret-Vert's touch of green. After some idle rambling they arrive in Brussels which both knew, Rimbaud from having come there at the conclusion of his second attempt to run away (he remembers Paul Durand, Izambard's friend who gave him shelter); Verlaine from having come there in August 1867 to greet Hugo, when the master was staying at the the home of his son Charles. He had stayed with his mother at the Grand Hôtel Liégeois[102] at 1 rue du Progrès, and undoubtedly it is not by chance that the couple now chooses to lodge at the same place facing the Station du Nord.

They have some money at their disposal, which they happily dissipate on meals, shows, and bar hopping. However, Verlaine sends Mathilde several letters on the sly. The first, which his wife finds quite strange, hypocritically reassures her: "It is a bad dream, I shall return one day."[103] In another sent several weeks later, he invents some likely excuses: if he is in Brussels, then it is because he wishes to write a book about the Commune (like so many others, after all!). Indeed, the people with whom the two poets are spending their time are precisely the same hotheads Verlaine knew in Paris when he held a position of little responsibility in the rebel-held Hôtel de Ville. But what serves to explain his conduct? If he so dreaded being prosecuted for his connections with the communards, why would he seek them out specifically in Brussels? The same recklessness will lead him to ask Mathilde to look in a desk where he stored his papers for some documents useful for the preparation of his book. By way of documents Mathilde fell exactly on the correspondence he had maintained with Rimbaud over the past months. From these she deduced the true nature of their relationship. Certain drawers were perhaps *locked* (this is what Verlaine will assert and she will deny).[104] Their locks would then have been picked in the hope of finding compromising material and they would have quickly given up their disastrous secrets.

Far from rue Nicolet, Verlaine, whom Rimbaud had whisked off as if by magic, goes through periods of doubt: Mathilde or Rimbaud, who should he choose? He tells his mother to write her letters to him in two parts, one he can show to Rimbaud and the other that will keep him informed about his "poor marriage." This fundamental ambivalence—it is necessary to keep emphasizing this—will continue to trouble his relationship with the "malicious genius"; it explains its alternations, its reversals, and its sometimes apparent absurdity.

However, in Brussels, the two men have put together a makeshift existence. In the cafés and fast-food restaurants on the Grand-Place, they have soon managed to connect to former insurgents. There were some great figures among them: Jean-Baptiste Clémont, the author of *Les Temps des cerises*, Leopold Delisle, Gatineau, Arthur Ranc, Francis Jourde. In a later text devoted to Rimbaud, Verlaine will also note the presence of Georges Cavalier, known as Pipe-en-Bois,[105] who has"a rough-hewn face, like a door handle over a body that is long and dry like a holly branch," as Vallès would say later. Yet the eternal student Pipe-en-Bois had hissed the 1865 premiere of the Goncourts' *Henriette Maréchal*, that the Parnassians had so valiantly supported. The communard exiles formed an ardent, anti-establishment milieu, full of lively hopes and fomenting numerous journals of fanatic opposition, such as *La Bombe*. From this frequentation was born not only the project for a *Histoire de la Commune*, announced by Verlaine to fool Mathilde, but also some poems by Rimbaud, which struck just the right note with these recalcitrants: "What are they to us, my heart, these sheets of blood?"[106] Rimbaud asks, taking his "romantic friends" to task. Creating a sequel to his texts from the spring of 1871, such as "Les Mains de Jeanne-Marie" or "L'Orgie parisienne," these skillfully composed quatrains demonstrate his anarchistic proclivity that longs for a general violent upsurge, a social upheaval that will overturn the entire world. "Perish! Down with power, justice, history!" Doesn't this sound like something out of *Les Incendiaires* which Vermersch wrote in the same period but wouldn't publish until a year later in London? Seen from afar, the Third Republic entrusted to the power of Monsieur Thiers appears like an authoritarian government assuring the triumph of the bourgeoisie. Rimbaud, who wished to radically "change life," knew that it also was necessary to change men. His *Illuminations* to come (already in the planning stages with some even roughed out?) will imagine new battles, will summon apocalypses and floods that will tear down what has for now irreparably remained in place. "Madame *** installed a piano in the Alps," the "Hotel Splendide" was built in "polar night."[107] The "same bourgeois magic" shines from the four corners of the horizon.[108]

However, the anger sometimes subsides within his rebellious heart. The summer has its charms. Certain hours of pure paradise are granted to him. He shapes from them a fable of many mysteries, without title, with the "Boulevard du Régent" its sole tangible landmark.

—Boulevart sans mouvement ni commerce,

Muet, tout drame et toute comédie,

Boulevard with no movement nor commerce

Mute, all drama and all comedy,

The architectural elements placed beneath his eyes take on a strange, crazy air, while the words blink their syllables: "*—La Juliette*, that reminds me of *l'Henriette*, / Charming railroad station." Obviously no rail station in Brussels bears this name; but women's names (legend or comedy? Shakespeare or Molière?) are pulled along by the thread of an active reverie in which emotion strengthens the powers of vocabulary. On another page, two more quatrains, an impression: "Is she Almeh? . . ." Rimbaud asks, imagining an Oriental dancer, an Arab seeress. And happiness momentarily and inexpressibly engulfs him: "It's too beautiful! It's too beautiful!, but it's necessary!" Elsewhere he noted: "It's too beautiful, too! Let's hold our silence."[109] The desired silence was not maintained. He had too much to say about it, even if just to confess it might be nothing. The curious necessity he asserts seems to coincide quite closely to that "fatality of happiness" mentioned in *Une saison en enfer.* Verlaine sings in unison with him. He traces simple "frescoes" in his weightless "romances"[110] that are also oriented by a perspective, an edge.

However, it wasn't said that this honeymoon would last long without mishap. Monsieur Mauté had come into possession of the compromising letters. He had put them in the hands of a lawyer, Guyot-Sionnest, so that he could make use of them if need arose, which he did not hesitate to do. Meanwhile, Mathilde, with a courage for which she should be given credit, attempts to save her marriage, encouraged by what she senses of Verlaine's indecision. She then proceeds to a final step, "more out of a sense of duty than affection,"[111] she will write, with all the coldness of her future disappointment. She announces to Verlaine that she is going to rejoin him in Brussels to pull him out of the bad fix he has gotten himself into. Her mother will accompany her. Verlaine liked Madame Mauté very much and it was clever of her daughter to bring her along. But when they arrive at the Grand Hotel Liégeois in the early morning they find no one. The suspicious Verlaine had left them a message. He would be there at eight o'clock. The tender reunion hoped for by Mathilde wasn't taking shape under the best auspices. For Verlaine, who must have been tempted momentarily by her woman's body, there was no question of leaving Rimbaud, with whom he had discovered a solar life, illumination, and self-controlled idleness. Mathilde has a scheme, though, that at first glance appears insane, at least if it doesn't smack of the most touching foolishness and blind passion. She believes that they could leave together on a long journey, after entrusting their child to the care of Monsieur and Madame Mauté, who have agreed to watch him. They could go to New Caledonia, for example! They would find acquaintances there, Louise Michel, Rochefort, Alphonse Humbert (the husband of Laure Lepelletier), all deportees of the Commune. This proposition leaves one speechless. Even though Verlaine had escaped prosecution, Mathilde imagines a "pleasure" jaunt for them to that remote isle inhabited by political prisoners. For a moment he truly wants to display his attraction to such a long-running adventure and, giving in to Mathilde, even goes so far as to promise to leave for Paris with her and her mother. A rendezvous is made for that very afternoon in the neighborhood of the station. Between time he sees Rimbaud, whom he informs of his decision. For Rimbaud it is a new failure, glaring proof that he has been burdened with a "pitiful brother." But what can he do without Verlaine's money? In the blink of an eye he imagines his return to Charleville, the marasmus of future days shipwrecked on quai de la Madeleine. The two men drink. Defeat on the very brink of happiness! At the appointed hour, Verlaine, tipsy, rejoins his wife and Madame Mauté. They take the train. Rimbaud, with no alternative solution, takes it as well, in another compartment and without necessarily having told his friend. Each sees again the landscapes that had enchanted them several weeks previously. The irreperable moment accelerates with the speed of the train. When they cross the border at the station of Quiévrain[112], all the travelers get off the train for the verification of their passports. Departure is then announced. The two women grow anxious. Verlaine isn't there. They lean out the door while the train is pulling away and see him motionless on the platform with Rimbaud next to him. With an angry fist he jams his hat on his head and waves them an ironic good-bye. And so Rimbaud has triumphed, and with him the adventure of poetry over the probable stagnation of a snug, infinitely morose existence. That very day Verlaine sends Mathilde an odious letter, which she will make certain to quote in her *Memoires*:[113]

Miserable carrot fairy, princess mouse, bug waiting for two fingers and the jar, you've done all you can to me; you have perhaps killed the heart of my friend; I am going back to Rimbaud, if he will still have me after this act of betrayal you've forced me to commit against him.

However he will quickly be overcome by remorse. While he still believed he was free to choose between Mathilde and Rimbaud he maintained a futile correspondence with his wife; sometimes he wished for her to come back to him and even—in an impressive display of inconsideration—that she would accept sharing his life with Rimbaud.[114]

Rimbaud, for once at ease, frequents the milieu of the political refugees. They sense the insurgent and maniac in him, ready to take over from the rebels of an earlier time. His clear eyes are a source of fascination. Following the example of Charles de Sivry, he now dresses in heavy velvet like the workers, despite the summer heat. Far from lying women, the two men spent more pleasant hours—a vagabonding of heart and body. Seated in the tavern of the Jeune Renard,[116] they watch the endless avenue where respectable gentlemen stroll. For a change of amusement and to mingle with the common folk, they stroll around the Saint-Gilles fairground where the "good wooden horses"[117] spin around. They venture out to Malines or Liège. "The wagons file by in silence/Among these pacified sites."[118] There will be discoveries, a pleasant change of scene. All their pilgrimages within the land of the later Baudelaire are still unknown. In Belgium they capture pleasures where the author of *Spleen de Paris* found nothing but heartburn. But soon they feel the need to go further. They decide to leave the Continent and put the sea between them and the stale things of the past, to go to the England of modernity following the example of the majority of the Communards. They push on to Ostend. Rimbaud sees the sea for the first time, a sombre mass that seems to breathe in the night without "singing phosphors," without "dazzling snows."

THE SEVEN- OR EIGHT-HOUR CROSSING IS MADE IN HEAVY WEATHER.
Whipped by the salt air and heading into the unknown, "a youthful couple
withdraws." It would be futile to try to reconstruct their impressions, but
whoever thinks back to this moment in Rimbaud's life might easily imagine
the amorous encounter of the author of "Le Bateau ivre" with "his" element.
Yet during this autumn of 1872, hasn't he already left the complex splendors of
his first poems? He will make a very furtive allusion to this crossing later in
Une saison en enfer.[119]

I had to travel, to distract the enchantments assembled over my head.
Over the sea, which I loved as if it were washing a stain from me, I saw the rising of the consoling cross.

Obviously, no reliable chronological record exists that would allow this
passage to be dated. A persistent theme connects "Le Bateau ivre" to the *Saison*, however—that of the sea erasing pustulent discharges and signs of guilt.
True to himself, Rimbaud repeats:

> *L'eau verte pénétra ma coque de sapin*
> *Et des taches de vins bleus et des vomissures*
> *Me lava [. . .]*

> Green waters penetrated my hull of spruce
> And washed me of vomit and stains of
> Blue wine [. . .]

The boat lands in Dover in the middle of the night.[120] The companions
find a hotel. Early morning finds them up and walking about the town, full of
curiosity, but everything appears singularly empty. In fact, they arrive on Sunday, a strict Sabbath day for the English, and they have all the trouble in the
world to find breakfast. They are already filled with wonder and irritation at

having to speak a foreign language. Rimbaud doesn't know any English at all. Verlaine possesses only the barest rudiments of the tongue. With no further delay they leave deserted Dover and take the train to London from which they discover the autumn landscape of England. Then they enter the suburbs. Little by little the immense city, under a sky clouded with thick fumes, opens before them. They alight at Charing Cross Station. London, like Dover, presents a deserted appearance on Sunday. Not a restaurant or pub is open. The streets are empty. If one wants to find any people, it is necessary to go to Hyde Park, where speakers try to outdo one another in eloquence before a crowd of gaping onlookers. It is not known what the two did this first day. Everything was still waiting to be discovered. Their first consideration is to find lodging. On leaving Brussels they had some good addresses in their pockets, but it isn't reported that they managed to navigate the dense urban infrastructure on this particular September 8.

Over the following days they hasten to renew ties with some French exiles. They find their way to the home of Félix Régamey, whose studio looks out on Langham Street. Régamey was well known by Verlaine. He had illustrated Vermersch's books, the invitation cards of the Vilains Bonshommes, and collaborated on many resistance journals such as André Gill's *La Parodie*. Like many other French citizens who found themselves endangered because of their participation in the Commune, he had come to London, where he continued to pursue his vocation as a draftsman and provided *The Illustrated London News* with caricatures. Régamey will later recount the arrival of the two men in his reminiscences.[121]

On September 10, 1872 [. . .], Verlaine, who had just arrived from Brussels, knocked on my door. He was handsome in his way, and though caught quite short in the matter of linens, didn't have the air of someone beaten down by fate. We spent some delightful hours together. But he was not alone. A mute companion accompanied him, who didn't shine by his elegance.

It was Rimbaud.

Naturally we spoke of absent friends.

While watching me paint and draw, inspiration seized Verlaine and . . . my album was enriched by two gems.

They depicted Napoleon III following Sedan and the imperial prince.

Each drawing is accompanied by some absolutely comical verses that parodied the style of Coppée, impudently signed with an elaborate flourish à la Joseph Prudhomme, in which the three Freemason marks were replaced by a little cross, a frisky allusion to the evangelical sweetness of the poet who wrote *Les Humbles*.

In fact, Rimbaud, despite his silence, will also collaborate on the album and was actually the one who wrote the piece concerning the little imperial prince, "the child who gathered up the bullets" at the victory of Sarrebrucken. Régamey will do a drawing of the exhausted Rimbaud, "suspect sign of an inn." The visitor is drowsing on a chair, his head leaning so far over his chest that his face is almost completely concealed by his top hat.[122] The host soon brings the newcomers up to date on the refugees in London, especially Vermersch.[123] Convicted in absentia following the Bloody Week, he had fled to Belgium, Holland, and Switzerland, before finally coming to London, where he had founded *Qui vive?*, a short-lived revolutionary journal. At least it was enough time for him to get to know the printer's daughter, whom he wed on September 5. Following this wedding, he was looking to leave his apartment. Verlaine and Rimbaud see it as theirs for the asking and, shortly afterward, pay him a visit. Rimbaud, who admired the first issues of *Père Duchêne* in March 1871, could only be delighted by this meeting. He establishes a good rapport with this caustic, scoffing mind, whose delectable opuscule, "La Lanterne en vers de Bohême" had inspired several verses of "Ce qu'on dit au poète à propos de fleurs." Vermersch, a "rather stout blond"[124] whose face gleams with health, reminds Verlaine of certain episodes of the recent past when he directed *Le Hanneton, journal des toqués*, and both of them frequented the cafés of the Latin Quarter. He also confirms he is leaving his lodging at 34–35 Howland Street in Soho, a working-class neighborhood. The building's owner is a Frenchman who, on the recommendation of his former renter, gladly allows Rimbaud and Verlaine to rent the now vacant apartment. The building is an Adams-style house, notable for its tall, decorative windows, but the interior is gloomy.[125] The apartments have been transformed into narrow rooms that are easier to rent. They aren't slum-like, however. And the money Verlaine has on him, as well as that he receives regularly from his mother, will allow the couple to live free from want for some time.

To speak of Rimbaud during this time in his life calls for a bit of imagination on the part of the narrator. Indeed no traces survive, nor the slightest bit of testimony. At most we can glean a few bits of information from the correspondence Verlaine then maintained with his friend Edmond Lepelletier, a correspondence in which he rarely mentioned his acolyte for the very reason of Lepelletier's lack of esteem for Rimbaud, who sarcastically ridiculed him on more than one occasion.

If London first represents a discovery for the two companions, a time of freedom, they remain no less yoked to the past. The surprise, even wonder of the first days will soon be replaced by reality: vague searches for employment, Verlaine's anguish concerning his matrimonial situation, and Mathilde's demand for a separation. Their existence will be fashioned from this blend and will cart these impurities along. Rimbaud has to support the "pitiful brother" who can't forgive himself for abandoning the "little wife," whereas he (Rimbaud) would like to see him cut all ties in order to embrace a new life wholeheartedly. Verlaine's weakness becomes undeniable, he still doesn't understand that love is "to be reinvented." He obstinately turns his head back toward the woman-child he still celebrates in the disturbing quatrains of "Birds in the Night."[126] He also continually brings up the little Georges who his mother no longer has the right to see, and he constantly sifts through the doings of the Mautés of rue Nicolet. *"Never again* will I enter *there*,"[127] he declares to Lepelletier, whom he has charged to look after his affairs as his attorney, for he has no doubt that the locks on the drawers where he kept his correspondence were picked. He makes a list[128] of everything he left there, which will subsequently be irrevocably lost (either given to Mathilde's lawyer, Maitre Guyot-Sionnest, or burned by Mathilde, scandalized by such "horrors"). These include four self-portrait caricatures by Rimbaud; two photos, a dozen letters containing verses and poems in prose, and the famous manuscript of La Chasse spirituelle, "in a sealed envelope also from Rimbaud"; three or four extremely crude drawings by Bretagne, not to mention Favart's Ninette à la cour, two works by Petrus Borel, the lycanthrope of the 1830s; all Vermersch's opuscules: "Testament," "Binette rimées"; the two volumes of Les Hommes du jour, drawings (with dedications) by André Gill on the Commune, and the two "dykes" by Forain that adorned the walls of the room on rue Campe. These treasures formed an entire world. Verlaine and Rimbaud henceforth found themselves free, but destitute. However, poetry continued to envelop them with its tutelary magic.

Verlaine is swarming with projects. He dreams of making a living from his pen—necessity knows no law—and grows tempted by journalism. He thinks first of entrusting his impressions of London to Blémont, his friend and the director of *La Renaissance littéraire et artistique*.[129] Rimbaud, for his part, seems to disdain such expedients. He stays mum while Verlaine steps up his efforts to place his prose, for example, entering into negotiations with Vermersch (a tireless publicist who, after the failed *Qui vive?*, has just started *L'Avenir*), to write book reviews.[130] Meanwhile, they establish contact with other political exiles: Lissagaray, "haughty, curt, authoritarian, and quarrelsome," a journalist during the Commune who once had the distinctive honor of fighting a duel with the Bonapartist Paul de Cassagnac; and Jules Andrieu, a fat, extremely composed, one-eyed man who is a former colleague of Verlaine at the Seine préfecture and is extremely well read.[131] He had been promoted to head of administrative services during the Commune. He now makes his living by giving Latin lessons and teaching literature, a means of subsistence much like the one to which Verlaine and Rimbaud will soon turn.

In October 1872, however, the versatile Verlaine, momentarily sick of the milieu of the Communards, "all scattered throughout the suburbs where they live peacefully," declares, not unspitefully, "I don't give a damn about them, having decided to spend as little time as possible with these gentlemen"[132]—which doesn't stop him from attending the meetings of the Circle of Social Studies founded by Lissagaray, nor from going to a conference given on November 1 by Vermersch at 6–7 Old Compton Street, on the second floor of a pub. The subject was not particularly political in nature, as the speaker discussed Gautier.[133] Did Rimbaud accompany Verlaine to such evening gatherings? We should assume so, though it is hard to picture him complying with any sort of social duty, all the more as the audience was made up of very distinguished French and English individuals, who were "not Communards at all."[134] That really took the cake! In spite of Verlaine's cool opinions of them, it would be an error to minimize the influence of these exiles (who were "intellectuals" rather than rebels) on Rimbaud, for whom the quest for the absolute must pass through a catastrophic transformation of society. Though the *Illuminations* cannot be dated, everything leads us to believe that several of them were composed at around this time. They were cleaned up in 1874, but this means simply that they were already rough drafts. Some of them definitely smack more of utopianism than oneirism. "Après le Déluge," which can be read like a legend in which the elements of the famous Biblical tale have been transposed and disassembled, implies a profound disappointment before the automatic restoration of the ancient order and issues again the call for an earthquake—like revolution capable of overturning the shapes of the past once and for all. "Barbare" and "Guerre" inscribe this new world, "far from the old retreats and the old flames." Rimbaud dreams of a war "of might and right," "of a logic completely unlooked for." Several of these texts seem inspired by libertarian visions. The necessity for a complete mutation of individuals, mores, and love belongs to his innermost thought, but it also mirrors the most idealistic concepts of the Communards in London. The origin of *Illuminations* cannot be reduced to just this vein, although it is certainly one of their auriferous lodes. Through political prudishness or extreme formalism, people have refused to take this into consideration. It so happens that right up to his very last poems, Rimbaud will demonstrate his fidelity to a kind of libertarian mentality seeking a total change of humanity, that goes far beyond any partisan or factional consideration. Is there any need to mention that Verlaine, on the other hand, had overlooked such possibilities, even though he had considered reprinting (for publication in *L'Avenir*) certain ideological poems that he had composed at an earlier time, the "Vaincus,"[135] for example, around which he had the intention of organizing an anthology. Rimbaud's relationship with Vermersch, Andrieu, etc., is more than certain. But there is nothing specific we can deduce from it. Our only recourse is to listen to certain "voices" in the heart of *Illuminations* that testify to an incendiary atmosphere, a violent gaze brought to bear upon the past, and the vision of an incandescent, absolute, almost theological future, like that "Reason" imagined by the poet who, with a stab of his finger, would "start the new harmony."

The exiled French citizens obviously counted for much in the life of the two fugitive poets. Their ignorance of English provides an even better explanation for their necessarily limited field for relationships. In November Verlaine states to Lepelletier "We are learning a little English, but we have enough of our *quatrezieux** for finding this city absurd once and for all . . ."[136] Barely two months after their arrival, disenchantement is already setting in. The fact is, London seems to have held as many disappointments as discoveries in store for them, at least for Verlaine. Nothing could be more banal, incidentally, than his first impressions of the journey that he wishes to send to Blémont and which, for the moment, he is transmitting to Lepelletier. His observations are of a piece with the tourist clichés of the time: gigantism, motley crowds, oddities, and idiomatic expressions. The *Voyage à Londres* (1875) by one De Amicis,[137] for example, bears out the same themes. As a reminder one may also leaf through the marvelous album written by Jerrold and illustrated by Gustave Doré in 1872[138] in which can be found an overpopulated, mutifaceted, and heteroclite world. Rimbaud, far from plagiarizing it, used it to craft some of the magic slides of his *Illuminations (painted plates)*,[139] colored plates that retain from this immense city only its dynamic drive, its mixed population, its incongrous contiguities, and the impression it gives of a visual and auditory strangeness that is perhaps also born from the misunderstood language. Certainly Rimbaud and Verlaine, left to their own devices, their eyes sharpened by a foreigner's curiosity, have traversed *miles* of streets; they have seen the Londoners with their fads, their singularities, "guilds of singers," "bands of rare music,"[140] and overall—what Verlaine found most amusing—"Negroes, as if it were snowing with them."[141] Next to formidable misery, frightening wrecks of humanity, clouds of beggars, the urban landscape reveals some beauties:[142] the bridges over the Thames, docks where the two enthusiasts for dubious encounters loved to stroll, "Carthage, Tyre, and all reunited!"[143] They take the Metropolitan Railway, venturing on more than one occasion into the suburban areas, going by boat up as far as Wolwich. Like everybody else, they use the Tower Subway, a metallic tunnel that passes beneath the river, and visit the famous Crystal Palace whose magnitude and modernity surprise them. Nothing will remain of it though in the texts of Verlaine, who is all ready to elaborate a "modernist poetics" the following year. But when he gets around to explaining it, it will be to suggest a design from which man would be banned.[144] We should be thankful he never followed up

---

* A pejorative term meaning four-eyes—translator's note.

on it. Nothing could be more opposed to his particular genius, and it is possible that these are some deformed and poorly understood reflections emanating from Rimbaud himself. Rimbaud, having no money, was living on the handouts from his companion, who received the necessary funds and perhaps then some, from his mother. But what continues to pose a problem concerns the poet's activity. Verlaine—as is known—was overflowing with ideas. He wished to publish his *Romances sans paroles*, he also planned to write some kind of novel of self-justification, and perhaps some small dramatic work. Faced by this effervescense, is it necessary to imagine Rimbaud living in the most perfect idleness or should we believe—which is much more likely—that he did a little work on some of his prose poems? This second hypothesis deserves consideration, although there is no way to determine a sure date for the appearance of such texts. Among the significant indications, however, are the numerous features of *Anglicinity*,* which several of these poems include.

A dozen of the prose poems indeed reflect a certain number of visual, cultural, and linguistic references to England. This reflection is certainly only a glimmer. Could Rimbaud's work be inspired by what falls before his eyes (but does his work stem from inspiration?) or did he make use of a material identifiable to the London landscape and language when elaborating his writings, without necessarily inhabiting the places these writings suggest? We stumble here upon the acute and often insoluble problem of *mimesis*. No reader that has gone through the entire (open) collection of these texts has remained unaware of a referential aura there, the many precipitous images going back to an urban, composite, mixed atmosphere that thrives on numerous interactions. Where Verlaine essentially found in London a city favorable for his sentimental ramblings, Rimbaud extracted the elements of an aesthetic of contiguity, relationships, and hybridization. It is as if the neighborhoods in their variety and juxtaposition, the races brushing past one another, and the things facing each other or becoming entangled in their heteroclite forms, taught him a lesson, proposed a model, a sketch, in the same way that the urban space had let Baudelaire discover the bizarre nature of modernity. Baudelaire based *Spleen de Paris* on his contact with the city's shuffling

---

*I risk the use of this neologism whose prolongation appears greater to me than anglicism, which only extends to matters of language alone.

—

together the ephemeral and eternal. Rimbaud, in turn, captures from London, in more precise fashion, the lines and tonality of an aesthetic. Despite the uncertainties concerning exact dating, it must be stated that this journey revealed to him a crossbred universe and a new language simultaneously. The series of *Villes* transposes a presumable reality, while rendering it unrecognizable, but bursts of a primal reality remain in this new tableau, which has been worked and reworked: "The official acropolis outdoes the most colossal conceptions of modern barbarism." "Nothing recognizable here," but here there are "premises twenty times more vast than Hampton Court." The city, its textual fabrication, is little short of astounding and in this forge the urban substance increases enormously in a fashion that is visible to the eye. London is more incomprehensible than Paris, with its streets and suburbs extending as far as the wandering vagabond can see. An unheard-of impression comes out of this, quite in tune with Rimbaud's foreign nature. In these landscapes and on these city plans no key is given to the passerby; he recognizes nothing; he is in the presence of the unusual; he goes down into the circus, he walks around the squares; he follows the embankments; however, a white ray may annihilate this comedy. Further afield, the suburb can strangely fade into the countryside: the "County." The people of cosmopolitan London include Indians, Norwegians, and so forth. Interlaced ribbons, conjugation marks, railway junctions, brotherhoods. The bridges straddling the Thames in Rimbaud's eyes become startling pieces of modern and medieval architecture. Some hold houses, such as the famous London Bridge, while many noises circulate between them—such as the pedestrians crossing them—causing a formidable din from which themes and identifiable melodies sometimes break loose. The metro stations (existing since 1868) are also elsewhere. Where Verlaine describes, Rimbaud *hallucinates*, and creates an epic. It is not the re-creation of a decor that matters to him, but the shaping of one from the starting point of a few elements bestowed by reality. Authentic magic, a spell-casting gesture. From the familiar he extracts the quintessence of the unknown, according to a style of transfiguration beyond any obligatory modernity or modernism. "Raise your head, arched wooden bridge; those last kitchen gardens of Samaria." The metro line becomes a trajectory to wonderland, far from any silly fairy scene. However, thick smoke weighs over these allusive landscapes, the one that envelopes the monuments and had so struck the two travelers when they entered the city. A fatality can be read in these gloomy clouds, the Erinyes of the modern world operating above the city.[145]

Rimbaud's life is therefore not idle. He is selecting the motifs for a new poetry, while at his side Verlaine, prey to heavy remorse, ruminates on his illegal situation and kicks his heels in "epistles" to Lepelletier. In "Vagabonds," which should also be considered an autobiographical memorandum, Rimbaud will recall these times of cruel uncertainty. He and his companion were nothing less than vagrants. Before carrying off Verlaine, he had entered into a strange contract with him in which he undertook to "restore him to his primitive state as a child of the sun," "to find the place and the formula." Supposing that the place was London, the formula was yet to be discovered. Oblivious to this magical path, Verlaine was not at all purified of the past, an essential condition for this initiation to be successful. The face of Mathilde ceaselessly held him back. As prey to his "idiot grief," he created nightmares, dreamed with his eyes torn out (Rimbaud will attribute such a fictitious delirium to him), that is to say castrated, impotent, punished as an example because of his flight. Gazing upon the almost deserted street from his window, Rimbaud continued to dream of the perfect formula that would deliver the world's secrets into his hands. Since Brussels, he knew he was advancing solitarily on a fabulous path. The pusillanimity of his companion in exile was daily made more and more evident. Since November 8,[146] Verlaine had been envisioning writing a memoir intended for his lawyer, Maître Pérard. He planned on explaining the true nature of their relationship: "In it I explain, in a psychological, but extremely clear and sober analysis, the highly honorable and admirable motives for my very real, very deep, and very *persevering* friendship for Rimbaud—I will not add *very pure*—for shame!" Such a lovely excuse does not, in truth, argue well for the one writing it. It was too ostentatious not to raise suspicions that it was hiding a very real indiscretion. There was nobody left to believe in Verlaine's "very pure" friendship for Rimbaud. He wouldn't label it as such except out of preterition. It was he who suffered from constant shame and never erased the original stain; for his part Rimbaud exempted himself and placed himself beyond morality, far from the "fogs or personal regrets, for which the discovery is already the affliction," and the poem "Honte," which he wrote at an unknown date, should not be placed in his mouth, but that of Verlaine or Mathilde who accuse him as a "trouble-making child," "the stupid beast," but are prepared to bless him with a prayer on his dying day. Verlaine sought to destroy the "vile accusation," to "pulverize" it. It is true that criticism of his scandalous and inexcusable flight had not come to an end in Paris.

On November 10, 1872, still obsessed, he thinks that this memoir for which he is presently organizing material, would make a good model for a novel. Hardly any notice has been given this effort because nothing remains of it. Rimbaud was made aware of it (it no doubt annoyed him). It may even be tempting to think that the autobiographical project of *Une saison en enfer* owes something to this quasi-"analytical" novel that Verlaine came back to many times but never managed to finish. From November on, in any case, Verlaine struggles to relate the story about his odd relationship, "lying couples," and his brother in misfortune—toward whom he showed less ill will than Rimbaud will display later in his regard. Precautiously, for Lepelletier is not ready to excuse his escapades, he assures:[147] "My situation with Rimbaud, too, is quite odd—equally and *legally*. I will *analyze* us in this soon forthcoming book—and he who laughs last laughs best!" In truth, nobody had anything to laugh about. Verlaine tries to get out of it with an evasive answer, a word game that doesn't make anything clear. On what legal grounds could he justify his life with Rimbaud? And one would certainly like to be given more details about the "odd" but "licit" nature of this liaison that he vainly strove to exonerate.

In London, life continued for good and ill. Literature and walks. The daily complaints of the "widower" and the sometimes shameless intrigues of the seer. However, in these unhappy times, there was always some public event that came as a distraction such as the inauguration of the lord-mayor, which took place with a lot of fanfare and a great display of splendor. On other days they would wander the halls of Madame Tussaud's famous wax museum, an unusual site, or attend Vermersch's lectures. On November 8, it was on Blanqui (a poem of Verlaine's, "Les Morts" was read on this occasion), and one on Vigny November 15. A fine surprise awaited them at the Durand-Ruel Gallery, where they saw the famous *Coin de table* exhibited, still lacking the brave Mérat, who had been replaced by a useless vase of flowers. "We leave to see ourselves," Verlaine jokes. It had been purchased for £ 400 (10,000 francs [approximately $2000—translator]) by a moneybags from Manchester. Fantin *for ever*! [English in text—translator]"[148] But their situation appears quite precarious to them, despite the money sent them by Madame Verlaine. Rimbaud, away from the family home since May 1872, sometimes sends them news of his doings. Despite his own intention of depravity, strictly determined for all that by a poetic requirement, Verlaine's instability disturbed him. He sums up his present situation for his mother. What's the use of lying! If he confessed to what he had been up to, didn't he do so under duress? In fact, that November, maybe even earlier, several anonymous letters brought the debauched life of her son to the attention of the *mother*. We know this through Verlaine's correspondence with Lepelletier, in which he mentions the existence of these denunciations about which Madame Rimbaud had personally written him.[149] Everything leads one to believe that the Mautés had been discreetly investigating the young Ardennes lad who had destroyed their daughter's marriage. Perhaps advised by a lawyer, the number of steps they were taking increased. "People" had come to Madame Verlaine about Rimbaud. Soon the other mother, the *daromphe*, weighed down by worries and wishing to avoid the worst—Arthur's reputation forever soiled—goes to Paris and the rues Lécluse and Nicolet.[150] Strong in her unfailing morality, armored in her infrangible principles, certainly old fashioned, pigheaded, and narrow minded, she is a figure who inspires respect rather than mockery for her unshakable austerity and deep-rooted convictions. As a woman of conscience, she attempts not to save Arthur but to spare him from absolute disgrace, and we can see how courageously she attempted the impossible. Verlaine informs Lepelletier at the end of November: "Madame Rimbaud is concerning herself quite vehemently with this case. She believes that by separating me from her son, I *will weaken* it. What do you think? But I believe that this would be giving them their *only weapon* [. . .] they are guilty—while we are ready, Rimbaud and I, to show, if need be, our (virgin) assh . . . to the whole band—"and justice will be done"!"[151] Verlaine was too sure of himself. A more disagreeable examination before the court doctor in Brussels awaited him! Naïve in his love, though not without still sometimes desiring Mathilde, he didn't dare accept the single real solution that would have quieted all the suspicions: leave Rimbaud. However, Madame Rimbaud sent him letters giving him that advice, and Rimbaud himself, less enchanted by London than he had expected, felt it was necessary to put the brakes to their insoluble escapade.

—

Nearly convinced by his mother's arguments and seeing the impasse his life had reached, Arthur decides to return to Charleville in December—a return that would be all too habitual over the following years—as if it were customary for him to return home to celebrate Christmas with his family, but even more as if in unconscious obedience to a kind of inescapable command or secret ritual. He removes all his belongings and takes leave of their common friends. He leaves Verlaine. They will write. It was not, in any case, a question of splitting up. Verlaine, coming around to these arguments, also takes the trouble to tend to appearances. He engages his mother to come live with him. They plan on renting a small house in London like quiet people of independent means.[152]

Rimbaud, returning to Charleville, wasn't therefore doing it reluctantly, as was the case when he returned from Paris in March 1872. He had now assessed the path taken and could not help but take note of the tight spot he gotten himself into under adult surveillance in a society ever ready to hunt down those who desire "the place and the formula" and who wish "to reinvent love."

Crossing the threshold of the family apartment, he finds Isabelle, Vitalie, and the good-for-nothing Frédéric. Of course he goes back to haunting the cafés on place Ducale and spending time with Delahaye and his other friends. However, Verlaine, who had adapted to the idea of this departure in his imagination, could no longer stand his solitude. He spends a detestable Christmas despite the exquisite goose ("with apple sauce") he ate in the company of exiles. He complains about Rimbaud's absence: "Frightful emptiness! The others mean nothing to me,"[153] he assures Lepelletier, while declaring that he is the only person who truly knows his companion. But what did he really know of him? A lot of base deeds and dreams of being a seer. His memories will show his fascination as well as his inability to grasp, other than in dazed terms, the literary crossing his unusual friend had attempted, and his amnesia concerning *Illuminations*, which most likely was written at his side, remains troubling. Thus forsaken, he who later would give himself the nickname "poor Lélian,"* experiences a serious crisis during which he considers killing himself. Certainly he was second to none in complaining and causing

---

Pauvre Lélian (Poor Lélian) is an anagram for Paul Verlaine.

---

alarm to his entourage. He will act exactly the same in Brussels in July 1873. Incapable of facing himself directly and harassed by his desire for love, he addresses several close friends (Forain, Blémont), and as a last resort sends them a sort of "death notice letter."

> "I am *dying* of grief, illness, ennui, and desertion. Rimbaud will send
> this on to you. Excuse this brief note from a *very sick* man.
> Good day, or perhaps farewell!"[154]

He also speeds a word to his mother and Mathilde, and begs Rimbaud to return. Madame Verlaine doesn't hesitate to reunite with her son who, perpetual spoiled child, knows how to convince her to send Rimbaud the fifty francs necessary to return to London, a sum that will first be expedited to him care of the loyal Delahaye. Rimbaud, suffocating in the narrow world of Charleville and who hasn't forgotten all Verlaine had done for him, doesn't hesitate to play the guardian angel. Still it isn't necessary to credit him with only magnanimous sentiment. His role as a sister of charity will soon be colored with satanic retorts. Arriving at Howland Street, he quickly measures up the situation: the crisis was less serious than he had thought. Refusing to choose among those he loved, Verlaine has also appealed to his wife (who wants nothing more to do with him) and Madame Verlaine, who has come to his bedside accompanied by a niece, Victorine Dehée, whose role here is not at all clear.[155] Soon, on the suggestion of Rimbaud, who is little inclined to tolerate such weepers, the two "pietas" return to the Continent.

Again the companions in exile would confront each other in a trying private conversation. Rimbaud, who had tasted the marasmus of Charleville, momentarily resigned himself to this empty life. Verlaine's health, truly shaken, was slowly restored. He knew it was thanks to his gesture to his refound friend. He even had the intention of dedicating his *Romances sans paroles* to him, at the time still lacking a publisher.[156] Nonetheless he sometimes felt a desire to return to Paris, encouraged by Nina de Callias, who advised him to snap his fingers at the rumors that had been spread about him, but he also still feared the prosecutions incurred by former Communards there.

Blémont's review, *La Renaissance littéraire et artistique*, came to 34–35 Howland Street on a regular basis. If Verlaine read it attentively, Rimbaud flipped through it disdainfully not even dreaming of participating in it. The publication of his poem "Les Corbeaux" the year past in September 1872 had hardly gratified him. He saw nothing there but stale ideas. Now their study sessions for learning the English language are the most constant activity for this makeshift couple. They spend hours at the British Museum leafing through Robertson's manual of everyday conversation and, moved by a laudable scruple, "give each other oral exams in order to aid pronunciation" in the pubs and bookstores.[157] Sometimes they go on "long walks"[158] in the suburbs and countryside. London no longer holds any secrets from them. Drury Lane, Whitechapel, Pimlico, Angels, the City, and Hyde Park are all so many quarters through which they walk about as regulars. One of Rimbaud's poems[159] perhaps recalls these long strolls. On a "warm February morning," a couple of workers, a man, who may be the narrator himself, and a certain Henrika are walking near the city, where they can hear the noises from the nearby weaving factories. Verlaine later mentions a young London girl whom Rimbaud knew.[160] But all the women attributed to him appear to be only *effects* of his texts. In fact, the most frequent presence at his side was none other than Verlaine himself, "at the hour of the *dear body* and the *dear heart*," a very tender expression[161] borrowed from Baudelaire that the "poor Lélian" loved to use lavishly in his various "sentimental seminars." Despite the angry outbursts of the one or the soulful states of the other, the reunited couple, for the moment, hasn't even considered separating. Verlaine, although seriously worried about his wrecked marriage, thinks they will continue to live together for some months yet and makes plans for the future: "This summer we will probably go to Brighton, and perhaps to Scotland, Ireland . . ."[162] It is a kind of honeymoon voyage, in short, to celebrate a simulated reconciliation! Meanwhile, Madame Verlaine continues to send consequential sums of money. As for the inheritance from his Paliseul aunt, only crumbs remain.

If nothing precise is known concerning the life of the two friends during the first months of 1873, certain likely forms of behavior can be deduced from reading the part of *Une saison en enfer* entitled "Délires I." Of course as a precaution these pages can be attributed purely and simply to Rimbaud's imagination. But what need is there for us to replace the masks on the actors in a scene he has defined so clearly? Even if all this bitter comedy takes place in hell, it is not difficult to sense the quintessence of a liaison lived daily and to consider Verlaine as the "Foolish Virgin" and Rimbaud himself as the "Infernal Bridegroom" in the characters of the biblical apologue used by the author. A thoroughly sarcastic and astonishing transposition. What personal diary could better describe the state of their daily relationships? Certainly, there is no indication of location or time frame to be grasped there. On the other hand, we do witness the monologue of one voice citing the other at need, interpreting the demon to which the unfortunate "Foolish Virgin" was bound. Under Rimbaud's pen there is no concession. He does not paint a flattering self-portrait. It is also malicious on his part to put in his lover's mouth the portrait he claims to be showing of himself. But how can we not hear in the cruel game he engaged in, for days at a time, a "relational" verity on the quick. He thus freed the most demonic aspect of his being (as once upon a time he heard an angelic voice murmuring within). His negative tendency came true, as if to fulfill the terms of a contract, a hundred leagues from the notions of good or evil, far from any constraining ethic and the idea of sin. It was Verlaine who thought to see a demon in this mortal partner, there where there was only liberty unleashed. Rimbaud radiates the insolence of youth, violence, timidity, and purity despite all opposition, and he exercises a formidable attraction over the "Foolish Virgin" who he realizes is cowardly and submissive.

"I go where he goes." Verlaine, though upset by the separation demanded of him by Mathilde, follows him with surprising servility. He *attends to* Rimbaud. He considers him a force in becoming, an unexpected and dreadful dynamic, and Rimbaud doesn't cease to amuse himself with this stupefied companion. "I understand you," Verlaine repeats to him relentlessly, getting nothing in return from the sardonic magician but an ironic shrug of the shoulders. The *Saison*, a redirected confession given focus by means of the *other*, a testimony that is no less disguised thereby, gives us entry into the gloomy skies of "the child of anger" (the expression is Verlaine's, see *Sagesse* I–IV), in the very fabric of his daily life, with his frenzied choices, his will to depravity that goes way past any Bohemia or gangsterocracy: a fascination for the infamous and cruel, even if nothing very tangible remains of it. It is actually Verlaine who will be considered especially at fault. He had abandoned his family (like Captain Rimbaud left his wife and children) and will premeditate a murder. Furthermore, to Rimbaud, infamy is only a word that he has put in

Verlaine's mouth and from which he—being beyond morality—is miraculously exempted. Cruelty, on the other hand, is closer to his heart, as is that kind of teasing, well known to Sade, whose touchstone is the causing of pain to others. Hence its constant application, for example, such as when the two men wound each other in the "loves of the tiger," and throw themselves into the basest intoxications. However, Rimbaud regains a strange primitive purity there, that of his savage, barbaric Gallic or Scandinavian ancestors. Using Verlaine as subject in an experiment, he takes pleasure in terrifying him from the shadows or by proclaiming his affinity for crime, a crime he will never commit, but which the other, taking the metaphor literally and definitely not grasping this new brand of gospel, will attempt later, at the risk of killing his idol. Verlaine—as Rimbaud desired—was constantly thrown off balance by his apparent contradictions, his habit of charity, his compassionate manner, his startling inhuman humanity. In the streets that they walked out of curiosity as much as for pleasure, the evil angel helps drunks back to their feet and plays with the children of the poor, those whose sad solitude he had perceived so clearly in "Les Effarés" or "Les Poètes de sept ans."

However, their "season in hell" was placed under the sign of an anxious exile that the miasma of the past did not cease to haunt. Mathilde still occupied their conversations, even if Rimbaud forbade Verlaine any sentimental inflation. "I don't like women," he said. The phrase isn't a physiological condemnation. It refers to then current motives for marriage in which all too often the marvelous risk of love and the demands of the absolute were dissipated.

Such were the observations of the two men late at night, Rimbaud sometimes speaking profusely, Verlaine trying to adopt his views, but basically still wounded by the memory of the woman-child (a poem from *Romances sans paroles* entitled "Child Wife" is addressed to Mathilde), while before him another "child of anger" developed the sophisms of his folly, dragging him into dreams from which he himself would not emerge unscathed. Because Rimbaud was progressively leading Verlaine into another world to which the poor Lélian could not adapt, accustomed as he was to the pleasures of an almost ornamental evasion, a "familiar" and "penetrating" dream. With one blow Rimbaud knocked reality ajar and put worn-out, weary life to the test of violent pleasure or grief. He claims to know everything, for he has found the means, a method—just as before in his letter of the seer—

ARTHUR RIMBAUD : PRESENCE OF AN ENIGMA

that contains the most effective magics and the potion of an enchanted char-ity with which he strives to change life. He is within this enlargement of him-self, touching the ends of the world with his hands and capable of every enchantment as witness and sorcerer. The hour of the *Génie* has come, "done, being," who lifts the "ancient kneelings" imposed by Christianity and pro-claims affection and love in the present, the future, and—even better—eter-nity. A new Reason is born into the world that, with a simple turn of the head, changes all assumptions.[163] It is difficult to say at what time he exhumed such treasures from his nourishing heart. Everything leads us to assume that it was during the time the *season* was lived, in those confused and vertiginous months in which his fanatic idleness also composed another sky over the backdrop of an absolute vacancy. But already a distance is widening between the visions of the more than real and the everyday things and people repre-sented by Verlaine. "He wishes to live like a sleepwalker," says the Foolish Vir-gin whereas Rimbaud refines a perhaps untransmittable method, but whose splendors he intends to share out of an unexpected bounty and unheard-of charity, and which he gives to Verlaine—perhaps as a total loss. Verlaine (as Rimbaud sees him) did not cease envying the benefits of domestic bliss, wish-ing to confiscate for his use alone, the "friendly embraces" and dreamed of a quiet future, "two good children in the paradise of sorrow," at the very moment they confronted a very decisive hell. However, the movement in *"Génie"* is prompted by goodness, after he's offered to remove himself, to efface himself: "It is necessary for me to help others." This phrase prevents any attempt at appropriation. And, in fact, we will see Rimbaud propagating his gesture of awakening, even when, as a being of silence, he will be prey to every disgust.

Still, as in a very bad melodrama, he has to listen to the jeremiads of the other in his company. His mad adventure doesn't thereby escape the most common measures. The wretched companion, but also the fragile poet of *"Romances sans paroles,"* harped on and on about the reasons for his grief. *Une saison en enfer* won't seek to cleanse itself of such an old tune, plaguing the superb vision. On this very occasion, Rimbaud, without pretense, plays the part of Mathilde: "A woman has devoted her life to loving that wicked idiot." So even as Verlaine was persisting in writing his famous memoir for his lawyer, Maître Picard, Rimbaud was performing the autopsy on the botched couple that "Paul, his eyelids red, / Wandering alone at Pomelo,"[164] formed with his carrot fairy.

However, the future could be neither one of laziness or drunkenness. The two men are now racing to find work. They now know English sufficiently well to give some private lessons in French or Latin, like their friend Jules Andrieu. But no student seeks them out. Moreover, news from the Continent continues to worry them relentlessly. Mathilde is pursuing her demand for a legal separation. Yet Verlaine hasn't despaired of seeing her again. Periodically he makes plans to leave. Finally on April 3 he embarks at Newhaven on a boat headed for Dieppe. An hour before leaving land, he chances to hear a conversation between some gentlemen who look like policemen[165] that persuades him to put off his journey. He wasn't mistaken, incidentally. His movements, like those of Rimbaud, were the object of constant surveillance. The next day, however, he makes a renewed attempt and boards a steamer for Ostend in Dover. Aboard the *Comtesse-de-Flandre* in the open sea, he writes the strange "Beams"[166] in which the person he is addressing is perhaps reminiscent, despite the blondeness of her hair, of a certain idealized image of Mathilde as an intercessor. Is he alone on the boat? Does Rimbaud accompany him? Whatever the case, this latter doesn't remain in London, and while Verlaine continues on to Namur, where he has asked Mathilde to write him care of general delivery, Rimbaud takes the train for Brussels and Charleville, long enough to establish that his family is no longer there, and to meet with Delahaye. In Namur, Verlaine has indeed received a letter from his wife, but she forbids him from trying to correspond with her anymore. This piece of bad news affects him so cruelly that he suffers a kind of brain spasm.[167] In desperation he goes down as far as Jehonville, a small locality in the Belgian Ardennes where he is given hospitality by one of his aunts, Julie Evrard.[168] Intentionally or not, he thereby finds himself in close proximity to Rimbaud. They will sometimes meet at Bouillon, a very tiny village on the banks of the Semoy that is halfway between his village and Charleville. Rimbaud, still destitute and momentarily weary of the vagabond life, resigns himself, not without some pique, to going to Roche like someone fleeing into the desert.

ROCHE, MECCA OF ABSENCE

ROCHE, THE NATAL HAMLET (IT SHOULD BE WRITTEN ROCHES[169]), IS A PAR-
ticularly mysterious site, perhaps because of the startling emptiness the traveler feels there arriving there on an illusory pilgrimage. Today everything that
gave the village its distinction has disappeared. Rimbaud certainly viewed it as
a "sad hole" in which his life was bogged down and where his enthusiasm for
roaming found its harshest imprisonment. But Vitalie's diary portrays a place
that is not without its charms. Claudel, a rare witness personally invited by
Isabelle before everything was destroyed, spoke little of it, even though he
grasped the geographical tenor of the surrounding lands in poetic terms and
briefly described "the large house of worn stone with its high peasant roof
and the date 1791 above the door."[170] Today only a handful of charmless farms
greet the eyes; the site is flat and treeless, looking as if fate had summoned
absence to this spot. You can go right through Roche without realizing it. A
walker coming from Attigny will feel his greatest surge of emotion at the
junction of Departmental Highway 983, and the Rilly-sur-Aisne and Chesne
road, where a highway sign reads: Roche 3, Vouziers 13. A hideous single-
story, half-abandoned dwelling is now erected on the site of the former farm
of Madame Rimbaud, with a monument or memorial (how else would one
describe it?) in front of it that is in little better condition. It consists of two
miserable pillars on which some metal letters are affixed, several of which are
missing today. A sort of pedestal separating them bears the inscription:

Here

RI BAUD

wrote

The rest of the sentence that we should be able to read on each of the pillars
would be UNE SAISON EN ENFER. This is a plausible though uncertain assertion.

Such desertification ends up quite seductive—as if it were necessary that everything be erased, as if it were forbidden for even the smallest stone to become a credible relic. The visitor to Roche will find no welcome there. Nothing opens before one except the earth and sky, a naked space almost as far as the eye can see, although the fields sloping toward the neighboring Aisne Valley, the canal, and the Voncq station can be seen in the distance. Another road leads to Chuffilly, an underprivileged village, with an unattractive, almost patchwork church, rough as the debris from a medieval fortification. However (and certainly rather), because of this visible desertion and all these omissions, we pass through here as if through a poetic mirage. The "bleak countryside" spreads far beneath the sky. Because this place offers nothing but its emptiness, it exposes the desire for an unimaginable encounter. We finally discover beyond Rimbaud's physical absence in Roche that Rimbaud was an absence: "Arrived from all time," he "will go everywhere." For purely circumstantial reasons, Roche was the place after Charleville to which he ceaselessly returned, and no doubt where some of his strongest work was written. For the seven-year period between 1873 and 1879 he will return here on a regular basis. He will see this countryside for months at a time under the hardships of winter and the high heats of summer while the work in the fields goes on, sometimes with his participation. Much later on Roche also will be the site of his final return just before his death in 1891, in unending pain and delirious suffering.

Since childhood, he had heard talk of this land of the Cuif's that had finally come down to his mother after the death of his grandfather in that her elder brother, Charles Cuif, was incapable of managing it (his share of the inheiritance was quickly squandered drinking, and he now hung around the vicinity as a simple farm worker, his sister not caring if she ever saw him again). The Cuifs had their roots here. In "Comédie de la soif," Rimbaud had already reinvented this countryside, the willows, the moats, "the horrible scum" of the pond in Chuffilly, and the castle of Monsieur Flamanville in Méry (there is a small chapel there surrounded by the very cemetery in which his ancestors are buried). Vitalie, his elder sister who would die two years later, appears at this point in Arthur's journey as a touching and unlooked-for witness. All that remains of this well-behaved young girl who marveled at the slightest thing, this extremely naïve individual whose simplicity is nothing other than simple-mindedness, are the painstakingly handwritten pages of her diary.[171] It is these pages that transform the arrival at Roche into a fabulous moment of joy. Thanks to these lines, we discover little by little Madame Rimbaud's farm as seen when approached from Attigny (the nearby subprefecture). These were the same images captured by Rimbaud himself when he came a week later on foot. The house was surrounded by trees, but its high roof rose above the foliage. A dovecote was erected on one side. It consisted of a story and a large attic. One part was reserved for their lodger, the rooms of Madame and her daughters were on the ground floor, and Arthur's was on the second floor. The outbuildings are numerous and extensive, and include granges and stables. It was surrounded by gardens of flowers in season, some hemp fields, and several kitchen gardens. Vitalie's description takes the tone of eclogues. This simple soul doesn't pretend to be totally objective and her writing is distorted by naïve happiness, an emotion that to Rimbaud was always foreign:

> Enormous poplars sway at the slightest breeze [. . .] The terrain is flat, rich, and fertile. Scattered here and there are small woods and groves, and in the distance the windmills of Vaux-Campagne can be seen. At the foot of the village a cool and limpid stream flows [. . .]

However, the whole town had around only one hundred inhabitants; it had neither a church nor a school. To attend Mass it was necessary to go to either Méry or Rilly-aux-Oies.

On April 5 the entire family had left Charleville. In turn Rimbaud arrived on the eleventh. Vitalie will note they had no "forewarning" of his arrival, "so to speak." It is presumable that he had advised his mother of his return by a letter, but it was also quite customary for him to arrive or leave unexpectedly. "I can still see myself," Vitalie notes, "in our room where we were as was our habit, rearranging some of our things; my mother, my brother, and my sister were with me when there was a discreet knock on the door. I went to answer it . . . and imagine my surprise when I found myself face-to-face with Arthur." Obviously his arrival causes a sensation, but he says only few words, and if he mentions his recent impressions of London, he makes only discreet mention of Verlaine. He is perhaps more talkative when in the presence of his mother alone. Then he visits the farm, "making its acquaintance" (as it is clumsily expressed in Vitalie's diary), which shows he must not have been there for three years, a time in which a portion of the buildings had been damaged by a fire. He saw them now almost definitively restored to their former state.

It was Good Friday. The major concern of Madame and her daughters was to celebrate Easter appropriately. They attend services every day without fail. Rimbaud quite certainly makes do without them, but he cannot escape the religious climate filling the surrounding countryside. He is again caught up in the circle of habit and the constricting chains of ordinary life. He finds himself back in the rustic as well as excessively religious world of his family. For three days he hears talk of nothing but Easter feasts and the priesthood, and Roche is teeming with peasants in their Sunday best. Hadn't the moment arrived to sum up the situation in his isolation? He recalls the pages of *La Chasse spirituelle*, probably confiscated, alas! because neither Verlaine nor his mother has been able to obtain them from Mathilde. They are undoubtedly in the hands of the Mauté's lawyer, Maître Guyot-Sionnest. He also keeps in mind Verlaine's curious project, a "great intimate novel," although not at all autobiographical, in which he would have been depicted. Alone, nourished on disgust, even though surrounded by the cautious affection of his sisters and the momentarily regained solicitude of his mother, there was nothing else to do except write. It is without doubt at this time that despite his own denials, he believes most strongly in literature as a means of "getting out of his difficulties." He is actively seeking a solution. The immense boredom of the Ardennes countryside and its false festivals sharpen his plaguing sense of urgency. There is not a single cabaret in the neighborhood where he can renew ties with blessed drunkenness. Any images and visions will have to be pulled out of himself. However, as a pastime, he pages through one of the only books in the house (along with the dailies and the inevitable *Imitation of Jesus Christ*), a Bible, perhaps the one with the "cabbage green edging" that was read out loud on rue Bourbon during the "wan Sundays of December," Le Maistre de Sacy's translation, Berrichon will tell us later on.[172] Rimbaud confronts the greatest mystery of Christianity: the resurrection of Christ and all these bodies "who will be judged." For a long time Christ served as his inescapable foil. He saw him crucified in the Charleville church, a statue of indifference before the poor. He covered him with filthy blasphemies by calling him "the eternal thief of energies," but he certainly pondered on more than one occasion the power of miracles and the potency of an efficient word that would change everything from one day to the next. Rimbaud was already aware of the formidable recourse to words and the magic powers of writing offered by the intolerable and the irrevocable. In London he had elaborated in endless nocturnal discussions a superb world made from an insane vigor and unpredictable logic before a dumbfounded Verlaine. Paging through the Bible in this paschal ambiance in which the bells of resurrection are ringing in all directions leads him to the life of Christ. He admires the Gospel for its language and the range of its storyline. Perhaps he does not find insipid charity or pity, but great leaps of kindness, as well as the sense of a duty to accomplish, a place and a formula to be found. Christ rises far from base hacks. He is the thaumaturge, the awakener of drowsy life. Rimbaud starts to write about the other he simply calls Jesus, like Renan during this same time, but it is against the terrifying Renans that he fights, and those people thirsty for proofs that caused the ruin of Christianity, a religion of causality and reason. From the holy history that he retranscribed into hexameters at the *collège*—as a well-behaved Latin student—he now pulls out pages that could be his own story, if he too had all the powers. He follows the text closely, but transforms it, laying down colors and asking questions. He creates three narratives in the margins of the Gospel of John, three paraphrases.[173] Jesus performs his miracles but nobody recognizes him or no one finds them astonishing. In similar fashion, Rimbaud was the one who went unheard: "Those I've encountered perhaps haven't seen me," he will recall in *Saison*. But he knows damnation exists in proportion to this thaumaturgy that he admires. He experienced it early on, first—like a romantic theme—from his heritage, then as an inevitable reality to be learned for the same reason as those monstrous deformations he wished to impose upon his mind, following the example of the *comparachicos*. In the last of his discovered evangelical paraphrases (and nothing forbids the thought he may have written others), Jesus enters the pool at Bethsaida lit by the prodigious light from a storm created by the passing of the angel of the Lord. The paralytic regained the use of his limbs merely from his presence, but close at hand were the troop of the damned sticking out their tongues. A gesture of scorn toward Jesus, a challenge hurled at salvation? It is among them that Rimbaud wished finally to take a place, in the midst of these "children of sin."

However, over the following weeks he conceives a completely different project, even if it doesn't appear senseless to see it preceded by these odd evangelical prose works in which people have thought to find more blasphemies than they actually contain.[174] It is necessary, in fact, to take into account retrospectively the composition dates indicated at the end of *Une saison en enfer*: "April–August 1873." Nothing forces us to believe Rimbaud. But nothing allows for a systematic challenge to the information he provided, either. The project would thus have taken shape in the second half of the month of April, if we are to believe the letter he sent to Delahaye at this time. The composition of the book would have been under way, though not without the probable gropings indicated previously. Rimbaud wished to relate "atrocious stories"[175] (he would have already written three, he wanted to write six more). Strange idea which—if we were not familiar with the result—would seem to foretell criminal stories instead. Now if we accept that the "stories" about which he is speaking conform quite nicely to several passages in the future *Saison*, we should agree that their atrocity touches the narrator himself first of all, caught in the tourniquet of a harsh martyrdom and portraying himself without smugness as a damned one. His scandalous ambition is to create a *Livre païen*, or a *Livre nègre*, just a few short days after the Easter celebration, as if, saturated by religious enchantments, he wished at all costs to react against their deleterious influence and shake off forever the authority of anesthetic sermons that turn their audience into automatons, like his mother, his sisters, and all the other "Rocheux."[176]

In their fashion, the first pages of *Une saison en enfer* following the prologue form a war machine against France and the West, hammering out phrases of pure revolt and disgust. In one go, Rimbaud escapes the hold, loosens the vice, chooses a young folly, and becomes the person who cannot be appropriated. He expresses his rancor for the entire sequence of disappointments he's suffered or will suffer up to and including the appointed time of his death, and for all time. Out of the picture, an *outlaw* [in English], though he is himself buried in a remote corner of the country, he expatriates himself through thought. He casts his mind back to the Gauls who have nothing in common with our colonized, Romanized race. A quarrelsome people, inept scorchers of grass, who testify to the most perverse sentiments. Confined to his room in Roche, he cuts himself off from everything. He wants to have "bad blood' that he will carry in his veins like a poison, even if, mindful of the Cuifs of an earlier time, he recalls that they owed everything to the Declaration of the Rights of Man. But his desire for atrocity carries him even further, and he now wishes to be one of those Negroes he saw in London, those savages still displayed as strange beasts in the different World's Fairs of the era. Without being unaware of the religious foundations from which the beginning of his "notebook" seems to have originated, he uses them for his own ends, like a Satan full of malice. Here he enters the African kingdom of the "children of Ham," where he will later alight—as if to become what he had written, to be born from his own works. Negro book or pagan book? Rimbaud is definitely a hundred leagues from what is commonly believed then, though he remains loyal to his screaming Red Skins who kill the enslaved haulers of his drunken boat. He speaks for the innocence of the Negro—mocked by the West—as a being exempt from the fault of original sin. Madame Rimbaud, Vitalie, Isabelle received communion from the chapel in Méry. Rimbaud is infuriated around these pious, no doubt too pious women, quite safe from temptation, whereas he is nothing but desires and gluttony. It is too easy to behave. Watched by the irreproachable family falling all over one another to be repentant and think good thoughts, he finally clearly detects the source of evil. Its specific source is that very Christianity that defines evil as belonging to man's nature when he was banished from Paradise. Rimbaud feels branded by this innate culpability as if by a red-hot poker, and not because he recognizes it as possessing some truth. He singles it out as one of Christianity's ruses, one that has rendered man guilty since the dawn of time in order to impose the next coming of a Messiah upon him. The "Negro" stories do exist and their panting, violent staging recalls the stranglehold of the colonizers over "innocent" peoples who, ignorant of the consecrated host or baptism, quite simply buried the dead in their bellies through an act of reverential cannibalism that honors the ancestors. Rimbaud was never more Negro than during this springtime of 1873 in which he was cured in the fires of hell. Later, he will less appreciate the "dirty Negroes" of Harar, the idlers and thieves who cause the failure of his undertakings. But who will he like in this extremity? Nobody will find grace in his eyes, least of all himself.

So he is writing his book. His fate depends on it. He states it through his belief that such a spiritual confession, revisiting the past, will permit him to enter a new lucid and disabused life. However, he is not yet thinking of quitting literature. The great poets have provided him a model. He knows himself preceded by them on the path below that plunges into the abyss. An entire theater of excess, in which souls are placed on the grill, constitutes the antecedent of his history or stories. When he asks Delahaye to send him Shakespeare or Goethe in a mass-market edition costing twenty-five centimes per volume,[177] he has in mind not so much transposing them as finding an answer to his fundamental anguish. Every enchantment files past his eyes in turbulent visions about which he may already have read in the *Tentation de saint Antoine* by Flaubert, published in *L'Artiste*.[178] He is also a man in the mold of Faust. Unwittingly, though, in that no tangible tempter has come to seduce him. All the magics have swept through him, all was granted him in the blink of an eye—yet all around the world remained as before, desperately "pale and flat."[179] Despite this intimate odyssey that leads him to the very borders of his self, Rimbaud's boredom (the true keyword to his existence despite his dedication of his life to the solar adventure) knows one of its definitive sites at Roche, an alchemical retort in which a diamond of hate and anger is forged. Roche, whose flatness enchants Vitalie, has for him all the merit of a *hole*, in which he sinks until he reaches the very Hell he has shaped inside these last few months. Later he will land in other similarly unlivable *holes* in which he will strive to endure as if out of defiance: Cyprus, Aden, Harar. No distraction, except (like for Verlaine) the daily walks, the jaunts toward Attigny or Voncq, for slaking his "unhealthy thirst" in some café, that most definitely does not serve "buttered" absinthe. Once he goes as far as Vouziers, a small subprefecture of three thousand people inhabited by a plethoric occupant. Hardly keen on "patrolling," he takes a bratty pleasure contemplating the Prussians pacing up and down the town as if they were in a conquered country. He views this as the consequences of the war. For the moment during this pleasant spring that he finds suitably irritating, he gives little thought to plunging back into the delights of nature. Long haired like a savage, staff in hand, he traverses the countryside. This lukewarm enthusiast of nature's felicities misses the cities. He also wishes to be as little like a peasant as possible and keep his distance from any kind of sedentary lifestyle. To him the country signifies certain death by slow asphyxiation. The cities, on the other hand, give him an illusion of life. Now, in the intolerable solitude (a solitude spitefully inhabited by "wily peasants"), he is about to create the tortured, torturous movement of *Saison*.

However, Verlaine, in Jehonville, has not delayed to send word to Delahaye for him to come with Rimbaud to meet him some Sunday in Bouillon ("Boglione"!) a border town on the Semoy, and, in fact, several "rendezvols"[sic] will be made, several of which were missed. One unfortunate May 18, Verlaine is left alone at the inn waiting for his friends who don't show up.[180] "It is a somber feast" during which he is forced to content himself by making casual conversation with a pupil from the Charleville *collège* sitting at a neighboring table. Other meetings will witness the reunion of the three pals. One of them will provide the opportunity for them to exchange certain texts, similar in form, in that Rimbaud will designate them (in the same letter to Delahaye and with no further explanation) under the common and intentionally deformed name of "fraguemants in prose." Just enough information to inconvenience whoever tries to follow the poetic trajectory of the "seer." Everything would be coherent if he didn't attribute such "fraguemants" to Verlaine as well as to himself. For if, yielding to a reasonable intuition, we imagine several prose poems of *Illuminations*, under this name, it is very hard to see what in Verlaine's known work would correspond to them. Verlaine, in any case, knew what was going on, in that he asked Rimbaud several days later to send him back "Explanade" (meaning "explanation"), a text that would figure—under this title, at least—among his works.* The perplexity surrounding this bizarre exchange remains; the term "fraguemants" itself seems to indicate parts of a whole in formation. Nonetheless we don't know the nature of the work conceived by Rimbaud. To perceive *Illuminations* therein is on the side of probability. In the final analysis, we will bear in mind especially the presence of other texts being worked on at the very time the *Livre païen* was being composed.

As can be seen, Verlaine and Rimbaud's relationship had not unraveled at all. Though Verlaine was deeply annoyed that Mathilde was not answering his letters and was instituting legal proceedings against him from which he would not emerge unscathed, he held a loving tenderness for his London

---

* Reprinted in *Parallèlement* (in the series *Lunes*), 1889, with an epigraph in verse from "Le Poète et sa muse": "I tell you that it was not what one thought."

companion that allowed him to give free rein to the most smutty allusions. Going one better than the dissolute argot of Rimbaud and Delahaye's pornographic inventions, he didn't hesitate to label himself an "old sow" completely submissive to his lover, of course. Such vocabulary would only be amicable language after all, if he didn't exacerbate it further on with a very distinctive expression, written in English this time, but one that leaves little room for ambiguity: I am *your ever open* or *opened old cunt* [in English]."[181] "Cunt" doesn't have a multitude of meanings and one can clearly imagine how Rimbaud could have used it, an inverse practice in which the *erastus* seems to have been the adolescent with the face of an "exiled angel," while the man with the Mongolian features played the role of the consenting *eromenus*.[182] At the same time he *opened* himself so completely to Rimbaud, Verlaine was nevertheless still dreaming of a reconciliation with Mathilde and—too obvious an example of an unresolved Edipus complex—wished his mother to accompany him to London to live with him. But a true literary and emotional complicity continued to unite the two poets. Verlaine vainly trying to get his *Romances sans paroles* published, Rimbaud had made inquiries to Delahaye, who proposed to the printer of *Nord-Est* (the journal of Henri Perrin, a former professor from the *collège*) to print it on their presses.* For his part, Verlaine meant to dedicate them to Rimbaud: "First as a *protest*, then because these verses were created, in his presence and his having urged me quite strongly to write them, especially as testimony to my gratitude for the devotion and affection for which he has always given me evidence [. . .]"[183] However, *Romances sans paroles* were meant to know another fate, and this dedication would be omitted on the hardly well intentioned advice of Lepelletier, who could not help but remember Rimbaud's conduct toward him.

Close, despite the distance separating them, the friends thus remained faithful to their world. Different, often ready to oppose each other's ideas, infatuated with the absolute, Verlaine seeking the body and Rimbaud the idea, they now maintained between them the elements of a connivance that was as spiritual as it was carnal.

Despite their meetings, the exchange of missives (which could cost them their reputations) and numerous literary occupations, both however re-

---

*The *Nord-Est* would cease to appear in September 1873.

mained moping in their separate corners of the countryside. Weary, Verlaine finally renounced his intention of going to Paris to make his final farewell to Mathilde (he also feared being apprehended by the police) and decided to depart for England, in Rimbaud's company, of course. His plan was all set. On May 24, he left Jehonville and rejoined his inseparable "camaraux"[184] in Bouillon. Rimbaud, who thought he would have to stay in Roche or Charleville the whole month of June, joyfully welcomes the idea of such a departure. After a final carousal during the course of which they made their final good-byes to "Delapompe," who was extremely vexed at not being able to accompany them, they made their way to Liège, which they crossed through like the wind. From there, "training" through Flanders, they reached Antwerp where they embarked for their destination, "Leun'Deun." The crossing, "unheard-of beauty," lasts fifteen hours.[185] Reconciled and happy, they think to henceforth live a conflict-free life. They have made good resolutions: to give lessons, for example, which will supply them with pocket money. Rimbaud has the intention of finishing his *Livre nègre* and places his hopes on this "notebook" of such disarming singularity, in which he does not yet have the intention of displaying his intimate quarrels with Paul. As for Verlaine, reassured by Lepelletier, he believes the publication of his *Romances sans paroles* is well on its way.[186] Everything was thus turning out for the best, and it is with the illusion of new happiness in their future life that they get off at Charing Cross Station, all shames erased.

FALLOUT

ON THEIR ARRIVAL THEY FIND LODGING IN A NEIGHBORHOOD CLOSE TO where they'd lived previously, at 8 Great College Street, Camden Town. Their landlady, as in the best English stories, is named Mrs. Smith. Her several-story house dominates the neighboring cottages and their neat little gardens. The urban fabric is ventilated everywhere by small squares. Vermersch, who perhaps brought this choice situation to Verlaine's attention, remains quite nearby in Kentish Town. Andrieu is also hardly any further away. The spot pleases them and Verlaine writes to Blémont, not without paradox: "You would think we were in Brussels." He adds: "I have firm intentions of working here."[187] In fact they are going to try to improve their basic situation, still assured by the money of Verlaine and his mother, by giving French and Latin lessons. They even contemplate teaching poetry! Heeding the advice of Andrieu, they place small advertisements in several papers: on June 11, 12, and 13 in *The Echo*, and on June 21 in *The Daily Telegraph*.[188] They portray themselves as "two Parisian gentlemen," which their appearance certainly doesn't reflect. It is known that Verlaine had several students, enough to afford him tobacco and old clothes. Rimbaud doesn't seem to have enjoyed the same success.

However, each of them continued to pursue his work in progress. Verlaine still had in mind a drama, his bizarre novel, and his next volume of verse:[189] *L'Île* or *La Vie au grenier* or *Sous l'eau, Le Sable* (none of which would ever appear in print). Rimbaud must have been continuing work on *Le Livre nègre*. But could he have then guessed the extent of his torture and the fate that awaited him? This work will not only include atrocious stories in its final appearance. He would also interrogate himself about a crucial period of his life, a highlight that perhaps hadn't received its full meaning yet in this month of June 1873. Likewise, it is necessary to think of the double writing that Rimbaldian creation presumes at this time: prose poems on the one hand, and a tale of the damned, or "atrocious stories," on the other.

Their life together continued to evolve under the sign of the poem, despite new rifts, rages, and acrimonious feelings that sometimes led them to fight with one another to the extent of slashing each other's bodies and bloodying their faces. The absolute experience of the poem and the insoluble seductions of a love not shared equally. "Scenes," monstrous ironies still set them at each other's throats, all stirred up by the alcohol they drank without moderation. By glorifying it, they have made it an obscurely necessary poison that intoxicates their bodies. Arguments result that are not attributable solely to Verlaine's indecisiveness or Rimbaud's impatience. Their constant drunkenness prevents them from seeing clearly and finding solutions. This creates a temporary paranoia that magnifies their slightest gestures and takes their words greatly out of proportion. They nonetheless continue, during their calmer moments, to take long hikes through the city and the suburbs and, during the evenings, when they are not in the pubs or at the home of some exiled Communard, they attend productions such as those performed by two recently established French companies, one at the Princess Theater, the other at the Saint James Theater. Performing at the latter site were the artists of the Alcazar, whom they may have already seen in Brussels. "I go there every evening that I am not giving lessons," Verlaine notes in June,[190] without specifying if Rimbaud accompanies him. The Saint James puts on a lot of vaudeville shows, operettas, and bourgeois dramas there: *Les Cent Vierges* by Lecocq, *L'Homme-femme* by Dumas the younger, *Mme Aubray*, *La Princesse Georges*. It is possible that Rimbaud was receptive to such productions that are lighthearted and luminous breaches into ordinary life. Several poems at the heart of *Illuminations* seem linked to the theatrical space and to be dreaming of a new stage that contrasts with the old comedy. Rimbaud assuredly makes use of transposition, and the few characters he names would be difficult to identify. Here realism counts less than a dramatic vision in which individuals find themselves coinciding with roles and metamorphoses.

Madame Verlaine came to London for a certain period of time.[191] Little is known about this trip, whose apparent reason—overseeing Paul's move into his new quarters—may have responded to another design as well. The fact remains that shortly thereafter Verlaine seemed to be seized anew by his fixed notion of resuming ties with Mathilde and stopping her demand for a legal separation. Was Rimbaud aware of this? If so, he was hardly in any mood to regard it sympathetically. Authorized biographers, such as Ernest Delahaye, state that his relationship with Verlaine had begun to cause a scandal in the French exile community, strict Communards one and all even if they did advocate free love. In any case the couple's homosexuality was no secret to the French police, which kept them under constant surveillance, as is indicated by a report dated June 26: "A strange kind of liaison joins a former employee of the Seine prefecture (who remained at his post during the Commune) and sometime poet in *Le Rappel*, Monsieur Verlaine, and a young man who often comes to Charleville where his family lives and who was a member of the franc-tireurs during the Commune in Paris, the young Rimbault [*sic*]. Monsieur Verlaine's family is so certain of this degrading fact that they are basing one of the elements of their demand for a legal separation on this point." One day Rimbaud, arriving to visit Andrieu, is rudely shown the door.[193] Surrounded by such suspicions, the two men had arrived at the point in which daily relations, stretched to the limit, could only break. Camille Barrère, a young exiled Communard,[194] would later testify of the constant arguments leading to their rift. Finally Verlaine, reiterating in this manner his April 1873 departure, hit upon the only possible solution. But whereas once he would have perhaps warned his companion, he arranged matters this time so as to leave him point-blank. A week later, Rimbaud would give his own version of events:[195] "Following a discussion we had [. . .], a discussion born from the reproaches I'd made to him concerning his indolence and his manner of behaving with regard to our mutual acquaintances, Verlaine left me almost without warning, without even letting me know where he was going." But this Rimbaud reproaching Verlaine for his laziness seems quite sanctimonious, all the more so as Verlaine gave lessons to some students. The remark concerning their acquaintances seems more sincere; it perhaps provides an explanation in retrospect for Andrieu's sudden antipathy for Rimbaud. So how did Verlaine behave before the refugee Communards? Did he allow himself some familiarities that Rimbaud found particularly shocking? A letter from the latter, written immediately after Verlaine's departure, makes an allusion to such a situation:[196] "You want to return to London. You don't know how everyone would receive you there! And the face Andrieu and the others would make at me if they were to see me with you again!" Their rift therefore was of a nature to satisfy those who condemned in veiled terms the couple they formed together. But Rimbaud bore his share of responsibility in this matter; he would soon blame his own conduct on the friend on whom he had cynically imposed all his whims:[197] "If I was surly with you, it was only a joke, I couldn't restrain myself!" and again: "What! Haven't you yet recognized that our anger was as false for both our sides!" The discussions of this "odd couple" sometimes ended in dramatic scenes. Verlaine displayed some sense by leaving without looking back again; he certainly didn't do it without premeditation, for he imagined that Mathilde would still be able to save him. This weakling became attached to the affection others gave him, his life was fed on it, and he felt his existence was pointless without it.

He had the foresight to gather information on the departure times for the next boats to Belgium, the place where, nostalgic for the days of July 1872, he already had the ultimate design of enticing Mathilde. A mere trifle would provide him an excuse for a definitive split. The unsuspecting Rimbaud continued to quibble with him capriciously. Would you like to see the most pitiable scene that ever parted two poets and broke a friendship? One of those anecdotes that, rather than explaining a life, reveals its fragility and sometimes absurd character? Delahaye relates it in such a way that no one will ever forget it:[198]

> One morning, Verlaine returned from "shopping" bearing a fish in his hand that he was regarding with an air of pathetic awkwardness. Sniggers and sneers from Rimbaud. This goes over poorly, since Verlaine, who has just been subjected to the "sneers' of "naughty boys" and "impertinent maids" [quoted phrases in English] in the street, is thinking, quite rightly, that embarrassment is a dreadful thing and that he has had enough, enough, enough! . . . Furious, he hurls his purchase in his mocker's face and leaves the house. [. . .]

A charming story that tempts one to praise the narrator's talents (even though he did not witness this scene personally). A handful of biographers have wondered if this fish was a herring or a mackerel! What kind of fish it was changes nothing! What is clear is that Verlaine sneaked out without even taking his luggage and that Rimbaud followed him, panic-stricken, through the streets to the pier where the "pitiful brother" (who was the victor on this occasion) resolutely jumped aboard a boat heading for Ostend.

From this point Rimbaud's only option is to return to 8 Great College Street and take stock of his situation. He is out of money. Verlaine took it all. He can certainly hold out for a few days by selling the books and rags left behind by the other. But then what? After making the circuit of his friends in London and having exhausted his resources, it will be necessary to return to France. His appeals from the pier didn't cause the fugitive to waver. For the first time, perhaps, he loves the person who had just left him.

The days that followed this Thursday, July 3 are animated by his abrupt fatality. Rimbaud will witness the catastrophic conclusion of the plot almost like a spectator of himself. Each letter written by either him or Verlaine will soon be the equivalent of those cues in the fifth act that hasten the arrival of death. The experiment, whether tinkled out on the piano in moderato or created with violence, reaches the point where it will produce its most lethal potion, just as a certain pledge to existence would later unravel on a bed in Marseilles, burned out from an overdose of the absolute.

Meanwhile, Verlaine on board ship, takes stock of the good and bad aspects of the situation. He writes a letter to Rimbaud and mails it from Ostend at the other end of the crossing. His ambiguous sense of truth is fully exposed therein. He loves Rimbaud "immensely," but since nothing has worked out between them, he will live with his wife or blow out his brains. Such excessive resolutions could only leave their addressee skeptical. Verlaine had a habit of such intimidating behavior. It is not too farfetched to see in his attitude his submission to an obscure fate: "because it was necessary that I might peg out," he says humorously. The epistle[199] is sent to their London lodgings, but bears the note: "Or, in case of a departure, Roche canton d'Attigny, Ardennes, France [in English] (care of Madame Rimbaud,") the author sensing quite well that Rimbaud wouldn't last there for long and would soon have to fall back to his Vouzinoise countryside. For his part, Rimbaud, who knew at least that Verlaine had gone to Brussels, the turntable of their pilgrimages (perhaps Paul informed him at the last moment), addresses a letter to that city's general delivery. What is heard here is a man at a total loss who has abruptly dropped his sarcastic mask and is simpering—as Verlaine had formerly pleaded with him to do. A harshly critical Henri Guillemin[200] sees in this behavior the mannerisms of a "tart, abandoned by her guardian, because she has pushed her insolence too far, and who promises to be sweet and good, if only the man will take her back." We are tempted to attribute less selfish feelings to Rimbaud, even if it is obvious that he played with Verlaine and likewise *was played*, the prisoner of an adventure whose every subtlety his extreme youth prevented him from grasping. Rimbaud and Verlaine made use of their hearts as if they were soulless objects. They didn't realize that they were thereby destroying in themselves the very substance of love. By pledging to reinvent love Rimbaud would exclude himself from human love, since it is necessary to spread that of the Genius. Through weakness, Verlaine would dissipate passion's unique ray.

No sooner has he read Verlaine's letter, "written at sea," then Rimbaud regains the tone of superiority that was always his trademark. He gives no credence whatsoever to Paul's threat of suicide since he is fully cognizant of that individual's appalling spinelessness.[201] "So, while waiting for your wife and your death, you are going to thrash about, wander around, and annoy a lot of people." Having retrieved his self-possession, he doesn't hesitate to impose his views on his fugitive lover. First he shows him how, by merely his presence, he has completely transformed him: "Think back to what you were before meeting me," and proclaims his role as his awakener. What was Verlaine and, most important, what would he become? One of the most flagrant effects of his relationship with Rimbaud certainly would not be what his partner had hoped for. Conversion and mysticism do not figure in the tableau of promised enchantments. But he will always bear the mark left behind by this intimacy. He will never forget that he was the witness to a private miracle, the occasional participant in an uncommon adventure. Soon Rimbaud, sensing that Verlaine is still a lover under his spell, does not hesitate to overdo it. He blends authority—"As for me. I will not return to my mother's. [. . .] If you wish to write me in Paris, write me care of L. Forain;"—seduction— "Return, I want to be with you "1I love you"—and threat—"If your wife comes back, I will not compromise you by writing you. I will never write you."

In Brussels, Verlaine moped while waiting for something to happen, annoyed by the very misfortune he had meticulously woven like a true Saturnian poet, almost dazed by his talent for creating misfortune. He has settled, so as not to break with tradition, in the Grand Hotel Liégeois, where he

—

was haunted by all manner of memories. There he put his plan—both complex and obsessed—into operation. He hasn't relinquished the thought of winning back Mathilde and he sends her letters and telegrams ordering her to come to him. An expert in blackmail by threatening suicide, true in the very falseness of his words, he appears moving by dint of being confused. One who has ideas but never follows through on them, yet disdaining the tragic asides of the suicides who don't fail in their attempts to end their lives, he insists on what everyone already knew. And though he hasn't yet procured a weapon, he is already imagining the fatal gesture with which he will do away with himself. He alerts Madame Rimbaud, whom he had already importuned previously during the winter of 1872, of his intention. He addresses another epistle to his mother[202] in the hope that she would immediately come to his side. In short, to use Rimbaud's polished expression concerning him, "He annoys a lot of people."

My mother,
I have resolved to kill myself if my wife doesn't come in three days! I have written of this to her. I am currently at this address: Monsieur Paul Verlaine, Hôtel Liégeois, rue du Progrès, room 2, Brussels. Farewell, if need be. Your son has loved you much. Paul Verlaine. I left London deliberately.

Alarmed, Madame Verlaine takes the first train to Belgium. She will arrive on July 5 or July 6. For her part, Madame Rimbaud spells out a very moral missive from Roche[203] perfectly phrased for calming the cloudy mind of a candidate for suicide. This Vitalie Cuif will always be the final authority in this world of ours—which is fundamentally her world. Our world, even the most topical, is made up of these individuals who argue for security and routine morality. She reveals there, moreover, a singular strength; she resists what she calls adversity (in which Rimbaud, for better or worse, will later resemble her):

Monsieur, I don't know what the nature of your disgraces with Arthur are, but I have always foreseen that the conclusion to your liaison would not be a happy one. Why? you may ask. Because whatever is not authorized and approved by good and honest parents cannot bring happiness to their children.

Her logic is simple and infallible. It is certainly quite clear that she is ignorant of nothing concerning the very unusual love binding her son to Verlaine. She recalls it with frankness and that confident, almost Louis XIV era vocabulary still used by folk in the country. In my opinion, her use of the term "disgraces" or the expression—banal in itself—"conclusion to your liaison" are quite admirable.

Meanwhile, having received nothing from Rimbaud, Verlaine remains all the more obsessed with him. He writes to Matuszewicz,[204] one of the London refugees who knows the Communard milieu quite well: "I had to leave Rimbaud in the lurch, what terrible pain, in all frankness! (and whatever one may say) this has given me—leaving him my books and rags to sell off in order to get home." But he also announces (though it is only the fifth) that, without waiting for the expiration of the ultimatum sent to Mathilde for her to rejoin him, he has renounced his intention to commit suicide ("I am beginning to find it very stupid to kill myself like that") and has come up with a new scheme: to enlist in the Spanish volunteers called Carlists because they supported the cause of Don Carlos, rival claimant with future king Alphonse XII for the throne of Spain. Verlaine, so to speak, wishes to enter the ranks of a foreign legion, the customary steps taken by other desperate men of his stripe. We will see Rimbaud having similar recourse to this expedient. The letter to Matuszewicz was dated July 5. Now, Sunday July 6, Verlaine posts a letter[205] to Edmond Lepelletier in which he speaks of his decision to kill himself: "I plan to do myself in if Mathilde isn't here by tomorrow afternoon." This is only a lie since the day before he had already abandoned his intention of suicide. Indeed, through a chance event such as only history can hold in store, he had met, while wandering the heart of Brussels with death on his mind, a distant friend from earlier times, the painter Auguste Mourot,[206] Madame Verlaine's godson. This latter individual, who knew all about Verlaine's flight with Rimbaud and now saw him in an alarmingly overexcited state, tried to comfort him and push him away from an overly fatal solution by suggesting he enlist with the Carlists. So by July 5 and 6 Verlaine had already been given this idea. He confirmed it to Matuszewicz but does not breathe a word of it to Lepelletier in the hope that the latter would convince Mathilde. Finally on July 8, he presents himself at the Spanish legation, without success moreover, as he is told foreigners are not eligible. That very morning, however— apparent proof of his resolution—he sped Rimbaud a telegram saying: "Spanish Volunteer come here Hôtel Liégeois laundry manuscripts if possible." He had to be thinking that his sudden display of courage would surprise its intended recipient. Furthermore, Rimbaud wrote him a singular and troubled letter[207] the day before, in which he alternately begs him not to return to London and to return anyway—where they will live despite what others may say. "Yes, my little dear, I will remain another week. And you will come, won't you? he asks, not knowing very well what role to play— the seduced or the seducer.

The laconic nature of Verlaine's telegram, received in London at 10:16 the morning of July 8, will cause something that a longer missive no doubt would not have encouraged. Rimbaud, short of money, decides to leave. The Hôtel Liégeois offers him a sure haven. With Verlaine he will be able to get the desired explanations. In addition, he was somewhat curious and was perhaps feeling a newfound compassion for the volunteer who had given in to some strange mental quirk. All the elements of what we have come to call the Brussels drama had now fallen into place. It is a well-known event belonging to legend. In these few days passion and love's incomprehensibility will reach their culmination resulting in, to parody a famous phrase, the shipwreck of poetry against ordinary life.[208] The retrospective chroniclers try to comprehend it. The depositions made by the victim (pronounced *victimne*[209]) and the accused are thought to provide an explanation. The irrevocable remains. Something had to give. Madame Rimbaud will always be right!

After a sea voyage Arthur arrived in the evening at the famous Hôtel Liégeois where they had lived happily despite, even then, some arguments. Did he know that Madame Verlaine would be there, the inevitable prop of her tottering son ever ready to rely on her support? As such she had already watched over Verlaine at the beginning of 1873 in London. Rimbaud is very quickly acquainted with the facts of the matter: Verlaine is not able to enlist. In this exhausted friend on the verge of a nervous breakdown, he finds the indecisive man always going with the flow, who is incapable of breaking with either Mathilde or him.

The next day will be wasted in fruitless discussions as they go from one café to the next. Rimbaud waits for a decision from his old lover. Verlaine hesitates. Sometimes, he speaks of returning to London and settling down there; sometimes—and he is leaning more toward this solution—he envisions going to Paris to see Mathilde one last time and heaping on her in one go all the reproaches she deserves. Rimbaud, who despises these beatings around the bush, feels that the time has come to leave his insufferable companion. But with Verlaine, everything must always be put off until later, as if patience and time would allow a promising development to occur in what had heretofore been seen as an unavoidable defeat. Rimbaud finally announces his departure. The "pitiful brother" cannot bring himself to see the "cunning genius" of Charleville abandon him. All night, spent by each other's sides, Verlaine repeats the stinging words of the "child of the sun." He can see nothing before him but a hermetically sealed world, emptied of love and lit by the leaden star of Saturn.

He leaves at dawn on July 10, having decided to buy a revolver. For five days he had been turning this idea over and over in his head; the weapon had become both a magical word and tool. He had probably already seen and coveted it, displayed in a window of the Passage of the Galeries Saint Hubert, where he finally bought it. Then he crawled from bar to bar until he felt a drunkenness mounting in him that, while giving him comfort, caused his mind to seethe and his anger to heat up. Toward noon he returns to the hotel and drags Rimbaud with him to the Maison des Brasseurs, where they have a meal that is washed down with copious amounts of alcohol. Rimbaud, deaf to the demands of Verlaine, who, to tell the truth, still hasn't chosen *him*, reaffirms his desire to leave. The revolver, which the other now shows him in a fit of bravado, hardly moves him. He plans to go back down to Paris, where he will go see Forain on rue Saint Jacques, as well as his few loyal friends. If there is nothing more to expect from them, he will go back to Charleville, where the *mother* will have to put him up. At around two o'clock the two men get back to the Hôtel de la Ville de Courtrai on rue des Brasseurs where they are now staying (they had moved there from the Hôtel Liégeois earlier). Madame Verlaine was waiting for them there. Rimbaud goes back to gather up his belongings. He intends to catch the train that afternoon and leave Paul to his fate. Suddenly, the latter, after locking the door behind him, places a chair in front of it, sits down, and pulls out his revolver. He hardly gives Rimbaud any warning: "Hold on! I will teach you to want to leave."[210] Two shots are fired, one bullet lodges in the wall, and the other strikes Rimbaud's left wrist. Taking stock of what he has done, Verlaine wishes to take his own life. But it is well past the time for such childish behavior. Rimbaud's wrist is bleeding. Madame Verlaine, present at the scene, cares for the wound as best she can, and then with no further delay, this strange and miserable group go to the Hôpital Saint Jean, where without saying that he was struck by a bullet, the wounded one has his injury cared for. Now Rimbaud is more insistent than ever on leaving. Verlaine's reaction has clearly shown him that Paul, with the help of alcohol, was ready to go beyond all limits and extend himself in scenes of cruelty, those that the seer had advocated in London as the paradoxical method and astrue black magic. But Verlaine was now a dangerous man, not a poet seeking the place and the formula. With no change to his plans, Rimbaud returns to rue des Brasseurs. While on their way there, Verlaine tries at all costs to convince him to remain. Madame Verlaine, definitely of the opinion that Rimbaud's departure is preferable, gives him the twenty francs necessary for the trip to Paris. That evening, still followed by the mother and her son, Rimbaud heads in direction of the Gare du Midi. He persists, even though Paul tries for the tenth time to change his mind with the most exaggerated arguments. Undoubtedly they were living through one of those hopelessly entangled moments in which love violently turns into hate as the sole antidote allowing a clean break from something that no longer offers anything but the colors of absurdity. And the story that could be made about it spreads an overly violent light on an intimate relationship suddenly open to all: detectives, and later on, exegetes, biographers, and pamphleteers. No one could wash away the shame. Neither the actors in the drama, nor the observers placed before a scene of human stupidity, weakness, running aground, and failure. Let's listen to Rimbaud's deposition as if we were there:

> We had reached the area of place Rouppè; Verlaine was a few steps in front of me, then he turned back toward me; I saw him put his hand in his pocket to get his revolver; I made a half turn and went back the way I had come. I met a policeman who I informed of what had happened to me and who then invited Verlaine to follow him to the police station.

Verlaine, for his part, gave a version that sheds a more favorable light on his actions, but each undoubtedly didn't see what the other really intended to do, only the interpretation of uncompleted gestures: "While on our way, I renewed my entreaties (for Rimbaud to stay); I stood before him, as if to prevent him from continuing on his way, and I threatened to blow out my brains; he thought perhaps that I was threatening him but that wasn't my intention." Rimbaud calling the police! Such a step could tarnish his memory. It would be a bad-faith gesture to hold it against him, though. He assuredly unleashed a fatal chain of events by this, but outside of heroism, what scruples remain when it is a question of life or death? From this point the agent Auguste Michel (of course all the names of these minor characters[211] whose paths crossed those of the two poets during this woeful time are known) leads the defendant, Paul Verlaine, arrested "on the petition of the honorable Rimbaud, Arthur, man of letters," before the police chief Joseph Delhalle. It is eight o'clock in the evening. Their depositions, as well as that of Madame Verlaine, were recorded. Madame Verlaine tries to blacken Rimbaud's reputation: "For two years the honorable Rimbaud has been living off my son, who has complained of his bad-tempered and wicked character," and to excuse Paul who "had no rancor against Rimbaud" and "acted in a moment of confusion."

Verlaine, now in the hands of the police, spends his first night in the lockup, in the *Amigo*,[212] as a cell was then called. Madame Verlaine and Rimbaud, according to their testimony, return to the hotel, without—one would thin—exchanging very many words. The worst has been avoided but the life of the irregular couple no longer belongs to the world of loose gossip. It has been made, in some manner, official. The next day, giving in to a quite understandable feeling of compassion, Madame Verlaine takes Rimbaud, who had shivered with fever all night, to the Hôpital Saint Jean so that the bullet can finally be extracted from his wrist. By doctor's order he has to stay in bed. He will remain for almost ten days here—a considerable length of time for such a mild wound—which leads us to believe that he was in a poor state of health at this time. This same July 11, Verlaine can see that his position is becoming serious, and his mother, who has decided to remain in Brussels (she rented a furnished room in Ixelles that she would not give up until the beginning of September), realizes that he has committed an irrevocable act. "Accused of attempted murder," he is imprisoned in the Petits Carmes Prison; on the twelfth the examining magistrate, t'Serstevens, comes to the hospital to record Rimbaud's deposition. The latter clearly sums up the atmosphere of the last days in Verlaine's company. He bluntly describes his companion as weak and versatile: "Sometimes he is desperate, sometimes he goes into rages. He never follows through on his ideas." In addition Rimbaud vehemently defends himself of the charges that he had amorous relations with the accused: "I don't want to go to the trouble of denying such slander." However t'Serstevens asks to be given the wounded man's wallet, in which he finds "a large number of letters and other writings in Verlaine's hand,"[213] the correspondence they had exchanged over these last few days as well as—a discovery which they would have done well to avoid—the inverse sonnet of "Le Bon Disciple," an obvious homage to their homosexual practices, an extremely free little work in which their respective roles are clearly portioned out and defined.

The bullet has not yet been extracted from the wounded man's wrist. Rimbaud has hours to spend sifting through the recent events of his life and thinking about his "final croak" while drinking in the unsavory odors of the hospital. On the thirteenth, Dr. Charles Semal makes a verification of the state of the wound that he describes with an almost laughable precision, and in so doing confers an almost surreal importance upon it.[214] "It is round in shape, its edges contused and torn, it's about 5 mm in diameter, etc." However, the bullet has still not been removed. That operation will have to wait until the seventeenth and the projectile, the irrefutable proof, will have to be sent to t'Serstevens wrapped up like a sacred relic. What frenzied bidding the sale of this projectile would inspire today if it hadn't been thrown away like a useless knickknack—which of course it was! Verlaine's offense, in which he had attempted premeditated murder, seems to have concerned magistrate t'Serstevens—who exerted himself quite a bit in this matter—more than is reasonable. The dossier abounds in legal minutiae: transfers, confrontations, cross-examinations, reports, down to the least savory item, the examination performed on Verlaine by Drs. Semal and Vleminckx "in order to ascertain if he carried traces of pederastic habits."[215] "O incomprehensible pederasts, it is not I who shall heap insults upon your great degradation, it is not I who will hurl scorn on your infundibuliform anus," says Lautréamont in the fifth canto of his *Les Chants de Maldoror*. "Infundibuliform"—such is the term in legal medicine that will be retained in the experts' report. An excess of guilt touched Verlaine, by virtue of an observation that is furthermore judicially regarded as nil, nowadays. Unable to confer with Rimbaud, he will however reply to t'Serstevens, who is definitely goaded by his base curiosity: "It is slander invented by my wife and her family to damage my reputation."

Interrogations continue one after the other while they wait for the trial. Madame Verlaine sometimes comes to the hospital to see Rimbaud. He himself has written his mother to tell her of all that has occurred and to announce his imminent return. On July 18 he makes another deposition in which he attributes Verlaine's action to drunkenness. "I can't think of any serious motive for the attack he made on me. Besides, he was not at all in his right mind; he was in a drunken state, he had gotten drunk that morning, as was his habit when left to his own devices." The next day he signs a release form in which he recognizes the fact that Verlaine's action was not premeditated.[216] A day later, restored to health and cleansed, so to speak, like Pilate of all responsibility toward his assailant, he leaves Saint Jean and, while awaiting his full recovery, lodges for several days at 14 rue des Petits Bouchers, in a furnished room kept by a tobacco shopowner, Madame Pincemaille. By the most extraordinary coincidence, an unknown painter by the name of Jef Rosman did a well-executed painting of him there.[217] Rimbaud is lying on his right side, wrapped in sheets covered by a shiny red eiderdown. His head rests on two pillows. His hair is tousled; his face, quite youthful-looking, is somewhat unusual for the way in which the eyes are portrayed: two somber almonds in which a speck of fever gleams. Once again Rimbaud is looking at us from the depths of secrecy. He will not stay long with this hostess. Once he's recovered his health, he catches the train to Charleville.

Meanwhile Verlaine is in the Prison of the Petit Carmes taking stock of his life. His incarceration has put him in the company of those excluded from society. He won there a negative sacredness, that which Rimbaud himself envied when he said he admired "the intractable convict on whom the prison doors are always closing."[218] On July 28, while Rimbaud was far away in his Ardennes countryside, Verlaine, for whom only his mother's affection remained, was brought before the Brussels criminal court by the royal prosecutor and accused of assault and battery "resulting in the personal inability of

Rimbaud to work." We didn't know he was left-handed! No matter! A writer is always a "hand with a pen." On August 8 Verlaine appeared before the court, a sordid courtroom—he will say so in *Mes Prisons*—in which a "scabby Christ" keeps watch, who "gazes at the defendants with an exasperated air." The day of the trial he is judged in the absence of the victim, who could have been summoned to appear, however. Rimbaud certainly had better things to do during that period of time, in that he continued to work on *Une saison en enfer*, roughed out over the previous months. In addition, he had provided the court with a legal document withdrawing the charges. T'Serstevens spoke there in his capacity as examining magistrate, then two witnesses were heard: Verplaes, the manager of the Hôtel de la Ville de Courtrai, and Auguste Mourot, subpoenaed to these galleys against his wishes. The deputy prosecutor with his "little handlebar mustache" fulminates against Verlaine and demands "the severest punishment allowable by law." Despite an excellent argument from his defense attorney, a Maître Nélis, the accused receives the maximum sentence: two years' imprisonment and a 200-franc fine. Rimbaud, however, had only been wounded. But the premeditated nature of the second offense, the suspicions of homosexuality that hung over Verlaine, the only one of the couple to be of legal age, were aggravating factors in his case. (Several years later, in 1895, Oscar Wilde, mentor and lover of the young Lord Alfred Douglas, would see himself similarly condemned by the prudish Victorian society and incarcerated in Reading Gaol.) Let me add that the court, its curiosity aroused about this foreigner, had gained information about his past in the most insidious fashion. It had been learned that he had participated in the Commune and frequented the company of the emigrant revolutionaries in Brussels and London. He now paid dearly for the precautions taken by Madame Rimbaud when, in 1872—almost a year before!—she had turned to the police for help in following her son.

Arriving in Roche with his arm in a sling, Rimbaud, even though besieged with questions, could find nothing better to do or say than collapse in a chair and murmur these simple words: "Ah, Verlaine! Verlaine!"[219] Normally hard and impervious to grief, he couldn't repress a long-overdue sob this time. These rarely shed tears of Rimbaud are precious. They will not be spilled save at times of mourning: the death of Vitalie and his own deathbed agony when he would witness the atrocious debacle of his own body. No doubt he was informed, in due course, of the excessively stiff penalty handed down on his friend. "The vision of justice is the pleasure of God alone,"[220] he would write soon, no longer maintaining any illusion about that dispensed by men. But a maxim of the purest egoism also echoes in his mind, as if it were of primary importance to be able to accept the fortunes life had in store until the bitter end: "Me, I'm intact, and I don't care."[221]

THE DAMNED ONE'S NOTEBOOK

UNE SAISON EN ENFER IS THE STORY OF AN INDIVIDUAL BREAKING OFF TO march alone in reaction to the great void that could, to borrow a simple expression, be called "adult life," or the "start of life." Of this there can be no doubt. "Real life" had been thrust upon Rimbaud ever since his total screw-up in London and Brussels. The "atrocious stories" he had wanted to invent during the month of April had ripened like fruit, right up to Verlaine's simultaneously failed and successful action. On July 20, he left the Hôpital Saint-Jean. Several days later he arrives in Roche, the "sad hole." However, the countryside is merrily animated by the harvests. During this time Madame Rimbaud and Vitalie, with the help of their servants, attend to the work in the fields. Isabelle, who is only twelve, takes over the domestic duties. Meanwhile Rimbaud is doing his part by devoting all his time to the *Saison*. Furthermore, his wound prevents him from taking on any jobs requiring strength. Perhaps he has also convinced his mother that it is imperative he finish his famous book begun in April on which, he claims, his future depends. Everyone knows that he is up in his room continuing to labor on a strange work, whose secret he keeps to himself. His sister Vitalie, a romantic soul drawn to this mysterious brother, will later note in her diary: "My brother Arthur did not take part in the farm chores; the work he did with the pen was serious enough that it didn't permit him to share our manual labors."[1] It is she who is creating literature, on this occasion, while he is impatiently exerting himself to breaking the overly beautiful inflexions of sentimental phrases, immured by four walls. For the first time, perhaps, they take him seriously and his prodigious aside develops invisibly, closely accompanied by useful and remunerative bouts of fatigue.

Rimbaud is not one to sit before a landscape, pen in hand, in order to better enter into the "feeling of nature." He writes cooped up, talking to himself, his thoughts ricocheting from one corner of the room to the next. Of his own free will he places himself in an exam room, in an experimental situation where he can no longer vacillate, where nothing can protect him from his own violence. Based on the length of time he himself will indicate it took for *Saison* to be set down: "April–August 1873," the rapidity of his writing is stupefying, despite the work's small size. In April–May he had enough time to draft his *Livre païen* or *Livre nègre*; in June he no doubt continued working on it, but all of July would have been disrupted by the Brussels incident and his prolonged stay in the hospital would have prevented him from working on his manuscript. How far along had he gotten with it at that time? It would be crazy to think that Rimbaud reconstituted it totally from memory on his return to Roche. It is more likely he brought it back with him from London, and that it had eluded the investigations of the examining magistrate who had taken his possessions, including his wallet, when he came to interrogate him at the Hôpital Saint-Jean. There is no proof that these pages were in his luggage, though. It is also possible that some of his papers were sent to him from London by Vermersch or someone else, even his landlady, Mrs. Smith, who will send back (this is almost certain) those belonging to Verlaine.[2] So it is over the last week in July and the entire month of August that he would have completed his extraordinary booklet. He composed its introduction in the light of what he had just lived through, "his last croak." He seems to have recovered from all his cruel experiences. He develops his retrospective through the accumulation of perfect tenses, but he is still not sure of anything, and fatal influences continue to constrain him: "You will remain a hyena." He wholly feels the demon he carries inside, it is the postulation toward Satan Baudelaire speaks of. It is Satan, moreover, to whom he dedicates the "hideous sheets" of his "damned one's notebook."

"Sheets." It could not be said any better. Sheets taken from a greater whole. After the narration of the "Délires," perhaps written down that June in London, the first part of his story was completed: "Today I know how to salute beauty" (the rough draft says "Hail to bounty"). It was most likely in Roche that the final four sequences were conceived: "L'Impossible," "L'Eclair," "Matin," and "Adieu." Verlaine is still traversing the countryside: I was right to despise those good fellows [. . .] parasites of the cleanliness and health of our women." But the hour belongs primarily to truth, sought with the impatience of one who thinks it exists transparently and translucidly in the real, and that it is only a question of seeing clearly. And the debate picks up again, at a very high altitude and on a global scale: West, East, modern era, or primitive country. Rimbaud trudges in impossibility. His phrases are violent shafts and arrows of a stripped-down interior debate devoid of hallucinations in a kind of constant, exhausting dialogue in which he speaks himself, as man (he says) *"deludes himself."* All of this polyphony has to be reconstructed at its natural site: the room in Roche, the attic as some will say.[3] Outside the harvests are continuing. Rimbaud returns from far away when he comes down the stairs for the evening meal. A formidable spiritual struggle takes place every day, like that of Jacob at Jaboq's ford. He reemerges worn out, unable to say anything of it to his mother, his sisters, or Frédéric. He brushes against madness in complete lucidity; he nears the truth. Even the most simplistic readers of *Saison* have perceived its vocalic percussion, no doubt to the extent of inventing Rimbaud's stampings on the floor and the cries he supposedly howled when he wrote these pages—just as imagination requires an Isidore Ducasse striking chords on the piano as he composed *Les Chants de Maldoror*. "Real" inventions suggested by fiction and the voice of his syncopations. Just as later the table on which Rimbaud would have written his book was discovered in the attic in Roche. A cross was carved into the wood![4]

Yes, Breton was well aware of this shortly after Claudel, and didn't accept it.[5] Christianity is in this book, as is God—who is never blasphemed in it—as well as the consoling, inaccessible cross, and ferocious damnation. It is a book written "under the sun of Satan," the image, but also the strength of misfortune here below, even if there isn't another world and it is quite sufficient that another one may not exist. *Saison*, devoted to the quest for the absolute, is also valid because reality hounds the individual writing it as he nears twenty years of age.[6] Working age, the age of majority. It is the story of a prehistoric time, before the entry into adulthood with the inevitable duties it incurs to the adult of the Western world: employment, military service, a world of citizens, not artists. He pants and gasps all this in "L'Eclair" with the temptation of suicide imminent: "my betrayal of the world." However, Rimbaud, having fallen without interruption, picks himself up. His "Matin" reverses the myth of the great revolutionary evening. There would now be a dawn; the three magi, the heart, the soul, the mind, that are tugging him in opposite directions, will find—who knows?—the site of a real adoration far from superstitions:

"Christmas on earth!" His phrases throughout *Saison*, which are those all men encounter, are nonetheless surrounded by the greatest solitude, persecuted by a doubt they strive to vanquish and which gives their movement all its cutting edge.

"Autumn already!" Rimbaud traces the beginning of "Adieu" to the end of summer. He sees the mists, the returning cold, the uncertainty that never leaves him—a harlot also, just like death, which brushes past him. Everything is consumed. The enchantments, the dreams of glory. All that is in the past. The words that he finds then are to be said over as he himself spoke them. And his voice reaches us, it is as intimate as Pascal's questions. It is audible, it is rage and lassitude, it is an immense force surging up out of complete isolation. The *we* of Rimbaud and *Saison* is his real act of charity, the example of his example. With him it is still permissible to march forward, on the side of an assured future: "And it will be permitted to me *to possess truth in one body and one soul*." The rest of his life will be the creation of the test of such a truth, one that doesn't necessarily accord with literature.

It remained for him to get his book published—as a secret justification and with no more illusions of being understood. He had been pushed, right to the bitter end, by the necessity of shouting, even in the desert. Although grumbling about it, Madame Rimbaud had respected his incomprehensible task. He convinced her now to advance him the sum that would allow him to assure its publication. The choice of a publisher was necessary, though the word *publisher* is an exaggeration in this case. Rimbaud knew he had been ostracized by the Parisian literary world. Lepelletier had repeated to Verlaine enough times what a scandal their departure had caused. So it would have been vain to turn to Lemerre, in whom, at the age of sixteen, his hopes had rested. Hadn't Verlaine himself, despite his growing notoriety, planned, following their flight, to publish his *Romances sans paroles* at author's expense? He had even thought of resorting to the *Nord-Est* printer in Charleville. Therefore it was toward a solution of this kind that Rimbaud directed his efforts. The one he chose shouldn't be so surprising, though. It resembles an act of provocation. Nonetheless, let's not look at it solely that way. It is a coincidence, rather, that it would be in bad taste to label "extenuating!" In fact, he made use of the services of a printer located at 37 rue aux Choux in Brussels. Monsieur Jacques Poot managed this establishment, known under the company name of the Typographical Alliance and which specialized in publications concerning law and the legal system, mainly the bulletin of *La Belgique judiciaire*. It is thought that Rimbaud took note of this address while reading such a pamphlet, but nothing serves to explain why it caught his eye, for it is not because he had a bone to pick with the legal system that he would have necessarily been made aware of its existence. It is also possible that Verlaine and Rimbaud had taken note of the Typographical Alliance during their first visit to Brussels, a time when finding a printer for *Romances sans paroles* was still a pressing concern. Did Rimbaud send *Saison* to Monsieur Poot? Did he travel to Brussels to discuss contractual terms for which he would have paid a certain sum in advance, the rest to be paid on the publication of the book? It had already been decided that a printing of five hundred copies would be made and that the book would consist of about fifty pages.

August 21, the court of appeals in Brussels confirmed the verdict condemning Verlaine, handed down on the eighth of the month. Verlaine had been transferred to the prison in Mons, which he would oddly call "the best of castles,"[7] and where he would rediscover his faith. Rimbaud probably had contact with him during this period, but there is actually no evidence they saw each other. Verlaine, too, had turned back to the past. The first week of his incarceration in the Petits-Carmes, when he was not yet housed "à la pistole," that is, in a moderately comfortable cell in return for a certain sum of money, he would have written with the means chance had left at his disposal—a little ink and a twig—the long poem "Crimen amoris."[8] It is a most appropriate counterpart to *Une saison en enfer* (that he only partially knew), a Satanic tale in which "the most beautiful" of all the "evil angels" figures, "sixteen years under a crown of flowers." The remarks of the damned soul recall the very ones Rimbaud will attribute to him when he causes the Foolish Virgin to speak for him:

> *Nous avons tous trop souffert, anges et hommes,*
> *De ce conflit entre le Pire et le Mieux [. . .]*
>
> *Assez et trop de ces luttes trop égales!*
> *Il va falloir qu'enfin se rejoignent les*
> *Sept Péchés aux Trois Vertus Théologales!*
> *Assez et trop de ces combats durs et laids!*

Et pour réponse à Jesus qui crut bien faire

En maintenant l'equilibre de ce duel,

Par moi l'Enfer dont c'est içi le repaire

Se sacrifie à l'Amour universal!

We have suffered too much, angels and men,

From this conflict between the Worst and the Best [. . .]

There has been more than enough of these too evenly matched struggles!

The Seven Sins are finally going to have to

Join with the Three Theological Virtues!

There has been more than enough of these cruel, ugly battles!

And in answer to Jesus who believes to be acting rightly

By maintaining the balance of this duel,

Through me Hell, whose lair is here

Is sacrificed for Universal Love!

All ends in a cataclysm, a Sardanapalish fire. The earthquake he has experienced was unfortunately more human in scale. In a later letter to Lepelletier, Verlaine will indicate that Rimbaud owned this poem, as well as three other "diabolical tales," a term reminiscent of earlier "atrocious stories." In fact, a version of "Crimen amoris" exists copied over in Rimbaud's own hand.[9] Did he receive this terrifying dithyramb written in his honor through the mail? Did he get it from Verlaine in person? And most important, why did he copy it over? There is presently no clear-cut answer that would permit any light to be shed on this enigma.

That September, he had only to wait for the proofs of his book. It isn't known if he corrected them. In fact, starting with the first page, some typos remain and questions have been raised by the strange quote marks that open the text and are never closed, as if by an irony of fate it is definitely forbidden to know who is speaking here. The following month *Une saison en enfer* appeared in as discreet a manner as possible. Rimbaud was informed of it by Monsieur Poot, to whom he announced his imminent arrival. In truth, nothing would be known of this trip if a note of the police, who were definitely quite intrigued by this former "franc-tireur" of the Commune, did not record his presence in Brussels on October 24.[10] It appears likely that he came to pick up a portion of the *Saison* print run. All the evidence shows, though, that after staying at the Hôtel de la Ville de Courtrai, he was content to just take the few author's copies that were contractually due him. For the moment, because of his lack of funds to pay off the rest of his bill, he left the bulk of them at the Typographical Alliance with a promise to soon pay the money he owed.

The same day his steps take him to the prison of the Petits-Carmes, where he most likely asks to see Verlaine but is informed of the prisoner's transfer to Mons. He then leaves one of his opuscules[11] for the absentee with this simple dedication: "To P. Verlaine, A. Rimbaud." The bare minimum. Without commentary. Should this autograph in which the initial letter P covers over an original R even be considered authentic? Let's grant him this gesture, however. Alone again, with one of the most troubling books of the West in his possession, misunderstood by everyone, just like Van Gogh who in this same era was painting canvases no one wanted, Rimbaud reached the Midi Station. Did he then return to Charleville? Did he go directly to Paris? The fact remains that, having only a dozen copies at his disposal, he gave one to Delahaye (he would ask for it back in 1875), and one to Millot, and he sent a small number to "Gavroche," the dear Forain who was entirely devoted to him, despite the Brussels drama. Forain, who now frequented the small group of the Vivants, distributed these brochures to Richepin, Ponchon, and perhaps Gineste,[12] who had just introduced a future friend of Rimbaud's into this non-conformist coterie: Germain Nouveau.

All writers opening their latest book subject themselves to a formidable test. They shall have to see themselves. *Verba volant. Scripta manent.* The text imperturbably faces them, like another self that has already passed over to the side of eternity. Rimbaud feels this shock for the first time, even if few illusions remain to him. (Hadn't he already noted in the rough draft of *Saison* "Art is an idiocy"?) *Saison* formed an unpredictable supplement to the "things of here below."[13] He experienced it as a raging disappointment, as if it provided him proof of literature's absurdity. Much later on Isabelle Rimbaud would recall several anecdotes pertinent to this topic, at least one of which has the ring of truth—these kinds of words can't be invented. When Madame Rimbaud expressed her astonishment at understanding nothing she read in *Saison* and asked her son what it meant, the latter allegedly responded: "It is to be read literally and in every sense!"[14] Vitalie Cuif had taught him his basic reading skills when he was a child, and he didn't want to remain in her debt! Another bit of information, again from Isabelle (she would have been only twelve then), shows Rimbaud casting his rough drafts and all his pamphlets into the fire.[15] The witness of this holocaust has long been taken at her word. However, in 1901, when Isabelle was still alive, it proved necessary to yield to the facts. A Belgian lawyer, Léon Losseau, who had bought up the business stock of Poot's print shop, got hold of several still-wrapped bundles (some of which were damaged). That day he would discover all of the copies of the *Saison*, excepting only those Rimbaud had taken away with him.[16] That Rimbaud may have surrendered to a purifying gesture with which he would have sought to destroy his books remains no less plausible. But he didn't display the radical determination of which Isabelle, definitely terrified by the fires of Hell, is speaking. Literature, whose limited powers had certainly prompted him to doubt it anew, was not yet completely useless in his eyes.

In October (a first visit or a second in the same month?) he had the audacity to return to Paris, more out of curiosity, certainly, than to proceed with some sort of launching of his *Saison*—which he had already decided to leave in the shadows (for the incredible ripening that we know). He most likely stopped by Jean-Louis Forain's, who was then living at 289 rue Saint-Jacques; one would think that he also saw Cabaner and his new Vivants,* who, by all evidence, were the successors to the Zutistes, even going so far as to continue the famous Album in the same scatological and parodic state of mind. Testimonies remain rare and uncertain. Forain has never supplied a recollection of this period. The worldly success that he subsequently enjoyed can explain his silence. Besides, there was nothing forcing him to talk about where he stood in this regard. Jean Richepin will be more verbose; nevertheless it will be years[17] before he decides to present several fragments of his memories that are perhaps muddled, and which, beyond their remarkable interest, nonetheless include their own shadow areas. Only two anecdotes survive concerning this Rimbaud's brave appearance in Paris. They complement each other to a certain extent, since both portray him in the same place, the Tabourey Café

---

*The Vivants group essentially consisted of Maurice Bouchor, Jean Richepin, and Raoul Ponchon.

near the Odéon, then frequented by numerous artists. The front room was willingly lorded over by Barbey d'Aurevilly, the dreaded critic of the *Nain jaune*. The back room was open to smokers and daring protesters against the establishment. The sudden appearance of Rimbaud in this place seems to have created great uneasiness. The distressing outcome of his cohabitation with Verlaine was known to all. His scandalous conduct had been held against him since the Carjat incident, still well lodged in everyone's memory. Thus no one was prepared to give him any sign of recognition and it called for the warm display of generosity by Alfred Poussin[18] (a large, strapping fellow with the air of a peasant and a newcomer who wanted to follow a career as a poet), for him not to be totally shunned. He refused Poussin's offer to dine with him and, after exchanging a few more words, withdrew back into his mute silence for the rest of the evening. On another occasion, he was allegedly approached by a small, brown-haired man, with a dull complexion, an Arab nose, and an air of mulish nonchalance.[19] Recently arrived from his natal Provence, this interlocutor sometimes signed the poems he submitted to *La Renaissance littéraire et artistique*[20] with the pseudonym P. Néouvielle but his name in reality was Germain Nouveau. He had been leading a bohemian lifestyle in Paris for about a year. His tastes and style placed him in the school of the Verlaine of *Fêtes galantes*. One of his *Fantasies parisiennes* summons up the "carnivals of Boucher and the dances of Watteau," "Un peu de musique" is reminiscent of "Guitare," "En forêt" copies "Colloque sentimental." He also admired Rimbaud, whose rare poems circulating in the Latin Quarter he knew by heart: the "Voyelles" sonnet, "Les Chercheuses de poux," "Les Corbeaux." Tradition maintains that Rimbaud and Nouveau talked together for a long time on this occasion and that the seeds for a journey to England would have been planted during this conversation. This is not at all certain, though, and we will see that many things argue in favor of a later meeting in 1874 alone.

Rimbaud's stay in Paris was cut short since he was shunned by everyone, and he soon returned to Charleville. There was no question of him resuming courses at the *collège*. He was no closer to deciding on a profession. Idleness took hold of him and crushed him like a stormy sky. "Let's pretend, let's laze," he said in *Une saison en enfer*. Most likely in order to laze he had to pretend to his mother. But epics were taking shape in his thoughts, mirages of a future in which the world gave itself to him: engineer, traveler, a sharp intelligence traversing Europe at a dizzying speed. We know nothing of this transit to emptiness that could just as easily have elicited a surge of writing in other *Illuminations*, the most desperate and often most audacious of these poems, the famous, deliberately delayed "base acts,"[21] whose ultimate magic power he saved for himself.

We are once more entering into a realm of pure hypothesis. Rimbaud's time eludes us. How did he live these days? How did he spend these days at his disposal during which he refused so much? The second poem of the series entitled "Vies," appears to reconstruct this moment in which he was constrained by uncertainty, just as he was at the time he wrote down the notebook of *Saison*. "At present a country gentleman in a bleak countryside under sober skies, I try to be moved by the memories from my beggar's childhood." This has the tone of a report. How many times was Rimbaud the man of a time "at present" that is in no way reducible to a bustling modernism! Waiting. In suspense. On the borderline. In the breech. And nothing better describes his state of mind on his return to Roche than this "gentleman" of another age forcibly subjected to the sobriety of the sky . . . and the absence of any nearby cafés. Thus cloistered in the room full of memories and still enamored of his marvelous escapes, it is necessary for him to realize the dead end in which he is a captive: "The sober air of this harsh countryside feeds my atrocious skepticism quite actively. But since this skepticism cannot, henceforth, be put into practice, and since, besides, I am devoting myself to a new disturbance—I expect to become a very wicked lunatic." Skepticism has become indispensable after the dreams, enthusiasm, and the useless *Saison*. This has a bearing on literature and it is not far from spilling over into life, in that—Rimbaud seems to be saying this—nothing else can be ventured, as was the case during the time in which he put into practice the sophistries of his folly before Verlaine. Does he now dare believe in "the putting into practice"? Quite a few mysteries are hovering here, skillfully supported by the narrator, the only person, of course, who understands them; and we know nothing whatsoever of the enigmatic "new disturbance" to which he feels devoted, except to hear in it as ingenuously as possible the name of Nouveau ["new" in English–translator's note] himself, either clearly spoken or as a play on words. I like to imagine that during this time of compulsory idleness, Rimbaud returned to the *Illuminations* but to go even further. He proceeds in a very distinctive manner that consists of not finishing in order to finish. He produces several texts announcing a radical conclusion: "Solde," in which it is a matter of selling off all his marvelous discoveries, the astounding beauties that unfortunately remained dead letters; "Barbare," convoking the catastrophes: and let's hear no more talk about them! "Depart," which bids farewell, breaking the mooring that delays the definitive undoing of the drunken boat and celebrates the "affections and new noises"; "Democratie," a disturbing prophecy in parentheses that has to be attributed to the dreadful mercenaries of modern times, "at the service of the most monstrous exploitations, industrial or military," a vague Foreign Legion in which one hotheadedly enlists to travel the world in fierce anonymity; and "Devotion," which takes inventory of the secret adorations—what little of these remain—and reflects on Verlaine in his hermitage at Mons, the castle-prison of the soul.

Several times Rimbaud reaches a conclusion, releasing bits and pieces from his "spiritual hunt," for want of a radiant begetting that would bring forth the Genius, his genius. The cruelest bitterness grates in the opening lines of "Vies," the harsh accent of a prediction that threatens all of us: "My wisdom is as scorned as chaos. What is my nothingness compared to the stupor that awaits you?" The final phrase is shouted at large. Rich with his negative experience, it ensures that he will necessarily have to pass through many ordeals before experiencing even the smallest bit of the troubling odyssey that is poetry.

A "YOUNG PARISIAN" IN LONDON

TOWARD MARCH 1874, HOWEVER, RIMBAUD EMERGES FROM WHAT MAY have been a fecund period of hibernation. The moment has come for him to go to Paris and leave Charleville, where time has slowed to a crawl. He courageously goes back on a road he guesses will be lined with snares and wreckage. He joyfully finds Forain again, whose talents as a draftsman are beginning to earn him recognition, and stays at his house. But it seems Rimbaud also spent an equal amount of time with the painter Jolibois, called "the Apple" (an ironic nickname he was given making fun of his turniplike complexion), whose studio was located on rue Saint-Jacques. The Vivants gladly hang out there. It isn't unusual to find Ponchon, Mercier, and Keck there, and Nouveau also puts in a frequent appearance. Richepin states he saw Rimbaud for the first time there with "his gauche peasant appearance, his large hands and feet, his thatch-like hair," and "his unforgettable angel's eyes."[22] It is no doubt wiser to place Nouveau's first meeting with Rimbaud at the famous Tabourey Café in this time frame. Richepin, late in life, provided a good characterization of the temperaments of the two men: "The energetic and brilliant Rimbaud—at the time still much more famous for his affair with Verlaine than for his works—soon exerted a visible influence over Nouveau, who had a weak character prey to enthusiasm, with all the agitation of a sensual woman surrendering to someone stronger."[23] We can almost recognize all the elements of Verlaine's character in this portrait. Rimbaud knew how to find *his* men. Wouldn't Nouveau's sensuality have reminded him of the impressionable sensitivity of the "pitiful brother," whose feminine bent was often concealed beneath the worst kinds of bawdy comments? Another motive, which does him no honor, permits a possible explanation for his sudden affection for Nouveau. In fact, Nouveau, who had lost his mother the previous year, had a small inheritance at his disposal. Rimbaud, who had profited off Verlaine's money (and would not forbear to do so again), may have thought (who knows?) that the convenient wealth of this impromptu companion would assure him yet another "season." As a counter to such unimaginatively materialist explanations, we should take note of the retrospective high esteem in which writers such as Breton and Aragon held Nouveau, not at all averse to viewing him as Rimbaud's equal.[24] Breton felt that this encounter was highly significant and that Rimbaud advisedly deemed it worthwhile to make Nouveau his "mystic confident." There was assuredly no one closer to Rimbaud the "illuminator" than Nouveau himself, who was witness to the final phases of a mysterious creation in which he sometimes collaborated.

In any event, Nouveau and Rimbaud quickly decide to leave for England together, a fact that tends to weaken the hypothesis of an earlier preparatory meeting during the autumn of 1873. Nouveau reveals in a letter from March 26, 1874, addressed to Jean Richepin[25] that he "left Paris at the moment he least expected to," so unexpectedly in fact that he took the key to the room he rented from a certain Madame Cordelle, a wine merchant on rue de Vaugirard. He also left all his papers there, which he asks his correspondent to retrieve for him. However, Richepin, hardly a prude, hasn't forgotten Rimbaud's particular moral standards and leaps to the conclusion that it is a case of abduction. Rimbaud—according to him—used his fabulous power to bend the fragile poet to his will. But wouldn't it be better to admire Nouveau for having rushed off headlong like this, as one spontaneously seduced by a word of genius, a strange kind of password transmitted to him alone that would leave its mark on him his entire life, including the years he spent in mystic adoration and wretched asceticism begging by the portal of a church in Aix?

We know little about the couple Rimbaud and Nouveau formed in London: definitely enchantment and seduction for the elder of the two (Nouveau); for the other the resumption of a life still marked by uncertainty. At least he had escaped the "hand on the plow" of Roche just as he evaded by working abroad that false "path of honor": inevitable military conscription. The two men rent a room at 178 Stamford Street[26] near Waterloo Station in southeast London. The young man of the house, who knows a little French, converses with them every day for an hour. Other than that, their occupations are the same as during the time spent there with Verlaine, the difference being that Rimbaud now has a better grasp of the English language and can hope, with a little luck, to give lessons. He introduces the city to Nouveau, an appreciative audience. They go to cafés that offer musical entertainment and where black-faced minstrels delight them; they take long walks, sometimes wandering from one bridge to the next for miles to find the right place at which to cross back over the Thames. By March 26 they still haven't seen Vermersch—"at least I haven't,"[27] says Nouveau. Nonetheless, there is no evidence that Rimbaud desires to see the Communards again following his recent disappointments and the Brussels incident of sinister memory. Nouveau, though, holds high hopes of meeting the most illustrious of all the exiles, Vallès, and is thinking of asking André Gill for a letter of introduction. This year, much like the other, certain behaviors are repeated: Nouveau, like Verlaine, intends to write some kind of London chronicle for the *Renaissance littéraire*. Unfortunately, Blemont's review, which had welcomed the best contemporary poetry for the last two years, is falling apart and will cease publication on May 3. However, as if to replace it, the *Revue du monde nouveau* comes into being under the prodding of Charles Cros and the direction of Henri Mercier.[28] It publishes a prose contribution from Nouveau, "La Sourieuse," in its April 1 issue.

The two comrades led a secret life over the space of several months. Poetry was certainly what gave shape to their world. Nouveau composed several poems of a Rimbaldian tone during this time. His "Rêve claustral" and his "Hôtesses," most definitely written before his cohabitation with Rimbaud, already testify to that latter individual's influence. For his part, Rimbaud seems to have experienced one final burst of creative energy. It would appear incontestable that the copies of two of the *Illuminations* date back to this time.[29] One of these, "Villes I," is entirely written in Nouveau's handwriting save for the title spelled out by Rimbaud; the first two paragraphs of the other are written by Nouveau, then continued by Rimbaud. This discovery leads us to believe that Rimbaud had not yet completely renounced his desire to publish his texts, despite his resolutions to the contrary flaunted in *Saison* and his gesture of burning several copies of that work. In March-April-May, the sole period during which he lived with Nouveau, he gives an impression of having wished to make neat copies of some of his poems, with an eye—one would think—to making a collection of some "little overdue infamies." Certainly, the manuscripts of the *Illuminations*, such as they have come down to us, display pages of varying quality; their very content attest to the fact that there were several different times and places involved in their creation. But here in the spring of 1874, it is necessary to impute to Rimbaud the awareness of an overall intention and affection for literature. A year later he will still be taking the time to send his poems to Verlaine and will exhibit a surprising confidence in Germain Nouveau, to whom he entrusts the task of getting them published. It is certain that all we have left at our disposal are copies, no rough drafts have survived. We can thus imagine that 1874 was a time for reflection, not invention, and that this gathering together and copying over of texts at least signify that his literary ambition had not been dulled and that his "atrocious skepticism" had been temporarily overcome.

In addition, a poem remains from these ill-defined months of their life together that is written in Rimbaud's handwriting. We still don't know to which of the two men to attribute the authorship of "Poison perdu."[30] It emanates a charm and rare delicacy that is closer to Nouveau's style and possesses a kind of Verlainian transparency.

In April, Rimbaud and Nouveau obtain their reading cards for the British Museum.[31] Both avow they are twenty-one years of age, the legal age for admission to the reading room. During this time, it is possible they took out small ads, a common procedure, to find some kind of suitable situation. However the exacting research of V. P. Underwood, an expert sleuth of these kinds of materials, has so far remained fruitless. As Nouveau's portion of his inheritance is close to running out, the friends will soon find themselves out of resources. Misery lies in wait for them. Nouveau, an adept at bohemianism, seems to have not resigned himself to his fate on this occasion. Unless this last close friend was alienated by Rimbaud's touchy nature. The fact remains that Nouveau decides to return to France, it is not known when exactly, before July in any case as it is toward the beginning of that month Madame Rimbaud and her daughter Vitalie will come see their son and brother, who is then sick and alone. Rimbaud and Nouveau will never see each other again, though they will continue to correspond. Soon Nouveau will make the acquaintance of Verlaine and Delahaye. For some time he will receive letters from the migratory Rimbaud crisscrossing Italy and Germany. In 1893, through an unwitting irony of fate, he will mail a letter to his old friend, who had died two years previously. Ignorant of the tragic end of the seer, he ingenuously contemplated going to meet him in Aden for the purpose of opening a "small shop for decorative painting!"[32]

With Nouveau gone, Rimbaud again finds himself in a solitude that he may well have cherished. In order to meet his needs, as he was out of money, he does not hesitate to take out classified ads, just as he did in the past. It is perhaps him in *The Times* of June 8 describing himself as twenty-five years old and a "French Gentleman of excellent family, well educated, possessing a French degree, excellent knowledge of English," seeking a position as "a Private Secretary, travel companion, or tutor." This text is signed "A. R.," which leads us to believe it really is him—but the address given indicates a place, 25 Langham Street, where he never seems to have lived. The fact remains that Langham Street was the street on which Régamey had his studio and could also be the location of an employment agency through which Rimbaud was seeking a job. Another advertisement appears three times in *The Echo* of June, 9, 10, and 11, that is his beyond the shadow of a doubt, as it is clearly signed "Rimbaud."[33] The address refers one back to 40 London Street on Fitzroy Square, and the contents (it doesn't concern a job search) gives a more realistic description of his abilities. Whereas the previous advertisement mentioned a diploma, the one from Rimbaud of Fitzroy Square makes do with simply noting:[34] "a YOUNG PARISIAN—speaks *passablement* [Rimbaud used the French word here—translator's note]—seeks conversations with English gentlemen; in his own home; preferably afternoons." Indeed Rimbaud was still far from knowing all the subtleties of the English language.

We find him busy and anxious about his situation during this month of June. Furthermore we have to satisfy our curiosity with conjectures. But the arrival of his mother the following month proves that he asked her help and had to give her some serious reasons for it. On July 6, Madame Rimbaud, accompanied by Vitalie (during this sojourn Isabelle was entrusted to the care of the nuns at Saint-Sépulcre), arrive at Charing Cross Station in the morning. Rimbaud is there to greet them. They had left Charleville two days before but Rimbaud's letter requesting his mother's presence must have been dated from the previous month. We can be sure that this parsimonious and hard-to-please woman would not have made such a move without a very good reason. Rimbaud seems to have been going through a disheartening time, caused by either lack of money or—more likely—illness. Verlaine, in the "Rimbaud" chapter of his book the Les Poètes maudits,[35] will remark concerning this period: "London again, some problem, hospital momentarily." If we go by the advertisements mentioned previously, Rimbaud wasn't ill yet on the ninth, tenth, and eleventh of June, and on the sixth of July he is well enough to wait for his mother and sister at the station. He would therefore have been sick during the second half of June. The fact is that Vitalie, still continuing her valuable diary, notes on the very day of their arrival: "Arthur is feeling so much better." On July 12 she specifies: "Several people have advised him to go to the countryside by the sea to recover completely."

The pages so sensibly written by this young girl[36] still provide a testimony of the first order. Of course they are entirely dependent on the gaze of the writer, who is first astonished by this large city, then very quickly feels bored and misses her native Charleville. She tells us only a few things about Rimbaud. Full of solicitude for the travelers, he takes pains to stroll with them through the most touristic spots of the city. With great simplicity and—one may say—"blind" objectivity, Vitalie records these various comings and goings. There is nothing extraordinary here. Profound genius does not always illuminate daily life. Nobody saw Rimbaud during this time for there was nothing to see. They visit the Parliament at Westminster, the palace of the Duke of Northumberland, the Alhambra Theater on Leicester Square where a bust of Shakespeare had just been erected; they go hear a sermon at Saint Paul and stroll through the rooms of the National Gallery. Rimbaud attentively instructs his fellow family members in the rudiments of everyday English. He likes to drag them along through the large, impossibly crowded streets along the banks of the Thames and up to the docks, whose bustle and activity he has always admired. He finds them comfortable lodgings (a spacious room with two beds), at 12 Argyle Square but the heat is oppressive during the summer month, even at night, and he often takes them to the closest park to enjoy a little relief in the shade. But what was he doing on his own? After the two days he devoted to them, he had to "return to his concerns," according to the too obvious words of Vitalie, who says nothing more about them, but clearly records how her brother used his time: leaving in the morning around nine o'clock, returning in the evening toward six. In all likelihood he was going most often to the British Museum (to which he will twice bring

Vitalie). For almost the entire day the exile would transform himself into a "sitter" in the reading room with its three million volumes (the figure he gave his sister). He undoubtedly goes over the Robertson Manual for the umpteenth time and skims through the great classics made available to the public. To suspect him of writing some additional *Illuminations* in this place would fall under the jursidiction of evidence that is far too disappointing. How could anyone imagine so many colors surrounded by all that gray?

In fact he isn't following any strict timetable. On Friday, July 10, he receives a letter most likely coming from an agency in which he is offered three different positions. He is overjoyed and the next day visits the English "to arrange something," as Vitalie notes in a phrase of obscure banality. To obtain a position, in other words. And his sister, now wishing to return to France, muses somewhat trivially that he is going "to get fixed up with a job." The phrase will reappear under Rimbaud's own pen when he is seeking work in Africa. But the various offers he has been made do not suit him. His mother is so depressed by this she falls ill. Recovered two days later, she remains no less saddened by Arthur's needs. In addition she resolves to leave in the upcoming week, "no matter what happens." Meanwhile Rimbaud has regained his peace of mind following a gloomy period. "Arthur has taken a turn for the better," Vitalie declares. Reading this journal, we can feel how high his hopes were for a favorable letter finally offering a job to his liking. On Saturday June 18, he goes to place more ads with another employment agency. That Monday he receives a letter, but the offer it includes is still displeasing. Hence Vitalie's disillusioned conclusion: "Positions are available! If he wanted to, he would have found something and we would have left." As it happens he doesn't want to, for reasons that obviously elude us, but which no doubt stem from the lack of any real enthusiasm he could muster for this kind of work.

Madame Rimbaud has to leave. Before Arthur's pleas and display of grief however, she allows herself to be swayed. Here he is as a child again, lost if he is pushed from his mother's lap and subjected to an endless misery: life. In London as in Roche stagnation claims its due. The impossibility of getting out of his difficulties is also accompanied by the deeply felt futility of any efforts to do so. Vitalie is also bored in this strange London, where she doesn't speak the language. On July 27 Rimbaud again takes her to the British Museum, among whose collections she admires are the remains of Negus

Theodore, the former king of Abyssinia who committed suicide in Magdala following his defeat by the English army. Isabelle, who will later piece Vitalie's diary back together, makes this comment: "It is likely that the objects noted and remarked on by Vitalie were brought to her attention by Arthur." It is even more likely that Isabelle, through an act of hindsight, saw an additional example of the curious premonitions she thought she could pick out of her brother's work in the attention paid by Arthur to Theodore's remains. We are certainly witness here to an encounter, a confrontation that will be burdened by all the weight the future can give it. But Rimbaud's calling to the East could not have originated in such a fleeting coincidence.

Rimbaud, who does not try to conceal his actions, is still an individual who creates a mystery around himself, even to those nearest him. Vitalie finds his behavior puzzling on Wednesday, July 29. Toward nine o'clock, "gloomy and nervous," he leaves, saying he will not return until noon. But an hour later he returns to announce that he is leaving the next day. An advertisement had appeared in *The Times* the day before that was phrased as follows:[37] "A FRENCH PROFESSOR seeks POSITION in London or anywhere else, as TUTOR or TRAVEL COMPANION. French, German, Spanish. Good references." Signed "R." There is nothing to prove that it was placed by Rimbaud. But we have seen the tone of the ads he happily placed. It is not likely that his rapid decision can be explained by the receipt of a letter. Our best guess is that, forced to make a decision (his mother had waited long enough and would be leaving at the end of the month), he went to a placement agency and finally chose a position. Vitalie does not really know. During that afternoon she cleans Arthur's pants and jacket. On the next day, July 30, Rimbaud postpones his departure for want of his shirts, that have not come back from the laundress. Finally on Friday, July 31, at four in the morning, while his mother and Vitalie prepare to return to Charleville by the long route he has drawn up for them, Rimbaud sadly leaves them. Once again he disappears into the shadows.

His first biographers, C. Houin and J. Bourguignon, assert that he left London for "a sojourn in Scotland."[38] At present no proof has emerged to confirm their belief. There has been no lack of inventive minds, though, to fill in this embarrassing gap. As there is a complete absence of testimony they have gone back to the poetic texts themselves. The very peculiar name of Scarbro' in "Promontoire" caught the erudite V. P. Underwood's attention.[39]

From the moment Rimbaud made use of this name, belief that he actually saw the port in question has been an attractive proposition. In fact "Promontoire" describes the layout and architecture of this place in Yorkshire, located about 250 miles from London, quite faithfully. But Rimbaud's concern was never any accurate depiction of a familiar spot in his *Illuminations*. To the contrary, he strove to deconstruct coherent groupings and fashioned many never before seen assemblages. "Promontoire," which boldly blends the Peloponnesus, Brooklyn, Japan, Italy, and so forth, provides an excellent example of this style. However, if Rimbaud did not necessarily reach Scarborough July 31, there are reasons to believe he undertook a journey of equal length that day: the extremely early hour at which he left his mother and Vitalie leads one to believe that he had to catch a train at dawn for a relatively long journey.

His trail vanishes and it is not known if he continued to reside in England. In fact, three months later a request for employment is found in *The Times* of November 7 and November 9 that is formulated as follows:[40] "A PARISIAN[20] of high literary and linguistic attainments, excellent conversation, will be glad to *accompany a Gentleman* (artists preferred) or a family wishing to travel in the southern or eastern countries. Good references.—A.R. no. 165, King's Road—Reading." The signature "A.R.," despite earlier proofs, would remain subject to caution if the specific rough draft for this advertisement written in Rimbaud's handwriting and corrected by someone else, had not been found.[41] This is conclusive evidence he then lived west of London, in the city of Reading, the very location where Oscar Wilde would have to serve a stiff sentence in prison from 1895 to 1897, when condemned for his notorious homosexuality. Investigations have established that a large house was at the indicated address. It was called Montpellier House and belonged to a certain Camille Le Clair who taught French there. Given the large number of students it could hold, it is not forbidden to think that Rimbaud momentarily assisted him in that task. This would have been the actual destination of his journey when he left London on the morning of July 31. In November, for reasons that escape us (Le Clair had no more need for an assistant? Rimbaud wished to travel?), the "man with soles of the wind" would have tried his luck to leave for faraway lands with a small advertisement. He must not have received any positive response in that a month later he is still in England living precariously enough to cause alarm about returning to France.

December 1, Vitalie, much loved by that "heartless" Rimbaud, receives a letter from him that she mentions in her diary. She sends him a long reply the very same day. She has another letter for England at month's end that she has her mother post from Mézières. Quite a few reasons necessitate Rimbaud's return. As he was born in October 1854, he would have to appear before the draft board. During his absence the mayor of Charleville had drawn the number twenty-four, which was not in his favor. It had been recorded on the census rolls[42] that he was a professor of French and English and someone had marked him down as being of average height (five foot six), which does not seem to have been his true height. He had demanded and obtained an exemption since his brother Frédéric, a patriotic good-for-nothing, had enlisted for five years in 1873, which would not free Rimbaud from having to serve regular periods of military instruction. "To do my twenty years since others do twenty years." The question of military service had already troubled him when he was writing *Une saison en enfer*. Far from wishing to be a conqueror, he had taken the part of the victims of colonial imperialism in "Mauvais sang," those blacks who the whites, landing with their gospel, wish to subjugate, all while adorning their enterprise with the colors of a false humanism. Rimbaud, hostile to soldierly things, will evade his military obligations up to his final hour, although obsessively fearing them and at times—a strange paradox—mixing in with the shady world of the legionnaires. His numerous voyages far from France are of course explained by his profound desire always to go farther, but also more opportunistically by his constant desire to escape military service—an irritating duty that only forced him to see again, and more than he would wish, the image of a father he had never kept in his heart.

At nine in the morning on December 20, during an extremely cold spell ("snow and ice are everywhere," Vitalie notes in her diary), he arrives unexpectedly at 5 bis quai de la Madeleine, having left England for good.

1875: A YEAR IN TATTERS

THE MOVEMENT OF RIMBAUD'S LIFE OBEYS A PERSONAL IMPULSE—DEPARTURES and reintegrations, divergences and reconciliations. To understand it demands that we not be satisfied with simply recording such phenomena. Rimbaud doesn't limit himself to returning, what he achieves here is a gesture representative of his subjective economy. He places himself under the yoke of his future fate. Until this time he had not perfected the means of rupturing and leaving, to which he would devote himself. Perhaps this is how he compensated his impatience. But it is easy to picture his stubborn refusal of the circular voyage of the "drunken boat" and the anguished anchoring of "Mémoire." For this reason he appears condemned to a repetitious automatism, even in his constant attempts to escape.

The same evening of his arrival, through an operation of parallelism that seems to have been foreseen for all eternity, Frédéric returned on leave from the city where he was garrisoned. Thus the entire Rimbaud family is gathered together for Christmas, and it's a happy occasion for Vitalie, whose sickly body is beginning to suffer from the attacks of the illness that will soon carry her off. There is no doubt that Rimbaud resumed contact with Delahaye, Millot, and Pierquin during this holiday season. This isn't enough to win him over to the charms of Charleville and he has already confided to his mother that he wishes to leave again. His plans were more detailed than one would think. They would be better understood if we were familiar with his acquaintances from the previous months. Otherwise, it is hard to explain his reasons for choosing to learn German and momentarily settle in Stuttgart. The closer cities of Aix-la-Chapelle, Koblenz, and Mainz would be another story. In any case, he had already decided on the destination of his next journey before he left, as shown by an abbreviated notation in Vitalie's diary from Saturday, February 13, 1875, that says: "A. has left for S."

In Stuttgart, Rimbaud finds a place to live in a boardinghouse on Wagner Strasse,[43] perhaps he gave French lessons as he did in London. Still he needed to learn German which was the specific reason he had gone to study there, no doubt with the ultimate aim of acquiring a skill. Engineer? Interpreter? Whatever the case may be, he planned to acquire a thorough knowledge of several subjects ("I am trying to infiltrate myself into the customs here") that would allow him to travel across Europe and finally be free.

On January 16, the prison doors at Mons swung open for Verlaine. Given his exemplary conduct—hadn't he converted?—he was freed sooner than anticipated. However, the gloomiest kind of existence lay before him. On January 3, Mathilde had won her case for a legal separation. He now had to pay her a monthly stipend of 100 francs—a considerable sum of money for him as he had no work. Furious, he decided to go to Paris, after a short stop in Fampoux, to attempt to soften the ruling against him. As should have been expected, this was trouble for nothing. Following this setback, he felt an irresistible desire to see Rimbaud again. This was a predictable step, love and curiosity, combined with a formidable interest in the "genius" and the duty to convert him, for he too had had his illumination and would not hear of the "child of anger" ignoring it. In turn, he didn't wish to restore himself to a state of a "child of the sun," but to reveal to Rimbaud another more inner light: the radiance of grace. When informing Delahaye of his anticipated release, Verlaine asked him for news of the "other." He then learns that "Thing" is no longer in Charleville. Intrigued, he demands the traveler's address and announces his intention to resume corresponding with him. He even entrusts Delahaye with a letter to send on to Rimbaud.[44] It is filled with religious figures of speech, healthy resolutions, a great deal of moralizing, and the plan to love one another in Jesus Christ.[45] Delahaye immediately forwards it and a short while later receives from Rimbaud a page full of snickers and unkind comments concerning this person who was now proclaiming himself an apostle of virtuous conduct. Obviously Rimbaud had no illusions about this new Verlaine. Nevertheless, Verlaine, surprisingly confident in solely the powers of his evangelical word, would not delay leaving for to Stuttgart after finally obtaining Rimbaud's address. He arrives with "a rosary in his paws."[46] Rimbaud is forced to welcome him, albeit reluctantly. The two men have much to say to each other. Verlaine recites his sermons and attempts to convert the "Infernal Bridegroom." The person to whom he speaks, hardly a gullible sort, sums up this first and last encounter in terms of the most biting irony: "Three hours later he had denied his god again." What could the recent convert oppose to the satanic dialectic of the evil angel? A crawl through bars where beer was poured in generous portions dulled the edge of his overly new faith. According to some accounts,[47] a brawl soon erupted between them. At the end of the afternoon, the friends left to take a walk along the banks of the Neckar, the river of which Hölderlin sang. A discussion fueled by alcohol put them at odds. Rimbaud became incensed and delivered a sound blow to Verlaine, who collapsed senseless into a ditch while his aggressor returned to the city without a backward glance. Some peasants would have found the injured party in a sorry state early the following morning. Barely after his arrival, Verlaine would have quit the city. Delahaye, an often quite reliable witness, draws here a scene from a popular novel which spices up Rimbaud's life with an additional villainy. Whether or not this brawl took place, we have to think that the two friends must have had the time to make up, as Rimbaud will take pains to write, again to Delahaye: "For two days and a half he remained quite reasonable and at my urging returned to Paris, in order to later finish his studies *over there on the island.*" Rimbaud is certainly providing his version of events here. Calm was so well restored between them that at the end of the short visit he entrusted Verlaine with an important mission. Two months later Verlaine deems it wise to remind Delahaye of it in terms that remain ambiguous:[48]

> If I insist on getting details about Nouveau, this is why, Rimbaud having asked me to send some "poems in prose" (his) that I had to this same Nouveau, who was then in Brussels, to be printed (I am talking two months ago) I sent them (2 Francs 75 postage[*] !!!) pronto.

Certainly, the attentive reading of the phrase these 'poems in prose' (his) would retain an ambiguous attribution if Verlaine had not explicitly stated

---

[*] This 2.75 francs' postage is relatively close to the cost for sending a package weighing 95 grams.

that they were in his possession. As it happens we can imagine a certain number of the *Illuminations* figured in the papers that had been sent to him from London and that they had remained in the hands of Madame Verlaine during his imprisonment. Nonetheless, why would Rimbaud be seized by this late desire to see them published? And what is the point of giving Nouveau, then in Belgium, this responsibility? Belgium, it's true, was the land of forbidden publications. It was obviously out of the question for him to seek the services of the Typographical Alliance, where the bill for *Saison* still remained partially unpaid. Many years later, in 1888, Verlaine would present the facts of the situation in a different light[49] (though not removing all obscurity with his effort) when he says that "in Stuttgart the manuscript for *Illuminations* was delivered to someone who had had it in his care." This "someone" leads us to believe it could of been Verlaine himself, but what was the point of using such a twisted periphrase? This time, moreover, it would have been Rimbaud in person who had handed over these texts; in this case we could ask why Rimbaud—if he was planning on having them printed by Nouveau—did not mail them directly to him without passing through Verlaine, who did not even know Rimbaud's most recent companion's address. To further complicate this thicket of hypotheses, let's note that Isabelle will believe that Rimbaud would have given his precious poems to Charles de Sivry, then in Stuttgart to attend some Wagner concerts.[50] And it is certain that Sivry had this manuscript in his possession later, as Verlaine would demand it back in 1878[51] (but because—it seems—he had lent them to the musician in the first place).

March 1875. So it was over. Rimbaud had rid himself of the last weights holding him to the world of literature. Henceforth he would fly on other wings, leaving those of an Icarus burned by the fires of a dangerous sun to Verlaine, Nouveau, or Sivry. Whether given the responsibility or not of this noteworthy burden, Verlaine returns to Paris, then reaches England, where he finds employment in Stickney, at a *grammar school* [English] where he will start teaching in April. In the meantime Rimbaud changes address. He forewarned his family of this move. After spending one or two months on Wagner Strasse he relocates on March 15 to a nice room, *"eine freundliches Zimmer"* in the center of the city: 2 Marienstrasse.[*] The room is well furnished and

---

[*] The address is actually Mariensbadstrasse, according to D. A. de Graaf.

—

inexpensive. He could even take meals there but his sense of independence advises against having recourse to such facilities: "These little arrangements are always a trick and an enslavement, no matter how economical they appear," he writes to his mother. As for his activities, they have hardly varied: "I am frantically whipping the language so that I'll have finished in two months at most." What will he have finished? Completing his study so that he speaks German fluently? No doubt. And this gives us a good idea of his gift for languages. But the time frame he provides implies a more concerted program about which one of his letters (that of April 14) allows us to have some idea. In fact, he was giving himself another month to "get off to a good start," unless he was already placing "advertisements" seeking "a position." There are no specifics concerning this last point but it can be assumed that he continued to do in Stuttgart what he had in London and that he was still hoping to find a position as a tutor. Madame Rimbaud, rightly convinced he is seeking work, is sending him the necessary funds for the moment. He also asks Verlaine for financial support, as he is aware of the latter's fond feelings toward him. But Verlaine refuses[52] and Rimbaud finds nothing better to do than to boldly threaten him with blackmail—a terrifying prospect to "the poor Lélian" already exiled from the society of Parisian writers and now threatened in England, at the very place he worked, for Rimbaud would perhaps have been capable of speeding a revealing letter to the *grammar school*, at least if he knew its exact address.

Furthermore, the student worked at 2 Marienstrasse with a relentless drive worthy in every respect of his "philomathy" (his excessive love for knowing everything), interspersing his hours of study by allowing himself some breaks in the inns on the riverbank; he drank some excellent glasses of Riesling by himself to the *"imperbédueuse"* (an echo of the *pioupiou* Boquillon!*) health of former friends. However, around April 15, he decides not to renew his rent. The future rent money coming from Charleville could be put to a better use. The famous "two months" were up. Though he now possessed a sufficient grasp of German it had not gotten him employment

---

* *La Lanterne de Boquillon*, published in 1868, had as its main character a soldier from the countryside who makes false liaisons in his every remark. "Imperbédueuse" means "impetuous," and is a word of superlative value in the language of this character.

—

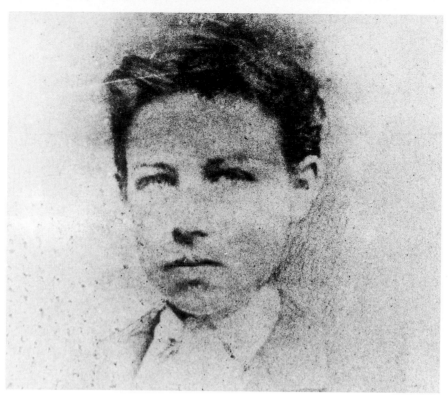

Portrait of Arthur Rimbaud, c. 1870. Photograph by Etienne Carjat.

Rimbaud with long hair. Drawing by
Ernest Delahaye, 1872.

Portrait of Paul Verlaine, 1871.

Arthur (right) and Frédéric Rimbaud's First Communion, 1866.

left: Rimbaud as drawn
by Paul Verlaine, 1872.

right: Rimbaud by Louis Forain,
"Stings on contact," 1871.

above: "Un Coin de table" by Henri
Fantin-Latour, 1872. Seated, from right to
left: Verlaine, Rimbaud, L. Valade, E.
d'Hervilly, C. Pelletan. Standing: E.
Bonnier, E. Blémont. J. Aicard.

right: Portrait of Rimbaud after the
"Brussels affair," 1873.
Painting by Jef Rosman.

"Ma Bohème (fantaisie)," 1870.

Verlaine and Rimbaud in London, Sept-Dec 1872.
Drawing by Félix Régamy.

Bottom: "Nouveau Juif errant," by Delahaye.

Portrait of Germain Nouveau, 1874-75.

right: A page from the *Illuminations*.

Self-portrait of Rimbaud, 1883.

A merchant in Harar.
Photograph by Rimbaud, 1883.

Rimbaud "in the depths of the sea," 1875. Drawing by
Delahaye taken from a painting by Nouveau.

Rimbaud playing an Abyssinian harp.
Drawing by his sister Isabelle Rimbaud, 1891.

Portrait of Constantin Sotiro.
Photograph by Rimbaud, 1883.

"La Tronche à machin," by Delahaye, 1875.

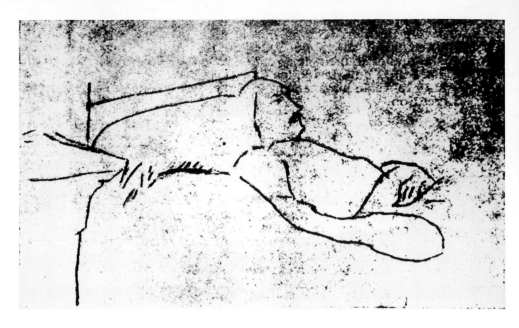

Rimbaud on his deathbed. Drawing by Isabelle, 1891.

Portrait of Rimbaud
by Isabelle, 1891.

and he now had another scheme in mind. Perhaps it was one he'd been nurturing for some time. The fact remains that he took a train south, as if summoned by a secret command. Delahaye furnishes—and ever so casually—some stupefying information whose validity presently remains unverifiable. A former Zutiste, Henri Mercier (whom Rimbaud had come across again that same year in Paris), being an industrialist, owned a soap works in Greece on the island of Ceos (Zea) and Rimbaud allegedly planned to go there.[53] Would his trip to Stuttgart in this case simply be one step on a longer journey? The distances here are considerable, the information chancy.

Rimbaud goes quite quickly. He is that "meteor" that Mallarmé will use as a metaphor to describe him. He takes off, disappears, and pops up again. And we have to be content with the leftovers from his forward march. Let some unpublished documents crop up—rough drafts, torn papers—and we may find ourselves obliged to add several thousand more miles to his travels! The biographer on this uncomfortable quest can console himself with the fact that he was preceded on this route by Rimbaud's immediate contemporaries: the faithful trio of Verlaine, Nouveau, and Delahaye, who were equally curious to acquaint themselves with the pilgrimages of their ungraspable friend, and equally vexed at learning only bits and pieces—even if he sometimes condescended to make them the gift of a letter sent, as if sarcastically, from one of the four corners of the globe.

For lack of certainty, they will begin to create a strange kind of comic strip through the exchange of letters, and their sketches[54]—which need to be described as well as seen (because of the symbolism in the caricatures)—and their poems—namely Verlaine's "Vieux Coppées" that rain curses on each of the traveler's escapades—all forming a strange patchwork, a Western, a game of snakes and ladders revised by Alechinsky. Through these Rimbaud tells his story. While escaping himself he has become one with the *effect* he has on others. Furthermore, under their pen he has become "Chose" [Thing], "the Philomath," "Homais,"* "L'Œstre" (meaning the Gadfly sentenced to sting poor humanity relentlessly). His life cannot be imagined without some sort of mythification. Of course behind this word the less complimentary one of

---

* "Homais" is the name of one of Flaubert's characters, a narrow-minded rationalist—translator's note.

mystification can be heard. Better though to maintain that this life derived constantly from myth, not at all from the later interpretations others gave to it but by the very existence of the man who lived it and even more because it was ceaselessly transmuted by the pens of its witnesses (not critics) who were obviously tendentious but all impassioned, industrious artisans of an awe-inspiring saga centered around their *hero*.

So it isn't enough only to record documents here. They have to be read either between or around the lines. The very tone they disseminate offers the assiduous commentary of a life. Impossible, from this moment forward, to reconstruct a "Rimbaud such as he was." It seems preferable to accept a construction desired by Rimbaud himself and completed by his acolytes. The Rimbaud of the years 1875 to 1879 (until his entry into his African adventure) is woven from multiple points: voices, personal writings, letters, little mocking poems, satiric drawings. His friends, those who were tied to him by eroticism and literature—Verlaine at the head of the list, but also Nouveau and Dela-haye—constructed and imagined it while he retreated into the silence of his actions.

Rimbaud was known to be traveling southward because Delahaye had received a recent letter from him informing him that he had just crossed the Alps. Immediately he alerted Verlaine of this and drew a sketch[55] showing "our hero" clad in an Italian hat with tears in his eyes and falling over backward while a plump monk is vehemently speaking to him. Its title: *Le capuchin folâtre* [The Frisky Monk]. Its legend: ("This is true or it's not true") On what facts would the alternate suggestion be based? Rimbaud's remarks recounting his escapade? In a letter to his sister Isabelle (its authenticity is disputed),[56] he describes the immediate aftermath of his trip: "I am in a beautiful valley that will take me to Lake Maggiore and old Italy. I slept in the heart of the Tessin, in a solitary barn where a bony cow was chewing its cud; it let me borrow some of its straw." Once he crosses the border he goes as far south as Milan. He no longer has even a sou in his pockets. Once again thirst and hunger are at his heels. But his youth gives him the power to evoke compassion in a charitable soul. On this occasion did the good deeds of Izambard's maiden aunts, the Gindres, cross his mind? The fact remains that it is in Milan he receives the hospitality of a woman who is not very young and with whom he will stay several days on the fourth floor of 39 Piazza del Duomo, enough time to regain his strength. He profits from this time to write to Delahaye, who is thereby privy to everything about this adventure. The conversations with his hostess are not confined to polite commonplaces, as Rimbaud discusses literature with her—a rare thing. He will even go so far as to bring up his sole published book and will, when sending Delahaye his visiting card,[57] ask back for the copy of *Une saison en enfer* that his friend had in his possession. This year 1875 is definitely troubling because there are at least two instances that reveal Rimbaud to be still concerned for his works. He detached himself from literature with less precipitation than commonly believed, even if his essential gesture was henceforth inscribed in walking and the ever more distant geographical beyond. Verlaine will later take this Milanese episode for true and will mention—eternal mystery!—the *"vedova molto civile."*[58] But on May 7 he brings another of Rimbaud's schemes to Delahaye's attention. "Through him [Nouveau], I have news of Thing, who is in Milan expecting money for Spain."[59] It so happens that Delahaye will subsequently report that Rimbaud was planning to travel down to Brindisi from where he could disembark for the famous Greek island where Mercier's hypothetical soap factory was located. Did he however have some intention of leaving for Spain? In this era the elliptical expression "expecting money for Spain" could evoke only something that had earlier tempted Verlaine himself, to wit, enlistment in the Carlist forces who were recruiting volunteers throughout Europe. And we will soon see Rimbaud actually resort to a similar solution. But between the intention reported by Verlaine in May 1875 and the probable deed in June, a month will elapse, during which time Rimbaud will leave Milan and the hospitable widow to traverse Liguria on foot. On the road to Siena he collapses, suffering from sunstroke. He is then transferred to the French Consulate in Livorno [Leghorn] which undertakes his return to France. On June 17, he sets sail on the steamship *Général Paoli.*[60] Several days later he arrives in Marseilles. But his health remains fragile. Countless hardships as well as the aftereffects of sunstroke have exhausted his robust body. Sick, he is admitted into a hospital, where he must stay in bed for several weeks, little suspecting it will be this same city (he will see it several times again) where he will end his days as a martyr to the gates to the East.

However, Delahaye had several new pieces of information from him that he immediately transmitted to Verlaine. "At present Rimbe is in Marseilles, having made, it seems, a tour of Liguria on foot. After assorted marvelocer-ous and miserable adventures, he appears to have gotten himself repatriated by a consul. Whatever the case may be, he declares his intention of going and enlisting with the Carlists! Just a question of learning *español* and continuing, while he waits, to attempt to swindle money out of his few remaining friends."[61] Verlaine will soon record this fact in one of his most vengeful "Vieux Coppées":[62]

> *Carlisse? Ah! non, c'est rien qui vaille*
> *À cause de l'emmerdement de la mitraille!*

> Carlisse? Ah! no, it's not at all
> worth the damned nuisance of being shot at!

This enlistment could be considered the final straw, as Rimbaud hated nothing as much as military service. However, it will be observed that over the following years he sometimes chose this expedient for lack of anything better. Moreover, it is not certain that he was recruited. It is believed, though, that he deserted, once he was paid the bonus for enlisting, and headed in the direction of Paris. Once in Paris, did he have the sense of completing a new cycle? His life, bizarre as it was, was made up of a chain of regularly occurring odysseys that were ultimately circular in nature. The large city now offered him a temporary stopping point before the distressing return to Charleville, the inescapable umbilicus. The correspondence he maintained with his mother, whether he wanted to or not, had no doubt informed him of Vitalie's illness that now required consultation with a specialist. On July 13, in a weak-ened state, she records the preparations for their departure to the capital in her diary. Later, Isabelle, who accompanied them, would say that during this visit they saw Rimbaud, who then held a position as a tutor in Maisons-Alfort.[63] Even though the information she provides is often subject to cau-tion, it is almost certain that Rimbaud met his family during this time and this tutor's job is well matched (perhaps too well matched!) with the kind of employment he was seeking. This wouldn't have provided any hindrance to the renewal of ties with his old bohemian friends. In fact a letter from Nou-veau to Verlaine mentions that he was living in the company of Mercier and

Cabaner and also spending time with Forain.[64] A familiar story. It was as if years hadn't gone by and the Brussels drama had no more consistency than a bad dream. Rimbaud rediscovered his intimates who were incapable of holding any grudge against him and for whom he continued to radiate with his suspect renown.

He was not alone, as an inveterate dromomaniac, to follow an unpredictable course. The long vacation period of 1875 would give rise to many journeys. Nouveau had just left England, where he had finally met Verlaine on May 20 at Charing Cross Station, both recognizing each other on account of their friendly faces.[65] A wandering Jew in his own right, he had returned to France, passing through Paris on his way back to his southern Pourrières, where several years later, he would live the life of a beggar, a poetic and naive disciple of the flea-ridden saint, Benoît Labre.[66] As for Verlaine, he was now spending peaceful days (in which prayer barely pulled him out of the taverns) at his mother's house, 2 impasse d'Ellbronne, in Arras. He invited Delahaye, who was happy to have finally passed his baccalauréat. The friends took strolls through the countryside, bringing up "the Gadfly," whose fate they tried to guess on more than one occasion. In their opinion, Rimbaud was beyond recovery. The alcohol and smoke dens would land him in a lunatic asylum. But several admirable verses echoed in their minds, and the magic plates of *Illuminations* continued to give off their light. In whose hands were these famous prose poems? Did Nouveau take them with him to Pourrières? That is a likely possibility. The thought of such superb pages lost forever is maddening!

However, Delahaye soon returns to Charleville and resumes his correspondence with Verlaine, who sends him a letter to forward to Rimbaud as well as a "Vieux Coppée," with the title in the form of a barbarism: *Ultissima Verba.*[67] In this dozen-line strophe of a Zutiste nature, Rimbaud is supposedly speaking his normal argot, which he punctuates with an insistent "shit." More aggressive than the melancholy Romantic dreamers, he is the preeminent example of one who gets damned bored where others sorrowfully empty their spleen and delude themselves with elegies. It should be listened to at close range. Or recited with the obligatory Parisian-Ardennais accent. On this August 22, 1875, Verlaine, imitator of a dear voice that has not been completely silenced, intones:

Épris d'absinthe pure et de philomatie
Je m'emmerde et pourtant au besoin j'apprécie
Les théâtres qu'on peut avoir à la Gatti.
Quatre-vingt-treize a des beautés et c'est senti
Comme une merde, quoi qu'en disent Cros et Tronche
À l'Academie où les Murgers boivent du ponche.

Smitten with absinthe and philomathy
I bore myself and yet as the need arises, I appreciate
the theaters that can be found at the Gatti.
Ninety-three has some beauties and it feels
Like shit, whatever Cros and Tronche may say
At the Academy where the Murgers drink *ponche.*

By all evidence Verlaine knew Rimbaud was in Paris, since he evoked the former Zutistes, Cros and Tronche (Cabaner) and the Academy of Absinthe on rue Saint-Jacques, the venue of their drinking binges. Despite such mocking sentiments he was no less curious for news of the always unpredictable "Gadfly." Delahaye, who knew the "dirty beast's" address, maintained the thread of a somewhat intermittent correspondence between them. "Have you received the *epistomphe* of the man with the Spanish grammar?"[68] he inquires of the poet of *Romances sans paroles.* Now the Gadfly seemed to want to plant his stinger in Verlaine's poor past. One day he showed up at Verlaine's mother's house on rue Lecluse where he asked to see her but was told she had left for Belgium.[69] Thus he had not abandoned his malicious intentions— which were of even greater concern to the "poor Lélian," as he had just returned that September to the grammar school in Stickney where he taught.

At the very beginning of October, Nouveau reappears on the Rimbaldian horizon. After a stay in Pourrières, he is in Charleville (this takes the cake!), at the former Institution Rossat, which is now the Institution Barbadaux—a name that seems to have been invented for a Topaze. Rimbaud, as will be recalled, had earned his first scholarly successes there. We should undoubtedly discern no act of chance in the fact that "the smallest of the bipeds"[70] had chosen to establish himself in the home town of his London companion. Rimbaud, informed by Delahaye, is made uneasy by this. While he is premeditating the revelation of certain things to Madame Verlaine, he may also be worried that Nouveau is contemplating similar revelations to his own mother. The monitor of Barbadaux (who is going by the name Monsieur Germain), moreover, conducts himself very freely with the students. He set up several smoking parties, watered by various alcoholic beverages with the older students in their dormitories, or "digs." A chamber pot had even served as a goblet in these schoolboy orgies.[71] It doesn't take long for him to be dismissed from his post. Shortly before, Delahaye had supplied Verlaine with the additional information:[72] "But note this; Nouveau's conduct inspires anxiety and distrust in him, he knows that he went to his home and is going to write him to demand an explanation. You'd do well to warn him." Verlaine immediately warns Nouveau, who, alarmed, answers,[73] "Absolutely no knowledge of what could have aroused R's anger? No correspondent in Paris." How could he speed a letter to this Parisian Rimbaud who suspected him of villainous steps against him? In fact, Delahaye, the confidant of many, was the only one at the time to know just what was going on, but his prudent recollections shed no light on these shadowy zones subject to the law of emotional secrecy. His scruples compel him to alert Verlaine of Rimbaud's intentions in his regard:[74] "As for you, you're just a skinflint. He went to your mother's in Paris. He (the monster) knows that you have gone to someplace called Boston, but supposes you have returned to London for the moment, where you continue to get abominably plastered, he's sure of it. But of course I don't know anything about anything. I've completely lost sight of you." For his part, Delahaye, who thought highly of them both, preferred to take refuge in the position of an observer and impartial go-between.

Rimbaud, left to his own devices and going to the dogs, and not truly knowing just what to do, was on the verge of depraving himself once and for all. He sought expedients, turned around and around in a circle of old friends with whom he wished to break off relations but whom he found on his path again and again, because he had never made "the big break." Hence the emergence of an enraged conduct that was again heated up by alcohol. Delahaye describes it to Verlaine by its most repellent aspect:[75] "This *end* we were arguing about over there [when they were in Arras during the summer] will be in some insane asylum—it seems to me he is headed for it now. The reason is simple enough: alcohol. The wretch brags with a volubility, which is quite

surprising coming from him, of having kicked everyone up the ass in Paris."
Such was the "Gadfly's" attitude during this stay. The last of those who still
remained attached to him had to incur his vilest sarcasms. Without admitting
that he had been defeated by events, he increased his provocative actions—as
he did during the days of the Vilains Bonshommes—with a heavy instinct of
loss and the energy from a strange despair as profound as his dreams of
genius. Meanwhile Verlaine continued to write him long letters that were
truly confessional diaries. He lectured him in extremely crude terms about
what he should do. Rimbaud called these "Loyola's vulgarisms."[76] Eventually,
worn out from his fruitless fits of rage and moved by a vague sense of anger,
he resigns himself to returning to Charleville. He establishes his winter quarters on an embankment near the Meuse; bogged down, he abandons himself to a sterile idleness, that far from delighting him, stimulates his hate and
lycanthropy. The others spend their time in obligatory occupations as unusual
professors and bizarre teachers, Verlaine in Stickney, Nouveau, for a flash, in
Charleville, and Delahaye in Soissons, where he held the boisterous position
of class monitor while preparing for the second stage of his baccalauréat.[77]

On a Thursday or a Sunday during that October, Delahaye, back in
Charleville, is strolling the familiar streets of the ducal town. As he passes
before the Hudréauxs' grocery store he feels a hand on his shoulder. He turns
around to see Rimbaud, dressed like a dandy with cuffs, tie, cane, and bowler,
and grown enormously since they last saw each other.[78] They quickly fall
back into the language of their old friendship, and Rimbaud, prolix for once,
recounts his story. Already a legendary aura is emanating from that ungraspable friend and surprising undesirable. However Delahaye has to return to
his collège in Soissons, to his "kids" and "Wolf Fart (meaning the principal).
On October 14 Rimbaud, who doesn't forget him, sends him a letter of an
inspired comic nature,[79] in which he inserts—as a sequel to the pains caused
by the thought of completing his military service—a small enigmatic poem
composed off the cuff. This "Rêve" may well constitute the ultimate de-
graded replica of the famous "Coeur supplicié" from the first letter of the
seer. It is no longer a simple recollection of the barracks room, as it first
appeared, but the disillusioned resumption of a scene in which genius, like
the "heart" previously, finds itself desacralized and commingled with the vulgar crowd. André Breton would see this as a veritable "testament" and place it

in his *Anthologie de l'humour noir.*[80] The genius of *Illuminations* here becomes a secular figure stating the names of cheeses. He offers no gift other than stench.

RÊVE

On a faim dans la chambrée—
C'est vrai . . .
Émanations, explosions. Un génie:
'"Je suis le gruère!—
Lefêvre: "Keller!"
Le Génie: :Je suis le Brie!—
Les soldats coupent sur leur pain:
"C'est la vie!
Le Génie.—Je suis le Roquefort!
—"Ça s'ra not' mort! . . .
—Je suis le gruère
Et le Brie! . . . etc.
—Valse—
On nous a joints, Lefêvre et moi . . .
etc.

(Dream)
One is hungry in the barracks room—
It's true . . .
Emanantions, explosions. A genius:
"I am the gruyere!—
Lefêvre: "Keller!"
The Genius: "I am the Brie!—
The soldiers hack at their bread:
That's life!
The Genius.— "I am the Roquefort!
—It'll be th'death of us
—I'm the gruyere
And the brie! . . . etc.
—Waltz—
They've paired us up, Lefêvre and I . . . etc. . . . !

———

While Rimbaud wrote so freely to his comrade Delahaye, he had, on the other hand, to follow quite a detoured route to answer Verlaine. Verlaine didn't dare give him his actual address in Stickney, and had sent him two alternatives, to either general delivery in London or 12 rue de Lyon at the home of his friend Istace.[81] Rimbaud, it is true, had renounced neither his demands for money nor his threats of blackmail. Hence Verlaine's prudence concerning his actual location. The threatened "Loyola" reels off his misfortunes in a letter to Delahaye and illustrates them with a new drawing.[82] Wearing a suit and a vindictive look while dropping a book entitled *Philomathy* from his left hand and making a reproving gesture with his right, Rimbaud has a balloon emerging from his pipe that says: "If ever I get him in my pincers." A vigilant eye, surely that of conscience in the style of Hugo's *La Legende des siècles* is gleaming on his back. On the left side of the picture Verlaine is on the ground with a terrified look on his face, seated between two saddles, one of which is marked "Rue de Lyon," the other "*posse* [sic] *restante*" (the two addresses!). Another balloon is emerging from his pipe that says: "Dear friend, etc." Between the two men is the crude depiction of a piano on whose keyboard is planted a label as if on a piece of meat in a butcher's display case which reads: "Fee: one hundred sous." The title of the drawing is "The Dream and Life" (an unexpected reference to Nerval's *Aurélia*). Its legend is "His Things." The letter accompanying this caricature couldn't have been any clearer. It was a reaction against the little schemes hatched by Rimbaud, the bitter "sweet things" that he had sent to rue de Lyon, for example, and it contained a threat against this sneaking "Homais": "Concerning this have you told him of my republicatory intentions in the event his little schemes take shape?"[83] But the former lover, simultaneously furious and piqued, continued to be curious about the child of anger; his derision here masks his disappointment: "With whom is HE staying? I imagine some angelic relative awakened every night by him returning on all fours, vomiting (I've been there!) and other anti-toilet-training exploits! And the mother, the *daromphe*, what does she say about that? Is it still my fault? Is she still at 5 *bis* quai de la Madelomphe?" We can see that if Rimbaud could imagine Verlaine in London "getting abominably plastered," for his part Verlaine thought that his drinking buddy had not changed his habits and was still disturbing the peace of those around him. Rimbaud's counterparts to Verlaine's letters are, alas, missing and it is only permitted to infer their contents by the rare quotes from them provided by their addressee. Their dialogue continued uselessly, the one talking religion, the other laughing at a sudden conversion in which he saw only the "modification of the same sensitive individual" and guessed only too well that beneath the new preacher was a man who remained enslaved to his carnal desires.

At the age of sixteen Rimbaud wished to cultivate his monstrous nature. Now other concerns demanded his attention. At 31 rue Saint-Barthélemy, where his mother had just moved, he gave German lessons to the building owner's son, Charles Lefèvre, to make some pocket money.[84] And a new obsession took hold of him: playing the piano. He didn't hesitate to ask for some money with which to rent an instrument from Verlaine, who wouldn't hear of it! But he didn't delay to satisfy his desire as he arranged to have a rental piano brought up to their apartment, without his mother's knowledge.[85] Madame Rimbaud started to protest but when a neighbor protested louder than she, the *daromphe* allegedly reacted favorably in order to assert her rights and took the instrument under her roof to the satisfaction of Arthur and the affliction of the other tenants. At the announcement of this event Verlaine couldn't resist the temptation to compose a satiric drawing:[86] Rimbaud, frenzied and disheveled like a Liszt, is pounding on the keyboard; his mother is fleeing the scene; the ground-floor occupant, coiffed in a dignified Greek skullcap, is plugging his ears shut, while the enraged pianist, sweat pouring down his face, is exclaiming: "Camels, semiquavers, let's go then." The legend (obligatory): "Music hath charms to soothe the savage beast." This Rimbaud the musician who appears one moment as if seen through a lattice fence in the biographical landscape, awakens more than one memory in every reader. If we think back, of course, to the oompahs of "À la musique," we are even more likely to recall the "sigh of the harmonica" that accompanies "Les Chercheuses de poux." And it brings back Cabaner with whom he shared a room at the Hôtel des Étrangers. During hours of boredom he had been able to do his scales on the piano of the scrawny musician and with his large, reddened hands, inventory harmonic treasures. Several *Illuminations* make mention of "cunning music" (that falls short of our desire). Yet another path for gaining access to the impossible. Yet another attempt to violate the narrowness of words.

Willingly or unwillingly, his mother consented to his taking lessons.[87] But nothing could keep him completely amused. Anguish, "the Vampire that makes us behave" watched his path; it mounted in the alembic quick of his body, causing him dreadful headaches that laid him out for hours. In a neighboring room the immobilized Vitalie continued to keep her journal. The visit to the specialist in Paris had served only to establish the harshest diagnosis: the invalid suffered from a tubercular synovitus, an affliction of the bones that Rimbaud was later believed to be suffering from when hospitalized in Aden in 1891. Death slowly made its presence felt. On December 18, Vitalie passed away at the age of seventeen. Rimbaud attends the funeral with his head shaved.[88] He had his abundant locks cut not as a sign of mourning, but because he thought he might thereby prevent the terrible neuralgias that sometimes laid him out. In a letter from this time, Delahaye depicts him in profile,[89] his head a sugar loaf like a young pharaoh, the upper lip shaded by a thin mustache and a cigarette in his mouth. Its legend: "Thingummy's noggin!"

On Sunday December 12 Verlaine had sent a letter to Charleville from London,[90] never dreaming that it would arrive during Vitalie's death throes. This missive was an attempt to make his point. The two men hadn't corresponded for more than a month. Very much the mentor, Verlaine expands himself in edifying tirades, perfectly constructed for exasperating his ironic reader. "Loyola" hadn't changed since Stuttgart. No more than the "Gadfly" had "mellowed" in his eyes. The recent convert now expresses, in all seriousness, the arguments of a preacher: "The Church created modern civilization, science, and literature; it made France, in particular, what she is and France is dying from having broken with it. This is quite clear! And the Church also forms men, it creates them." But certain passages betray a natural sympathy for the thought of Rimbaud and manifest the solicitude of a protective love for want of being clairvoyant: "I call into evidence your disgust for everything and everyone, your perpetual anger against everything—which is basically truly justified, though quite unconscious of the reasons why." Yes, Verlaine has taken the measure of Rimbaud's temperament, his sense of revolt, when he writes the two words that explain the course of a destiny: *anger* and *disgust*, by virtue of which had come the moment, for the person who loved him, to leave everything or to attempt a bizarre existence far from all poetry. The rest of the epistle touches on money matters and is filled with ceaseless, indelicate reminders of the past, the "enormous chunks taken out of my capital by *our* [Verlaine's emphasis] absurd and shameful life three years ago." As for the troubling partner's threats of blackmail, they will be punished if need arises. The end seems to seek to erase so many long paragraphs full of discontent: "Come now! Make a nice gesture and show a bit of kindness, hell, a bit of consideration and affection for someone who will always remain—and you know it—very cordially yours, P. V."

To expect a "nice gesture" from Rimbaud was obviously to believe in chimeras in that the "nice gesture" in question would have consisted of his conversion (as well as the abandonment of any inopportune demands for money). It doesn't seem that the epistolary exchange was pursued after this letter. As of October 14, Rimbaud reminded Delahaye that he had "no more energy to spare in that direction!" As for Verlaine, he had attempted the impossible. Their reunion in Stuttgart had been illusory and troubled. Since then Rimbaud had followed strange paths with no more concern for him, except as someone to swindle. Both now had the feeling of a failed relationship. Verlaine's religion and Rimbaud's *libido sciendi* were evolving in opposite directions. But Verlaine, despite the sarcasms he heaped on the person who had abandoned him, will long devote a veritable worship to this unsurpassable passerby—a devotion motivated by a fabulous encounter in which he had the sudden breathtaking revelation of the intact and integral strength of poetry and action (not simply writing) in which it was just as easy to radiate as dissolve.

THE JAVANESE

DATING FROM THIS RIFT, IN WHICH HE RADICALLY RID HIMSELF OF VER-laine, who for him embodied poetry irrevocablye, Rimbaud penetrated deeper into the solutionless zone of a non-literary space. Assuming that he once believed in the recourse represented by a literature equipped with the most magical powers through the power of his will, he now advances into the real world that has been stripped of the consolations of art and its sorceries. However, the episode with Germain Nouveau demonstrates how much remorse he felt abandoning all poetic creation and, as we've seen, the year 1875 still bears the traces of an aborted dream: the probable transmission of certain prose poems in Stuttgart, and his desire in May when he was in Milan to get back a copy of *Saison*. After this time and the derisory poem "Rêve" written in mockery, Rimbaud no longer believes in literature. He forsakes this "practice" for other, more effective ones that permit him to be "absolutely modern." The story of his mind and body having become others corresponds to the image of modernity he has created for himself. In this sense he is fabricating a lifestyle. His modernity (although conquered in *Illuminations*) in the end refuses to entrust itself to the text. It repulses what it deems illusion. Far from considering—as did Baudelaire—that the union between the eternal and the ephemeral would provide an explanation, he entrusted himself wholeheartedly to the ephemeral and to the moment, precisely by abandoning eternity, that's to say a transcendent value sought by art, philosophy, meditation. Nevertheless his gesture will never include a single moment's enjoyment or evoke even the tiniest bit of a quotidian happiness. He will perpetuate himself in a forward thrust, "thought hooking on to thought and pulling," a march that takes on the appearance of a quest, through setbacks and repetitions. What repeats for Rimbaud is his attempt to disengage. And by the same token, the glaciation and the running aground, the modalities of a shipwreck.

Existence in Charleville was open to every dream in that it included every manner of disappointment. For several months Rimbaud was in a state of waiting. No benevolent Providence was watching over him now, nor did he benefit from any stroke of good fortune. His only remaining recourse was study, which he did relentlessly, piano lessons, drinking binges, countryside excursions. What parts of the Rimbaldian legend can be believed? By the same token, how is one to escape it? He created something there unknowingly, through the insistence of his temperament that was so disturbing to others and so mystifying to him.

This explains how so many scattered (and always later) witnesses think to remember his ferocious study habits. One person met him in the woods near Charleville with a Russian grammar book in his hand;[91] another person (Louis Pierquin), the same who will manufacture a Rimbaud as a victim of a great unrequited love, erects an almost Beckett-like scenario for us:[92] Arthur would spend days enclosed within an "old closet of olden time" (one admires the pleonasm: it was thus a *very old* closet!) and would study there for twenty-four hours in a row without eating or drinking. Was this the best means of preparing for the Polytechnic or the more modest degree in science (in his letter of October 15, 1875, he had asked Delahaye to tell him what books he should get with an eye to passing this exam). Delahaye fortunately sets our minds at ease when he shows us the "Philomath" is still a hearty drinker tempted to wander.[93]

Delahaye will retain a memory from these hikes that I don't hesitate to number among the most valuable recollections concerning the poet. With an extraordinary accent of truth and a gift of presence, he successfully describes Rimbaud's "supple" and "strong appearance," "that of a resolute and patient walker who can go on forever." "His large legs would take calm and formidable strides, his long arms dangling in rhythm with his regular movements, torso and head erect while his eyes stared off in the distance, his entire face bore an expression of resigned defiance, an air of being ready for anything without fear or anger."[93bis] We couldn't get any closer to a body going forward and no film could render with such fidelity what was—very well then, appearance!—but also, in the final analysis, a style of thinking, a fashion of coping, even if resignation modified to some extent this defiance we love.

Despite a long rainy period, the friends take their habitual walks on the outskirts of Charleville, often in the "violet forests" and as far as the frontier.

These take place on Thursday and Sunday especially, when Delahaye, the monitor at Soissons, returns to the ducal town. They walk from village to village following an itinerary planned in advance. Rimbaud left it to his walking companion to arrange a stopover in the best café of the neighborhood. There they settle in and drink large tankards of beer. The aim of their excursions is not at all cultural. Simply a stop watered with beer or small glasses of "pequet."* Rimbaud hardly speaks. Sometimes, though, when exhilarated by alcohol, the two strollers emerge from the tavern and joyfully launch into a tune from Lecocq's *Les Cent Vierges*, a "catch-tune" for the party animals of that era. This pair are sometimes joined by former classmates from the *collège*, the "sweet, joyful, and ardent" Ernest Millot, who Rimbaud had known well since 1871, and Louis Pierquin, an intellect, but also a bizarre witness whose memories most often do not correspond at all to Delahaye's.

When the friends are not rambling through the Ardennes countryside they arrange to meet in the principal cafés of Charleville: the Café de la Promenade or the Café de l'Univers facing the station. As in the past, Rimbaud takes delight in recounting atrocious and scandalous stories. Sometimes he consents to recalling literary memories, as well, as if he hadn't renounced anything. But can we rely on Delahaye? Quite often there seems to be a strange superimposition of his memories. Furthermore, Rimbaud's life, so rich in reiterated experiences, could not help but give rise to such confusion.

In the beginning of spring, April 1876, the erratic individual appears to want to reattempt what he'd tried the previous year. He leaves again for Germany, provided with some money that once again was generously granted him by his mother. No doubt he's kept her abreast of his scheme, which is quite likely similar to the one he had in mind in 1875. This time he doesn't set his sights on Stuttgart or on an apprenticeship in the German language; he is looking much farther afield.[94] He plans to go to Austria, from where he will strike out to Varna in Bulgaria. There he will embark to that famous Greek island where a position (more or less implied by Mercier) would be waiting for him in a soap works. Rimbaud and Greece! This is a subject that deserves further study. For preamble we would note, for example, the manner in which his first poems utilized Greek mythology. Greek poetry "rhythms

---

* Grain alcohol in the Ardennais dialect.

action" in the letter of the "seer." Now here is Rimbaud the realist, denying his fleeting adherence to the Parnassian aesthetic, who wishes to go to Greece, not with the touristic intention of admiring antiquities, but with the hope of finding a modern kind of job: making soap, for example! This spring 1876 expedition is soon cut short. On his arrival in Vienna he is robbed of his money by a coachman. He was allegedly drowsing in a horse-drawn carriage from having drunk more than was reasonable; the coachman, seeing what state he was in, quickly relieved him of his wallet. On receiving this piece of news, Verlaine composes an unkind "Vieux Coppée" and scribbles an illustration as the next installment for the ongoing comic strip.[95] Rimbaud, stark naked, has only his pipe in his hand from which puffs a voluminous balloon: inside are the ten verses of the "Vieux Coppée." The coach driver is seen fleeing in the distance. Behind the scene of the crime there is a street sign: VINGINCE STRASSE, Vengeance Street (an Ardennais accent is a must).* In Vienna, Rimbaud, who had made a scene that nobody understood (the thief having slipped off in the meantime), is quickly taken to the police station, and then brought to the French consulate where, when they determine he is without means, it is decided that he will be escorted back to the border. It is the repetition of a familiar scenario. From one country to the next until he reaches his inevitable Ardennes again. A drawing sketched by Delahaye[97] highlights this episode perfectly. Rimbaud is advancing with great strides. He is dressed elegantly, but his pants cuffs are threadbare. His ever-present pipe is in his mouth and he is holding a gnarled staff in his hand, a real *bousingot's* cudgel, and a roll of paper marked "passe-porc" is sticking out of his pocket. His head bears the famous top hat bought for ten shillings in London that has over time become a crumpled, broken piece of headgear that is creased like an accordion. An entire landscape in the background reproduces the different stages of his journey. On the right is the Black Forest covered with pines. In the center is the steeple of Strasbourg, and on the left, Charleville. Various figures are greeting him—uniformed customs agents, peasants, even a tiny being that is every bit a sylph: "That's a Wallachian, if you like," Delahaye mentions for

---

* "Therefore Vienna is emphasized and placed in the list of vengeful places of which Artichas (and Brussels) take first place in chronological order—TO THE FAITHFUL COACHMAN!" Verlaine writes in his jargon to Delahaye on March 24, 1876.[96]

Verlaine's benefit. Rimbaud is walking from right to left, thus in the direction of his return trip. Legend: "The New Wandering Jew." The label was all the more appropriate as it was how Rimbaud and Verlaine had seen themselves during their earlier Belgian ramblings.

This hardly glorious adventure must have been a great disappointment to him. It had wasted his time and given Verlaine fine sport making jokes at the expense of the enraged traveler who is always pushed far back from the world he so strongly wishes to attain. Rimbaud, though, is used to backsliding. He knows how to add some prodigious variations to it when he needs to. It was no longer a question for him, after five wasted months in Charleville and this recent disappointment, to rot at anchor in the inept ducal town. Whatever the cost, he seeks to escape this slow death, to experience a life for want of "the real life." Here the links are lacking for reconstructing the chain of his actions. Most likely, following some days spent moping in the family apartment, he made an impromptu disappearance, like Romulus in the middle of the Senate. Nevertheless, it is perhaps appropriate to relate here one of his preparatory conversations, in which he would have shown a glimpse of his intention to leave for the East. To do this, he had momentarily envisioned joining the Brothers of the Christian Schools,[98] who were then teaching in China, Japan, and so forth. Rimbaud, provided that he achieved his goals, was little distressed by contradicting his personal convictions. We imagine that on arrival in these faraway lands he would have left his employers high and dry and led a life to his liking as the adventurer he dreamed of being, not far from his "cherished hut," a gourd of kava within reach, whether as a gold digger or a comet finder. Delahaye informed Verlaine of this whim in a few words and Verlaine, who hardly credited the demon's conversion, questioned "Rimbaud's entry into religion," in return. "Keep me informed of these beautiful mysteries,"[99] he asked his correspondent.

As Rimbaud had left Charleville, any and all conjectures were permitted to explain his departure. Verlaine and Delahaye were most inclined to imagine him in an African country, which allows us to assume the existence of some sort of prior information provided by the errant one. The saga grows, proportionately, with the addition of several fabulous drawings.[100] Delahaye deploys here all the treasures of humor. First there is "A missionary from Charleville": Rimbaud dressed only in a loincloth, his body tattooed with pipes and glasses. He is wearing a heavy Hottentot dictionary on his belt and a hat pierced by an arrow. With his right hand he is brandishing a good-sized bottle while with his left he is dragging quite a carnival of scantily clad women who have—as female savages should—bones through their noses. They are dancing a wild dance that somewhat resembles the French cancan. Several rudimentary palm trees make up the landscape. Another drawing shows him stretched out in a chair, crowned and smoking a pipe. Two savages are venerating him, prostrated on their bellies before his serene highness. Another caricature portrays him from the front wearing a tie, though he is otherwise naked and covered with tattoos (a bottle, a glass and pipes: his inveterate habits). Words: "These Kaffirs, yet more famous pelvises!" a sad conclusion to the *Livre nègre*, in short, since even the savages bore him.* For his part, Germain Nouveau skillfully draws[101] a hirsute Rimbaud (as in the *Coin de table*), correctly dressed and running through the open desert after his wind-blown hat. In the distance a small figure that could be Nouveau himself is contemplating the scene. The legend reads: "Negro Landscape." Nothing was unthinkable on the part of the one they from now on would call the "flaky traveler."[102] Soon, with a certain prescience for the truth (at least if they hadn't received some vague piece of news), Nouveau and Delahaye draw a half-symbolic composition depicting Rimbaud beneath the waves: a steamer is sailing on the ocean, while the moon over the marine horizon stretches out the contours of his submerged hat. Nouveau is watching this spectacle from the distance with the aid of a spyglass.[103]

However, the reality was even more stupefying. In the spring of 1877, Rimbaud wished to go far, very far, and flee Europe. As the Greek scheme was definitely unworkable he thought of other means to satisfy his vagabond fancy. Two years previously he resorted to the Carlist connection. This time he heard talk of recruitment for the Dutch colonial army, which had recently put down a revolt in the former sultanate of Achin, on the isle of Sumatra.[104] Another end of the earth! Transported there at the army's expense, he could desert once he got there and live in this land "where freedom shines." Who had told him about it? "Touts" as they were called then, mentioned in several

---

*The French word *bassin*, which means "pelvis" is also slang for "to bore" when used as a verb—translator's note.

documents as having an active presence in France, in Lille as well as Paris. Rimbaud accepts their offer with no hesitation. His name is registered at the Dutch consulate in Brussels. He receives a train ticket for Rotterdam, where he introduces himself to the garrison commandant. From there he goes by train via Gouda and Utrecht to Harderwijk, where the colonial recruiting center is located. He arrives on May 18 toward the end of the afternoon. The troops destined for the Indies are billeted in this port town of five thousand souls. After being judged fit for service and their civil status has been verified, the soldiers-to-be wait in secondment for the day of departure. They are taught to handle arms and to obey military commands (spoken in Dutch); they perform the indispensable drills and other duties. But from 5:00 to 9:30 in the evening they can go into town, where they frequent the taverns or several brothels (the small town's population includes around forty prostitutes). From May 18 to June 10,[105] Rimbaud remains barracked in an old monastery, surrounded by "lost souls," delinquents, vagabonds, mercenaries, the living whose only reality stems from the "Present" they shout out each morning during roll call. The true "moderns" perhaps. Individuals of a terrifying banality, pure adventurers, with whom he merges. A solitary soul, he disappears in their midst. He is back in the barracks rooms, just as he was at the time of the Paris Commune or during his passage with the Carlists in Marseilles, and in his last poem, "Rêve." Beyond recall, save for his name, "Arthur Rimbaud," which means nothing to anybody. He breaks his ties with poetry and philomathy. Unless his poetry now shares his clandestine nature. An unknown leaving for the unknown. The contract he signed offers a perilous future: "Six years to serve the Dutch army"; six years as a legionnaire during which time death is all too foreseeable. In return, he has received three hundred florins, a small fortune in that era. But how can he spend this money? Rimbaud forces fate, provokes it. This time he has gone too far to retreat, he has become the other, an heresiarch replica of the father "in the service of the most monstrous industrial and colonial exploitations." At times the idea of deserting crosses his mind. People around him have talked about it. However, he holds his own in Hardewijk for twenty-five days. And he knows full well that after they set sail it will be too late for regrets.

June 10, 1876, the day of departure, arrives. The evening before, the men had spent part of their pay in the red-light district. To the beat of drums the soldiers march to the station in orderly ranks. They return by train to Utrecht, then Den Helder. Still to the beat of the drum, they reach Nieuwe Diep and climb aboard the ship, the *Prins van Oranje*, which soon casts off. There is no one on the wharf to miss these departing loners. The next day, they take on several months' worth of provisions at Southampton, their first port of call. Tobacco, pipes, parlor games, and black soap are distributed to the men. On that same day the first desertion takes place. It is a Frenchman, a certain Marais, aged twenty-eight, who throws himself overboard and is fished out of the water. The long voyage begins. It is a mixture of discipline and promiscuity. The schedules are rigorous, but the men are left to a boring idleness. Time passes en route to the unknown. The Rimbaud who lives these hours is a simple roll call number among legionnaires. For the first time he is confronted by pure exteriority, we may also dare say by meditation in its pure state. Enslaved and free at the same time. An unoccupied mercenary and a potential deserter.

Several days after passing through the Straits of Gibraltar, the *Prins van Oranje* reaches Naples in the afternoon. It remains in port just long enough to take on additional provisions, and the vessel casts off again that evening. The Italian recruits are kept under close watch since it is known that some have enlisted only to repatriate themselves. No desertion is mentioned, however. The ship pursues its voyage off the shores of places Rimbaud will see again: Cyprus, for example. The Mediterranean, *mare nostrum*, will also be "his" sea, which he will cross on more than one occasion. The *Prins van Oranje* now takes the Suez Canal, opened only seven years earlier. The men themselves are affected by this transit, as they are leaving Europe and entering another world of deserts and incomprehensible languages. It is at this crucial (critical) moment that several choose to take off, especially the Italians, who were unable to escape in Naples. Some succeed, others, who fall into the sea, drown. Rimbaud waits. Leaning on the rail, he sees, with the others, the rocks of Aden surrounded by barren lands on the horizon. Then the ship hits the open sea. Now, everyone aboard will have to wait for the end of the voyage. On July 19, the *Prins van Oranje* docks at Padang on the coast of the isle of Sumatra. Three days later, they enter Batavia Harbor [present-day Jakarta— translator], the capital of Java, an island of dream. The city is surrounded by high ramparts. Boats of every nationality are moored in its port. The most mixed population passes through its streets. The arrival of the Indies troops is an event. To the beat of drums, the volunteers grouped in columns march on foot to Prinsenstraat, then climb into horse-drawn trams that take them five miles farther on to the Meester Cornelis quarter, where their barracks are located in a former tea manufacturer's warehouse. They proceed to the distribution of the soldiers. Rimbaud is assigned to the Fourth Company of the First Infantry Battalion, which is under orders to go to Salatiga. He leaves July 30 for Semarang, arriving on August 2. After Batavia, Semarang is the second most important city on the island. In 1876 this large town and its surrounding area counted seventy five thousand inhabitants. Next to the Javanese were a Chinese community of fourteen thousand souls and some five thousand Europeans of different nationalities. Business is flourishing, the port receives considerable traffic: vessels from Europe as well as the traditional junks and sampans. Rimbaud has just enough time to see the richness of the city. On August 2 his company takes the train for Kedong Djati, then Tintang. The heat is stifling–98 degrees in the shade. All activities cease during the afternoon. From Tintang the volunteers reach Salatiga by a two-hour march, and their journey's end is a mountaintop village. The climate here is milder. Exhausted, the men finally arrive at their campsite. Some of them, fallen ill since Batavia, are transported by special vehicle. During the journey, Rimbaud has no doubt noted for later reference the villages, the woods, and the places where the makeshift restaurants of the indigenous Warongs are hidden. In Salatiga the men are settled in barrack rooms. No doubt they are grouped by nationality. There are not many French—six in all, including Rimbaud. Over the long voyage they have gotten to know one another. The majority of them are young: Dourdet has not yet reached his legal majority, he enlisted at the age of nineteen; Louis Durant and Brissonnet are twenty-two and twenty-three respectively; Auguste Michaudeau is twenty-eight. He will die the day following their arrival in Salatiga, no doubt from a malignant fever. Prothade Monnin, the elder of the group, is thirty-two. Nothing is known about any of them. Rimbaud's contemporaries momentarily crossed paths during his adventure. These witnesses, though unconscious of their role, were the actors of his last "barracks room," as ignorant participants in one of his dreams.

The men soon grow familiar with harsh military discipline. Exhausting drills are imposed on them—and people begin to talk about war, deaths, and the dangers of the nearby jungle. On August 15, Assumption Day, a mass is celebrated for the Catholic community by a Jesuit priest, but Rimbaud does not attend. That evening he misses roll call, and the next day he is declared a deserter. Leaving behind almost everything the army had given him, he departs wearing a flannel undervest and white pants, dressed as a simple settler.[106] His uniform would have attracted attention. Most likely he had prepared for his flight in advance. He had seen the journey from Tintang to Semarang only from his seat on the train. He now has to travel this route on foot (about thirty miles). He takes care to go around the jungle. There are numerous villages and hamlets where he can take shelter. During the period between August 2 and 15 he had no doubt learned enough basic vocabulary from the Javanese soldiers of the camp to know the essential words for food, resting places, and directions. Moreover, the surrounding vegetation is abundant with fruit trees that allow him to satisfy his thirst and hunger at any time.

Rimbaud's desertion appears totally natural, just like the later desertion of Jacques Vaché (who viewed it paradoxically as he envisioned only his inner desertion[107]). Should we, in memory of the hero of Alfred Jarry's *Les Jours et les Nuits* ask ourselves if Rimbaud should be Vaché or Sengle? Rimbaud had deserted ordinary life a long time ago. His activity over the last two years merges with a perpetual flight that has the search for employment as its alibi, whereas it was primarily a matter of getting away. But what was he waiting for before giving this company of mercenaries the slip? Did he wish to follow the journey through to its conclusion just to satisfy his own curiosity about the true nature of the areas he traveled? We can't imagine Rimbaud in quest of perpetual wonders. Alain Borer rightfully said: "Rimbaud doesn't physically see the countries through which he travels and it probably serves us nothing to calculate their beauties. There is nothing in him of the bourgeois tourist. He isn't interested in remarkable sites. His escapade in Java is exclusively contractual, the contract he had signed before the military authorities, and what's more, the one he had imposed upon himself, through inner bravado, with a very distinctive sense of excelling. It is a heroism against the grain, when the hero acts for himself alone, in the name of a personal necessity that others are incapable of comprehending."

He manages to get back to Semarang, where he loses himself in the crowd, no doubt happy to be an indistinguishable individual, just one of the some five thousand Europeans who walk through the streets, make transactions, and drink in cafés. His knowledge of languages—English, German, and bits of Dutch—allow him to put any pursuit off the scent. But time is pressing and everywhere in the crowd he sees those he guesses to be searching for him. Thus it is necessary for him to find, in as brief a time as possible, a boat that will take him back to Europe. Once more he readies himself to carry out the voyage of the drunken boat. From among all the craft at the wharves, he soon has picked out the boats flying the British flag. Indeed, returning on a British ship would offer greater security. He has to avoid any contact with the Dutch, who accounted for the largest numbers of Europeans in Java. He doesn't wish to meet any French, either, with whom he would have to speak and thereby run the risk of giving himself away. By wandering around the port and talking with crewmen he finds a ship aboard which he could find hire.

The patience of the researchers is admirable, their resources almost infinite. On the trail of Rimbaud, they allow us to gain entry not into the exotic marvels of an adventure but in the equally impressive secrets held in archives. As with the best police matters, maritime voyages are supervised from beginning to end. Nothing—or little—is lost. However the flair of one such as Enid Starkie is required[108, 109] to think to examine the maritime archives concerning the boats that cast off from Semarang for Europe in August to September 1877 and arrived in France in the neighborhood of December (based on the later statements by Ernest Delahaye attesting to the fact that he saw Rimbaud at this time). Furthermore, it calls for the perspicacity of V. P. Underwood[110] to uncover new documents where Miss Starkie had left off. Certainly no new information resulted concerning Rimbaud's state of mind during this voyage, but we are informed in a much more precise manner of the world in which he lived and the dangers he was running.

Let's first recall the facts. On August 15, Rimbaud had been declared a deserter because he had missed evening roll call. Five months later, on December 9 (the date is quite precise), Delahaye would state that his presence was noted in Charleville. However, in informing Millot of this news he added a "Silence about this," and Isabelle, who certainly is not always to be believed, would state that her brother did not return to the family home until the end of the year.[111] Between these dates of August and December a long voyage from Asia to Europe took place in different stages for which Delahaye provides a list. Few boats follow such a course. In truth, only one ship corresponds to the specific information provided. The tale that may be deduced from this is based on probability for want of absolute certainty. This probability remains troubling. Let's accept this probable Rimbaud for now, as an intimate companion of the real Rimbaud who, in the final analysis, is always someone who cannot be found.

So Rimbaud seeks passage in Semarang on a boat setting sail for Europe. Then and there he offers his services. He certainly has some money at his disposal—the wages he had put in his pocket—but he wouldn't dream of paying for his passage. After several fruitless attempts, he has dealings with a certain Brown, the captain of a small-tonnage Scotch vessel, the *Wandering Chief*, that had left South Files, a northern English port, in February for a projected three-year voyage. Brown, after knocking around the seas of Java, decided—it seems—to return sooner than originally intended. He is carrying a cargo of sugar. The crew consists of a dozen hands: the captain, two officers, a cabin boy, a cook, and seven sailors. However, one of these men had drowned shortly before. Two others, among them the cook, were discharged due to illness. Thus, at the time he is contemplating a return voyage Brown has to fill out his crew. On August 8 he takes on a new cook, a Dane; on the eleventh a certain Holmes, and on the twenty-ninth, a certain Hinghston, who formerly served on the *Cleveland*. On that same day the British vice-consul at the port authorized all these men to be part of the crew. The name Rimbaud appears nowhere, nor does it appear on the rolls of ships departing Java at that time. But—and Underwood's hypothesis deserves to be taken into consideration on this account—it would have been quite bizarre if he had casually given his own name; it is rather more likely that he chose another English-sounding name, in accordance with the captain himself, who at the same time, would have knowingly faked the date on which he would have hired this sailor for his ship. All of this assumes that Rimbaud spoke perfect English (which isn't certain), or else that Brown, in need of sailors, didn't look too closely into the identity of his new recruits. Hinghston's case was perfectly clear. Holmes, on the other hand, when asked to furnish information about his previous employment, had indicated that he had worked on board the *Oseco*, a ship that (everyone knew this in Semarang) had been found abandoned in the Indian Sea on July 4. It so happens that in the Register General of Shipping and Seamen the name Holmes does not appear on the roll of the *Oseco* or on that of any British ship that had come to the East. Thus a lie can be inferred on the part of this unplaceable Holmes. Rimbaud, under the circumstance, would not have hesitated to assume a new identity and represent his age as nineteen. As for the patronymic Holmes he allegedly adopted, this is a widespread name in England, a name of exemplary banality, called upon to triumph in countless detective mysteries in later years!

The *Wandering Chief* left the port of Semarang in September. Rimbaud had escaped the search of the Dutch army. He was free. With the shores of Java disappearing in the distance, the adventure continued. On board he had to work, for which he received a small wage. Sailor Holmes drew pay of only seventy-five francs a month, while his comrades got eighty-seven. Perhaps his job was less onerous than theirs. Isabelle would declare later that he was the on-board interpreter, but it is hard to imagine any negotiations for which his services would have been useful under these conditions. Indeed, the ship, having a complete cargo, would be making no ports of call, except for several-hour stopovers at certain points on the journey. The journey was not exempt from the perils of the sea, the common lot of adventurers. At the end of September the *Wandering Chief* rode out a terrible storm. Rimbaud would tell Delahaye that he saw the crew, believing their final hour had come, kneel on the bridge and pray. A report sent by Captain Brown to Lloyd's of London would effectively sum up this sinister event with no unnecessary circumlocutions: "At 31° latitude south and 31° longitude east, we rode out some heavy weather in which an adverse swell swept away everything from the bridge that hadn't been nailed down and caused the boat to keel over so that it remained listing for thirty hours, with the hatches and the ends of the yards in the water. We had to pull down the mizzen mast and the big and the little top gallants. Since water had entered the hold, a certain amount of sugar was washed away." The crippled *Wandering Chief* repaired its damage. On October 23 the ship put in at Saint Helena, the "little island." Continuing on its course, it crossed the path of another vessel on November 18 at 19° latitude north by 30° longitude west. It therefore was not following a direct course to reach its destination, Queenstown, but was heading toward Ascension Island in order to benefit from certain favorable winds and currents. There is nothing that says Rimbaud paraded "his disgusting mug in Senegal," as Verlaine would subsequently write in one of his most ferocious "Vieux Coppées."[112]

The sailor Holmes (still him. Was it him?) applies himself to his shipboard chores. Calm has been restored. The passing time draws him irresistibly toward Europe. Waves and the stars, "The drifts rolling back into the distance, their shutter-like shudders." How could one not dream of "Le Bateau ivre." But by then Rimbaud was the last person to dream or remember it. His choice of reality forms part of a tough hygiene that doesn't know the complacency of poetry and is strong like the winds of the sea. Meanwhile, the British coast emerges in the distance after three months of sailing. It's Queenstown, the *Wandering Chief's* main port of call. At this moment Rimbaud leaves without warning. It is the evening of December 6 or the morning of December 7. Then begins a positively frenzied race as if he wanted to be on time for his future biographers! "He was—a depressing state of affairs—in Charleville since the ninth of December," Delahaye maintains in a private letter (he cannot be suspected then of seeking to cause trouble for hypothetical researchers). V. P. Underwood, who follows on a map the stages of the journey later specified by Rimbaud, recapitulates in order the names of the locales: Queenstown (where, for the moment, we have left the sailor), Cork, Liverpool, Le Havre, Paris, Charleville. Then he gets hold of a train and boat timetable, the *Bradshaw's Monthly Railway Guide* from December 1876. He now must equate the times and places. A tour de force of the most delicate nature that shows it would have been possible for Rimbaud to catch the train from Queenstown to Cork at seven in the morning (twenty-one minutes), and from there a ferry to Liverpool (arriving on the eighth at dawn), then a train to London, where he hops into a train for Paris, via Dieppe. He arrives at two in the afternoon, enough time for him to be seen in his English sailor uniform by Germain Nouveau who promptly dubs him "Rimbald the sailor."[113] Finally he sets off for Charleville from the Strasbourg station, which he reaches that evening, thus fulfilling the terms of his contract as elegantly as Philéas Fogg, the bettor from *Around the World in Eighty Days*. It is also easy to imagine much less haste on his part. After all what urgency was pressing on him? The prospect of hearing the inevitable reprimands from the *daromphe*? Underwood himself, troubled by the presence of the city of Le Havre in the itinerary indicated by Delahaye, also thinks that Rimbaud may have taken the ferry going to Le Havre from Southampton. But these schedules do not agree, Rimbaud could no longer be in Charleville at the hour of his imaginary rendezvous. Another fact allows some doubts to hover over the speedy hypothesis reached by this excellent researcher. In fact, after it made port in Queenstown, the *Wandering Chief* would later reach—but very much later—Le Havre, where it puts in on December 11. The muster sheet indicates that on December 20 eight men legally left the boat. Among them, Hinghston and the mysterious Holmes. Nothing, however, forbids us from thinking that the earlier departure of some of these men may have been registered only at this time. Captain Brown would only have pushed that of Holmes ahead two weeks before it was logged. Certainly to live in Rimbaud's shoes is to travel, but also to form parallel escapades, to let oneself be seduced by the possibilities. The reality, presuming that it isn't the one we just reconstructed, was no doubt as fabulous. Here Rimbaud becomes a ship, like the *Argo*. But he doesn't sing. He has become the voyage, the odyssey completely, he becomes the *other* completely in order to meet the truth he constantly has been seeking.

There remains the enigmatic suspended time in which he reappeared in Charleville, where—if we take Delahaye at his word—he would have remained secretly. But how could he live concealed in this town where everyone is watching everybody else, where rumor spreads through people like fire through oakum? We assume, at least, that he returned to the family apartment where his mother lived with Isabelle having abandoned all hope in her son Frédéric, the enlisted man, who would soon return with no occupational skills in exchange for his trouble, and the incomprehensible Arthur, who was intent on ruining all his talents (as Verlaine already believed). While waiting, Delahaye, who saw him and to whom he recounted his story with a certain precision, alerted their common friend Ernest Millot from where he was teaching in Rethel:

He has returned!!!

from a small voyage, almost nothing, really. Here are the stops: Brussels, Rotterdam, Den Helder, Southampton, Gibraltar, Naples, Suez, Aden, Sumatra, Java (a stay of two months), the Cape, St. Helena, Ascension Island, the Azores, Queenstown, Cork (in Ireland), Liverpool, Le Havre, Paris, and, as always, to conclude . . . Charleville.

By what series of splendid tricks he has performed these skedaddlings would take too long to explain.

Delahaye's relative epistolary laziness, which is quite excusable after all, has only encouraged Rimbaud's biographers to guess at what these "tricks" were. No doubt the future holds yet more fantastic inventions in store for us. Meanwhile Delahaye, in a lampooning state of mind, completed the ongoing comic strip:[114] in one Rimbaud is lazing on the ship that carries the volunteers; in another, clad in rags and clutching a gnarled staff in his hand, he is walking with great strides across an exotic landscape with palm trees, grass huts, and natives. A third image shows him with Delahaye sitting at a pedestal table that is holding the usual glasses; they are smoking their pipes, "sprawled" in their chairs and chatting, while quite clearly above them, as if an emanation of their remarks, is a vessel with sails pitching in a rough sea. The legend: "When are you leaving again?—As soon as possible." Verlaine, in turn, will spread himself to his heart's content in a "Vieux Coppée" whose opening offers an ironic summary of the deplorable state of the pilgrim exhausted by his long journey:[115]

> O là là, j'ai rien fait du ch'min d'puis mon dergnier
> Coppée! Il est vrai que j'en suis chauv' comme un pagnier
> Percé, que j'sens queut'chos dans l'gosier qui m'ratisse
> Que j'ai dans l'dos comm' des avant-goûts d'rhumatisse
> Et que j'emmerd' plus euq jamais

> Oh la la, I 'aven't traveled t'all sinch my last
> Coppée! It is true that it leff me bald as a pierced savage
> and I'm feeling sumthin' in my throat that's cleaning me out
> and sumthin' in my back feels lik' the first stirrings of rheumatisse
> and I'm a bigger pain in the ass than ever

The boredom and annoyance, these were the words that, far from any overly elegant spleen, he repeated to himself and whose meaning he felt deeply. Against this formidable grievance that ballasts every hour of human life, he still had but one resort available: to leave, ready to face the worst, to dare to be movement itself, at war against despondency and vain patience.

THE FLAKY TRAVELER*

FROM ONE YEAR TO THE NEXT THE EXPERIENCES ADD UP, EACH ONE JUST as disappointing and as if contrived for that very purpose.

Around Easter 1877, the man who returned has taken off again. Mother Rimbe has given him some money. He heads off again in the direction of Germany. Not to Stuttgart this time, or Vienna, but to Cologne. He has been forced to abandon the "Greek scheme" because Mercier is now a stage manager for the Comic Opera. Again, the only thing that lets us get our bearings in this instance of Rimbaud's wandering is Delahaye's testimony.[116] It remains vague, but portrays Rimbaud in a plausible role, that of a recruiter for the very Dutch army he had just deserted. At first it is hard to imagine him in this job that he had gotten to know firsthand, at his own expense. Yet he now knows what it takes to get the job done. Formerly enlisted in the Carlists, then the Dutch colonial army, he becomes a skillful craftsman at pulling a con in turn. He will earn a commission for each person he enlists. Rimbaud is fully cognizant of the anxiety felt by young men his own age who, refusing any occupation and ill at ease with themselves, see their lives slipping away. The bars, cafés, and public places are where he now searches for recruits. With his skilled way with words he paints them a gleaming picture of a "gloomy sky" colored by fate. But he is not the type to settle in one city, he soon feels a need to go somewhere else, not for the purpose of seeing the world, but to flee, *flee from himself.* Scenes from novels can easily make up for those we are missing. The same analogous texts are always brought to mind by this period of his life: the short stories by Mac Orlan about the ports of Europe, depicting individuals living a totally clandestine existence and humorists of misfortune; as well as several pages from *The Picture of Dorian*

---

*This nickname given to Rimbaud by Delahaye, Verlaine, and Nouveau no doubt came from d'Hervé's operetta *Le Compositeur toqué.*

Gray in which the young lord haunts low dives, opium dens, and taverns where crimes are plotted, without losing his beauty.

Risking his all while in Bremen and recalling his work on the *Wandering Chief*, Rimbaud sends a letter to the American consul[117] asking to enlist in the American navy. He then produces a veritable identity card in which he explains his situation. Following the "seven-year-old poet" and "the Infernal Bridegroom" appears another of his selves, no less surprising, and reduced to the most elementary and sometimes the most truncated bits of information:

> Bremen, May 14, 1877
>
> The untersigned Arthur Rimbaud
> Born in Charleville (France)—Aged 23
> 5 ft 6 height—Good healthy—Late a teacher of sciences and languages.
> Recently deserted from the47th Regiment of the French army, Actually in Bremen without any means, the French consul refusing any relief.
> Would like to know on which conditions he could conclude an immediate engagement in the American navy.
> Speaks and writes English, German, French, Italian, and Spanish.
> Has been four months as a sailor in a Scotch bark, from August to December 76
> Would be very honored and grateful to receive an answer.
>
> John Arthur Rimbaud.

This introduction from Rimbaud, which the American consul could only turn down, as it was necessary to be of American nationality to enlist in the American navy, is his personal confirmation of certain suppositions concerning his past activity. He was certainly a sailor aboard a British ship (the English word *bark*, used in the written original, is an indication of its small tonnage) whose voyage ended for him in Queenstown—and not in Le Havre, where—as we have seen—a certain Holmes reportedly disembarked. And the recent occupations he attributes to himself definitely corroborates the jobs he held over the last few years in Germany and England. We didn't know, though, that he had taught the "sciences," even if he did confide to Delahaye in 1875 his intention to pass the *baccalauréat* in this field. More disturbing is the detail about his desertion from the French army, an offense for which he does not

have to take responsibility in that, with the exception of periods of mandatory military instruction, he had been exempted from service. But Rimbaud
will always have the feeling that his situation is not in order with the authorities, even later, when he is completely crippled. His desertion from the Dutch
colonial army is transformed here into desertion from the French army, to
which he adds, in an irony he alone would understand, the "47th Regiment,"
the one to which his father belonged! No doubt we should not make his conduct dependent on recollections of this kind. They do provide clues, though,
to what stuck in his memory. The repetitive nature of Rimbaud's departures
and returns never cease to weave and "unweave" the temporary bonds that
existed between a remote father and a sedentary mother, a military traveler
and a peasant wife. We can read in his claim of desertion a mocking revenge
upon his sire, the soldier ever faithful to his garrisons where he never missed a
roll call while shamelessly abandoning his own hearth and home.

Thus in Bremen, at the end of his resources, Rimbaud admits his failure.
His bounty as a recruiter no longer gives him enough to survive. His request
rejected, he is forced back into the world of the streets and small expedients—
no doubt of the light-fingered variety. However, his polyglot skills, it seems,
will allow him to find, *in extremis*, a job. For several months he finds employment with the Loisset Circus, which travels across Europe and for the
moment is in Stockholm, where the traveler has arrived. The Loisset,[118] long
established in Holland, tours regularly in the great tradition of equestrian cir-
cuses. The milieu in which Rimbaud now finds himself (perhaps he fulfills the
duties of cashier and clerk) is not, properly speaking, that of traveling folk,
those "sturdy fellows" he evoked in "Parade." The two stars, Emilie and
Clotilde, are widely sought after by European aristocracy. Two years later,
Emilie, a circus equestrian, will marry a prince! Rimbaud must have remained
working for the Loisset for two or three months. But circus touring bores him
because of its regular itinerary between Stockholm and Copenhagen. From
there, according to a tradition tacked together by Delahaye, he has himself
repatriated by the French consulate.

Delahaye had also sent a letter on June 16, 1877[119] to his old friend Millot
to tell him that he knew nothing about the recent movements of the "Flaky
Traveler" and that he must be far away—far, far away. On August 9 he wrote a
letter to Verlaine and, as was his habit, accompanied his words with a draw-

ing:[120] Rimbaud, wearing a long fur coat, a shoulder pouch, and his ever-present top hat, bearing a cane as well, is clinking glasses with a standing polar bear; both are smoking pipes. From Rimbaud's pipe a balloon emerges with the words "Oh la la, it's not Javanese men I need here," an obvious allusion to his last caper. There is a tall bottle marked "ABSINTHE" between Rimbaud and the bear. The legend reads: "On the 70th parallel." On the back of the sheet of paper are several, more explicit lines: "No one has heard anything more about Rimbe, and I have seen nothing: *abeat proditor!* as Lhomond says, 'how the rascal gets around'! I send you, with a Siberian view, a little incident that has just stirred up the honest folks "of these places.'" The expression "no one has heard anything more" clearly shows that they did know at a certain point (for example, that Rimbaud had taken off for Nordic "places"). Perhaps he sent a postcard to Delahaye, who in another letter to Ernest Millot,[121] dating from the same period, repeats almost exactly what he said to Verlaine, but with the addition of these details: "He whom [I have known since] childhood and whom you see clinking glasses with a [Polar Bear] you will recognize easily enough (on the back of the paper), I tell you that he was lately seen in Stockholm, then in Copenhagen, and no news since. The best-informed geographers suppose him around the 76th parallel. so I humbly make myself their interpreter." Thus some people had received news of this Rimbaud now making his way toward the polar regions like a hero out of Jules Verne in quest of the North Pole. We don't know how Millot reacted to this information. Verlaine couldn't resist composing a "Vieux Coppée"[122] in which Rimbaud, after crossing Sweden (which makes him miss the warmth of the Café de Suède in Paris), has reached Norway; a dreamer, though (the tone is indicated by Verlaine himself), he now wants to return home:

> Si j'rappliquais pour un trimess' à Charlepompe
> (A merde)? Histoire eud'faire un peu suer la darompe?

> If I were to turn up for a trimest' in Charlepompe
> (in deep shit)? A story that'd cause the *daromphe* to sweat?

In fact, by one means or another, Rimbaud did "turn up," either repatriated at the expense of the state or as a traveler with long strides on soles of the wind.

———

No doubt he returned in autumn. As any real documentation is lacking we are forced to rely on even more debatable testimonies in that Delahaye, now teaching in Orléans, didn't know what was going on in Charleville. Verlaine had succeeded him at the Institution Notre-Dame of Rethel. Returning to his detested town for the winter soon was turning into a habit for Rimbaud. His pilgrimages cruelly brought him back to his chilly Ardennes at the harshest time of the year. Although they subsequently claimed to be his close friends, neither Millot nor Pierquin provided the slightest bit of information on this most recent stay. The often credible Delahaye grafts a "plausible" story[123] that could just as easily respond to the desire for fiction that Rimbaud inspires in those seeking to reconstruct his life, as if it were necessary to add any additional episodes to his real odyssey. Thus it is impossible not to reproduce here, word for word, the remarks of Rimbaud's La Boétie:

> A new attempt at the East, this time direct and fruitless as well, marks the end of autumn 1877. Rimbaud, embarking in Marseilles for Alexandria, fell ill at the beginning of the voyage with gastric fever and inflammation and exhaustion of the walls of the abdomen, caused by the rubbing of his ribs against his stomach as a consequence of excessive walking; such was the doctor's diagnosis, word for word. The unlucky traveler was left for treatment on the Italian coast. Once recovered, he took advantage of it to visit Rome, and returned by way of Marseilles to spend the winter of 1878 in Saint-Laurent, where Madame Rimbaud owned a country house.

Nothing else confirms this long journey. If it took place, it seems to have primarily paved the way for the one that will take place the following year. Rimbaud has accustomed us to such repetitions. In 1876, he passed through the Suez Canal, on board the *Prins van Oranje*. From that time he held the notion of returning to Alexandria for the purpose of commerce. Verlaine's "Vieux Coppée" on the voyage to Java[124] ends with these verses:

> *Mais tout ça c'est pas sérilleux: j'rêve eud' négoce,*
> *À c't'heure, at, plein d'astuc', j'baluchonn' des viell' plagu's*
> *D'assuranc', pour revend, cont' du rhum, aux Canaqu's.*

—

But none of all tha' was serious; I dreamt I t'was a trader,
at tha' time, and, full of trix, I packed up ol' reliabl'
tins, to resell, full o'rum, to the Kanaks.

But the Egyptians aren't Kanaks, and Verlaine went far afield to endow Rimbaud with a demoniacal ubiquity. In any event, not a trace survives of this abortive expedition.

It seems logical to assume that Rimbaud, in order to economize on the little money he had at his disposal, didn't take trains often. Thus he crossed the largest part of France on foot—which would explain his exhausted state and the illness he experienced at sea that forced him to disembark in Italy. This demonstrates how his body, endurable though it was, could betray him at times. He would always demand too much of it and push himself to the end of his strength. In 1876 he was struck by sunstroke on the road to Siena; in 1877 he was still not in perfect health. He was treated in Civitavecchia; the ensuing visit to Rome, mentioned only by Delahaye, falls into the realm of probability, but it is not evident that he was ever drawn to these prestigious sites. Nothing of what charmed the gaze of the Romantics held his attention, and the Eternal City, a memory of school essays and translations, had no reason to attract him, unless he wanted to verify if they really had preserved several prelates' noses filled with "schismatic powder" in richly decorated caskets at the Sistine Chapel—something he had farcically written in a poem of the *Album zutique!*[125] The return to Marseilles was self-evident—by what means?—and the ascent back to Roche like a penitence.

Around the time of Easter 1878, his presence is once more noted. It is true that this piece of information would be given only months later, in a letter to Verlaine composed by Delahaye on September 28:[126] "It is certainly true that Rimbe was seen in Paris. One of my friends saw him in the Latin Quarter around Easter." The "it is certainly true" has the value of a confirmation. Hadn't Verlaine himself announced in an earlier letter that "the man with soles of the wind" strolled the streets of the capital? If this true, it is easy to guess what activity he undertook over those few days. On his arrival he would have resumed contact with Cabaner, Mercier, and Richepin, and stayed with them. They had no recollection of it as his transit there was so swift. But his silhouette always lurked in the Latin Quarter of his rebellious youth, in sudden and futile appearances.

The inevitable return to Charleville takes place at the end of spring. Madame Rimbaud now lives in Saint-Laurent,[127] not far from Mézières, in a house that had belonged to the Cuifs. She will soon settle, once and for all, with Isabelle at the farm in Roche. During the summer Rimbaud accompanies them there; he shares the work of the harvest. This is no longer the time for writing *Une saison en enfer*. This book, far from being an exorcism, has taken on the value (he now realizes) of a prelude to all his future disappointments. However, the images of his last long trip surge into his memory and he feels the call of a pointless liberty, as useless and raging as the wind. Stretches of seas, jungles and wildernesses, "vertigo, collapse, routs, and charity" as "the seven-year old poet" said. No longer poetry, certainly, with its constraints and weaving of words but a "rough" or profoundly unpredictable reality. Once again, Roche is the site of an apparent work and a profound meditation—like a prayer before departure or a knightly vigil. In the course of his discussions with his mother, it is impossible that he does not mention certain things, even if only in grumbling, such as the necessity for him to live in hot lands, Africa especially, where he no longer will have to suffer from winter or unhealthy mists. He will make money there and return to Charleville later as a wealthy man. Madame Rimbaud lets herself be half convinced. However, she certainly wants to believe that all is not lost. Her son has no diploma, it's true, but he speaks the majority of European languages and she has no doubt of his genius. Finally he almost wins her over to the idea that he will become an engineer in faraway lands. This time—he promises—he will find a position and send her news regularly.

On October 20, 1878,[128] he goes back on the road. He will not pass through Marseilles, the detour to getting back to Italy is too great. With the money his mother has given him, he makes a direct line for Altdorf, where the Saint-Gothard tunnel is being dug (its inauguration will take place the following year). There he intends to go south to Genoa, where he will catch a boat for Alexandria, Egypt, as in the year just passed. He has asked his mother and Isabelle to send their letters there, general delivery. Leaving Charleville, he takes the train as far south as Remiremont in Lorraine. He then crosses the Vosges on foot, with an eye to getting back to the German station of Wesserling. But he hasn't taken the premature snowfall into consideration. A freezing wind is whistling through the mountains, the bed of snow on the ground has reached depths of twenty inches. He finally boards the train that runs along the lake of the Four Cantons and reaches Altdorf, the end of the line. The letter that he will send to his family from Genoa on November 17 (his father, Captain Rimbaud, had died the day before in Dijon), narrates the series of events of this journey in picturesque terms in which again we see the confident prose writer: his sense of composition, the energy of his style, the precision with which he looks at things, and the perfect dose of humor. But we also can hear the voice of the person he wishes to become: the geographer, the man of science who places more stock in exact measurements than ephemeral notations.

That's when the real ascent begins—in Hospenthal, I believe; first it is almost a climb, by way of traverses, then plateaus, or simply cart roads. Because you have to figure we can't follow them all the time, as they ascend in zigzags or by extremely gradual terraces, which would make the ascent interminable, considering the peaks are never less than 15,000 feet high on each side, although less than 15,000, when taking into consideration the height of the surrounding area. People no longer climb over the peaks but follow well-worn, if not actually cleared ascents. People not used to the sight of mountains will also learn that a mountain can have peaks but a peak is not a mountain. Given that, Gothard's summit is several miles in area.

The road, hardly even six yards wide, is filled all along its right side by a snowfall almost two yards deep, which, at every moment, spreads over the road in a yard-high barrier, which must be plowed through under an atrocious tormenting hail. Here it is! Not a shadow above, below, or around us, although we are surrounded by enormous objects. No more road, precipices, gorge or sky: nothing but white to think about, to touch, to see or not see, for it is impossible to raise your eyes from the white annoyance you think is the center of the path. It is impossible to raise your nose against such a biting wind, with your eyelashes and mustache like stala[c]tites, with your ears torn, your neck swollen. Without the shadow that you have become and without the telegraph poles that follow the supposed road, you would be in as big a fix as a sparrow in an oven.

Here's something we have to plow through that is more than a yard deep and almost a mile long. We haven't seen our knees in ages. It's irritating. We're panting, for the storm could bury us in half an hour without too much trouble; we encourage one another with shouts (one never makes the ascent alone but in groups). Finally there is a roadman: it's 1.50 francs for a bowl of salted water. Back on our way. But the wind grows violent, the road is visibly filling up. Here a convoy of stragglers, there a fallen horse half-buried. But the road has vanished. Which side of the telegraph poles was it on? (There are telegraph poles on only one side of the road.) You swerve, you plunge in up to your ribs, up to your armpits . . . A pale shadow behind a ditch: it's the Gothard hospice, a civil, charitable establishment, an unsightly building of wood and stone; a bell turret. When the bell, is rung a shady-looking young man receives you; you climb up to a low, dirty room where you are treated to the regulation bread and cheese, soup, and drop of wine. You see the beautiful big yellow dogs known in story. The laggards from the mountain soon arrive, half dead. By evening there are about thirty of us, and after the meal we are given hard mattresses and inadequate blankets. During the night our monkish hosts can be heard giving vent to sacred chants to celebrate their delight at having once again robbed the governments that subsidize their hovel.

We leave in the morning, after the bread–cheese–drop of wine and fortified by the free hospitality that can be extended for as long as the storm allows. This morning the mountain is marvelous in the sun: no more wind, all downhill through the traverses, with leaps and kilometrical tumbles that bring you to Airolo, on the other side of the tunnel, where the road resumes its circular, swollen alpine character, but descending. It's the Tessin [. . .]."

At this moment when he crosses the frontier that carries him to the other side of his life for good, far from any possibility of return, he remains in some respects ardently the same: the observant adventurer, the *Zutiste* who will infuriate the mother with his Gothard monks giving vent "to sacred chants to celebrate their delight at having once again robbed the governments," the individual threatened by boredom, who sees in the piles of snow not the "great white silence," but quite simply a "white annoyance" (so as not to say more).

Once he arrives at the cosmopolitan port of Genoa he boards a steamship headed for Alexandria and scrupulously pays off the fare. Having come there rather than to Marseilles has otherwise served him no purpose. "The passage to Egypt has to be paid for in gold; in other words, it's quite expensive, so providing no advantage," he is forced to realize. The crossing takes about a dozen days. It is probable that he was one of those who slept on the bridge, stretched out in deck chairs. The boat makes a call in Cyprus; Rimbaud again passes by familiar places, when he disembarks in Alexandria, he feels that this land had put its claim on him long ago, even if, detached from his battered past, he is now far from everything. Nerval had come there earlier, at a time when the Suez Canal did not yet exist: "Egypt is a large tomb, this is the impression it gave me when landing on the beach of Alexandria, which, with its ruins and mounds, offers a view of tombs scattered across a land of ashes."[129] The melancholy impression of a traveler in 1843! The city, whose population had clearly diminished since the time of its ancient glory, had been newly developed when Mehmet Ali had made it his virtual capital and the traffic created by the nearby canal had given it a renewed existence. During a two-week period Rimbaud sought employment and spent time with the Europeans of the city. He made the acquaintance of a French engineer there, "an obliging man of great talent." In the beginning of December—he says when writing to his family[130]—he doesn't yet know if wants to enter into a large agricultural enterprise, find employment with Anglo–Egyptian customs (Rimbaud a customs agent! For God's sake, nothing doing!), or leave for Cyprus as the interpreter for a work camp. For the first position he needs a certificate of ethics declaring he is free of all military obligations, so he asks his mother to send him all the necessary papers. He comes to a decision quite quickly, perhaps he was given advice on this matter by Ernest Jean or the son Thial, the engineer with whom he has become friends: he will go to Cyprus. On December 16 he starts his job. He is not an interpreter as he first thought he would be, but the foreman of a crew working a quarry. He has command over a crew of workers of every nationality: Syrians, Arabs, Maltese, etc.

Under his supervision the quarried and carved stones are loaded onto low-tonnage steam tugs or iron barges. Cyprus had belonged to the Turks, who had let it fall into neglect since the sixteenth century. But it was placed under British control with the recently signed accord of June 4, 1878. The English, who highly valued this key site, from where they could oversee commercial transactions in the Mediterranean and the Suez route, had been leading a policy of large works since that time in order to modernize the island and exploit its natural resources. The French had already constructed important buildings in Lanarca (a slaughterhouse, an Anglo-Egyptian bank). Rimbaud was arriving at an opportune moment. The same December he arrived, around twenty Europeans had come to take care of the work site. The harshness of the climate and the unhealthy air had already caused the death of several. In February, Rimbaud would inform his mother that he was the only person spared from fever.

This is definitely the point at which the years of exhausting labor begin that he will experience until his death and to which he submits as an acceptable punishment. He was spared from the edict pronounced by the God of Genesis less than any other human being: he would truly earn his daily bread from the sweat of his brow.

The closest village is an hour's walk from the encampment. The port of Lanarca, a large city on the south of the island inhabited by 20,000 people and housing the main consulates, is six leagues (15 miles) away. A riverbed, most often dry, ran through the side of the quarry. The sea is nearby and its shoreline is barren. "No cultivated lands, no gardens, not a single tree."[131] A desert of sorts. One he would come across again on his path. Arid, even during these winter months. Despite his good health, he knows full well that his situation is precarious. Another company can take the place of the one he works for. Despite the contract he has signed, he himself hasn't seen a bit of the one hundred fifty francs he is owed. He then addresses his family members with this astounding phrase: "Would you rather that I returned?" Is he going to abandon everything one more time? However, with rare tenacity, perhaps encouraged by his mother, who always had a similar toughness toward herself and was able to transmit this character trait to him, he doesn't give up but sticks to his task. Nevertheless, in two months the conditions of his life worsen. The heat becomes intolerable, he must sleep on the beach that is so plagued by fleas and mosquitoes that he asks for a tent to be sent to him with all haste. What's more, the workers are quarreling among themselves. It is necessary for him to intervene and he requests a dagger be sent. Faced by these inconveniences and dangers a great lassitude overwhelms him. He refrains from complaining, though. Such is his habit: rage or mute silence, and exhibiting as little despair or sorrow as possible. But the failure of his latest endeavor is obvious to him, despite his desire and will to rise above it. Furthermore, the illness that had spared him up to now strikes him in insidious fashion with vomiting and nausea. What was not yet the desire to return to France soon became a necessity. On May 28, he obtains a certificate from his employers attesting to the quality of his work. He has to return. He does.

In June 1879, he gets off the train at the station in Voncq,[*] three kilometers from Roche. Someone is waiting for him. His latest letters had announced his return and the poor state of his health. No doubt stricken by typhoid (this, at least, was the diagnosis of the doctor who treated him[132]), he slowly recovers. He's truly riding at anchor now and doesn't foresee the moment to leave, although he knows it is inevitable. For the time being he is caught in a snare of his own making, a snare forged so meticulously by fate. Does he still have the courage of his anger sometimes? Is he at risk of drowning in resignation? Considered after the fact, this "borderline" period takes on a distinctive vividness. It covers his final prolonged stay in France before a departure he wished to be definitive. He would reappear eleven years later. But for the moment he knows nothing of this future. What future could he foresee for himself, back again in the peasant world? Nothing had changed, nothing would ever change. He repeated such phrases to himself continually. The voyage to Java, the long journeys, the months spent near Lanarca always brought him back to his mud-stained starting point. Irony, following the most unimaginable detours, forces his return to Roche, his permanent desert, to which, later, he could only compare the most forsaken regions of Africa. The "hole" with no depth reclaims him. The flat horizons of the hamlet that reflect the imperturbable passing of the seasons. The family he suffers (after having cursed them). The obligatory labor that wears out the body and atrophies the mind.

---

[*] The Amagne-Vouziers line with a stop at Voncq, three kilometers from Roche, had been opened on February 17, 1873 (see *Le Courrier des Ardennes* of February 21, 1873).

Rimbaud rediscovers the neurotic space at the heart of which, in splendid rebellion, he had the strength to erect *Une saison en enfer*. But there is no longer any question of picking up the pen again. He is enclosed and held captive here, morning, noon, and night. The *daromphe* now dins into him over and over: "I told you so. Everything had to turn out this way." But do these Rimbauds talk very much about the states of their souls? It's necessary to keep an eye on the farmwork and the accounts. A severe life, a life of duty. And the mother, the widow, lives surrounded by her children in the hamlet where everyone, hungry for imaginary scandals, knows everything about everyone else. Madame has always kept her distance. All those in the neighborhood are familiar with her misfortune, an unhappy, incommunicative woman who, out of a kind of profound dignity, also refrains from making any conspicuous displays of sorrow. Frédéric has returned from the service. He couldn't make a career in the military like his father, so he is looking for work in Charleville, where he will hawk newspapers for a while before finding a job in Attigny driving a horse-drawn bus. Isabelle is now nineteen. Marriage appears an unlikely possibility, despite the good education she received from the nuns of Saint-Sépulchre and the beautiful blue Rimbaud eyes that light up her face. She will spend years in Roche, a loving and resigned daughter, showing little interest in her peasant neighbors. A difficult person, she will later refuse to become engaged to a rich landowner, and it won't be until the dead Arthur has become famous that she marries a reformed bohemian, Pierre Dufour (whose alias is Paterne Berrichon[133]), destined to become the poet's first biographer. During this month of June 1879 in which she celebrates her birthday, she could hardly imagine the incredible posthumous destiny of her brother. And when the latter returns exhausted from a day of work in the fields, she hasn't any thought of capturing these moments of life that make up an individual's reality. Hours pass unseen, and not even the slightest froth is harvested from them. These neutral hours count, though. It is regrettable we cannot talk of their slow pace, the strange flavor of a time that is almost immobile.

At the beginning of September, before parting for the town of Quesnoy in the department of the Nord, where he performs the duties of a head supervisor, Rimbaud's old friend Delahaye decides to make a brief visit to Roche.[134] He arrives on a beautiful afternoon and, without further ado, is put to work unloading a cart. Everyone is working enthusiastically, Madame Rimbaud, Isabelle, their old Luxembourgian servant Father Michel, and Arthur himself. Delahaye, while tending to his work, stares at the prodigal son returned to the fold. His emaciated face retains a tan from his faraway journeys; a scraggly beard adds a blond cast to his cheeks; his voice, which had been shrill until this time, now has a deep tone. That evening, after a day's labor, they unwind at dinner. Arthur is calm and cheerful. They talk about this and that. As their conversation continues, Delahaye, out of curiosity, throws out the question that Verlaine would not have failed to ask: "So, no more literature, then?" Rimbaud, with a "gay, somewhat surprised laugh," simply responds: "I don't think about all that anymore." Another version of the same scene relays an almost identical reply: "I no longer concern myself with *that.*"[135] Is Rimbaud, with his customary terseness, trying to say that literature (*that*) was now powerless in the modern world and that it did not deserve any effort devoted to it?

Late into the night the friends recall scenes from the past. They speak softly from their beds in the large room where, six years ago already, part of *Une saison en enfer* was written. They devote the next day to a long walk reminiscent of the long strolls they took during their days at the *collège*. They chat along the way and Rimbaud surprises his companion by the ease with which he speaks of everything with equal knowledge: culture, industry, commerce, engineering. He reasserts his scheme of becoming an engineer, one of those world-conquering heroes he admired in the books of Jules Verne. On their route they stop at some inn or other to drink rosé. The hours fly by on this sunny day. Just one last moment of happiness before the harshness of pitiless years. But Rimbaud will not be staying at Roche for long (he confides this to Delahaye). As soon as he has fully recovered (for he is still knocked out by daily attacks of fever), he is taking off. He plans to return to either Cyprus or Alexandria, where men like him find work easily. Delahaye reminds him of the idea he had once of going to the United States, but Arthur admits he has given up on that. "Le Bateau ivre" will not touch the shores of the "incredible Floridas." The sun begins to fall toward the horizon. The visitor has a train to catch. Their final words are exchanged on the road to the station, for soon, shaken by an attack of fever, Rimbaud must part from his friend and return to Roche at great strides.[136]

He will spend the winter—of the harshest kind—on the oppressive family farm. Long cold spells and large snowfalls, everything he detests. The minor daily tasks that followed the hard labors of summer are of little use in overcoming his deadly boredom. Dare we imagine him leafing through some book? His disdain of literature, no doubt, refuses to allow any such concession. So he carefully reads the local newspaper, as peasants still do during the long winter evenings. There is no longer any possibility of his leaving in the immediate future; he was surrounded by a tenacious snowfall everywhere, the "great white annoyance" that he had seen in the Saint-Gothard pass. Does he sometimes go to Charleville as a break from his dismal solitude? It is possible. He no longer sees Delahaye, who has left for Quesnoy, or Bretagne, who was assigned to the Bistade sugar works in the Pas de Calais in 1872. No doubt he still chats with Deverrière at the Café de l'Univers and meets with Millot and Pierquin. These latter, in their nebulous memories, easily confuse dates. Pierquin[137] recounts that he supposedly met the traveler in a small cafe off Ducal Square in the summer of 1879. Millot would have arranged this meeting. Rimbaud had just bought a suit, a sure sign of an imminent departure. It so happens that during the summer of 1879, Rimbaud had returned quite ill from Cyprus and was thinking only of restoring his shaky health. Pierquin would make note of other memories: as he was enumerating the list of books of poetry he had recently purchased in front of the unusual Jean Arthur, he was struck by this reply: "Buying books, especially books like these, is completely idiotic." In an anti-establishment vein, the former grind would even provide the vaguely aesthetic advice to make use of them, arranged on shelves, to "hide the leprous condition of old walls."

In Roche, Rimbaud does not seem to have spent any time with the other inhabitants of the hamlet. Everyone remained at their own farms, wearing away the weft of their lives. No doubt he knew through Delahaye (how could he not have known?) that Verlaine often came to within six kilometers of there to visit the home of the Létinoises[138] in the small village of Coulommes. A professor at the *collège* Notre Dame in Rethel, Paul was infatuated—discreetly, at first—with their son Lucien, who was one of his students. He would soon give agriculture a try and buy a small concern for his protégé in the outskirts of Juniville. This good Catholic certainly fell back easily into the rut of sin, even if he disguised his actions behind the best intentions. He still persisted in his role as Rimbaud's inconsolable "Mad Virgin," but quickly sought to replace him with the most drab partners for satisfying his carnal cravings in total hypocrisy.

In the first days of spring 1880, Rimbaud, as promised, announces his departure. It is not possible to hold on to this prodigal son. The *mother* truly feels another vocation has awoken in him, one as imperious as poetry, that is now dragging him toward the East. His itinerary is set in advance. For the third time (and this is the bare minimum), Rimbaud goes down as far as Marseilles. A strange yet familiar journey. What hopes does he have on the steamship taking him to Egypt? He is again escaping from Europe but is still ignorant concerning the material from which his truth will be forged. At the end of the voyage, will he finally touch not the ideal image dreamed of his poems, but reality, urgency, and daily fortunes?

PART IV

RIMBAUD THE AFRICAN

ADEN: "A FRIGHTFUL ROCK"

UPON ARRIVING IN ALEXANDRIA, RIMBAUD QUICKLY DISCOVERS THAT THE jobs on which he is relying have been taken. He has no recourse but to leave again for Cyprus in hopes of finding his former employers there. Upon landing in Lanarca, he learns that E. Jean and Thial have gone bankrupt. Despite these depressing circumstances, the idea of giving up does not occur to him. Many adventurers are taking their chances in Cyprus. He quickly finds a job that, this time, takes him to Mount Troodos, the highest point on the island, with an altitude of 6,000 feet, where the governor wishes to have a summer home built. Rimbaud will oversee the construction; while waiting for the workers to arrive he moves in with the engineer. The site is picturesque, dense with high ferns and shadowed by pines, but the nights are freezing and Rimbaud, who did not foresee the need for warm clothing, has to spend part of his financial reserve to outfit himself against the cold. Furthermore, he has difficulty obtaining food, even the most basic kinds. Fortunately English troops would soon establish an encampment nearby and the men on the work site would henceforth lack for nothing.

Rimbaud, far removed from everything, sometimes spares a thought for his family. He sends them letters that end with the pompous phrase "I commend myself to your memory."[1] In a show of generosity he offers to send some of the fine wines of the Commanderie—certainly because he does not wish to be in their debt for the demands he has made upon them. In fact, from now on his correspondence will always (or almost always) contain orders for books and things—in which it is not hard to hear a secret cry for affection. Rimbaud forces his mother and sister to take care of him. If he is "making amends," it is also necessary for those in Roche to share in this symbolically discharged atonement. Appearing as postscripts are lists of books: a regular enumeration of perfect little handbooks every reader of his African correspondence notes first with astonishment, then weariness. The literary works

257

his mother once refused him have been transformed into a vast utilitarian commodity. She clearly sees that there is no longer a question of the stupidities of poetry—all those wild imaginings she doesn't understand one whit. Arthur reads valuable guides to the road of life from now on. In the vein of Bouvard and Pécuchet, he becomes a polymath who believes that everything can be learned from endless reams of printed pages: practices and professions. Didn't he already dream all the enchantments? Books will always accompany his life quest, even these that are quite disappointing and almost totally lacking in style, but still provoke reading and pull the reader toward the other world of words, even if they are the poorest and most strictly referential kind.

Overseeing the Mount Troodos work site was not exactly a sinecure.[2] At the end of a week, though he had planned to remain there through September, Rimbaud wishes to quit. What happened? On June 4 he is contemplating leaving for an "ashlar and lime firm."[3] As it happens, nothing occurred as planned in that toward mid-June he took ship from Limassol for Egypt. Several hypotheses provide a possible explanation for this precipitous departure. According to a letter he sent his family, he had a falling-out with his employers, who were clever at exploiting manual labor for which they offered only slender guarantees of payment in return.[4] But an Italian, Ottorino Rosa,[5] would later declare that Rimbaud left Cyprus for a more serious reason: in fact, he allegedly killed one of his workers with a hurled stone. Was it an accident? A premeditated act? All suppositions are permissible, but the hypothesis of an act of anger carries more weight than that for an unfortunate accident.

Thus he had the choice of returning—the usual scenario—or of sinking deeper into the improbable, to take another step further into the hell of his life, with his only satisfaction being the thought that he is far from Roche, far from France, far, quite simply, from his native tongue. He was soothed—I am convinced of this—by no longer hearing the drone of French, the "colossal June bug"* in his ears. He was thereby no longer *guilty of poetry*. The horizon of the unknown was opening before him (even though it was a rerun), of which all possibilities had not yet been exhausted, despite so many setbacks.

---

*Such as the one drawn by Delahaye in his sketch of Rimbaud entitled "The New Wandering Jew."

He rediscovers, though with less innocence, of course, the wind, heavens, and starry nights imagined in "Ma bohème"; but life has burdened him with painful memories: his miserable time in the Latin Quarter, the disappointing experience with Verlaine, and death, both Vitalie's and his own narrow escape.

He doesn't stop at Alexandria again. Following the path of his voyage on the *Prins van Oranje*, he crosses into the Suez Canal. He was told earlier that work was available in the ports on the Red Sea. He passes by Port Saïd for the second time. These semi-desert regions are now exciting the lust of Europeans. A great spot for transit, the Suez Canal (inaugurated in 1869), not only opened a direct route to the Far East but facilitated access to closer, previously inaccesible regions that were rich in rare goods. Rimbaud arrives in this part of Africa at the very moment the English, French, and Italians are nursing many schemes of conquest, even though the Turkish empire and the Egyptian khedivate maintains temporary supremacy over these territories.

Slowly the ship enters the canal,[6] sometimes it has to dock in order to allow a heavy liner returning from China to pass through. Above the desert-locked Lake Menzaleh, the passengers momentarily admire a flight of flamingos. Farther on in El Kantara, they see a newly constructed bridge for a boat, the two halves of which rest on either bank. Here the numerous caravans from Egypt to Palestine continue to cross over. All along the banks, as far as the eye can see, are high dredges that remove the ceaselessly windblown sand from the shallow waters. Next they pass, in these solitary regions made less hostile by civilization, the pavilion—outlined against the sky—constructed by the canal company for sheltering the Khedive Ismael, during the official inauguration ceremonies—the very ruler who finally gave de Lesseps authority to begin the work, following years of discussions. They then pass near Lake Timsah, a tugboat anchorage. Finally Suez appeared—as did the vast horizons of the Red Sea that were later much loved by Monfreid, the old salt on the "Cruiser of Hashish." On the port side are the biblical lands of the Sinai Peninsula, which no doubt did not arouse any emotion in Rimbaud. He didn't have the soul of a crusader and was forever excluded from the Christian religion. On the starboard side is Egypt. It is very likely that he now knows he will go no farther than the end of the Red Sea. China and Japan can be saved for another time! However, this taciturn passenger on the bridge consents to talk to other adventurers like himself. His intention, though vague, sticks to several schemes: supervising construction work or engaging in trade. "Merchant! colonist!, medium!," such was the ironic program to which he devoted himself in "Ce qu'on dit au Poète à propos de fleurs." He was maybe a medium at the time of *Illuminations*. Now it was the turn for other duties that were less mysterious and more lucrative.

Europe has been left far behind. Passing through the canal is not a mere formality, it truly opens onto a new world. And Rimbaud feels that he has crossed an imaginary line, on one side of which the universe of the Vilains Bonshommes and the "miserable women of drama" is erased and lost in its unhealthy mists. A new, detached (in the best sense of the word) man, traveling incognito, he is on the brink of becoming another person, with the appreciable difference this time of not having to desert. He finds himself alone, the bearer of his freedom, master, in some respect, of what we will later call his fate. He gets off at one of the first ports: Suakin, the port where the roads out of the Sudan end, but there is nothing for him here. Further down he takes his chances in Massawa and sets foot for the first time on the soil of ancient Abyssinia, again in vain. He next stops in Hodeida,[7] in Arabia, at the edge of Yemen, still finding no work—he does not have a good command of Arabic and the large construction works on which he has pinned his hopes do not exist in these regions. Furthermore, the heat during this July is more and more oppresive, and as a result his health is deteriorating. Sick, he is forced to remain in bed. Luckily, a certain Trébuchet, a French merchant representative of the Maison Morand et Fabre based in Marseille takes care of him.[8] In several days he has recovered from his fever, and Trébuchet, who has shown an interest in his fate, lets him look into the possibility of a job in Aden, where he knows all the European merchants, notably the Bardey brothers, who settled there after exploring the coast and establishing trading posts. For Rimbaud, the trip to be accomplished is still a long one, some 470 miles, but he has the presentiment that he is coming to the end of his woes. Trébuchet's words have reassured him. He can now imagine an exit from his unhappy pilgrimages. From Hodeida the boat follows the barren coast of Arabia, passing offshore of Mocha, the coffee town that has been abandoned for forty years following its invasion by desert Bedouins. The boat reaches the southern end of the Red Sea, enters the straits of Bab el-Mandeb—a fateful name meaning the Gate of Tears—then, following the littoral, arrives in Aden.

The ship casts anchor at Steamer Point, the new port. Several European buildings have been constructed there: the Messageries Maritime (a shipping agency), the bungalows for British officials, and the governor's residence. Aden is a British dependency. There is also a French consulate, to which Rimbaud would resort on more than one occasion over the following years. A half circle of white dwellings surround Twaie Beach. The arcades on the ground floor support the large verandas on the second floor, themselves topped by terraced roofs. A little boat brings the passengers to the landing stage—the Bender, as it is called. From there, if he likes, Rimbaud may take a horse-drawn carriage. But having almost no baggage, he first makes his way to the Grand Hôtel de l'Univers where the majority of foreigners—European merchants and explorers—stay. It has an imposing sign. Its rooms look out over the sea, the view of which enchants him (this is before boredom conquered him). Rimbaud asks to see Jules Suel, a close acquaintance of Trébuchet and a friend of the recently arrived Bardeys. He is a cheerful, alert man of about fifty. He wears the colonial attire that Rimbaud himself would soon adopt: pants and shirt of white cotton and canvas slippers. Suel soon gives the newcomer, who has told him his story, ample information about the Bardey brothers, Alfred and Pierre. For the moment Alfred is away in the region of Harar in Africa to set up a trading post, but one may always see M. Dubar, his associate. There is work available. However, life is expensive, the heat is terrible, and daily life is nothing to write home about.

Leaving the hotel, Rimbaud hails a coach to take him to Aden. About five miles separate the city from the port. At the pace set by its team, the carriage follows a well-traveled route, passing enormous piles of coal where each day the liners stock up; four amounts of merchandise wait on the old wharves: skins, gum arabic, sacks of coffee. They skirt a village of straw huts inhabited by Somalis, astonishing-looking individuals with their hair tinted in violent colors: red, yellow, or green: they are walking vowels! The naked, grassless landscape is constantly crossed by long caravans, the *gaflah*, out of Arabia; they form an almost unbroken line that is both picturesque and noisy; men, women, and children shouting in a cloud of dust; the camels reeling under the weight of their heavy burdens, often secured by whatever means were available at the time of loading. But then the team labors up a steep climb where at the summit a passage opens: the Main Pass Gate. Beyond it Rimbaud will enter into the city proper, which has been established in the crater of an extinct volcano. *Cipayes* check the entries and exits. After these formalities, the carriage enters a narrow corridor, a veritable crevasse cut straight through the rock. The city appears colorless, like a kind of mirage. Before reaching it they have to cross a bridge over a river that is most often dry. The animal market is held in its arid bed: goats, sheep, and camels. An intolerable odor and waves of golden dust emanate from it. Soon they enter the city, right next to the bazaar. The variety and richness of the Orient. All its races brush past one another: Somalis, Arabs, Indians. The world of the cities imagined by Rimbaud in *Illuminations.* Trade is flourishing; the traveler is momentarily dazed by these numerous activities that seem to have emerged straight out of the pages of *A Thousand and One Nights.* Every occupation can be found here: Jewish jewelers are hammering out gold and copper, water bearers are offering their water jugs, the weavers hang their warps in the middle of the street. The vehicle soon reaches the Main Square, where a minaret crowned by a gold crescent rises. Next to it is a building covered in tile (a rare material here). This is the court. The coachman points out the Maison Bardey facing it: on the ground floor are the traditional arcades that support the second-floor veranda. It contains many rooms and is an attractive dwelling. Rimbaud, knowing that Alfred Bardey is absent, asks to see the person taking over for him while he is away on his journey. He is received by Monsieur Dubar who is well known to Trébuchet and a close relative of Jules Suel, the manager of the grand Hôtel de l'Univers.

The agency had just been created; it exported more or less rare items of merchandise, especially coffee, and also sold or bartered European products to the indigenous population. At the opening of the canal, a number of merchants and adventurers, smelling a windfall, had established themselves in these regions through which the wealth of Arabia and Eastern Africa flowed by caravan. Three other agencies were already in business in Aden: that of César Tian, for whom Rimbaud would be a trading representative in 1888; the association of Morand, Fabre, and Company; and the Italian firm of V. Bienenfeld. Rimbaud's hiring doesn't seem to have posed any problem. He pleased Dubar at first sight; Dubar was a former army officer, then an administrative employee in a trading house in Lyons, and now served the Bardey house, also of Lyonnaise origin. Asked to give his personal particulars, Rimbaud indicated that he was born in Dôle[9] (his father's birth place), in keeping with his private sense of humor that had prompted him in Bremen to say that he was a deserter from his father's 47th Regiment. His most secret attachments are confirmed by such details, as if, having abandoned the world of poetry, he wished to reconnect with one of another adventure and place his feet back in old footsteps in repetition of someone else's fate. We cannot learn any more about this aspect of his character, but his reserve and silence allow glimpses of the elements of a personal game, a tacit contract that he entered into with himself in the name of an inner truth that cannot be determined.

He is first hired on a trial basis with a daily salary of seven francs (the equivalent of two hundred ten modern francs[10]). His job is receiving the bales of coffee bought by two native brokers. After purchase, the coffee is stored in warehouses, where it is hand-sorted by their Indian female employees, verified, weighed, and placed doubly wrapped in sacks, and is then finally ready for exportation. Rimbaud supervises a *harim*—an ironic word, since the word *harem* here simply means a workshop of women and not a group of concubines! During that time he appeared as "a large and friendly young man who spoke little and accompanied his brief explanations with small, sharp, uncoordinated gestures of his right hand."[11] This is the "captured image" of him that remains. A Rimbaud we didn't know? It is rather a complementary portrait of one who will always be for us a person in flight and a mirage assaulting our daydreams. The Rimbaud arriving in Aden is a man who, though in the prime of life, has already been worn down by his futile peregrinations. His face has grown thinner, his hair is short, a small mustache emphasizes his upper lip. His blue-white eyes no longer dare dream . . . For the moment he is living in a makeshift time. Day after day, from seven in the morning to five in the evening, he works without a break for a salary he knows is mediocre. But he displays an obvious goodwill and Dubar quickly recognizes his mental quickness and remarkable ability to adapt. In very little time he has learned the rudiments of popular Arabic; he can then give orders, a function that hardly earns him any affection. He is nicknamed *Karani*, "the nasty guy."[12] He knows it and also knows that this nickname is currently popular for the person who is second in command. In his rare rest periods, which are evenings (because Sunday is not a day off), he strolls the streets of the city. Aden is really at the ends of the earth despite its fourteen thousand inhabitants of every nationality. There are few Europeans: an unchanging community exchanging visits among themselves, discussing business over cups of tea, playing billiards, or smoking with a melancholy air while reading the week-old newspapers. Another Charleville? Yet everything is different. The heat is intolerably heavy and at night it is necessary to sleep in the open air on the verandas with a water jug in arm's reach to refresh oneself from time to time. Moreover, drinkable water is the object of genuine trade; it is expensive, since it has to be distilled from seawater.

Rimbaud will describe these woeful regions in several letters:

Aden is a frightful rock without a blade of grass.[13]

The crater of an extinct volcano whose bottom is filled with sand from the sea. Thus one sees and touches absolutely nothing but lava and sand that is incapable of producing the thinnest kind of vegetation. The surroundings are a desert of absolutely arid sand. But here, the walls of the crater prevent air from entering, and we roast at the bottom of this hole as if it were a lime kiln.[14]

Here combined more closely than one would think possible are Rimbaud's "season in hell" and "comedy of thirst," as if to validate the writing that had already labored in an exhausting universe. Also Rimbaud, ever faithful to his desire to take off, soon takes it into his head that he must get away to—the indispensable ever farther beyond—Zanzibar.[15] The name will reappear constantly under his pen when he wishes to get away from everything. An unhoped-for magical Open Sesame, like the Blessed Isles of the Ancients. What did he expect to find there? Flourishing trade, an amiable populace? Some kind of happiness? For him, Zanzibar signifies one of those extreme points that he will never see. It is no doubt enough for him to dream about it indefinitely.

Completing the metamorphosis inaugurated several years previously, he is now a "positive" man who feels dedicated to human labor and is already dreaming of amassing enough money so as not to be a tramp or bohemian pulling another fast one on his mother. The true modern man is the merchant and the engineer who, strong with a youthful energy, makes his way to those spots in the world where gold and money are flowing. If he once believed that "real life" was absent, he now thinks that another kind of life deserves to be attempted in risks and ventures.

As the agency conducted "business tolerably well" and Dubar allowed him hopes for a secure position, he decides to remain, despite his disgust. Although his situation is improving, over the following months, seized again by his ambulatory mania, he thinks of leaving the house to go "probably to Zanzibar, where there are possibilities." "There are possibilities"—a favorite expression of the African and Arab Rimbaud. His correspondence of the time initiates us into this sort of language and the mutant forms of his desires. He has less curiosity for seeing unknown lands than a desire to draw money out of them: buying and selling, profits and losses. His relationship with money characterizes all of these years and it is not a question for him of exploring a world, but of triumphing *over* this world. He lives more and more with the idea of building his personal fortune as if to prove he is capable of doing that, at least. "I will have gold." Gold should be seen here as the secular substitute for the sun he once sought as the ideal in a poetic quest.

In October 1880,[16] Alfred Bardey returns from the long expedition that had taken him as far as the province of Harar to establish a factory in the heart of the mountains. Since May, at which time he and "Colonel" Dubar had left the parent company of Lyon known under the corporate title of Viannay, Bardey, and Company, he had not spared any pains. Having established a trading post and workshop in Aden, he had first gone on a reconnaissance mission that took him all the way to Bombay, India, then, on his return, had set off on a fairly perilous venture into Africa, where he had crossed through the hostile lands of the Issas before finally reaching the city of Harar, a center of coffee cultivation, where he had founded a commercial firm. Now back in Aden, he had gone by the Grand Hôtel de l'Univers to see Jules Suel and enjoy some of the amenities of civilization. Dubar, who is there to meet him, brings him up to date on the agency and describes the new recruit, Rimbaud, with whom he is quite pleased. Shortly after, the two men will meet each other. Both form good impressions of the other. Bardey knows how to judge an individual for his true worth. At first glance he sees in Rimbaud a reserved individual, little inclined to share memories of his past, but also a man with a quick mind and great learning who has run aground there for obscure reasons about which he won't seek to enlighten himself. As in the Foreign Legion, the people who come to these lands don't have to give an account of their past. They are judged on their actions. Rimbaud finds in Bardey a man of his age with an athlete's build. A heavy black beard shades his face. His eyes sparkle with honesty and determination. Ernest Delahaye was the accompanist of the Charleville *collège* student during the years 1870 to 1871. Bardey, in turn, though totally ignorant of the literary importance of Rimbaud, whom he first regards as only a respected colleague, will be the eyewitness of the places now traversed by Rimbaud and the people he frequents. By writing his *Barr–Adjam*, he will keep the diary[17] that the deserter of Europe and poetry would have been able to write, had he not renounced all writing so radically.

Here Rimbaud enters into the most astonishing part of his life.[*] He certainly couldn't have known he was doing so. For what later takes on the figure of fate is actually shaped by what he now does day by day. From 1875 to 1880, he wandered ever farther and, burning with dissatisfaction, threw himself into a headlong search for the "region where to live."[18] Now, one slope he encounters on his almost blind quest will lead him to the worst possible outcome.

---

[*]Another Rimbaud was in Aden at the same time he was: "Be sure to write my address clearly because there is a Rimbaud who is an agent for the Messageries Maritimes," he points out in a letter of September 22, 1880, in bringing up this coincidence that is an inopportune variation (through the homonym) of "I is an other."

BACK FROM HARAR, ALFRED BARDEY KNEW "THERE WERE POSSIBILITIES" there and foresees a worthy colleague in this young, intelligent, thoughtful man with no ties, who could work wonders alongside Pinchard, who had been left alone as head of the African factory. Learning this, Rimbaud immediately sees it as his possible ticket out of Aden and the terrible dry climate he could no longer tolerate. On November 10, he signs a three-year contract[19] agreeing to "become one of the personnel of the house employed by the agency of Harar [. . .] or in any other trading post or agency on the coast of Africa or Arabia where the service needs and the interests of the house require his [your] presence." He will be paid fifty rupees a month, which is a substantial improvement on his former salary; he will receive a one percent commission on all profits; finally he will receive room and board. Rimbaud is happy with these conditions. Thus he has made his choice once and for all. He postpones the idea of Zanzibar to some future journey, but is already aware he is going deep into untamed regions and, somewhat boastfully, declares to his mother: "One can only go there armed [. . .] there is a danger of losing your hide there at the hands of the Gallas."[20] In fact, this people of cruel reputation had recently cut a caravan passing through its territory to pieces.

Before leaving, he made certain to send his family[21] a long list of the utilitarian works, manuals, and guides he wanted, no doubt under the illusion that everything could be learned by carefully following recipes. This Rimbaud the handyman wasn't close to ending his litanies of books that could be purchased at M. Lacroix's shop: *Manuel du Charron, Manuel du Tanneur, du Verrier, du Briquetier, du Faïencier, du Potier, du Fondeur en tous métaux, du Fabricant de bougies, Guide de l'Armurier, Le Parfait Serrurier, L'Hydraulique urbaine et agricole,* etc.*

---

*These are manuals for wheelwrights, tanners, glassmakers, bricklayers, potters, smelterers (for all metals), candlemakers, gunsmiths, locksmiths, and on urban and agricultural hydraulics, respectively—Translator's note.

One would imagine a Robinson Crusoe foreseeing his future shipwreck on a desert isle and taking all necessary precautions for reconstructing the civilized world. Over the coming years he would complete this bibliography of the man who can do everything. He is under the impression that everything will be possible if only such books could be sent him, and that provided with their viaticum as if they were alchemical treatises, he would transform the order of reality. He believes nothing can stand against human ingenuity and displays the powerful drive of a Jules Verne hero. Harar would be the equivalent of *The Mysterious Island*, and the exile from Ardennes would imitate Cyrus Smith, the inventive engineer who had pulled through the Civil War. With the purchase of books soon followed by money to be deposited, there are no small number of letters requesting his distant family take an active interest in his solitary life. Thus it is necessary that his mother go to the bookstore in Attigny, consult catalogs, forward the orders, and package them. Rimbaud makes his demands and, in a roundabout manner, it is love he demands, all while demonstrating he has become a new, unrecognizable man cleansed of his faults and enduring here beneath the punishment he deserves.

Rimbaud in Harar, Rimbaud in Abyssinia. All his biographers have perceived the homogenous nature of this final stage of his life. A novel could be constructed from several rediscovered documents, but given Rimbaud's stubbornness in that regard it would refuse any fantasy element. A precise and detailed history, attentive to his constant financial pressures, may also be erected. However, in the final analysis, such literary regimens appear insufficient: fiction or reconstruction, *a posteriori* coherence or a sparkling of anecdotes. It appears just as dangerous to shadow Rimbaud, in his most minor gestures, as to draw out of these few years some facts that recur, "themes" that when put together would run the risk of creating a unique and unvarying portrait of him.[22] All we can do is understand his correspondence by reading between the lines, but sometimes it may also express violently the struggle of a body and mind in revolt against their deterioration, and the pure, simple energy of the life he pursued there, in the face of all opposition and in the greatest kind of isolation, even if figures are constantly appearing around Rimbaud, protagonists that momentarily give him his cue or accompany him, actors in an often interrupted act, in which he himself fades into the shadows of a room with the odors of leather and green coffee or among the people of a caravan.

At the end of November 1880, provided with all the necessary recommendations, he takes a dhow to Zeila, an African port and terminus for all caravans out of Harar. He brings cloth, trinkets, and a large sum of money. For once the future appears in a propitious light, even though he is fully aware of the dangers of the road ahead and the total isolation incumbent upon anyone settling there. The boat crosses the Gulf of Aden in a straight line: 190 nautical miles. Arriving in Zeila, it pulls alongside a jetty recently constructed from the ruins of the former city wall. In fact, the town consists of straw huts and two white houses: one is occupied by administrative services, the other is a *kouba*, a modest building serving as a mosque.

Rimbaud does not explicitly state if he made his way to Harar with a caravan,[23] but simply tells his family on December 13 that he spent twenty days on horseback through the desert to reach the city. But one would think Bardey took advantage of this opportunity to convey goods to the trading post. Rimbaud takes part in the organization of a *gaflah*[*] for the first time; he became acquainted with Abu Bekr on this occasion, the powerful pasha of Zeila and Tadjoura, who had been given authority over Somalian territory. Any trade with the interior was dependent on his goodwill and that of his eleven sons. He controlled—to his own great profit—the traffic in slaves then rampant in this part of Africa. Soon the *abbans* (the guides), the *sepians* (the porters), and camel drivers are assembled. A troop of "savages," as one would say in the West then. But Rimbaud marvels at the sight of them. The majority belong to the ethnic group the Issas, tall individuals who wear their hair braided in long locks coated with butter and held in place by large combs. They carry the traditional weapons: a javelin, a long spear, a small buckler, and a short sword in their belt. Before leaving,[24] all go to the wells of Tococha to fill their spacious *gherbes*, which will provide water for the men of the convoy for several days. Next the caravan reaches Warambot, five miles away and where the real journey begins. It is one in the afternoon. Despite the sun the *gaflah* sets off. For a

---

[*] A caravan. The larger part of this small *gaflah* must have been put together before Rimbaud's arrival in that it seems to have been ready several days after he disembarked in Zeila.

duration of seven hours it will traverse the arid plain of Mandao. "Fool who stops here," the natives say. Escorted by a guide, Rimbaud takes the front position with Constantine Righas, a Greek who will be his assistant in Harar, and moves off at horse pace. He welcomes the respite at evening; the first day has been quite an ordeal. Rimbaud doesn't yet know the rhythm of the desert. However, he has discovered its harsh beauty and everything that a slow march across a mute landscape can teach: it resembles a progression into his own heart. Late in the evening they resume their journey under the starry sky. All through the night the march continues in order to take advantage of the cool night air. At dawn the men stop. From eight until noon they rest before departing again. At dusk they reach Hennessa, forty-five miles from Zeila. In Hennessa both men and animals race for the wells, and an encampment is set up. The animals graze on the scarce grass. After Hennessa the terrain becomes rocky. A five-hour march and they arrive at Las Maneh, the "wells of combat," a place in the bush where the Somalis traditionally demand a fee for passage. The caravaners light large fires that night at their camp. They will then stay up a good portion of the night singing their tribal songs. Rimbaud will be the stubbornly silent witness to all of this: he alone will benefit from it, perhaps thinking to speak more of it at a later date. He will do nothing of the sort, however. Soon the howls of hyenas rise, troubling the silence. These detestable companions of death will remain with the travelers constantly from here on. They follow them at a distance to eat their refuse and will reappear each evening in ironic and lugubrious fashion. On the next day the caravan crosses through several encampments of Somali nomads, who are feeding their herds on the meager grazing lands of the desert. Gradually the trail climbs higher; they are now entering the Samadu, the "black country," formed from volcanic rock. Five hours and fifteen miles later the team reaches Arowena in Wardik territory, followed by their arrival the next day in Biokaboka, the halfway point between Zeila and Harar and also the location of some "excellent water." There are numerous wells as well as a wadi in which Rimbaud bathes. They make three-day stopover in this water-rich region before entering the bleak and rocky terrain of the next leg of their journey. There was once a tomb built there for a sheik, a man of god, whose memory is still venerated. From there they can see two peaks in the distance between which, though still invisible, lies Harar. The caravan then

begins a series of painful stages of the journey in that there was no sure
source for replenishing their water supply. The trail climbs to three thousand
feet in altitude. After a three-hour march they reach Ali Bini, at the foot of a
hill where, despite the dryness, a few *gherbes* can be filled with water and afterward they enter onto the plain of Dahelimaleh. They resume their nighttime
marches by starlight. Ten miles later they reach Kotto, the "land covered by
scrub"; a wadi, which is not completely dried up, passes through here and
groundwater favors the growth of vegetation. Large tortoises hide in the tall
green grass. The caravan remains in Kotto for two days before departing for
Wordji. This stage of the journey is so short that the camel drivers joke that
one can speak at one end and be heard on the other, but they know full well it
is the echoes caused by the now more hilly terrain that is the explanation
behind this bizarre phenomenon. The animals labor to ascend the uneven
ground. They finally arrive in Wordji, a pass that sits at 3,300 feet in altitude.
From here the trail snakes across a plateau obstructed by stony terrain; the
vegetation (especially the thorny mimosas) grows thicker. Nearby mountains
emerge. The temperature, stifling until now, becomes almost tolerable. A
new encampment is established in Boussa. But the caravaners warn Rimbaud
that the next leg won't be without danger, as they will have to cross through a
wadi infested with mosquitoes whose sting could be fatal. As a precaution,
some of the men chew asafetida as an anti-toxin. However, they will emerge
from this leg of the journey unscathed. A region of forests, trees, thickets,
and vines opens before them now. The vegetation thins out as they approach
Gueldessa. A wadi descends from the mountainous massif. A barracks of a
Sudanese detachment has been set up there under the administration of the
Egyptian khedivate. The *effendi*, their leader, has a brief conversation with
Rimbaud. He had seen Alfred Bardey's caravan two months earlier. At this
point the caravan has now reached the foot of a volcanic massif. Its passages
are narrow and its slopes quite steep, and the animals often experience difficulty making their way forward. The *gaflah* crosses through the first Galla villages where it causes a sensation. Rimbaud looks at and listens to everything.
Does he find all this cause for wonderment? In any event, he finds himself in
the unknown. He passes by the *guimbes*, the round houses with walls of reed
and dried mud, erected on platforms. Jugs are placed on the summit of their
conical roofs to drive away evil spirits. The villages are surrounded by small

fields of durra, a variety of sorghum, the basic food of the Gallas. A few shepherds are watching over their flocks. Beyond Bellawa, the road narrows and climbs. Even the mules stumble through the rocky passes. Not without difficulty, the caravan makes its way to Egou Pass at 7,000 feet: on one side stretches the vast Somali plain, with its arid yellow lands; on the other are countless peaks, many reaching 9,000 feet in height. The men and beasts of the caravan cross the plateau, then make their way down a gentle decline to a grassy region where herds of zebus are grazing. Their path now often crosses that of the ever armed, proud, and inscrutable Gallas. Footpaths now cut across the trail. After Sbillou and Komboultcha, the caravan reaches a summit. All at once the city appears, encircled by ochre walls with towers. Gardens and coffee plantations can be seen on the outside. After the fatigue of spending twenty days in the saddle, Rimbaud enjoys the short pleasure of having reached the end of his journey. "We will enter splendid cities," he had written in *Une saison en enfer*. Harar was not his Jerusalem, however. He found himself there through a series of circumstances. Harar, Hazar, a dice game invented in Syria by knights crusaders. On a notarized writ attributing ownership of a piece of land bought in his name, isn't he mentioned as "a professor in Hasar?"[25] And his brother Fréderic, who has a vague grasp of the word, will transform it into "Horor,"[26] an astonishing slip of the tongue that speaks volumes about the fright such countries invoked.

The caravan halts outside the walls but Rimbaud enters the Bab el-Ftouh, the "gate of conquest." His arrival had been announced by a messenger. The Egyptian soldiers require him to go through the necessary formalities. He is now entering the most astonishing place of his exile. Projected at his feet is his shadow, the "old serpent,"[27] the only thing to be irreparably faithful to him.

A poetic truce, one will say, and at whatever it costs him. Rimbaud doesn't lay it on thick. He shows no desire to do so when writing to his mother and Isabelle. Literature does not concern him. Besides, literature no longer exists! Let's take a good look at the impressions recorded by the new arrival:

> Harar is a city colonized by the Egyptians and dependent upon their government. The garrison is several thousand men. This is where our agency and warehouses are located. This country's products for trade are coffee,

ivory, and skins, etc. The land is high but not infertile. Its climate is cool and not unhealthy. They import all merchandise from Europe here by camel. Furthermore, this land offers many possibilities. We don't have regular mail service here. We are forced to send our mail through Aden, on rare occasions.[28]

One could not be more precise or more impersonal. Rimbaud does not describe. He furnishes information about an administrative situation and about his work. It is Bardey who saw Harar like a "reddish mass" on the horizon. Under Rimbaud's pen, on the other hand, the place is made humdrum, a pure point (almost geometrical) of transactions and exchanges (army, colonization, commerce, and mail). He thereby proceeds by effacement, by voiding what remains of style in everything he writes: a smoothed-down letter, a model of transparency and quasi-objective dullness.

No doubt he was welcomed on his arrival by Pinchard, the director of the agency. They now advance through the steep, narrow streets of the city.[29] Rocks poke through their surfaces and very few are suitable for vehicles. The houses with their earthen walls have no second story. Their open doors reveal gloomy, smoke-filled interiors. Minarets are predominant in every neighborhood. Several large squares have been contrived in this maze of overpopulated spaces. Rimbaud crosses through the *faras magala*, the horse market, packed with a mixed populace of dark-skinned Hararis, Abyssinians, Gallas, and Somalis. The majority are swaddled in *tobes*, a large piece of cloth, whose different drapings have symbolic meaning. The colors share none of the clarity or violence that we would expect in the East: dirty whites, ochres, a deep blue that in the case of women's clothing has a separate red triangle that starts at the throat and opens outward as it goes down to the middle of their breasts. Rimbaud rubs shoulders with these bodies, these unusual peoples. He appears to them in all his foreignness. Today it is no longer possible, even when coming to places such as this, to understand what he felt and experienced. The era of worldwide communication and circulation of images has forever destroyed the mystery of the faraway. Rimbaud discovered the unknown step by step, another world with different faces, clothing, and customs, almost like the Englishman Burton, the first European to have entered the city, which he did disguised as an Arab traveler in 1854. Sometimes he had close brushes with horror, such as when he brushed past the pale and bloated lepers who were begging in the alleys at every turn, or the sick who were abandoned outdoors and where some were slowly dying. In addition, when he passes by the meticulous piles sold by the squatting peasant women of the neighboring villages, he doesn't recognize these "curious goods": sesame seeds, hot red peppers, green coffee beans that people eat like olives, citron, jujubes, and the almost liquid butter that is blended with foods and which is used to grease hair in order to make those astonishing plaits that decorate their heads like jewelry. There are slender women with smooth-skinned, golden faces; the beauty of the men, the desert runners. Also enveloping all this is a wide array of noises and rumblings: the guttural speech with the accent of Oromo or Amharic, of which he has only a confused impression, whereas at times he can make out bits and pieces of Arabic, the administrative language; the brouhaha of the surging crowd in which the falsetto tones of women's voices can be heard in monotonous chanting or bickering; the hammering of blacksmiths; the barks of the dogs that wander everywhere in search of carcasses; the braying of donkeys; and the crowing of roosters and clucking of hens who are pecking in the dust. However, over all (and tenacious in the memories of all travelers) are the indescribable, suffocating odors of rot, excrement, and sugar, pierced by perfumes that are strong and voluptuous like musk. Harar is a city without water, where women constantly come and go between the wells in the gardens and their smoke-filled homes. The filth is left to pile up and livestock is slaughtered in the middle of the streets. The stench of rot, the rosy sickliness of leprosy. Drawn by this stench, hyenas wander along the ramparts all night and sometimes gain entry where walls have collapsed. Also, every night, once the herds that graze the surrounding area have returned, the five monumental gates are closed. At dawn they are opened, triggering the slow, almost processional movement of the women bearing local fruits, vegetables, and grains, and the young sprouts of *khat*, a hallucinogenic shrub that the residents of Harar chew and rechew to deaden a little the life pain that Rimbaud will never pacify in himself.

Pinchard leads him over a bumpy path to the elevated section of the city where the barracks, the palace of Nadi Pasha, and the grand mosque are located. They arrive in a large square in front of "a large square construction with a terrace" that dominates the neighboring roofs. This is the former residence of Raouf Pasha, who conquered the city in 1875 in the name of Egypt and where the agency's employees are now housed.[30] The back looked out over a spacious interior garden. Rimbaud and Constantine Righas were installed on the second story in rooms supplied with the most rudimentary furniture: *angarebs** "in straps of uncured leather stretched over wooden frames mounted on four legs and covered by a thin cotton mattress." Through the windows that had no glass but were furnished with wooden bars, they had a view over the Medina. Soon, before taking delivery of the caravan cargo that will be carried *intra muros* on the next day, Rimbaud is introduced to the personnel that he will have under his orders: Dimitri, the brother of Constantine Righas, and Sotiro, an enterprising man who is extremely knowledgeable on local customs. Then he strolls through the warehouses where goatskins, leathers, and elephant ivories purchased in the neighboring brush for salt or cotton fabrics are piled; a corner is reserved for gold dust, for musk, and for civet (the *zebad*), which is sold by a specific measurement: the *okiete*. He turns the talers over and over in his fingers, those coins bearing the image of Maria Theresa of Austria that are the most widespread currency here. Greek and Armenian merchants have also established trading posts in the city. Rimbaud will frequent them but without maintaining any relationships closer than what commerce requires.

From the outset the climate seems to suit him; despite the great heat of the afternoon, the nights are cool. The hope for a new life restores the energy he had lost in Aden. The former inventor of language, who described unheard-of lands, becomes the person who desires to wander in virgin lands. In January he forms the intention of journeying into the desert to purchase camels[31] and making a reconnaissance of the territory of native tribes with whom he would like to trade. He quickly plans this transformation into that poet of modern times: the explorer. He even envisions his metamorphosis with a professional consciousness that lends itself to laughter. How does one enter into this career? The answer he gives is formidably simple: by reading a *Manuel théorique et pratique* and skimming the *Guide du voyageur*.[32] Consequently it is these two books that he begs his mother to send him most quickly, as if it were prohibited to discover on his own the hazards of expeditions in

_____
*Camel saddles.

unknown regions. Similar requests would be constant, for want of more obvious testimonies of affection. On January 30, 1881, doesn't his brain, "an ever new vapor" give birth to new schemes, for example that of creating a tremendous scientific bazaar? We can imagine a sign or, better yet, a visiting card sent from port to port: "Monsieur Rimbaud, merchant of precision instruments in general throughout the Orient!"[33] Intellectual bulimia plays these kinds of tricks on him! Thus his realm would be "precision in general"—which conforms well with the absolute belief in progress held by the people of that era. Under the banner of Toussenal, Flammarion, and Monsieur Figuier,[34] that great popularizer published by Hachette and read from Paramaribo to Harar, Rimbaud would like to know "the totality of what is best manufactured in France (or abroad) as concerns mathematical, optical, electrical, meteorological, pneumatical, mechanical, hydraulic, and mineralogical instruments." You would think the list exhausted, but, since no branch of science should be overlooked, since it is the Western world that he wishes to import into Africa, as well, he would like them to add "catalogs from manufacturers of physical toys, pyrotechnics, prestidigitatory toys, mechanical models, and miniaturized constructions." What the hell could he be thinking? To spread these apparati for which sales are unlikely throughout the East? Or else even keep them for his personal use as a veritable magician? Imagine him arriving in the villages and launching great fireworks displays into the heavens. With such he could pass himself off as a magician of high science. But he cannot have held this belief in the future for these "physical toys" for very long, it was a dream that scintillated momentarily in the sky of one of his sleepless nights in Harar.

To tell the truth, his temporary enchantment comes to an end during the following month (February). Without being too specific, he tells his family he has "caught a disease, not very dangerous in itself."[35] Alfred Bardey, who would see him in April, says Rimbaud contracted syphilis[36] and that, concerned about infecting his guests, he took pains not to mix his dishes with theirs or to let them drink from his glass. There is nothing to say that he didn't surrender to the attraction of Harari women, famed for their beauty, and that he soon suffered the worst kind of setback because of it. The verb he uses—"I have caught"—corresponds closely to the customary expressions in use then to refer to venereal diseases. However, this syphilis, even if poorly treated, cannot be blamed for the bone deterioration that would cause his death.

Linked to this secret disease or not, the irresistible temptation to get away then appears under his pen: "I don't plan to remain here long."[37] "I haven't found what I thought I would." He has now made the complete tour of the city, tightly enclosed by its ramparts, and he who had suffered the horrible heat of Aden now observes that he is in a climate that is too cold and possibly unhealthy. As for his life, he judges it as "extremely stupid and extremely annoying, as " silliness and boredom. The worst is that, even a thousand leagues from Europe, he has again found everything he had thought he'd left behind for good. One doesn't change. People don't change; once again he is surrounded by "dogs and bandits." Nevertheless, this malcontent keeps a secret energy within; he is far from having renounced everything and curiosity hasn't stopped sharpening his mind, no matter how much at a loss he is. He continues to pass on his orders for dictionaries; he is perfecting his grasp of Arabic and, recalling the papers left by his father in Charleville, gives Frédéric the responsibility of finding and sending them to him.[38] In this way, laden with resentments, his needy existence flows like a Styx with leaden waters. How far he is from "real life"! Sometimes his boredom becomes intractable and his anger erupts; he takes it out on those around him, just short of coming to blows with the nonchalant, shortsighted natives. He realizes that Harar was just one more illusion. "There are no possibilities here"— the same old insipid song. As a consequence he erects another mirage, a deeply felt living fantasy that he keeps close at hand: "If I leave this region, I will probably go down to Zanzibar."[39] At least if he doesn't go to the large lakes discovered by Burton and Speke in 1858 or even leaving Africa to sail to Panama, the other Suez, where the piercing of the isthmus had just begun. Rimbaud wishes to take himself to those places where science is modifying the earth, where engineers are triumphing. But he always finds himself back in a hole; the variations of Roche are legion, just like the names of Satan. From February to May he confirms his plan to go to Central America: "Write me with news of the work in Panama: as soon as it is opened, I will go."[40] But he knows that he should be wary of his violent need for haste. The boredom of life radiates over all parts of the globe. It is just as well that he content himself with being on the lookout for another thing—the other thing—and to mark time when he is not en route, a suspended time such as precedes an inescapable leap. Perhaps I will next embark on a campaign in the country,"[41] he thinks, not without reason. Hardly moved in, halfway settled, he has a true Gypsy-like need to leave the place. And to tell the truth, the place that tempts him doesn't coincide with any spot that can be located on a map. Under his gaze, all fixed locations are commanded to vanish completely. The profound appeal comes from farther away. He wonderfully makes note of it in a letter: "to go traffic in the unknown"; assuredly a recollection of Baudelaire: "To the depths of the Unknown to find the *new*." He once was well acquainted with this verse that is the closing line to "Voyage." But is it the new so much that he desires to discover? He plans on going over there to "traffic." One has to live well. And this time the unknown isn't a go without money and commerce. Rimbaud is a "capitalist." He will say so to his family with pride. This is a source of satisfaction to his mother, who sees him as an ambitious and responsible son who is now making up for his youthful misconduct.

Yet Harar was an extremely active city, animated by the constant movement of the caravans. During the second half of April, Alfred Bardey returned from Europe, and with Pierre Mazeran, brother of one of the associates in the agency, headed toward the city followed by a new *gaflah* they had chartered. They were also accompanied by the members of a French Catholic mission: five Franciscan priests headed by Monsignor Taurin-Cahagne, named as the vicar apostolic of the Galla country. Rimbaud came to Gueldessa to meet them and shared their journey back to Harar, where Bardey and Mazeran settled themselves on the first floor of the Raouf Pasha house, which they were happy to find waiting for them. Several days later, the priests, who had remained in Gueldessa to rest, in turn reached the city of five gates. While waiting to find a place to live, they took up residence in the factory. Rimbaud would subsequently maintain a friendly and discreet relationship with them. He would show them all proper esteem, but he won't attend the services they courageously perform in this Muslim country in which there are Christian Abyssinians, though of Coptic allegiance.

The arrival of the French pulls him out of his solitude for a while (in fact, Pinchard, stricken with malaria, had gone down to the coast, leaving him alone with three employees to oversee the trading post). With Bardey and Mazeran, the evenings were now spent in long discussions enlivened by anecdotes. Bardey revealed the importance of the French Geographical Society, of which he had been a member since December, to Rimbaud. There was great interest then in the little-known ethnic populations of Abyssinia. A promising future was awaiting prospective explorers. However, at the beginning of May Rimbaud, who had a poor tolerance for the climate, which was extremely humid this time of year, had to take to his bed for a fortnight. Once recovered, and wishing to put himself to the test and toughen up his treacherous body, he made plans to go to Bubassa, thirty miles to the south. Cattle and goat skins were available there for sale in quantity. With Bardey's assent, although Bardey was reluctant to endorse the idea that someone take such risks for such common merchandise, Rimbaud set off on his journey. At the time of departure, "he wrapped his head with a towel for a turban and draped a red blanket over his usual clothing." Everyone laughed, he the loudest, but he thinks this would help him be mistaken for a Muslim, a "rich Mohammedan merchant."[43] Gestures, facial expressions—thanks to Bardey the storyteller, Rimbaud's appearance, which we all too often must leave to our imagination, comes alive and becomes familiar—in the time it takes for him to disappear over the horizon, followed by some beasts of burden and camel drivers. His expedition will last about two weeks, at the end of which he returns exhausted but not without having created two markets out in the middle of the bush. In turn, Bardey and Sotiro will reach Bubassa while he remains lying on the second story of the vast edifice, vainly seeking some rest in that noisy environment.

Other expeditions would follow: a campaign for ivory that entails a six-week journey in totally unexplored country. But this bit of news doesn't bring him anything; this activity resembles a bad fever. For the *daromphe*, completely occupied with her little jobs at the farm in Roche, he reels off the commentary of his life, the same one he would repeat over the years, with the same words obstinately hollowing out the infinite nature of time: "Alas! me, I don't expect much out of life; and if I live, I am used to living with fatigue, but if I'm forced to wear myself out as I do at present, living on nothing but griefs as vehement as they are absurd in these atrocious climates, I fear my life will be shortened."[44] The phrase has an echo, and the expression "to feed on griefs" gives to Rimbaud's real thirst and hungers their just spiritual extension. The mother reading these lines will see not the blue gaze "that lies," but a burden of sobs that refuse to pour out. These griefs of Rimbaud, an exhausting psychological duration beneath the apparent and proud toughness of the character he plays, really do exist. "Finally, may we enjoy a couple of years of real rest in this life; and happily this life is the only one, and that is obvious, since one cannot imagine another life more boring than this one!" This is the definition of hell experienced: a boredom which could be that of eternity (and not uniformity). Real life is no longer desirable, it figures as a nauseating delusion. Christianity announced it but only for the beyond. Once Rimbaud had wished it for this world, but what he covets now is quite simply rest, which he guesses will be only what death provides: the *requiem*. Life merges into a purposeless activity, a slavery, a duty that is imposed upon one to the last and has no reason to be heeded. As for his mania for moving, it is simply changing location for the sake of changing location, a flight forward to flee himself, while boredom lies in wait everywhere, the partner of nothingness.

Peut-être un Soir m'attend
Dans quelque vieille ville
Où je boirai tranquille.[45]

Perhaps an evening awaits me
In some old town
In which I will drink peacefully.[45]

What does he drink? Abyssinian tea mixed with liquid butter, coffee—and overall an inexhaustible disgust, in little mouthfuls. What does he discover? Absurdity. The work I do is absurd and exhausting, and the conditions of life as well. are generally absurd"[46] "The world is full of nastiness."[47]

The only tangible result of so many "extraordinary exhaustions:" is money. As he is housed and fed by the company he puts aside some fairly considerable sums, from which he despairs he may realize nothing, so he finally decides to have them forwarded to his mother by the Maison Bardey in Lyon so that she can invest them profitably. Furthermore, he had long thought that his first savings had gone astray[48] or that they had been stolen, and without taking much time to reflect on the matter, will accuse his employers until the day the agreed-upon sum arrives, minus, it is true, several hundred francs deducted by the exchange. Madame Rimbaud, a sensible peasant woman, will find no better solution than to buy land with this money, which first angers the wanderer whom no land has been able to hold. He soon changes his mind, though, and finds this investment as worthy as any other. His indestructible desire to leave thwarted, he retreats into excessive resignation: "If you have need, take what is mine," he tells his mother and Isabelle. As for me, I have no one to think of but myself, who require nothing."[49]

The year 1881 was eaten away by concerns he deemed useless, and countless dangers; trade did not meet his expectations and people were exploiting and taking advantage of him. Even the letters from Roche only brought worries. He was even briefly considered a deserter in France because he still hadn't fulfilled his periods of military instruction and had never furnished any papers that would allow him an exemption.[50] This illegal situation would preoccupy him for months and years and his mother would never lift a finger to spare him this idle worry. He was definitely a crushing burden upon himself because he always felt he was inhabited by the same unspent force that neither poetry nor activity had ever succeeded in exhausting. At the beginning of September, in disgust and desperation, he handed in his resignation,[51] despite the protestations of Alfred Bardey, who left Harar to sail for Europe the following month. On December 6, his brother Pierre arrived to replace him as the head of the factory.[52] At the end of the year Rimbaud leaves again for Aden,[53] where he would have to assist Dubar again in order to honor the terms of his contract. As he leaves Harar through the Bab el-Ftouh gate he thinks that it is "very unlikely that he'll ever return here." Definitely a case of forecasting the future badly.

THE "MIND-NUMBING TASKS"

HAVING HANDED IN HIS RESIGNATION, RIMBAUD CONTINUES TO LIVE IN Aden in hope. He is still with the Bardey Agency, waiting out the rest of his contract. This is the timeframe in which he holds another project close to his heart for several months. He would actually like "to create a work for the Geographical Society with maps and engravings on Harar and the Galla country." His discussions with Bardey have borne their fruits and his frequentation of the two Italian explorers Count Antonelli and Captain Cecchi in December, while still in Harar, could not help but stimulate schemes of this kind. His plan does not lack ambition, especially if we recall he was only an amateur. But Rimbaud rarely doubts himself when launching into a new venture. Confident in his intelligence and savoir-faire, and armed with the information of some instructive books for which he will soon put in an order, he believes he can assume this new avatar of his personality that is always in a state of becoming: the geographical explorer. At once he requires some impressive paraphernalia, which he charges his mother to procure for him— or rather the stouthearted Delahaye, who has just sent Madame Rimbaud a letter for her son. Seizing this opportunity, Rimbaud responds: "I received your news with pleasure. Without further preliminaries, I am going to explain to you [. . .]"[55] and his missive pours forth a long list of objects to buy: a traveling theodolite, a sextant, a compass, an aneroid barometer, a surveyor's measuring tape, a mathematics case, and so forth, all in the avowed design of adding a new tome to his complete works, that were actually quite limited then, as they included only the single booklet of *Une saison en enfer*. The end of the letter hardly shows any consideration of his correspondent, his old friend from Charleville now living in Paris. In extremely terse fashion, Rimbaud limits himself to making a single promise: "Details by the next post, which leaves in three days. Meanwhile, hurry. Cordial greetings." In fact, alarmed by the order this letter contained, Madame Rimbaud would neglect to forward it. Rimbaud definitely placed too much confidence in her. For the moment at least, he continues to dream of his book: he will no longer talk of chimeras and bizarre poetic illusions, but of reality, what little of it that can be grasped or—what matters more to him now—measured. The "objective" writing of science. Thus he could inform his contemporaries about the unknown without dragging them into dangerous phantasmagoria. As proof he will take photos of these strange lands. (He and Pinchard had already thought to have a camera brought to Harar in January 1881.)

Over the following months, however, he gives proof of a great uncertainty, and though he continues to work at the agency, he nonetheless increasingly plans to leave. Sometimes he muses on returning to Africa to organize elephant hunts.[56] Sometimes he envisions going down as far as Zanzibar— a tenacious whim.[57] His boss, Dubar, gives him a letter of recommendation for Monsieur Ledoulx, the French consul for that island.[58] He will remain attached to this scheme for two months.[59] Then, finally, having made up with the Bardeys, he signs a new contract with them, which does not prevent him from complaining and hurling from the depths of his daily hell some imprecations tinged with black humor: "I am still employed at the same dump and I am wearing myself out like an ass in a country for which I've an invincible horror. [. . .] I hope this existence comes to an end before I have the time to become a complete idiot."[60] In his fashion, he too feels the wing of imbecility grazing him.[61] But this isn't the abrupt physiological sensation that Baudelaire experienced. On the contrary, he has the impression that his mind is dwindling away, his intelligence is coming undone, and his thoughts are disintegrating.

Thus he sinks into the point of no return at a very slow pace. With lucidity and his most desperate smile, he says: "I am spending a lot of money in Aden and this gives me the advantage of tiring myself out much more here than elsewhere." Strange benefit, that life may exhaust itself more quickly! Exhaustion and work are breaking this still young man, placed in a furnace or lazeret of boredom, in which he refines a new language beyond all muteness and reserve. "If I complain, it's just a way of singing."[62] He had once been a rebel intoning the "Chant de guerre parisien" or making fun of elegiac sufferings. He now feels he cannot escape complaining—vehement protests without a prayer of being understood. Thus a "way of singing," just as he had plucked his resentments with bizarre old hackneyed melodies in 1872.

The Bardeys, who appreciate this withdrawn, harsh, but enterprising man, ultimately convince him to return to Harar. He knows the place and its European and native residents well; he has already "trafficked" there. Furthermore, they promise him a more important and better-paying position, that of manager. During the summer of 1882 he hopes to depart and repeats his scheme to create some erudite works; in order to do so it is necessary that someone send him a precise map of the regions from France, that of the Peternam Geographical Institute.

But Dubar, who manages the agency in Aden, having serious health problems, plans to leave in six months. Rimbaud then begins to hope that he may take his place, in which case, benefiting from a substantial increase in his salary, he would keep that position for five or six years, the time necessary to amass sufficient savings to allow him to later live in France off his private means—verification of the prophetic phrase he had inscribed in the "Narrative" at ten years of age: "I will be a stockholder." However, he wasn't a man to delude himself with illusions. "Finally we will see where these swings will land me,"[63] he notes talking to himself. "O swing! O lilies! Silver enemas!" he exclaimed in the *Album zutique* to mock the worthy Armand Silvestre and his profusion of ornamental flowers.

Several weeks later he has again changed his way of thinking: "I plan to part [yes we know this formula, this open-sesame for the ailing imagination of the sedentary merchant stuck in the black soil of Aden] at the end of the year for the African continent, no longer for Harar, but for Shoa (Abyssinia[64])." Here is finally a mention of this Abyssinia where he didn't live for as long as one would like to believe. Why Shoa on this day of September 28, 1882? No doubt because of the information he has obtained about these regions. Perhaps he is already scheming to sell arms as certain Europeans were doing with the king of that country, Menelik. Pierre Labatut had just proposed an expedition of this nature to Bardey, and we have to believe that Rimbaud would have been informed about it.[65]

However, he claims it is for a more "poetic" reason (if one could call it that). Indeed, while waiting to receive the famous camera[66] that Monsieur Dubar, who had left Aden and returned to Lyon, is going to obtain for him, he believes that it will be enough to transport such a fantastic instrument into this Shoa at the ends of the earth to make a small fortune. Photography being unknown there, he imagines the success this process of "white" magic will bring him among the natives. A new version of Rimbaud as an illusionist with—on his part—a good dose of naïveté. As for the functioning of the apparatus and the development of the photos, he has no doubt that he will be able to handle it. Then success would crown his undertaking, and everyone— as Baudelaire said—would dash "like a single Narcissus to contemplate his trivial image upon the metal."[67] However, Rimbaud would not simply be (as he wrote in "Ce qu'on dit au Poète à propos de fleurs") a "very peaceful pho- tographer,"[68] he would offer remote populations the portrayal of their faces.

In November a letter from Dubar informs him that all his photographic equipment has been purchased.[69] The cost was considerable, some eighteen hundred francs, and he couldn't conceal such an expenditure from his mother because she settled the bills for all his purchases from the savings that he regu- larly sent her. A reprimand wasn't late in coming from the woman who viewed all of this as some puerile fantasy. Arthur going so far away to do just what their neighbor, old Jacoby on rue Forest did, and to photograph Negroes! We don't know what tone these letters were written in, but we can easily imagine the remonstrations they contained. For this thrifty peasant woman, who trusted only revenues earned from the land, Rimbaud was being robbed and was the victim of a shameless fraud. In his reply he is set upon proving to her that all his expenditures aren't pointless:[70] "Instead of getting upset with me, you should be sharing my happiness. I know the worth of money and if I risk something it's advisedly so." He refers to his Cuif ancestors, farmers for whom a sou was a sou. But he no doubt says more than he should seeking to please his irascible *mother* at any price. How could she have taken any pleasure in his latest folly? Then, stripping away all pride, he allows the grief of his isolation to be heard. He strips himself bare in his astounding exile.

> What is especially saddening is that you end your letter declaring that you won't concern yourself with my affairs anymore. This is no way to help a man a thousand leagues from home, traveling among savage peoples and having not a single correspondent in his own country. I hope you will soften this hardly charitable intention. If I can't turn to my family for my commissions, who the devil can I turn to?

One would think it was a simple matter of money to invest or spend. But it does show the strength of a bond he did not wish undone and which continued to exist in the most intolerable tension and torsion.

The famous apparatus and its escort of cards, glass, basins, flasks, and various ingredients will follow a somewhat fantastic path and it will be necessary for Rimbaud to arm himself with patience to await the day (surprise) of its arrival. The baggage will finally arrive around March 1883, after an unforeseen detour by way of Mauritius; everything, well packed, reaches him in perfect condition.[71] He seems to have been waiting for just this moment to leave.

After much beating around the bush and, in fact, for the lack of any better possibilities, Rimbaud resigns himself to remaining attached to the Maison Bardey. He has been given to understand that he could become manager of the factory in Harar and his departure was set for the month of March 1883.[72] As Alfred Bardey is ill and forced to leave Aden, his brother is coming to replace him. In turn, Rimbaud will be Pierre's successor in Harar. During this time he is still fondly attached to his book project for the Geographical Society, in that he is requesting treatises on topography ("and not photography,"[73] he specifies) and geodesy, for he intends to make surveys; in addition, he needs a graphometer and a treatise on practical astronomy.[74] Furthermore he plans, once he has become somewhat conversant with the specific techniques, to make "reproductions of these unknown countries and the unusual types inside them," in order to "sell them in France."[75] But other orders he puts in lead us to believe that his ingenious and versatile mind has formed quite different designs. This is why we think he most certainly had the idea of railway constructions, as he wants someone to obtain for him[76] Couche's *Traité complet des chemins de fer*, Salin's *Manuel pratique des poseurs de voies de chemin de fer*, and Debauve's *Tunnels et souterrains*, a title that falsely suggests a gothic novel! In 1887 he would mention possible "railways" from Harar to the sea. Others would think along these lines: Menelik's councilor Alfred Ilg, for example, who will soon make his appearance in these pages. We will have to wait until 1917 for the inauguration of the Franco-Ethiopian railway linking Djibouti to Addis Ababa that, moreover, bypasses Harar using the easier route through Diredawa.

At the beginning of 1883, Rimbaud the Adenian, more and more irritated by the nonchalance of the native personnel, had a serious altercation with a shop clerk, Ali Chemmak. Rimbaud slapped the latter for refusing to obey him—a gesture he will call a *"soufflet"*[77] in his correspondence (the word is very seventeenth century) and he mitigates it still further by declaring that it was done without violence. But Chemmak did not take it that way at all. After ripping Rimbaud's clothes and striking him in the face, he lodged a complaint with the municipal police while his friends threatened to kill his aggressor. Worried, Rimbaud alerted the French consul, Monsieur de Gaspary, of the situation. As for Bardey, courageously taking his side, he fired Chemmak, who was one of the oldest employees of their house. It was time Rimbaud left, as he now had to fear an act of deadly vengeance that the authorities would certainly be powerless to prevent.

He sets sail for Zeila on March 22, 1883, with his chest of scientific books and photographic baggage. His contract runs through December 1885. For the first time he is thinking more concretely of the future, perhaps because of the remarks made by his mother in her recent letters. It is now almost three years since he left and, because of the difficulties he has encountered, she has tried to persuade him to return to France for better or for worse. But as early as November 1882 he had responded: "As for returning to France, what would I look for there at present?"[78] To this contingency he was inclined to oppose the all-powerful freedom that ceaselessly motivated his actions (and paradoxically reduced him to slavery). The desire to return is foreign to him, the sole tie connecting him to the times and to life—at least he likes to repeat this in his correspondence—consists precisely of these letters he sends his family, however little the love he shows them therein. The hole of Roche aspirates his distant life. Back there is where the principal witnesses to his incomprehensible odyssey are to be found, those who can size him up and figure him out, and whom he keeps informed no matter what. They constitute his eyes and ears across the sea, permit him to live, attest to his presence, and give him consistency. Also Rimbaud the adventurer is entertaining the hope (insane on the surface) of marriage. A new and fairly unusual preoccupation that, appearing under his pen, marks this year of 1883[79] and one he will not abandon. Did this start as just an accommodating reply to his mother, who was worried about him, or to encourage Isabelle, who had recently received a marriage proposal which she rejected? Still this objective was a pretense he adopted for a time. For him it is not a matter of amassing money so much as starting a family. Ought we be deceived by this Rimbaud? To the future "families, I hate you" of Gide, he appears to oppose a conventional reply in advance that is in absolute contradiction to his vagabond instinct and erratic tendencies.

Arriving in Harar after the long caravan trip through the now-familiar hostile regions, he tried as much as possible to get off on the right foot and temper his natural misanthropy. Business was doing well, for what it was worth, and the climate suited him. And the camera was causing a sensation. At least this is what he claims: "Everyone wants to be photographed here; they even offer a guinea per photograph."[80] We can imagine him for a brief moment on the main square with his paraphernalia, and the gawkers clustering around him as if around a montebank. The reality was no doubt less pleasant. The apprentice photographer had to learn everything by himself and the photographic chemicals that had deteriorated in the heat made printing on paper an even more delicate procedure. However, by way of proof and as a souvenir, he added three cloudy and clumsy photos of himself to his letter of May 6, 1883.[81] "All this has turned white because of the dirty water I used to wash them."

We can only regret the out-of-focus appearance of these documents. Though we look at them with a close attention that we would exchange for clairvoyance if we could, they hide away in their details. Rimbaud appears as if through a fogged window that nothing can render transparent. The features of his distant face have lost all their roundness, his cheeks are emaciated. We can barely make out the fine mustache he has allowed to sprout since 1875. His severely cut hair leaves his temples clear. His eyes are staring at us and he doesn't smile. In each one he assumes a pose. In one of the photos he is clad in a black (or dark-colored) jacket and white pants. In the other two he is wearing the cotton clothes that constitutes the usual dress for Europeans in the hot countries and which Claudel, overdoing it, would see as similar to the uniforms of convicts.[82] The photo in which he is wearing the black jacket is more solemn. With one hand he is holding the post of a fence, and with the other he is holding the right lapel of his jacket. Behind him, in the distance, a mountain can be made out. He will explicitly state that he is "on the balcony of the house" (this is how he designates the Bardey establishment, the former dwelling of Raouf Pasha). Two self-portraits show him profiled against a background of plants, banana or coffee trees such as are grown in Harari plantations. It would be too much to say we are gripped by a strong emotion when looking at these images. They tell us nothing, despite their evidence. Rather, they bear before our eyes the presence of a secret, and also throw back in our faces the almost scandalized questions: Why are you trying to see me? What do you still want from me?

Three other photos similarly due to Rimbaud have come down to us: one that is much sharper shows his employee Sotiro coiffed in an Egyptian fez in a grove of banana trees, wearing a finicky expression, with one hand on the muzzle of his rifle, whose stock is resting on the ground; the superb photo taken of a coffee merchant: the man is squatting in an airy room supported by fat Doric-style pillars. On the right, hanging from the ceiling by long ropes, are the large plates of a scale. Some utensils are in front of the merchant: the measures for selling his merchandise. The contrast between the light and shadow offers the truth of an instant, and other realities become visible, as if we were entering the room ourselves—such as the little padlock that closes the door in the background. A final photo shows an almost spectral view of the market in the main square in which a dense crowd can be seen along with the stores, the earthen homes, and the tall minaret that dominates the city.

Full of goodwill but with little confidence in the future, Rimbaud enters into a new contract with the "dump" (this is how he refers to the agency). He signs on for three years this time, until May 1886.[83] Nothing is certain, though. But his deep-seated sense of revolt has calmed. To restore serenity to his ailing mind he now repeats the precepts of the Koran: "Like the Muslims, I know that what will be will be, and that's all." *Mektoub*, it is written!

However, he advises Isabelle to marry. "Solitude is an evil thing here below."[84] So, too, thought Jehovah, the God of Genesis, when he spied Adam alone in the terrestrial paradise: "It is not good for man to be alone."[85] Rimbaud is nothing less than the person who has provided us with the lesson about the greatest kind of solitude. In the evening, after he has finished his tasks, when he has read "all his [technical] books," when he has taken leave of the vaguely friendly wholesale merchants who are interested only in the pelt and ivory trade, he finds his thoughts turning back to his family, to the "house," as he puts it. "I am always happy to contemplate the picture of your pastoral work."[86] The label is well chosen; it conjures up an ancient world of Arcadian tranquillity, a primal vision in which a perfect balance is established between work and rest. It is quite permissible for him to dream, and at times it isn't of traveling but of quite simply a life that hasn't been lost and would finally be finding its reason to exist:

> As for myself, I regret being unmarried and not having a family. But, at present, I am condemned to roam, associated with a distant business, and every day I lose my taste for the climate and way of life, and even the language of Europe. Alas, what good are these comings and goings, these exhaustions and these adventures among foreign races, and the languages with which we fill our memories, and the endless discomforts, if I couldn't one day, after several years, settle down in a spot that pleases me and start a family and have at least one son whom I will spend the rest of my life raising in accordance with my ideas, embellishing and arming him with the most complete education that can be found at that time, and whom I will see become a renowned engineer, a man made rich and powerful by science?

When his bitterness grows too strong, Rimbaud forgets he should be writing in a dry, soulless style; he unintentionally turns back into the troubled thinker of *Une saison en enfer*. With a few words, the news he provides is transformed into a quest for self; current events take on an undreamed-of dimension. A wandering Jew, he sees a condemnation within the profound impulse that pulls him along; he pushes past the point of no return on an infinite itinerary that he visualizes as a "distant business." Certainly, the Bardey Agency itself was also, strictly speaking, that "distant business." But what he really intended by that was his personal itinerary marked by an unknown expiration date. What kind of bizarre life edifice did he build this way? What was the real invisible building site in which he figured as the "predestined" foreman? His own legend on the martyr's rack? In the Harar evenings with hyenas howling at the walls and the smell of putrefaction simmering, he reassess his journey thus far, and it forms a strange kind of negative whole. Yes, he is struck by his own foreignness as he is by that of his surroundings. Life, "a tale told by an idiot," said Shakespeare. Thus idiocy and absurdity. And the idea that such a mess isn't possible, causes him to perceive another version of himself, in which he perhaps doesn't believe, but can momentarily imagine and which numbers among his secret tawdry rags: the father of a family (better than his own), having finished all his journeys, outdistanced his shames, and who "returned from the hot countries," wants nothing more than a son destined to succeed where he, Rimbaud, has failed, a son who will be the engineer that he could not become despite short, unformed attempts such as his scheme to prepare for a *baccalauréat* in science, and the technical manuals he read frenziedly. A dissatisfied autodidact, he only supervised a few work projects in Cyprus, sent his men packing, slaved in a quarry, and built a house in the country. In several sentences and a mirage, he now expresses his ideal, a narcissistic projection in which the former hooligan refines himself into a hero of modern times: a man made rich and powerful through science," one of those insistent, providential figures who are the bearers of vast learning, active, living encyclopedias, who are experts in the new secrets of the world, no longer the impalpable alchemy of the word, but profound chemistry that alters matter and mechanical, electrical, and magnetic forces. "The world marches on! Why shouldn't it turn back?"[87] Once the shop is closed, he dreams of large and unrealizable future projects in a darkened room still reached by strong odors, shouts, the uproar of the crowd, and the "din of the neighborhood."

He puts his life in order for several months in Harar. His situation is better than before, even if the political situation is worsening. He dreams about concluding his business deals successfully. It is enough for time to pass and perhaps he will attain the moment when his dream becomes a reality. He has again renewed ties with the cosmopolitan tradesmen who were the neighbors of his trading post during his first sojourn; his subordinates, the Righas brothers and Sotiro the Greek, who is highly knowledgeable of native ways; and Ahmed Wadi, the colonel of the garrison, who understands French; not to mention the Franciscans of the mission directed by the excellent Monsignor Taurin, whom he sometimes honors with brief visits.

Rimbaud enjoys photographing all his close acquaintances. With satisfaction he declares to his mother: "I will soon send you some well-executed things."[88] He had also managed to have a certain number of other photos sent via Aden to Alfred Bardey, who was back in France taking the waters at Vichy. Bardey, with whom he had settled his differences a long time before, thanks him for these photos but not without pointing out some of their technical imperfections. In addition, he would like to send him a gift, but he knows Rimbaud's character quite well: "You are a little bizarre,"[89] he admits quite straightforwardly. Perhaps he had already learned in France something about his employee's literary past. The two men, notwithstanding, had not only discussed trade in Aden and Harar. Books had also demanded their attention. Not *Une saison en enfer* (we very much doubt it), but a curious narrative about an Abyssinian campaign, written by a certain Ahmed Guirane.[90] Rimbaud, Monsignor Taurin, and Bardey had rediscovered this old book of great historical interest. They had examined it, read what they could decipher of it, and now Bardey had the intention of having it translated. Rimbaud had not forgotten this precious text; soon he will announce to his correspondent the existence of a second volume that is "much more interesting than the first geographically."[91] With such details, an unexpected light is cast on the people who surrounded him and whom he could treat as "asses" and "boors" as easily as he could esteem for being extremely well read.

However, most of his time was spent involved with commercial operations. The season, alas!, is not too good. There is no coffee, and the price for cowhides is prohibitive. Fortunately goatskin stocks are still piled in the warehouses and hopes are high for a profitable elephant hunt, though they are short on men and rifles. Out of a sense of adventure and no doubt in answer to Pierre Bardey's suggestions, Rimbaud mounts some short expeditions, like the one that took him earlier to Bubassa. He explores the trading regions. His caravans carry all kinds of cotton fabrics to the Galla villages (often spun and imprinted in Marseilles with native tastes in mind); in exchange he receives pelts or sponsors wild-animal hunts from which he would obtain the pelts of leopards, lions, and cheetahs. Other Europeans, more ambitious and propelled by the desire to discover new lands and make the presumptuous claim of being first to do so, had much less success than he did. One such example was Pietro Sacconi of an Italian agency in Harar, who dressed in European-style clothing, openly ate ham (the meat of pigs is expressly forbidden by Islamic beliefs), and "had his little drinks"—a novice explorer in short. He was massacred along with his expedition before reaching the Wabi, which he planned to take credit for discovering.[92] As for Rimbaud, he had long since adopted native customs. He spoke their language, dressed as a Muslim when he traveled in the surrounding lands, thereby following the example of his employee Sotiro, who had not hesitated to take an Arabic name and to assimilate native practices, to the extent of being considered a *wodad*, one of those men in every tribe who improvises poems, knows how to write, and interprets the Koran.

Sotiro undertook a trade-motivated foray into the southeast part of the country, the unexplored regions of the Ogaden. On his return at the end of August 1883, Rimbaud had him write down a long report on this expedition, to which he added some corrections when he had it transcribed in proper French. Recognizing the great significance of this document, Bardey sent it on to the Geographical Society when he received it in France. They would publish it in the account of their February 1, 1884, meeting.[93] It was obviously with the idea that it would be read by this eminent assembly that this informative, concise text had been written. The predominant "we" that also responds to the impartiality required in the scientific style of writing only better conceals the principal witness, to wit Sotiro, for there is nothing that establishes with any certainty that Rimbaud took part in this expedition, even if he did write: "we have returned," "we have seen," etc. In fact his duties as agency manager prevented him from leaving the city. The main strength of certain descriptions is the sober precision with which they are written:

"The Ogadens, at least those we have seen, are tall, and more generally red than black; they keep their heads bare and their hair short; are clad in fairly clean robes; carry a *sigada* over their shoulder, a saber and a washing gourd on their hips, a cane and a large and small spear in their hands; and walk wearing sandals." However, there is nothing there that contrasts sharply with the normal tone taken by the popularizers of the time. This report, so valuable for its ethnographic observations, ends, though, in its original version, with an extremely prosaic conclusion. The exploring note coincides with a market survey: "Indeed this is our goal. One of us, or some energetic native acting for us, could gather a ton of ivory in several weeks that could be exported directly through Berbera by franchise."[94]

Constantly commandeered by the preparation of new expeditions, Rimbaud sought to establish links with tribes that still had little contact with whites. He also sent caravans on a regular basis to the port of Zeila loaded with goods for Aden: five thousand goatskins and cowhides. These materials were certainly not rare but they assured the continuance of trade at a sufficient pace.

However the political situation was becoming of greater concern. In January, Rimbaud begins speaking of "war troubles"[95] that have even been felt in Harar. Since 1882 and the bombardment of Alexandria by the British to punish Araby Pasha's military revolt, England had occupied Egypt, whose army was now under its command. The government of Harar had to suffer the consequences, as the English were more and more prone to taking upon themselves the right to intervene in all states dependent upon the Khedivate. Furthermore, in the Sudan, administered by these same English in the name of Egypt transformed into a protectorate, a visionary leader, Mohammed Ahmed Abdallah, proclaiming himself Mahdi, that is to say the envoy of Mohammed, had launched a holy war, the revolt of the Dervishes. This affected all the neighboring countries, and Emperor John (Yohannes), who ruled over Tigray, in northern Abyssinia, was striving to protect his threatened borders. Although Harar, as an independent province, had been spared until then, these multiple military confrontations had repercussions on the local administration. Soon the Egyptians, who had already been forced to abandon the ports of Berbera and Zeila, were going to leave the city, and the English would install a governor of their choice. All at once, the Maison Bardey, which had just established trading posts in Algeria, Greece, and the Indies at great expense, deemed it wise to momentarily close those it had put together in East Africa. Rimbaud, on the scene, could only concur with the rightness of such a decision. He himself saw how alarming the situation was becoming, since the new emir, Abdellahi, was exhibiting signs of an intolerable xenophobia.

At the end of March he regretfully organizes a final caravan with Sotiro to take the road down to Zeila, then with Charles Cotton, the Bardey agent for this area, catches the boat to Aden. When the black rock that dominates the city appears,[96] he can't help but reflect on the fateful coincidence taking him to the worst possible outcome, the frightful hole that won't even swallow him as Etna did Empedocles, but imprison him forever. He knows the Bardeys will be forced to lay him off. He does receive a certificate full of high praise from them, commending his good and loyal service; his needs will be taken care of until July.[97]

The only favorable event in this whole series of annoyances is a letter from the Geographical Society[97bis] asking him to send them a photo of himself and some personal information, as they would like to gather together in a volume "portraits of the people who have made a name for themselves in the geographical sciences and travel." The letter was flattering (thus they had remembered his "Report on the Ogaden") and honored him with an unexpected celebrity. "Oh! science [. . .] Geography, cosmography, mechanics, chemistry!" These words from *Une saison en enfer* had carried him much further than he would have believed possible; but what irony could be read in them now if he conjured up his past as a poet and his momentary renown in an art he once had ambitions of conquering! He would henceforth no longer be an explorer of elsewhere except in random walks confined to the streets of Aden and its nearby sun-scorched surroundings. Less than forty years later, Paul Nizan, when visiting these regions, would say about this taste for nothingness: "In the life of men reduced to its state of uttermost purity, in other words the economic state, one never runs the risk of being fooled by the deforming mirrors that reflect existence in Europe: art, philosophy, and politics are absent for want of employment, and there is no correction to be made. We can see the foundations of Western life; people are stripped bare as if they were anatomical models.[97ter]

The days wear away in waiting. Perhaps Alfred Bardey, who has gone to Marseilles seeking funds, will succeed? In this case, Rimbaud would resume his work for the agency. For the time being he is living in Aden-Camp, in the former company building; life is expensive but he has considerable savings, 12,000 or 13,000 francs, which he cannot invest anywhere. His "intolerable" existence once again appears to him as a condemnation and a punishment: "absurd climates," "insane conditions." And all this useless money he carries around with him like a wound! "My life here is thus a real nightmare."[98] Aden was the place where Rimbaud reflected most obstinately on his life. It was no longer himself he looked at but the indecipherable drifting that carries him along: "Personally, I have no idea where I will find myself dragged to next [his words are hesitant and stumbling. Does he act? Is he acted?] and by what roads, and to where, and for what reason, and by what means!"[99] In the fever of uncertainty, the questions come out in bursts. So he constructs some small dreams that are within his reach: he will return to Harar to set up a small business; buy some gardens and set up some plantations. Rimbaud corrects his rough drafts in a frenzy. This is how, in a life that is always being propelled forward, he is always going back over his footsteps and imagining a more positive outcome. But each time it is necessary to resume his adventure at another point.

His idle state leads him to brood over old themes of desperation. What he writes to his family is a perpetual examination of conscience: "It is obvious that I haven't come here to find happiness."[100] Again one of those phrases that can be claimed to translate the meaning of a destiny. Some have asked if his running all over the world was not a stubborn search for happiness. But where could this illusory felicity be concealing itself? Behind him, no doubt. Indefinitely. Before "black gravel" fills up the sky forever. And his future is becoming unavoidably obvious. He sees it picking up speed. Despite his anchorage in Aden and his vegetation in its torrid weather, he sees his life on a precipitous course toward old age and death: "I will be thirty-two or thirty-three by those dates. I am starting to grow old."[101] Yet this is a young man writing this. But his capacity to resist and the powers of illusion were wearing away within him. Then, out of lassitude, he conjures up, as he did a year before, a semblance of conjugal happiness; striking a peasant note, he dreams of "getting wed in the country," without believing for a minute that a young and pretty woman would be able to love him: "Only widows would still have me!" as much to say someone like his mother, who, since her husband abandoned her, prematurely (and obstinately) signed her name as "Widow Rimbaud." To top it off, his wrangles with the military authorities have returned to flood his memory. He still doesn't know if his situation is in order, he restricts himself to conjectures. The future opens before him like a black corridor! "But who knows what tomorrow will bring, and what will follow in its wake!" Rimbaud starts singing the litanies of a gloomy eternity.

At that moment, Bardey returned from Marseilles with enough money to reestablish the Aden agency. Rimbaud is hired for six months, until December 31, 1884.[102] Alarmed by his sadness, his mother proposed that he return to France, where she would provide him a place to stay; he would soon find a job. At least this is what she thought. But temporarily cheered by the new situation, he prefers to remain in order to "amass a few sous"[103] (these are his words). It is only too obvious that he will never have enough of his hell and that his contract with the Bardey brothers is the equivalent of a personal pact concluded with his own destruction. Business in Aden resumes, without giving him any reason to hope for a brilliant future, however. Aging frightens Rimbaud and adds a new color to his palette: "I feel as if these idiotic jobs and this company of savages and imbeciles are making me very old, very fast."[104] He turns everything black, with no respite. Work. Other people. What had been strangeness in Harar was now an object of disgust. The natives were transformed into savages and his close acquaintances into imbeciles. In advance of Cioran, he hurls a few syllogisms of bitterness: "Every man is a slave of this miserable inevitability";[105] work, in other words, the punishment that evicts him from Paradise, even if an ancient tradition places Eden precisely in the high regions of Abyssinia. But he repeats the maxims of Mohammed to himself more often than the verses of Genesis, the *Mektoub*, the "So it is written," which he translates again (quite far from the text) as "That's life: it's not funny!"[106] He momentarily accepts his lot without grumbling. He makes himself over according to the laws of the Prophet. Morning and evening, he hears the muezzin of the nearby mosque calling the faithful to pray, and as his father once did, applies himself to the Koran. When he was still in Harar he had ordered a translation of it with the Arabic on the facing page; he had then wished to understand the minds of the savages surrounding him and, who knows, maybe become a *wodad* like Sotiro. Later, and no doubt also to facilitate commercial transactions, he would have a seal engraved in the name of "Abdo Rimbo," Rimbaud the servant of the Prophet.[107]

However, the *Mektoub* of Islam does not prevent him from howling in pure rage, and it is most often a universe abandoned by God that he delights in describing, as if everything has to suffer, labor, and groan in total absurdity. "The entire littoral of this filthy Red Sea is thus tortured by the heat. There is a French warship in Obok that has a crew of seventy men; sixty-five are ailing from tropical fevers and the commander died yesterday." The existence he describes with his pen is deprived of life and color; it is bloodless and devitalized. The tone recalls that of his letter from Cyprus in which he recalled the ravages of fever with an almost boastful voice. As for describing a landscape, he does not venture to try, except to portray a null location, the "sad French colony of Obok," for example. Its governor Léonce Lagarde attempted, however, to establish a commercial base of operations there and his efforts would bear fruit a decade later with the development of Djibouti. "But," Rimbaud incorrectly predicts, "I don't believe anything will ever be made of it. It is a deserted, burning beach, with no foodstuffs or trade, good only for making a coal depot for the warships on their way to China and Madagascar,"[108] a place where one does not stay, a place that one forgets. He himself is at a standstill in Aden, that other port, on the outskirts of the Gate of Tears.

It is in this state of mind, gnawed by bitterness and whipped by resentment, that he receives a letter from Roche in October alerting him to the curious actions of his brother Frédéric. His mother informs him that the latter, married and married badly, is making disturbing remarks about the family and him, Arthur, in particular. Accused, but not too sure of what, Rimbaud doesn't hide his thoughts on the subject: "He is a perfect idiot, we have always known it, and we have always marveled at the thickness of his head."[109] Certainly there was no reason for people to still be ranting about him in the hamlet of Roche or the surrounding area as far as Attigny. Wasn't Frédéric getting mixed up remembering those painful years in which Rimbaud wandered in Belgium and England with Verlaine? *Les Poètes maudits* had just been published in 1884. This book grouped together three studies due to the "poor Lélian," one of which was devoted to Rimbaud. On this occasion the past had certainly resurfaced, and Frédéric's remarks had perhaps been motivated by this publication or its preparations, when Verlaine, curious about Rimbaud, had inquired of his present whereabouts. But cleansed of the past and redeemed through work, Rimbaud wishes now to be to be exempted of such arrears: "If I had some unhappy moments in the past, I have never tried to live at the expense of others or by wrongdoing."[110] Thus he forgot the wrong he had caused Mathilde and his troubled relations with the saturnian poet, sometimes stained by the most shameless extortions. What was Frédéric hoping to gain by spreading these rumors? The simple cart driver in Attigny was no doubt jealous of Arthur (who now sent money home regularly), and claimed to have some right to the lands that Madame had bought with his younger brother's nest egg. In December 1884, the *mother*, as she did at the end of every year, conjured up the improbable return of her faraway son. While he admitted the possibility of returning there for a rest, Rimbaud rebelled at the thought of settling in these regions, which, in any event, he found so inhospitable and where the long winters are worse than the oppressive sun of Aden: "How could I bury myself in a countryside where no one knows me, where I couldn't find any opportunity of earning something?"[111] To return, he is clearly saying, is to "bury himself," to take his place *under the earth*. In contradiction to any presumable kind of rest we should rather be hearing his sentence and punishment here: "Thus I am condemned to follow the trails to where I can find the means to live, to where I can scrape together, at the price of exhaustion, enough on which I can rest for a moment."

At the beginning of 1885, he found nothing better to do than sign up for another year, to the great satisfaction of the Bardeys. With room and board he would earn a salary of one hundred fifty rupees a month (equivalent to about nine thousand modern francs[112]). At this time he had amassed together a capital of thirteen thousand francs in gold, but he could not live off the income this would earn him in such a country. His position is the same as it was five years ago, shortly after his arrival. He makes various purchases of coffees and cured leathers, to which were added many other products in lesser quantities, such as ivory, ostrich plumes, gum, incense, cloves, words that prompt dreams and are sufficient on their own to evoke an exoticism dear to Baudelaire. For Rimbaud, however, not a bit of evocation.

Little concerned with politics previously, he now comes to criticize the different events whose effects touch his business directly. He had become quite aware of this subject in 1883, when he was forced to leave Harar. Egypt's difficulties and the colonization attempts by England, France, and Italy hold his attention. His conversations with Bardey, his reading of the papers that come from Cairo—*Le Bosphore égyptien*, for example—and the news from the port let him glimpse the complexities of history whose thread he is not always capable of untying.

Entirely placed under British influence, Emperor Yohannes rules over Tigray in northern Abyssinia. The recent Mahdist troubles have affected that part of his country bordering Sudan. In southern Abyssinia, Menelik, the king of Shoa, does not conceal his expansionist objectives. Meanwhile, since the opening of the Suez Canal the Europeans have been dreaming of dividing up these poorly known regions and are actively seeking to gain the good graces of the various sovereigns in order to bend them to their will and profit from their territories. Rimbaud sums up the situation with evident Anglophobia: "The Somali and Harar coast are in the process of passing out of the hands of poor Egypt into those of the English. [. . .] English occupation ruins all the trade on the coasts from Suez to Gardafui (the easternmost part of the horn of Africa). He observes that everything is disorganized. Following the insurrection of the Mahdi, Mohammed Ahmed, the whole of the Sudan had fallen into the hands of the dervish fanatics. Without much discrimination he calls Major Gordon, heroically slain during the taking of Khartoum on November 26, 1884, an "idiot," and sees Wolseley, whom he had known, by reputation at least, when this latter was administrator of the island of Cyprus, as an "ass." He takes no greater delight in the development of the French colonial empire. The conquest of Madagascar and Tonkin appear problematic. These are, he says, "miserable lands." As for French plans for Abyssinia, he disapproves of them:

> France has also made blunders on this coast: they have occupied the entire bay of Tadjoura for a month so as to possess the beginnings of the roads into Harar and Abyssinia. But these shores are absolutely desolate; the expenses they will go to there will be for absolutely nothing, if they don't next march toward the interior plateaus (Harar), which are quite healthy, productive, and beautiful lands.[113]

If he does not condemn colonialism in the name of a humanism that would respect native identity, on the other hand he judges such undertakings as futile. He misjudges the motivation behind these struggles to conquer zones of influence. However, every day teaches him to measure their consequences on business, the only thing that truly interests him. Either hegemonic English authority, for want of respecting native ways of thinking, will put commercial trade with the local populaces at risk or else trade will prosper anew, if one continues to enter African lands by the traditional method of caravans, a human and animal river that is the veritable link between the desert civilizations and the outside world.

Rimbaud, who so easily criticizes the establishment of the French in Tadjoura, from which the Somali trading post will be formed, will not delay, though, to take advantage of this new state of things. Over the following months he notes the evolution of the situation in Khartoum, Suakin, Obok, Massawa, in constantly sarcastic terms.[114] Since Egypt is in collapse, all the

European powers are seeking to divvy up eastern Africa. "In the Sudan, the Khartoum expedition has beaten a retreat, and since I know these climates, it must have melted down by two-thirds," he says sarcastically after learning of the defeat of the English and the definitive capture of the great Sudanese city by the Mahdists. As for the French in Obok, he does not hold a special place in his heart for them; he sees them concerned with feasting and battening on government money that won't earn a sou in return from this frightful colony, colonized up to now by only a dozen freebooters." Finally, he notes the advance of the Italians, who "have become mixed up with Massawa" and doesn't seem to foresee their future importance in the years to come, although he had already met several of their explorers, Antonelli and Captain Cecchi, in Harar. The entire Red Sea at this moment is the prey of various European "missions." In Aden, where one fears the worst, "the fortifications are being rebuilt." With the same ill will he already demonstrated when he witnessed the Prussians as masters of Mézières and Charleville, he now writes: "It would give me pleasure to see this place pulverized—but not when I'm here!" The imprecation of a secular Isaiah with the no doubt involuntary memory of a passage from *Une saison en enfer.*

> *Général, s'il reste un vieux canon sur tes remparts en ruines, bombarde-nous avec des blocs de terre sèche. [. . .] Emplis les boudoirs de poudre de rubis brûlante.*[115]
> General, if there is a cannon remaining on your ruined ramparts, bombard us with lumps of dried mud. [. . .] Fill the boudoirs with the powder of burning rubies.

Rimbaud will continue to sit in judgment of the politics of his time. The war in Sudan has come to an end. France is mired in the conquest of Tonkin and he prophesies that the Chinese are going "to flank the remaining troops by sea." Madagascar is in no better shape. Furthermore, there is the good possibility of a Russo-Anglo war breaking out.

Outside of these hardly pleasant news items on which commerce in this part of the Red Sea and the prosperity of the Bardey firm depend, Rimbaud still suffers from the depressing stagnation that is customary for him. While he desires to take off and leave his untenable situation, at the same time he senses it is not something from which he can extricate himself. Furthermore, he knows his instability, he has made it into a law. And the idea of returning to France that he jiggles like a pet obsession before his mother and sister is no sooner said than contradicted in no uncertain manner: "In any case, don't count on my temperament becoming any less vagabond; to the contrary, if I had the means to travel without being forced to work and earn a living, I wouldn't be seen two months in the same spot."[116] Thus it isn't rest he is seeking, unless it comes as a break in a series of countless miseries. The adolescent of "Ma bohème" has become a tireless traveler, always driven to discover new places. Rimbaud, prisoner in Aden, has dreams of being a rich adventurer. A superior Barnabooth going from port to port: "The world is quite large and filled with magnificent countries that the lifetimes of a thousand men would not be enough to visit." Like a break in the clouds of a rancorous letter shines this hope: splendid countries, immense cities, the deep wild breath of poetry. His life is too narrow to contain so many hopes for beauty, as well as the possibility of living a thousand and one lives, which he attempted in the past and would like to attempt again. But the corners of the roads he raced had shrunk and he himself was tending to assume the role of an adventurer without adventure, a vagabond pursued by the eternal ill luck of a vile sojourn in a filthy country where one set down roots to earn sterile and absurd money for lack of anything better. Previously he repeated the law of the Muslim *Mektoub*. Here he now enunciates an acrid maxim of disenchantment: "After all, the most likely probability is that we go where we don't want to go, do what we would rather not do, and live and die quite differently from how we wanted, without hope for any kind of compensation."[117] Such is his assessment of life: a series of vexations, a stray letter that never reaches its true addressee. This is how it was in appearance. But Rimbaud did not take into account the negative force that compels individuals unconsciously, the death impulse that necessarily drags them to an abyss. And how can we refuse to believe that in turning to the East, he didn't fail to reach his final destination, even if it did end at the extinct crater of Aden? How can we not accept that he was, to the contrary, there where his instinct of loss and inner justice wished him to be? Reduced by his own hand to slavery and subjugated by his own desire to mind-numbing tasks. His astounding trajectory contains a logic that is the reverse side of success, the conquest of failure—because failure is the form life takes when it subjects itself too deliberately to the impossible.

We could dare say his situation deteriorates from January to May 1885. He now remains in the lowest possible state with sometimes, as a crowning blow, alarms about the state of his health: "I can no longer digest anything, my stomach has become very weak."[118] "A year here equals five elsewhere."[119] Reckoning by these calculations, one would speedily enter an "eternity of hot tears" and aging becomes mandatory, rushing headfirst toward death, even if one has the illusion of a slow, inexhaustible death. No distractions, Rimbaud has given up his camera; he has sold it, but "not at a loss." He refuses himself any pleasures, as if in accordance with a secret oath: "I drink absolutely nothing but water," "I never smoke." He reads nothing except for a few newspapers that are always several days old, the time it takes for them to arrive from Cairo. And his sole entourage is composed of pariahs like himself, who will soon leave "cursing" the place, the idiots who spend their time playing billiards in the Aden cafés. Sometimes the tone of his letters climbs higher, sparkling with the facets of a poetry of denigration: "The skin glistening with sweat, stomachs turning sour, brains fogging over, business affairs are revolting, the news is bad."[120] What more could he say? What could he *even* say? This is why, faced with experiencing this void, he seems to have renounced writing to his family. In October 1885, Madame Rimbaud complains of not receiving anything for eight months. She is no doubt exaggerating but it is true that his letters were becoming increasingly rare.

However, several letters come to him from France—and not only from his family. In 1885, Verlaine, following the publication of his *Poètes maudits*, partially devoted to Rimbaud, set off in quest for the *Illuminations* that he initially believed irretrievably lost. The project of publishing the works by the author of "Le Bateau ivre" was germinating in his mind. Having stayed in touch with Delahaye, the poor Lélian had no trouble in obtaining the address of the African traveler. A curious testimony—late, it's true—by Alfred Bardey[121] certainly seems to indicate that he had sent a letter and maybe several. Rimbaud would have responded, once and for all and in very terse fashion, by begging their author to cease a correspondence he found undesirable. Nothing confirms or denies this memory (which we can, however, fear was suggested by the questioner, Jean-Paul Vaillant) except a curious postcard sent by Rimbaud to Delahaye in the first half of May 1885.[122] On it we see a humorously retouched drawing, representing two "Armenians" (Rimbaud has corrected this to "Adeniens") sitting cross-legged and facing each other over a game of backgammon. Rimbaud has added this legend: "Jean-Arthur and his boss." In the portion reserved for correspondence he has written these few words: "Dear Delahuppe, Enclosed my portrait and that of my boss, after our naturalization. Greetings/Yours/A. Rimbaud." The nickname Delahuppe is one of those that Delahaye's friends (Verlaine, Nouveau, Rimbaud) bestowed on him during the times they were living large on little means.[123] The word "naturalization" refers to the animal-like retouching made to the characters on the card and mocks their "stuffed" nature. Rimbaud and Bardey, two people at home in Aden! This little note contains some surprises. No epistolary exchange was reestablished, it seems, between the two men; the only time Delahaye had written to Rimbaud, in December of 1881, the latter had addressed him a letter that essentially was composed of an endless list of objects to buy for him, and Madame Rimbaud had not forwarded it. Now the brief word to Delahaye in May 1885 has all the air of a response to some new letter from the old friend. It would not be exaggerated to think that this latter had just contacted Rimbaud for a very specific reason, to wit, not so much for reestablishing contact but to lay the groundwork for a subsequent letter from Verlaine asking for information about the famous *Illuminations*.* But, whereas Rimbaud retained a friendly tone with Delahaye he avoided any show of friendship toward the "pitiful brother." If we take Bardey at his word, he would have answered Verlaine with an extremely curt letter, reaffirming his complete lack of interest in literature.[124]

The year lengthened. Rimbaud put up with a life in damnation: "frightful country," "deplorable climate." "There is no social life, outside of the local Bedouins, and one becomes a complete idiot in a couple years."[125] Such were his estimations of the inevitable metamorphoses. The remembrances of an old idiot! The Bardeys are "vile louts"[126] who exploit him more than is permissible. Outside the human contacts made necessary by his business, he sulks in his solitude. He sends away a woman he had in his employ and gives his reasons to Auguste Franzoj, an Italian journalist who had procured this servant-concubine for him. "I've had this masquerade in front of me long

---

* Some people (Paul Gribaudo, *Parade sauvage*, April 1986, pp. 103 and 106) have deemed this card to be a hoax.

enough,"[127] he notes unsympathetically. Several testimonies indeed do indicate that a woman lived with him during this period. She was a Christian Amhara he had known in Harar and brought back to Aden. Slender and light complexioned, she is reputed to have lived beneath his roof for this entire period; she dressed in European-style clothing, smoked cigarettes, and Rimbaud had taken pains to teach her French.

Alfred Bardey's servant, Françoise Grisard,[128] who went to Rimbaud's every Sunday, claimed to have even taught this woman certain sewing techniques. He went out with her every evening—she says—adding that Rimbaud always treated this companion with great kindness. Alfred Bardey would also testify to this feminine presence, even going so far as to provide dates (from 1884 to 1886). He would specify that "the union was intimate" and that "Rimbaud, who first lodged and took his meals with us, rented a special house to live in with his companion during those hours he didn't spend in our offices." The most complete account concerning this Abyssinian woman comes from the Italian O. Rosa who—noting this with no great elegance himself—"kept the sister of that woman," but "rid himself of her after several weeks." He also pushes this liaison back to 1882. Such information, as we see, is somewhat in contradiction with the letter sent to Franzoj. So should we confuse this native woman with the "masquerade" from Shoa whom Rimbaud decided to send back to Obok in September 1885? What is the meaning of masquerade, in this instance? An appearance? A decoy? One will recall that many Europeans settled in the Middle East had, with respect to the customary polygamy of Islamic society, to take with them one or more women who were both servants and possible companions. Such was the case for Nerval in Cairo.[129] But in this case, why would Rimbaud have sent her packing? The most troubling thing in this somewhat muddled history remains the photo of a *Dama abissina*, published in 1913 in Rosa's book *L'Impero del Leone di Guida*, and the note at the bottom of the page indicating that said person "lived in 1882 in Aden with the brilliant poet Arthur Rimbaud."[129bis] How are we able to cast any doubt on such a proof? Certainly the portrait is disappointing. Wrapped in her *tobe*, she appears more robust than slender. She is not dressed in European fashion (exoticism oblige!) and her hair is covered by a scarf. Her facial features aren't very delicate and she almost gives the impression of being a young man. Nothing else can be said.

In fact we don't know anything at all about Rimbaud's sexual demands and desires during this period of his life. He already had in his employ a young boy, Djami (if we rely on Isabelle's later statements[130]). Monsignor Jarosseau, a good Catholic soul, would assert that Rimbaud was chaste; this didn't prevent him from contracting a venereal disease during his first stay in Harar. Françoise Grisard's account definitely casts doubt on the homosexual reputation that quickly became attached to his memory. Berrichon even seems to have taken possession of this document with a certain zeal, but when he brings it forth at the end of his biography, we cannot help but think that it is in obedience to his evident decision to destroy all the "legends of perverse and natural lassitude" for which his brother-in-law was already the object. In clumsy decadent style, he asserts quite loudly that Rimbaud "was, in Aden, considered the attentive husband of an Abyssinian woman intellectually and morally educated through his efforts, according to her sex."[130bis] An excellent alibi that actually corresponds only to a brief episode. It is certain, though, that Rimbaud desired to marry. At least this is the appearance he gives in several letters to his mother, but most of the time he lived as a bachelor. His "It is bad for a man to live alone" certainly resonates like a sigh of regret, yet the remote marriage he envisions contracting from time to time has too close a resemblance to those mirages with which he liked to delude himself according to his current needs. We shouldn't attach too much importance to it. At the very most, he had a companion to fulfill all his needs, with whom he behaved tenderly, in accordance with the human respect he showed for deserving, plain folk, but he perhaps grew weary of her, and nothing will subsequently attest to her presence.

ARMS MERCHANT IN SHOA

RIMBAUD'S PRINCIPAL WORRIES CONCERNS AND MAIN CARES HIS BUSINESS, which he calls "his affairs." In 1885, he is again contemplating departure from Aden, that "dirty spot" where he is earning and saving money with great pains, but also "spending" his life. He thinks that if his capital were invested in Bombay, it would bring him a return of 8 pecent, whereas here it earns him nothing. This momentarily inspires thoughts of embarking for India about which he's been told by Alfred Bardey, who journeyed there for business reasons in 1880. Despite this he has no clear intentions in mind: "I could also go to Tonkin."[131] However, the Tonkin expedition appeared as folly to him several months earlier, but he must have learned in the interim of the success dearly paid for in human lives by the French army in Tuyen Quang. Tonkin will be restructured into a protectorate this very same year. Furthermore, Rimbaud still hasn't given up on the idea of "pushing through as far as the Panama Canal, which is still far from finished."

However, during this period in which he appears to be hesitating before his future, he seems to have made the major decision that would weigh so heavily on his fate. Aware of the various kinds of commerce prospering in the Red Sea, and abreast of the current situation in Abyssinia, his attention was caught by the arms traffic in which some European nations were indulging. Menelik, the king of Shoa, intended to expand his empire at the expense of the Emperor Yohannes, who held Tigray. Following the Mahdi affair, Egypt had lost all its influence in these lands. Henceforth, England, Italy, and France would try to curry the favors of the two sovereigns, thinking they would then be in a position to circumvent them quite nicely. Menelik and Yohannes skillfully took advantage of this situation, without dreaming of giving in to these specious allies for a single minute.

Quite knowledgeable about Abyssinian matters, the French merchant Pierre Labatut had lived in Shoa for fifteen years. He had married a native woman and adopted the local customs. He was in favor with Menelik, who received him frequently at his royal *guebi* and had made him a gift of several parcels of land. Rimbaud got along well with this shrewd man, who knew the king's military needs. Labutut had an ambitious plan in mind. He wished to mount a caravan that would transport a great number of weapons: rifles and shells from the coast to Ankober. The deal could pay off big: "The payments would be made in merchandise given up by the king at Shoa prices that would in return give them a 50 percent profit in Aden." (Already in September 1881 Alfred Bardey and Labatut had been in contact about sending a similar caravan to Zeila.) The rifles to be sent were not modern Remingtons; they consisted essentially of rifles with primers, an already obsolete model (the preferred model since 1866 was the chassepot with central percussion) that, bought in large quantities in Europe for a laughable price, would ensure immediate and considerable profit if sold in Africa.[132]

Rimbaud thinks he is getting his hands on the deal of a lifetime. He hopes to earn 25,000 to 30,000 francs in gold at the very least—in addition to the savings he'd invest. In this year's end of 1885, he considers the future in a more tranquil frame of mind, even though he suspects the difficulties that lie ahead. He knows that the journey will be long, two months through "frightful deserts," but in Shoa the climate will suit him. Living totally in this pipe dream, he finds pleasure in describing this part of Abyssinia to his family as a little Switzerland: "The weather is neither hot nor cold, the population is Christian and hospitable: they lead an easy life, it is quite an agreeable rest stop for those turned to idiots by several years spent on the burning banks of the Red Sea."[133] Two months later, he paints the same idyllic picture, quite convinced that he is finally reaching the promised land: "The climate is excellent; life there costs absolutely nothing at all; all the produce of Europe grows there; one is highly regarded by all the populace. It rains six months of the year."[134] In short, a kind of Eden obligingly provided to him by his associate Labatut. But he isn't ignorant of the trials that await, the least of which would not be the crossing of the territory of the Danakils, those "Bedouin shepherds and Muslim fanatics"[135] ready to kill any whites they found passing through their lands, especially with the recent English ban on the sale of slaves. This was one of the principal resources of these natives, who collected tolls from the caravans coming out of the heart of Africa en route to the Red Sea ports, from where all this human livestock would be shipped to Arabia. Assured of making a fortune (but isn't he placing too much confidence in his star that until then had shone only with the most baneful of gleams?), Rimbaud broke his contract before it had expired with the Bardey brothers, who have unjustly exploited him in their "frightful house" and their "dirty city."[136] However, it was they who introduced him to Labatut and who, without suspecting the temporary aversion he would display toward them, provided him with an excellent certificate praising his services and his integrity.[137] Such ingratitude was in keeping with the logic of his behavior. He had his own path to follow, which did not include showing any consideration for others, and certainly not burdening himself with the ties of any possible friendship. Alfred Bardey, for his part, would calmly write in his book *Barr-Adjam*: "In 1885 [Rimbaud] left us to join with Monsieur Labatut, our former agent in Shoa. We remained in touch with Rimbaud and, at his request, sent him camping equipment for Menelik's troops."[138] This shows that Rimbaud, after his fit of ill temper, had not delayed renewing ties with his former employers. He was definitely—according to Bardey's prudent phrase seeking to depict him—"a little bizarre."

After breaking his contract, he stays for several weeks at the Grand Hôtel de l'Univers, still run by Jules Suel, while waiting to cross the Gulf of Aden. He is then nourishing the wildest hopes and imagines the course of the upcoming operations with a surprisingly carefree attitude. He has the idea that he will be able to put a caravan together immediately once he arrives at the port of Tadjoura in early January. Fifty days will suffice to reach Ankober. The delivered rifles will be duly paid for. All that will remain will be for him to return. After the success of this problem-free expedition he would give himself a vacation. So he announces to his mother the possibility of his coming to spend the summer in Roche. The phrase is charming and full of urbanity: "Such that you could well receive a visit from me toward the end of the summer in 1886."[139] He will certainly be taking off from there again, for if he returns to France it would also be with the intention of procuring new merchandise to support his Abyssinian business.

In November 1885, a dhow takes him as far as Obok territory, which had been colonized since 1862.* He sets up his winter quarters in the port of Tad-joura, where caravans entering the heart of Abyssinia are organized. Tad-joura, principal village of the Danakils, is built on a small plain at the foot of high volcanic mountains. Several groves of palm trees cast their shade here and there in the surrounding area. The only buildings of note are two mosques built of solid stone and a fort formerly constructed by the Egyptians that now serves as a shelter for six French soldiers under the orders of a sergeant.[140] The spot is considered a protectorate and governed by a local sultan, Ahmed ben Mohammed. Paul Soleillet had bought these lands in August. Immediately upon arrival, Rimbaud finds a cabin to live in and contacts the local authorities to mount his caravan—which requires intensive activity and endless discussion. It is at this time he is spotted by the Italian explorer Ugo Ferrandi, who leaves us a short but gripping description:

> Tall, scrawny, with hair graying at the temples, he was dressed in European style but in quite rudimentary fashion, with rather wide pants, a sweater, and a roomy, grey khaki jacket. On his head he wore only a small skullcap, also gray, and he braved the torrid sun of the Danakils like a native. Even though he owned a small mule, he never rode it during the treks, and with his hunting rifle, he always preceded the caravan on foot.

A moving photo in which we see Rimbaud, prematurely aged, but quick, enduring, and seemingly compelled by the intoxication of walking and the desert horizon.

At the end of January the merchandise has been unloaded; it consists of 2,040 piston rifles and 60,000 cartridges and all the camping equipment furnished by the Bardey brothers. But, as Rimbaud declares, no camels were to be found."[142] The procrastinations were beginning, the slow pace appropriate to these lands of infinite discussions that teach patience. "You need superhu-

---

*Henri Lambert and Fleuriot de Langle had acquired it from a chief of the Danakil tribe for the sum of two thousand talers (5 million francs of that era, which would be 500 million in today's francs [close to $100 million at today's exchange rates—translator]).

man patience in these countries."[143] "Those who are always repeating that life is hard should spend some time here, to learn philosophy!"[144] What good listener was Rimbaud thinking of when writing this word to the wise if not his mother, to whom he thus addressed a late lesson? He thinks all is going well. In fact, he should be paying closer attention to the actual evidence. The expedition is in a lamentable state of stagnation. He himself is anchored in another hole on these cursed coasts. What's worse is that a missive has arrived, countersigned by Léonce Lagarde, the governor of Obok, from the French government henceforth forbidding the importation of any arms into the Shoa. The sultan of Tadjoura is given the order to halt the formation of the caravan. We can imagine no more damning news for Labatut and Rimbaud, who invested considerable sums of money in the purchase of their merchandise and who have to pay the men they hired for every day that goes by before their big departure. Indeed, in February, the English minister Hunter, citing an accord concerning the limitation of weapons imports, had prevented the famous French traveler Paul Soleillet from unloading a cargo that had to pass through Aden. Finally, thanks to Monsieur de Gaspary, the French consul in this city, an arrangement had been reached. Unfortunately for Rimbaud and Labatut, it was stated quite explicitly that such an authorization would not be renewed.

At the thought of what he risks losing, Rimbaud pulls himself together and, *in extremis*, sends a long letter to the secretary of foreign affairs,[145] clearly setting out the validity of his enterprise and denouncing the injustice striking him, for the French government had first given him an authorization in good and due form, then gone back on its decision. He gives a detailed list of the merchandise he has to deliver. He shows the improbable nature of the alleged dangers represented by the import of these weapons. First there was no possibility that a certain number of these arms would fall into the hands of the Danakils (a specious pretext advanced by the English, who claimed they feared that Menelik would thereby be threatened in those regions where he was extending his influence). No more could anyone claim that this commerce masked a traffic in slaves. Rimbaud, who would later be suspected of engaging in such a trade, shows with exemplary lucidity in a letter written to Monsieur de Gaspary[146] that the two businesses were without any close ties, and we should emphasize the explanations he provided at that time, certainly not with the intent of skillfully exonerating himself, but in order to bring full light to bear on what was a somewhat confusing situation, even for those in authority: "Our affairs are quite independent of the obscure traffics of the Bedouins. No one would dare suggest that a European has ever sold or bought, transported or helped to transport a single slave either to the coast or to the interior." The slave trade was the doing of Arabs, Bedouins, "Islamics."[147] No caravan mounted by Europeans would have ever tried to combine the products of trade with this human commodity! The letter would be sent on to the Ministry of the Navy for an opinion with a detailed note requesting a concession.[148] Rimbaud and Labatut have cleverly displayed how such bans give a trade advantage to their primary foreign competitors. The English and the Italians would have a clear path through the other ports of Massawa and Zeila, which would thereby allow them to establish relations with the interior of Abyssinia. Excessive strictness here runs the risk of causing definitive harm to French merchants. Resuming the argument according to which the authorization had been granted on a date on which the French and English accord had not yet been passed, the government would ultimately advise Léonce Lagarde to let them go ahead with it one more time.[149] For the moment, Rimbaud finds himself extricated from a tight spot.

In this month of June 1885 in which they had finally been given satisfaction, Rimbaud and Labatut seem to have entered into a business arrangement with Jules Suel, the owner of the Grand Hôtel de l'Univers in Aden. He had no doubt provided the financing for the arms purchase that Paul Soleillet, another French merchant, planned to import into Shoa, and who was likewise waiting in Tadjoura. Another caravan was also to be found there, that of Franzoj the Italian journalist and correspondent for *La Gazette de Turin*, to whom we have seen Rimbaud send a letter on the subject of his woman/servant. It so happens that in June, for reasons that aren't exactly clear, Suel asks Rimbaud to take on a thousand piston rifles and transport them as quickly as possible into Shoa.[150] A month later, he asks him to take "the whole thing" but then enumerates only six hundred rifles.[151] They must be delivered to a certain Éloy Pino, who will take receipt of them at their destination. We don't really know what pushed Suel to take this action, but in September Rimbaud would announce that he has to join with Soleillet's caravan.[152] Thus it would seem that Rimbaud, who had put together quite a large caravan during the summer of 1886, thanks to his perseverance and tact when dealing with the indigenous populace, was responsible not only for the transport of the 2,040 capsule rifles originally bought by Labatut, but also for another shipment: the rifles entrusted to Soleillet.[153]

The evolution of events will become particularly dramatic over the following months. In fact, Labatut becomes gravely ill and has to leave for France to be hospitalized. Stricken by cancer, he will die at the end of the year. Thus Rimbaud finds himself alone to make a journey on a route with which he is completely unfamiliar. He momentarily contemplates leaving with Soleillet, so that there would no longer be a question of leaving before him under these circumstances. Now, on September 9, by an unfortunate coincidence that any superstitious individual would view as a sign from fate, Soleillet collapses in an Aden street, stricken by an embolism. Momentarily despairing because nothing is going as planned, Rimbaud then displays that second wind that has saved him in critical moments on more than one occasion. Confronted by the worst, he fully exposes himself to it, an almost anonymous hero. The caravan is of considerable size: a hundred camels, a hundred men—Abyssinian *sepians* and camel drivers—and a large amount of cargo to which had to be added the foodstuffs necessary for a minimum fifty day's march in the desert, with the only hope of relief being a few almost dried-up wadis, scarce grass, and whatever hamlets they chance upon. The population is hostile; the Danakils have the cruelest reputation. In June, Barral's caravan, which had left for Shoa before that of Rimbaud, had easily reached its goal but on the return trip, for want of vigilance, had been cruelly carved to pieces.[154] Happening upon the site of the ambush, another traveler, Léon Chefneux, would see nothing but scattered rifles and corpses half-eaten by wild animals. Rimbaud refers to these as "disagreeable incidents." Phlegmatic, when not consumed by anger, he decides to take to the road and thus embarks on a most perilous adventure. When the caravan gets under way and Tadjoura disappears on the horizon, he needs all his strength to believe in any possibility of success. The trip will last two months at the rate of twelve to twenty miles a day. In Sajalo, he hires thirty-four Abyssinians with whom he signs a contract granting each a sum of fifteen talers[155] upon arrival in Ankober, the capital of Shoa. In six short stages, after having crossed regions "recalling the presumed horror of lunar landscapes"[156] (this notation is in his handwriting), the caravan reaches Lake Assal, encircled by volcanic mountain chains. A thick layer of salt fringes its shores. Aware that a corporation is being formed to exploit this resource and that the French government had granted the concession to Chefneux and Brémond, Rimbaud will later advise against any efforts in this direction, thinking that the construction of a narrow-gauge railway linking the lake to the coast would be more expensive than any profits realized from the sale of the salt. Their march continues on a difficult and inhospitable route. The Danakil members of the expedition, despite their reputation as formidable warriors (in order to be considered an adult in their society it is necessary to have killed an enemy and cut off his virile member), equally dread the Issas, who are always seeking fights with them. They reach Herer in twenty-three legs, after passing through "the most frightful country-side of Africa." Around them, various tribes wait for the slightest excuse to battle one another or plunder the travelers. Herer, located at 2,400 feet in altitude, finally offers grazing land where the expedition can rest. It is only a village of around fifty *gourbis*. The cabins are grouped into two zones: one inhabited by the Issas, the other by the Danakils. Another nine day's journey and they will be out of these unsafe regions where one is constantly at the mercy of traps set by the natives. The Awash River cuts across their path. Beyond it begins the territory of Shoa, placed under Menelik's rule. For a moment Rimbaud is disappointed. He had expected to find a much larger watercourse. The camels, in water up to their bellies, cross it with no problem, and he can only smile thinking of the unfortunate Soleillet who had wanted to have a special craft constructed in Nantes to cross what in truth was only a winding ditch that from all evidence was impossible to channel. Rocks and tree trunks impede its flow through its high banks. They will cross this river on several occasions. Once they would make use of a fine footbridge constructed on Menelik's orders by Alfred Ilg. They finally reach Farre, the last stop for caravans coming from the coast. Hardly has Rimbaud arrived when the *azzaze*, one of the royal stewards,[157] comes before him and, no doubt informed of Labatut's death, as there are no secrets in the desert, tells him that he has a debt owed him by the deceased and that this debt is huge. Obviously Rimbaud suspects this claim is exaggerated; he is no less pressed by the difficulties ahead and guesses that Labatut's death is going to cause more than one problem for him. However, he succeeds in calming the *azzaze* by making him a gift of some field glasses and several laxative pills! Too simple a solution for calming the animosity of such an acrimonious nature.

On February 6, 1887, after a difficult mountain march along veritable precipices, he enters Ankober. The king's capital is a collection of about one hundred conical-roofed huts dominated by the sovereign's *guebi*, placed on an elevated site surrounded by several concentric walls. There is a magnificent view of the neighboring heights from the city. Through the *azzaze*, Rimbaud is already aware that Menelik is away on a remote expedition. Following a military intervention by Abdellahi, the emir of Harar placed in power by the English after the departure of the Egyptians, Menelik had decided to rid himself of this pretentious "kinglet" with no fear of his collusion with British agents.[158] Having left with 30,000 warriors, he defeated the less numerous and poorly equipped troops of his enemy, in the village of Shalenko, thirty-five miles from Harar. Abdellahi's 3,000 men, armed only with blades, had been crushed. His Sudanese, Turkish, and Egyptian mercenaries were massacred and, according to Amharic custom, castrated. Strengthened by this success, Menelik entered Harar as a conquering hero and, climbing to the top of minaret, publicly urinated all over the roof of the great mosque to show what little regard he, a Christian, had for the law of the Prophet. After pillaging the goods of the natives and confiscating those of several Europeans who happened to be there, he is now preparing to return to Shoa, after leaving 3,000 riflemen camped outside Harar's walls and entrusting the administration of the city to the emir Ali Abu Bekr (the nephew of the same Abdellahi he had just defeated in Shalenko).

Day after day, Rimbaud learns these bits of news and follows the progress of the king's campaign. So much time is wasted before he can deliver his merchandise. Outside of the curiosity it awoke, his arrival in Ankober had aroused many gestures of recrimination. A mob assails him demanding he pay off Labatut's debts. The widow, taking the role of weeping shrew, remains constantly at his heels seeking to obtain a nebulous inheritance at any price. Rimbaud is solvent. His prestigious caravan is proof enough of that. He already realizes that he will have much trouble getting out of such a situation that he guesses to be inextricable and over which he has little purchase. He can only argue that he had received power of attorney from the deceased to sell these weapons in his stead. He has no knowledge whatsoever of all the debts he is being presented. He sees people are trying to swindle him and that all are leagued against him. The widow even decides to bring an action against him with the support of a French national, Monsieur Hénon, a former cavalry officer who had come to Abyssinia to make topographical surveys (in 1888 he would be given the responsibility for this task by the French government). Hénon himself is assisted by two Amharic lawyers, two ill-natured and chattering magpies, ready to deploy their weapons of eloquence in defense of their client. Rimbaud momentarily believes he has prevailed. He even obtains a writ of scizurc for the dead man's houses, but as the wife prudently removed all items of value from the premises, he finds only (as he will say in a later letter to Monsieur de Gaspary[159]) "several old pairs of underpants," which the widow seized with "hot tears," and several pregnant slaves. The Abyssinian woman's litigation did not stop there. Eventually, she would obtain a verdict ordering all the Europeans of the community to contribute a certain amount of money into a common fund for her inheritance. But she is not alone in demanding her rights. A veritable horde of creditors, each greedier than the next, and all presenting the best reasons, press Rimbaud to give in to their demands. He will hear out a certain number of these claimants. Later, he would recount the visits of these vultures in quite a picturesque manner. The guest drinks *tej* (a kind of mead) in his company, calls up the merits of the old "friend," then works around to stating his demands. Anything can serve to insinuate that the deceased was his debtor. An ass passes nearby, he believes he recognizes "the mule he gave the good Monsieur Labatut." Rimbaud, overrun by these beggars, no longer knows what to think. Sometimes, pushed over his limits, he acts precipitously. Such as when he hastily burned the notebooks found in Labatut's shack (his "Memoirs" he called them, ironically) in which the deceased had inscribed his "confessions," which lightly skimmed through at first appeared worth hardly a more serious examination. He would later realize that property titles had been included therein and that his thoughtless gesture would cause him irreparable harm. But he would also sometimes give in to well-founded demands: he pays the wives of the servants who had died in Labatut's caravan the wages they were due; he wipes out the debts that this same Labatut had contracted with the peasants at the time he lived in Ankober; he even went so far as to perform an act of charity, when, reimbursing a certain Monsieur Dubois—a Frenchman, no doubt—he offers this miserable beggar enough to buy himself a pair of shoes. At this rate his money is melting like snow under a hot sun. Furthermore, he hasn't yet received a thing for the rifles he has transported. Falling victim to such a downturn in his personal fortunes, he could still rely on Jules Borelli, a zealous explorer and an affable man, although somewhat full of himself and his discoveries, who, like Rimbaud, was staying in Ankober. Rimbaud had already seen him in Aden, and then in Tadjoura where he was organizing his own caravan. Borelli, for his part, has left of this compatriot and arms merchant not a portrait but rather a descriptive note: "He knows Arabic and speaks Amharic and Oromo. He is tireless. His aptitude for languages, his great willpower, and patience for every ordeal place him among the accomplished travelers."[160] Under the gaze of this specialist, the Ardennais pedestrian becomes a traveler in savage lands, shattering all obstacles, and endowed with heroic qualities; the stiffened arm no longer drags a "dear image"; the former polyglot, emerged from the overly conventional Indo-European domain, now speaks mysterious languages whose very names are unknown.[161] Borelli will later speak of the attraction he felt for Rimbaud's personality and will attempt to reconstruct its psychology: "His ways of being that some found grotesque and others thought a studied originality were simply the result of his independent and somewhat misanthropic nature."[161bis]

Waiting in Ankober for Menelik's return was not the ideal solution. So Rimbaud decided to leave the area, under the curses of the ever-growing crowd of beggars. His and Borelli's caravans departed in convoy, with the intention of reaching Intoto, a magnificent site in the mountains where the king had decreed his residence would henceforth be established. Former Ethiopian sovereigns had resided there in the past. Mindful of reconnecting with that illustrious tradition, Menelik wished to settle in this spot. In 1891, he will have constructed further below on the mountain, at the instigation of his wife, Taitu, Addis Abbaba, the "new flower," as the intended capital of his empire. After his victory in Harar, he had made a triumphant entry into the new royal city led by musicians playing Egyptian trumpets. The parade was worthy of the ceremonies reserved in antiquity for the *imperator*. The king, carried by slaves, was followed by soldiers, the riches he had won, and—an even greater wonder—two Krupp cannons taken from the enemy that were each pulled by forty men. Perhaps Rimbaud and Borelli were there as spectators. But while Menelik had plenty of reason to be intoxicated by his taking of Harar, which, it is true, had provided him with many weapons, he had not forgotten the important order he had sent to Labatut. His schemes of conquest could be satisfied only by the delivery of such material.

Soon Rimbaud is presented to him in accordance with the customary rituals. The European enters the *guebi*[162] and is led into the counsel chamber where Menelik is waiting. The sovereign is a robust man with very black skin, keen eyes, and a face scarred by smallpox that is framed by a short, thick beard. He wears the traditional Amharic headgear, the *rass masseria*, a light scarf knotted in the back, on top of which, out of vanity, he has placed a black Quaker's hat. His shoulders are wrapped in a silk burnoose with gold decorations. He is seated cross-legged on a divan covered with rugs and cushions. He is surrounded by his counselors, among whom is a white man wearing glasses, a crew cut, and a thick mustache: Alfred Ilg. Menelik, of course, had been informed of Rimbaud's misfortunes. He knew of Labatut's death and the swarm of creditors that had bothered the newcomer in Ankober. But he lets his visitor speak to see how this loser, this traveler with too much baggage, would refer to his desperate situation. Rimbaud testifies with his habitual sang-froid but also bemoans his bad luck. Then, without dwelling any further on the death of his associate, he asks the king for the agreed-upon sum. The crafty Menelik is fully aware he can swindle this merchant as he pleases, especially if he uses the vexing chain of circumstances that are overwhelming the adventurer. He also claims to be one of Labatut's creditors, in that he has granted him lands and houses, and he estimates that his debts at the very least are as high as 3,500 talers, a fortune. Moreover, he claims he will only pay a lump sum for the all the rifles and will not accept them sold by the piece. He offers 14,000 talers for everything, whereas Rimbaud is expecting 40,000 talers. Furthermore, as reimbursement for the alleged debts of the deceased, he proposes to subtract the famous 3,500 talers which, after discussion, he consents to reduce to 3,000. For his part, Rimbaud, if he had done his arithmetic, would be thinking that he would also have to subtract 2,500 talers from the money Menelik is going to give him, for the rent of the camels and various other expenditures. He would thus find himself again with 9,000 talers, the equivalent of the sum he had invested for the entire expedition. Also (currency being demonetized in all the king's states) it would be paid only in drafts, in Harar, by the new governor of that location, Ras Makonnen, a cousin of Menelik who has just driven his insipid predecessor from power. The palavers over *tej* last several days. Seeing that he will not be able to obtain anything more, Rimbaud ends up accepting these conditions that are so disadvantageous for him, and with no further delay, starts thinking of leaving again. He shares with Borelli his intention of not going back by the horrible path that traverses the country of the Danakils from Ankober to Tadjoura. It was, in any case, necessary for him to get back to Harar, where he should get paid. From there, he would go to Zeila, a route he knows quite well, having taken it several times, and which appears more reliable to him.

During the several weeks he had spent in Intoto, Rimbaud had all the time in the world to enjoy long discussions with Alfred Ilg, a man of the modern world who had come into these regions not to "traffic in the unknown," but to make something new.[163] The future, which he had believed sealed forever, now seemed opened anew by the example of this Swiss engineer who was taking his chances there[*] and appears to be succeeding according to his wishes. Ilg did not displease Rimbaud with his reassuring corpulence, his drawling accent, and his remarks slightly tinged with humor. The two men promise to write each other and make plans to work together.

On the eve of his departure, a little genre scene, wonderfully "sketched" out by the main party involved, was able to delight the residents of Intoto. While Rimbaud was climbing the path toward the royal palace with Ilg, he spots behind him "the helmet of Monsieur Hénon" and behind that, "the burnoose of the frenetic widow snaking along the precipices."[164] The description deserves a comic strip, an unexpected supplement to the misadventures of Private Boquillon lost among the savages. However, these recalcitrant creditors who have come to plead before the king on the merits of their case,

---

[*] It was on the advice of Pierre Labatut that Menelik, in 1877, had engaged Ilg, Zimmermann, and Appenzeller in his service. Ilg, born in 1854 like Rimbaud, had first worked in Europe as an engineer of public works. He had some important achievements to his credit: the cupola of the Bern observatory, the installations of water conveyances in that city, and so forth. Ilg had been defined by Furrer, the Swiss consul in Aden, as "the man who knows everything," a perfect polymath, in short (from Michel Barthe, *Rimbaud en Abyssinie*, thesis from Saint-Augustine, La Trinité, British Antilles: n.d.).

will obtain nothing for their trouble. As for Rimbaud, tired of so many set-backs, he takes to the road. His projects are not lacking in ambition, in that he plans to plunge deeply into regions where Europeans have never gone, and it is with the care of an explorer that he intends to note all the particular circumstances of this itinerary. Borelli is not mistaken in his estimation of Rimbaud and immediately falls into step with him, noting in his journal on April 30, 1887: "Finally, I have been authorized (by Menelik) to get started on my journey without waiting for anything or anyone. It is midnight. I write these lines ravaged by fatigue, but I am determined to depart with Monsieur Rimbaud at dawn, without letting myself be delayed by false promises or the organization of a team more suitable to my plans."[165] Rimbaud seems to have taken the initiative in this operation. He intrepidly drags along the experienced explorer who, moreover, will later try to attribute himself with all the merit of this "first." "On May 2, 1887," he would write with fine self-assuredness to the minister of public education, Monsieur Fallières, "I left for Harar. [. . .] I am the first European who has followed the road opened by the Amharic invaders from Intoto to Harar."[166] In this type of adventure, there are always predecessors and it actually seems that neither Rimbaud nor Borelli were the first whites to discover this trajectory, which had already been followed by Vincenzo Ragazzi and Raffaele Alfieri,[167] two Italians attached to Menelik's court who had escorted him on his recent campaign. At least Borelli would have the honor of making the geodesic survey before anybody else.

How great the sense of discovery must have been for the travelers on this journey! Sensation! "On the blue summer evenings, I will follow the paths." It was certainly no longer a question of a poetic promenade, but an eighteen-day march[168] with asses, mules, camels, averaging fifteen miles a day. The men advance over a high plateau and cross the Akaki River. On the second day, with a longer march (forty-four miles), they reach the village of Abitchu before descending to the Minjar Plain, a magnificent country "fully cultivated and one of the richest provinces of Shoa," Borelli asserts, "although water was somewhat scarce at that time" (the peasants collected it in enormous ditches against times of drought). That night several of their servants fled back to Intoto. The crossing of the Minjar was done in several stages, until they reached more rugged terrain where cottonwood grew. This was followed by the descent over Cassam, which they made using a road opened by Menelik. They pass through mimosa forests that shelter wild beasts, and the path they are following runs along an elephant trail. At Fil-Uaha, they pass near a hot spring. Farther on the Awash is flowing. Beyond it extends a land covered by stunted trees and gum trees. The wretched plain, out of which point giant agaves, is furrowed with elephant tracks. The path then starts climbing again until Itu in the highlands, and emerges over the Galamso Post where several hundred soldiers of the *dejash* Walday Gabriel are bivouacked. The next day they arrive twenty miles farther along, at the Boroma Post, which contains a thousand soliders. The first plantings of durra, the preeminent Abyssinian cereal plant, start to appear. The expedition now starts advancing into the Tchertcher. The plant life is incomparably beautiful and awes Borelli. Rimbaud contents himself, in his account of the trip, with a "magnificent forests," without lingering any further over the superb flora of these regions: zygbas, centuries-old olive trees, candelabra-like euphorbias of colossal proportions. After a stop in Watcho, they arrive, twelve miles farther down the road, at the large village of Goro, the most important commercial center for the Itu people. Traders come here from great distances to sell chammas* and slaves. Next, on the Hernay side, are again beautiful forest-filled valleys, planted with coffee trees and *khat*, a country of great fertility. The torrential Burka River descends out of the mountains. A pine forest extends over a distance of sixty miles. The highest point of the journey is reached at Shalenko (7,900 feet). The remains of the Emir Abdellahi's army, which was defeated there, are rotting beneath their weapons: "Skeletons are lying everywhere and we are treading human bones underfoot."[169] The next day, after ten days of travel, they emerge at the lake region, within sight of Harar. Borelli, exhausted, decides to get some rest.[170] But the indefatigable Rimbaud continues on. The two men will meet again in the city. Rimbaud enters on May 21. He has not seen Harar for three years. He is aware that numerous political events have profoundly shaken it. The little he says about it reveals his disappointment, not to mention his disgust. The houses have been burned. The city has become a cesspool.[171] The invaders have left corpses in the streets. Borelli, for his part, will insist on the stench of the city,

---

*Abyssinian robes.

the human waste that soils it, the countless remains of cattle where "cruel flies" drone. Rimbaud is struck even more by the misfortunes of this populace he knew in happier times and who now, pressured by Menelik, are subject to incredible extortions and are raided for furniture and jewels. Under his pen a catastrophic vision is reconstructed, as if it were always necessary to arrive at this kind of truth: "Famine and plague are imminent." Despite this deplorable situation, Menelik led 13,000 Abyssinians and their slaves into the city; his troops (3,000 riflemen) are camped in the nearby area.

On his arrival, Rimbaud, whose first thoughts were obtaining the money owed him, hustled to solicit an audience with Makonnen, the new governor, who was the only person with the ability of paying the I O U s promised by Menelik. The *ras* lived in the *salamlik* and harem built by the Egyptians at an earlier date. A skilled general of the royal troops and cousin to the king, he himself belonged to an old aristocratic family and one of his ancestors, Shaile Selassie, had been *Negus negusta* at the beginning of the century. After his conquest of Harar, Menelik had placed Emir Ali Abu Bekr at the city's head. The troops commanded by Makonnen had remained outside the city walls. But after a short while, on the pretext that Harar was being managed in defiance of common sense, Makonnen had come down with his men from the neighboring heights and invaded the city, imprisoning the emir, whom he later had brought before Menelik bound hand and foot. The king, convinced that such conduct could only have been inspired by the greatest loyalty, had then given him charge of the government. When Rimbaud is received by the *ras*, he finds himself in the presence of an affable man with tender, expressive eyes and fine hands that are almost feminine; he is a well-educated individual who is shrewd but difficult in business matters. He also could obtain nothing from him but some pieces of paper that had a certain value in talers but not a cent in real money. In any event, all trade was rendered impossible by the absence of an actual currency. Menelik had forbidden the use of the old Egyptian piasters, which he first replaced with copper coins of no value.[172] He was now preparing to strike a coinage bearing his image.

Several days spent in Harar were sufficient for Rimbaud to judge the state of commerce. After the conquest, the majority of Europeans were forced to leave. All that remained was the Catholic mission of Monsignor Taurin. However, Makonnen, mindful of the importance of alliances, considered international business indispensable for the growth of Harar, which was the closest Abyssinian city to the sea, despite the two-week journey separating it from Zeila and Djibouti. It formed the most favorable site for receiving the riches from Shoa and expediting them to Arabia and Europe. The other route, that of Tadjoura, remained dangerous and crossed non-annexed territories. With the idea of turning this situation to his advantage, Rimbaud takes his leave of the *ras*. He also parts with Borelli, determined to make the ascent back to Shoa. The two men had established solid bonds of friendship. Despite the disparity between their two personalities, their common liking for science had drawn them together, and Borelli's technical knowledge had awed Rimbaud, who wished he had such knowledge (and such instruments) at his disposal when he still had the idea of writing a book on the Gallas in mind. His conversations with the explorer would leave a vivid imprint on him; they would reawaken the old projects that he had dropped out of lassitude; they would cause the rebirth of various hopes in this unlucky tradesman. Borelli frequently conversed with the reserved and silent Rimbaud. So much time spent in each other's company had allowed him to assess the nature of this bizarre traveler who was all too often taciturn and gloomy:[173] "He entered his tent, sat without saying a word, remained for half an hour, then took off." Such is the man he spent time with: "a sarcastic spirit," an irascible and embittered man, but one who knows how to control himself when necessary." Borelli, convinced of his travel companion's capabilities, had suggested to him that he make a request of the minister to obtain a grant for an exploration project. He had also passed on to him the address of his brother Octave, editor at *Le Bosphore égyptien*, the great daily paper of Cairo.

Rimbaud, now on his return trip, is thinking about the several solutions open to him as well as still chewing over the failure of his most recent expedition; he looks back at at the "frightful" countries crossed despite all dangers, the new faces he has met, all set over a backdrop of trickery and piracy. A fine disaster. He will never find serenity, he will never find rest. A stronger disgust stirs him up. And, if he is still going forward, then it is in the name of an obscure duty that forces him to walk until he dies.

FROM REST IN EGYPT
TO THE RETURN TO HARAR

ON JULY 25, 1887, AFTER AN ABSENCE OF A YEAR AND A HALF, RIMBAUD disembarks at Aden with eight thousand talers in I O U s and six hundred talers in cash.[174] With him is Djami, his young servant from Harar. Again he spends his time with the Europeans with whom he had relations before his departure: the Bardey brothers, Jules Suel. He stays at the Grand Hôtel de l'Univers. But he can't stand that frightful crater Aden for long, with its crushing summer heat, where life stretches on and on; it is a useless neoplasm. And the *idea* of rest (as in *Illuminations* he had an idea of "The Deluge") resurfaces. He had hoped to return to France following his expedition, to spend the summer or fall in Roche. He contents himself with Egypt, whose more temperate climate would be more tolerable than the scorching midsummer heat farther south. Perhaps he is also thinking of investigating—from port to port as the case may be—what work is available and the possibility of finding a change of scene. In Aden, Tadjoura, and Harar he is a familiar figure, just another part of the scenery. Henceforth he refuses to be assigned to a residence.

When he sets sail on the weekly packet out of Aden with Djami, he is carrying a leather valise in his hand (the one that can still be seen today in the Old Mill Museum in Charleville), and his belt weighed down with several pounds of gold and silver pieces, will soon increase when he is finally able to convert the I O U s given him by Makonnen into cold cash. We know his appearance at this time: "Tall, thin, gray eyes [where are the blue eyes of an earlier time, now washed by torrid suns?], almost blond but small mustache." In fact he was arrested in the port of Massawa, on the Sudanese coast, for having no passport. The *carabinieri* brought him to the French consul. Alexandre Merciniez, the consul, finding him a somewhat shady character, addressed a letter to his colleague in Aden, Monsieur de Gaspary, to get more information about this "honorable Rimbaud, so-called businessman in Harar and Aden."

Rimbaud had to wait several days for the requested information to come. The few papers he carried on him, for want of a passport, had only strengthened the consul's suspicions. What exactly did these two I O U s signify: one for 5,000 talers drawn on a certain Lucardi, the other for 2,500 talers on a certain Indian trader in Massawa? Rimbaud—as can be assumed based on this clue that is often overlooked by his biographers—had no doubt landed in the port to cash in the I O U s given him by Makonnen. Thus he planned to see the "Indian trader" who would have repaid him 2,500 talers and likewise Monsieur Lucardi, debtor for an even larger sum. In 1887, Massawa was largely occupied by the Italians. They had fairly close relations with Menelik, whom they wished to take a stand in Abyssinia and whose rivalry with the Negus Yohannes they were trying to stir up.

A week goes by. The passport finally arrives, accompanied by a note from Monsieur de Gaspary that speaks of the high esteem he has for his compatriot and stands as surety for his honesty. In the meantime Merciniez has realized he isn't dealing with a shady adventurer hanging around the ports. He will even draft Rimbaud a letter of recommendation to the Marquis Grimaldi-Régusse, a lawyer at the court of appeals in Cairo.[176] Did Rimbaud intend to have him plead the merits of his case in the Labatut affair?

Toward mid-August, after a short stopover at the home of Lucien Labosse, the French vice-consul of Suez, he arrives in Cairo. He plans to stay in this unfamiliar and enormous city several months and quite quickly learns to find his way through its mazes. He takes note of the high cost of living. The rhythm of city life doesn't suit him at all. He is now too habituated to the very distinctive pace of Arabia and Abyssinia. Here each minute counts; the bustling, rushing crowd and the swarm of restless passersby disturb his temperament, which while lively is used to the siesta hour and the slow pace of palavers. During his stay he lodges at the Hôtel d'Europe. The address he gives his correspondents simply reads "General Delivery" or else "Consulate of France." This period of relaxation would provide him his last opportunity to write. Not simply letters but several retrospective pages concerning his activity over the last few years. Nothing emotional, of course, not even descriptive. Just what's strictly necessary. Perfect, refined information that is stylized to the point of indigence. Nevertheless, he somehow remains faithful, outside of fiction, to one of his oldest desires and to his tracking instinct that pulls the words onto the paper in the image of the trails he followed. Shortly after his arrival, he rediscovers his innermost demon; he plunges back into a fundamental element he knows well and out of which he never ceased recharging himself. In a few days he fills up a good several dozen pages. Count them yourself: on August 20, he sends a letter to the director of *Le Bosphore égyptien*, eleven cramped pages recounting his most recent long trip; August 23, a letter to his family; August 24 and 25, two letters to his mother; August 26, a letter to Alfred Bardey describing the famous Intoto-Harar itinerary; on the same day, a letter to the Geographical Society.

What an unforeseen resumption! After *Une saison en enfer*, his letter to Octave Borelli on August 20 will be the sole text that he will see appearing under his supervision and published during his lifetime. *Le Bosphore égyptien*, "a daily paper on politics and literature," would insert it in their issues of August 25 and 27. No attempt at style, of course. These are notes on the state of things in a region, sagacious observations with a bearing on contemporary geography and history, and commercial perspectives. This text of an epistolary nature ends with a very formal: "Cordially and hastily yours." It is signed with only the name "Rimbaud." For the sake of Alfred Bardey, always curious about things African, Rimbaud also exerts himself to write a dry, precise account describing the route he has discovered. He adds some remarks concerning "business possibilities": the purchase of ivory, musk, gold, the sale of arms (8,000 Remingtons but this would require chartering a boat in Suez). Bardey, a correspondent of the Geographical Society, would send a copy of this text to Paris. Furthermore, simultaneously and no doubt advised to do so by Jules Borelli, Rimbaud had made certain to address said society to request a mission.[177] Thus he staked his all, in hopes that he would be granted the funds to travel through unknown regions. His letter will be taken under consideration, but finally they would respond (October 4) that he has little chance of being given a satisfactory answer, as the ministries are now under orders to practice strict economies.

Left to his writing activity, the obscure Cairo tourist did not forget his family, the Roche residents to whom he must once more confess: "I find myself with the 15,000 francs I started with, after exhausting myself in a horrible manner for two years. I have no luck!"[178] The brilliant conclusion of a grand saturnian display! Rimbaud, who believed in destiny, was quite com-

pelled to conclude that his was marked by misfortune. However, he refused
to make any grandiloquent statements and resort to his arsenal of old curses.
He is simply someone to whom the chain of events brings nothing but heart-
break. Thinking of the evil fate that weighs him down, he resigns himself to
obligatory alternatives imposed upon him by the most miserable kind of life:
work, exhaustion, work, exhaustion. For once he recognizes that the latter
has triumphed. Despite his will, his body no longer follows through. He feels
a great weakness from way back crossing his body. He is now struck by his
first serious physical ailments. These herald the first sufferings that ultimately
will take his life: a rheumatism in his lower back that makes [him] curse,
another in the left thigh that paralyzes him at times; an articular pain in the
left knee; and another rheumatism in the right shoulder. He guesses they
were caused by his exertions over recent months, his "exploits" as he calls
them, and he concludes that they have placed his "life in jeopardy,"[179] an
observation that could not be any truer but is one he refuses to consider with
all the gravity it deserves. This is the first appearance of Rimbaud in decline.
The expedition to Shoa has given him nothing in return, save this accelerated
pace toward death, this hastening to his own end.

However, there is no way to fix this and the weeks he spends in Cairo convince him even more irrevocably that he can no longer tolerate the European
lifestyle, to which he opposes some miraculous words like an incantatory
open sesame: "The wandering and free life."[180] Rimbaud has known what he
wanted since 1870; he hears it obscurely in his very depths. Every gesture was
made with the purpose of breaking his moorings and freeing himself of any
haulers, the passenger of an astonishing, terrifying freedom. This is what he
loves above all else during this summer of 1887, in which he briefly resumes
contact with civilization only to recognize almost with amazement that he no
longer owes anything to it and that it is his sickness. Once again, he feels
the pull of the indefinable call of the void, the unknown zone, the self-same
unknown that he himself signifies, yet with more than seventeen pounds of
gold at his belt,[181] weighing down each of his steps, gripping him like a torturous yoke to which he consents, as if in sacrifice to the remote devotions of
the Cuifs for leasable and profitable lands whereas he takes no rest anywhere.
Obedient to his very strange and perfectly monomaniacal frenzy, he still envisions making a number of trips. Obedient to the fundamental injunction of

his "wandering life," he becomes a compass card, spinning between the south and the Far East: "Perhaps I will go to Zanzibar [he is the one who grows pale hearing the name Zanzibar[182]] from where long voyages into Africa can be made, and perhaps to China, Japan, and who knows where?" He is unconsciously resuming the same program, or almost, of "Soir historique." Perhaps he also realizes that he has reached the evening of his personal history or that history is on the downward slope of time. "Center of the Celestial Empire"? Tintin in Tibet! Rimbaud in Japan! Can you picture the bizarre etching? He will land there later, carried in the head of one man: Paul Claudel in the land of the Rising Sun.

However, on August 24, he performs an essential act of jettisoning some ballast. He now weighs seventeen pounds less, in that he has finally deposited the 16,000 francs he has been carrying in his belt in the Credit Lyonnais for six months at 4 percent interest.[183] What purpose did this lightening of his load serve? To continue a life of pain and forced labor? His obsession to go to Zanzibar does not lessen, either, and he makes plans around September 15 to take the boat there.[184] There are jobs in Zanzibar. If not, he will bury himself in the heart of Africa or head to Madagascar. Yet over the following days his plans take on such a different twist that when he leaves Cairo after a period about which we know nothing (perhaps he visited the pyramids?[185]), he limits himself to returning to Aden, as if he could not escape those "satanic countries"; nevertheless, he nourishes "the hope that things will turn out better,"[186] even if knows he is wasting his time in the midst of privations and unimaginable sufferings. His fleeing movements always bring him back to the center, back to the worst possibility available. A traveler who willfully hurls himself to the peripheries, he is cruelly pushed back toward a hollowed-out hub that is called either Roche or Aden. The hole. He will never get through to the other side. Or else the two holes are connected, one equivalent of the other, and his life dwindles away, flowing from one vial of sand to the other. His horizon, his world as he sees it, are "desperate regions"—as if he had crossed through the gate of Hell. And humor rattles in his words: "You must think me a new Jeremiah, with my perpetual lamentations."[187]

Having made his way to Aden, he hesitates before several different prospects offered him by the future. His imagination never reaches the ends of its resources. This is how he first comes up with the idea to create a superior race of mules—the true means of transportation in these lands—for the mountainous region of Shoa. To do this he requires four or five strong jack-asses of the best breeding. So he turns to the French consul in Beirut, the viscount of Petiteville, to obtain information about the costs for the animals, their transport, and insurance to cover them.[187bis] He seems to have abandoned this project quite quickly, though two months later he did receive a letter encouraging him to go through with it. Between times, it is true, he had been troubled again by the consequences of the ill-advised Labatut matter. Antoine Deschamps had lodged a complaint with the Aden consul accusing Rimbaud of not having paid off his debts. At once Rimbaud is obliged to furnish a detailed account of the caravan's liquidation—which he did, but not without demonstrating an obvious irritation: "I thus have the honor to declare to Monsieur the Consul that henceforth I refuse to answer in any way to any demand on the subject of said matter."[187ter] Such a display of insolence would now preclude, as would be expected, any indulgence in his regard.

Continuing his search for work, he soon deems that in Massawa, where he knows the French consul Alexandre Merciniez, "there is perhaps some possibility"[188] (reading between the lines: selling arms*). However, at the end of November 1887, he remains in a state of uncertainty. Is he going to request a concession in the French colony of Obok, which he previously considered a vile place, or else solicit authorization to import military materials into Abyssinia?[189]

In addition, journalism has a new appeal for him, through which he realizes an old dream he's nourished since 1870. His article in *Le Bosphore égyptien* has given him confidence and he now plans on informing several French newspapers of his discoveries. He asks his mother for the name of the largest local periodical,[190] for he would like to publish an account of his journey; he mentions that he has sent "some articles to *Le Temps*, to *Le Figaro*, etc.," and that he would like to do the same with *Le Courrier des Ardennes*.[191] Is there any need to add that all the researchers have rushed to go through the old files in the newspaper morgues? Only to find nothing, not even the slightest suspect text adorned by some pseudonym or veiled by an anonymous author. Just

---

*Jean Voellmy has suggested to me that he wished to find a position as a war correspondent.

because Rimbaud sent some pages to these daily papers does not mean they were published. There is nothing attractive about his particularly dry prose, stripped of any picturesque elements. Nevertheless, a note by Savouré to Alfred Ilg on February 13, 1888, whom we will see again in the following pages, gives us a troubling clue. Savouré, in Paris at the time, notes laconically:

> I only know that the gossip in the papers is always more and more un-likely and contradicts on the morrow the news of the day before.
>
> It's Rimbaud in Aden who amuses himself by writing hoaxes for the press.[192]

Rimbaud the hoaxer! This clearly defamatory epithet was applied to him by the illustrious pen of François Coppée.[193] Who knows if Savouré, then a Parisian, hadn't gotten wind of his associate's literary past? There was much talk then—in a small circle, it's true—about *Illuminations*, which had just been published by the review *La Vogue*.[194] More likely an article signed "Rimbaud" in a widely distributed newspaper—but which one?— had fallen under his eyes, proof that the persistence of the Aden trader had finally been rewarded.

Furthermore, all this seems to have originated in a very specific event that is customarily given very little exposure. Paul Bourde, a former resident of Charleville, met Alfred Bardey aboard a shipping line freighter en route to the Orient. The conversation turned to the personnel of the Aden trading post and Rimbaud. Bourde, an ironic expert of some of Rimbaud's verses recently published in a review, would have revealed to his interlocutor the literary past of his strange employee. Subsequently, and no doubt encouraged by Bardey himself, he suggested that Rimbaud give him articles for *Le Temps*,[195] the newspaper for which he worked as a specialist in colonial matters:

> This would in no way be a business proposition for you, but a link by which you may reconnect to civilized life, a relationship from which you may be able to draw a moral profit. You would be paid fifty centimes a line.

The same letter clearly announces to its addressee his budding celebrity:

> You no doubt are unaware, living so far away from us, that for a small cir-cle in Paris you have become a kind of legendary figure. [. . .] Your first

works, prose and verse, have been published in Latin Quarter reviews and even collected together in a book; several young people (who I find naive) have tried to base a literary system on your sonnet about the colors of letters.

Paterne Berrichon, the first to have partially cited this letter, asserts that Rimbaud demanded an exorbitant fee of 4,500 francs for his reporting—the reason his offer was rejected. It seems, though, that he wasn't satisfied by this lone attempt and had envisioned other places to be published. The way remains open for those who would try the archives!

In all likelihood he was too demanding and soon had to abandon such projects. Fairly quickly, he deemed it preferable to fall back on the arms trade, in which he has experience and to which he now intends to devote all his efforts. He knows that Menelik and Makonnen would have need a for extra weapons in the near future. However, the prohibition on importing arms has not been lifted and would need to be skillfully skirted. Rimbaud thinks he may have found the solution by having the military materials sent in separate pieces. A means of playing on words and things. It would not be rifles transported to Shoa by camelback the entire distance between Intoto and the coast, but rather all the pieces and equipment necessary to assemble them. This is an almost brilliant idea, which he sets forth in a letter to the minister of the navy and colonies, enticing him with the establishment of a French industrial enterprise 440 miles from the coast for the benefit of a Christian power that is friendly to France.[196] He has the backing of Monsieur Fagot, deputy of the arrondissement of Vouziers, to whom Madame Rimbaud, a constituent of his district, had transmitted this request without fail. The official answer arrives in January 1888. The legislator wasn't duped. Because of the accord reached with England, Félix Faure, then undersecretary of state of the said ministry, responds that he refuses to give any authorization.[197] Rimbaud, still stuck in Aden, has no delusions: "This will happen if it happens, or it won't happen at all, which is more likely."[198] However he takes pains on behalf of his plan to interest a certain number of "capitalists"[199] (his term for them): Savouré, the Bardeys, and Ilg, whom he has seen again in Aden and with whom he maintains a correspondence. The situation is exceptionally favorable; Menelik is buying. But the Europeans, greedily intent on dividing up the western banks of the Red Sea and, even more so, Abyssinia and the neighboring lands, control the arms supply to the Abyssinian sovereigns, Menelik and Yohannes, depending on what their needs are at the moment. Rimbaud, a lucid observer of these manipulations, which furnishes additional fuel to his constant anger, draws the moral from this situation: "All the governments have sunk millions (and even billions) along these accursed, desolate coasts, where the natives wander for months without food or water, in the most dreadful climate on earth; and all these millions that have been thrown into the stomachs of the Bedouins* have brought nothing but wars and disasters of all kinds!"

"What do they mean to us, my heart, these sheets of blood?"[200] he shouted when the hours of the Commune still haunted his desire for freedom. To him, Europeans appear as despicable as Bedouins. The only ones to find grace in his eyes were the pitiful natives, born in these underprivileged lands and threatened by constant famine while fortunes are being spent all around them. The Abyssinia he envisions was already the Ethiopia of our time, with its thirsts and famines that temporarily touch the whole world. However, the words of the shrewd trader he was are unavoidably at the heart of the struggle for life that takes place there more than elsewhere: "All the same, I will perhaps find something to do there."[201]

At this time Rimbaud seems to have been in cahoots with Armand Savouré, an arms trafficker well known throughout the entire Red Sea region. In the beginning of 1888 Savouré writes him from Paris with some instructions.[202] For a fee, and at Rimbaud's own proposal, he gives him the responsibility of bringing two hundred camels to the coast, taking care to avoid the port of Zeila, then in the hands of the English, who strictly forbid this kind of commerce. Rimbaud was to make his way to a point along the coast between Dorale and Ambadu. There, a dhow laden with three hundred packages containing Remingtons and cartridges would be waiting for him.[203] The animals would only have to convey this precious merchandise to supply either Ras Makonnen or Menelik. So there was no question of Rimbaud returning with this caravan. In fact a great deal of uncertainty hovers over this matter. Rim-

---

*The Bedouins took care of the caravans. Rimbaud is thinking here of the numerous families of Abu Bekr, whom he doesn't hesitate to label as "bandits."

baud, it seems, participated in it only from a distance. It appeared that a certain *Mauconel* (as written by Rimbaud, but this no doubt is Makonnen), took a much closer hand in its operation. In April, Savouré, having come to Aden, wrote to Rimbaud to express his dissatisfaction at not having found the requested animals at the designated site. He felt his acolyte had failed in his mission.[204] In fact, Savouré had a longer stay ahead of him in Obok with his munitions and rifles piled on a boat anchored off the coast. He would be able to charter his caravan only toward the end of the year. However, his undertaking did conclude successfully in October 1888—but what a delay![205] Rimbaud certainly intervened on his behalf, but is not yet free of his commitments. Nevertheless the two men would reconcile because this was a difficult matter to bring to a successful conclusion. Indeed, the French government did not adhere to any single doctrine in this domain and would show itself by turns to be helpful and reticent. At the beginning of May, Rimbaud would receive a letter from the minister of the navy telling him that the terms of a new treaty with England allow the transport of arms through Obok, on condition their destination is Shoa,[206] but two weeks later, following new negotiations, this authorization would be jeopardized.[207] This state of affairs would prompt him to write Ilg—on June 25—to relate the difficulties encountered by Savouré: "Authorization and prohibition alternately swell [swelling] the sails of the satanic tartana jam-packed with the cursed pipes"—a pretty picture of its kind that includes allegory and metonymy ("pipes" meaning rifles). Rimbaud had experienced a similar beaching in the past when he had waited months on the beach of Tadjoura for the departure of Labatut's caravan. Soleillet's caravan was still waiting there!

The political situation in the opening days of 1888 was of an alarming nature to those who took an interest in the fate of Abyssinia. In the north the Italians continued to make their raids out of their possession Massawa. In Dogali on January 25, 1887, an armed column had been destroyed by the troops of Ras Alula. Since that time their relations with the Negus Yohannes had deteriorated considerably. Elsewhere the dervishes continued to threaten the frontiers of the empire. Because of the defeat they suffered in Metema, they had attacked the king of Gojam on January 21, 1888, in reprisal. They had taken the city, burning the churches and massacring the populace. Menelik, on the orders of his suzerain Yohannes, had come to the aid of the besieged city, but with the sole purpose of preserving his own state. Rimbaud then thought, and for good reason, that he should not undertake any new enterprise in Abyssinia except in Harar. He clearly explained his reasons in his correspondence with Ilg.[208] For the time being this later individual was no longer in Africa. Like many Europeans exhausted by spending several years in this climate, he had returned to Europe for several months—in his case Zurich. The letters of the two men testify to a great complicity between them that was not overly familiar, however. Outside of the commercial interests that drew them together, a certain humor—mixing lucidity and disillusionment—can be heard. This delectable dialogue would last for several years. Alfred Ilg's style is clumsy but singularly receptive to Rimbaud's opinions. That of Rimbaud, whose trust has been won, frees small doses of the bitter despair smoldering inside. Rimbaud Celine? Here are the sham and pangs of war, colonial stupidity Italian style: "They are going to conquer all the volcanic hillocks scattered in a thirty-mile radius around Massawa, connect them by a jury-rigged railway, and, having reached these extreme points, they will let fly at the vultures with several volleys from their howitzers, and launch a balloon beribboned with heroic slogans."[209] Ilg, on reading these words, bursts out laughing and sends back to Rimbaud the true picture he has of him: "Behind your mask of a horribly severe man is hidden a great sense of humor for which many people would have good reason to envy you."[210] He has clearly seen that Rimbaud has something to hide. No doubt he hasn't guessed that literature is the cause of that secret wound, but he refuses to believe in just the impassive face of the traveler from Aden; he senses the deep currents within. The game growing on him, he amuses himself echoing Rimbaud's jeering. This is how at the beginning of the year he announces to his correspondent the return of his two "nightmares personified," his "two terrible children": Monsieur Hénon, who had pursued Rimbaud as far as Intoto in defense of the interests of Labatut's widow, and Savouré, in Marseilles ready to depart for Africa. Mockingly, Ilg makes as if Savouré would return from France directly by rail and remarks: "I fear that the line may be somewhat interrupted [. . .] not by avalanches, but by gluttons" [avaleurs in French—translator's note].[211]

For many objective reasons and perhaps also by virtue of a certain attachment to this city at the end of the earth, Rimbaud will finally decide to conduct business in Harar again. Certainly the city appeared to be in a deplorable state the last time he was there, but more recent tidings have informed him that the situation has since improved. Accordingly, in February 1888, he makes a reconnaissance journey there, accompanied not by a caravan but alone on horseback save for one guide, and reaches the city in six days—a record. He remains there for a little more than a week and returns in five days. On March 17 he is back in Aden.[212] In such a short amount of time he has made all the most necessary connections. The news he brings back to Ilg is relatively reassuring: "Peace and silence upon the earth and under heaven. The doctors are doctoring." What does he mean by that? Not that people are striving to heal various illnesses but that the different members of the Italian scientific missions, i dottori, are sticking their noses everywhere. Alfieri in Shoa continued to perform his duties as a doctor for Menelik. Il signor Traversi was hunting hippopotamuses on the Awash; Antonelli, the Italian political representative to the sovereign's court and quite skilled in intrigue, was in Lit-Marefia, stricken with smallpox; il signor Viscardi was headed toward Aussa in the north.[213] Other characters were still coming out of the wings, henceforth they would be a part of Rimbaud's life. Brémond, who has married a native woman, "suckles his children in Alin-Amba." Bidault travels in the neighboring mountains, dragging a camera behind him (Rimbaud is recalling his own similar obsession). Appenzeller, the carpenter, and Zimmerman, the mechanic, called Zimpi, are doing their jobs for the king in Intoto (both, Swiss nationals, were friends of Alfred Ilg.[214])

Having recognized his Harar, Rimbaud returns to Aden, only to obtain supplies with which to open a trading post. He soon reaches an understanding with César Tian, one of the most reputable traders of the port. Sympathetic, loyal, quick-witted, this older man, with an imposing white beard, places his full confidence in Rimbaud, who will be his new business correspondent.[215] The "new wandering Jew" embarks on a small steamship with the Righas brothers (Dimitri and Athanasios), Ugo Ferrandi (who will relay the facts to us), and a young Greek, Christos Mousaia. They make a direct route to Berbera, where they take a rest; three days later they reach Zeila. In Zeila, an indispensable relay point for his commerce, Rimbaud installs the Greek Sotiro, with whom he had already worked during the days when he was employed by the Bardey brothers. Then, at the beginning of May, he takes the road to Harar. After a detestable journey under a driving rain,[216] he finally enters the old city.

A strange document, discovered by Enid Starkie in the Foreign Office archives, mentions the presence during these months of a certain "M. Rembau" (or "Remban"), "merchant," "one of the most intelligent and active agents of the French government."[217] This "Rembau" was reported to have accompanied a caravan of ivory and slaves that arrived in Ambos around May 10. It was led by Ibrahim Abu Bekr, one of the sons of the pasha of Zeila, who controlled this kind of traffic throughout this entire part of the coast. The name "Rembau" gives every reason to believe that it clearly designates our Rimbaud. But the date of the caravan's arrival leaves us perplexed since, at this time—as we are about to see—Rimbaud was specifically in Harar since May 3. We recall that he had made a quick trip lasting from mid-February to March 17, the date on which he returned to Aden, but there is nothing guaranteeing that on this occasion he may have gone down as far as the coast with Abu Bekr's caravan, which was proceeding at an extremely slow pace, besides. The dates, in any case, do not coincide. What should we think of this official document (for which there is a duplicate in Italian)? It would seem on this occasion that it was simply a matter of hearsay. Mr. Matucci believed it was possible to attribute this error to British informers, who were generally ill disposed to the French traders.[218] Rimbaud's activity at this time, his two trips to Harar, could only promote such confusion. We see also that his skill as a trader and the numerous initiatives he took had earned him some notoriety, giving rise to many of the rumors that were inevitable in such a case.

On his arrival in Harar, Rimbaud establishes his trading post; he rents a small house where he will live with his servant, Djami Wadai, until his final departure. When the Tharaud brothers made their way there in 1936 they found only a pile of fallen stones.* In Harar, where the European community

---

*But they say that Rimbaud inhabited this house between 1881 and 1891. Now Rimbaud's residence in 1881, then undoubtedly in 1883 1884, that of Raouf Pasha, was— according to O. Rosa (1930)—destroyed on the orders of Lijd Yassu, Menelik's grandson, who had become governor of Harar. That of 1887, on the other hand, stands out in the background (especially noticeable is an ostrich crossing a dirt street) of a photo in Rosa's work, *L'Impero del Leone di Giuda* (op. cit., p. 145). According to the author, a post office was subsequently constructed on this site.

---

numbers no more than several dozen individuals, Rimbaud claims to be the sole Frenchman;[219] at least he proclaims to be so in[220] his quickness to overlook the priests of the Catholic mission. Free and in good shape for the first time in a long while, he finally allows a slightly optimistic tone to be heard in his letters, which is surprising, coming from him: "I am doing well. I have much to do, and I am all alone. I am in a cool place and content to take a rest, or rather refresh myself, after three summers spent on the coast." How his happiness can momentarily depend on so little. In the evening a soothing breeze cools the city. The stench of decay it stirs up is of little import. Rimbaud is once again seated in the shadow of his trading post, near his scales, and has products stacked in his warehouse. There is the strong odor of dried leather and musk; the sparkle of ivory and gold. He sticks to his lair, wearing canvas clothes, with his gray hair and an attentive eye for the quality of his commodities. Or else with his head bent over his writings, not verses, but accounts, calculations, business letters, while waiting for his capital to inflate, a useless treasure. There is no question of him returning to Europe, like the others, to restore his morale: "I find myself settled back here for a long time" (letter to his family of May 15). "I have settled down here again for a long time" (letter to his family of July 4). Self-persuasion? Sacrificial premeditation?

Quickly, though, and by an all-too-familiar process, his fine hopes deteriorate and boredom reappears like an inexpugnable truth that remains sealed to his heart: the very substance of existence, for the little he feels to have one: "I am still extremely bored; I have never known anyone who is as bored as I am."[221] Rimbaud was not only a very great poet and a worthy explorer, but someone whom boredom will have reduced for a long time to its mercy and whom it will have molded into its very quintessence. And the report will not be late in coming, the judgment of his heart of hearts on the image of himself as seen in other's eyes, a result in the form of nothing:

And then, how miserable this life is without family, without intellectual occupation, lost in the midst of Negroes whose lot I would like to improve, but who seek to exploit you and make it impossible for you to complete your business quickly. Forced to speak their lingo, to eat their filthy foods, and to be subjected to a thousand aggravations resulting from their laziness, their disloyalty, their stupidity![222]

How far away now are the *Livre nègre* and the vices of the depraved raised to the rank of cardinal virtues. But it isn't hard to see that behind these "Negroes" it is the entire world he is accusing, and the obstacle that this world always opposed to his superior celerity and his metamorphic mobility. August 4, 1888: Rimbaud feels like the most isolated of men. Robinson Crusoe at the ends of the earth on the isle of Harar. He holds the desire to speak and not become stupefied within, and enjoys a new taste for his returning intellect. Rimbaud is a thinking adventurer, not simply an instinctive march. A mind that walks, and with this walk, pushes himself well beyond the point to which his body can take him.

Business goes on; he organizes caravans, prospects for commodities, and sells and barters musk, ivory, gum, coffee, and gold. The talers pile up; the native populace sometimes surrender him treasures for trifles. Thus César Tian has no cause for surprise when Rimbaud places orders for "strange articles" for which at first he does not see any necessity.[223] But quick to return is the hour of dialogue with himself every day, and every night when he cannot find sleep. Did they really understand what he was saying over there, in Roche, when he talked about trading in arms? Once again he'd received a lecture from Madame Rimbaud in a quarrelsome response and has to defend himself from accusations that strike him to the quick. "Please believe that my conduct has been beyond reproach. It is rather I who have been exploited by others in all that I have done."[224]

The emphasis on misfortune is repeated like an epic formula: "My life in these countries, as I've often said, but can never say enough, and I have hardly anything else to say, is painful, made short by boredom and exhaustions of all kinds."[225] Yes! Like a song of misery Rimbaud utters a few incantatory words that in no way exorcise but simply speak in black and white, to be over and done with. Identical to reality, they are the excretory sap of that reality. This gaze brought to bear upon life, this never-ending interrogation, is ceaselessly present. As is the glare of the evidence—against which nothing can be done. In his poems and in his last letters he always invoked the bare facts.

The movement of foreigners coming to the city becomes particularly important toward the end of 1888.[226] He estimates this city to hold 40,000 inhabitants, one of the most commercial centers of eastern Africa. Its annexation by Menelik had created a new situation. In October, Jules Borelli, who with Rimbaud had been one of the first to have traveled the route from Intoto to Harar, and subsequently reconnoitered other regions, made a stop at the trading post. We can guess that the two men talked more about exploration than business. Exhausted and gnawed by cruel fevers, Borelli was preparing to return to Europe. He will not get that far, though, and must be satisfied reaching Cairo, where his brother would put him up. He would write a letter from there to Rimbaud in January 1889. Several weeks later Savouré arrives with his caravan of 250 camels, loaded with weapons. His undertaking has finally been crowned with success. For several days he rests up at Rimbaud's. On October 17 he starts off toward Ankober, the ancient royal residence and terminus of his journey. That December in turn, Ilg, back from Europe by way of Zeila, accompanied by forty camels loaded with machinery intended for the king, will make a long stay at the factory. He remains there for so long (a month and a half) because it takes him until then to find camels ready to make the trip into Shoa. He would not leave the city until February 5. His intention, directly inspired by a recent plan of Rimbaud's, is to establish a cartridge factory permitting him to manufacture munitions on location instead of buying those made elsewhere for top dollar. In addition, Harar would now see the transit of a good number of other foreigners. Among them are Count Teleki, a Hungarian explorer who has just crossed Kenya, and Nerrazzini, Count Antonelli's correspondent who will remain there some time.

However, considerable political changes were about to leave their mark on the history of this part of Africa. Abyssinia was part of the realm of two sovereigns: in the north, Emperor Yohannes, and in the south, Menelik. This latter was the vassal of the emperor, who held the title Negus Negusta, but he was constantly extending his own power and Yohannes could not remain blind to such an open display of ambition, all the more so as he knew Menelik was Italy's favorite. Conflict was inevitable. To settle some rulership problems in the kingdom of Gojam (whose former king had rebelled), the emperor had intervened personally; on this occasion, Menelik had—it was said—lent rifles to the rebels. Yohannes threatened to invade Shoa in retaliation. War was imminent. Both sides massed their troops on the opposite banks of the Abbai River. Makonnen, Menelik's general, held himself ready to intervene. However, after a long period remaining on the alert, both sovereigns decided to make peace. In fact, the Mahdists—those Muslim integrists who now were the dominant power in the Sudan—were ceaselessly harassing the imperial army. Yohannes took a courageous stand in opposition to these hordes spilling over his borders. On March 8, in Metemma, he was on the brink of defeating them when, seriously wounded by a stray bullet, he died of his wounds. In mourning, his army abandoned the field. Menelik, who had hardly shown his solidarity with the emperor on this occasion, found himself much more powerful after this unexpected death. Mangash, the son of the Negus, had little hope of asserting his claims. The king of the Shoa, on the other hand, made a constant show of his military power, which was partially financed by the Italians who were nurturing some long-range plans with which they hoped to circumvent him eventually. These apparently friendly relations with Italy would be strengthened over the course of the year 1889. This was grist for the newspapers and Rimbaud paid particularly close attention to the columns on the subject. Count Antonelli and his assistants, Traversi, Ragazzi, etc., were hindering commercial operations planned by the other European traders based on arms sales. In fact, the Italians, in order to gain the goodwill of the king, did not hesitate to heap presents of a very special kind upon him. This was the reason they gave him 5,000 rifles and large amounts of ammunition in January 1889, no doubt hoping he would put their gift to good use against Yohannes, who was still alive then and whose empire included the section around Massawa that they coveted. That same year, after the death of the Negus and the coronation of Menelik, they signed with the latter, on May 2, the ambiguous Treaty of Ucciali, which reserved for them a territory surrounding Massawa. Quickly occupying this neighboring fringe beyond its assigned limits, they rapidly turned it into a colony: Eritrea. There was now question of Ras Makonnen going on a visit to Italy with Count Antonelli. The governor would thereby once again be leaving Harar and leaving his city in the hands of the *choums* (a kind of police authority), who were strongly inclined to exercise their authority well beyond reasonable limits. This splendid Shoan mission would have the added gift of provoking Rimbaud's hilarity. On more than one occasion he would evoke it for the delectation of his correspondent, Alfred Ilg: "Poor *tota*," he writes about Makonnen!"I can see him from here, puking on his boots between Alexandria and Naples, and the *djanos** of

---

*Tota—a small Abyssinian monkey. *Djanos*—clothing.

---

the Shoan Embassy floating on the planks."[227] For his part, Makonnen expected mountains and marvels from this journey: machine gun batteries, bundles of silk (what Rimbaud sold!), enormous sums of money. Once again there was a risk trade would suffer as a result; the situation deteriorated, subject to—as Rimbaud amusingly puts it—the alternatives of being raised up or flattened."

However at the beginning of 1889, business matters had not yet taken such a downturn. In the space of several months, Rimbaud had been able to establish himself as the best trader in the area. The prices for ivory, *zebad* (musk), etc., were calculated in Abyssinia on the basis of his estimations. Of course he had to take into account direct competitors—Antoine Brémond, for example, the doyen of the French in the country, who sought to establish a rival trading post. "This place is very bad for people like him who *wish to earn a lot and work a little*,"[228] notes Rimbaud without batting an eyelash. He is speaking as one who had made his warehouse the key point and pivot for trade in the region with his persistence and intense activity. Kept abreast of all operations by his barefoot messengers, controlling the movement of caravans, he took receipt of merchandise, packaged his own before shipping it back out, and set the price for goods. Such was the substance of his daily life.

Soon, though commercial transactions would become particularly delicate; there would be neither coins nor talers, not even those withdrawn from circulation. In addition the king decides to levy an extraordinary tax that affects not only the natives but all the European merchants as well. "Here we are sentenced as *gabares*,"*[229] Rimbaud states indignantly, planning to lodge a protest in Obok with Léonce Lagarde, and in Aden with the French consul. To Menelik any means that refill the vaults of his treasury are good. A caravan arrives in Zeila carrying 10,000 talers for Rimbaud. This money is immediately requisitioned by customs officials,[230] and it calls for the intervention of Monsignor Taurin with the authorities for the money boxes to be restored finally to their true addressee. Such procedures would multiply to the point that English soldiers, brought specially from Zeila, would be necessary for the transport of any money. "Instead of paying [meaning, what they owe] they steal,"[231] Rimbaud remarks tersely when thinking of the money owed

---

* *Gabares*—taxpayers, individuals sentenced to forced labor.

Savouré by the king, who until now has been reimbursed only by some partial I O U s. Rimbaud, writing to Ilg, doesn't beat around the bush. Reading what he said about Makonnen and Menelik, we are forced to conclude that these gentlemen held no special place in his heart. How could he have felt otherwise if we believe the picture he paints of the situation: "an odious tyranny, that needs must stain the name of the Amhara in general for a long time.[. . .] For a month now they have been sequestering, beating, dispossessing, and imprisoning the people of the city, in order to extort from them as much of the sum demanded as possible."[232] The payments for the merchandise he has received and the amounts he owes to Savouré, Ilg, and some others, can only be settled under the form of equivalents—coffee, for example (at its sale price in Harar or Aden). As for real talers, they are rarer than a white crow, and to see the color of one "you would have to strangle the cashiers and smash open the cash boxes."

Nonetheless, Rimbaud continues to keep some merchandise circulating. Constant exchanges take place between the coast (Zeila) and Harar (where goods manufactured or warehoused in Aden are transported), and between Harar and Intoto or Ankober: ivory, gold rings and chains, civet, gum, coffee, or coming from Europe, fabrics, cotton, yarn, and different textiles: silk for the *matebs*,* blue thread for the *djanos*; coarse silk of red, yellow, and violet; pearls and *birilles*, the jugs for mead that Rimbaud had had the idea to have manufactured to his design in France and with which he is now flooding the Abyssinian market. He launches out with typically European items, the 1,400 saucepans, for example, that he sends to Ilg[233]—who can hardly picture what use they would serve in a land where everyone has at their disposal traditional utensils perfectly suited to his or her purpose. But his bazaar is nothing next to his emulator and competitor, Antoine Brémond, whose boutique reveals bric-a-brac worthy of the antique dealer from "La Peau de chagrin": hairbrushes, sculpted oysters, julienne for soups, slippers, macaroni, nickel chains, wallets, boleros, cologne, peppermints, and so forth,[234] the perfect panoply of the useless.

As the months passed, Rimbaud found the ideal correspondent and almost a confidant in the person of Alfred Ilg. The letters he sent to Roche

---

* Silk laces or ribbons that Abyssinian Christians wear around their neck to show that they have been baptized (from a note by J. Voellmy).

---

grew further and further apart. What did he have to talk to them about, except his nullity! Ilg, on the other hand, shared his vexations, was informed of the slightest doings of the kingdom, and knew how to let someone in on a secret. A great complicity existed between them. The engineer, Menelik's counselor, liked to tease Rimbaud affably: "Thus you will give me your kind assistance in earning my first 100,000 francs of principal. I will endeavor to do as much for you so as to have the pleasure later of eating in your company and passing on lugubrious ideas."[234] Resolutely optimistic, Ilg is eager to profit from Rimbaud's wise words and gives him perfect cues. If necessary, he prods him: "You know how to tell a story so well when you want to, but it appears that your splendid business deals have completely deprived you of what little good humor you had left."[236] "Splendid business deals!" The term was certainly an exaggeration. Rimbaud did not cease to storm about the shameless taxes that struck the items he traded both upon entering and exiting the city. In fact, all merchandise transported through his trading post fell under the blow of double taxation. In irritation he lodged a complaint and asked Menelik to intervene—which the king did, almost magnanimously, by sending him a letter with superb calligraphy in Ge'ez letters and signed "the lion of the tribe of Judah, the Lord's chosen, king of kings of Ethiopia,"[237] But in fact this solemn epistle advised him to await the return of Dejash Makonnen for the matter to be settled.

Makonnen, for his part, continued on his prestigious journey. The Shoan Embassy had received a triumphant welcome first in Naples, then in Rome. In October an additional clause to the Treaty of Ucciali was signed, one that rolled back the frontiers of the Italian colony and granted Abyssinia a loan of 4 million lire. After having seen the eminent figures of Italy, who were no less curious to see him, Makonnen was—it was said—en route to the Holy Land. Rimbaud, who informed Ilg of this, added to the planned itinerary the cities of Sodom and Gomorra[238] and, finding again the amicable idiom he used with Delahaye, insinuates that the ras must presently be in Solomon's city: "Je rusalème à le croire!"* [239] He viewed the Shoan mission somewhat like a large-scale farce, and for him it remained the funniest event of the year. Receiving the old newspapers that came out of Aden, he collected all the articles that

---

* A pun that turns *Jerusalem* into the first-person pronoun and a verb—translator's note.

alluded to the voyage of the governor,[240] for whom he could easily imagine the upcoming reception in Harar: "We will be waiting here, waving our bills with a choir of curses."[241]

However, in Paris another event was holding everyone's attention, the famous Universal Exposition with which the Third Republic wished to assert all its prestige. Greatly admired there were the Hall of Machinery, the Central Dome, and most of all, the metallic "shepherdess"[242] of the bridges across the Seine: the Eiffel Tower. Madame Rimbaud and Isabelle had spoken of it to the exile, who was, in his fashion, also sharing in the prodigious prosperity of France at this time. Rimbaud would regret being unable to attend. But his business forbids him from making such distant journeys: "At the next one I could perhaps exhibit the products of this country," he remarks, "and maybe exhibit myself, because I believe I will have an excessively baroque air after a long stay in lands such as these."[243] He knows all too well that he has become an "odd duck," another kind of man even more bizarre than the adolescent he once was who wished to make himself monstrous in the example of the children tortured by the *comparachicos*. However, in this year of 1889, he had no need to exhibit himself for people to judge him "baroque." Another word then in vogue among literary circles is certainly much more appropriate, the word *decadent*. *Les Déliquescences d'Adoré Floupette*, a small volume due to Gabriel Vicaire and Henri Beauclair, published immediately after Verlaine's *Les Poètes maudits*, recalls in its pages "the consent of large heliotropes" from "Oraison du soir," turned into "the consent of your callybistris." Other pastiches had circulated since, parodying—in the inevitable return of things—the former *Zutistes: Le Limaçon* by Laurent Tailhade, "L'Oméga blasphématoire" by Ernest Raynaud, etc.[244] But Rimbaud couldn't or rather didn't want to know. While he may not have gone to the Universal Exposition, Savouré, who had left Africa for several months, on the other hand, did make the rounds. On this occasion he announced a strange visit to Rimbaud: "You are going to see coming to your house a charming boy bearing you this letter, Monsieur Georges Richard. He is much more up on the Exposition than I, who saw only very little of it. He will tell you of all its wonders. He has, I believe, friends that were once your friends."[245] The past, over which Rimbaud had cast a veil, was threatening to come back to the surface. Periodically letters to which he failed to respond would arrive recalling those undesirable times: a letter from Delahaye, a missive from Verlaine, a word from Paul Bourde, and now the announced arrival of this Georges Richard, a friend, we may assume, of someone like Richepin, or Forain, or any number of others. In truth no one has shown any interest in this individual mentioned only by Savouré, but he was assuredly one of the last people to speak of literature with Rimbaud, at the risk of being sent packing on the spot by the person who repressed such memories.

In Abyssinia, political events followed their course. Having eliminated Yohannes's weak successors, Menelik had himself proclaimed *Negus Negusta*, "King of Kings." He was crowned emperor on November 3, 1889, in Intoto, at the church of Marium, which had been built on his initiative two years previously. The *abouna*, the head of the Coptic community of Abyssinia, presided over the ceremony. Alfred Ilg was in attendance but no evidence of this can be found in his letters.[*] Perhaps he knew Rimbaud cared little for such details. The supremacy of the Negus did not prevent serious skirmishes in the territories inhabited by the independent tribes. During the night of December 23, a caravan out of Zeila that was camping near Emsa was attacked. The merchandise that it was transporting was stolen, along with 25,000 talers, 10,000 of which had been sent by César Tian to Rimbaud. In addition, two French Capuchins and two Greeks had been murdered. The press was buzzing over this event. César Tian, wishing to reassure Madame Rimbaud, quite kindly informed her that her son had not been a member of the convoy and that the incident was exceptional in nature.[246] The announcement of this carnage alarmed all the Europeans living in Harar. The exchanges with Zeila were interrupted during the end of 1889. A certain quantity of merchandise sent from the interior remained stuck in Gueldessa. The English attempted to mount reprisals but the tribes of the Issas and the Gadiboursis, authors of the Emsa massacre, would remain impregnable for a long time.

Rimbaud, still doing business with Ilg, could not pull as much as a simple franc out of these dirty coffees (the "filthy stuff," the "rubbish") he was given by way of payment for the merchandise with which he had been entrusted.[247] Furthermore, Ilg had left with the emperor for Boroda, where he would be staying for several months. All the Europeans, with the exception of Rimbaud,

[*] See Conrad Keller, *Alfred Ilg*, p. 174.

frequently moved from place to place. They often accompanied their caravans going down to the coast. Rimbaud, however, remained in his factory to
which he was attached by his work and the need for constant supervision—
which didn't prevent him from making his daily rounds, on foot or horseback,
outside of the city, over rough terrain, where there were not even any well-
marked paths. In January, the Frenchman Chefneux, whom he had met in
Tadjoura at the time of the Labatut expedition, came to see him.[248] Rimbaud
was going through a new period of bitterness and resentment. His letters
home express quite well his state of cold distress. "I never have anything interesting to say,"[249] he declares. This is the man who drew the definitive portrait
of these picturesque lands that for him have now become "filthy countries"
and "accursed zones." "Deserts inhabited by stupid Negroes, with no roads,
no mail, no travelers: what do you expect me to write about that? That one is
become vexed, that one is bored, that one is growing stupider and stupider;
that one has reached one's limits but one cannot give it up, etc. etc.!" The conclusion is inevitable: "It's necessary to shut up."[250] He repeats the same
words; pleonasm hammers out fact. The torture goes on. A taste for a peni-
tent infinity breaks loose from all that. And the necessity for muteness in
which he wishes to seal himself.

However—we know this for a fact—he dedicated himself each day to his
writings: accounts, business letters (in which he sometimes distilled a few
drops of humor for Ilg, his sole confidant thus privileged). The testimonies
concerning this stage of his life are at odds with one another. Rimbaud seems
to have created several different personas. Bardey, with whom he had words,
declares that "his caustic and biting spirit made him many enemies" and that
he "was never capable of getting rid of that wretched, wicked, satirical mask
that concealed, however, the true qualities of his heart."[251] This judgment,
formulated after Rimbaud's death, echoes one that Alfred Ilg wrote to Rimbaud himself: "Behind your terrible mask of a horribly severe man hides
[. . .]."[252] Yes. Rimbaud wears a mask just as in 1871 he had chosen to play a
perfectly thought-out role that was completely exaggerated and significative
of his desire to deprave himself. It is difficult to determine his true nature,
although we constantly hear its truth, which is the effort of his search.
Because it pleases him—as if he were affected by a very strange form of
dandyism—to present contradictory aspects of himself. His truth stems from

346

the secret osmosis that reattaches the opposing parts of himself. His "I is an other" is not a futile phrase, but the expression of his consciously dilacerated being. The Bardeys and Alfred Ilg, who spent time with him personally, always sensed a sort of dissimulation in him that was not so much a ruse as a personal decision not to speak, to keep his mouth shut. Rimbaud's "it's necessary to shut up" utterly belongs to the adventure of a life voluntarily linked to silence. However, other witnesses, such as the Italian Robecchi-Brichetti, whom he welcomed into his home in Harar,[253] show him in a more affable light. Rimbaud, without ever laughing, though, would recount a great many anecdotes and entertain his guests with his banter and sometimes blunt humor. Robecchi-Brichetti recalls evenings in the factory, where served by the faithful Djami, discussions took place in all languages and on the most diverse subjects between joyful table companions.

Such accounts would be corroborated later on by those of Savouré, for example: "I have never seen him laugh, whereas he can make you laugh until you cry with his ways of one of the most charming storytellers I have ever met."[254] And Pierre Bardey would describe the antagonistic sides of his personality: "He appeared a little odd to me. Sometimes he was morose and silent, seemingly seeking to avoid the company of his fellows; and sometimes he opened up, becoming a pleasant conversationalist with a slightly caustic verve that led him to ridicule the doings and gestures of the people he depicted in his stories."[255] This was no doubt the real Rimbaud—a personal work just as his poems were—a rebel, a loner, yet never disdaining to share the harsh vision he had of people and things. Difficult to grasp because he concealed himself, not out of cowardice or shyness, but out of an inner necessity that remains short of consenting laughter to which he prefers the stinging irony that reduces creatures to an automatic behavior pattern and gestures of nullity. However, in his letters to his family he would never allude to the few gatherings that sometimes procure for him, for the space of an evening, a brief image of happiness. No doubt he preferred putting the worst face on his life, as a means of making an impression on the *mother*, who, over there on her lands in Roche, was helpless to do anything about it. He is perfecting his portrait and discreetly suggesting his future hagiography: "In the countryside and on the road, I enjoy a certain consideration on account of the way I treat people. I've never caused anyone any harm. On the contrary,

I have done some good when the opportunity has arisen, and it is the sole activity from which I derive any pleasure."[256] It is difficult to assess such remarks at their true measure. What was the reason behind this brief apology? In several previous letters Rimbaud had already emphasized his irreproachable conduct. Didn't his mother have ambitions of getting him married on his projected return to the Ardennes for a summer sojourn? The fact is that 1890 marks the year in which, again, he conjures up this possibility he had already envisioned in 1883. During his last stay in Harar he does not seem to have entered any sort of relationship and the only mention of anyone at his side is that concerning his young and faithful servant, Djami. But other, later accounts, put forth by merchants in Djibouti (where he never went), which were collected by Pierre Mille in 1896, attribute an entire harem to him, a "series of dictionaries bound in skin,"[257] thanks to whom he was allegedly able to learn a number of native dialects! We won't put much faith in this gossip, especially if we keep in mind that Rimbaud was once the head of a *harim*, by which we mean a workshop of women—coffee sorters in this instance, and not beautiful concubines.

Rimbaud's identity remains a secret. Intense activity and laziness. Anger and wisdom. He certainly learned to judge others with some degree of commiseration: The people of Harar are neither more stupid nor more unscrupulous than the white Negroes of the so-called civilized countries; they are not of the same order, and that is all. They are even less wicked and in certain cases can even show sentiments of gratitude and loyalty. It is just a matter of treating them like human beings."[258] Was he recalling certain pages from *Une saison en enfer?*" "I am a beast, a Negro. But I can be saved. You are fake Negroes, you maniacs, savages, misers. Merchant, you are a Negro; Judge, you are a Negro; General, you are a Negro."[259] It would be out of place to talk of negritude with regard to Rimbaud. A better way of understanding this would be to say that in each of us there is *a Negro* and we are all oppressed by our condition as slaves of life. He is seeing the "white Negro" that hides behind the honorable roles assumed by the European. Later, in a display of marvelous sympathy, Verlaine, would evoke this Rimbaud of the difference:[260]

Toi mort, mort, mort! Mais mort du moins tel que tu veux,
En nègre blanc, en sauvage splendidement

Civilisé, civilisant négligemment . . .
Ah, mort! Vivant plutôt en moi de mille feux.

Dead, dead dead! But dead at least as you wanted
as a white negro, a splendidly civilized
savage, nonchalantly civilizing . . .
Ah dead! Rather you live in me with a thousand fires.

Nevertheless, what did this humanitarianism, of which he can show proof, matter to the natives who spent time with him and sometimes gave him their confidence? It was said that the people of Harar did not hesitate to speak to him. Furthermore, he was one of the rare individuals who knew their language and whom they ranked as a member of their society. He sometimes signed his name with a seal that bore his name in Arabic letters "Abdo Rimbo." Rimbaud Abdullah, the servant of God, the transporter of incense. There is nothing in all this that implies he embraced the Islamic faith. Along with these generous actions toward some poor wretches whom he sometimes helped as a Good Samaritan, it is important not to overlook his acts of brutality and the scorn he displayed for those he ceaselessly accused of laziness and causing obstacles in the course of his business.[261] In February 1889, he had poisoned some of the dogs that haunted the city in huge packs and soiled the sacks of coffee piled up along the walls of his warehouse on a regular basis. This caused a scandal. The specifics of the case pursued the guilty party who was summoned to account for his actions before the court. He earned a nickname from this, and Savouré would recall it in a letter to the main party concerned: "It appears at present that people are saying Rimbaud, or the terror of dogs"[262] (in Aden he had been the "nasty guy"). As an epilogue to this story of dead dogs that had been the talk of the town, two years later Rimbaud will mention a certain Banti (in his status as a grazmatch*), "the dog's protector,"[263] who was then leaving Harar to settle much farther south in the Ogaden. Was this the person who had him hauled before the judges by lodging a complaint about his actions? In any case, it would be false to claim that he was unanimously appreciated by the Hararis. If he was

---

* Grazmatch: Commander of an army's left flank.

honest and straightforward in his business dealings, he displayed, on the other hand, only a mitigated sympathy for these "Negroes," whom he considered to belong to an inferior race—which doesn't imply that he had any greater admiration for the Europeans.

The broken connections with the coast were finally restored in March 1890. The conflict between the English and the Issas had been resolved. The 10,000 talers César Tian had sent to Rimbaud and which had been held up in Zeila made their way to him. In the other direction his merchandise that had been detained in Gueldessa was now leaving by caravan for the Red Sea.[264]

The emperor had beaten his adversaries in his expedition to Tigray in northern Abyssinia. However, Makonnen, who had assisted in these operations, still had not returned to Harar, thus preventing Rimbaud from being completely reimbursed. As for Ilg, he had accompanied Menelik, and the letters addressed to him in Intoto had been received by his friend, the engineer Zimmerman, who had taken over his affairs during his absence. Other than this, the news wasn't good. Nothing was selling. Rimbaud is worried about all the money that he should be taking in, but his merchandise finds no takers. His impatience is further increased by César Tian's demand for 4,000 talers from him (the sum Rimbaud had been compelled to lend to the Abyssinian government).

Furious, he sends a sharp letter to Menelik in which he demands, in addition to what he is owed, 2,000 talers interest[265] and threatens to lodge a complaint with the French consul in Aden. Eventually this matter would be settled and the municipal treasury of Harar would reimburse him for the debts it had contracted with him almost a year previously.

During March 1890, he seems to have seriously contemplated breaking his work relationship with César Tian, who he thinks exploited him.[266] Here again we see the mistrust he displayed earlier toward the Bardeys. His idea is not so much to leave Harar but to start over on a new foot the following year, after he has liquidated all his merchandise. Over the next months he would continue to press Ilg to sell off his wretched saucepans, for which the native populace has no use. Ilg, concerned with larger schemes, truthfully devoted little attention to the sale of this cumbersome stock. At least he offers reassurance to Rimbaud, whom he still esteems: "Again I tell you, don't worry yourself sick, that won't do you any good, we are already aging quickly enough."[267] Rimbaud knows this all too well; he has just written his mother: "I am doing well, but one of my hairs turns white every minute. Given the length of time this has been happening, I fear I will soon have a head like a powder puff. This betrayal by one's scalp is depressing; but what can you do?"[268] What his "scalp" is betraying is precisely the verity of the troubles accumulating under his skull. At less than thirty-six years of age, Rimbaud is turning whiter in the land of the "Negroes." We don't know him under this real light; the black-and-white photos give only an imperfect image of his pre-maturely hoary head, a sign that depressed him, the staging and rehearsal before death (which he little suspected was so close). His mother still doggedly hoped to get him married if he returned to Europe. Without expressing much regret, he replies: "I have neither the time to get married, nor even think about getting married."[269] Yet marriage would remain one of the key words in the letters he sends to his family during this period. In August 1890, he himself becomes the one asking that question: "Could I come home and get married next spring? [. . .] Do you think that I will be able to find someone who will consent to travel with me? I would like to have an answer to this question as soon as possible."[270] There is no reason to doubt that he was worn out from his life of solitude. He is haunted by banal dreams, though they are marked by the seal of the impossible: return to France— something he will never do, unless compelled by mortal urgency—find a wife, and finally take on an image of respectability.

He kept harping on these familiar themes at the end of 1890, though mod-ulating them with serious reservations: "In speaking of marriage I've always meant to say that I intend to remain free to travel, living abroad, and even continuing to live in Africa. [. . .] If there is one thing I find impossible, it's the sedentary life."[271] He had perceived the truth of this quite clearly in Cairo when he had resumed contact with civilization and spent hours in his room at the Hôtel d'Europe. In fact, marriage for him consisted of a word that he restricted himself to speaking as a kind of exorcism, for strictly personal use, intended for his mother, for example, who wished to see him on the straight and narrow path, and for his sister, whose own plans of finding a husband have been shelved. Yet in a letter dated November 10, 1890, he lays out a series of personal details worthy of a matrimonial agency. He soberly describes his work, mentions the honorable nature of his employer, and points out that the

French consul can furnish the best references about him. He ends with a short laudative couplet: "No one in Aden has anything bad to say of me. To the contrary. I am well known to everyone in this country and have been for the last ten years." His purpose is clear. He makes it even clearer: "If anyone's interested!" The terrible sufferings that are going to strike him will prevent us from ever knowing what the upshot of all these attempts would have been. What person did Madame Rimbaud have in mind for him? What young girl of Roche or Charleville was ready to go into exile with the prodigal son?

More worrisome to him than a hypothetical marriage was the state of his accounts with Savouré. This latter had just returned from Paris with his head brimming with ideas. As in the past he was possessed by a mania for construction. He had had a "palace" built in Ankober large enough to contain two hundred camel loads, flanked by a stable for forty donkeys. In admiration of the Universal Exposition he had visited in October 1889, he had bought dozens of small iron girders in France. Arriving in Obok, he was thinking of building a trading post there: "He built a scale model of the Eiffel Tower with the help of fifty masons,"[272] Rimbaud informs Ilg. Rimbaud had tried to get the best price for the goods entrusted to him by Savouré. Now the latter was demanding his money, but Rimbaud had been paid only in coffee with an equivalent value to 8,800 talers. Eventually, though not smoothly, things would work out and Savouré would obtain his due in good hard cash and not in trade goods.[273] Other matters didn't cease to trouble Rimbaud: the repercussion of the Labatut affair. The "dirty bitch" and her son felt he owed them an additional sum and applied to the king, who had taken their complaints under consideration. We will recall, that in the press of events, Rimbaud had at first dealt with his accusers somewhat lightly. He was far from being free of them. In addition, Zimmerman continued to recount the difficulties he was encountering trying to dispose of the famous stock of 1,400 saucepans sent to Intoto. That August, however, Zimmerman came to Harar to bring the money thus earned, but there were still several hundred units to be sold before the entire lot was disposed of.[274]

On his return from Tigray with Menelik, Ilg again concerns himself with some absorbing tasks. He nonetheless takes the time to seek out a good *saggar* (ambling) mule for Rimbaud, who had insistently asked him for one. In one of his letters in which he states he has not yet procured the animal, he apolo-

gizes for not being able to furnish some merchandise of a completely different nature: "As for slaves, I'm sorry, I cannot help you, I have never bought any
and don't wish to start. I recognize your good intentions absolutely, but I
would never do it, even for myself."[275] Indeed, Rimbaud put in such a request
and took pains to renew it December 20, 1889: "I quite seriously confirm my
order for a very good mule and two slave boys." These few lines have incited a
lively polemic among Rimbaud's biographers. Enid Starkie, strengthened by
new documents recently discovered in the Foreign Office archives, believed it
was possible to affirm that Rimbaud had participated in the traditional slave
traffic that was rampant in the ports of the Red Sea, of which the Abu Bekrs
of Zeila had arrogated the control for a long time. We have seen that this traffic, quite distinct from the arms trade, was always controlled by the Bedouins.
Mario Matucci would later contest the majority of arguments put forward by
Enid Starkie and will, by that fact, even clear Rimbaud of the accusation of
having been a slaver that has all too often been charged against him after his
death.[276] Yet we cannot deny that he had no hesitation about wishing to
acquire two slaves for his personal use, going so far as to explicitly state to the
already reticent Ilg: "I confirm," as a man perfectly aware of the scandalous
interpretations his request risked provoking. However, his actions did not
make any distinction between himself and the native populace who still made
use of this ancient custom. Furthermore, slaves were not mistreated. They
were considered as servants who were housed and fed by their masters. The
fact remains that Rimbaud concurred with an African custom that Europeans
generally condemned. Moreover, everything leads us to believe that he finally
renounced his request—unless he had satisfied it through other avenues. On
the other hand, he would still harass Ilg for months to obtain the famous *saggar* mule, indispensable for the long daily journeys he made in the mountains.

In the midst of such concerns, literature, which he had left far behind,
caught up with him again. So Rimbaud would never truly be done with it. He
had maintained his silence, though, as if to fulfill a secret vow. But his
anonymity was increasingly threatened. The success of *Illuminations* in some
small literary circles had won it a wider readership. Decadents and Symbolists
unanimously claimed him as their absolute initiator. On July 17, 1890, a certain Laurent de Gavoty, director of a small Marseillaise avant-garde review, *La
France moderne*, did not hesitate to write to him:

Monsieur and Dear Poet,

I have read your beautiful verse: this is to say how proud and delighted I would be to see the leader of the Decadent and Symbolist school contribute to *La France moderne*, of which I am the director.

I hope you will join us.

Many thanks in advance and my ardent admiration.

Such perfectly courteous phrases should have flattered their addressee; however, they roused only bitterness and disgust in him. He found some incredible scribblers there, truer than life, who retained only his "beautiful verses," whereas he "sat Beauty upon his knees" and "cursed" her.[277] Was Rimbaud, when reading this letter, at the point of not being aware of what was hatching on his account (like Cézanne fearing that his sudden admirers were plotting "a nasty surprise")? Despite the distance and his own oblivion, it appears more than likely that he didn't mistake the strange glory that was going to befall him. Even during his lifetime, Tian, Bardey, and several others had caught wind of his past activities. Bardey, notably, had questioned him on this matter,[278] and for a response got only a series of curses: "Absurd, ridiculous, disgusting." Later, Maurice Riès, who worked at the Tian Agency in Aden, mentioning Rimbaud's waxing celebrity to him, brought down only the sharpest sarcasm and the final reply : "Hogwash!"[279] an appreciation which was certainly not judged on its true merits, for it should undoubtedly be taken as spoken with more sincerity than one might think by Rimbaud when measuring the little he had left behind in comparison to a Hugo, a Baudelaire, or even a Théophile Gautier. What was the worth of his few poems, including a tour de force like "Le Bateau ivre," next to the real books he had once admired? The year before, Savouré had announced the arrival of a Georges Richard, an acquaintance of his old friends. Did this Richard come to Harar to confirm what he probably already knew from other sources such as the publication of *Les Poètes maudites*, in which Rimbaud figured at the sides of Mallarmé and another completely unknown poet, Tristan Corbière? We should at least regard as certain that he didn't reach the end of his life without sensing the unforeseeable glory that would soon become attached to his name. His trail had been followed. His "hogwash" lived on in reviews and anthologies. He had definitely not washed his hands of that stain, that ridiculous presumption, literature. We will certainly not find any correspondence with a writer in the papers he would bring from Harar. Presuming that Verlaine had tried to renew epistolary ties with him, he must have thrown away the letters. But by all evidence, people had a vague idea of his address, the great informer on this occasion being Ernest Delahaye. How did the almost forgotten Laurent de Gavoty manage to reach Rimbaud? The mystery remains unsolved. The fact remains that Rimbaud saved this impersonal, almost official letter, which no doubt did not come directly but made its way on a roundabout route, through the French consulate in Aden, for example. Didn't Verlaine then assume he was dreaming up or participating in "gigantic works of art" over in Cyprus, and then Aden?[280] The following issue of *La France moderne* (February 19–March 4, 1891) proves, in fact, that the principal party concerned neglected to respond (if he had, it would have been truly astounding), but that they had really discovered his true lair: "This time, we have him! We know where Arthur Rimbaud, the great Rimbaud, the real Rimbaud, the Rimbaud of *Illuminations* is. This is not a decadent hoax. We are declaring that we know the hiding place of the famous missing poet." Overcoming his irritation, Rimbaud stores away this unexpected letter. A final burst of pride on his part for escaping human stupefaction? Astonishment at the sight of these few "marvelocerous" lines? This simple piece of letterhead at least provides positive proof that he *knew everything*. What crazy news, people were reading his verse. For one moment, sitting between his cash box and his scales, he embraces the strangeness of his destiny. He is constrained to accept the thread—which escapes him. He sees his "other" taking shape. He sees his double—precursor of his death. Transformed into the leader of a school by Laurent de Gavoty, a third-rate alchemist, did he have any more reason to live, now that he had already survived himself?

SUFFERING AND DEATH

HIS INCONGRUOUS CELEBRITY AND THE VAGUE MARRIAGE PROJECTS THAT provide him a semblance of listening to the *mother* do not prevent Rimbaud from devoting his energies to a step he now thinks essential. He has resolved to liquidate his business with César Tian and depart before the end of 1890.[281] To do this, he absolutely must obtain the money for the merchandise he has entrusted to Ilg; he is ready to sell it all at a discount to Menelik, the only person with enough cash to buy everything in bulk. But every day counts. Because of a rise in the value of the exchange, and consequently the rupee, the taler ceaselessly declines in value. The year had been disastrous. He was now ready to leave these lands as soon, and with as little loss, as possible. Rimbaud cancels all his most recent orders. His primary concern is to inventory everything he still has. Such steps don't mean that he wanted to leave once and for all. To the contrary. Free of his arrangement with César Tian, it is probable that he contemplated settling again in Harar—though under completely different conditions.[282]

Nevertheless, the end of the year arrives before he has been able to draw up a balance sheet for his business. He anxiously presses Ilg to dump everything, but the satanic saucepans won't sell. "I've bent over backward to get rid of them," Ilg says sarcastically, "and almost everywhere today you see people walking with polished, white saucepans on their backs to attract public attention."[283] The Swiss engineer wasn't lacking in a sense of humor. Rimbaud sulks. He has quite a number of other worries pestering him. The Labatut affair, for example. On January 8, Chefneux, on the emperor's orders, had placed a writ of seizure on his merchandise in proportion to 1,800 talers, the sum owed him by Rimbaud.[284] Not only can Rimbaud no longer recover the money earned from his sales, but must again spend more if he wants his stock to be disposed of down to the last item. He is now forced to bow to the goodwill of his creditors. He agrees to pay 600 talers.[285] The seizure is lifted. He then admonishes Ilg: "End it, just end it!"[286] It is indeed time to end it. He couldn't have said it any better—or any worse. The injunction occultly hastens his end. He wishes to leave with all his affairs settled and to turn over a new leaf. Starting over at zero, of course, although he has *returned from everything*.

At the moment, amid his daily exhaustions, his journeys to sell off everything and close up shop, he begins to feel a pain in the right leg that feels like a hammer striking his kneecap once a minute. He believes it is caused by the joint drying out. He had suffered from such attacks in Cairo and Verlaine, at the time of the "Vieux Coppées" in 1877, when he wanted to make fun of him, brought up his *"rhumatisses."* This time, however, the ailment is more tenacious. It even indicates its presence by an abnormal swelling of the veins in his knee, which he first mistakes for varicose veins.[287] Hardened to pain, he nonetheless continues to work like a damned soul, making daily journeys in the mountains without conserving his strength, and still believing in the omnipotence of his body, which wouldn't dare betray him. He walks, even if it feels as if a nail were going into his leg with every step. He then rides a horse. But his difficulties are not lessened as every time he has to dismount, he is struck by pains that make him scream. The illness moves in and takes over his life. Yet he wants to hear nothing about it. He needs to sell off all his merchandise and only then will he go to Aden for treatment.

Starting from the beginning of February 1891, his suffering is so great he can longer sleep. This worries him and he asks that he be sent a stocking for varicose veins from Aden, without truly believing such an item would be found there. Soon the pain has spread and races through his leg like burning lines from ankle to waist. Nonetheless he continues to toil, fearful of losing everything. Only money matters: he refuses to believe that his failing health will be a hindrance. He bandages his leg and, as there are no doctors in Harar and he won't even dream of seeing a native bone setter, he relies on basic medications: baths and rubs—with no apparent results. He loses his appetite and grows thin. Toward the end of the month he has to alert his family of the new illness by which he's been stricken. In a letter to his mother,[288] he goes over all the reasons that might explain this endless suffering. He is no longer thinking of the "it is written" of the Koran he so deliberately accepted before. He prefers to become the man who has brought his punishment down upon himself. Multiple reasons flow from his pen: exhausting marches, interminable horseback rides. They spread, becoming commingled with the state of the world, the whole of Harar. Unhealthy living quarters, poor food, vexations, "a constant rage amid Negroes who are as stupid as they are villainous," everything that is abject, frightful, and unacceptable becomes concentrated in his ailing knee, the proliferations within a botched life. Today we would call this a psychosomatic effect. Care and anguish prevent him from walking—just as they would one night strangle Mallarmé, who would be gripped by a spasm of the glottis while at his retreat in Valvins.

Faraway, in Roche, Madame Rimbaud keeps watch over her prodigal child. This woman of duty stands firm in an attitude of proud resignation. No doubt on receipt of her son's letter, she regarded it only as the natural result of the course of things, a catastrophe she saw in advance. But she had a Dr. Poupeau come from Attigny to render a diagnosis from what the patient said in his letter, then carefully wrapped the medications and signed her letter with a disturbing *"Au revoir, Arthur,"* in which an *"Adieu"* can almost be heard. However, these Cuifs are of a resistant stock. Still they need roots. What life substance will now nourish the Harar exile? Each night he is kept awake by a fearful insomnia. During the day, he may find the strength to sell his merchandise and work on his accounts, but he remains totally incapable of walking. He has his bed placed between his cash box, his "writings," and a window looking out over the courtyard that houses the scales and where all the products bought from the surrounding area are weighed: coffee, ivory, *zebbad,* incense. However, the illness progresses, pursuing its autonomous life in Rimbaud's body. There is him and there is his illness, which he looks on like a stranger that has grafted itself to his flesh. His knee swells up, becoming a ball as large as a fist; his kneecap is immobilized. In several days he watches with terror as his knee and ham ossify and his leg becomes emaciated. He is struck as if by a metamorphosis created by a curse. There is no longer but one solution available: liquidate everything at a loss, then, after collecting his money, get out of there like an outlaw, a victim. All the Europeans in Harar are alarmed by his condition. Certainly it is common knowledge that serious illnesses threaten anyone who remains for long periods in these countries. The majority—Italians, Greeks, French—are in the habit of returning to their native lands after spending one or two years in Abyssinia. Rimbaud is the sole person who persevered in not returning to his homeland, remaining there tied to his cash box and riveted to his work. Constantine Righas, Brémond, Chefneux, and the Italian traders bestow on him what little care they have within their power to give him. Quite a commotion fills the factory. Soon he announces his intention of leaving. The cargo for the future caravan is packaged and food for the journey is collected. Rimbaud will be guided by one of the *abbans* accustomed to making the descent to Zeila. Djami accompanies him, prepared to do whatever it takes to ease the sufferings of his beloved master. Joining the caravan are Mr. MacDonald, an English merchant from the region, and his wife, and their two children. Given the weakened state of the invalid, he will be transported on a stretcher manufactured according to his own design.[290] To protect him from the sun and, more important, from periods of bad weather (it is now the middle of the rainy season), it is covered by a canvas curtain. Rimbaud hires sixteen porters who will convey him in relays of four men four times a day.

At six o'clock in the morning of April 7, 1891, he leaves Harar. He sees the house he had rented two years earlier for the last time. The porters pass through the main gate of the city. Though worried and in pain, he has firm hopes of returning there, on his way toward a harsh ordeal that he can't know will be his last. He gathers within himself that precious energy that has allowed him to triumph over the worst so many times before. Outside the walls, the caravan begins to get under way. Half-dead in his stretcher, Rimbaud feels the cruelest pains climbing through him, imposed upon him by each step of the porters' jolting march. He sums up in advance the long route he will have to travel before reaching the port. He knows it well from having traveled it so many times. He is especially apprehensive of the passage through the mountains, and the miles of desert awaiting them. The ascent to the Egou Plateau is particularly painful. On the descent, pulled by the weight they are carrying and stumbling over the rough terrain, the men barely avoid bouncing him off the stretcher. He then attempts to mount a mule, "his sick leg tied to the neck," but pushed well beyond the limits of endurable pain, he quickly gives up on this idea. They arrive in Ballawa that evening, where a campsite has been established. It starts to rain. A furious wind makes the chilly night even colder. After a dawn departure—this will be the rule during the ten-day expedition—they reach Gueldessa, on the border of Somali territory, four hours later. The men take a rest break for the afternoon; on the next day the porters reach Grasley in two hours but the caravan is trailing far behind. They have to wait. Their route that afternoon, still under rainy skies, takes them as far as Boussa. The wadi, swollen by the torrential rains, is uncrossable and Rimbaud camps close by with the MacDonalds and their children. As he is incapable of moving at all, the tent is set up above him after he has been laid down on the ground. As an added physical humiliation he must roll over to the edge of the stretcher to excrete into the sand, like a cat in ash—a detail of his misery he will later write down for his sister Isabelle when recounting his final journey. It is still raining on April 10. The cargo is reloaded on the camels, who refuse to leave. The porters then take the lead. They arrive in Wordji, located at 3,300 feet in altitude, at the beginning of the afternoon. There they wait in vain for the arrival of the camels loaded with their food and camping equipment. Under a driving rain that falls nonstop for sixteen hours, Rimbaud and his porters spend the night exposed to the wind. The invalid on his stretcher is protected only by a cowhide. Water leaks in everywhere. That morning the camels have still not finished this leg of the journey and will arrive only that afternoon. It is finally possible to eat. The rest of the journey, despite the obstacles it encounters, will not experience any more such critical phases.

But Rimbaud regularly has to tolerate the nocturnal cold, the delays of the caravan, and the exhaustion of the worn-out porters who, one time, at the end of a leg of the journey, throw him down like a lifeless package. Furious in his pain, he curses them and imposes a fine on them. Each day, though, he scribbles a summary of that day's travels on a few sheets of paper. Nothing literary about this at all. A simple account of his trip with the thought, no doubt, such notes might later prove useful. It is also a means of maintaining contact with reality, of recapturing to his satisfaction the different moments of what could only have been a nightmare absorbing him into its vertigo. Everything is jotted down in this daily log: dates, distances, timetables, fines, and even—on April 16—notes on a region to prospect in the future as a possible market. Friday, April 17, they enter the last large leg of the journey that takes them from Dadap, where they had camped for the night, to Warambot, the customary arrival point of the caravans. They are now near the coast. All the same, Rimbaud does not feel the end of his sufferings are in sight. At least he has hopes of finding some remedies soon. In Zeila he visits his old friend Sotiro, César Tian's agent for the area, then has himself hoisted aboard a steamer ready to cast off for Aden. A mattress is laid down on the bridge for him. He will remain there for three days, barely eating a thing, his body immobilized and shivering with fever.

There was no doubt forewarning of his arrival in Aden, where he is first taken to the home of César Tian. Tian, who regards him as an honest if difficult employee, is momentarily dumbfounded by the unfortunate man's condition. With no further delay he takes him to the hospital where he is entrusted into the hands of an Englishman, Dr. Nouks. On seeing the size of Rimbaud's knee, Nouks provides a most alarming diagnosis: an acute synovitus;[292] his intention is to cut off the leg. In a flash Rimbaud sees himself crippled for life and refuses. The doctor then decides to wait a week to see if, with rest, the tumor shrinks. However, nothing of the sort occurs. Rimbaud is forced to accept his diagnosis, but prefers to return to France, where more advanced procedures and equipment for operations of this type are available. He remains for several more days in the Aden hospital, sleeping in the room reserved for paying patients. Before returning to Europe he intends on settling his accounts and desires to have everything in order before the big departure. Sometimes he is visited by the Bardey brothers or César Tian. Most of the time he is left facing only himself with no dissimulation possible. He doesn't hem and haw: "I have become a skeleton; I scare people." His leg lies before him, "bandaged, bound, rebound, enchained," a vampiric limb annihilating his body.

Finally, on May 7, he sets sail on a steam-packet of the Messageries Maritimes, *L'Amazone*. The voyage lasts thirteen days, which he spends in pain and the greatest uncertainty concerning his future. A year earlier he had planned to return to France rich, healthy, and ready to buy goods to invest in his African trading post. He is returning now stricken by an inexplicable disease and the 37,450 francs[293] he is bringing with him, earned amid countless pains, are first being used to pay the fare for an unwanted journey and ineffectual health treatments. He perhaps had hopes of going straight to Roche from Marseilles. Instead he has to enter the hospital immediately. He is transported there "very gently." A doctor examines him immediately, astonished by the extent of his illness. In cases like these the spoken medical name is akin to a fatal baptism and the patient attaches himself to it like a double, the bearer of his most intimate truth. The apparently anodyne term "synovitus" comes out of the doctor's mouth, and the doctor quickly pairs it with other, more obscure names, such as "hydrarthrosis,"[294] and one that Rimbaud didn't recognize at first: "neoplasm"—in other words, cancer. In his mind "synovitus," already spoken by the doctor in Aden, couldn't help but evoke the death of his sister Vitalie in 1876. Some sort of family death was beating a path toward him. Who at that time didn't know Dr. Lucas's theories about heredity?

Rimbaud's obsessive fear at this moment (have you noticed how he always needs an obsessive fear?) is centered on the amputation of his leg. His body has taken the upper hand in formidable fashion. The essential instrument has shrunk and broken down, dropping him after he reposed total trust in it and imposed the worst kinds of exhaustions upon it, from which he no doubt thought he would emerge unscathed. "I have my thighbone,"[295] he puts in the mouth of one of his grotesque characters in a poem of which only fragments have survived. Will Rimbaud now have his leg? This man who walks constantly is struck at the heart of his very functioning. It is all the more depressing to him as it takes away his very reason to exist. "To operate living on poetry"[296] had been only a vaguely hygienic thought process for him. But he holds on to his leg like a fragment of thought. This is the means by which he advances, by which he progresses in the mental world itself: "Life has become impossible. How unhappy I am. How unhappy I've become!" All his despairs from Aden and Harar resurface. The mask mentioned by Bardey and Riès is taken off, unbridled. There is nothing left to do. To speak about Rimbaud's life is to accompany him to the very end in the trials of his flesh, in the nosology that confiscates him and the state of being at a loss carried to the very quick: the shamelessness of despair. There is no longer any dignity here, any exalted attitude when facing the inevitable, but a physical disintegration lived day after day; a fear, a nameless terror, that is spoken, that is screamed, when nothing permits it to be dominated anymore, when there is no more need for courage or heroism. There is no cowardice in Rimbaud, however. Rather the most human kind of distress, which once again brings him close to us, and the strength he had in that weakness to watch his departing body with eyes wide open. We cannot now refuse to evoke the "history" to which he briefly sends us back by the sequence of his sufferings and the stations of his agony. Would Christ, "thief of energies," steal this man's death? Whatever Isabelle's efforts to transform him into a saint on his hospital bed, we certainly have no need of this sacrificial Rimbaud. But we Westerners reflexively see it *like* a Calvary. Rimbaud's great strength is having, whether consciously or not, achieved an exemplary journey. He took precautions not to attach any importance to it, though. He didn't suffer for humanity or, in the example of Socrates, listen at the last moment to the prosopopoeia of the Laws. He was merely someone who would endure a misery consubstantial to our own. "Alas, how miserable our life is!" The phrase of the old maid with the wobbly head *and* the phrase of Rimbaud, still at the height of his powers, revolting against absurd misfortune. In following him to the bitter end, we are not performing an autopsy on the complications of one man's suffering. We see absurdity at work—and it is a matter of some importance that this absurdity finished him off with an irrevocable blow, while his poetry was beginning to survive him.

An urgent decision will be quickly made at the Hôpital Conception, one against which he had rebelled several weeks previously: the amputation of his right leg. There was no time to lose. On May 21, so that someone would see him while still intact and unscathed, he sends a telegram to Roche: "Today, you or Isabelle come to Marseilles by express train. Monday morning, they are amputating my leg. Danger of death. Serious matters to be settled. Hôpital Conception. Reply." The next day at 6:30 in the evening, Madame Rimbaud, who had someone take her to Attigny, responds with these simple words: "I am leaving. Will arrive tomorrow evening. Courage and patience." The moment of the dénouement approached. The long, foreseeable confrontation between mother and son would take place. On the one side, him waiting in his hospital bed and his tapping pain, forgotten only when he wrote letters putting all his affairs in order before the end. On the other, Madame Widow Rimbaud, whose daily life was abruptly hastened and who, during the hours she was crossing France, had in mind the image of Arthur such as he had become, the man in the cotton clothes in the photos from Harar, the trader whose hair was turning white, and soon this distraught and emaciated individual she went to see in Marseilles. Nothing is known of their reunion after a ten-years absence. The ties that bound them were woven with hate and love. The woman of duty and the man of desire could only look at each other with incomprehension.

—

Scheduled for Monday, the operation would eventually be delayed. It does not take place until May 27, and is temporarily successful. A colleague from Aden, Maurice Riès, who is in Marseilles at this time, attends.[297] Rimbaud, at first in despair about being crippled, regains confidence but needs encouragement. His doctors apply themselves to this task, holding up the sparkling possibility of an artificial leg before his credulous imagination. Madame Rimbaud herself is a believer. Hasn't she seen crippled veterans of the War of 1870 perfectly "able-bodied" despite their amputations in Roche and Charleville! Despite his condition, Rimbaud still has hope. He will one day return to Harar. Despite everything he said previously about the inhabitants of this cesspool of a city, he remains passionately attached to them in an unhealthy and exhausting way. He writes to one of his employees, Dimitri Righas, and informs him of his condition. Righas will be quite touched by this letter. His response,[298] written in very broken French, testifies to his deep compassion: "I woold haf preferd my own be cut off stead than yourn. [. . .] Me, since you leaving Harar, I is thinking my world am lost." Rimbaud also alerted Makonnen of the fact. Indeed his intention was to return for business purposes and from this point of view he wished to procure the favor of the ras, who held him in esteem and called himself his friend. Madame Rimbaud, who has taken a room in the city near the hospital, remains by her son's bedside for a week. When she sees that he is on the point of recovering, she feels it is high time for her to return to Roche to watch over the work in her fields and even more because Isabelle, also in poor health, has need of her care. In tears, Rimbaud begs her to stay. Hasn't he told her enough times that she is all he has in the world? Confronted by the invalid's pleas, she reverses her decision, and it isn't until June 9 that she tears herself from his clutches and leaves the hospital, where he still must remain for some long days.

He now finds himself alone. The days pass by in agony and expectation. He keeps watch over his body; he notes that the healing process encounters no difficulties. He soon hopes to be able to walk with the aid of a crutch, but he feels an ache at the site of the amputation. "Finally I've resigned myself to everything, I don't have any luck!"[299] For the moment he is stuck in bed. His entourage is reduced to the nuns who care for him and the doctors who visit him. Otherwise—as he will bitterly say later—the doctors, when they don't have any "knife cuts"[300] to perform, are totally disinterested in him. He spends his days in endless boredom. Nevertheless he writes several letters to César Tian, to Righas, who can keep him up-to-date on life in Harar, to Isabelle, with whom he maintains an even more regular correspondence in that, having seen her, he now knows there is nothing more to be expected from the *mother*. He continues to resent her departure. Once again, and in the worst circumstances, he has seen what little real affection she has for him. Thus Isabelle becomes his interlocutor of his final days, the person in whom he will confide *in extremis*. They recognize each other to the extent that their letters are in accord. From this final fraternity will be born, after Rimbaud's death, the figure of the sister depository, the unique judge of a work and a man that have become untouchable, because of her excessive affection.

At the Hôpital Conception the days flow by with that slowness so bitterly felt by patients, placed far from life in an isolation that creates suffering. For Rimbaud, hardened in his own created image, sealed shut as a wall, a great fissure of tears opens. Here is where his tears rise up and overflow. Up to his final hour, they will be his sole refuge, since revolt and rage are no longer permitted him. He then likes to pound out unassailable truths: "I am a dead man."[301] He is left to large patches of boredom and a detested inactivity, and the same question that had been posed to him from Stuttgart to Java, from Cyprus to Aden comes back up: "So why do we exist?"[302] He provides his own terrible answer: for an endless suffering, a "season in hell"— this cannot be expressed any better. He isn't thinking of religion, of an illusionary Christianity. There is never the hope of another life glittering in his phrases. And when he takes on the appearance of an agonized being, he no longer remembers what they kept harping on at catechism: that Christ had come to earth to endure such sufferings and redeem them. As a crowning blow, foolish worries about his military service were now pestering him. They further darken this July 1891 spent in the hospital without being able to take a single step, except briefly with a crutch that cuts into his right armpit and quickly forced him to abandon it. In Roche, gendarmes from the Attigny subprefecture visited Madame Rimbaud to make inquiries about her absent son. Though exempted since 1875, he still was obliged to complete his twenty-eight days of military training. The new law of 1889 could not be any stricter on this point. In the absence of any certificate from an employer proving that he worked abroad, he was at risk of being declared a draft dodger. However, he had anguished about this problem numerous times since his arrival in Aden, but he had no doubt never supplied the necessary documents. Military service signified an obligation for Rimbaud in which the shadow of his father and the necessity to bow to it could be read. We have seen the ruses with which he surrounded this relationship: desertion, false claims of desertion, enlistment, flight to the East. For weeks in Marseilles he is fearful of being caught in a snare[303] (an utterly absurd fear as his leg was amputated and physically he can't take even the slightest step!). It testifies to a tenacious fear, linked to his past as a marginal individual, that can always be held against him like an inexpiable crime. Rimbaud decidedly has an overly strong tendency to assume the role of a hunted man. He also spots among the other patients "a police inspector" who is preparing—at least this is what he thinks—to play some sort of trick on him.[304] Alarmed, Madame Rimbaud and Isabelle make a trip to the military headquarters in Chalons and ascertain, furthermore, that his name does not appear in any records. They finally obtain a certificate from the head of recruitment in Mézières attesting to the fact that Arthur is "on a renewable deferment until his return to France." Obviously it was necessary that they did not find out he had already returned unless he could produce a certificate of disability. The matter would finally be settled before he gets out of the hospital, but it was the source of painful worries at the very moment the after-effects of his surgery were causing him other terrifying anxieties.

He is now the one, sitting outside on a chair, who has withdrawn from life. Crutch, wooden leg, articulated leg, aches, immobility, such is the restricted circle of words around which his mind turns, broken sometimes by the feverish ascent of the temptation to end it all: "Perhaps a new evil will now happen to me [. . .] on that occasion I would know to rid myself of this miserable life quickly.[305] But his life force excludes such solutions. He still spies a means of "getting out of his difficulties." He also has the impression that a new illness is awakening inside him; he feels it and almost welcomes it during his nights of insomnia: "Now it's my other leg that feels very weak." It so happens that this is not only the limb he rests on but the one on which he depends. His left leg. The ancient "wonder," the pillar of the universe: "At present it's my only support in the world!" A dull pain begins to take shape. Despite the terror it causes him, he can no longer hide from the reality: "I'm still standing, but I'm not doing at all well. [. . .] I greatly fear some sort of accident."[306] Rimbaud is en route to death with celerity, sitting motionless on his chair "motionless with great strides." His regrets are wearing him out. While vaguely looking out over the courtyard in which he sits, he dreams of the cherished, imaginary silhouette of the person he had been, the astounding traveler: "What boredom, what exhaustion, what sadness in thinking of all my old journeys and how I was still active only five months ago! Where are the brisk journeys over mountains, the rides on horseback, the walks, the deserts, the rivers, and the seas?"[307] A brief spurt of lyricism is reborn in this phrase of a perfect euphony. The "dirty country," its inhabitants, the "dirty Negroes," were deep down what he truly loved from Europe, in healthy isolation. And his mad journeys of an earlier time would henceforth nurture his dreams and orient his desires: "I spend night and day reflecting on means of getting around; it's a real torture! I would like to do this and that, go here and there, see, live, leave."[308] His writer's instinct is reawakened by this memory of the recent past and, as if setting down what he had been through in black and white, will allow him a better understanding of it, he writes a long letter to Isabelle, in which he makes himself the historian of his illness. The account extends for several pages,[309] and is carried out in the past tense. His style is precise. The self-pity can be discerned but is not emphasized. He restrains his tears while narrating how his life has come undone. At the end he draws a completely physical portrait of himself mocking his silhouette as a grotesque man on crutches: "The head and shoulders hunch forward and you bulge out like a humpback." He purposely avoids using the first person in this impasse. It is replaced by *you*, as if everyone should take part in his sufferings. *Ecce homo:* "Sitting down again, you have weakened hands, an aching armpit, and the face of an idiot." He has become that "old idiot" whose memories he recounted in the *Album zutique*. After the human brutalization in Aden and Harar, here is his station on the chair: "like a complete cripple, sniveling and waiting for night, which will bring perpetual insomnia." Something of which he is proud has been left to him: the accuracy of his writing. No fiction here but the power to speak the real and stress the angles, the capability of hearing at the heart of taciturn heroes what makes them speak. "Sequel in the next issue," he notes at the end of the letter, thereby picking up again, without truly remembering it, the end of his schoolboy "narrative" that ended with "the sequel, coming soon." Isabelle will hardly get the humor behind such an expression in that she will write to him, "You said to me yesterday: the sequel in the next issue; I made a note of your words and am impatiently awaiting your news." Now, what he had said was meant to signify his abhorrence of this miserable serial with its repetition of useless gestures, the reiteration of his pains, and news about the incurable and irreparable.

In his extreme solitude he receives several letters from Harar, from Aden, from Zeila. They are most often sent to him to Roche, the address he left behind on his departure, and then reexpedited by Isabelle. Tian, Righas, and Makonnen sympathize with his fate, and without having a true measure of the seriousness of his condition, await his return and declare their hopes of resuming their business relationships with him. It is surprising not to find among this correspondence any letters from Alfred Ilg, to whom he was bound by a great intellectual complicity outside of their common commercial interests. But it would seem that Ilg had returned to France during that time, since he would later declare that he visited the amputee at the Hôpital de la Conception right after his operation.

Looking over the letters Rimbaud received over this period, we see the appearance of old acquaintances who provide a sudden demonstration of their unsuspected attachment. One of those most dismayed by the announcement of his bad news is assuredly Sotiro, with whom he had worked when he was first assigned to the trading post in 1880. Sotiro now conducts business in Zeila. On several occasions[310] he provides Rimbaud detailed information, speaking to him of Aden, Harar, and the recent events that have occurred there; he passes over a number of their friends in review and thus reveals a world with many players: Dimitri Righas, Rimbaud's former *abban* Farahli, Ilg, Brémond, the Mousaïas, the Ras Makonnen, Djami the young servant who had followed Rimbaud to Aden and who on his return to Harar had entered into the employ of a certain Felter, an employee at the Italian Bienenfeld Agency. The situation in Harar was catastrophic. The famine, foreseen at the beginning of the year, was decimating the populace. The Ras Makonnen was forced to punish several natives who, in order to survive, had resorted to cannibalism. However, on the coast, the European trading posts were gaining in importance. Djibouti was in full expansion. On his return from Europe, Ilg had begun prospecting the subsoil, and had discovered a coal mine in Samado; in Berbera platinum had been discovered. The entire world Rimbaud had just left was rebuilt in his mind; he raged at having to lie around useless and inactive.

Finally, he surrendered to Isabelle's arguments advising him, for better or worse, to come to Roche. He had enough of being stuck between the four walls of the hospital where he also fears catching some disease. He is determined to part, despite his pitiful state, by July 20 and on the twenty-third he is transported on a stretcher to the Gare Saint Charles. Whatever it may have cost him, he has rented a *coupé-lit* (a sinister pun!*), because he knows the length of the journey ahead of him: it will take two days to go as far as Ardennes, but he has experienced worse, such as when he was carried from Harar to Zeila through the desert.

Despite the comfort of the compartment, he did not manage to find a favorable position that would allay his pain. Through the window he could see the French countryside to which he had become unaccustomed. Mentally he compared it to the barren plains of the Somalis or the profuse vegetation of Harar. Whether he likes it or not this journey is a return to the past. No virgin territory to be discovered here, rather, at the end of the road, the primal soil on which he had bungled his adolescent attempts at running away. The value of an entire life is found in such moments. These are the ones that cannot be reconstructed, these interstices where time and space tremble in between memory and the present. Once the leg to Paris has been completed the journey takes on an air of inevitability, the train channels him toward those unfortunate spots he returned to year after year. Outside the countryside is rustling with the sounds of the harvest. At six in the evening, the train—after running alongside the poplar-lined canal he knew so well—stops at the Voncq station, at the bottom of the valley where the Aisne folds back into numerous meanderings. Rimbaud is helped down from the train with the greatest care. The cart is waiting hitched to the mare Countess. Their old servant picks his emaciated body up in his arms and deposits it into the vehicle. Exhausted, Rimbaud gives a sad smile to Isabelle, who has changed so much since he left and is now living the life of a drudge at the farm. The distance separating the station from Roche isn't far. A steep climb. A wide turn in the

---

* In French *coupé* also means "cut," thus the term could also read as "cutting bed"— translator's note.

road. Then the hamlet appears with the familiar farm in the distance. The peasants watch the cripple getting down. The mystery of this misfortune strikes them momentarily, even if they are whispering among themselves of its good reasons: the misconduct of the son, his debauched life, his Communard airs. His mother waits, almost impassively. Inside the furniture is gleaming; and the familiar smells—wax, food, dairy products—embrace Rimbaud like an old friend. For a moment there is rest, the true rest that comes late in life, when it is too late. He eats a little, says a few words about his trip, and he is then taken up to sleep in the chamber on the second floor that had been prepared for him, the exam room of *Une saison en enfer.*

He would remain with his family for a month,[311] plunged against his will into his past, but also at the mercy of a terrifying future. In the beginning, despite the suffering he is experiencing, he likes to be taken around in the cart and have it stop in the neighboring villages, where he can watch people, as he has taken an interest in daily life that has changed so much since the time he left France. But the awful weather of that summer often prevented him from taking such excursions, which quickly wore him out, besides. He would have enjoyed some sun and hot temperatures, instead there was so much rain falling in the fields that the wheat was rotting underfoot: the crops were ruined. On August 10 an extremely rare phenomenon took place: an early "frost stripped the fruit trees bare." Thus he found himself constrained for the most part to remain in his room. Displayed around him are some curios he bought back from Abyssinia, as well as some beautiful fabrics. As if to escape the sight of the soaked and desolate countryside, he asked that his shutters be closed and there as a recluse, but protected, he repeats his memories of Harar for Isabelle. Inside his room is lit by lamps and candles for these strange vigils he had personally wished for. He sadly turns the crank of a small barrel organ someone had bought him, as if thereby saying his prayers and soothing his pain. However the illness progresses. Dr. Beaudier comes regularly from Attigny to see him; he can't help but notice that his condition is growing worse. None of the treatments used offers him any relief and he soon hits upon the notion of turning to simple "old wives remedies." Thus he has concoctions made from poppies picked from the garden prepared for him. The opiated potion eases his suffering and loosens his tongue. Isabelle declares that during these moments he recounted his life story: memories of child-

hood, "personal thoughts," "future plans and projects." His speech is embell-
ished with terms from Arabic and Amharic, which were now as familiar to
him as French. Among his involuntary remarks, one (reported by Isabelle)
appears most surprising: he would have abandoned literature "because it was
evil."[312] Madame Rimbaud was always of this opinion. But when was he ever
hindered by such moral considerations? In his eyes, literature was only "evil"
because of its inefficacy, it was too deep a dream to be realizable. Perceiving
that under the effects of the drug he was saying more than he should, he soon
resolves to take no more of these potions, these "truth beverages."

At the rare times the sun pierced through the clouds, he sometimes tries
to take a few steps with his crutch, but as his right arm is becoming more and
more paralyzed, he must content himself with his bed or chair. Later the
inhabitants of Roche would claim they saw him. Now, what was there for
them to see, if not someone who was already a phantom who though back
had nonetheless gone for good? In Roche, news was coming to him from
Africa and Arabia, letters from Tian, Righas, Sotiro. Sotiro advises him, with
no ill will intended, to make up with his mother and regain her affection
("nobody loves like a mother") and reminds him that "God is good and always
thinking of us." Savouré repeats how highly esteemed he is by Makonnen and
informs him that now all the Europeans are bringing women to Harar: blacks,
mixed-bloods, and whites. Maurice Riès sends him a missive apologizing for
not visiting him in Marseilles before he left the hospital, to which Rimbaud
responded with a letter, which has since been lost, but which its addressee
remembered because it was curiously dated from "Roche, Den of Wolves."[313]

In a short time, the deplorable weather, the resumption of inveterate
habits, the European lifestyle, and domestic annoyances all served to irritate
the invalid. His mother has certainly remained the curt and intransigent
woman he has always known. It is she who to a certain extent—he believes
this, he knows this—created his misfortune. He loathed the people of the
area as wily peasants and men tethered to their native soil whereas he wished
to be always marching further, to the very limits of the world. And he is
gripped by the horror of what he has become. Weary of the tenacious rain,
paralyzed by the cold, and knowing also that the affection that surrounds him
serves no purpose, he hears only the folly of his desire, before which, until his
death, all obstacles should fall. He attempts the impossible. Toward the end of

August, numb and broken by the incessant pains that wrack his body and are paralyzing him little by little, he wants, in one last jump, to leave again for the East. Abyssinia has now become a faraway paradise to be attained. What's common sense against such an appeal? His mother's protests hardly matter to him. He is compelled to obey this final secret injunction out of a supreme instinct for loss or sublimated life. It is obvious to everyone that he won't get far. Crippled, a motionless trunk, he finally consents to Isabelle accompanying him to facilitate his travels in this desperate expedition.[314]

He has to catch the train in Voncq, at the bottom of the valley, at 6:30 in the morning. At three o'clock in the morning, impatient and feverish, he demands that the early preparations be made and that his clothes be given to him. However, this early start would cause him to be late. Ready too soon, he grows languid and falls back to sleep; the hours go by, and when he is lifted into the cart there is just enough time to make it to the station. But the horse is restive and will not trot fast enough; it has to be whipped (Rimbaud himself is supposed to have done this with his belt in a fury) to get it to move forward and finally bolt its way to Voncq, at the risk of overturning the vehicle. However, when they get there the train has already left. This failure carries a sort of truth in itself. It is possible to read in it the strength of the unconscious bonds attaching Rimbaud to Roche that he could not break by will alone. On the platform, swallowing his bitter disappointment, he first wishes to wait until noon for the next train; then, ceding to Isabelle's pleas, he lets himself be taken back to the farm. After a nap to vainly try to restore his strength, he wakes up, anxious about the time. For a moment he sees that he could remain there and end his days in that bed, surrounded by the few friends he has remaining in Charleville. A touching picture. One requiring a handkerchief. And reconciliation with French "reason." But he recovers. He finds the energy to not betray his vocation as a traveler, ambulatory poetry, and the desire to go beyond every horizon. He will wait another two hours at the Voncq station with Isabelle and two servants. To soothe the sufferings of his body, he periodically drinks a few drops of a bromide elixir. Isabelle will recall that he made a joke "about the miniature flower bed kept by the station master." We would like to know what this bit of black humor may have been. Did he think there was something there with which an appropriate funeral crown could be woven?

Finally the train arrives and he is settled into a seat with great care. During the entire trip to Paris he experiences intolerable pain from the rhythm of the car's vibrations. Other travelers, despite their horror of the invalid, are soon crowding the compartment and encroaching on the space he needs. Isabelle has left us a definitive portrait of him from this final journey: "He is seated on a red cushion and has placed his valise next to him on which he supports his right arm; his burnoose and blanket relieve a little the hardness of the support of his diseased limb; with his left elbow he holds himself up on the edge of the window in the door." Outside on this August 23, 1891, the sky is clear over a smiling countryside. Nothing is in harmony with Rimbaud's sorrow. "O Nature, o my mother!" He knows an indifferent sky, marked by the absence of God. A young married couple sits near him. He sees his dreams again: a wife, an engineer son. . . . They reach Paris in the evening. At first there is thought of stopping there and sleeping at a hotel. But once he and Isabelle are in the cab, Rimbaud abruptly changes his mind. They will go straight to the Gare de Lyon and wait the time necessary for the express train to Marseilles. In this way he still obeys the great haste that rules his life and the urgency that always prompts him to take action, as time is now so measured. To gain a half day would perhaps enable him to set sail the following day, and thus in ten days reach, even if on death's door, the port of Aden to see everyone there again. Around eleven o'clock that evening he was stretched out in a *coupé-lit*. All the rest of the journey, Isabelle, "kneeling and curled up in the most cramped space" will witness "the most dreadful paroxysm of despair and physical torture that can be imagined." Finally on the evening of August 24, Rimbaud alights at the Gare de Saint-Charles. While waiting for his condition to improve, a hardly likely prospect that would enable him to take a boat to the East, he has himself taken once more to the Hôpital de la Conception, where he registers under the simple name of Jean Rimbaud—thus avoiding being taken for the homonymous poet with the first name of Arthur! The doctors who treated him several months previously recognize him and take note of the alarming progression of his illness. Isabelle, who has taken a room in a nearby hotel, no doubt the same one where her mother stayed in June, will now become the witness of his slow death throes. Over the coming weeks she would remain at his bedside, listening to his complaints, and collecting his dreams, hopes, and rages that he expresses in bits and pieces. We have to satisfy ourselves with the account she has left of these terrible days, even if we sense how the moral principles of her Christian faith could have inspired her beliefs and tainted her testimony. "Rimbaud is Isabelle's novel," Marguerite Yerta-Méléra would say with good reason.[315] It remains to interpret this "novel," the sole means of access we have to the reality it deformed.

Following his admittance to the hospital, a brief period elapsed in which he experienced the semblance of a remission. Then the illness, as often occurs in such cases, came back even stronger and raged throughout his entire body. His right arm became entirely paralyzed. Now Rimbaud could no longer write. His words and thoughts would come to us only as transcribed by the hand of Isabelle. Out of anxiety she questions the doctors. Dr. Trastoul tells her to abandon any hope: "He's a poor boy who's going to go little by little," is what he tells her.[316] As for the illness torturing the invalid, it was certainly a cancer that they now expected to spread through his marrow to the rest of his body, an "osteosarcoma," as would be specified years later by Maurice Riès,[317] who had been present at Rimbaud's amputation and discussed the matter with the doctors.

In his despair Rimbaud sometimes takes leave of his senses and raves, maddened by his pain and by life itself, which he must endure, come what may, even when he would like to end it. All his limbs are now paralyzed and he has grown yet even thinner because he eats almost nothing and vomits what little he does eat. "His eyes circled by rings,"[318] he rarely sleeps. At times he wakes up with a start from terrifying dreams, nightmares whose nature Isabelle would not tell us, but they seem as atrocious as those with which he afflicted the Verlaine of London, "the eyes torn out," "the heart filled with worms."[319] Rimbaud is no longer a text at this moment but a body. This is what he is reduced to, plunged into "relentless enchantment." Speech that is strangled by the misfortunes of the body, a mind annihilated by the burden of his sufferings. It is rather not words that emerge from him but humors: tears (he is always crying), and sweat, the copious water of agony. Diminished this way, he becomes like a child, divesting himself of adult courage because he feels it no longer serves any purpose to take a stand against his misery. He takes Isabelle into his arms, looking at her with bewilderment. He needs a mother, any mother, except his own, who now, bolstered by her fortitude, is waiting in Roche for the final news of his death. "I always told you so." Yes, there are mothers who predict a bad end for their adolescent sons. How is it they can't understand that such prophecies, over the long haul, will carry their poison into the body? Under Isabelle's pen, some harsh comparisons are born; despite their naiveté they provide a shudder: "He is treated like a condemned man to whom nothing can be refused."[320] Furthermore, Rimbaud rebuffs any indulgence or pity. Even if he cries, he is beyond the cries of others. This is not the beginning of the death throes of one of the world's greatest poets in a Marseilles hospital, but an individual over whom a reflection of the sacred is passing. Harcamone! Gênet saw a death row prisoner at the main prison of Clairvaux radiating a marvelous aura, a halo. This is how Rimbaud at the Hôpital de la Conception carries the mystery of his illness before which soon "all the doctors remain mute," "terrified by this strange cancer." His completely inert right arm starts to swell. His left arm is now three-quarters paralyzed. He experiences painful burning sensations in his chest and back. His heart sometimes beats as if about to burst, while his organs are congealing. We encounter here the horror of the body, like a useless wound, becoming an object of repulsion even for the person who inhabits it. We are in the presence of Rimbaud's disfiguration, which is almost unacceptable because of the admiration formerly evoked by his beauty, the marvelous gaze captured in the photo taken by Carjat, the tenderness of the portrait by Fantin-Latour, and even as a trader in Harar, in which he displays a severe elegance in his cotton clothing. Isabelle has left us some drawings depicting this final Rimbaud. Two reproduce his face with its emaciated features and his eyes half-closed; the last one[321] portrays him stretched out on his deathbed, hardly recognizable, his right arm swollen with bandages; the only identifiable feature remaining is the short mustache he wore for the last ten years of his life.

To believe Isabelle—and in this instance we have to—he was seized by profound fits of despair that went well beyond boredom to the point of suicide. He wished to strangle himself. He was also recaptured by certain fantasies, his fixation on persecution—for whoever suffers overmuch necessarily always needs to understand the illness that affects him, this atrocious injustice, this absurdity. Rimbaud suspected the nurses and nuns of "abominable things."[322] Such as? Isabelle doesn't provide any details. But we guess that these "things" were not foreign to the pains that had wiped him out, and it is possible he thought they had grown worse because of the malice of those claiming to treat him. In any event, nothing will cause him to abandon his foremost obsession: leaving Europe for Algiers, Obok, Aden. He is apprehensive of winter, "the season of comfort," as he once wrote. "Autumn already." It is now September. Outside the sun is shining in a clear sky. " I am going under the ground and you will walk in the sun,"[323] he says to Isabelle, who will hold on to this phrase that is as pure as his poem "Éternité." Despite his misfortune, he would still like to live under this large light that interrogates all humanity. To give himself to the sun, "god of fire."

A helpless, immobile trunk falling toward death, he soon attained, two months after his departure from Roche, those moments in which the body has reached the limits of its endurance and for which the word *torture* is not too strong to express the overstepping of these bounds. As we have seen, the life of Rimbaud was not lived to be easily comprehended. True as a man's writing may be, his life outstrips it. It confers his destiny. The final enigma posed by Rimbaud specifically concerns his death, "his good death,"[324] as Isabelle will say. From his arrival at the Hôpital de la Conception in August, he had been visited by the chaplains of the establishment, before whom he no doubt exhibited a predictable indifference. Isabelle had already considered it useless to speak about this to her mother, who was already vexed by the irreverence her son displayed during his last stay in Roche. However, as "death approached in great strides," she wished at any price for her brother to die a Christian. During the week of October 19 to 25, Canon Chaulier and Abbé Suche, the chaplains, try to converse with the patient. He finally consents to receive their visit, more "out of lassitude and discouragement"[325] than by any hope in the beyond. However, on Sunday, October 25, he gives in to their suggestions and finally accepts confession. The sequel to this would merit belief if Isabelle—more a hagiographer than a biographer—hadn't later taken pains to transform so openly the life of her brother into an edifying existence worthy of posthumous beatification. However, the account she provides in this instance contains important contradictions that allow us to think that it isn't pure invention, since it sometimes runs counter to the narrator's own intentions. Thus one of these chaplains allegedly took Rimbaud's confession and when leaving the room where he had been alone with the invalid, he supposedly told her: "Your brother has the faith, my child, what did you tell us? He has the faith and I have never seen faith of this quality." This sole witness—

and regrettably so—subsequently kept his silence and no one at the time ever sought to reawaken his memories. What kind of faith could the Rimbaud of his final days have possessed, he who never showed the least sign of piety, for Isabelle would admit that she forewarned the priests of Arthur's lack of belief? Yet she would declare that over the days following his confession, he "did not blaspheme ever again" (whereas previously he swore like one of the damned) and he started to pray to "the Crucified Christ." It doesn't prevent the fact that even after this major action, Rimbaud—still according to the opinions uttered by Isabelle—seems to have been prey to the worst doubts. In fact he will insistently ask her if she believes, as if his own faith depends on the answer. He will also murmur, as if vexed by a terrible suspicion: "Sure they say they believe and pretend to have converted, but that's so people will read what they write, it's speculation,"[326] as if he wanted to evoke the Verlaine of "Sagesse," the person who had tried to indoctrinate him with "a rosary in his paws." The fact still remains that Rimbaud will not take communion, even if everything was prepared for such a ceremony. Not out of refusal on his part, but because the spasms contracting his throat would prevent him from swallowing the host.*

At this end of October, his body uses up its final resources—as if against his own wishes—to resist death. In order to ease his suffering he is now given injections of morphine. The doses being particularly strong, visions resulted that were described by the invalid in terms that astonished the doctors as much as Isabelle. "Extraordinary," "bizarre things" that he recounted very tenderly. At the time, Isabelle would comment on them with quite singular remarks: "One would say, and I believe it is so, that he did it on purpose." Or else: "He blends everything . . . and with art."[327] She would modify these reflections in 1892, exaggerating her beliefs to the point of making them hardly credible: "His mind retains the distinctive charm I've always known, but lifted into regions that are so rich and beautiful they completely dazzle me. . . . He expressed his feelings in terms that were so angelic and otherworldly that I don't believe anyone, even among the Saints, had such an edifying end."[328] Rimbaud, in this final phase, becomes a Catherine Emmerich! He lacks only a Brentano to immortalize him. Nevertheless, everything shows

---

*We may ask if this is a perfectly valid reason.

that he had no confidence in the beyond; to the contrary, the fear of dying drowned him; it was constantly growing with his tears. He even possessed so little sensible acceptance of his fate that in his state of despair he still wished to leave. As for the visions he recounted, it is necessary to see—and Isabelle concurs—that, blending past and present, they concern his African life exclusively: sales and purchases, writings, caravan plans, and the appearance of Djami Wadai, with whom he sometimes confused her.[329] For hours at a time, despite his exhaustion, Rimbaud speaks in little clipped phrases that obey the rhythm of his panting breath, until the moment his fatigued head falls back on the pillow and tries to abandon itself to sleep.

As death was inevitable, his thoughts turned to drawing up his will. On this occasion, Isabelle, freed for the first time from her mother's control, shows signs of an almost vindictive independence: "I am absolutely determined to respect his wishes," she writes to Madame Rimbaud, who is worrying about her son's inheritance. "We have to take into consideration that his holdings will revert to others,"[330] she adds gallantly. Certainly, Rimbaud had brought back a considerable sum from Africa, around 37,000 francs in gold. But the expenses incurred by his illness had made a dent in it. We have no additional specific information. A part of his legacy reverted to his sister, who, on this matter, sent several unambiguous letters to César Tian and the French consul in Aden.[331] Tian, an honest but prudent businessman, took his time to reckon his accounts and settle those of his former associate that were still left hanging in Harar. The most certain information we have concerns the sum that Rimbaud wished to bequest to his young servant, Djami. Isabelle shows him particularly concerned during his final days that a significant bequest be given this twenty-year-old man who had been in his service for almost ten years and whom he would even have liked to bring with him if Djami had not had to remain behind with his wife and newborn son. Isabelle would make efforts to pick up the trail of this faithful servant and give him the money intended for him.[332] But Djami, as if contaminated by Rimbaud's bad luck, would not profit from the 3,000 francs that came down to him[333] and would soon die from unknown causes.

From October 28 to November 10, date of Rimbaud's death, a new sheet of silence is extended in which we can only imagine this body grappling with its pain. No matter how much Isabelle says about a strange kind of calm that came over him, we need to understand the relentless struggle signified by the end of the death throes, when the individual, pushed to the limit, holds on, fragile and threatened, to the edge of time. Nonetheless, he continued to depict superb visions. Isabelle will tell us they resembled *Illuminations*.[334] But wouldn't she have unconsciously charged these fits of delerium with the content of the texts she read later and was too quick to confuse with feverish hallucinations? In fact it appears more likely that Rimbaud, under the influence of the morphine with which he was injected daily, but also because his lucidity was abandoning him, drew further and further away from an intolerable reality and into the realm of a deep dream.

As the final evidence of this madness, which now took him out of himself, there remains a letter that he dictated on the eve of his death that we know of, thanks to Isabelle, who preserved it as if it were some kind of incomprehensible relic—words that aren't truncated this time, even though written by the hand of one who, in any case, would have been incapable of improvising their apparent absurdity. Rimbaud is addressing the manager of the Messageries Maritimes who would assure the voyage from Marseilles to the East, by way of the Red Sea:

Marseille, November 9, 1891

One lot: a single tooth.
One lot: two teeth.
One lot: three teeth.
One lot: four teeth.
One lot: two teeth.

To the manager, Dear Sir,

I am writing to ask whether I have anything left in your account. Today I wish to change from that service, whose name I don't even know, but in any case let it be the Aphinar service. All those services are there, everywhere, and I, an unhappy cripple, can find nothing, the first dog in the street will tell you that.

So send me then the prices of the Alphinar service to Suez. I am completely paralyzed: so I want to get aboard in good time. Tell me what time I should be carried aboard. . . .

In these simple yet sibylline phrases are blended all the elements that made up the framework of his recent life in Africa. The series of lots, their litany, ressembles a final clearance sale. These teeth—in other words, the elephant ivory he traded in Harar—take on the air of human remains that are arriving just ahead of the future skeleton. The merchant worried about his most urgent tasks. He wants to liquidate his merchandise and draw up a definitive balance sheet. Almost all the letters he had sent from France to Ilg, Tian, and Savouré testify to the same concern. But the former merchant doesn't succeed in forgetting the illness that tortures him. A prisoner of the hospital, he sees himself changing service. In this instance does this word designate the staff of a medical or naval service? Will we ever know who or what Aphinar is? Was he one of the people Rimbaud frequented during his brief stay in Suez when he was welcomed there in 1887 by the vice-consul Lucien Labosse? Or should we understand this to be the name of a boat: *Al Fanar*, "the beacon"?[335] Rambling? Lucidity? it doesn't matter. His resolution was unshakable. He wished to leave Europe one last time.

One thinks of funerary barques and the stories of mythical voyages to the land of the dead. In his delerium, Rimbaud achieved the ultimate passage. By way of the isthmus of Suez, he enters the other side and opens time and space to the beyond, yet for all that not placing any credence in any sort of Promised Land.

On the morning of November 10, 1891, he breathed his final breath. During this last second he experienced an absolute sensation of joy, the amnestying bounty of the irreversible. The body, given up to its own devices, ceases to struggle. The traveler, in the desert of Marseilles, reaches the definitive stage of his journey with Djami Wadai at his side, wearing the appearance of his sister Isabelle. He enters again the "green inn" in Charleroi, the one at which he had stopped around five one happy evening. Unless he had the impression he was entering the shadowy warehouse of Harar, where the plates of the scales are slightly stirring—before the weighing of souls. It is ten o'clock in the morning. That very day in Paris, *Reliquaire*, the soon-to-be-contested edition of his old poems, is being released.[336] With Rimbaud dead, the sequel belongs to that same literature from which he had exempted himself in order to assert in the most violent fashion the thing that, even beyond love, calls all people to his mirage: "the real life."

ENDNOTES

FOREWORD

[1] "À une raison" in *Illuminations*. The final phrase of this prose poem reads: "Arrived from all time, you'll go everywhere."

[2] *Contre Sainte-Beuve* (Paris: Gallimard, 1954), (chapter 8, "La méthode de Sainte-Beuve.")

[3] Mallarmé, from an article in *The Chap Book*, May 15, 1896.

[4] A distinction made by Tzara in "Essai sur la situation de la poésie," in *Le Surréalisme au service de la revolution*.

[5] H. Miller, *Rimbaud* (Lausanne: Mermod, 1952). New translation by F. J. Temple, *Le Temps des assassins* (Paris: P. J. Oswald, 1970), then C. Bourgois, coll. "10/18." In English *The Time of the Assassins* (New York: New Directions, 1961).

[6] Félix Fénéon, *Le Symboliste*, October 7, 1886, "and probably superior to all [works]," he adds.

[7] I am referring to the henceforth classic article by Tzvetan Todorov, "Une complication de texts, les *Illuminations*," *Poetique* 34, April 1978, republished in *Genres in Discourse* (Paris: Éditions du Seuil, 1978).

[8] Maurice Blanchot, "L'Œuvre finale," in *L'Entretien infini* (Paris: Gallimard, 1969).

[9] "The strange and legendary life of Rimbaud, his mangled fate, and the mysteries he gave forth constitute a veritable provocation to identifications," Alain de Mijolla, "Rimbaud multiple" in *Rimbaud multiple*, Colloque de Cerisy, Gourdon, D. Bedou, 1986, p. 223.

[10] Étiemble, *Le Mythe de Rimbaud* (1952–1968), 5 volumes (Paris: Gallimard). See especially volume 1, *Genèse du mythe* and volume 2, *Structure du mythe*.

[11] P. Berrichon, *La Vie de Jean-Arthur Rimbaud* (Paris: Mercure de France, 1897); Isabelle Rimbaud, *Mon frère Arthur* (Paris: Bloch, 1920); and *Reliques* (Mercure de France, 1922).

[12] Letter of Isabelle Rimbaud to Louis Pierquin dated January 3, 1892 from Rimbaud, *Oeuvres*, (Bibl. de La Pléiade, Paris: Gallimard, 1972), p. 721.

[13] Enid Starkie, *Rimbaud en Abyssinie* (in French), (Paris: Payot, 1938); *Rimbaud* (first biography) (London: Faber and Faber, 1938); *Rimbaud* (last biography), (London: Faber and Faber, 1961) (translated by Alain Borer, Paris: Flammarion, 1983).

[14] Pierre Arnoult, *Rimbaud* (Paris: Albin Michel, 1943). Revised edition, 1955.

[15] Pierre Petitfils, *Rimbaud*, Paris: Julliard, coll. "Les Vivants," 1982, p. 10.

---

¹⁶ Alain Borer, *Rimbaud. La Terre et les Pierres* (Paris: Lachenal et Ritter, 1984; republished by Livre de Poche, "Biblio/Essais," 1990) and *Rimbaud en Abyssinie* (Paris: Éditions du Seuil, coll. "Fiction & Cie.," 1984). The two books are markedly identical as far as concerns the text.

¹⁷ Victor Segalen, *Le Double Rimbaud* (Paris: Mercure de France, April 15, 1906, then Fata Morgan, 1979). Also see *Les Deux Rimbaud* by Jean-Marie Carré (Paris: Les Cahiers libres, 1928).

¹⁸ The edition of his works published by Paris: Garnier-Flammarion (1989): vol. 1, *Poésies;* vol. 2, *Vers nouveaux, Une saison en enfer;* vol. 3, *Illuminations.* Two groups of studies on Rimbaud by Jean-Luc Steinmetz have been published in his books *Le Champ d'écoute* (La Baconnière, 1985, pp. 107–76) and *La Poésie et ses raisons* (Corti, 1990, pp. 13–70).

¹⁹ See the clarification made by P. Petitfils in "Lumières et ombres dans la biographie de Rimbaud," in *Rimbaud multiple,* op. cit., pp. 17–28. The diary of Alfred Bardey, Rimbaud's employer, was published only in 1981: Barr-Adjam. *Souvenirs d'Afrique orientale (1880–1887)* (Paris: Éditions du C. N. R. S.)

²⁰ Verse 74 of "Le Bateau ivre": "I who pierce the sky reddening like a wall."

²¹ Yves Bonnefoy in his admirable *Rimbaud par lui-même,* Éditions du Seuil, coll. "Ecrivains de toujours," 1961, leaves this part of his life to the side: "But someone who determines to change his life encloses himself in a destiny and has the right that its private nature be respected. I find it indecent that someone would strive to follow on the trail of someone who has returned to an anonymous existence" (p. 173).

²² "If, in contrast to received ideas, men had only the life they deserved?" Sartre, *Baudelaire,* Paris: Gallimard, coll. "Idées," 1963, p. 18.

PART I
A SCHOOLBOY IN CHARLEVILLE

PIECES OF CHILDHOOD

¹ Currently 7 quai Arthur Rimbaud.

² According to an expression in "Mauvais sang" (from *Une saison en enfer*).

³ Charleville. Civil Records. Births, 1854, #188.

⁴ Paterne Berrichon, *Jean-Arthur Rimbaud. Le Poète* (Paris: Mercure de France, 1912), pp. 12–13.

⁵ All the information concerning Captain Rimbaud's military career were furnished by Colonel Godchot in his *Arthur Rimbaud ne varietur* (Nice: self-published, 1936), Vol. 1, pp. 21–30.

⁶ For Borel, see my *Pétrus Borel, un auteur provisoire* (Lille: Presses universitaires de Lille, coll. "Objet," 1986).

[7] General Daumas, *La Grande Kabylie* (Paris: Hachette, 1847); *Le Grand Désert*, N. Chaix, 1848.

General E. Pellissier, *Mémoires historiques et géographiques sur l'Algérie* (Paris: Imprimerie royale, 1844).

[8] Bourguignon and Houin describe them in their article on Rimbaud published in the *Revue d'Ardenne et d'Argonne*, Nov.–Dec. 1896. But when Colonel Godchot personally asked them if they had seen the documents with their own eyes they responded: "We saw nothing, neither works, nor copies, nor documents, nor service records." They were satisfied with a "verbal testimony" provided by Isabelle (*Arthur Rimbaud ne varietur*, p. 6). See also Isabelle Rimbaud's letter addressed to Charles Houin and Jean Bourguignon in Rimbaud's *Oeuvres complètes*, Bibl. de la Pléiade (henceforth noted as *Pl.*) (Paris: Gallimard, 1972), p. 813 14.

[9] Rimbaud asked his brother to find and send these to him in one of his letters from Harar, dated February 15, 1881.

[10] "She was thin, with long, gnarled hands and had a proud and energetic air about her," as described by Paterne Berrichon, op. cit., p. 15.

[11] For more on Vitalie Cuif see Suzanne Briet, *Madame Rimbaud, essai de biographie* (Paris: Minard, 1968) and Françoise Lalande's *Madame Rimbaud* (Presses de la Renaissance, 1987).

[12] *Arthur Rimbaud ne varietur*, op. cit., pp. 60 and following.

[13] Details supplied by Colonel Godchot, op. cit, p. 58. In 1854 the farm was the property of Charles. In 1855 it passed into the hands of Jean-Félix, her brother, who died on December 3, 1855. It was then repossessed by their father, who then died in July 1858. At this time Vitalie had to share her inheritance with Charles, who for his part, eagerly urged her to give him his share with no delay.

[14] See my edition of *Poésies* (Paris: Garnier-Flammarion, 1989), p. 119.

[15] According to P. Berrichon, op. cit., p. 13.

[16] For the most part my references to Ernest Delahaye are taken from the edition of *Delahaye témoin de Rimbaud* (denoted as *D.*), which gathers together his principal texts and is edited by Fréderic Eigeldinger and André Gendre (Neuchatel: La Baconnière, 1974). Here, p. 30.

[17] Letter of June 6, 1907, to Isabelle, *Pl.*, p. 810.

[18] In a much more realistic manner, P. Berrichon, (op. cit., pp. 66–71) will see Rimbaud's transcription of his first runaway attempt in 1870 in this poem. He oddly says that this text is "of a retrospective sadness at the same time it is prophetic." On Rimbaud's relationship to his father, see Alain de Mijolla, "L'ombre du capitaine Rimbaud," reprinted in *Les Visiteurs du moi*, Les Belles Lettres, coll. "Confluents psychanalytiques," pp. 35–80 and my interpretation of the poem "Mémoire" in my book *Le Champ d'écoute* (Neuchatel: La Baconnière, 1985), pp. 107-26, "Exercice de mémoire."

[19] "Apes of men tumbled from their mothers' vulvas" in "Credo in unam . . ." poem sent to Theodore de Banville in his letter of May 24, 1870.

[20] An expression borrowed from Hugo's poem "What the mouth of shadow says" (in *Les Contemplations*) and later applied by Rimbaud to his mother (letter of April 17, 1871): "But I have pacified the mouth of shadow for a while."

THE HUMANITIES

[21] Stéphane Taute, "La scolarité de Rimbaud et ses prix. La fin d'une légende," Centre culturel Arthur-Rimbaud, *Cahier no. 6*, Nov. 1978. [It should also be noted here that in France the classes are numbered inversely to that of the American school system; that is, the first grade in the United States is equivalent to the twelfth grade in France and so on. Rimbaud at this time is beginning the French equivalent of the third grade—translator's note.]

[22] Notebook presented by Suzanne Briet in *Rimbaud notre prochain*, Nouvelles éditions latines, 1956.

[23] E. Delahaye, *D.*, p. 63 (in *Souvenirs familiers*).

[24] E. Berrichon, op. cit., p. 31.

[25] In "Roman," a poem from 1870.

[26] Pierre Petitfils, *Rimbaud*, op. cit., p. 35, feels that Madame Rimbaud didn't appreciate "either the modern and scientific direction of the teaching [of the institute], nor the lukewarm nature of its religious instruction." See R. Robinet, "L'institution Rossat de Charleville . . . ," *Actes du 88ieme Congrés national des Sociétés savantes*, modern and contemporary history section (Paris: Imprimerie nationale, 1964), pp. 173–80.

[27] E. Delahaye, *D.*, p. 62 (in *Souvenirs familiers*).

[28] Ibid., p. 66.

[29] Ibid., p. 67.

[30] See *Album Rimbaud*, Bibliothèque de la Pléiade (listed henceforth as *Album Pl.*), 1967, p. 20.

[31] E. Delahaye, *Rimbaud*, 1905, pp. 20–21.

[32] Text analyzed and published in the review *Nota Bene*, Spring 1984, pp. 19–28. Rimbaud made use of the *Études littéraires sur les ouvrages français* by E. Geruzez (Paris: J. Delalain et fils).

[33] Jolly was assuredly from the family that owned the Jolly Bookstore on place Ducale. This letter was published in the *Mercure de France*, April 1, 1930, and reprinted in *Album Pl.*, p. 19. It is dated May 26, 1868.

[34] From rue Bourbon she moved the family on St. John's Day 1862 to 13 cours d'Orléans, then, in the first third of 1865, to 20 rue Forest.

[35] The Rimbaud soirée, December 1982.

[36] E. Delahaye, *D.*, p. 74 (*Souvenirs familiers*).

[37] Ibid., p. 71.

[38] E. Delahaye, *Rimbaud*, 1905, p. 26.

[39] See "Un témoignage tardif sur Rimbaud," *Mercure de France*, May 15, 1933.

———

[40] Colonel Godchot states quite explicitly that this was the subject of the competition, *Rimbaud ne varietur*, p. 88, in accordance with the note in Delahaye's *Rimbaud, l'artiste et l'être moral* (see D., p. 32). The exam took place on July 2, 1869, and was published in the *Bulletin* of November 15, 1869. For the Latin text see *Pl.*, pp. 185–86.

[41] Quotes from the poem *Rages de Césars*, summer–fall 1870.

A TEACHER NAMED IZAMBARD

[42] Izambard himself expressly stated in his *Rimbaud tel que je l'ai connu* (Paris: Mercure de France, 1963 [first edition 1947]), that he had been born on December 11, 1848 (in the section *Arthur Rimbaud à Douai et à Charleville*, originally published by Kra in 1927). I will henceforth refer to this text in the notes as *Iz.*

[43] In this May 4, 1870, letter (*Pl.*, p. 235), she wrote Hugot, moreover, with a *t* as if she saw in him one of the revolutionary bousingots of 1830. (For the orthography, see *Iz.*, p. 59.)

[44] See *Album Pl.*, pp. 21–29.

[45] For more concerning this situation see *Iz.*, p. 57, and Delahaye, *D.*, p. 75 (*Souvenirs familiers*).

[46] Albert Glatigny was in fact one of those who inspired Rimbaud's first poems. There is a strongly possibility that Izambard hadn't found him on his own but thanks to Bretagne, whom he already knew. For more see p. 73. Glatigny (1839–1873) published *Les Vignes folles* (1857) and *Les Flèches d'or* (1864). He was an ardent champion of the bohemian lifestyle.

[47] Indeed, in his letter of August 15, 1871, to this same Banville, Rimbaud pointed out: "You were kind enough to respond."

[48] See *Album Pl.*, p. 36, where this dedication can be clearly read: "In acknowledgment of the satisfactory performance of the student Rimbaud of the rhetoric class for his class notes, March 12, 1870, Principal Desdouets." See also R. Robinet, "Le Collège de Charleville de 1854 à 1877," *Actes du 95e Congrès nationales des Sociétés savantes*, Modern and Contemporary History section, (Paris: Imprimerie nationale, 1974), pp. 845–66.

[49] *Iz.*, p. 63.

[50] Rimbaud's love relations have given rise to several legends, none of which are verifiable. The only trace here is that in the texts. The poem relating a possible adventure of this sort was specifically titled "Roman."

[51] See *Iz.*, p. 65. "One of the aunts from Douai . . . was close to me in Charleville during the last days of the school year.

[52] This apartment was located at the first "sous les Allées (that's to say cours d'Orléans, which was planted with chestnut trees), Izambard specifically states, p. 65.

[53] All of these next books were mentioned by Rimbaud in his August 25, 1870, letter to Izambard.

[54] Between September 23 and October 18, 1870, Captain Rimbaud published four articles in *Le Progrès de la Côte d'Or* castigating the defunct imperial regime and calling for a war

of national defense. See "Captain Rimbaud in Dijon (1864–1878)" by Lubienski-Bodenham in *Rimbaud vivant*, 18–19, 1980, pp. 4–24.

[55] In *Rages de Césars*.

[56] See P. Berrichon, op. cit., p. 68.

[57] For everything concerning this sojourn see *Iz.*, pp. 97–132, "Arthur Rimbaud in Douai and Charleville."

[58] Ibid., pp. 120–21. Only Izambard signed this letter shortly before leaving Douai with Rimbaud.

[59] This text is found in *Iz.*, pp. 125–26.

[60] *Les Glaneuses* (Paris: Librairie artistique). In-12, 176 p. A reading of this tome will confirm the little interest it deserves.

[61] Letter of September 24, 1870, first published in "Lettres retrouvées d'Arthur Rimbaud," *Vers et Prose*, 1st trimester 1911.

[62] For the follow-up to this story, I drew my inspiration from *Iz.*, pp. 71–76 (first publication in *Vers et Prose*, 1911).

[63] *Iz.*, p. 74. Izambard, who doesn't quote it, confines himself to saying that it contained the order of giving the duty of returning him home to the police, and that without cost. "Expressly forbidden to seek other means."

HISTORY

[64] November 2, 1870, letter from Rimbaud to Izambard: "My mother won't be sending me to boarding school until January '71."

[65] Delahaye recounts their reunions in his *Souvenirs familiers*, D., p. 77 ff.

[66] *Jean Baudry*, a four-act comedy performed in 1863. August Vacquerie (1819–1895), dramatist and unconditional admirer of Victor Hugo, was the head editor of the daily *Le Rappel*, created in 1869 under the aegis of the famous exile.

[67] This is the name given Paris by Rimbaud in the version remembered by Verlaine of "Paris se repeuple," in the text of *Poésies* (Paris: Mercure de France, 1912), edited by P. Berrichon.

[68] E. Delahaye, D., p. 105 (*Souvenirs familiers*).

[69] April 17, 1870, letter to Demeny: "As for what I asked you, was I stupid! Knowing nothing of what should be known, resolved to do nothing that was necessary to do, I was condemned, for ever and ever." August 28, 1871, letter to the same individual: "I am not asking anything. I am only asking for some information. I wish to work freely; but in Paris, which I love."

[70] E. Lepelletier, *Verlaine* (Paris: Mercure de France), p. 253.

[71] In *Une saison en enfer*, the fifth part of "Mauvais Sang."

[72] Izambard (*Iz.*, p. 228) cites a letter from one of his students, Charles Gillet, dated April 16, 1871: Concerning the day students, only Raimbaud [*sic*] is missing, who has great ambitions to be a newspaper editor, according to what Billuart told me."

[73] See E. Delahaye, *D.*, pp. 108–12 (*Souvenirs familiers*) and the important clarification provided by F. Eigeldinger and A. Gendre (*D.*, pp. 304–22) quoting from the first drafts of Delahaye's letters to Colonel Godchot. Also see P. Berrichon, *La Revue blanche*, August 15, 1896 (pp. 165–73), Verlaine "Arthur Rimbaud 1884" in *Les Hommes d'aujourd'hui*, January 1888, Henri Guillemin, *A vrai dire* (Paris: Gallimard, 1956), pp. 194–200 (Rimbaud fut-il communard?").

[74] Verlaine "Arthur Rimbaud 1884," art. cit.

[75] P. Berrichon, *Jean-Arthur Rimbaud*, op. cit., p. 100 ". . . these scenes caused great suffering to someone of his warmhearted and sensitive delicate nature, if we should rely on these symbolic verses that they inspired." With the epithet "symbolic," the author is obviously taking every precaution. In his first *Rimbaud* of 1897, Berrichon said nothing of this.

[76] *Iz.*, p. 158, and Delahaye's December 19, 1927, letter to Izambard, *D.*, p. 179.

THE NEW POETRY

[77] On Rimbaud's loves, the testimony given by his best friends remains confused (see the balance sheet established by F. Eigeldinger and A. Gendre in *D.*, pp. 322–31) and I have preferred to dispense with all anecdotes here. Delahaye in his *Rimbaud*, 1905, pp. 134–37, speaks of a young girl with violet eyes (she who is evoked at the end of "Voyelles") with whom he would have gone to Paris in February 1871. He makes clear in *Rimbaud, l'artiste et l'être moral*, 1908, pp. 96–97, that Rimbaud nicknamed her Psuké (in reference to the heroine of a poem by Mendès) and that they arranged a rendezvous at the square de la Gare. She came, but accompanied by her governess and he was "as bewildered by it as thirty-six million newborn lapdogs." This passion quickly burned out. Louis Pierquin corroborates this memory (see his testimony in J. M. Carré's *Lettres de la vie littéraire d'Arthur Rimbaud* [Paris: Gallimard, 1931], pp. 154–55) and goes so far as to say Rimbaud would still remember this lover on his deathbed.

[78] See the poem that bears this title and dated June 1871. But the underlined expression "sister of charity" was used in an April 17, 1871, letter to P. Demeny: "Sure, you're happy. I say this to you—and miserable is he who, in woman or idea, doesn't find his *Sister of charity*." (Demeny was married on March 23, 1871.)

[79] In the poem "Accroupissements," which he will soon send to Demeny, letter of May 15, 1871.

[80] Verlaine in his Rimbaud of the *Poètes maudits* (Paris: Vanier, 1884) will evoke this head librarian who reproached Rimbaud about the books he was asking for and advised him to reread the classics, hence the famous poem "Les Assis" that targeted this highly visible personage of Charleville in particular.

[81] This is the first letter known as "the seer." Izambard introduced it with abundant commentary in his style in *Iz.*, pp. 132–36, "Arthur Rimbaud pendant la Commune. Une Lettre inédite de lui. Le voyant."

82 On this period and the rejection of Musset's poetry by the new writers, see Luc Badesco, *La Génération poétique de 1860* (Paris: Nizet, 1971).

83 P. Petitfils, *Rimbaud*, p. 117.

84 Date of its publication in *La Nouvelle Revue française*, October 1912, pp. 570–76. It was republished in the review *Le Grand Jeu* in spring of 1929 with commentary by the review's coordinators, André Rolland de Renéville, Roger Vaillant, and Roger Gilbert-Lecomte.

85 Issue no. 18 of *Littérature*, March, 1921.

86 The word "seer" already used by poets had been mainly enhanced in value by Théophile Gautier in the introductory Notice he had provided for the 1868 Michel Lévy edition of *Les Fleurs du mal*, the edition of Baudelaire quite likely read by Rimbaud. It had already appeared in Balzac's *Louis Lambert* (1832).

87 Delahaye mentions it in his *Rimbaud*, 1905, pp. 30–33. Rimbaud read this text to him in August 1871. "It was also communicated to this group of professors (Messieurs Izambard, Duprez, Deverrière, Lenel, etc.) who so intelligently encouraged the young poet. . . . It formed the contents of a notebook of cramped writing. It was an obviously considerable work, as much for its strength as for its spirit."

88 The expression is found in *Illuminations*, "Soir historique."

89 Izambard provides this poetry in *Iz.*, p. 154.

90 *Le Parnassiculet contemporain. Recueil de vers nouveaux*, J. Lermer, 1866. Second edition in 1872. Its principal authors were Alphonse Daudet and Paul Arène.

91 Rimbaud finished "Le Bateau ivre" by conjuring up "the horrible eyes of the hulks." Political prisoners were then incarcerated in the hulks, that is to say old boats that were out of service.

92 This is what he wrote to Izambard in his May 13, 1871, letter.

93 See Delahaye, *D.*, pp. 115–16, which quotes several verses and is especially reminiscent of another poem in which a sitting man attacks a journalist professor:

> *"Parce que vous suez tous les jours au collège*
> *Sur vos collets d'habit de quoi faire un beignet . . .*
> *Et quand j'apercevrai, moi, ton organe impur,*
> *À tous tes abonnés, pitre, à tes abonnés*

> Because every day at the *collège* you sweat
> Enough on your shirt collar to make a doughnut
> And when I see, I see your unclean organ,
> to all your subscribers, buffoon, to your subscribers.

It is understood that "unclean organ" here designates *Le Nord-Est*.

94 *Iz.*, pp. 109–10. "After his departure . . . one of us noticed on the front door a short piece of verse in his handwriting . . . written in pencil on the dark green door . . . the following week painters came one morning and gave it a touch of the brush."

[95] *D.*, pp. 117–22 (chap. 8, "le clocher," from *Souvenirs familiers*). Delahaye gives too much importance to this anecdote. He recalls Rimbaud's eight octosyllabic verses drawn on the support of "the louvred window" (see *Pl.*, p. 219). Rimbaud was still using the name of Jean Baudry then.

[96] August 28, 1871, letter to Paul Demeny.

[97] *D.*, pp. 127–30.

[98] For more about Bretagne, see *D.*, pp. 132–36, and the brief study by P. Petitfils in *Le Bateau ivre*, no. 14, November,1955. Verlaine mentions this individual in "Nouvelle notes sur Rimbaud" (*La Plume*, 15–30, November 1895) "A great beer drinker, poet (Bacchic) in his moments, musician, draftsman, and entomologist."

[99] Bretagne had stayed at Fampoux from January 20, 1868, to September 29, 1869. Verlaine had seen him during his vacations of 1868 and 1869, when he had come to spend them at the home of his cousin Julien Dehée. During those of 1869, Charles de Sivry the musician and his future brother-in-law, had joined him there and made Bretagne's acquaintance.

[100] Julien Dehée had married his daughter Zulma in spring of 1871. Verlaine had not attended this wedding but Bretagne could have gone. In any event, the Verlaines arrived at their uncle's in Fampoux shortly after and stayed there during the summer of 1871.

[101] A facsimile published in *La Grive*, July-December 1963 and introduced by M. Pakenham.

[102] Letter to Banville dated August 15, 1871, and containing this poem.

[103] *D.*, pp. 135–37.

[104] Verlaine, "Nouvelle notes sur Rimbaud."

[105] Ibid.

[106] He had mentioned several in a letter to Izambard (August 25, 1870) in which he advised his correspondent to read *Les Fêtes galantes*.

[107] *D.*, p. 136.

[108] Phrase quoted by Delahaye, *D.*, p. 136.

[109] Ibid. Verlaine reutilised the term in "Arthur Rimbaud. Chroniques" (*Les Beaux Arts*, December 1, 1895): "People were stupefied at the sight of so much youth and talent blended with so much savagery and positive lycanthropy."

[110] Printed clandestinely in Brussels by Poulet-Malassis in 1868, this sixteen-page opuscule was later republished in *Parallélement* (1889).

[111] Phrase quoted by Delahaye, *D.*, p. 39. Delahaye has recounted it on many occasions with several variations.

[112] Poem published in one of the installments of the second *Parnasse contemporain* (pp. 283–84 of the collected anthology).

[113] Isabelle Rimbaud, August 21, 1896, letter to P. Berrichon (*Pl.*, p. 758).

[114] The former Madame Paul Verlaine, *Mémoires de ma vie* (Paris: Flammarion, 1935), p. 180: "Verlaine sent a money order for the voyage."

PART II
WITH THE "PITIFUL BROTHER"

IN THE LAND OF THE *VILAINS BONSHOMMES*

[1] Verlaine, "Nouvelle notes sur Rimbaud," *Les Beaux Arts*, December 1, 1898.

[2] The former Madame Verlaine, *M.V.*, p. 180. *M.V.* will henceforth denote *Mémoires de ma vie*, Paris: Flammarion, 1935.

[3] Beginning of "Mauvais Sang" in *Une saison en enfer.*

[4] Montmartre was made part of Paris in 1860 and belonged to the eighteenth arrondissement. The Mauté family had lived in their town house since that time; the mayor of Montmartre, M. de Trétaigne was a friend of theirs. Rue Nicolet is near rue de Mont-Cenis and rue Saint Vincent. See Romi, *Amoreux de Paris*, 1961, pp. 254–70.

[5] Verlaine's ugliness was striking. E. Lepelletier will speak of his "baboon-like originality" *Verlaine* (Paris: Mercure de France, 1907), p. 212.

[6] Word reported by Verlaine in his "Nouvelle notes sur Rimbaud."

[7] On the Parnassians see Catulle Mendès, *La Légende du Parnasse contemporain*, 1884 (republished Geneva: Slatkine Reprints, 1983), Louis-Xavier de Ricard, *Petits Mémoires d'un Parnassien* (a series of articles that appeared in *Le Petit Temps* between 1898 and 1900), and Adolphe Racot, *Les Parnassiens*, (a series of articles that appeared in *Le Gaulois* in 1875), these last two collections were introduced and published by Michael Pakenham in *Avant-siècle*, vol. 1 (Paris: Minard, 1967).

[8] "Les Vilains Bonshommes et Rimbaud" by M. Pakenham in *Rimbaud multiple*, collective, D. Bedou, 1986, pp. 29–49.

[8 *bis*] Decree of the Seine Prefect, July 11, 1871. See Gianni Mombello "The Verlaine Dossier in the Archives of the Department of the Seine and the City of Paris," *Atti della Accademia della Scienze di Torini*, vol. 96 (1961–1962).

[9] For more on this period see *M.V.*, pp. 172–77.

[10] Ibid., p. 181. Mathilde adds that "he broke several things, *on purpose*" that she valued.

[11] Ibid., pp. 183–84.

[12] For more on the life of Verlaine, one can read the biography by François Porché, *Verlaine tel qu'il fut* (Paris: Flammarion, 1933), not to overlook that by Edmond Lepelletier (Paris: Mercure de France, 1907) nor that by Ernest Delahaye (Paris: Messein, 1923).

[13] Anecdote relayed by H. Mercier. See M. Pakenham "Un ami inconnu de Rimbaud et Debussy" in the *Revue des Sciences humaines*, July–August 1963, p. 403.

[14] A Zen practice in which the apparent absurdity of a reply or a behavior comes in to play in order to provoke the disciple's thought.

[15] *M.V.*, p. 185. Mathilde cites this phrase incompletely, no doubt deliberately. The expression *"saturnian* poet" establishes an ambiguity between the Verlaine who is the author of *Poèmes saturniens* and the licentious Verlaine, at home in the saturnalia of antiquity.

[16] Anecdote relayed by Delahaye in a letter addressed to Colonel Godchot. See *Arthur Rimbaud ne varietur*, op. cit., vol. 2, p. 141.

[17] Léon Valade had given him this nickname because he was a mulatto. [*Bamboula* means whoopee as in "making whoopee"—translator's note.] Cochinat exercised his talents as a critic for *Le Nain jaune*. See his article of January 17, 1869.

[18] Letter to É. Blémont of October 5, 1871 (Municipal Library of Boudeaux, ms. 1786, piece 3).

[19] Ms. from the E. Buffetard collection. Delahaye speaks of an encounter between Rimbaud and Claretie, *Rimbaud*, 1923, p. 43. footnote.

[20] F. Coppée, "Ballade des Vieux Parnassiens," *Annales politiques et littéraires* of March 5, 1893.

[21] Work published in 1903 (Imprimerie nationale).

[22] "I didn't know him, but I saw him, once, at one of those hasty literary dinners, put together at the end of the war—the *Dinner of the Vilains Bonshommes*. . . ." Mallarmé then repeats several elements of the portrait of Rimbaud given by Rimbaud in his study *Les Poètes maudits*, then he completes it with the specific comment that I quoted. *The Chap Book*, May 15, 1896.

[23] Verlaine, "Arthur Rimbaud; chronicle," *Les Beaux-Arts*, December 1, 1895.

[24] Ibid.

[25] For more about Charles Cros see the book by Louis Forestier, *Charles Cros, l'homme et l'oeuvre* (Paris: Minard, 1969) and the *Oeuvres complètes* (Bibliothèque de la Pléiade, Paris: Gallimard, 1970). The collection *Le Coffret de santal* will appear in 1873.

[26] The title of a novella by Cros later published in *La Revue du Monde nouveau*, no. 2, April 1, 1874.

[27] Gustave Kuhn, "A. Rimbaud," *La Revue blanche*, August 15, 1898.

[28] Letter from the P. Berès collection bound in the manuscript of some of *Illuminations* owned by this collector. Its descriptions with several quotes were given by L. Forestier in *Charles Cros*, op. cit., pp. 98 and 100.

[29] Banville lived at 10 rue de Buci. Mallarmé relayed the anecdote in his "Arthur Rimbaud," art. cit. "It's because"—Rimbaud answered . . .—"I can't stay in a room that is so clean and virginal with my old clothes riddled with lice."

[30] Darzens, *Reliquaire* preface. Rimbaud would have slept, "totally dressed with his muck-covered feet *in the sheets!*" On the next day he would have broken several things and sold all the furniture!

[31] For more on the Zutistes and the *Album zutique*, see the edition, the preface, and the commentaries provided by Pascal Pia in this volume (Paris: Tchou, coll. "Cercle du Livre precieux," 1962, 2 vol.) and the review of this work by M. Pakenham in *R.H.L.F.*, January–March, 1964, pp. 135–37.

[32] D., p. 141.

———

³³ For more on Cabaner, one can consult the *Dictionnaire de biographie française*, vol. 7, p. 750. Verlaine's expression was given by Delahaye in his *Verlaine*, p. 143 (see also *D.*, p. 349).

³⁴ Sonnet entitled "Cabaner" and signed L. Valade and Camille Pelletan in the *Album zutique*.

³⁵ This sonnet is in the *Album zutique*. Verlaine in his account of Charles Cros in *Les Hommes d'aujourd'hui* will write: ". . . the likable Cabaner of whom I can still hear the sonnets in plain-chant and the sometimes abracadabraesque theories that leave you writhing at the time, then make you think "when heading down the stairs.""

³⁶ In *Champavert. Contes immoraux* (Paris: Renduel, 1833).

³⁷ A loose-leaf version was in Delahaye's possession in 1875. It bore the indication *Paul Verlaine fecit* facing two quatrains, and *Arthur Rimbaud invenit* facing two tercets. This version of the *Album* is signed "P.V.–A.R."

³⁸ Published in 1866 at *Luxuriopolis* [Brussels], *à l'enseigne du beau triorchis*.

³⁹ *L'Idole, sonnets*, 1869. See Verlaine's account of Mérat in *Les Hommes d'aujourd'hui*: "The first book of the Parnassian period and the following in which the antique, orthodox worship of the carnal Woman developed in total freedom."

⁴⁰ There is, indeed, an autographed manuscript in Valade's papers housed at the Municipal Library of Bordeaux.

⁴¹ P. Petitfils, op. cit., pp. 150–51.

⁴² *Dinah Samuel*, 1st Ed., 1882, Ollendorff. Definitive Ed., 1888, same publisher. Verlaine dedicated to Champsaur sonnet LII of *Invectives*, which ends significantly with this verse: "Little guy still lives and tells him: Zut!" [at society].

⁴³ *La Maison de la vieille*, contemporary novel (Paris: Charpentier, 1894).

⁴⁴ See the letter of May 15, 1871, to Demeny: "The weak-minded would begin by *thinking* of the first letter of the alphabet, and would soon rush into madness!"

⁴⁵ Verlaine "Arthur Rimbaud," *The Senate*, October 1895. He had already written in "Arthur Rimbaud 1884" (*Les Hommes d'aujourd'hui*): "The intense beauty of this masterpiece, in my humble opinion, bestows a theoretical exactitude upon it, about which, I think, the extremely spiritual Arthur Rimbaud no doubt hardly gave a damn."

⁴⁶ Verlaine, "Arthur Rimbaud" in *Les Poètes maudits*. Subsequently Verlaine will no longer mention this poem.

⁴⁷ We will see in the following chapters the manuscript described; it seems to have been part of Rimbaud's letters saved by Verlaine dating from March-April 1872.

⁴⁸ Recounted by Rodolphe Darzens in the preface he wrote for *Reliquare*, the first edition of Rimbaud's works (1891).

⁴⁹ Verlaine mentions more than once rue Campagne-Première: in the preface to *Les Poésies complètes* (1895) and in a letter to Rimbaud on April 2, 1872: "You are a tenant at rue Campe until the eighth. " For a more precise definition, see F. Caradec (*Parade sauvage*, no. 6, June 1989, pp. 97–100). This place would correspond to the current 243 boulevard Raspail. At this time there was still an entrance to the Montparnasse Cemetery facing

that street; it opened onto "a part of the cemetery reserved for the interment of the unclaimed bodies from the hospitals, whose processions proceeded along rue Campagne-Première."

[50] *M.V.*, p. 204. Mathilde recounts this remark of Verlaine's: "When I am with the little brown cat, I am good because the little brown cat is very sweet; when I am with the little blond cat, I am bad, because the little blond cat is ferocious." And she concludes simply: "I knew that the little brown cat was Forain, and the little blond cat, Rimbaud."

[51] Ibid., p. 189.

[52] Ibid., Mathilde says that "he only remained absent for three days," which doesn't seem to be confirmed by the mail he was then posting.

[53] Letter to Charles de Sivry, written from Paliseul on Christmas night.

[54] This word belongs to Verlaine's argot. He would also say "aller au bural," etc.

[55] In *Sagesse*, III, II. Poem intended for *Cellulairement*, under the title "Via dolorosa." For this period see *D.*, p. 142: "In January I had the surprise of receiving, in Charleville, a message from Verlaine stating that he would be at the Café de l'Univers during the aperatif hour."

[56] "Verlaine . . . was enraptured by hearing him explain that the greatest loss was that the Louvre Museum hadn't been burnt down . . . ," E. Delahaye, *Verlaine* (Paris: Messein, 1919), p. 142.

[57] See *Le Figaro littéraire* from April 28 to July 28, 1951 (for the discovery of the painting and the commentaries it inspired). Garnier spelled Rimbaud's name as "Raimbaut."

[58] *Le Poète et la Muse*, reprinted in *Jadis et naguère* (January 1885). Charles Donos assures us in his *Verlaine intime* (Paris: Vanier, 1898), that the manuscript of this sonnet, dated as Mons, 1874, bears the mention "À propos a room, rue Campagne-Première, in Paris, January 1872."

[59] *M.V.*, pp. 197–98.

[60] Ibid., p. 200. "We traveled by short stages, so as not to tire ourselves, until Perigueux. There we found a comfortable hotel."

[61] Verlaine, *Confessions*, 1895, final pages. See also Verlaine, *Oeuvres en prose complètes* (Bibl. de la Pléiade, Paris: Gallimard, 1972), p. 548. In *M.V.* (p. 202), Mathilde writes: ". . . Verlaine accused me of having been *jealous* of Rimbaud. I can state here in total honesty that I never gave that urchin black sheep the honor. I was also very far from the thought of accusing him of a vice that I had no idea even existed."

[62] For the detailed accounting of this party, see Verlaine, the preface to *Les Poésies complètes* by Rimbaud (Paris: Vanier, 1895), in which he corrects the errors of the anecdote as it was told by Darzens in his preface to *Reliquaire* (1891) and the reply to the article by Charles Maurras, "Poésie. Etude biographique, Arthur Rimbaud," *La Revue encyclopédique*, January 1, 1892. Richepin will provide another version ("Germain Nouveau and Rimbaud: Souvenirs et papiers inédits," *La Revue de France*, January 1, 1927, p. 125) in which Carjat himself is the reciter and is reading "one of his poems of the 'poet-citizen.'"

[63] According to Darzens, *Reliquaire* preface. *Le Sonnet de combat* will appear in *La Renaissance littéraire et artistique* of April 12, 1873. Creissels extolled in it the rigor of the sonnet form, the double quatrain "Straight, severe, properly laid out" and the "serious and rigid" tercet. In turn Jean Richepin would recount the anecdote in the *La Revue de France* of January 1, 1927.

[64] Verlaine seems to remember it in his letter to Rimbaud of April 2, 1872, in which, designating himself, he writes "the friend of toads" that can be understood as saying "the friend of one who has been treated as a toad."

[65] The anecdote will spread and cling to memory. Nouveau, in a letter to Richepin of April 17, 1875, will still remember it: "But you who know more of nothingness than Carjat" (who was thus not dead as a result of the scratch he had received from Rimbaud!), Nouveau, *Oeuvres complètes* (Bibl. de la Pléiade, Gallimard, 1970), p. 821. Verlaine in April 1872 will mockingly write to Rimbaud: "The late Carjat embraces you!"

[66] On É. Carjat, see the recent book by E. Fallaize, *Étienne Carjat and "Le Boulevard" (1861–1863)* (Geneva: Slatkine, 1987).

[67] For the history of this painting, see *Fantin-Latour, Coin de table*, the dossiers of the Musée d'Orsay, op. cit.

[68] Verlaine, "Arthur Rimbaud 1884" in *Les Hommes d'aujourd'hui*, 1888.

[69] Banville in *Le National* of May 16, 1872, notes "M. Arthur Rimbaut [*sic*], an extremely young man, a child of Cherubin's age [Cherubin is the character from Beaumarchais's *Marriage of Figaro* who embodies adolescence at the first stirrings of love—translator's note], whose pretty head peers out in astonishment beneath its inextricable wild mane of hair and who asked me one day if it wouldn't soon be time to eliminate the Alexandrine!" This last remark is possibly less a reflection from a personal discussion than a memory of the letter of August 15, 1871, containing "Ce qu'on dit au Poète à propos de fleurs."

[70] *M.V.*, pp. 212–13. Mathilde asserts that according to the letters from Rimbaud she found later that he "had therefore departed, not for his mother's . . . but to Arras, where he was living at her [my] husband's expense while waiting for him to return."

[71] Expression that occurs in the last lines of the final section of *Une saison en enfer*.

MARTYRDOM, PRAYERS ,AND THE WAY OF THE CROSS

[72] Ernest Delahaye, *Note sur Rimbaud*, Fonds Ducet 7203–146, f° 242.

[73] D., p. 41. The whole would of been called *L'Histoire magnifique*.

[74] Letter from Rimbaud to Verlaine of April 2, 1872, in Rimbaud *Pl.*, pp. 261–62. As a postscript Verlaine writes: "Speak to me of Favart, indeed."

[75] The studies in *L'Art au XVIIIe siècle* by Edmond and Jules de Goncourt first appeared sketchily in reviews from 1852 to 1875.

[76] Notice on white virgin paper, 2 ff. recto-verso, *Correspondence* (Paris: Messein, 1922), vol. 1, pp. 67–70.

—

[77] *M.V.*, p. 211, "pieces of verse, all of which were published. I also insist on this point, for over the long years Verlaine has let his comrades *believe* that I stole and then destroyed a 'sublime' work by Arthur Rimbaud."

[78] Paterne Berrichon, *J.-A. Rimbaud*, op. cit., p. 187.

[79] Letter of April 2, 1872, *O. C.*, p. 262.

[80] As it appeared in Verlaine's letter to Rimbaud of April 2, 1872: "But when the devil are we going to begin this *way of the cross*, eh?"

[81] Quoted by Mathilde (*M.V.*, p. 212), according to the letter from Rimbaud she found.

[82] Verlaine, April 2, 1872 letter to Rimbaud: "having never abandoned your martyr-dom, think about it, if possible—with still more fervor and joy, as you well know, Rimbe." Another letter of May 1872: "*All martytesque letters* to my mother's but make no allusions concerning any meetings."

[83] See Edmond Lepelletier, *Verlaine*, op. cit., pp. 261–62. It was during the course of this meal that Rimbaud, who had seen Lepelletier take off his hat at a funeral, called his host a "saluter of the dead," an expression that was all the more ill chosen as Lepelletier had just lost his mother September 29, 1871.

[84] The two following dreams can be found in the letter of May 1872.

[85] Letter of May 1872, *O.C.*, *Pl.*, pp. 264–65.

[86] For more on this curious character, see Jean Raspail, *Moi, Antoine de Tounens, roi de Patagonie* (Paris: Albin Michel, 1981).

[87] See his letter to Delahaye of "Junphe" (June) 1872. "The past month, my room on rue Monsieur-le-Prince, looked over a garden in the Lycée Saint-Louis." See also Jean Richepin, *Revue de France*, January 1, 1927.

[88] Anecdote recounted to Mathilde by Charles Cros, *M.V.*, p. 214.

[89] Ibid., p. 205

[90] Ibid., p. 207.

[91] First publication in Vol. III of Verlaine's *Oeuvres complètes* (Paris: Messein, 1929). The reproduction of this manuscript figures in *Verlaine, Rimbaud, ce qu'on présume de leurs relations, ce qu'on en sait* (Librairie de France, 1931).

[92] Jean Cocteau, *Les Enfants terribles* (Paris: Grasset, 1989).

[93] May 22, 1872.

[94] *M.V.*, p. 208.

[95] *M.V.*, p. 209. "He [Monsieur Mauté] went to the Lloyd's office, where he was told that [Verlaine] hadn't been seen for eight days."

[96] Fragment of a verse from Baudelaire's poem, "Le Voyage."

[97] Poem reprinted in *Parallèlement*. It was composed later at the Tenon Hospital in 1887, at the erroneous death announcement of Rimbaud.

[98] Verlaine, *Mes prisons* (Paris: Vanier, 1893), writes "The much missed Arthur Rimbad and me, keenly interested in the masculine mania for voyages, departed on a beautiful day . . . of July 187 . . . , by A . . ." First publication, *Le Chat noir* of January 23, 1892.

[99] On this sojourn, see Louis Pierquin in the J. M. Carré edition of the *Lettres de la vie littéraire de Rimbaud* (Paris: Gallimard, 1932).

[100] De Graaf, "Autour du dossier de Bruxelles," *Mercure de France*, August 1, 1956, in the report said Verlaine lodged at the Province de Liège Hotel on the rue de Brabant à Saint-Josse-Ten-Noode, when he was at the Grand Hôtel Liégeois.

[101] "Walcourt" and "Charleroi" in the *Paysages belges*, reprinted in *Romances sans paroles*.

[102] The coach took us [Verlaine and his mother] in front of the station du Nord, to the very first house of the Faubourg de Saint-Josse-Ten-Noode, then called Grand Hôtel Liégeois, a very comfortable and unpretentious place." *Croquis de Belgique*, 2, published in *Oeuvres posthumes* (Paris: Vanier, 1903), vol. 2.

[103] *M.V.*, p. 210.

[104] Ibid., p. 211. "I insist on the words 'unlocked,' because Verlaine, in a letter to Lepelletier, speaks of picking the locks on the drawers." See this letter quoted in chapter 3 of this section.

[105] Verlaine, "Arthur Rimbaud 1884," art. cit. "Rencontre avec quelques Français dont George Cavalié dit Pipe-en-bois, étonnés." For more on this individual see J. Jacques Lefrère: "Qui était ce Pipe-en-bois?" in *Parade sauvage*, no. 6, 1989, pp. 86–91.

[106] First verse on an undated poem by Rimbaud, traditionally classed with the "Vers nouveaux," but first published in the *Illuminations* collection of *La Vogue*, June 7–14, 1886, which grouped together only texts in verse, besides.

[107] "Après le Déluge," in *Illuminations*.

[108] "Soir historique," in *Illuminations*.

[109] In a titleless piece that begins with: "Plate-bandes d'amaranth jusqu'a" (Flower beds of amaranth up to). First publication in *La Vogue*, no. 8, June 14, 1886.

[110] This title groups together two poems. It is preceded by the one entitled "Bruxelles" that is also subsequently found again bringing "Chevaux de bois" and "Malines" together.

[111] *M. V.*, p. 215.

[112] Ibid., p. 218.

[113] Ibid., p. 219.

[114] Ibid., p. 221: "He also offered to have me come live with him and his friend."

[115] According to a passage in a letter from Verlaine to Mathilde, quoted in *M.V.*, p. 221: "Rimbaud who is clad in velvet like a simple Sivry, has found much success in Brussels and will be quite happy to have you with us."

[116] "Simples fresques II" dated "August, 1872" in *Romances sans paroles*.

[117] "Bruxelles," "Chevaux de bois," dated "August, 1872."

[118] "Bruxelles," "Malines," dated "August, 1872."

TWO ENGLISH "SEASONS"

[119] In *Délires II.* "Alchimie du verbe."

[120] Verlaine, "Notes on England. Myself as a French master" in *The Fortnightly Review*, July 1894, republished in *Oeuvres en prose* (Bibl. de la Pléiade, Paris: Gallimard), p. 438 (French text) and p. 1084 (English text).

[121] Félix Régamey, *Verlaine dessinateur* (Paris: Floury, 1896).

[122] This drawing is undoubtedly after the first visit of the two men, for it was in London that Rimbaud bought this top hat, which cost him ten shillings. He was quite proud of it and kept it for a long time. See Delahaye's caricature drawings described in part three of this book. A drawing by Regamey is reproduced in *Album Pl.*, p. 146.

[123] On Vermersch, see the *Dictionnaire biographique du mouvement ouvrier*, Ed. Ouvrières, 1971, vol. 9, pp. 298–300 and the Vermersch Collection at the International Institute of Social History in Amsterdam.

[124] Verlaine, preface to Vermersch's *L'Infamie humaine*, published posthumously in 1890 by Lemerre.

[125] According to Jean Aubry, *Verlaine et l'Angleterre* in the *Revue de Paris* of October 13, 1918.

[126] Collected in *Romances sans paroles* and significantly dated "Brussels-London, September-October 1872."

[127] Letter to Lepelletier, September 1872, *C.* (will henceforth designate the *Correspondance de Verlaine* (Paris: Messein, 1923, 3 volumes), vol. 1, p. 39.

[128] List of the objects belonging to Paul Verlaine left at rue Nicolet (who is asking for them from London), ibid., p. 67.

[129] Letter to É. Blémont of September 22, 1872, ibid., pp. 291–93. "I will keep myself at your disposal for a series that I am going to call: *De Charleroi à Londres.*"

[130] Letter to Blémont, ibid., p. 292.

[131] For Andrieu, see Verlaine's letter to Lepelletier of May 23, 1873, ibid., p. 106.

[132] Letter to Lepelletier, October 1872, ibid., p. 51.

[133] Letter from Verlaine to Lepelletier of November 1 or 2, 1872, ibid., p. 54.

[134] Ibid.

[135] The first two parts of this piece appeared in *La Gazette rimée*, then in *Le Parnasse contemporain* (1871). Verlaine will add others to it in 1871–1872. He planned on providing an assemblage of works on the Commune that would be dedicated "to some proscribed friend." Letter to Lepelletier of May 23, 1873, ibid., p. 105.

[136] Letter to Lepelletier of November 10, 1872, ibid., p. 66.

[137] Edmond De Amicis, *Souvenirs de Paris et de Londres*, trans. in 1889 (Paris: Hachette).

[138] London, a pilgrimage, by Jerrold, illustrated by Gustave Doré (London: Grant, 1872), in-fol., XII–192 p.

[139] We know that Verlaine seems to be indicating an English pronounciation of the word: "et les illuminécheunes, donc!" (Letter of October 27, 1878, to Charles de Sivry in

Verlaine, *Œuvres complètes*, Club du meilleur livre, 1959, vol. 1, p. 1143). In his preface to *Illuminations*, Éditions de la revue *La Vogue*, 1886, he specifies *Coloured plates*. In other letters to Sivry, Verlaine will write "painted plates." On the connections of these texts with the art of photography or the cinema, see "La lanterne magique de Rimbaud" in Jean-Luc Steinmetz, *La Poésie et ses raisons* (Paris: José Corti, 1990).

[140] Expressions borrowed respectively from *Villes* [II] and *Vagabonds*.

[141] Letter to Lepelletier, October 1872, *C.*, I, p. 48.

[142] For the London that Verlaine and Rimbaud knew, V. P. Underwood gives a profusion of more or less useful references in his *Rimbaud et l'Angleterre* (Paris: Nizet, 1976).

[143] Letter to Lepelletier, October 1872, *C.*, vol. 1, p. 52.

[144] Letter to Lepelletier of September 24, 1872, ibid., vol. 1, p. 46 and of November 8, 1872, p. 58 and November 10, pp. 64–65.

[145] "New Erinnyes" who Rimbaud defined as: "Death," "a desperate Love, and a pretty Crime whimpering in the mud of the street," in *Ville*.

[146] Letter to Lepelletier, *C.*, vol. 1, p. 55.

[147] Letter to Lepelletier of November 10, 1872, ibid., p. 65.

[148] Letter to Lepelletier, December 1872, ibid., p. 84.

[149] Letter to Lepelletier of November 14, 1872, ibid., p. 73. "For her part Madame Rimbaud has written me that she has received several anonymous letters against her son."

[150] About this visit Mathilde will simply say (*M.V.*, p. 223): "The good woman came quite simply to ask me to renounce the separation because, as she said, it could hurt her son."

[151] Letter to Lepelletier of November 23, 1872, *C.*, vol. 1, p. 78.

[152] Letter to Lepelletier, December 1872, ibid., p. 82.

[153] Letter to Lepelletier of December 26, 1872, ibid., p. 80.

[154] Letter to É. Blémont, 1873, ibid., pp. 302–3.

[155] Letter to Lepelletier, January 1873, ibid., p. 86. "His good cares joined to those of my mother and my cousin." Van Bever's footnote mistakenly indicates Élisa Moncomble (she died in 1867).

[156] Letter to Blémont, 1873, ibid., p. 305. Verlaine is thinking now of having his book printed on the presses of *L'Avenir*.

[157] Letter to Blémont, ibid., p. 306.

[158] Ibid.

[159] "Ouvriers," in *Illuminations*.

[160] Verlaine writes in "Arthur Rimbaud 1884": "a rare if not unique Londoner—and that's all."

[161] Which can be found again emphasized like a quote (both of Verlaine and Baudelaire) in one of his prose poems, *Enfance*, vol. 1.

[162] Letter to Blémont, 1873, *C.*, vol. 1, p. 306.

[163] "À une raison," in *Illuminations*.

———

[164] Quote from a verse in *Images d'un sou* reprinted in *Jadis et naguère.* The beginning of this poem, that is the first fourteen verses, will be inserted by Verlaine in a letter to Lepelletier of November 23–24, 1873.

[165] Letter to Lepelletier of April 15, 1873, *C.*, vol. 1, p. 90. "An attempt to travel from Newhaven to Dieppe has provided me abundant proof of this sad truth, and it is thanks only to a providential chance, dare I say, and a conversation in kitchen English, overheard on the boat an hour before departure—said conversation held by gentlemen wearing frock coats and white mustaches(!!)—that I am not currently locked up and groaning in beautiful France. . . ."

[166] The last poem of *Romances sans paroles*, dated April 4, 1873, "Dover-Ostend, on board the *Comtesse-de-Flandre.*" "And in her blond tresses were rays of gold." *Beams* means "rays" in English. It is interesting to scrutinize the actors in this poem: a group formed of "us" and "she," who seems to be a fairy irresistibly encouraging us to follow her.

[167] Letter to Lepelletier, *C.*, vol. 1, p. 91 (April 15, 1873).

[168] Julie Evrard was one of the sisters of his father. In a letter of April 18, 1873, Madame Verlaine the mother announces his arrival and advises her to watch over her son (published by Th. Braun in *Les Marches de l'Ouest*, 1909). Jehonville, a small locality, was close to the border town of Bouillon, on the Semoy, about twenty kilometers from Charleville.

ROCHE, MECCA OF ABSENCE

[169] As it appears in Rimbaud's May 1873 letter (to Delahaye) and in several letters from Vitalie or Madame Rimbaud.

[170] Claudel, preface to *Œuvres: vers et prose* of Rimbaud, edition edited by P. Berrichon (Paris: Mercure de France, 1912). See also the footnote by Julien Gracq in *En lisant, en ecrivant* (Paris: J. Corti, 1981), pp. 267–68. "Five or six rural houses or farms, loosely strewn around a crossroads of byroads, trapped in a maze of orchards and hedges."

[171] Diary preserved at the municipal library of Charleville. Isabelle painstakingly copied it over. For the principal entries concerning the sojourn in Roche, see Rimbaud, *Pl.*, pp. 817–22.

[172] P. Berrichon, *J.-A. Rimbaud*, op. cit., p. 30. "A rebound copy of the French translation of the Vulgate, by Le Maistre de Sacy, of the Old and New Testaments, Éditions Hachette, Paris: 1841."

[173] "Bethsaïda" was published in *La Revue blanche* of September 1, 1897, under a false interpretation "Cette saison . . ." "À Samarie" and "L'air léger," in the *Mercure de France* of January 1, 1948.

[174] For their interpretation see mainly Pierre Brunel, "Rimbaud récrit l'évangile" in *Le Mythe d'Étiemble*, collective, Didier erudition 1979, pp. 37–46, and Jean-Luc Steinmetz, "Les proses johanniques" in *Le Champ d'écoute* (Neuchâtel: La Baconnière, 1985), pp. 127–45.

[175] Letter to Delahaye dated May 1873 and recently published in facsimile in Bulletin no. 1 of *Parade sauvage*, February 1985 with notes by Steve Murphy. See also *Une saison en enfer*, the critical edition edited by Pierre Brunel (Paris: José Corti, 1987), pp. 114–17.

[176] The word "Rocheux" as a humorous designation for an inhabitant of Roche will be used by Delahaye in a letter to Verlaine on December 31, 1881: "the hypothetically Rocheux monster" (in other words the possibility of Rimbaud being in Roche).

[177] Same letter to Delahaye, May 1873.

[178] Extracts published in *L'Artiste* on December 21 and 28, 1856, January 11 and February 1, 1857. But the book will only come out at the beginning of April 1874.

[179] "A little world pale and flat," an expression of Rimbaud's from "Soir historique," *Illuminations*.

[180] Letter to Rimbaud of May 18, 1873, Rimbaud, *Pl.*, pp. 268–69.

[181] Ibid.

[182] Erastus and eromenus designating the active and passive roles in male homosexuality among the ancient Greeks.

[183] Letter to Lepelletier of May 12, 1873, *C.*, vol. 1, pp. 101–2.

[184] Letter to Lepelletier (from Jehonville), May 23, 1873, ibid., p. 105. "I leave tomorrow for Bouillon where I have a rendez-vous with *camaraux* from Mézières-Charleville, and from there to Liège, a beautiful city with which I am unfamilar, and from Liège to Anvers and from Anvers to "Leun'Deun.""

[185] Letter to Lepelletier of May 30, 1873, ibid., p. 107.

[186] Letter to Lepelletier of May 19, 1873, ibid., p. 105. Verlaine called his "phameux manusse"[famous manuscript] "Gustave." He counted on Lepelletier to act as an intermediary for getting it published in Paris (Claye the printer, Lechevallier the publisher).

FALLOUT

[187] Letter to Blémont of May 30, 1873, *C.*, vol. 1, p. 312.

[188] V. P. Underwood, *Verlaine en Angleterre* (Paris: Nizet, 1965), p. 130. "French, Latin, Literature Lessons, conducted in French by two Parisian gentlemen; moderate fees. Verlaine, 8 Great College Street, Camden Town."

[189] Letter to Lepelletier of May 30, 1873, *C.*, I, p. 98.

[190] Letter to Blémont, June 25, 1873, ibid., p. 316.

[191] Ibid., p. 314. The letter to Blémont, hand-delivered to Madame Verlaine, had to have been posted by her on her arrival in Paris—this is a clear proof of her presence in London in June 1872.

[192] Auguste Martin, "Verlaine et Rimbaud. Documents inédits tirés des Archives de la préfecture de police," *La Nouvelle Revue française*, February 1, 1943.

[193] Delahaye, *Rimbaud* (Paris: Messein, 1923), p. 52. Delahaye dates the episode as occurring toward the end of 1873—which is impossible, Rimbaud no longer being in England—and he attributes other causes to it than those I put forth here (the care Andrieu gave then to his young and brilliant student Oliver Madox Brown who would die the following year). See P. Petitfils, *Rimbaud*, op. cit., p. 207.

[194] Testimony reported by V. P. Underwood (*Rimbaud en Angleterre*, p. 136) who heard it from the mouth of C. Barrère. In 1873 the Communard refugee Barrère was twenty-two years old. Verlaine mentions him frequently in his letters from that time.

[195] Rimbaud's deposition of July 12, 1873, *Pl.*, p. 280.

[196] Letter to Verlaine of July 7, 1873.

[197] Letter to Verlaine of July 4, 1873.

[198] Delahaye, *Verlaine*, Messein, 1923, p. 170.

[199] See Rimbaud, *Pl.*, pp. 269–70.

[200] Henri Guillemin, "Connaissance de Rimbaud" in the *Mercure de France*, October 1, 1954.

[201] Letter to Verlaine of July 5, 1873.

[202] See Maurice Dullaert, *L'Affaire Verlaine* (Paris: Messein, 1930), not paginated.

[203] See *Pl.*, pp. 273–75. Letter dated July 6, 1873, and seized from Verlaine on his arrest July 10.

[204] Letter of Verlaine to Matuszewicz of July 5, 1873, *Pl.*, pp. 272–73. Matuszewicz was an exiled officer who had played a role in the Commune. He would soon return to France secretly, but be arrested there on July 24.

[205] Letter to Lepelletier, published by Maurice Dullaert in *L'Affaire Verlaine*, op. cit. It was given to the examining magistrate by Madame Verlaine on July 17.

[206] According to Dullaert (op. cit.), Mourot, who lived in Brussels, was the son of a brilliant officer from the Metz garrison who had known Captain Master Sergeant Verlaine, the poet's father.

[207] Letter of Rimbaud of July 7, 1873 (Monday morning), *Pl.*, p. 275.

[208] Sentence written in the letter found next to Maiakovsky the day after his suicide, April 14, 1930. "The barge of love has broken against contemporary life."

[209] Verlaine, *Mes Prisons*, 8. Verlaine is making fun here of the Royal Proscecutor's Belgian accent.

[210] Rimbaud's first statement to the police chief on July 10, 1873. In his July 12 deposition before the examining magistrate the phrase becomes: "This is for you, since you are leaving!" See *Pl.*, pp. 277 and 281.

[211] Ibid., and A. Fontainas, *Verlaine, Rimbaud. Ce qu'on sait de leurs relations, ce qu'on en présume* (Paris: Librairie de France, 1931).

[212] Verlaine, *Mes Prisons*, 4. "This friendly word, a remnant of the Spanish occupation during the sixteenth and seventeenth centuries, is a good rendering of our French word 'violon' designating a police station."

[213] See D. A. de Graaf, "Autour du dossier de Bruxelles," *Mercure de France*, August 1, 1956.

[214] See M. Dullaert, *L'Affaire Verlaine*, op. cit.

[215] See F. Lalande, "Examen corporel d'un homme de lettres," *Parade sauvage*, no, 2, 1985, pp. 97–98.

[216] Rimbaud's dropping of the charges: ". . . because of the drunkenness of Monsieur Verlaine who was simply stuck on the idea of his clashes with his wife Madame Verlaine."

[217] Se *Le Figaro littéraire* of April 5, 1947. The painting now belongs to the H. Matarasso collection. A beautiful color reproduction can be found in *Rimbaud*, Hachette, collective, coll. "Génies et Réalités," 1968, p. 164. In the painting, written on the depiction of a shutter in the room, can be read: "Epilogue à la française. Portrait of the Frenchman Arthur Rimbaud wounded after drinking by his intimate, the French poet Paul Verlaine. From life by Jef Rosman, at Madame Pincemaille's, tobacco merchant, rue des Bouchers, Brussels."

[218] *Une saison en enfer*, 5th section of "Mauvais Sang."

[219] Anecdote related by Paterne Berrichon, *J.-A. Rimbaud*, op. cit., p. 278. Berrichon dates it July 20, but it has been seen that Rimbaud still remained in Brussels following his release from the hospital July 20.

[220] Expression from *Une saison en enfer* (last section of "Adieu").

[221] *Une saison en enfer*, 1st section of "Mauvais Sang."

PART III

HERE AND ELSEWHERE

THE DAMNED ONE'S NOTEBOOK

[1] Diary of Vitalie Rimbaud, *Pl.*, p. 820.

[2] P. Petitfils, "Les manuscrits de Rimbaud," *Études rimbaudiennes*, 2, 1969, pp. 51–52.

[3] P. Berrichon, *J.–A. Rimbaud*, p. 279. "Starting the next day, isolating himself in his grain attic where he had roughed it out during the spring, he continued to write . . . *Une saison en enfer.*

[4] Paul Claudel, "Un dernier salut à Arthur Rimbaud," preface for the CI Bibliophiles edition of Rimbaud's *Oeuvres*, 1942, republished in Claudel, *Oeuvres en prose*, Bibliothèque de la Pléiade, 1965, p. 527: "Paterne Berrichon told me, several days before the war of 1914, that the table from the grain storage room of the farm in Roche on which the *Saison en enfer* had been written had been rediscovered. Its top had been turned upside down. While replacing it in its original position, imagine the surprise of the witnesses to see a cross deeply carved there by a knife and surrounded by rays."

[5] *Second Manifeste du surréalisme*, 1930. See Breton, *O.C.*, Bibliothèque de la Pléiade, 1988, vol. 1, p. 784: "Rimbaud wanted to decieve us. He is guilty in our eyes . . . of not having rendered totally impossible certain dishonorable interpretations of his thought, of the Claudel variety."

[6] Which is particularly perceptible at the end of "Mauvais Sang" and in certain passages from "L'Impossible."

[7] In the poem "Ecrit en 1875" reprinted in *Amours* (1888).

[8] See *Mes Prisons*, 6, in which he writes: "The several diabolical tales that appeared in . . . "Jadis et naguère," "Crimen Amoris" . . . and several others, among which "Don Juan pipé," of which my friend, the excellent poet Ernest Raynaud, owns the original manuscript . . ." Verlaine mentions them in his letter to Lepelletier of November 24–28, 1873 in which he specifies: "Rimbaud has them."

[9] There is, copied over in Rimbaud's handwriting, a first draft of the "Crimen Amoris," subtitled "Mystère" and reproduced in facsimile in H. de Bouillane de Lacoste's book, *Rimbaud et les problème des "Illuminations"* (Paris: Mercure de France, 1949), p. 107. See also the sale of June 27–28, 1990, Bibliothèque du Château de Prye (Chaix d'Est-Ange), no. 269 in the catalog, expert: Madame J. Vidal-Mégret.

[10] Note of the Belgian police in a folder bearing the title "Ex-convict [crossed out] Freed convicts" (See D. A. de Graaf, "Autour du dossier de Bruxelles," *Mercure de France*, August 1, 1956: "A. Rimbaud . . . *profession:* man of letters, *domicile:* rue des Brasseurs, no. 1, *change of domicile:* left furtively on October 24." 1 rue des Brasseurs is the address for the Hôtel de la Ville de Courtrai.

[11] There is a reproduction of this dedication in *Album Pl.*, p. 180.

[12] According to J. Richepin and P. Berrichon, *J.-A. Rimbaud*, p. 294. Charles Maurras ("Arthur Rimbaud," *Revue encylopédique*, January 1892), added Gineste to the list.

[13] We should hear here the phrase that Valéry Larbaud, stricken with aphasia, rephrased as "Good evening, things of here below."

[14] Berrichon, in his preface to Rimbaud's *Oeuvres* (Mercure de France, 1898), relates that this phrase had been recalled for him by his wife Isabelle Rimbaud. In turn, Isabelle would write it down, specifying that Rimbaud spoke it "in a modest tone to his mother" (in "Rimbaud catholique" [1914]), reprinted in *Reliques*, 1921, p. 143.

[15] Berrichon asserts that Rimbaud brought back the edition "in its entirety to Roche" (*Rimbaud*, p. 294) and that "he tossed almost the entire pile of copies into the fire. . . . At the same time he burned all of his earlier manuscripts located in the house. " See also I. Rimbaud's letter to L. Pierquin of January 6, 1892, *Pl.*, p. 722: Several days after receiving the advice of the publisher, he gathered up what he believed to be all the copies and burned them all in my presence."

[16] See Léon Losseau, *La Légende de la destruction par Rimbaud de l'édition principe d'Une saison en enfer* (Mons: Léon Duquesne, 1914). According to the Poot business ledger, the balance of the debt remained unpaid.

[17] Jean Richepin, "Germain Nouveau et Rimbaud, souvenirs inédits," *Revue de France*, January 1, 1927.

[18] P. Berrichon, *J.-A. Rimbaud*, pp. 294–95: "Alfred Poussin, the poet of *Versiculets*, tells us he met him on November 1 . . ." *Versiculets*, prefaced by J. Richepin and accompanied with a note by A. Valette, was published by the Dentu house in 1887 (in-32, 144 p.). "An incurable dreamer," Valette de Poussin will say.

[19] See Delahaye, the preface to *Valentines et autres vers* by G. Nouveau, Messein, 1922, pp. 9–15.

[20] *Sonnet d'été* in the issue of November 30, 1872; *Style Louis XV* in the March 15, 1873 issue; *Un peu de musique* in the May 24, 1873 issue; *En forêt* in the September 14, 1873 issue.

[21] End of the prologue to *Une saison en enfer:* "And while waiting for a few small, overdue infamies . . . I will tear out for you some hideous pages from my damned one's notebook."

A "YOUNG PARISIAN" IN LONDON

[22] Richepin, "Germain Nouveau et Rimbaud," Art. cit.

[23] Ibid.

[24] "Germain Nouveau is without doubt the greatest unknown from the last century. . . . In truth Nouveau is the born deserter," André Breton says in "Rimbaud, Verlaine, Germain Nouveau d'après des documents inédits"; an article published in *Les Nouvelles littéraires* of August 23, 1924. See also the "Avant-propos à l'exposition G. Nouveau" (1950) reprinted in *La Clé des champs* (Paris: J.-J. Pauvert, 1967), pp. 297–99.

[25] Nouveau, *Œuvres complètes*, Bibliotheque de la Pléiade, 1970, p. 818.

[26] Address mentioned by Nouveau in his letter of March 26.

[27] Ibid.

[28] See M. Pakenham, "Les débuts parisiens de Germain Nouveau, " *Cahier Germain Nouveau*, Minard, 1967.

[29] See André Guyaux, "Germain Nouveau copiste" in *Poésie du fragment* (Neuchâtel: La Baconnière, 1985), pp. 109–33. The two texts are "Métropolitain" and partially "Villes."

[30] On the matter of "Poison perdu," see G. Nouveau, *O.C.*, Pl., p. 781. Published in Rimbaud's *Poésies complètes* in 1895 (Vanier), it was omitted from other editions and republished as an unpublished work in *Les Feuilles libres*, Sept.–Oct. 1923. André Breton then protested this inclusion in *L'Intransigeant* of October 23, 1923. Julien Gracq has wondered to whom this poem should be attributed on several occasions, whose beauty he admires in *En lisant, en ecrivant* (Paris: José Corti, 1980), pp. 151–53 and 164.

[31] See *Album Pl.*, p. 185. Nos. 2336 (for Rimbaud) and 2337 (for Nouveau) for the register entries that carry this printed acknowledgment: I declare that I am not under twenty-one years of age," that they (Rimbaud, at least) tacitly contravened.

[32] Letter dated from Algiers, December 12, 1894, and addressed "to the good offices of the consulate of France," Rimbaud, *Pl.*, p. 742.

[33] V. P. Underwood, *Rimbaud en Angleterre*, op. cit., p. 153.

[34] Ibid., p. 152.

[35] Verlaine, *Les Poètes maudits* (Paris: Vanier, 1884).

[36] Vitalie's diary. See Rimbaud, *Pl.*, pp. 822–33 (journey to London). The writing about the trip from July 9 through the fourteenth was revised and corrected by Isabelle.

[37] V. P. Underwood, *Rimbaud en Angleterre*, p. 169. Underwood doesn't specify if it appeared in the *Times*. The bulk of his text allows one to presume so.

[38] *Revue d'Ardenne et Argonne*, Sept.–Oct. 1897.

[39] V. P. Underwood, op. cit., pp. 174–93.

[40] On this discovery see Enid Starkie, "Sur les traces de Rimbaud," *Mercure de France*, May 1, 1947. [This text "On the Trail of Rimbaud" is now included as an appendix in the 1961 edition of the author's biography of Rimbaud published by New Directions—translator's note.]

[41] Rough draft published in the catalog from the Maggs Exhibition, Paris, 1937. Baudelaire-Verlaine-Rimbaud Exhibition. The catalog states, probably wrongly: "Advertisement written in pencil by Rimbaud, *corrected by Verlaine*."

[42] Charleville archives. Census roll for the class of 1874.

1875: A YEAR IN TATTERS

[43] This is as indicated in a letter to Delahaye of March 5, 1875, *Pl.*, p. 296: "I have only a week left on Wagner (meaning "on Wagner Street"). Rimbaud was a boarder at the home of a certain Wilhem Luebke, a professor at the Polytechnic in Stuttgart and an art historian. See D. A. de Graaf, *Revue de philologie et d'histoire*, vol. 34, 1956. For her part, Isabelle would declare (in a letter to the editor of the *Petit Ardennais* of December 15, 1891): "Their mother placed him in a Franco-German school in Stuttgart to learn the German language." (*Pl.*, p. 716).

[44] Delahaye, *Rimbaud*, 1923, pp. 58–59. In a note, Delahaye assures us that Verlaine said: "I have been thinking on this letter for six months." "Slim thinkings!" would have been Rimbaud's reply.

[45] D., pp. 46–47. On several occasions Delahaye would quote an expression from this letter: "Let us love each other in Jesus!"

[46] An expression of Rimbaud in recounting the fact to Delahaye (letter of March 5, 1875).

[47] And first of E. Delahaye in his *Verlaine* (Paris: Messein, 1923), pp. 210–11.

[48] Letter to Delahaye of May 1, 1875, *C.*, vol. 3, p. 107. Further on Verlaine asks Delahaye "to squeeze out of him the address of the Germain Nouveau in question without saying for whom."

[49] Verlaine, "Arthur Rimbaud 1884" in *Les Hommes d'aujourd'hui*.

[50] Isabelle Rimbaud in her "Rimbaud the Catholic" (*Reliques*, p. 133) unhesitatingly writes that her brother, "as was attested by Verlaine, would have given it back in 1875 to 'someone who had had it in their care'—in other words Charles de Sivry, momentarily in Stuttgart when Rimbaud was there, when the audition of Wagner's works began to attract numerous musicians from other countries to Germany."

[51] Letter to Sivry of August 8, 1878, *O.C.*, Club du meilleur livre, vol. 1, p. 1143.

[52] Letter from Verlaine to Delahaye of April 16, 1875. And I explained to him in detail my arithmetical reasons for not giving him any money."

[53] Delahaye, *Rimbaud*, 1923, p. 61. Delahaye explains in a note that he believes to remember Ceos, but adds: "It could rather have been Syra or Naxos, but it is certain he

named this isle as being part of the Cyclades." Isabelle, in contrast, would write in a letter to the editor of the *Petit Ardennais* on December 15, 1891 (*Pl.*, p. 716): "The soap works of the Cyclades and the Carlist enlistment are absurd and mendacious imaginings."

[54] They were collected together in the work of J.-M. Carré, *Autour de Verlaine et Rimbaud* (Paris: Cahiers Jacques Doucet, 1949).

[55] Cahier Doucet, plate 17. See also the *Album Pl.*, p. 197.

[56] Rimbaud, *Pl.*, p. 298. Fragment published by Maurice Métral in *La Tribune de Genève*, September 10, 1963. The entire letter would be in the possession of a Swiss collector.

[57] Delahaye, *Rimbaud*, pp. 60–61. In a note Delahaye mentions that Rimbaud was offered visiting cards in his name in Stuttgart, imprinted on a handsome Bristol board. One came to him from Milan, overwritten with his new address (which Delahaye incorrectly gives as 2 Piazza del Duomo). See the *Album Pl.*, p. 199.

[58] Verlaine, "Arthur Rimbaud 1884," art. cit.

[59] Verlaine to Delahaye, letter of May 7, 1875, *Lettres inédites à divers correspondants* (noted here as *LI*) (Geneva: Droz, 1976), p. 58.

[60] See the consulate's register for this date and the facsimile of it published in *Le Bateau ivre* of May 11, 1949 (a Rimbaldian review published in Charleville).

[61] Fonds Doucet, Verlaine dossier, vol. 2 (7203–155)

[62] In a letter to Delahaye of August 24, 1875, *LI*, p. 66. The "Vieux Coppée" is entitled "Ultissima Verba" and is accompanied by a drawing in which Rimbaud is seen sitting at a table reading a dictionary. He is smoking a pipe. In hand's reach there are two bottles one of which is marked PORTER.

[63] Letter from Isabelle Rimbaud to Paterne Berrichon of December 30, 1896, Pl., p. 774: "If there were any short-lived enlistments . . . they never came to anything or else the enlistees were dismissed or something of that nature. In any event, in June, July, and August of 1875, we (my mother, my sister, and I) were in Paris with him and when we left him at the end of August he had just obtained a position as an assistant teacher at Maisons-Alfort."

[64] Letter from Nouveau to Verlaine of August 17, 1875, Nouveau, *O.C.*, *Pl.*, p. 828.

[65] See Verlaine's "À Germain Nouveau" in *Dedicaces* (1890).

[66] During a stay with Verlaine at the latter's mother's home in Arras in August 1877, he would visit the house of Saint Benoît Labre whose disciple he will call himself.

[67] Letter from Verlaine to Delahaye of August 24, 1875, cited above. The title "Ultissima Verba" is a parody of Victor Hugo's poem "Ultima Verba" (in *Les Châtiments*).

[68] Bibliothèque Doucet, Verlaine dossier, vol. 2, 7203–165.

[69] Bibliothèque Doucet, Verlaine dossier, 7203–152.

[70] Nouveau was of small height. Verlaine had designated him by this expression in a letter to Delahaye accompanied by a drawing in which he portrayed the three friends and himself as professors. Rimbaud is called "Thing," he is holding a "Traduzione" in his hand and is dressed like a Calabrian bandit. See *LI*, p. 60, and the *Album Pl.*, p. 100.

[71] Letter from Delahaye to Verlaine, Bibliothèque Doucet, Verlaine dossier, 7203–171. " In particular, there is a story about a shocking punch in a chamber pot, in the company of the sly devils of the boarding school, that would have prevented the Other from sleeping if he had known about it."

[72] Letter from Delahaye to Verlaine, Bibliothèque Doucet, Verlaine dossier, 7203–152.

[73] Letter from Nouveau to Verlaine dated from "Paris, October 20, 1875" in Nouveau O.C., Pl. p. 832.

[74] Letter to Verlaine already cited (Verlaine dossier, 7203–152). From "where you continue" to "he is even sure of it," the text has been rubbed out either by Verlaine or one of the later owners of this document who by that sought to erase the phrases incriminating the conduct of the poet.

[75] Ibid.

[76] This expression, which should be understood as a paradoxical use of the phrase that designates either Verlaine's edifying recommendations or the religious poems that he sent to Rimbaud, can be found in Rimbaud's letter to Delahaye, dated October 14, 1875, and quoted later in this chapter.

[77] In October Delahaye was an assistant teacher in Soissons. In February 1876, he would perform this duty at Notre Dame collège in Rethel. He would obtain the second part of his baccalauréat in March 1877.

[78] I am describing here a drawing by Delahaye entitled "Rencontre." Bibliothèque Doucet, Verlaine dossier, vol. II, 7203–152. See the Album Pl., p. 202.

[79] For the facsimile of this letter and his commentary see Steve Murphy "La faim des haricots" in Parade sauvage, no. 6, June, 1989, pp. 14–54.

[80] Anthologie de l'humour noir (Paris: Éditions du Sagittaire,1940).

[81] Letter from Verlaine to Delahaye of November 27, 1875, C., vol. 3, pp. 112–13.

[82] Drawing reproduced in the Album Pl., p. 203.

[83] Letter from Verlaine to Delahaye of November 27, 1875, C., vol. 3, p. 112. These words have been scratched out by Verlaine.

[84] See Bourguignon and Houin, Revue d'Ardenne et d'Argonne, Sept.–Oct. 1897, p. 177.

[85] See Delahaye, Rimbaud, 1923, pp. 62–63, note 1.

[86] See the Album Pl., p. 208.

[87] Louis Létrange, choirmaster of the church Notre-Dame of Charleville gave him piano and organ lessons. He lived in the same building. See Ernest Létrange, "Les Leçons de piano" in La Grive, October 1954, pp. 31–32. Louis Pierquin in J.-M. Carré, Lettres de la vie littéraire de Rimbaud, pp. 146–47, places this epsiode when Rimbaud was twelve—which is highly unlikely.

[88] Delahaye, Rimbaud, 1923, pp. 63–64.

[89] See the Album Pl., p. 207.

[90] It can be found in Rimbaud, Pl., pp. 300–301. It was published for the first time by Armand Lods in Le Figaro of April 2, 1932.

THE JAVANESE

[91] Bourguignon and Houin, *Revue d'Ardennes et d'Argonne*, Sept–Oct. 1897, also impute to him the ambition of learning Asiatic, Hindu, and Amharic languages. Delahaye declares he applied himself to Arabic.

[92] Ibid., p. 177.

[93] Delahaye, *Rimbaud*, 1923, pp. 65–66, note 2.

93 *bis*. Ibid.

[94] Ibid., p. 64.

[95] Cahier Doucet, plate 10, reproduced in the *Album Pl.*, p. 212. Title: "Dargnières nouvelles." See Delahaye, "Rimbaud" in *Revue littéraire de Paris et de Champagne*, 1905, pp. 174–175. The "Vieux Coppée" and the drawing can be found in a letter from Verlaine to Delahaye of March 24, 1871, see *LI*, pp. 71–72.

[96] "Vienna" here means "Rimbaud" (since he is in Vienna). "Artichas," is Arras and echoes their July 1872 arrest in that town; "Brussels" obviously refers back to the unhappy days of July 1873.

[97] Drawing by Delahaye in a letter to Verlaine. Dossier Verlaine 7203–166. There is a facsimile in the *Album Pl.*, p. 214.

[98] Delahaye, *Rimbaud*, 1923, pp. 66–67.

[99] Letter from Verlaine to Delahaye. A fragment of it is cited on page 1203 of Verlaine's *Oeuvres poétiques complètes*, Pl. (1954). See the description in no. 187 of the Blaizot et fils auction catalog for March 12, 1936.

[100] Drawings by Delahaye, reproduced in E. Starkie, *Rimbaud*, 1982 French translation, between pp. 334–35: *Farondole nègre*, *Le Roi nègre* (inspired, incidentally, by a drawing from *La Lanterne de Boquillon*), and *Rimbaud cafre*, in the *Album Pl.*, p. 214.

[101] Drawing by Nouveau in a letter to Verlaine dated August 4, 1876. See Nouveau, *O.C., Pl.*, p. 843.

[102] Expression used in a letter from Delahaye to Verlaine dated June 16, 1877. Doucet, Verlaine dossier, vol. 2, 7203–198.

[103] Drawing by Delahaye after a picture by Germain Nouveau, with instructions on the colors and explanations about the characters. *Album Pl.*, p. 221.

[104] The entire tale that follows is based on the documents gathered together for a remarkable program that was broadcast by Dutch radio and France Culture on February 26, 1983, and the file that was made from it, *De Charleville à Java, Arthur Rimbaud, soldat et déserteur de l'armée des Indes néerlandaises*, par Jean Degives et Frans Suasso.

[105] See the facsimile of Rimbaud's enlistment papers in the *Album Pl.*, p. 216.

[106] The list of deserters has been rediscovered. We also know what clothing Rimbaud left behind (Dr. Marmelsteim, *Mercure de France*, July 15, 1922, p. 501). "The sale of the property left by Rimbaud has earned the sum of 1.81 florins, said sum being donated to the regents of the orphanage in Salatiga."

[107] See André Breton's commentary on Jacques Vaché in the *Anthologie de l'humeur noir*, 1940: "In the place of outward desertion during wartime . . . Vaché opposed another kind of insubordination that could be called desertion within oneself."

[108] See Enid Starkie, *A. Rimbaud*, French translation, 1982, pp. 396–99 and appendix III from the same edition, "Sur les traces de Rimbaud," pp. 531–34 (which first appeared in the *Mercure de France* of May 1, 1947).

[109] Claudel called her "an English bluestocking" in his preface to Rimbaud's *Oeuvres* (1942). It is true that he then considered her chiefly responsible for erecting the image of Rimbaud as a slave dealer.

[110] V. P. Underwood, *Rimbaud en Angleterre*, op. cit. pp. 202–15.

[111] Delahaye's tale about this entire voyage was long regarded as unlikely. This is not at all the case and his quality as the primary witness should only be enhanced by later discoveries that have all confirmed what he said. See his *Rimbaud*, 1923, pp. 67–68. On Rimbaud's return to Charleville, Isabelle Rimbaud's letter to Paterne Berrichon of December 30, 1896 (*Pl.*, p. 774), can also be read: "It was during June of the year 1876 that he left for Java (Batavia) and he was back in Charleville on December 31."

[112] "Vieux Coppée" in Verlaine, *O.C.*, vol. 2, p. 1422.

[113] Reported by Delahaye in his book *Les "Illuminations" et "Une saison en enfer" de Rimbaud* (Paris: Messein, 1925), p. 16, note 2. It should be noted, though, that it was 1871 that Cabaner dedicated his *Sonnet des sept nombres* "to Rimbald."

[114] Five previously unpublished drawings illustrate the January 28, 1877, letter to Millot (Bibliothèque de Charleville, AR–284 [72])" on board the *Prince Orange*" (*Album Pl.*, p. 218), "to Java" (*Album Pl.*, p. 222), "at the home of a Javanese mayor," "a small storm during the return trip," and "Delahaye and Rimbaud at a bistro table" (*Album Pl.*, p. 225).

[115] "Vieux Coppée" in Verlaine, *O.C.*, vol. 2, p. 1422.

THE FLAKY TRAVELER

[116] *D.*, p. 51.

[117] The facsimile of this letter written in English can be found in the *Album Pl.*, p. 227. The detail "five feet six inches" is the equivalent of 1.69 meters. It is no doubt a mistaken estimate on Rimbaud's part. On his enlistment sheet for the colonial Dutch army he measured 1.77 meters.

[118] An article, that is hardly enlightening, moreover, by Henri Thétard appeared in the *Revue des Deux Mondes* of December 1, 1948: "Arthur Rimbaud et le cirque."

[119] Letters from Delahaye to Verlaine and Millot, see the Bibliothèque Doucet, Verlaine dossier, II, 7203–198 for the letter to Verlaine and the Bibliothèque de Charleville for the letter to Millot.

[120] Reproduced in the *Album Pl.*, p. 228. Bibliothèque Doucet, Verlaine dossier, 7203–187.

121 Published by D. A de Graaf in the *Revue des Science humaines*, Oct.–Dec. 1951, pp. 325–32: "Deux lettres d'Ernest Delahaye à Ernest Millot sur 'l'homme aux semelles de vent.'" The sketch accompanying the second letter is reminiscent of the one in Verlaine's letter mentioned above (of August 9, 1877).

122 Verlaine, *O.C.*, vol. 2, p. 1422.

123 Delahaye, *Revue d'Ardennes et d'Argonne*, Sept.–Oct. 1907, pp. 180–81.

124 "Vieux Coppée," Verlaine, *O.C.*, vol. 2, p. 1422.

125 "Les lèvres closes. Vu à Rome" (parody of Léon Dierx) in the *Album zutique*, folio 3 recto.

126 Fragment of a letter to Verlaine dated "Charlepompe, September 28, 1878," Verlaine dossier, II, 7203–201.

127 Delahaye, "À propos de Rimbaud, souvenirs familiars," *Revue d'Ardenne et d'Argonne*, Sept.–Oct. 1907, pp. 180–81. Rimbaud "returned via Marseille to spend the winter of 1878 in Saint-Laurent, where Madame Rimbaud owned a country house." In *Rimbaud*, 1923, p. 70, Delahaye tells us that Rimbaud, "applied himself to the sciences; he was seen with an algebra manual, a geometry manual, and an engineer's manual in hand."

128 See the letter from Rimbaud to his family dated from Alexandria, December 1878, in which he indicates that he had left Roche on "October 20, 1878" (*Pl.*, p. 307).

129 Nerval, *Voyage en Orient* (Paris: Charpentier, 1851), "Introduction." See Nerval, *O.C.*, vol. 2, (1984), *Pl.*, p. 259.

130 See letter cited above, *Pl.*, pp. 306–7.

131 Letter to his family dated from "Larnaca, Cyprus, February 16, 1879," *Pl.*, p. 308. See also *Nota Bene*, spring 1984, the article by R. Milliex, "Le premier séjour d'Arthur Rimbaud à Chypre," pp. 75–86, for specifying Rimbaud's location then: the Potamos Quarry.

132 According to Delahaye, *Rimbaud*, 1923, p. 72 and the letter of the same cited in *D.*, pp. 22–23 in "Biographie d'Ernest Delahaye" by Y. and L. Delahaye.

133 She wed Pierre Dufour in 1897. Madame Rimbaud will write Mallarmé a letter on March 23, 1897, with questions about the moral character of Pierre Dufour (alias Paterne Berrichon) to which Mallarmé will respond on March 25, while recollecting the "troubled beginnings of her [your] admirable son."

134 See the letter cited above (*D.*, pp. 22–23) and the story in *Rimbaud*, 1923, p. 72. Delahaye will recall this day to Madame Rimbaud (letter of March 16, 1897, *Pl.*, p. 784): "I have kept a very fine memory of your friendly welcome in Roche in September 1879 when I saw, for the last time, my dear friend Rimbaud.

135 "I no longer concern myself with *that*," in *Rimbaud*, 1905; "I don't think about *that* anymore" in *Rimbaud*, 1923, p. 72, in which his tone is described as containing a certain nervousness. In 1905 (Delahaye–Cazals manuscript, Fonds Doucet, folio 29), Delahaye speaks of a "little half-amused, half-exasperated laugh."

[136] Pierre Petitfils believes a possible departure for Alexandria took place during the following months. But Rimbaud, stricken with fever, couldn't get any further than Marseille and was forced to return (*Rimbaud*, Juilliard, p. 283).

[137] Louis Pierquin, "Souvenirs" in J.–M. Carré, *Lettres de la vie littéraire d'Arthur Rimbaud* (Paris: Gallimard, 1931), p. 161.

[138] There was no encounter, but Delahaye found pleasure in imagining one in a satiric drawing (see Charles Donos, *Verlaine intime*, 1898, and the *Album Pl.*, p. 296). It seems impossible that Rimbaud wouldn't have been informed of the nearby presence of Verlaine. Isabelle (letter to P. Berrichon of August 21, 1896) remarks: "Our family doctor, precisely the same one who cared for Verlaine, already stricken in 1879 when he was here (that's to say in Coulommes, located two kilometers from Roche) told me, without supplying any specific details, that Verlaine's illness was the result of overindulging."

PART FOUR

RIMBAUD THE AFRICAIN

ADEN, "A FRIGHTFUL ROCK"

[1] Letter of May 23, 1890.

[2] In 1981 this outrageously commemorative inscription was placed on the front of the Mount Troodos cottage: "Arthur Rimbaud, poet and French genius, despite his renown, contributed to the construction of this house with his own hands."

[3] Letter of June 4, 1890.

[4] Letter of August 17, 1890.

[5] Ottorino Rosa worked in Harar from 1884 to 1896 as an agent of the merchant house of Bienenfeld. He wrote a book of recollections: *L'Impero del Leone di Guida. Note sull'Abissinia* (Brescia: Lenghi, 1913). See the translation of the passages concerning Rimbaud in the *Étude rimbaldiennes*, no. 3, 1972 (Minard): "He [Rimbaud] set off for Cyprus in 1880, where he had previously spent some time, and he found work with a construction firm. There he had the misfortune of throwing a stone and striking a worker with it in the temple, causing his death. Frightened, he took refuge on a parting ship and this is how fate led him to Aden."

[6] I have taken my inspiration here from Bardey's text describing the passage through the Suez Canal on to Aden, *Barr-Adjam, souvenirs d'Afrique orientale, 1880–1887* (henceforth referred to as *B.A.*) (Paris: Éditions du C.N.R.S., 1981).

[7] Letter of August 17, 1880.

[8] *B.A.*, p. 219.

[9] *B.A.*, ibid. "It was not until long afterward—Alfred Bardey makes clear in a note— that I learned he was born in Charleville (Ardennes)."

¹⁰ 7 francs he says in a letter of August 17, 1880; 6 francs in another one of August 25, then 5 francs a day, but including board, lodging, and laundering, he announces in a letter of September 22, 1880.

¹¹ *B.A.*, p. 219.

¹² *B.A.*, p. 220.

¹³ Letter of August 25, 1880.

¹⁴ Letter of September 28, 1885.

¹⁵ "I will probably go to Zanzibar, where there are possibilities." Letter of September 22, 1880.

¹⁶ For these dates see the introduction of *B.A.*, p. vii, in "Le patron de Rimbaud" by Joseph Tubiana.

¹⁷ A typed manuscript of 277 pages that remained unpublished until extracts of it appeared in the first issue of *Études srimbaldiennes* (1969). It will subsequently appear under the title *Barr–Adjam* (see note 6 above).

¹⁸ An expression of Mallarmé's from his poem "Le vierge, le vivace et le bel aujour-d'hui."

HARAR, THE CITY OF HYENAS

¹⁹ Contract dated November 10, 1880, and signed Dubar, *Pl.*, p. 320.

²⁰ Letter of November 2, 1880.

²¹ Ibid.

²² If it was a work of an author and not a biography, Alain Borer's *Rimbaud en Abyssinie* (Paris: Éditions du Seuil, coll. "Fiction & Cie," 1984), could be subject to the same criticisms.

²³ But Bardey in *B.A.* (p. 233) will note: "Messieurs Tramier-Lafarge have written to Suel that Messieurs Rimbaud et Constantine had left with our number 3 caravan on December 16 carrying almost all of our merchandise."

²⁴ All the subsequent part of this chapter has been inspired by Bardey's tale in *B.A.*, chapters 7, 8, 9, 10, 11, and 12.

²⁵ See Colonel Godchot, *Arthur Rimbaud ne varietur*, Nice: 1936, vol. 1, pp. 62–63 for this property purchase by Madame Rimbaud: "A parcel of 37.70 acres acquired in 1882 and put in the name of Jean-Nicholas-Arthur Rimbaud, professor in Hazar (Arabia).

²⁶ Letter from Fréderic Rimbaud to Rodolphe Darzens on December 10, 1891: "My brother had to remain in Harar, or Horor, and, from what I know, concerns himself with business." *Pl.*, p. 713. Verlaine says "Herat" in his "Arthur Rimbaud" in *The Senate*, October 1895.

²⁷ "Ô mon ombre, ô mon vieux serpent," verse in "La Chanson du Mal-Aimé" from Apollinaire's *Alcools*.

²⁸ Letter of December 13, 1880.

²⁹ We have several different sources from which to reconstruct such a description of the city. They don't necessarily coincide. See *B.A.*, chapters 13, 14, and 15; the accounts by

Jules Borelli in *Ethiopie méridionale* (Paris: Librairies-imprimeries réunies, 1890); Ugo Ferrandi, *Lettera dell'Harar* (Milan: 1896); L. Robbecchi-Brichetti, *Nell'Harar* (Milan: Galli di Chiesa, 1896); Henri de Monfreid, *Ménélik tel qu'il fut* (Paris: Grasset, 1954), etc.

[30] Bardey situates the first installation of the agency near the *Faras magala* on August 22, 1880; on his return in April of 1881, he seems to be describing another, larger, building, see *B.A.*, pp. 262–66.

[31] Letter of January 15, 1881.

[32] Ibid. Reading *Barr-Adjam*, one will note that Bardey, in France in January 1881 and accepted as a member of the Geographical Society, had received the advice (on the part of the secretary Monsieur Charles Maunoir) to obtain a copy of Kaltbrunet's *Manuel du Voyageur* and that same author's notes. Thus it seems obvious that Rimbaud was repeating titles of which Bardey had informed him by letter, without having mentioned their author's name. Rimbaud will again ask for them on May 4, 1881, this time specifying the name of Kaltbrünner and the publisher (in Zurich).

[33] The letter addressed to a certain Monsieur Bautin indeed begins like this: "Desiring to concern myself with the placement of precision instruments in general in the East . . ."

[34] Figuier is named in "Ce qu'on dit au Poète à propos de fleurs," a poem addressed to Banville on July 14, 1871.

[35] Letter of February 15, 1881.

[36] Letter from Bardey to Berrichon of July 7, 1897, in "Nouveaux documents sur Rimbaud," *Mercure de France*, May 15, 1939, p. 14 and pp. 18–19: ". . . he had recently contracted syphilis and . . . he had the unmistakable signs of it about his mouth."

[37] Letter of February 15, 1881.

[38] Ibid. It concerns a notebook entitled *Plaisanteries, jeux de mots, etc.* in Arabic and a "collection of dialogues, songs, or I don't know what that are useful to those learning the language."

[39] Letter of March 12, 1881.

[40] Letter of February 15, 1881. And in a letter of May 4 in the same year: "Are they working in Panama?"

[41] Letter of April 16, 1881.

[42] Letter of May 4, 1881.

[43] *B.A.*, p. 274.

[44] Letter of May 26, 1881.

[45] In *Comédie de la soif* ("Vers nouveaux").

[46] Letter of September 2, 1881.

[47] Letter of July 22, 1881: "Are not health and life more precious than all the other foul things in the world?"

[48] A first sending of 2,468 francs is mentioned in his letter of August 5, 1881.

[49] Letter of November 7, 1881.

[50] Letter of July 2, 1881: "I am not in infringement with military law? I never know where I stand in this regard." Letter of July 22, 1881: "It is quite necessary for me to be certain that I am not in any way contravening military law." Letter of September 2: "I continue to believe that I am not at fault concerning military service, and I would be quite angry to find I am. Inform me of the true state of this matter. I will soon have to take out a passport in Aden and I will have to provide explanations on this point." Letter of November 7: "I'd like to think that this twenty-eight-day business will be settled quietly. . . . How the devil do you expect me to chuck all my work to the side for these twenty-eight days?"

[51] Letter of September 22, 1881: "I handed in my resignation twenty days ago. . . ."

[52] Letter of Pierre Bardey to his brother: "I had an admirable journey and arrived without feeling the slightest fatigue . . . ," *B.A.*, p. 318.

[53] Letter of December 9, 1881. "Don't address anything else to me in Harar. I am leaving in the very near future. . . . I plan on finding another job immediately on my return to Aden." In a letter of January 18, 1882, Rimbaud says that he is "waiting for his engagement with the house to be broken. . . ." In March 1882, Alfred Bardey, on his return to Aden, will write in *B.A.*, p. 321: "I have Arthur Rimbaud as my assistant in Aden."

THE "MIND-NUMBING TASKS"

[54] Letter of January 18, 1882.

[55] Letter to Delahaye (who lived in Paris), included with the letter to his family cited above.

[56] Letter to the Parisian gunsmith Devisme, included with the letter to his family of January 22, 1882.

[57] Letter of February 12, 1882.

[58] Letter from F. Dubar to Ledoulx of March 6, 1882.

[59] Letter of April 15, 1882: "In a month I will be either returning to Harar or on my way to Zanzibar."

[60] Letter of May 10, 1882.

[61] "I have felt the wind from the wing of imbecility passing over me"; fragment dated January 23, 1862 in *Fusées*, Baudelaire, Bibliothèque de la Pléiade, *O.C.*, 1975, vol. 2, p. 668.

[62] Letter of July 10, 1882,

[63] Letter of September 10, 1882.

[64] Letter of September 28, 1882.

[65] See the letter from Pierre Labatut to Alfred Bardey dated from Ankober, September 30, 1991, quoted in *B.A.*, p. 298.

[66] He already had this scheme in mind in that he wrote to his family from Harar on January 12, 1881: "We are having a camera sent, and I will send you pictures of the country and the people." For his part, Pinchard, on January 9 had written A. Bardey from Harar: "A camera would be of great usefulness here, there are so many interesting things that I could

send to you. I have also written to Monsieur Dubar, who is so expert in these matters. He will be able to inform you better than I." Letter quoted in *B.A.*, p. 234.

[67] *Salon de 1859 (II. Le Public moderne et la photographie)* reprinted in *Curiosités esthétiques*, Michel Levy freres, 1868. Baudelaire was then speaking of daguerreotypes. Rimbaud worked with a classic camera and made prints on paper.

[68] *"De vos forêts et de vos prés,*

Ô très paisibles photographes,

La Flore est diverse à peu près

Comme des bouchons de carafes!"

In your forests and meadows

O very peaceful photographers,

The Flora is almost as diverse

As the stoppers on carafes.

[69] Letter posted from Lyon on October 20 of which he will speak in a letter to his family of November 3, 1882.

[70] Letter addressed only to his mother, of December 8, 1882.

[71] Letter of March 19, 1883.

[72] Letter of March 19, 1883: "I leave tomorrow for Zeila." And this letter of March 20, 1883: I alert you with this letter that I've renewed my contract with the *maison* until the end of December 1885."

[73] Letter of January 15, 1883.

[74] Letters of March 14 and March 19, 1883.

[75] Letter of January 6, 1883. Rimbaud adds: "And, furthermore, I will even derive an immediate benefit over there [meaning Harar] from all the seesawing back and forth."

[76] Letter of March 20, 1883.

[77] Letter to Monsieur Gaspary, French consul in Aden, of January 28, 1883. Alfred Bardey will support Rimbaud in this matter and not hesitate in firing Ali Shamok [*sic* in his letters]. See "Nouveaux documents autour de Rimbaud," *Mercure de France*, May 15, 1939.

[78] Letter of November 16, 1882.

[79] Letter of March 19, 1883: I would like to rapidly make, in four or five years, around fifty thousand francs; and then I will marry." See also his letter of May 6, 1883: "As for me, I regret not being married and having a family."

[80] Letter of May 6, 1883.

[81] Very good reproductions of these can be found in A. Borer's work, *Un sieur Rimbaud se disant négociant* (Paris: Lachenal & Ritter, 1983).

[82] Claudel will describe him this way: "An individual all in black, with bare head and bare feet, in the clothing of the convicts that he formerly admired." Preface to Rimbaud's *Œuvres complètes* (Paris: Mercure de France, 1912).

[83] Letter of May 6, 1883.

[84] Ibid.

[85] Genesis: 2, 18.

[86] Letter of May 6, 1883.

[87] Second section of "Mauvais Sang" in *Une saison en enfer*.

[88] Letter of May 20, 1883.

[89] Letter from Alfred Bardey to Rimbaud, dated July 24, 1883 (Vichy), Rimbaud, *Pl.*, pp. 366–67.

[90] Bardey will lend this book to the conservator of the Algiers library. It will not be returned to him, although he had planned to make a gift of it to the Geographical Society. However, the first installment of the French translation will be published in Paris in 1897 (Leroux), translated by René Basset. See *B.A.*, pp. xv and xlvii.

[91] Letter from Rimbaud to Alfred Bardey (in Marseilles), dated "Harar, August 26, 1883."

[92] Letter from Rimbaud to Messieurs Mazeran, Viannay and Bardey, August 25, 1883.

[93] The report is dated December 10, 1883. A. Bardey will speak of the "detailed report 'Notes on the Ogaden,' drawn up by Rimbaud from the information gathered and the notes brought back by Sotiro," *B.A.*, p. 328.

[94] The report sent to Bardey by Rimbaud was more complete and Bardey later published some unpublished details from it in *B.A.*, p. 329.

[95] See the letters from Rimbaud to his family on January 14 and April 24, 1884.

[96] Letter of April 24, 1884: "I have arrived in Aden after a six-week journey in the desert."

[97] Letter of May 5, 1884.

[97bis] Letter of February 1, 1884, signed "C. Maunoir" and "James Jackson," general secretary and archival librarian of the society. It had been addressed to Marseilles, "to the gracious cares of Messieurs Mazeran, Viannay, and Bardey."

[97ter] Paul Nizan, *Aden Arabie* (Paris: Maspero, 1960).

[98] Letter of May 5, 1884.

[99] Ibid.

[100] Letter of May 29, 1884.

[101] Ibid.

[102] Letter of June 19, 1884.

[103] "It is better that I stay at my job and amass a few sous." Letter of July 10, 1884.

[104] Letter of September 10, 1884.

[105] Ibid.

[106] Ibid.

[107] Reproduced in the *Album Pl.*, p. 254. "Everyone in his circle said that Rimbaud was a Muslim," Ugo Ferrandi noted; see "Des souvenirs inconnus sur Arthur Rimbaud," published by Pierre Petitfils in the *Mercure de France*, January 1, 1955. Léonce Lagarde, former governor of Obok wrote in a letter to Paul Claudel (quoted by I. Rimbaud, *Reliques*, 1921, p. 89): "he next dreamt of things that were beyond the comprehension of the natives and the head Muslims of the emir's entourage. They considered him, however, as being

heavenly inspired, so much so that the faithful flocked to his presence." It seems more likely that Rimbaud read the Koran (as he spoke Arabic) to better reach and understand the natives.

[108] Letter of October 7, 1884.

[109] Ibid. A probable allusion to the time Frédéric ran away in 1870 when he followed a regimental troop as far as Metz.

[110] Ibid.

[111] Letter of December 30, 1884.

[112] Contract reproduced in *Pl.*, p. 395.

[113] Letter of December 30, 1884.

[114] Letter of April 14, 1885.

[115] Passage quoted in parantheses in "Alchimie du verbe," *Une saison en enfer.*

[116] Letter of January 15, 1885.

[117] Ibid.

[118] Letter of April 14, 1885.

[119] Ibid.

[120] Letter of May 26, 1885.

[121] Letter of Bardey to P. Berrichon, "Nouveaux documents sur Rimbaud" published by H. de Bouilland de Lacoste and H. Matarasso in the *Mercure de France* of May 15, 1939.

[122] Dated May 3–17, 1885. A facsimile can be seen in the *Album Pl.*, p. 259.

[123] In a letter to Verlaine of November 7, 1877, Nouveau calls Delahaye "Delahupette"; see Nouveau, *O.C., Pl.*, p. 849. See also the letter Nouveau sent to Rimbaud from Algiers on December 12, 1893: "Haven't seen Verlaine for two years, nor Delahuppe, either." (Rimbaud, *Pl.*, p. 743.

[124] See Bardey's remarks to Jean-Paul Vaillant, *Rimbaud tel qu'il fut* (Paris: Le Rouge et le Noir, 1930).

[125] Letter of September 28, 1885.

[126] Letter of October 22, 1885.

[127] Letter to Monsieur Franzoj, September 1885: "I would not have been so stupid to bring her out of Shoa, I will not be so stupid as to incur the responsibility of returning her there."

[128] Letter of Françoise Grisard to P. Berrichon, Marseilles, July 22, 1897, reprinted in *La Vie de Jean-Arthur Rimbaud* (Paris: Mercure de France, 1897), pp. 158–59. Bardey (letter of July 16, 1897 to Berrichon) will supply other details: "The liaison with the Abyssinian woman took place in Aden from 1884 to 1886. The union was intimate and Rimbaud, who first lodged and took his meals with us, rented a special house to live in with his companion outside of the hours he spent in our offices" (*Mercure de France*, May 15, 1939, art. cit.).

[129] Nerval, *Voyage en Orient*, "Les femmes du Caire," chap. 4, "Inconvénients du célibat." "Your neighbors have women and . . . they will be troubled if you do not have one. Moreover, it's the custom here," a sheik tells Nerval, who, on hearing this, acquired a slave.

[129bis] *L'impero de Leone di Guida. Note sull'Abissinia* (Brescia: Lenghi, 1913), edition of one hundred copies printed, not for sale to the general public, 235 pages with 148 photographs. The photo and the note are on page 207. It was reproduced in *Études rimbaldiennes*, no. 3, 1972, p. 6, Minard, colle. "Avant-siècle." It can also be found on page 56 of *Rimbaud d'Arabie* (Paris: Éditions du Seuil, coll. "Fiction & Cie," 1991) by Alain Borer.

[130] Letter from Isabelle Rimbaud to the French consul in Aden, February 19, 1892: "He had a native of Harar named Djami for a servant over the last eight years."—this pushes Djami's hiring back to the year 1883, since Isabelle is speaking here in context of Rimbaud's last year of life (1891).

[130bis] P. Berrichon, *La Vie de Jean-Arthur Rimbaud*, op. cit., p. 256 (the next-to-last page).

ARMS MERCHANT IN SHOA

[131] Letter of September 28, 1885.

[132] All these details are provided in the letter that Rimbaud and Labatut addressed to the secretary of Foreign Affairs on April 15, 1886.

[133] Letter of November 18, 1885.

[134] Letter of December 3, 1885. See also the letter of February 28, 1886: "The African Switzerland, without summer and winter: spring and perpetual greenery, and a free and easy life!"

[135] Ibid.

[136] Letter of October 22, 1885.

[137] Certificate delivered on October 14, 1885, see *Pl.*, pp. 404–5.

[138] A. Bardey, *B.A.*, p. 340: "Cooking pots, cast-iron goblets, and plates of round sheet metal intended for the roasting of seeds or waffles," clarifies Bardey.

[139] Letter of November 18, 1885.

[140] For the description of Tadjoura, see Jules Borelli, *Ethiopie méridionale* (Paris: Librairies-imprimeries réunies, 1890). See also Rimbaud's letter of November 18, 1885.

[141] U. Ferrandi in *Lettera a Ottone Schanzer* published in *Il Corriere italiano*, September 16, 1923, by A. Soffici and reprinted in French by Benjamin Crémieux in *Les Nouvelles littéraires*, October 20, 1923.

[142] Letter of January 31, 1886.

[143] Letter of January 2, 1886.

[144] Letter of January 6, 1886.

[145] Letter of April 15, 1886.

[146] Letter of November 9, 1887 to Monsieur de Gaspary, French consul.

[147] On this question, see Mario Matucci's *Le Dernier Visage de Rimbaud en Afrique*, reprinted in *Les Deux Visages de Rimbaud* (Neuchâtel: La Baconnière, 1986), chap. 2. Matucci also cites the letters of the Marquis Antinori, Menelik, and Jules Borelli (March 21, 1939), all invalidating the assumptions concerning the slave trade made by Enid Starkie.

[148] Published in Suzanne Briet, *Rimbaud notre prochain*, Nouvelles Éditions latines, 1956.

[149] See E. Starkie, *Rimbaud en Abyssinie* (Paris: Payot, 1938), p. III.

[150] Authorization by J. Suel for Rimbaud dated June 4, 1885, *Pl.*, p. 420.

[151] Letter of J. Suel to Rimbaud, July 3, 1886.

[152] "I will leave alone, Soleillet (the other caravan I could have accompanied) also being dead." Letter to his family of September 15, 1886.

[153] However, Soleillet's rifles will remain a long time on the coast, as Rimbaud will say in his letter to the director of *Le Bosphore égyptien* (August 20, 1887): "The thousand Remingtons brought by the late Soleillet on the same date are still sitting after nineteen months under the only grove of palm trees in the village."

[154] Letter to his family of July 9, 1886: "A caravan has been attacked en route, but because it was poorly guarded."

[155] Letter to Monsieur de Gaspary, November 9, 1887.

[156] I describe the entire expedition based on the information provided by Rimbaud himself in his letter to the director of *Le Bosphore égyptien* (August 20, 1887) and Jules Borelli's account in *Ethiopie méridionale*, op. cit.

[157] These details are provided in the November 9, 1887, letter to Monsieur de Gaspary. The *azzaze*, or *hazage* is the head servant of the household.

[158] Abdellahi contested the border between the Shoa and the province of Harar. He had chased off the men of an Abyssinian post who, according to him, were encroaching on his territory. He had also massacred an Italian mission, that of Count Porro, when it was in transit over his land.

[159] Letter already cited of November 9, 1887.

[160] J. Borelli, *Ethiopie méridionale. Journal de mon voyage au pays amhara, oromo et sidama* (Paris: the former Quantin publishing house, Librairies-imprimeries réunies, 1890), p. 201.

[161] Letter of November 18, 1885. Rimbaud asks that he be sent "the *Dictionnaire de la langue amhara* (with prononciation in roman letters) by Monsieur de Abbadie, of the Institute." Amharic is spoken in northern Abyssinia, Omoro in Gallaland. In addition, a special dialect was spoken in the city of Harar.

[161] *bis.* After a letter of J. Borelli cited by P. Berrichon in his *Vie de Jean-Arthur Rimbaud*, op. cit. p. 183.

[162] The description that follows is inspired by the one provided by J. Borelli in *Ethiopie méridionale*, op. cit. p. 99.

[163] For Alfred Ilg, see Jean Voellmy's preface to the *Correspondance avec Alfred Ilg*, 1888–1891 (Paris: Gallimard, 1965).

[164] Letter to Monsieur de Gaspary (already cited) of November 9, 1887.

[165] J. Borelli, *Ethiopie méridionale*, p. 219.

[166] J. Borelli, ibid., p. 412.

[167] See M. Matucci, *Les Deux Visages de Rimbaud*, op. cit., p. 140, footnote 68.

[168] I describe this itinerary from the succinct description provided by Rimbaud in his letter to A. Bardey of August 26, 1887—which will also be sent to the Geographical Society

and published in the minutes of their November 4, 1887, meeting. Compare this with the description given by Borelli in his *Éthiopie méridionale*.

[169] J. Borelli, op. cit., p. 234.

[170] J. Borelli, op. cit., p. 235: "Rimbaud has gone ahead. He wishes to arrive this evening. A six-hour march will take us to the edge of the Oborra and Metta forests, on the edge of Yabatta, the smallest of the three lakes neighboring Harar. . . . A five-hour march from the lake, I established my camp at the place called Arro (lake)."

[171] Rimbaud to the director of *Le Bosphore égyptien*, August 20, 1887: "The Abyssinians, having entered the city, reduced it to a horrible cesspool. . . ." Letter from Rimbaud to Bardey of August 26, 1887: "The city has become a cesspool."

[172] Letter to the director of *Le Bosphore égyptien*.

[173] Letter of J. Borelli sent to Enid Starkie in September 1936 and included in her *Rimbaud en Abyssinie* (Paris: Payot, 1938).

FROM REST IN EGYPT TO THE RETURN TO HARAR

[174] Letter from Rimbaud to Monsieur de Gaspary, July 30, 1887.

[175] Letter from the Massawa consul (Alexandre Merciniez) to the Aden consul (Gaspary), August 5, 1887.

[176] Letter from Merciniez to the Marquis of Grimaldi-Régusse, August 12, 1887.

[177] For his part, Bardey had provided some "interesting extracts" from the journey log, sent to him by Rimbaud, to the Geographical Society. This society's secretary, C. Maunoir, will inform Rimbaud of this in a letter dated October 4, 1887.

[178] Letter to his family of August 23, 1887.

[179] Ibid.

[180] Ibid.

[181] Ibid. "Figure that I am constantly carrying sixteen thousand and several hundred francs in gold in my belt; it weighs around eighteen pounds and gives me dysentery."

[182] To parody a verse by Marcel Thiry: "Toi qui pâlis au nom de Vancouver [You who pale at the name of Vancouver]," that also served as title to one of the collections of his works that appeared in 1924 (Liège: Thone).

[183] Letter to his mother of August 24, 1887.

[184] Rimbaud (same letter) asks his mother for 500 francs "or else I will miss the steamer that leaves only once a month, from the fifteenth to the eighteenth."

[185] Rimbaud's name appears carved in high capital letters on the west wall of the birth chamber of Amenophis III. Its discovery was made simultaneously by Jean Cocteau (*Maalesh. Journal d'une tournée de théâtre* [Paris: Gallimard, 1949], p. 115), Henri Stierlin (*Formes et couleurs*, March 1949), and Théophile Briant (*Le Goéland*, no. 90, March 1949). Alain Borer has given us some very beautiful pages imagining this journey (chapter 13 of *Rimbaud en Abyssinie*, op. cit.).

¹⁸⁶ Letter of October 8, 1887.

¹⁸⁷ Ibid.

^{187bis} Letter of October 12, 1887. The consul's response will reach him dated December 3, 1887.

^{187ter} Letter of November 3, 1887 to Monsieur de Gaspary.

¹⁸⁸ Letter of November 5, 1887.

¹⁸⁹ Letter of November 22, 1887.

¹⁹⁰ Letter of November 5, 1887.

¹⁹¹ Letter to his family of November 15, 1887. See also the letter to Ilg of October 7–10, 1889: "If I wasn't settled here, I would send to *Le Temps*, on the occasion of the Shoan Mission some interesting details on the economic situation of these countries. . . ."

¹⁹² Letter from Savouré to Ilg, February 13, 1888.

¹⁹³ François Coppée spoke of "Voyelles" in this way in "Ballades des vieux Parnassiens," *Annales politiques et littéraires* of March 5, 1893.

¹⁹⁴ First published in review in 1886, no. 5 (May 13), no. 6 (May 29), no.7 (June 7: texts in verse), no. 8 (June 13), no. 9 (June 21). At the end of 1886, these texts would be regrouped and published in a different order in booklet form by the publishers of the review.

¹⁹⁵ Letter dated February 29, 1888, Argelès, and placed on sale December 15, 1983, Nouveau Drouot, expert: Theodore Bodin (no. 264 in the catalog). It was published in part by P. Berrichon, *La Vie de J.–A. Rimbaud*, p. 203, and in extenso in *Un sieur Rimbaud se disant négociant* by Alain Borer, op. cit., p. 79.

¹⁹⁶ Letter from Rimbaud to the Minister of the Navy and the Colonies, dated December 15, 1887 and included with a letter to his family bearing the same date.

¹⁹⁷ Response dated January 18, 1888, and communicated to Rimbaud by Monsieur Fagot, deputy for the Ardennes.

¹⁹⁸ Letter from Rimbaud to his family of January 25, 1888. He had not yet received the note from Félix Faure then.

¹⁹⁹ Ibid.

²⁰⁰ An untitled poem traditionally included in the "Vers nouveaux."

²⁰¹ Letter to his family of January 25, 1888.

²⁰² Letter from Savouré to Rimbaud of January 14, 1888, in response to a letter of December 22, 1887.

²⁰³ Letter from Savouré to Rimbaud of January 27, 1888.

²⁰⁴ Letter from Savouré to Rimbaud of April 26, 1888 (sent from Obok).

²⁰⁵ Letter from Rimbaud, then in Harar, to J. Borelli, February 25, 1889: "Thus we have received by way of Djibouti the 250 camels of M. Savouré, whose enterprise has finally succeeded; he arrived here some weeks after you. . . ." (Borelli had left Harar in the beginning of October 1888.)

²⁰⁶ Letter from the Undersecretary of State to Rimbaud of May 2, 1888.

[207] Letter from the same individual, May 15, 1888.

[208] Letter to Ilg, February 1, 1888.

[209] Ibid.

[210] Letter from A. Ilg to Rimbaud of February 19, 1888.

[211] Ibid.

[212] These details are provided by Rimbaud himself in the letter he sends to Ilg on March 29, 1888, and the one he sends his family on April 4.

[213] From a letter to Ilg of March 29, 1888.

[214] See the letter to Ilg of June 25, 1888.

[215] Letter from Rimbaud to Ilg, sent from Aden and dated April 12, 1888.

[216] Fragment of a letter from Rimbaud to Bardey, May 3, 1888, cited by Bardey with the information that he sent to the Geographical Society June 4, 1888 (presented in the meeting of July 15, 1888).

[217] See E. Starkie, *Rimbaud en Abyssinie* (Payot, 1938), pp. 154–55.

[218] See the reproduction of these two texts in M. Matucci's "Le dernier visage de Rimbaud," in *Les Deux Visages de Rimbaud*, op. cit. pp. 172–74.

[219] Ibid., p. 158.

[220] Letter of August 4, 1888: "There are hardly twenty Europeans in the whole of Abyssinia. . . . Harar is still the place where there are the most: around a dozen. I am the only one of French nationality. There is also a Catholic mission with three priests, one of whom is French like myself and who educates the pickaninnies." Among these "pickaninnies" educated by Monsignor Jaroseau will be Haïle Selassie, future Negus of Ethiopia and son of Makonnen. He will be born in 1892.

[221] Ibid.

[222] Ibid.

[223] Letter from Rimbaud to Ilg of June 25, 1888: "My repeated orders for strange and odious articles is exasperating my correspondent in Aden, Monsieur Tian."

[224] Letter to his family of November 10, 1888.

[225] Ibid.

[226] Rimbaud summarizes all these movements in a letter to Jules Borelli of February 25, 1889.

[227] Letter to Ilg of July 1, 1889.

[228] Letter to Ilg of August 24, 1889.

[229] Letter to Ilg of August 26, 1889.

[230] Letter to Ilg of September 7, 1889.

[231] Ibid.

[232] Ibid.

[233] Inventory of the merchandise mentioned in a letter to Ilg of October 10, 1889.

[234] Letter to Ilg of July 1, 1889.

[235] Letter from Ilg to Rimbaud of June 16, 1889.

[236] Letter from Ilg to Rimbaud of October 26, 1889.

[237] Letter of September 25, 1889, published for the first time in facsimile in *Lettres de Jean-Arthur Rimbaud: Égypte, Arabie, Ethiopie* (Paris: Mercure de France, 1899).

[238] Letter to Ilg, October 7, 1889.

[239] Letter to Ilg, December 20, 1889.

[240] Letter to Ilg of October 7, 1889: "Included herein is a collection of short pieces concerning the Shoa mission. I will send you everything else of this nature that I receive."

[241] Letter to Ilg of November 16, 1889.

[242] An expression by Apollinaire in his poem "Zone."

[243] Letter to his mother and sister, May 18, 1889.

[244] *Les Déliquescences d'Adoré Floupette* will have two printings, both in 1885, one by the review *Lutèce* (May 2) and one by Vanier (June 20). The sonnets subsequently quoted appeared respectively in *Le Décadent* of May 15–31 and September 15–30, 1888.

[245] Letter from Armand Savouré to Rimbaud, dated Paris, December 10, 1889.

[246] Letter from César Tian to Madame Rimbaud, January 8, 1890.

[247] Letter to Ilg of December 20, 1889: "I have only been paid in coffee that is valued at least $\frac{1}{4}$ talers above the going rate, and . . . this coffee, that is always dirty and quite impure, only sells in Aden at $\frac{1}{4}$ or even $\frac{1}{2}$ taler below the current price." Another letter to Ilg of February 24, 1890: "I've earned nothing from the filth received on your account under the name of coffee."

[248] Letter to Monsieur Deschamps, January 27, 1890: "Monsieur Chefneux, passing through here . . ."

[249] Letter to his mother and sister, February 25, 1890.

[250] Ibid.

[251] Letter from Alfred Bardey to Paterne Berrichon, July 7, 1897, published in the *Mercure de France* of May 15, 1930.

[252] Letter from Ilg to Rimbaud of February 19, 1888.

[253] Robecchi-Brichetti, "Ricordi di un soggiorno nell'Harar," *Bollettino della Società geografica italiana*, 1891, series 3, vol. 4, section 1, pp. 23–45.

[254] Letter from A. Savouré to Frédéric Rimbaud, dated "Addis Ababa, April 12, 1897"; a facsimile can be found in *Un sieur Rimbaud se disant négociant*, op. cit., pp. 73–75.

[255] Pierre Bardey, letter of August 10, 1897, to Berrichon (sent from Aden), *Mercure de France*, May 15, 1939, p. 21.

[256] Letter of February 25, 1890.

[257] Pierre Mille, "Un aspect du cas Rimbaud," *L'Age nouveau*, 1, January 1938. P. Mille recounts a memory about Rimbaud gathered by Paul Bourde in 1896.

[258] Letter of February 25, 1890.

[259] In "Mauvais Sang," fifth section of *Une saison en enfer*.

[260] "To Arthur Rimbaud, from a drawing by his sister depicting him in Eastern dress" and accompanied by this legend: "Lost climates will tan me.

A. Rimbaud, *La Saison en enfer.*"

First publication in *La Plume*, February 15, 1893. Reprinted in *Dédicaces*, 2nd ed., 1894.

[261] Let's cite the previously unpublished testimony (quoted by Henri Guillemin in *A vrai dire*, Paris: Gallimard, 1956, p. 196) gathered by the author from the mouth of a Mr. Paddock, a member of the American delegation in Addis Ababa who was repeating the opinions of a Capuchin friar who had known Rimbaud: ". . . a normally sad and even quite gloomy character, with fits of enthusiasm, Rimbaud had made himself detested in Harar, because he indicated certain people he had problems with to Ras Makonnen as enemies of the state; he openly practiced homosexuality with the Somalis and the Issas."

[262] Letter from Savouré to Rimbaud, April 11, 1889. L. Brémond in a letter to Rimbaud of February 10, 1889, had already said: "We will discuss it when I see you, and decide if there is the possibility of doing something together, as long as you don't continue poisoning all the dogs of Harar, starting with the hyenas, the sheep, and even the Greeks."

[263] Letter to Ilg, February 5, 1891.

[264] Letter to Ilg, March 16, 1890.

[265] Letter to Menelik, April 7, 1890.

[266] Letter to Ilg, March 16, 1890: ". . . send me the product at the earliest, I have a great need of it, having to liquidate an earlier operation with Tian in order to make other arrangements."

[267] Letter from Ilg to Rimbaud, May 9, 1890.

[268] Letter to his mother, April 21, 1890.

[269] Ibid.

[270] Letter to his mother, August 10, 1890.

[271] Letter to his mother, November 10, 1890.

[272] Letter to Ilg, June 6, 1890.

[273] Rimbaud to Savouré, April 1890, and the letter from Savouré to Rimbaud, May 4, 1890, posted from Djiboutil [sic].

[274] Rimbaud's letter to Ilg of September 20, 1890, provides an account of these steps.

[275] Letter from Ilg to Rimbaud of August 23, 1890.

[276] See M. Matucci, "La malchance de Rimbaud," reprinted in *Les Deux Visages de Rimbaud* (Neuchâtel: La Baconnière, 1986), pp. 189–200.

[277] At the beginning of *Une saison en enfer*: "One evening I sat Beauty upon my knees. And I found her bitter. And I cursed her."

[278] "Nouveaux documents sur Rimbaud," published by Bouillane de Lacoste and Matarasso, *Mercure de France*, May 15, 1939, p. 19.

[279] André Tian, "À propos de Rimbaud," *Mercure de France*, October 1, 1954, p. 21.

[280] "Arthur Rimbaud, '1884' " in *Les Hommes d'aujourd'hui*, 1888, ". . . on the date of 1885 he was known to be in Aden, pursuing there, for his pleasure, concerns with gigantic works of art that had been begun earlier in Cyprus. . . ."

SUFFERING AND DEATH

[281] Letter to Ilg of November 18, 1890.

[282] Ibid.

[283] Letter from Ilg of March 15, 1891.

[284] Note sent by Chefneux to Rimbaud, dated Intoto, January 30, 1891. The order of seizure had been given by the emperor on January 8, as Ilg informed Rimbaud in a letter of January 30, 1891.

[285] See the receipt of Monsieur Teillard dated February 19, 1891, made out in Harar.

[286] Letter to Ilg, February 20, 1891.

[287] Rimbaud will recount the rapid development of his illness in the letter he will later send his sister on July 15, 1891, from Marseilles. See also the letter to his mother of February 20, 1891.

[288] Letter to his mother of February 20, 1891.

[289] Letter from Madame Rimbaud to Rimbaud of March 27, 1891.

[290] See the sketch of Rimbaud, *Album Pl.*, p. 292.

[291] This entire itinerary is described from the daily log notes taken by Rimbaud. Autograph, Fonds Doucet.

[292] Letter to his mother, dated Aden, April 30, 1891: "The English doctor, once I showed him my knee, cried out that it was a *synovitis that has reached a dangerous point.* . . ."

[293] Invoice spelled out in Tian's letter to Rimbaud of May 6, 1891, and that of Rimbaud acknowledging its receipt, dated the same day.

[294] Letter to his mother and sister, Marseilles, May 21, 1891.

[295] See the first part, p. 69 and note 93.

> *"J'ai mon fémur! j'ai mon fémur! j'ai mon fémur!*
> *C'est cela que depuis quarante ans je bistourne*
> *Sur le bord de ma chaise aimée en noyer dur;"*

> I have my thighbone! I have my thighbone! I have my thighbone!
> It's what I 've been twisting for forty years
> On the edge of my much-loved hard walnut chair.

[296] An expression used by Mallarmé in his article on Rimbaud published in *The Chap Book*, May 15, 1896.

[297] Maurice Riès, César Tian's proxy. There are two letters from Riès to Rimbaud, one of August 3, 1891, the other addressed to Madame Rimbaud, from Paris, September 10, 1891.

[298] Letter from Dimitri Righas, dated Harar, July 15, 1891 (Fonds Doucet). An extract from it is provided in *Rimbaud, Pl.*, p. 686.

[299] Letter to his sister Isabelle of June 17, 1891.

[300] Letter to his sister Isabelle of July 10, 1891.

[301] Letter to Isabelle of June 23, 1891.

[302] Ibid.

[303] Letter to Isabelle, June 20, 1891: "I am awaiting news of your inquiry concerning military service, but whatever the case may be, *I fear snares* . . . ;" letter to the same person of July 2, 1891: "For me, I have great fear of a snare and would greatly hesitate to return under any circumstances."

[304] Letter to his sister, July 10, 1891: "Right at my table there is a sick police inspector who is always getting on my nerves with his stories of service and who is trying to play some sort of trick on me."

[305] Letter to Isabelle, June 29, 1891.

[306] Letter to Isabelle, July 10, 1891.

[307] Ibid.

[308] Letter to Isabelle of July 15, 1891.

[309] Ibid.

[310] Letters from Sotiro of June 21 (Aden), July 10 (Zeila), and August 14 (Zeila).

[311] For this month, see Isabelle Rimbaud's testimony, "Le dernier voyage de Rimbaud," dated from "Charleville, 1897" and reprinted in *Reliques* (henceforth referred to as *Rel.*), Mercure de France.

[312] *Rel.*, p. 108.

[313] Letter from M. Riès to Emile Deschamps, March 15, 1929, and partially quoted in *Un sieur Rimbaud se disant nègociant*, op. cit.: "He wrote me from there, one final time, dating his letter *Lair of the Wolves*, instructing me on some new business schemes. . . . He couldn't continue writing and his sister finished his letter under his dictation." See also *Pl.*, pp. 815–16.

[314] She will provide a detailed account in "Le dernier voyage de Rimbaud," op. cit., pp. 11–123.

[315] Marguerite Yerta-Méléra, *Rimbaud* (Paris: Firmin-Didot, 1930).

[316] Letter from Isabelle to her mother, September 22, 1891.

[317] Letter to E. Deschamps, already cited: ". . . killed by the disease diagnosed by the head doctor Trastoul at the time he was first admitted, who confided to me this would be how he would die. . . ."

[318] Expression of Rimbaud's from "Les Assis." In her letter of September 22, 1891, to her mother, Isabelle says of Rimbaud: "His eyes are sunken and have black circles."

[319] Same letter: "He has terrifying dreams." Rimbaud in "Vagabonds" (*Illuminations*) had recounted a terrifying dream of the "pitiful brother."

[320] Ibid.

[321] See *Album Pl.*, p. 309.

[322] Letter from Isabelle to her mother, October 4, 1891.

[323] Ibid.

[324] Letter from Isabelle to her mother, October 5, 1891: ". . . I only ask one thing: that he has a good death."

[325] Letter from Isabelle to her mother, October 28, 1891. Isabelle will publish this letter in "Rimbaud mourant," first publication in *Mercure de France*, April 15, 1920. The autograph (3½ pp.) was recently put up for sale (June 27–28, 1990, library of the Château de Prye, expert Madame J. Vidal-Mégret, no. 233 in the catalog). It has no erasures. Claudel and André-Suares made a copy of this document (see Fonds Doucet). On "la mort de Rimbaud," see H. Guillemin, *À vrai dire*, op. cit., pp. 201–8.

[326] Ibid.

[327] Ibid. The publisher deemed it wise to explicitly state in a footnote (p. 67 of *Rel.*): "It should be recalled that on the date this was written, Isabelle Rimbaud knew nothing of her brother's literary works."

[328] Letter from Isabelle to Louis Pierquin, December 18, 1892 (*Pl.*, p. 737).

[329] Letter from Isabelle to her mother, October 28, 1891: "He thinks to see everyone. Me, he sometimes calls Djami, but I know it's because he wants to, and it fits into his dream as he wants it to be."

[330] Ibid. "Concerning your letter and Arthur, don't count at all on his money." As early as the end of 1888, Madame Rimbaud had become concerned about her son's will arrangements, as is shown by a letter from Arthur to her and his sister of January 10, 1889: "It's my full intention to make the donation of which you speak. Indeed, it doesn't please me at all to think that the little I've carefully put together would serve to provide a feast for those who have never even written me a single letter!" No doubt, Rimbaud was thinking of Frédéric here.

[331] Letter from Isabelle to the French consul in Aden, February 19, 1892.

[332] Letter from César Tian to Isabelle, March 2, 1892. Monsignor Taurin-Cahagne was put in charge of the transaction.

[333] Letter from César Tian to Isabelle, Marseilles, November 23, 1893, in which he announces that Monsignor Taurin-Cahagne had given the sum "to those it rightfully belonged."

[334] "Several weeks after his death I shivered with surprise and intense feeling when reading *Illuminations* for the first time." Remark of Isabelle Rimbaud's cited in the appendix of *Rel.*, p. 199. A footnote specifies that it was through the articles of Charles Le Goffic that appeared in *L'Ouvrier* and *Les Veillés [sic] des chaumières* that Isabelle learned of the position her brother held in literature.

[335] See "La signification d'Aphinar dans les dernières paroles de Rimbaud," article by Duncan Forbes in *Parade sauvage*, 6, June 1989, pp. 144–46, in which he thinks that a ship of this name, *Al Fanar* ("the beacon" in Arabic) could have been thus indicated.

[336] *Reliquaire*, presented and prefaced by Rodolphe Darzens (Genonceaux Editions), vol in-16 of 184 pages, preface i–xxviii, was printed in 550 copies. A portion of the edition (119 copies) was seized on November 11, at the request of Rodolphe Darzens, who complained he had been unable to revise his text. The copies with the preface deleted were put back into circulation in 1892. Outside of the presence of a few apocryphal texts, the preparation of the poems had been carefully executed.

1854 October 20. Birth of Jean-Arthur Rimbaud, at six o'clock in the morning in Charleville in the department of the Ardennes. His father, Frédéric Rimbaud (born October 7, 1814), is an infantry captain. His mother, Vitalie Cuif (born March 10, 1825), is the daughter of rural landowners who own a farm in Roche, in the canton of Attigny. Rimbaud has an elder brother, Frédéric, born in 1853.

1855–1856 Captain Rimbaud takes part in the Crimean campaign from March 14, 1855, to May 28, 1856.

1857 The birth on June 4 of the poet's sister, Victorine Pauline Vitalie, who dies in July.

1858 The birth of Vitalie Rimbaud on June 15.

1860 The birth of Isabelle Rimbaud on June 1.

1861 Rimbaud enters the ninth form of the Institution Rossat in October.

1865 Rimbaud, having finished the first two trimesters of the sixth form at the Institution Rossat, transfers to the *collège* of Charleville at Easter.

1868 Rimbaud "secretly" sends a letter in Latin verse to the imperial prince on the occasion of the latter's first communion (May 8).

1869 On January 15 the *Moniteur de l'enseignement secondaire special et classique. Bulletin de l'Académie de Douai*, no. 2, publishes a piece of Latin verse by Rimbaud, "Ver erat . . ." ("The Schoolboy's Dream").

The same bulletin, no. 11, on June 1 publishes another piece by Rimbaud, "Jamque novus . . ." ("The Angel and the Child").

On November 15 the *Moniteur de l'enseignement secondaire*, no. 22, publishes another composition by Rimbaud in Latin verse, *Jugurtha*, which earns him first prize in the academic competition of Latin verse.

At the end of the year Rimbaud composes "Les Étrennes des orphelins."

—

1870 In January the professor of rhetoric at the collège, M. Feuillâtre, is replaced by the young Georges Izambard (aged twenty-one) with whom Rimbaud will form a bond of friendship.

On January 2 the *Revue pour tous* publishes "Les Étrennes des orphelins."

On May 24, in the hope of being published in an upcoming issue of the *Parnasse contemporain*, Rimbaud sends a letter to Théodore de Banville containing three poems: "Sensation," "Ophélie," and "Credo in unam."

On July 19 France declares war on Prussia. Rimbaud writes the sonnet "Morts de quatre-vingt-douze."

On August 13 *La Charge* publishes "Trois Baisers." Rimbaud then writes a certain number of poems among which are "Vénus anadyomène" and "Les Reparties de Nina."

On August 29, Rimbaud's first attempt at running away. He leaves for Paris by way of Charleroi. He arrives in Paris on August 31. Arrested on his descent from the train, because he has neither money nor a ticket in his possession, he is led to the station, then to Mazas Prison.

September 2: The disaster of Sedan, Napoleon III capitulates to the Prussian army.

September 4: The proclamation of the Third Republic. On September 5, thanks to Georges Izambard's intervention, Rimbaud is freed. He goes to Douai, to the home of Izambard's maiden aunts, the Gindres. He remains there about two weeks and takes advantage of his time there to copy over his poems into a notebook, intended for a young poet, Paul Demeny, to whom he had been introduced by his professor and who had just been published.

On September 26 Rimbaud, accompanied by Georges Izambard, returns to Charleville. But on October 7 he takes back to the road, on foot this time, passing through Fumay, Givet, Charleroi, and pushing on to Brussels. Between October 20 and October 30 he is once more at the home of the Gindres, where he completes the "Douai notebook," which he entrusts to P. Demeny. November 1: Madame Rimbaud seeks the intervention of the police, and Rimbaud is obliged to return to Charleville. The *collège* has closed its doors because of the war. Rim-

———

baud then lives through a period of idleness. He reads and takes long walks with his friend Ernest Delahaye.

1871   On January 1 the Germans occupy Mézières and Charleville. On January 28 the armistice is signed. On February 17 Thiers becomes the head of executive power. On February 25 Rimbaud leaves by train for Paris. His life there is miserable and he returns to Charleville on foot March 10. March 18, the Commune of Paris is proclaimed. Rimbaud takes the side of the insurgents. He will soon write his first Communard poems: "Chant de guerre parisien," "Les Mains de Jeanne-Marie," "Paris se repeuple." He tries to obtain employment at the newspaper Le Progrès des Ardennes (which ceases publication on April 17).

Mid-April, the beginning of May, Rimbaud, according to E. Delahaye, (Entretiens politiques et littéraires, December 1891), allegedly went to Paris. There he would have enlisted in the national guard and stayed at the Babylon barracks. A police note from June 26, 1873, concerning Verlaine and Rimbaud in London points out that the young "Raimbault [sic] was a member of the francs-tireurs under the Commune." Let's note, however, that Rimbaud was in Charleville on April 17 and will be there also on May 13 and May 15, as shown by his letters. The Versailles repression, the Bloody Week, began on May 21. For his friends there was no doubt concerning Rimbaud's participation in the Commune. In Verlaine's biography of Rimbaud that appeared in Les Hommes d'aujourd'hui (1888), it is noted: "Return to Paris during the Commune and several sojourns at the barracks of Château-d'Eau among the vengeful waves of Flourens."

May 13: Rimbaud sends a letter to Goerges Izambard in which he reveals his new ideas on poetry. It contains the poem "Le Coeur supplicié."

May 15: he sends Paul Demeny the letter known as that "of the seer" in which he develops at great lengths certain elements of the preceding letter. It also contains "Chant de guerre parisien," "Mes Petites amoureuses," and "Accroupissements."

June 10: Rimbaud sends a new letter to Paul Demeny. He asks him to burn the notebook he sent him the year before and presents him with three new poems, "Les Poètes de sept ans," "Les Pauvres à l'église," and "Le Coeur du pitre."

———

August 15: Rimbaud addresses a letter to Théodore de Banville containing the ironical "Ce qu'on dit au Poète à propos de fleurs," signed "Alcide Bava."

Rimbaud forms a friendship with Auguste-Charles Bretagne, a head clerk of indirect taxation who is keen on occultism and no doubt a homosexual, as well as a friend of Paul Verlaine.

In September, Rimbaud sends two letters to Verlaine in rapid succession. He accompanies them with several poems, "Les Effarés," "Accroupissements," "Les Douaniers," "Le Coeur volé," "Les Assis," "Mes petites amoureuses," "Les Premieères Communions," "Paris se repeuple. Verlaine responds to Rimbaud with the suggestion he come to Paris.

At the end of September, Rimbaud arrives in Paris, "Le Bateau ivre" in his pocket. He is first welcomed to the rue Nicolet in Montmartre, at the town house of the Mautés, Verlaine's in-laws, who house their daughter Mathilde and Paul Verlaine, who had recently wed her, under their roof. The young couple's son, Georges, will be born October 30. Verlaine brings Rimbaud to one of the dinners of the Vilains Bonshommes (a gathering of his friends the Parnassian poets). There Rimbaud recites "Le Bateau ivre." His reading is received enthusiastically. During this entire period Rimbaud will frequent the Cros brothers, Léon Valade, Émile Blémont, Forain, known as "Gavroche," the draughtsman Étienne Carjat, former director of *Boulevard* and photographer (with whom he will have a serious altercation).

In October he is forced to leave the Mautés' town house. He lodges for a while in Charles Cros's studio, then in a room lent to him by Théodore de Banville. At the end of October, the so-called Zutist circle is founded on the suggestion of Charles Cros; they hold their meetings in a room of the Hôtel des Étrangers, on the corner of rue Racine and rue de l'École de Médicine. Rimbaud lives there while waiting for something better, in the company of the bohemian musician Ernest Cabaner. He contributes pieces on several occasions to the *Album zutique* (October 22, November 1, November 6, and November 9). Mid-November: Rimbaud resides in a garret located at the corner of boulevard d'Enfer (today boulevard Raspail) and rue Campagne-Première.

At the end of December Fantin-Latour begins his painting *Coin de table*, in which Verlaine and Rimbaud are depicted next to Jean Aicard, Léon Valade, Ernest d'Hervilly, Camille Pelletan, Pierre Elzéar, and Émile Blémont. The painting will not be completed until April 1872.

1872 Verlaine and Rimbaud scandalize the literary milieus they frequent with their behavior. Verlaine leading an increasingly irregular life, Mathilde Mauté decides to leave during the second half of January to stay with relatives in Périgueux and brings her young son. Alarmed by this situation, Verlaine advises Rimbaud to leave Paris. Rimbaud has no choice but to agree. He goes to Arras and spends some time at the home of Verlaine's relatives. Little is known about this stay. He next returns to the maternal residence in Charleville, where he spends time with Delahaye in particular. At the municipal library he reads all kinds of books; for example, Favart's ariettas. (Favart was a writer of the seventeenth century and the author of numerous vaudeville pieces and comic operas.) He corresponds with Verlaine, sending him letters his correspondent labels "martyresque." According to Delahaye, Rimbaud then had the idea of writing prose texts under the title *Photographies du temps passé* (he allegedly wrote several texts in this vein). According to Verlaine, he was working on the *Études néantes*. Mathile returned to Paris around March 15. She seems to have reconciled with Verlaine. But their relationship would deteriorate rapidly. At Verlaine's prompting, Rimbaud returned as well at the beginning of May. He would soon find lodging on rue Monsieur le Prince in a room looking out over courtyard of the Lycée Saint-Louis. There he wrote several poems, such as "Fêtes de la patience," or copied over those he had written during the previous months. There is little doubt concerning the sexual nature of his relationship with Verlaine, as is shown by the sonnet written by the latter, "Le Bon disciple," dated May 1872.

In June Rimbaud took a room at the Hôtel de Cluny, rue Victor Cousin, near place de la Sorbonne.

On July 7, as he hadn't been able to convince Verlaine to abandon his wife and child to follow him, he decided to leave France for Belgium by himself. When taking his letter of separation to Verlaine's home (whom he hadn't planned to see again), he ran into him. Verlaine then made the immediate decision to leave his family. Having gotten as far as Arras, they are arrested there for their eccentric behavior. They return to Paris but leave again immediately. On July 9 they stop in Charleville to see Bretagne.

They next go by train to Brussels (by way of Walcourt and Charleroi), where they take a room at the Grand Hôtel Liégeois.

On July 21 Mathilde and her mother come to Brussels to persuade Verlaine to return to Paris with them. He gives his consent, but on the return train, in which Rimbaud has also taken a seat, he sneaks away from them at the border station of Quiévrain. The two friends continue to live in Brussels.

On September 7 they take the boat from Ostend to England. They arrive in Dover the next day. They find a place to live in London at 34 Howland Street, in an apartment inhabited by Eugène Vermersch before them. They befriend the Communard exiles, the draughtsman Félix Régamey, Jules Andrieu, Lissagaray, etc. They visit "the immense city" that is a blend of misery and modernity. Verlaine continues writing his *Romances sans paroles;* Rimbaud perhaps composes certain texts of *Illuminations* (his poem "Les Corbeaux" had appeared on September 14, against his will, it seems, in *La Renaissance littéraire et artistique*, a review directed by Émile Blémont).

The couple Rimbaud-Verlaine live off the money Madame Verlaine sends her son. For her part, Mathilde pursues her demand for a separation; this causes anxiety to Verlaine, whose spinelessness becomes a little more obvious every day to Rimbaud.

Rimbaud informs his mother of his situation at the beginning of November. Madame Rimbaud comes to Paris and meets with Madame Verlaine, then Mathilde. She urges Rimbaud to return.

In December, Rimbaud is back in Charleville, where his presence is attested to on the twentieth of this month.

1873   At the beginning of January, Verlaine, sick and alone in London, makes a plea for aid. His mother comes to see him. In turn, Rimbaud comes and decides to remain. They resume their life as a couple. In order to give lessons that will earn them some money, Verlaine and Rimbaud

—

work on perfecting their English. They frequent the library of the British Museum.

On April 4, Verlaine, alarmed by the legal proceedings brought against him by his wife, decides to return to France. After a failed attempt to disembark from Newhaven, he takes the boat from Dover to Ostend, goes to Namur, then settles in Jéhonville (Belgium Luxembourg) at the home of his Aunt Evrard. On April 11, Black Friday, Rimbaud arrives in Roche (property of Madame Rimbaud), where his entire family is then living.

Around May 15 Rimbaud annonces in a letter to Delahaye that he wants to write a *Livre païen* or *Livre nègre*, "atrocious stories" (he has already written three).

On May 25 Verlaine and Rimbaud leave again for England. They visit Liège on May 26 and catch the boat from Anvers on the twenty-seventh. In London they rent a room in the home of a Mrs. Alexander Smith at 8 Great College Street, Camden Town. They are still seeking to give French lessons. But the couple is ill regarded by the refugees of the Commune. Verlaine, also anxious about his wife's separation demand and thinking he can again convince her to drop it, leaves, after a violent quarrel. On July 3 he catches the boat for Anvers. Rimbaud is a powerless witness to this departure. However, Verlaine soon regrets what he has done and sends a letter of explanation to Rimbaud.

Arriving in Brussels on July 4, Verlaine writes to his mother, to Madame Rimbaud, and to Mathilde, whom he asks to join him in three days time or else he will kill himself. Mathilde doesn't answer this appeal. But Madame Verlaine comes to Brussels on July 5. On July 6 Verlaine writes to Edmond Lepelletier to ask him to look after the publication of *Romances sans paroles* and confirms his desire to commit suicide: "I am going to kill myself." On July 7, although giving up on the idea of suicide, he sends Rimbaud a telegram announcing his decision to enlist as a volunteer in the Carlist army.

Rimbaud arrives that very evening. The two men make their way to the Hôtel de la Ville de Courtrai with Madame Verlaine. The day of July 9 is spent in discussions and quarrels as Rimbaud has mentioned his intention of leaving Verlaine and going to Paris or Charleville.

On July 10 Verlaine buys a revolver in the early morning. After another argument he fires a shot at Rimbaud, wounding him in the left wrist. Rimbaud goes to the Hôpital Saint-Jean for treatment. Then, around seven o'clock, persisting in his decision to leave, he heads toward the Gare de Midi, still accompanied by Verlaine and Verlaine's mother. While on their way Verlaine threatens to make use of his weapon (against himself or Rimbaud?), and Rimbaud seeks aid from a policeman. Verlaine is immediately arrested and imprisoned.

On July 11 Rimbaud enters the Hôpital Saint-Jean to have the bullet shot by Verlaine into his wrist removed. The next day he is interrogated by the examining magistrate and makes a deposition in Verlaine's favor. He will sign his demand to have the charges withdrawn on the nineteenth and leave the hospital the next day.

On August 8, Verlaine is brought before the sixth correctional chamber of Brussels. He is sentenced to two years in prison and a 200-franc fine. He is then incarcerated in the prison of the Petits Carmes in Brussels.

In August, Rimbaud, on his return to Roche, writes *Une saison en enfer*, which he no doubt had already begun. He entrusts his manuscript to Jacques Poot, a Brussels printer. Madame Rimbaud paid the down payment on the printing costs out of her own pocket.

On October 22 Rimbaud, in Brussels, takes his author's copies. The lion's share of the printing will remain at the printers until it is discoverd in 1901, still packed up on the premises of the Typographical Alliance. He leaves a volume to be sent to "P. Verlaine" at the prison of the Petits Carmes.

On November 1 Rimbaud is in Paris, where he gives his few friends the remainders of his copies of *Saison*. It is probable that at the Café Tabourey he met the poet Germain Nouveau, who had participated in the sequels to the Zutist circle, the group of the Vivants, and associated with Raoul Ponchon and Jean Richepin, whom Rimbaud had known in 1872. Rimbaud then returned to Roche or Charleville, where he stayed the winter.

1874 In mid-March Rimbaud comes to Paris, where he meets up with Germain Nouveau again. Together they leave for England. The two friends live at 178 Stamford Street, near Waterloo Station, on the south side of the Thames. Rimbaud places advertisements in certain newspapers offering French lessons. During this period he appears to have copied over, sometimes helped by Germain Nouveau, the majority of *Illuminations*.

In June, Nouveau decides to return to France. Somehow or other Rimbaud tries to survive. He seeks a job as a tutor.

In July, Rimbaud appeals to his mother for help out of desperation. Madame Rimbaud and Vitalie come to London (Vitalie has left numerous details concerning this stay in her diary). On July 31 Rimbaud leaves for an unknown destination. According to V. P. Underwood and Enid Starkie, he had taken in a job in the port of Scarborough, Yorkshire, a place mentioned in the poem "Promontoire," one of the *Illuminations*.

On November 9 Rimbaud places an ad in *The Times* seeking employment.

On December 29 he returns to Charleville to sort out his situation with the military authorities. As his brother Frédéric had enlisted for five years, he can obtain a deferment.

1875   On February 13 he leaves for Stuttgart. He lives on Wagnerstrasse in this city, then after March 15, at 2 Marienstrasse in a family boardinghouse. He is performing the duties of a tutor at the home of a certain Herr Lübner at this time.

On March 2 Verlaine, who had been freed on January 16 after eighteen months of captivity at the Petit Carmes Prison in Brussels, then at the prison in Mons, visits Rimbaud in Stuttgart. During the course of this meeting, Rimbaud is supposed to have given him the manuscript of *Illuminations* (see Verlaine, "Arthur Rimbaud '1884,'" *Les Hommes d'aujourd'hui*, 318, January 1888). The definitive falling out between the two friends took place over the following months. However, this didn't stop Verlaine from continuing to keep himself informed through Ernest Delahaye of Rimbaud's wanderings and occasionally making fun of them in "Vieux Coppées" about the person he called "the man with soles of the wind," but also "Homais," "the Philomath," "l'Oestre" (the gadfly), etc.

Rimbaud leaves Stuttgart for Italy in May. He is in Milan on the fifth or sixth. Then he crosses through Lombardy.

On June 15 he is stricken by sunstroke on the road from Livorno to Siena. The French consul in Livorno has him repatriated to Marseilles where he receives treatment for his condition in the hospital. Shortly thereafter, he intends enlisting in the Carlist army in order to get the signing bonus—which he perhaps may well have done; if this is so, he didn't waste any time to desert in that he returned to Paris in July and, over the vacation period, assumed the duties of a tutor at a summer school in Maisons-Alfort.

Around October 6 he is back in Charleville, where he again spends his time with Delahaye, Louis Pierquin, and Ernest Millot. At this time he is contemplating the idea of becoming a monk of the Christian Schools, in order to get sent to the Far East. He devotes time to study-ing several foreign languages and learns to play the piano.

On December 18 Vitalie dies of a tubercular synovitis.

1876   At the beginning of April, Rimbaud leaves for Vienna, where he is robbed of his money. He returns to Charleville.

In May, while in Brussels, he is recruited by "touts" and enlists in the Dutch colonial army. With all expenses paid, he goes first to Rotter-dam, then the garrison port of Harderwijk on the Zuyder Zee.

On June 10, the *Prins van Oranje*, carrying the ninety seven foot sol-dier recruits, casts off at Niewe Diep. The ship arrives in Naples on June 22.

On July 19, the *Prins van Oranje* weighs anchor at Padang (Sumatra), then casts off again for Batavia. On July 30 Rimbaud's company sets off for Semarang. On August 15 Rimbaud is classified a deserter. On August 30 he sets sail from Semarang under an assumed name (Edwin Holmes), on board the *Wandering Chief*, a Scottish vessel en route to England by way of the Cape and Saint Helena (October 23) and so on.

On December 6 Rimbaud disembarks at Queenstown in Ireland, then takes the train to Cork, where he catches another boat to Liver-pool. At Liverpool he books passage on a ship that takes him to Le Havre. On December 9 he is back in Charleville.

1877   During the winter, Rimbaud remains in Charleville or Roche.

In May he is in Cologne, recruiting volunteers on behalf of a Dutch agent.

On May 14 he is in Bremen, where he writes, without success, to the United States consul to enlist in the American navy. We next find him in Hamburg. Then he finds work as an employee of the Loisset Circus.

In July he accompanies the circus to Stockholm, then Copenhagen. He returns to Charleville at the end of the summer.

That autumn he disembarks for Alexandria from Marseilles, but illness forces him to break his journey at Civitavecchia in Italy. Following his recovery he goes as far as Rome then back to Marseilles, from where he finally returns to Charleville, where he remains for the winter.

1878   In January *The Gentleman's Magazine* of London publishes "Petits Pauvres" ("Les Effarés"), signed "Alfred [*sic*] Rimbaud."

His presence is indicated in the Latin Quarter of Paris around Easter.

Rimbaud spends the summer in Roche.

On October 20 he leaves Charleville. He crosses through the Vosges and Switzerland on foot and goes through the Saint-Gothard pass.

On November 19 he arrives in Genoa, from where he books passage to Alexandria, where he signs a contract of employment with E. Jean et Thial fils of Lanarca, a port city in Cyprus.

On December 16, he starts his job in Lanarca, where he works as the foreman of a quarry crew.

1879   Rimbaud continues his work under difficult conditions. He sometimes has serious altercations with his workers.

Stricken with typhoid at the end of May, he has to return quickly to France. He goes back to Roche to recover. He participates in the harvest work during that summer.

In September he meets for the last time with Delahaye, who has come to spend several days at the farm in Roche. During the Autumn, Rimbaud intends returning to Alexandria, but catching a fever in Marseilles he is forced to turn back and return to Roche.

1880   Rimbaud spends the winter in Roche.

In March he embarks for Alexandria, finds no work, and goes back to Cyprus. At this time he is hired as the foreman of a construction crew to build the governor's palace on Mount Troodos (6,400 feet).

In June he quits this job for one that is more lucrative, but deeming he is still badly paid, he hands in his resignation and leaves for Africa. It is possible this departure was also motivated because of the murder of a worker that he commited either accidentally or during a fit of anger. He finds employment with the agency Mazeran, Viannay, Bardey, and Co., which specializes in commerce (import and export) in the Red Sea port city of Aden, thanks to the recommendation he was able to obtain from a French trader in Hodeida, a certain Trébuchet.

On November 10 he is assigned to the Bardey branch in Harar, an eastern African city then consisting of around 35,000 to 40,000 inhabitants. He sails to Zeila, then crosses the Somali desert to finally arrive in Harar at the beginning of December.

1881   Rimbaud has difficulty becoming accustomed to this new post, despite its more favorable climate. He also undoubtedly contracts syphilis at this time.

In April, Alfred Bardey and Pierre Mazeran arrive in Harar, where they will remain until December.

During the months of May and June, Rimbaud makes an expedition to Bubassa, thirty miles south of Harar.

During the month of July, struck by a new bout of fever, he is forced to take to his bed.

In September, irritated at not being promoted to manager of the agency in Harar, he hands in his resignation. On December 15 he resumes work in Aden, still at the Bardey Agency.

1882   Rimbaud continues to work in Aden, where he has earned Alfred's Bardey complete confidence. Gnawed by boredom, he contemplates writing a "work on Harar and the Gallas" to be submitted to the Geographical Society (letter to E. Delahaye on January 18).

1883   On January 28, in Aden, Rimbaud slaps a shop clerk, Ali Chemmak. The French consul is informed of the matter. Alfred Bardey vouches for Rimbaud.

On March 20 Rimbaud signs a new work contract for two years with the Bardey Agency. On March 22 he starts his trip to Harar, where he will settle again, this time as the agency manager. He takes several photos.

In August he sends his associate Sotiro on a reconaissance expedition of the Ogaden (a region located between Harar and the Somali desert).

In September, on Sotiro's return, he organizes several expeditions into this region and participates in one of them.

On his return December 10 Rimbaud touches up the report made out by Sotiro and sends it to A. Bardey, who sends it on to the Geographical Society.

This year Verlaine publishes a study of Rimbaud in several issues of the young review *Lutèce* (from October 5 to November 17); this study will be republished during the following year in his book *Les Poètes maudits* (Vanier).

1884 Publication of "Report on the Ogaden" signed "Arthur Rimbaud" in the *Comptes rendus de la Société de Géographie* (report presented during their February 1 meeting).

Political events force the Bardey Agency to close their Harar branch.

On March 1 Rimbaud is forced to leave Harar. He arrives in Aden on April 23. He reveals his desperation in the letters he sends his family: "It is impossible to live more painfully than I do."

In June, Alfred Bardey creates a new corporation with his brother. He hires Rimbaud for six months (June 19). At this time Rimbaud is living with an Abyssinian woman who is either a servant or a concubine, and perhaps both.

In September Egypt is forced to evacuate its former dependent, Harar.

1885 On January 10 Rimbaud signs a new one-year contract with Pierre Bardey.

At the beginning of October he decides to quit his job with the Bardeys and make his fortune in the arms trade. On the eighth he signs a contract with Pierre Labatut, a trader in Shoa. It obliges him to lead a caravan of weapons to Shoa to be delivered to the king, Menelik, who is then busy with numerous schemes of expansion.

In November, Rimbaud lands in Tadjoura, the the caravan's departure point.

1886 Rimbaud is forced to remain in Tadjoura, because the French government has prohibited arms exportation into Shoa. However, he finally obtains a one-time authorization.

Labatut falls gravely ill and has to be repatriated to France, where he will die. Rimbaud then decides to join forces with Paul Soleillet. But this individual dies on September 9 from an embolism.

In October, Rimbaud decides to attempt this expedition to Ankober, capital of Shoa, by himself. He is delivering 2,040 rifles and 60,000 cartridges.

Published in *La Vogue* this year (May 13 and May 23, June 3, June 13, and June 20) are the majority of Rimbaud's *Illuminations* and some of his "Vers nouveaux." These texts are also published as a small volume with a preface by Verlaine, this same year.

1887 On February 6, Rimbaud reaches Ankober. He doesn't find Menelik, who is in Intoto. He journeys to that city, where he is forced to turn over his merchandise at bargain prices, for the debts incurred by Labatut in the Shoa have also become his responsibility.

On May 1, with the explorer Jules Borelli, he leaves Intoto for Harar. In Harar, Ras Makonnen, governor of the province and Menelik's cousin, gives him the money he's owed—but in the form of I O U s—for his arms shipment.

Returning to Aden on July 30, Rimbaud decides, after the setbacks of the previous year and the exhaustion he has suffered, to take a rest. He embarks from Obok, accompanied by his servant, Djami, for Cairo. On August 5, he is in Massawa, where he wishes to cash in Makonnen's I O U s he encounters difficulties with the authorities as his papers are not in order. The first impression he gives to the French consul in Massawa is "this honorable Rimbaud, so-called businessman in Harar and Aden. . . ."

On August 20, following a stop in Suez, Rimbaud is in Cairo. He remains there for almost five weeks. "I have totally gray hair. I figure that my life is falling apart," he writes to his family on August 23. Ready to do anything that will take him out of Aden, he forms the intention of leaving for the Far East. On August 25 and August 27, *Le Bosphore égyptien* publishes notes (that Rimbaud gave to Octave Borelli, brother of the explorer and manager of the newspaper) concerning his expedition to Shoa.

On October 8 he is back in Aden.

1888   On behalf of Armand Savouré, Rimbaud has the scheme of conveying a caravan of weapons from the coast to Shoa, but he will not obtain the necessary ministerial authorizations.

On March 14, after a month-long voyage to Harar for his own business, he is back in Aden.

On May 3 he sets up a commercial agency in Harar for the Frenchman César Tian, a merchant in Aden.

On August 4, in a letter to his family, he writes: "I am always very bored, I have never known anyone as bored as me."

During the period of September to December he receives visits from several of his friends of that time: Jules Borelli, Armand Savouré, Alfred Ilg.

1889   On May 18 Emperor Yohannes dies from the wounds he received in the battle of Metema, which took place between his army and the troops of the Muslim fanatic the Mahdi.

On November 10 Menelik, king of Shoa, becomes emperor of Abyssinia.

On December 2, in a letter to Ilg, Rimbaud asks for "a mule" and "two slave boys." This request will suffice for a long time as accreditation of the unfortunate legend of Rimbaud the slave trafficker, a legend destroyed once and for all by Mario Matucci in his book *Le Dernier Visage de Rimbaud en Afrique.*

1890   Rimbaud continues his business activity in Harar.

In a letter dated July 17 and which Rimbaud will bizarrely keep with his papers, Laurent de Gavoty, manager of *La France moderne*, a small literary review in Marseilles, asks his participation and tells him that he considers him to be "the head of the decadent and symbolist school."

1891   In the beginning of the year Rimbaud suffers pains in his right knee.

In March he can no longer walk and has to manage his affairs from his bed.

At the end of the month he decides to seek treatment in Aden.

On April 7, on a stretcher constructed according to his own blueprints, he is transported across 200 miles of desert to the port of Zeila, from where he sets sail April 19. His sufferings during this journey, from which he has left us a daily log, were practically unbearable. The diagnosis he receives in Aden is quite grim. There is talk of a cancer in the knee.

On May 9 Rimbaud embarks for France aboard the ship *L'Amazone*.

Landing in Marseilles on May 20, he is transported to the Hôpital de la Conception, from where he immediately writes his mother.

On May 23 Madame Rimbaud arrives in Marseilles, summoned by an urgent telegram, because Rimbaud has to have an operation. On the twenty-seventh Rimbaud's right leg is amputated. On June 9, Madame Rimbaud returns to Roche. On July 23, Rimbaud leaves the hospital and, placed in a special train car, travels as far as the Voncq station near Roche. His condition worsens by the day during his stay in Roche. Accompanied by his sister Isabelle, he leaves again for Marseilles, with the idea of catching a boat for Aden. But he has to be hospitalized immediately in Marseilles on the twenty-fourth. The cancer has spread and Rimbaud is totaly paralyzed.

On October 25 he accepts confession.

On November 9 Rimbaud dictates an incoherent letter intended for the manager of the Messageries Maritimes. He asks to be carried on board the next ship leaving for Aden.

On November 10 Rimbaud dies at ten o'clock in the morning, at the age of thirty-seven. This same day *Reliquaire*, *Poésies* by Rimbaud, with a preface by Rodolphe Darzens, appears under the imprint of Éditions Léon Genonceaux. But this edition will quickly be pulled from sale because of a disagreement between Darzens and Genonceaux.

1892 The publication in one volume of *Les Illuminations. Une saison en enfer*, with a preface by Paul Verlaine, Vanier.

1893 On December 12 Germain Nouveau, still ignorant of Rimbaud's death, sends him a letter from Algiers to Aden (in the care of the French consulate).

1895 *Poésies complètes* by Rimbaud, prefaced by Verlaine, is published by Vanier with notes by this publisher.

1898 *Les Oeuvres: Poésies, Illuminations, Autres Illuminations, Une saison en enfer*, preface by Paterne Berrichon (who had married Isabelle Rimbaud under his true name Pierre Dufour in 1897) and Ernest Delahaye, are published by Mercure de France.

I. Books and articles concerning the life of Rimbaud (these publications are in chronological order).

1883   Paul Verlaine, "Les poètes maudits, Arthur Rimbaud," *Lutèce*, October–November; reprinted as part of the book *Les Poètes maudits*, Paris: Vanier, 1884.

1886   Paul Verlaine, preface to *Illuminations* by A. Rimbaud, *La Vogue*.

1888   Paul Verlaine, "Arthur Rimbaud," *Les Hommes d'aujourd'hui*, vol. 8, no. 318.

1891   Rodolphe Darzens, preface to *Reliquaire, Poésies*, by Rimbaud, Paris: Genonceaux.

       Louis Pierquin, "Arthur Rimbaud," *Le Courrier des Ardennes*, November 30.

       Ernest Delahaye, "Sur Rimbaud," *Entretiens politiques et littéraires*, 21, December.

1892   Charles Maurras, "Poésie, Étude biographique. Arthur Rimbaud," *La Revue encyclopédique*, January 1.

1893   Louis Pierquin, "Sur Arthur Rimbaud," *Le Courrier des Ardennes*, December 24 and 31.

1895   Paul Verlaine, preface to the *Poésies complètes* of Arthur Rimbaud, Paris: Vanier.

       Idem, "Arthur Rimbaud," *The Senate*, London: October.

       Idem, "Nouvelle Notes sur Rimbaud," *La Plume*, November 15–30.

       Stéphane Mallarmé, "Arthur Rimbaud," *The Chap Book*, May 15, reprinted in *Divagations*, 1897.

1896   Jean Bourguignon and Charles Houin, "Poètes ardennais: Arthur Rimbaud," "Enfance," *Revue d'Ardenne et d'Argonne*, November–December. We will henceforth refer to this review as *R.A.A.*

1897   J. Bourguignon and C. Houin, "Rimbaud. Vie littéraire," *R.A.A.*, January-February and "Vie d'aventures," ibid., September–October.

      Paterne Berrichon, *La Vie de Jean-Arthur Rimbaud*, Paris: Mercure de France.

      Isabelle Rimbaud, "Le dernier voyage d'Arthur Rimbaud," *Revue blanche*, October 15.

1898   Charles Donos, *Verlaine intime*, Paris: Vanier.

1899   J. Bourguignon and C. Houin, "Vie en Afrique," *R.A.A.*, May–June.

1901   Idem., "Rimbaud. Son rôle en Afrique," *R.A.A.*, January–February and July.

1902   Edmond Lepelletier, *Paul Verlaine, sa vie, son oeuvre*, Paris: Mercure de France.

1906   Ernest Delahaye, *Rimbaud*, Paris–Reims: editions of the *Revue littéraire de Paris et de Champagne*.

      Victor Segalen, "Les Hors-la-loi. Le double Rimbaud," *Mercure de France*, April 15 (article republished under the title *Le Double Rimbaud*, Fata Morgana, 1979).

1907   Ernest Delahaye, "À propos de Rimbaud. Souvenirs familiers" in *R.A.A.*, March–April, May–June, July–August, October–November, December.

1908   Idem., *R.A.A.*, January–February, March–April, May–June, September–October, November–December.

1909   Idem., *R.A.A.*, May–June.

1911   Georges Izambard, "Lettres retrouvées d'Arthur Rimbaud," *Vers et Prose*, January–February.

1912   Paterne Berrichon, *Jean-Arthur Rimbaud le poéte (1854–1873)*, Paris: Mercure de France.

      Paul Claudel, preface to the *Oeuvres* of Rimbaud, Paris: Mercure de France.

1914   Isabelle Rimbaud, "Rimbaud mystique," *Mercure de France*, June 16.

1916   Léon Losseau, *La Légende de la destruction par Rimbaud de l'édition princeps d'*Une Saison en enfer," Brussels: L'Imprimerie, separate printing of an article from the *Annuaire de la Societé des Bibliophiles et Iconophiles de Belgique* for 1915.

—

Henri Deherain, "La carrière africaine d'Arthur Rimbaud," *Revue de l'histoire des colonies françaises*, 4th trimester.

1919   Ernest Delahaye, *Verlaine*, Paris: Messein.

1920   Isabelle Rimbaud, *Mon frère Arthur*, Paris: Camille Bloch.

1922   Idem, *Reliques*, Paris: Mercure de France.

J.M. Marmelstein, "Rimbaud aux Indes néerlandaises et à Stuttgart," *Mercure de France*, July 15.

1923   Marcel Coulon, *Le Problème de Rimbaud, poète maudit*, Nîmes: A. Gomès.

Ernest Delahaye, *Rimbaud, l'artiste et l'être moral*, Paris: Messein.

Ugo Ferrandi, "Lettre à Ottone Schanzer," translated and published in an article entitled "Du nouveau sur Rimbaud? in *Les Nouvelles littéraires*, October 20.

1924   Jean-Marie Carré, "Les souvenirs d'un ami de Rimbaud" (Louis Pierquin), *Mercure de France*, May 1.

1925   Marcel Coulon, *Au coeur de Verlaine et Rimbaud*, Le Livre.

Ernest Delahaye, *Souvenirs familiers à propos de Rimbaud, Verlaine et Germain Nouveau*, Messein (reprinted with commentary in Delahaye, témoin de Rimbaud, Neuchâtel: La Baconnière, 1974).

1926   Jean-Marie Carré, *La Vie aventureuse de J.-A. Rimbaud*, Paris: Plon.

Pierre Mille, "Un saint colonial" (on Pierre Bourde), *Revue de Paris*, April 15.

1927   Ernest Delahaye, *Les* Illuminations *et* Une saison en enfer *d'Arthur Rimbaud*, Paris: Messein.

Georges Izambard, *Arthur Rimbaud à Douai et à Charleville*, Paris: Kra.

Jean Richepin, "Germain Nouveau et Rimbaud, souvenirs inédits," *Revue de France*, January 1.

1928   Jean-Marie Carré, *Les Deux Rimbaud*, Paris: Les Cahiers libres.

Georges Izambard, "Arthur Rimbaud pendant la Commune. Une lettre inédite de lui. Le Voyant," *La Revue européenne*, October.

1929   Marcel Coulon, *La Vie de Rimbaud et de son oeuvre*, Paris: Mercure de France.

François Ruchon, *Jean-Arthur Rimbaud, sa vie, son ouvre, son influence*, Champion.

1930   Maurice Dullaert, "L'Affaire Verlaine-Rimbaud," Brussels: *Nord*, 4th
        notebook.

        Marguerite Yerta-Melera, *Rimbaud*, Paris: Firmin-Didot.

        Jean Paul Vaillant, *Rimbaud tel qu'il fut*, Paris: Le Rouge et le Noir.

1931   André Fontinas, *Verlaine, Rimbaud. Ce qu'on sait de leur relations, ce qu'on
        en présume*, Paris: Librairie de France.

1933   Jules Mouquet, "Un témoinage tardif sur Rimbaud" (Paul Labarrière),
        Mercure de France, May 15.

1934   Robert Goddin, *Sur les traces d'Arthur Rimbaud*, Paris: Éditions du
        Sagittaire.

1935   The ex-Madame Verlaine, *Mémoires de ma vie*, Paris: Flammarion.

1936   Robert Goffin, *Rimbaud vivant*, Corrêa

        Colonel Godchot, *Arthur Rimbaud ne varietur*, Vol. 1, (*1854–1871*), Nice:
        by the author.

1937   Idem, Vol. 2, (*1871–1873*), Nice: by the author.

        Enid Starkie, *Rimbaud in Abyssinia*, Oxford: Clarendon Press (published
        in French the following year by Payot).

1938   D. A. de Graaf, *Arthur Rimbaud homme de lettres*, Assen: Van Gorcum
        and Co.

        Vitalie Rimbaud, *Journal* presented by H. de Bouillane de Lacoste and
        Henri Matarasso, *Mercure de France*, May 15.

        Enid Starkie, *Arthur Rimbaud*, London: Faber and Faber (reprinted in
        1947 and 1961).

1939   Jean-Marie Carré, *Vie de Rimbaud*, Paris: Plon (1926 edition with addi-
        tional documents).

        Henri Matarasso et Pierre Petitfils, "Nouveaux documents sur Rim-
        baud" (mainly the letter from A. Bardey to P. Berrichon), *Mercure de
        France*, May 15.

1941   Jérôme et Jean Tharaud, "Rimbaud à Harar," *Candide*, November 19.

1942   Louis Piérard, L'édition originale d'*Une saison en enfer*," *Poésie 42*,
        January.

1943   Pierre Arnoult, *Rimbaud*, Paris: Albin Michel (new ed. 1955).

        Auguste Martin, "Verlaine et Rimbaud. Documents inédits tirés des
        archives de la préfecture de Police," *La Nouvelle Revue française*, Feb-
        ruary 19.

———

1946 George Izambard, *Rimbaud tel que je l'ai connu*, Paris: Mercure de France.
François Ruchon, *Rimbaud. Documents iconographiques*, Geneva: Pierre Caillier.

1947 Enid Starkie, "Sur les traces de Rimbaud," *Mercure de France*, May 1.
Henri Matarasso, "À propos d'un nouveau tableau de Rimbaud," *Mercure de France*, November 1.

1949 Henry de Bouillane de Lacoste, *Rimbaud et le problème des Illuminations*, Paris: Mercure de France.
Jean-Marie Carré, *Autour de Verlaine et de Rimbaud*, unpublished drawings, Cahier Jacques Doucet.
Jules Lefrance, "Roche. La maison de Rimbaud," *Revue palladienne*, April–May.
Pierre Petitfils, *L'oeuvre et le visage de Rimbaud, essai de bibliographie et d'iconographie*, Nizet.

1951 D. A. de Graaf, "Deux lettres d'Ernest Delahaye à Ernest Millot sur "l'homme aux semelles de vent"," *Revue des sciences humaines*, October–December.

1952 Henry Miller, *Rimbaud*, Lausanne: Mermod.

1953 Henri Guillemin, "Rimbaud est-il mort chrétiennement?," *Le Figaro littéraire*, May 9.
Idem, "Rimbaud fut-il communard?," *Le Figaro littéraire*, October 10.
(These two articles were reprinted in *À vrai dire*, Gallimard, 1956.)

1954 Idem, "Connaissance de Rimbaud, nouveaux documents inédits," *Mercure de France*, October 1.
André Tian, À propos de Rimbaud," ibid.

1955 Pierre Petitfils, "Des souvenirs inconnus sur Rimbaud, *Mercure de France*, January 1.

1956 Suzanne Briet, *Rimbaud notre prochain*, Nouvelles Éditions latines.
D. A. de Graaf, "Autour du dossier de Bruxelles, d'après des documents inédits," *Mercure de France*, July 1.

1960 D. A. de Graaf, *Arthur Rimbaud, sa vie, son oeuvre*, Assen: Van Gorcum.
Franco Petralia, *Bibliographie de Rimbaud en Italie*, Florence: Publications of the French Institute of Florence, Sansoni.

1962 Henri Matarasso and Pierre Petitfils,*Vie d'Arthur Rimbaud*, preface by Jean Cocteau, Paris: Hachette.

451

1963   Michael Pakenham, "Un ami inconnu de Rimbaud et de Debussy," *Revue des sciences humaines*, July–September.

1965   André Dhôtel, *La Vie de Rimbaud*, Paris: Albin Michel.

Roger Milliex, "Le premier séjour d'Arthur Rimbaud à Chypre," *Kupriakai Spovdai* (reprinted in *Nota Bene*, Spring 1984).

Jean Voellmy, preface to the *Correspondence de Rimbaud avec Alfred Ilg, 1888–1891*, Paris: Gallimard.

1967   Henri Matarasso and Pierre Petitfils, *Album Rimbaud*, Bibliothèque de la Pléiade, Paris: Gallimard.

1968   Suzanne Briet, *Madame Rimbaud, essai de biographie*, Paris: Minard, "Les Lettres modernes."

M.-A. Ruff, *Rimbaud, l'homme et l'oeuvre*, Hatier-Bovin, coll. "Connaisance des Lettres."

1969   Mario Matucci, *Le Dernier Visage de Rimbaud en Afrique*, Marcel Didier.

1970   Henry Miller, *Le Temps des assassins*, Paris: P. J. Oswald (translated by F. J. Temple).

1971   Jean Chauvel, *L'Aventure terrestre de Jean-Arthur Rimbaud*, Paris: Seghers.

Michel Decaudin, "Rimbaud et la Commune. Essai de mise au point," *Travaux de linguistique et de littérature*, Strasbourg: IX, 2.

Pierre Gascar, *Rimbaud et la Commune*, Paris: Gallimard, coll. "Idées."

1972   Yves Reboul, "Les problèmes rimbaldiens traditionnels et le témoignage d'Isabelle Rimbaud," Paris: Minard, Arthur Rimbaud series, 1.

1974   *Delahaye témoin de Rimbaud*, presented by F. Eigeldinger and A. Gendre, Neuchâtel: La Baconniére.

1975   Alain de Mijolla, "La désertion du capitaine Rimbaud," *Revue français de psychanalyse*, May-June (reprinted in *Les Visiteurs du moi*, Les Belles Lettres, 1981).

Henri Peyre, *Rimbaud vu par Verlaine*, Paris: Nizet.

André Thisse, *Rimbaud devant Dieu*, Paris: José Corti.

1976   Yves Reboul, "Les problèmes rimbaldiens traditionnels et le témoignage d'Isabelle Rimbaud," (sequel and end), Minard, *Revue des Lettres modernes*, A. Rimbaud, 3.

Vernon P. Underwood, *Rimbaud et l'Angleterre*, Paris: Nizet.

1978   Gérard Macé, "Rimbaud recently deserted," *La Nouvelle Revue française*, April–May (reprinted in *Ex-Libris*, Gallimard, coll. "Le Chemin," 1980).

—

1979   Duncan Forbes, *Rimbaud in Ethiopia*, Hythe: Volturna Press.

1980   Alfred Bardey, *Barr-Adjam, souvenirs d'Afrique orientale*, presented by Joseph Tubiana, Paris: C.N.R.S. Editions.

H. Lubienski-Bodenham, "Le capitaine Rimbaud à Dijon (1864–1878)," *Rimbaud vivant*, no. 18–19.

1982   Pierre Petitfils, *Rimbaud*, Paris: Julliard, coll. "Les Vivants."

Enid Starkie, *Rimbaud*, translation by Alain Borer, Paris: Flammarion.

1983   Alain Borer, *Un sieur Rimbaud se disant négociant*, Paris: Lachenal et Ritter.

Pierre Brunel, *Arthur Rimbaud ou l'éclatant désastre*, Champ Vallon, coll. "Champ poétique."

Jean Degives and Frans Suasso, "Arthur Rimbaud, soldat et deserteur de l'armée des Indes néerlandaises," *Nederlanse Omroepstichtting*.

1984   Alain Borer, *Rimbaud en Abyssinie*, Paris: Éditions du Seuil, coll. "Fiction & Cie."

1986   Mario Matucci, *Les Deux Visages de Rimbaud*, Neuchâtel: La Baconnière.

1989   Pol Postal, "À propos du dossier de Bruxelles," *Parade sauvage*, 6.

1990   Steve Murphy, *Le Premier Rimbaud ou l'Apprentissage de la subversion*, Lyon: C.N.R.S. Editions, Presses universitaires de Lyon.

1991   Alain Borer, *Rimbaud, l'heure de la fuite*, Paris: Gallimard, coll. "Découvertes."

Alain Jouffroy, *Arthur Rimbaud et la liberté libre*, Monaco: Éditions du Rocher, coll. "Les Infréquentables."

II. Editions of works (first publications in book form or first publications of certain texts, in chronological order).

Une saison en enfer, Brussels: Alliance typographique, Poot and Co., 1873.

Les Illuminations, with a note by Paul Verlaine, publication of the review *La Vogue*, 1886 (texts formerly published in the revue in different order).

Reliquaire. Poésies, preface by Rodolphe Darzens. Paris: L. Genonceaux, 1891.

Les Illuminations. Une saison en enfer, note by Paul Verlaine. Paris: Vanier, 1892.

Poésies complètes, preface by Paul Verlaine. Paris: Vanier, 1895.

"Cette saison . . .", ("fausse lecture" for "Bethsaïda"), *Revue blanche*, September 1, 1897.

Oeuvres, preface by Paterne Berrichon and Ernest Delahaye. Paris: Mercure de France, 1898.

Lettres de Jean-Arthur Rimbaud: Égypte, Arabie, Éthiopie, with introduction and notes by Paterne Berrichon. Paris: Mercure de France, 1899.

Les Déserts de l'amour in *Revue littéraire de Paris et de Champagne*, September 1906.

Oeuvres: vers et prose, preface by Paul Claudel. Paris: Mercure de France, 1912.

"Les Mains de Jeanne-Marie," in the review *Littérature*, 4, June 1912. Published the same year by the publisher Au Sans Pareil.

Letter of May 15, 1871 (called "of the Seer"), *La Nouvelle Revue française*, October 1, 1912.

Les Stupra (three erotic sonnets), sonnets, private printer, (false) date of 1871, placed on sale by Messein, 1923.

Un coeur sous une soutane, with a foreword by Louis Aragon and André Breton, Ronald Davis, 1924.

Ce qu'on dit au Poète à propos de fleurs, "Le Livre," 1925.

Letter of May 13, 1871, to G. Izambard (first of the letters of the "Seer"), text and facsimile reproduction, *La Revue européenne*, October 10, 1928.

Rimbaud's poems in l'*Album zutique*, under the title *Album zutique*. Lyon: Editions de l'Arbalète, Marc Barbezat, 1943.

"À Samarie, plusieurs . . .") and "L'air léger et charmant de Galilée . . ." (two "evangelical" prose pieces) in *Mercure de France*, January 1, 1948.

La Chasse spirituelle (apocryphal). Paris: Mercure de France, 1949. Text denounced as false in André Breton's pamphlet, *Flagrant délit*, Thésée, 1949.

Correspondence avec Alfred Ilg (1888–1891), preface and notes by Jean Voellmy, Paris: Gallimard, 1965.

III. Principal editions of the complete works currently available.

Oeuvres complètes, presented and annotated by Antoine Adam, Paris: Bibliothèque de la Pléiade, Gallimard, 1972.

Oeuvres, introduction and notes by Suzanne Bernard. Paris: Classiques Garnier, 1960. Edition revised and corrected by André Guyaux in 1981 and again in 1987.

I. *Poésies*, II. *Vers nouveaux. Une saison en enfer*, III. *Illuminations* and a selection from his later letters. Edition in three volumes, preface and notes by Jean-Luc Steinmetz, Paris: Garnier–Flammarion, 1989.

IV. Groups and Symposiums.

1. *Rimbaldian reviews*

Bulletin des Amis de Rimbaud: seven issues from January 1931 to April 1939.

Le Bateau ivre, twenty issues from January 1949 to September 1966.

Études rimbaldiennes (Minard publisher), three issues (1968, 1970, 1972).

Rimbaud vivant, twenty-two issues from 1973 to 1990.

Circeto, review of Rimbaldian studies, two issues (1983, 1984).

Parade sauvage, (1984 to the present), reviews or Rimbaldian studies accompanied by information bulletins.

2. *Special issues from reviews*

La Grive, October 1954; *Europe*, May–June 1973; *Littérature*, October, 1973; *Revue de l'Université de Bruxelles*, 1982; *Berenice*, Rome: 2, March 1981, and 5, 1982; *Revue des sciences humaines*, 1984, 193; *Revue d'histoire littéraire de la France*, March–April 1987; *Magazine littéraire*, June 1991; *Europe*, June 1991.

3. *Symposiums and Symposium Proceedings*

Symposium of Cerisy, August 1982. *Rimbaud multiple*, Gourdon, D. Bedou, 1986.

Symposium of Neuchâtel (Arthur Rimbaud Center), May 1983. *Le Point vélique*, Neuchâtel: La Baconnière, 1986.

Symposium of the École normale supérieure (rue d'Ulm), February 1984. "Minute d'eveil," *Rimbaud maintenant*, C.D.U.–S.E.D.E.S., 1984.

Symposium organized by the International Association for French Studies, July 1984. *C.A.I.E.F.*, no. 36, May 1985.

Symposium of Grosseto, September 1985. *Poesia e avventura*, Pisa: Pacini, 1987.

Symposium of Charleville, September 1986, republished in *Parade sauvage*, "Rimbaud et la liberté libre," 1987.

Symposium of Cambridge, September 1987, republished in *Parade sauvage*, "Rimbaud à la loupe," 1990.

Various symposiums are scheduled to take place in 1991, the centenary year of his death (Warsaw, April; Charleville, September; Sendaî (Japan), September; Cyprus, October; Marseilles, November; Amiens, December).

One can find the complete details for the bibliography given above by referring to the critical bibliography included in the the third volume of the complete works (see III).

V. General Bibliography

Aubry, Jean. "Verlaine et l'Angleterre," *Revue de Paris*, October 13, 1918.

Azema, Jean Pierre. *see* Winock.

Badesco, Luc. *La Génération poétique de 1860*. Paris: Nizet, 1971, 2 vols.

Baudelaire, Charles. *Oeuvres complètes*, Paris: Bibliothèque de la Pléiade, 2 vols., Gallimard, 1975–1976.

Beauclair, Henri, and Gabriel Vicaire. *Les Déliquescences d'Adoré Floupette*. Paris: Vanier, 1885.

Blanchot, Maurice. *La Part du feu*. Paris: Gallimard, 1949

———. *L'Entretien infini*. Paris: Gallimard, 1969.

Bonnefoy, Yves. *Rimbaud*. Paris: Éditions du Seuil, coll. "Écrivains de toujours," 1961.

———. "Madame Rimbaud" in *Le Lieu et la Formule*, collective anthology, hommage to Marc Eigeldinger. Neuchâtel: La Baconnière.

Borelli, Jules. *Éthiopie méridionale, journal de mon voyage au pays amhara, oromo et sidama*. Paris: Librairie–Imprimerie réunies, 1890.

Bouillane de Lacoste, Henry de. *Rimbaud et le problème des Illuminations*. Paris: Mercure de France, 1949.

Breton, André. *Oeuvres*, vol. 1, Paris: Bibliothèque de la Pléiade, Gallimard, 1988.

———. *Anthologie de l'humeur noire*. Paris: Éditions du Sagittaire, 1940.

Champsaur, Félicien. *Dinah Samuel*. Ollendorff, 1st ed., 1882, definitive ed., 1888.

Chastenet, Jacques. *Histoire de la Troisième République*. Paris: Hachette–Littérature, 1952.

Claudel, Paul. *Oeuvres en prose*. Paris: Bibliothèque de la Pléiade, Gallimard, 1965.

Cocteau, Jean. *Les Enfants terribles.* Paris: Grasset, 1929.

Cros, Charles. *Oeuvres complètes.* Paris: Bibliothèque de la Pléiade, Gallimard.

Davy, André. *Éthiopie d'hier et d'aujourd'hui.* Le Livre africain, 1970.

De Amicis, Edmundo. *Souvenirs de Paris et de Londres.* French translation of 1880. Paris: Hachette.

Demeny, Paul. *Les Glaneuses.* Paris: La Librairie artistique, 1870.

———. *La Flèche de Diane.* one-act play, Paris: La Librairie artistique, 1870.

———. *La Soeur du fédéré.* Paris: La Librairie artistique, 1871.

Dictionnaire de biographie française.

Dossier du Musée d'Orsay, no. 18, 1987: "Fantin-Latour: Coin de table."

Fallaize, E. *Étienne Carjat and "Le Boulevard" (1861–1863).* Geneva: Slatkine, 1987.

Ferrandi, Ugo. *Lettere dell'Harrar.* Milan: 1896.

Forestier, Louis. *Charles Cros, l'homme et l'oeuvre.* Paris: Minard, 1969.

Goncourt, Edmond and Jules de Goncourt. *L'Art au XVIIIe siècle.* 1873.

Guillemin, Henri. *À vrai dire.* Paris: Gallimard, 1956.

Gracq, Julien. *En lisant, en écrivant.* Paris: José Corti, 1981.

Guyaux, André. *Poétique du fragment.* Neuchâtel: La Baconnière, 1985.

Hureaux, Yanny. *Le Guide des Ardennes.* Lyon: La manufacture, 1986.

Jerrold. *London, a pilgrimage.* Illustrated by G. Doré. London: Grant, 1872.

Kahn, Gustave. *"Arthur Rimbaud," La Revue blanche,* August 15, 1898.

Keller, Conrad. *Alfred Ilg.* Frauenfeld and Leipzig: Uber and Co., 1918.

Maitron, J. *Dictionnaire biographique du mouvement ouvrier.* Ed. Ouvrières, 1971, 9 vols.

Mendès, Catulle. *La Maison de la vieille.* Paris: Charpentier, 1894.

———. *La Légende du Parnasse contemporain.* 1894; republished Geneva: Slatkine Reprints, 1983.

Mérat, Albert. *L'idole.* Lemerre, 1869.

Monfried, Henri de. *Ménélik tel qu'il fut.* Paris: Grasset, 1954.

Nerval, Gérard de. *Le Voyage en Orient.* In vol. 2, *Oeuvres complètes.* Paris: Bibliothèque de la Pléiade, Gallimard, 1984.

Nizan, Paul. *Aden Arabie.* Paris: François Maspero, 1960.

Noël, Bernard. *Dictionnaire de la Commune.* Paris: Hazan, 1971.

Nouveau, Germain. *Oeuvres.* Paris: Bibliothèque de la Pléiade, Gallimard, 1970.

———

Parnasse contemporain. Paris: Lemerre. 1st Series, 1866.

———.2nd Series, 1871.

———.3rd Series, 1876.

Poussin, Henri. *Versiculets.* Definitive Edition. Note by A. Valette and preface by J. Richepin. Dentu, 1887.

Racot, Adolphe. *Les Parnassiens.* Collected articles in *Avant-siècle,* 1. Edited by M. Pakenham. Paris: Minard.

Raspail, Jean.*Moi, Antoine de Tounens, roi de Patagonie.* Paris: Albin Michel, 1981.

Régamey, Félix. *Verlaine dessinateur.* Paris: Floury, 1896.

Ricard, Louis-Xavier de. *Petits Mémoires d'un Parnassien.* Republished in *Avant-siècle,* 1. Paris: Minard, 1961.

Robecchi-Brichetti, L. *Nell'Harrar.* Milan: Galli di Chiesa, 1896.

Robinet, René. "L'Institution Rossat de Charleville," *Actes du 88e Congrès national des sociétés savantes.* Paris: Imprimerie nationale, 1964.

———. "Le collège de Charleville et l'enseignement secondaire dans les Ardennes de 1854 à 1877," *Actes du 95e Congrès national des sociétés savantes.* Paris: Bibliothèque nationale, 1974.

Romi. *Amoureux de Paris.* Paris: 1961.

Rosa, Ottorino. *L'Impero del Leone di Giuda. Note sull'Abissinia.* Brescia: Lenghi, 1913.

Steinmetz, Jean-Luc. *Le Champ d'écoute.* Neuchâtel: La Baconnière, 1985.

———. *La Poésie et ses raisons,* Paris: J. Corti, 1990.

Verlaine, Paul. *Oeuvres poétiques complètes.* Paris: Bibliothèque de la Pléiade, Gallimard, 1954.

———. *Oeuvres en prose complètes.* Paris: Bibliothèque de la Pléiade, Gallimard, 1984.

———. *Correspondence.* 3 vols. Paris: Messein, 1922.

———. *Lettres inédites à divers correspondants.* Geneva: Droz, 1976.

Vermersch, Eugène. *L'infamie humaine.* Preface by Paul Verlaine. Paris: Lemerre, 1890.

Winock, Michel, and J.-P. Azéma. *Les Communards.* Paris: Éditions du Seuil, coll. "Le temps qui court," 1964.

Zola, Émile. *La Débâcle.* Paris: Charpentier, 1892.

INDEX